The Transformation of Ed...

Land, Property and Trust in the ...

This clear and lucid study explores the physical transformation of Edinburgh in the nineteenth century. It is based on a formidable amount of new archival research and is enriched with fascinating illustrative material. In a powerful analysis of how the law adapted to the new possibilities for profit created by urbanisation, Richard Rodger examines how the city of Edinburgh was transformed in the nineteenth century. A modern form of 'feudalism', he argues, was invented. It was the financial implications of this 'feuing' system, rather than an early form of town planning, that contributed much to the development of the Edinburgh New Town and, more significantly, to the character of urban development in nineteenth-century urban Scotland.

Richard Rodger shows how the Church of Scotland, famous schools and educational endowments, as well as private trusts and small investors, all contributed to and benefited from urban expansion. He also explains how interconnected rural and urban interests were with revenue from the countryside recycled through urban property incomes. These and other relationships associated with the building of the city are explored at various levels, including a study of the largest builder in Edinburgh, James Steel, in a rags to riches, bankruptcy to baronetcy story that unveils how the process of urban development actually took place.

Despite its genteel New Town and 'douce' suburbs Edinburgh, known locally as 'Auld Reekie' for its polluted atmosphere, experienced both environmental damage and congested living conditions. In the final section, Richard Rodger explores civic efforts to address these concerns. He also examines the achievements of a working men's co-operative to provide 'colonies' of houses in an innovative attempt to improve urban lifestyles. And, in an ethnological approach, the adornment and decoration of the tenement is examined in the context of ego, myth and national identity.

Historians – whether political, urban, economic, social or legal – will find challenging new insights here which have a resonance far beyond the confines of one city.

RICHARD RODGER is Professor of Urban History at the University of Leicester and Director of the Centre for Urban History. He teaches courses in economic and social history and is interested in the application of computing to historical analysis. He has written or edited ten books on the economic, social and business history of cities, including *Scottish Housing in the Twentieth Century* (1989), *European Urban History* (1993) and *Housing in Urban Britain 1780–1914* (1995). Since 1987 Richard Rodger has been Editor of *Urban History* (published by Cambridge University Press).

The Transformation of Edinburgh

Land, Property and Trust in the Nineteenth Century

Richard Rodger

University of Leicester

CAMBRIDGE
UNIVERSITY PRESS

PUBLISHED BY THE PRESS SYNDICATE OF THE UNIVERSITY OF CAMBRIDGE
The Pitt Building, Trumpington Street, Cambridge, United Kingdom

CAMBRIDGE UNIVERSITY PRESS
The Edinburgh Building, Cambridge CB2 2RU, UK
40 West 20th Street, New York NY 10011–4211, USA
477 Williamstown Road, Port Melbourne, VIC 3207, Australia
Ruiz de Alarcón 13, 28014 Madrid, Spain
Dock House, The Waterfront, Cape Town 8001, South Africa

http://www.cambridge.org

First published 2001
First paperback edition 2004

Typeface Plantin 10/12   *System* QuarkXPress™   [SE]

A catalogue record for this book is available from the British Library

Library of Congress cataloguing in publication data
Rodger, Richard.
The transformation of Edinburgh: land, property and trust in
the nineteenth century / Richard Rodger.
     p.   cm.
Includes bibliographical references and index.
ISBN 0 521 78024 1 hardback
1. Edinburgh (Scotland) – Social conditions.   2. Urbanization –
Scotland – Edinburgh.   3. Housing – Scotland – Edinburgh –
History – 19th century.   4. Edinburgh (Scotland) – History.
I. Title: The transformation of Edinburgh. II. Title.
HN398.E27 R63 2000
306′.09413′4–dc21   00–040347

ISBN 0 521 78024 1 hardback
ISBN 0 521 60282 3 paperback

Contents

Figures

Tables

Appendices

Acknowledgements

Subsidies underpin every book. In an age of audit and accountability, authors normally acknowedge first their research councils, colleges and universities, and even their colleagues. However, I wish first to acknowledge the priceless emotional support and practical help I have had from my wife and from my mother. For extended periods of research and writing they have provided a system of support which has released me from many daily concerns and allowed me to concentrate single-mindedly on this project. Their unselfish subsidies can never be acknowledged sufficiently.

Subsidies have been generously offered by a number of readers and I have benefited enormously on technical and interpretive matters from them. In the over-committed academic environment of the 1990s to read and discuss my work in draft has necessarily sidelined theirs and I appreciate their selflessness. Alan Mayne, Ken Reid, Dave McCrone, Bob Morris, Bill Luckin, Marjaana Niemi, Lucy Faire, Rose Pipes, Charlie Withers and Martin Daunton were particularly helpful, but there were many others, often in ways which I did not always appreciate at the time, whose suggestions subsequently proved helpful. This was especially the case at various meetings and seminars where I presented papers. Often, too, the technical advice and assistance I received on mapping matters from Donald Morse and Joan Fairgrieve in Edinburgh and on my various databases from Alex Moseley in Leicester made all the difference to the historical analysis. Toby Morris of Edinburgh University's computing service revived my laptop on occasions and gave real meaning to his call sign – 'sociable science'. Their efforts on my behalf went far beyond the call of their daily duties, and are deeply appreciated. From time to time, and on a casual basis, I have asked Sheila Hamilton and Amy Juhala to resolve particular research questions, necessarily involving them in hours of tedious work, and they like my daughter, Anna Rodger, put in more hours than modest research funds could cover. Long ago Jenny Newman preserved my sanity by undertaking an extended period working on property records in the Register of Sasines in Edinburgh, and this gave the project needed impetus.

Subsidies from public officials far exceeded what might reasonably constitute their job descriptions. In Edinburgh archives and libraries the expert and helpful assistance I have received should never leave the public in doubt as to the quality of service in these areas. In the Edinburgh City Archives, Richard Hunter was invariably supportive, and Alison Scott and, before his emigration to Ayrshire, Kevin Wilbraham fetched and found more 'dirty books', papers and files than I wish ever to see again; more recently Pam McNicol and Stephanie Davidson were just as willing. At the National Archives of Scotland, Alan Borthwick kindly showed me manuscript listings of the Heriot Papers which long ago persuaded me that the project was worthwhile, if also beyond the labours of a single individual, and Hugh Hagan and Alison Lindsay fielded particular queries and suggested avenues for research enquiries with the customary deftness of the NAS archivists in West Register House. The staff at the Royal Commission of Ancient and Historical Monuments of Scotland were always helpful; Miles Glendinning probed gently on areas which helped me refine aspects of the research, and Ian Gow and Jane Adams helped in tracking down plans and elevations of the Heriot Trust. Entire benches have been given over to the maps which I have consulted in the Map Library of the National Library of Scotland. I learned to trust the staff absolutely, just stating what my particular research problem was in the knowledge that if there was a map which even vaguely approximated my needs, then it would be found and produced. My enthusiasm for their service probably generated more enquiries from members of the public and other researchers than they realised. Margaret Wilkes was invariably interested in my progress and Chris Fleet helpfully discussed the problems of digitising maps when I was at the planning stage of the Geographical Information Systems approach adopted for business data.

I consulted immense numbers of Merchant Company records. Though their fragmentation and inaccessibility remains a disgrace to the venerable institutions involved, I could not have completed crucial elements of the research without the willing co-operation of John Lunn, solicitor with Morton, Fraser and Milligan. Under the usual daily pressures of a law office, he located volumes of records in which I was interested, withdrew them from lead-lined vaults and permitted me to read them at my own pace. Key elements in the mosaic of property ownership in Edinburgh became evident as a result of this arrangement.

Finally, but most importantly, I should like to acknowledge the work and co-operation of the entire staff of the Edinburgh Room in the Central Public Library. There are many aspects of the municipal library system under pressure, even in crisis, in Britain. Yet the Edinburgh Room staff deal adroitly and patiently with the most diverse questions about the city, past and present. The collection is a priceless yet under-appreciated resource, as are the efforts of the staff, and I benefited immensely from the endless supply of pamphlet literature on nineteenth-century Edinburgh which Andrew Bethune particularly, but the rest of the staff, too, helped me to locate.

Privately, often unconsciously, support has been forthcoming. Many friends have shown an awareness of the scale and complexity of my research, and of the loneliness of the long-distance researcher. David Stafford and Jeanne Canizzo have been particularly supportive, as have David Reeder, Barbara Morris, Peter Fearon and Ewan Colling; the doctoral students I continued to supervise while writing were particularly sensitive to my needs. Adrian Beck and Mark Maynard, my SMS business partners, shouldered additional burdens during my absence. My teammates understood that I was not always available and did not pressurise me to play, and so long as they are acknowledged here will welcome me back to the cricket nets at Grace Road, Leicester.

The Social Science Faculty Research Fund of the University of Leicester provided a small grant for a pilot project, the Nuffield Foundation made funds available for data entry and the Institute of Chartered Accountants of Scotland also funded some work on the Heriot Trust accounts which is incorporated here. Much of the research and writing latterly was undertaken while I was based as a Research Associate at the International Social Science Institute, University of Edinburgh, and their generous allowance of physical space provided the mental space essential to the project. Dilys Rennie's daily efforts to assist the smooth running of research projects there also added materially to the ISSI, and I should like to acknowledge this and the support of the University of Edinburgh.

Other acknowledgements are due to many individuals and organisations in Edinburgh for their permission to reproduce illustrations: Edinburgh City Archives (3.14, 3.19, 8.2, 8.6, 9.7, 9.8, 9.13); Edinburgh City Art Centre, People's Story Museum (11.6); Edinburgh City Libraries (1.2a, 2.13, 3.13, 11.9, 12.1 (Plate 25 by J. C. Balmain is reproduced by permission of Trevor Yerbury), 12.6, 14.2); George Heriot's Trust (2.1, 2.3, 2.4); National Archives of Scotland (11.1); National Library of Scotland (2.6, 3.15, 3.16, 11.10, 11.15); Rosemary J. Pipes (11.3, 11.13); the Reformation Society, Magdalen Chapel (11.5); Royal Commission on the Ancient and Historical Monuments of Scotland (2.11, 6.2, 8.5b, 9.11, 11.7c, 11.11, 11.20, 13.6a); Scottish National Portrait Gallery (2.2); University of Aberdeen, George Washington Wilson Collection (13.5). All other graphs, maps and illustrative material have been produced by myself.

Subsidies of a financial kind have been forthcoming principally from the Economic and Social Research Council and from the Leverhulme Trust, whose support I warmly acknowledge and without which the time to complete this project would not have been forthcoming. This financial support has enabled me to benefit from a period of extended research leave, and my intellectual batteries have been recharged. These research bodies enabled me to do this.

At Cambridge University Press, an international reputation for publishing urban history owes much to the vision of Richard Fisher. His support for my endeavours was invaluable. At key moments, Vicky Cuthill, Sophie Read and Elizabeth Howard also offered their advice and encouragement unstintingly. In the later stages of production it has been Linda Randall to whom I owe an even greater debt since, despite my years of experience as a journal editor, her acute reading of the typescript has resolved many inconsistencies in style and format.

Subsidies, then, from many directions and in a variety of forms have contributed to this book. To all, whether individuals or institutions, I am most appreciative of the support I have received.

The book is dedicated to Anna Rodger and Euan Rodger for whom Edinburgh also holds a fascination and whose affectionate encouragement has meant a great deal to me.

Abbreviations

ACC	accession number
BS	Building Society
DGC	Dean of Guild Court
ECA	Edinburgh City Archives
ECBC	Edinburgh Co-operative Building Company
ECL	Edinburgh Central Library, Edinburgh Room
GG	George Grindlay's Trust
GHH	George Heriot's Hospital
GPIC	General Property Investment Company
GWH	George Watson's Hospital
HL	House of Lords
JGH	James Gillespie's Hospital
MC	Merchant Company of Edinburgh
MMH	Merchant Maiden Hospital
MOH	Medical Officer of Health
NAS	National Archives of Scotland (formerly Scottish Record Office (SRO))
NLS	National Library of Scotland
PP	*Parliamentary Papers*
RCAHMS	Royal Commission on Ancient and Historical Monuments of Scotland
RHP	Register House Plans
RS	Register of Sasines
SL	Search List, Edinburgh City Archives
SLBS	Scottish Lands and Buildings Society
SLEC	Scottish Land Enquiry Committee
TCM	Town Council Minutes
TLC	Trinity Land Company
VR	Valuation Rolls

Part 1

Urban frameworks

1   Introduction

> The development of institutions like property rights . . . was critical to the rise of the West.
>
> F. Fukuyama, *Trust: The Social Virtues and the Creation of Prosperity* (Harmondsworth 1995), 223.

The construction of the state in nineteenth-century Britain relied heavily on the cities.[1] It was there that intervention in housing, health and public utilities and social policy generally first was tested once it was deemed necessary to ameliorate the adverse human consequences of laissez-faire capitalism. To implement social and environmental policies town councils formed boards and created commissioners to oversee the delivery of local services: gas, water, tramways and electrical power generation had their commissioners; sewers, cemeteries and slaughterhouses possessed their executives; and the civilising missions of libraries and museums, galleries and schools were administered by municipal agencies too.[2] This civic empire was supervised by a new breed of Victorian barons, the town clerks and city engineers, whose fiefdoms were extensive by the end of the nineteenth century. Their administrative tentacles were everywhere.

This dawn to dusk version of enlarged civic responsibilities harnessed local pride and preserved a strong measure of local autonomy yet bound, though did not shackle, the interests of the municipality to those of the state. Considerable autonomy was gained by newly constituted local councils from the 1830s in return for a degree of administrative conformity.[3] As a result, locally delivered services were decided locally as first middle-class and, much later, working-class candidates were elected and appointed to the executive machinery of boards of governors and

---

[1] A. Sutcliffe, 'In pursuit of the urban variable', in D. Fraser and A. Sutcliffe, eds., *The Pursuit of Urban History* (London 1983), 234–63.

[2] W. H. Fraser, 'Municipal socialism and social policy', in R. J. Morris and R. Rodger, eds., *The Victorian City: A Reader in British Urban History, 1820–1914* (Harlow 1993), 258–80; D. Fraser, *Power and Authority in the Victorian City* (Oxford 1979), 149–73.

[3] G. Morton, *Unionist Nationalism: Governing Urban Scotland 1830–1860* (East Linton 1999).

commissioners. It was a Victorian version of a 'stakeholder' society in which participation meant compliance with the decision-making process and policy goals.

The present study moves away decisively from public policy and the origins of 'municipal socialism' to put considerable emphasis on the legal and institutional structures within which urban development took place. Trusts, educational endowments and charities provided resources and leadership in the city and so contributed to its identity. These institutions operated in a time frame which was often two or three generations, centuries in some cases, and so provided a stability and strategic continuity within the social and political structure of towns and cities generally, and in Edinburgh particularly. Nor were institutions just a nineteenth-century counterweight of conservatism in a rapidly changing world. They were active, innovative and responsive economic agencies in their own right with resources which were often substantial, greater occasionally than even the town council itself.

So to presume that the family firm or joint stock company was the normal form of business development and wealth creation in Britain is to overlook the contribution of institutions to the economic climate of a city, to its infrastructure, to the social order, personal networks and the basis of trust which underpinned commercial activity. This is not unlike another line of argument, that clubs, societies and associations produced overlapping networks, formal and informal, by which influential individuals forged alliances in business and politics, and in so doing shaped the identity of the town or city. In church and chapel, at the 'Lit and Phil' or the subscription concert, different sub-sets of the middle class established cordial working relationships.[4] Pluralism flourished in the late eighteenth- and early nineteenth-century city, and institutional and trust-based relationships were instrumental in this.

The present study of trusts and endowments emphasises a consensual approach to social and economic relations rather than a conflictual one as previously embedded in class-based studies of towns and cities organised around tensions between capital and labour.[5] This is not to deny conflict,

[4] R. J. Morris, 'Clubs, societies and associations', in F. M. L. Thompson, ed., *The Cambridge Social History of Britain 1750–1950* (Cambridge 1990), vol. III, 395–443; J. Barry, 'Bourgeois collectivism? Urban association and the middling sort', in J. Barry and C. Brooks, eds., *The Middling Sort of People: Culture, Society and Politics in England 1550–1800* (London 1994), 64–112.

[5] See, for example, J. Foster, *Class Struggle and the Industrial Revolution: Early English Capitalism in Three English Towns* (London 1974); P. Joyce, *Work, Society and Politics: The Culture of the Factory in Later Victorian England* (London 1980); R. Price, *Masters, Unions and Men: Work Control in Building and the Rise of Labour 1830–1914* (Cambridge 1980); T. Koditschek, *Class Formation and Urban Industrial Society: Bradford 1750–1850* (Cambridge 1990).

nor to downplay market forces, nor to reject analyses of municipal intervention as public reactions to unacceptable private actions. It is to offer a corrective to the significant omission of trust-based institutions such as incorporations, charities and livery companies which were present throughout urban Britain during the nineteenth century.[6]

Institutions contributed significantly to the character of towns and cities because they shielded 'an unusually stable and diverse civil society from the arrogance of the politicians in temporary command of the state'.[7] Often, these institutions embodied values and followed principles at variance with market economics, and governors, trustees and commissioners, together with councillors, provided a countervailing ideology to the centralising tendency of Westminster. A British version of checks and balances existed in the nineteenth century, therefore, through the intersection of institutional, private enterprise and municipal or public agendas. The effect of this can be more clearly understood in our own recent experience, the 1980s and 1990s, when the decommissioning of boards and consultative bodies, and their replacement by unelected and unaccountable agencies, enabled a small group of powerful ministers to determine national policy.[8] An 'elective dictatorship' consciously diminished the checks and balances on its authority. This 'hollowing out' of the state by dismantling the institutional fabric of society was the converse of the nineteenth-century process by which the state was assembled through the creation of public bodies, institutions and pressure groups.

Pluralism and social cohesion in the city were powerfully influenced by the scale and nature of the institutions within it. A temporal horizon of generations and adherence to a set of principles established in a will or trust deed produced a sense of direction and a continuity of purpose which mediated changes in, say, the work practices and family structures associated with industrial change at the beginning of the nineteenth century. Whatever social and economic wreckage was wrought by war and technological change, trusts and charities resolutely pursued their benefactors' intentions. In a changeable world they were unchanging in their central characteristics. This was an externality in which all who inhabited the city participated and precisely why 'the development of

---

[6] M. Gorsky, *Patterns of Philanthropy: Charity and Society in Nineteenth-Century Bristol* (Woodbridge 1999); S. Yeo, 'Working class association, private capital, welfare and the state in the late-nineteenth and twentieth centuries', in N. Parry *et al.*, eds., *Social Work, Welfare and the State* (London 1979); R. J. Morris, 'Voluntary societies and British urban elites 1780–1850: an analysis', *Historical Journal*, 26, 1983, 95–118.

[7] D. Marquand, 'Commentary: after Tory Jacobinism', *Political Quarterly*, 65, 1994, 125.

[8] R. A. W. Rhodes, 'Hollowing out the state: the changing nature of public service in Britain', *Political Quarterly*, 65, 1994, 138–51.

institutions like property rights, contract, and a stable system of commercial law was critical to the rise of the West'.[9]

These long-term horizons and a steadfast adherence to the terms of the will ensured that institutions such as trusts and charities contributed to the climate of gradualism and tolerance in nineteenth-century Britain which enabled liberal political institutions to flourish.[10] Yet, conversely, the very persistence 'of a large number of very rich intermediate organizations [during] industrialization', it has been argued, 'balkanized British society' in the twentieth century since the same longevity associated with trusts, charities, clubs and churches also perpetuated fissures between different social classes and interest groups.[11]

Institutions were administered by trustees to execute the wishes of an individual. The trust was established to sustain the lifestyle of family members in the form of a private fund administered for their benefit, or, more expansively, for the benefit of the community, however defined. Procedures were developed, rules drawn up; minutes and accounts were presented and decisions ratified.[12] In short, institutions were the progenitors of bureaucracy and were based on defined jurisdictions and regulations. They were rule bound, as examples of trust administration in Edinburgh show.[13] Institutions were founded on order and procedure, epitomised rationality and ushered in an age of municipal administration based on the same principles. Bureaucracy in the twentieth century assumed a pejorative context synonymous with the inflexible application of procedures, yet in the nineteenth century this was its principal virtue, replacing trust which occurred naturally in kinship and family relationships with a framework of regulations by which strangers could transact business.[14] Indeed, Edinburgh trustees so sheltered behind procedures that when, or if, they dared contemplate some deviation then they sought to indemnify themselves against actions in court should they be considered subsequently to have transgressed their powers and duties. Individualism was subordinated to the will of the trust.[15]

The concepts of public service and civic duty, therefore, which permeated the town halls of Victorian Britain were carried over from the

---

[9] F. Fukuyama, *Trust: The Social Virtues and the Creation of Prosperity* (Harmondsworth 1995), 223.

[10] M. J. Wiener, *English Culture and the Decline of the Industrial Spirit* (Cambridge 1981), 13–14.   [11] Fukuyama, *Trust*, 251.

[12] As an example of manuals governing institutions see J. B. Wardhaugh, *Trust Law and Accounts* (Edinburgh 1928, 3rd edn).   [13] See chapter 4.

[14] B. A. Mistzal, *Trust in Modern Societies: The Search for the Bases of Social Order* (Cambridge 1996), 65–88.

[15] ECA Merchant Company, James Gillespie's Hospital, Box, 3/8, Memorial as to the Feuing of Colinton Estate 1877, f. 19.

principles by which institutions such as trusts and charities were governed. In Edinburgh, where professional employment was more than double the United Kingdom average and triple that in Glasgow, the code of trust was deeply embedded. From the 1850s, the town clerk's administrative tentacles reached ever further – voter registration, council housing, weights and measures, garden allotments, street lighting, reformatories, regulation of diseased animals, in addition to the responsibilities for sewers, slums and sanitation with which the councils first became involved – yet it is rare to encounter cases of malpractice concerning the award of municipal contracts, stealing or other misdemeanours. Probity in public service owed much to standards set, and enforceable in law, for trustees, governors and officials generally.

Trusts were designed to transmit wealth across the generations; trustees were obligated to administer the assets of the trust for the beneficiaries. Whether as a private trust set up by a father for his spouse and dependants, or as an endowed school, hospital or relief fund for the benefit of the public according to specified criteria, then the procedures and priorities were virtually identical. Property investments were central to trustees' objectives either in the form of land and buildings (heritable property) from which rents were obtained or, in Scotland, in the form of 'feu-duties', an annual payment created by and payable to the landowner or feudal superior. Alternatively, these rights to annual feu-duties (heritable securities) could be sold for a lump sum and the proceeds reinvested in other assets to generate an income from which to pay annuitants under the terms of the will.

The creation of successive tiers of feu-duties by a process of sub-infeudation meant trusts and institutions such as the Church of Scotland were active participants in financial markets, judging when to trade heritable securities and influencing, as a result, the flow of capital available to the building industry. In addition to property, gilts, municipal bonds, bank stocks including some foreign banks, debentures and certain classes of railway shares were admissible investment opportunities for trustees and institutional treasurers. In short, property investment and development was far from being a self-contained sector and switching between different types of investments had far-reaching consequences for the property sector as it had for a wide range of industries and services.

As property investments were an active area of trusts' activities then the detailed study of these contributes to an understanding of the workings of both the trusts and the property market more generally. In Edinburgh, trusts were particularly influential and an analysis of their activities enables the motives and methods of major institutions and small private trusts alike to be unravelled. Over two-fifths of Edinburgh landowners with more than a 1 acre holding were trusts and institutions. Six of the seven largest landowners in Edinburgh in 1872 were institutions of one kind or another – they were the Crown (437 acres), George Heriot's Hospital (180), Edinburgh town council (167), Charles Rocheid's trustees (96), Sir William Fettes' trustees (92) and Alexander Learmonth's trustees (83).[16] In view of these large slabs of landholding it was inconceivable that the institutions concerned would not have an important impact on the timing and nature of property development and building activity in Edinburgh, but that they would also define, in a significant way, the activities of private landowners too. Whether such a highly visible institutional presence necessarily produced an architectural coherence in the built environment is questionable, but because development was subject to the same principles and constraints, then it certainly was more likely to do so than under circumstances where ownership was highly fragmented.

The interface between trust administration and urban development was the lawyer's office.[17] Solicitors drew up the Trust Deed and Disposition, the will, and were represented almost invariably as one of the trustees. Solicitors drew up agreements concerning the tenure – feuing – of property; they arranged mortgages for a buyer. Where an individual had funds to invest then it was commonly solicitors who acted as a banker, taking deposits from diverse lenders and channelling them to borrowers as mortgages. Clearly, given this degree of involvement in property development and a considerable element of professional trust, lawyers acted as facilitators or 'lubricants' in the process of urban expansion.[18] They were not alone in this process, however, and the roles of building associations as highly localised institutions as well as heritable security and other mortgage societies were also significant, as was the role of accountants.

Institutional and legal influences on urban development assumed a varied, but not inflexible, character and as a social construct, the law was responsive in the longer term to changing priorities and societal needs. Nowhere was this better illustrated than in 1818 when the House of Lords decided to reverse several of its rulings over the previous fifty years concerning the legitimacy of James Craig's plan as a determinant of what could, or could not, be built in the New Town of Edinburgh. In this

[16] *PP 1874 LXXII* pt III, Owners of Lands and Heritages, 1872–3, 66–9. See also chapter 3. These acreages are those still at the disposal of landowners in 1872. In some cases they significantly understate the extent of land available in earlier years.

[17] J. D. Bailey, 'Australian borrowing in Scotland in the nineteenth century', *Economic History Review*, 12, 1959, 268–79.

[18] Mistzal, *Trust in Modern Societies*, 77, uses this term.

instance Contract Law proved to be an unreliable arbiter of property use in the future and consequently undermined present value. A landmark decision, the judgement meant that, thereafter, feu charters or deeds were to become the instruments by which to restrict certain types of undesirable development. In so doing, property law evolved to protect the interests of property owners and trusts since it reassured investors that obnoxious activities could not be undertaken on their neighbours' property. Without the Lords' decision in 1818, property investment would have been impaired, funds would have sought alternatives such as gilts and, unquestionably, the long-term effect would have been to undermine the visual coherence of many Edinburgh streets since, whatever their initial appearance, without the 1818 judgement they would have been raped over the decades by successive changes of uncontrolled use. This brief example, developed at greater length in chapter 2, demonstrates that property owners were assured that their investments would not be compromised by the actions of others and that they could trust a disciplined legal code which sanctioned transgressors. Put differently, once trust was embodied in social institutions, of which the law is one, then urban development could proceed.[19]

Far from the inflexible and invariable application of legal codes and institutional procedures it was their very existence which affected the actions of builders and developers in Edinburgh. The sanction that non-compliance with the building authority, the Dean of Guild Court, might result in the compulsory demolition of an unapproved building was a sufficient deterrent in most instances to impose discipline on developers. A departure from the landowner's feuing plan could result in 'irritancy', that is, the repossession and reassignment of the plot to another builder, without compensation. Not to maintain the steady pattern of interest payments at Michaelmas and Martinmas on bonds issued for loans might instigate bankruptcy proceedings and involve the trustee in bankruptcy in the liquidation of assets in order to pay creditors. In other words, as the daily dramas of urban development unfolded in Edinburgh, as elsewhere, the full weight of the law did not have to be applied since trust between parties in the normal course of business allowed for some elasticity in payment or delivery dates, designs or related matters. Rational choice dictated that few would go to court over the minutiae of an agreement given the expense and the distraction.[20] But in the background and secure in the knowledge about how, ultimately, a legal principle would be interpreted or how an institution would function, landowners and developers,

---

[19] N. Luhmann, *Trust and Power* (Chichester 1979), 88.
[20] N. Luhmann, 'Familiarity, confidence, trust: problems and alternative', in D. Gambetta, ed., *Trust: Making and Breaking Cooperative Relations* (Oxford 1988), 94–107.

like other citizens, knew the extent to which they could press an issue. The contours of business strategy, therefore, were defined by the implicit understanding between parties. These relationships were a powerful indicator and 'a required condition [for] a society to be a stable system in equilibrium'[21] and, where mutual trust operated, it can be seen as an important form of social capital since it reduced the cost of monitoring and enforcement.[22]

Building and property development were indissolubly linked to the legal and institutional framework which operated at several levels and, in the broadest terms, the nature of property rights was central to the political discourse of the nineteenth century.[23] Best known, perhaps, are the issues surrounding the 'Irish question' – fair rents and fixity of tenure were amongst the issues as well as compensation for improvements – but there was a wider geographical dimension to the nature of property rights in respect of Settler Acts and the 'rights' of indigenous populations in Canada, Australia, South Africa and indeed in most of the 'white dominions'.[24] There was, too, a strong Scottish strand following on issues raised in connection with Ireland as debates about property rights surfaced in the highlands and islands, led to the formation of the Crofters' Commission and the issue of tied cottages, and then spilled over in the early twentieth century to the condition of miners' housing before finally being taken up in a Royal Commission established in 1911 to review all aspects of housing and property rights, urban and rural.[25]

Fair rents in an urban setting were at the heart of Rent Strikes in the west of Scotland during the First World War.[26] They were a catalyst in the growth of socialism and of women's participation in direct political action in Scotland. Both movements were the product of alienation and class tensions between rentier landlords and tenants. Direct links have been made between this pre-1920 trend in housing politics with the growth of council

---

[21] T. Parsons, *The Structure of Social Action* (Glencoe, Ill., 1949), 389.

[22] J. S. Coleman, *The Foundations of Social Theory* (Cambridge, Mass., 1990).

[23] For recent contributions on various aspects of property law see J. Brewer and S. Staves, eds., *Early Modern Conceptions of Property* (London 1996).

[24] See, for example, J. Tully, 'Aboriginal property and western theory: recovering a middle ground', in E. F. Paul *et al.*, *Property Rights* (Cambridge 1994), 153–80; D. van der Merwe, 'Land tenure in South Africa', *Tydskrif vir die Suid-Afikaanse Regsgeleerheid*, 1989, 4, 663–92.

[25] *PP 1888 LXXX*, First Annual Report Crofters' Commission, 1886–7; *PP 1911 XXXIII*, Annual Report of the Local Government Board for Scotland for 1910, lxvii, and *PP 1912–13 XXXVII*, lix, for 1911; *PP 1917–19 XIV*, Royal Commission on the Housing of the Industrial Population of Scotland, Rural and Urban, Report; R. Rodger, 'Crisis and confrontation in Scottish housing 1880–1914', in R. Rodger, ed., *Scottish Housing in the Twentieth Century* (Leicester 1989), 25–53.

[26] J. Melling, *Rent Strikes: Peoples' Struggles for Housing in West Scotland 1890–1916* (Edinburgh 1983); S. Damer, 'State, class and housing: Glasgow 1885–1919', in J. Melling, ed., *Housing, Social Policy and the State* (London 1980), 73–112.

housing in Scotland between the wars when 80% of new housing stock was owned by local authorities – an exact mirror image of the situation in England.[27] The present study explores how a growing pattern of co-operative housing, owner occupancy and an emerging mortgage market in the forty years before the First World War familiarised Edinburgh residents with the trappings of capitalism and acquainted them with phased mortgage repayments, deposit and savings schemes. It was not such a remarkable step, therefore, for the city council in the 1920s to take advantage of Treasury subsidies for private owners rather than, as in Glasgow and other burghs, to build uniformly for the rented public sector.[28]

If, rather than Red Clydeside, Pink Lothian was the political result of the diversification of tenure in Edinburgh it is connected also to broader arguments about the nature of Liberalism.[29] The reason for undertaking a latter-day Domesday survey in 1910 was associated with Lloyd George's urgent need to raise revenue to pay for social welfare programmes.[30] Taxing property and land jointly, 'a single tax', was suggested by Henry George in 1881 as a means of removing capital gains which accrued to property owners and resulted from the effects of population increase and urbanisation and not from any conscious improvement undertaken by landlords.[31] A disincentive to escalating property prices, the knock-on effects were assumed to be a restraint on rents and so to the benefit of working-class tenants. Property taxes – rates – were also spiralling upwards in the final decades of the nineteenth century as local councils' ambitious plans for libraries, new town halls, and hospitals, as well as other expensive capital projects, increased local taxes, which were then, with rents, collected by landlords. Slum clearance and town centre redevelopment added to the taxpayer's bill, but in reality the central philosophical issue was unchanged: to what extent could an individual's property be subjected to the control of public policy in the name of the common weal? Jurisdictional issues were central to property relations

---

[27] R. Rodger and H. Al-Qaddo, 'The Scottish Special Housing Association and the implementation of housing policy 1937–87', in Rodger, ed., *Scottish Housing in the Twentieth Century*, Table 7.1, 185.

[28] A. O'Carroll, 'Tenements to bungalows: class and the growth of home ownership before the Second World War', *Urban History*, 24, 1997, 221–41; and A. O'Carroll, 'The influence of local authorities on the growth of owner occupation 1914–39', *Planning Perspectives*, 11, 1996, 55–72.

[29] U. Vogel, 'The land question: a Liberal theory of communal property', *History Workshop Journal*, 27, 1989, 106–35; A. Offer, *Property and Politics 1870–1914: Landownership, Law, Ideology and Urban Development in England* (Cambridge 1981), 283–313, 384–406; M. J. Daunton, *A Property Owning Democracy? Housing in Britain* (London 1987), 40–69.

[30] B. Short, *Land and Society in Edwardian Britain* (Cambridge 1997), 19–37; H. George, *Progress and Poverty* (London 1881).

[31] Offer, *Property and Politics* 184–200, 242–53. For a summary of the issues see R. Rodger, *Housing in Urban Britain 1780–1914* (Cambridge 1995), 52–62.

throughout the nineteenth century whether they were in the form of obligatory sewer connections, inspections by officials concerning the number of occupants in a tenement flat, amendments to building plans for approval or compulsory purchase for slum clearance purposes. It was one thing to require street alignment to aid the passage of traffic; it was quite another to insist upon the internal fitments and room arrangements of the flat itself. Intra-muros and extra-muros controls in relation to housing diverged fundamentally in their concepts of property rights and social responsibility.[32]

Squalid and overcrowded housing represented the unacceptable face of nineteenth-century capitalism. It was ameliorated by sanitary policy, slum clearance and the more caring face of municipal socialism, emerging into the twentieth century in the form of cloned council estates and semi-detached suburbia. This is a caricature of the history of housebuilding and property development over a two hundred year period but the detailed studies on which it is based need to incorporate a more sophisticated analysis located within legal and institutional frameworks. This study is a start.

Contexts

The transformation of the Edinburgh townscape in the nineteenth century was a combination of redefining the old and superimposing a new built environment. This did not occur independently. Buildings were the product of savings and investment, of potential yields calculated against risks for various parties. So the Edinburgh townscape was altered as a result of economic growth, part of which involved a workforce expanding as a result of either natural increase, or immigration, or both. That workforce needed housing and it was housing more than any other element which transformed the appearance of Edinburgh in the nineteenth century. So it is essential, as background to what follows in Parts 1–3, to outline the scope, scale and pace of economic, demographic and social change in nineteenth-century Edinburgh.

As a capital city and a city of capital, nineteenth-century Edinburgh inherited the power of the past. True, a measure of constitutional power had been conceded to London following the Act of Union in 1707, though any greater congruence with England was abandoned implicitly by the guarantees of autonomy extended in 1707 to the Scottish legal, educational, financial and religious frameworks.[33] Thereafter, these

---

[32] C. B. Macpherson, 'Liberal democracy and property', in C. B. Macpherson, ed., *Property: Mainstream and Critical Positions* (Oxford 1978), 199–207.

[33] N. T. Phillipson, 'Lawyers, landowners and the civic leadership of post-Union Scotland', *Juridical Review*, 1976, 97–120.

distinctive elements of Scottish society became even more deeply embedded, and influenced fundamentally the economic structure and social ecology of Edinburgh as a result.

At the apex of the legal and religious systems were the superior courts and assemblies which met only in Edinburgh.[34] The University, and the legacy of Hume, Robertson, Smith, Ferguson and Stewart – humanists and philosophers of 'European significance'[35] – attracted intellectuals from far and near, as did the international reputation of medical science in the city. The momentum of the Scottish Enlightenment also propelled the rationalist image of Edinburgh into the nineteenth century in what amounted to a sustained public relations coup for the city. By that time the company head offices and institutional headquarters which lined St Andrew's Square and displayed New Town brass plaques had replaced Edinburgh Castle and St Giles' Cathedral as the icons of Scottish strength and propriety.

In other words, a critical mass of professional expertise was concentrated in Edinburgh as a direct result of the guarantees enshrined in the Act of Union. The multiple administrative functions of a capital city converged like ley lines of economic and social power, none more so than in the area of financial services – banking, life assurance, insurance and investment – where Edinburgh's Victorian hegemony over Glasgow and the rest of Scotland owed much to formal relationships established in earlier centuries.[36] By the mid-nineteenth century, Edinburgh had become a high-ranking international financial centre 'engrossing all the top legal and much of the top financial business [of Scotland]'[37] and possessed a status which far outstripped the regional functions of, say, Manchester or Glasgow.

Cities were the information super-highways of the nineteenth century.[38] There the gentlemen's clubs, coffee houses and pubs offered

[34] HM Register House itself included legal and administrative headquarters as follows: General Record for Scotland; Crown Rents; Hornings; Extractor's Office; Bill Chamber; Court of Session Minutes; Edictal Citations; Fee Stamp; Great Seal; Privy Seal; Signet Office; Register of Sasines; Register of Deeds and Protests; Entails; Office of the Accountant of Court; and the General Registry of Births, Deaths and Marriages. For further military, religious, scientific societies and educational head offices located in Edinburgh, see listings in *Edinburgh and Leith Post Office Directories*.

[35] R. A. Houston, *Social Change in the Age of Enlightenment: Edinburgh 1660–1760* (Oxford 1994), 9.

[36] C. W. Munn, 'The emergence of Edinburgh as a financial centre', in A. J. G. Cummings and T. Devine, eds., *Industry, Business and Society in Scotland since 1700: Essays Presented to John Butt* (Edinburgh 1996), 127.

[37] G. F. A. Best, *Mid-Victorian Britain* (London 1971), 49.

[38] See D. Reeder and R. Rodger, 'Industrialisation and the city economy', in M. Daunton, ed., *The Cambridge Urban History of Britain*, vol. III (Cambridge 2000), 553–92, for an extended version of this argument.

information about local trading conditions, investment and work opportunities, and information about where work, materials and credit could be
obtained. Powerful informal Edinburgh networks based on lifestyle,
beliefs and family contacts reinforced liaisons based on membership.[39]
Not to be in touch with sources of commercial intelligence incurred an
unnecessary risk for business and from the second quarter of the nineteenth century the proliferation of trade directories, masonic lodges and
associations of employers was indicative of the need for business news.
Information concerning risk and uncertainty, key variables in business
survival, was evaluated more fully where bankers, insurance agents,
brokers, merchants and distributors co-existed in close proximity. Just
how significant these information-oriented professionals were has
recently been demonstrated in a study which claims that knowledge-
based human capital, as represented by professional groups, exerted a
systematic, positive influence on the long-run growth of British cities generally.[40] Thus the conventional role of commerce as a spur to the expansion of the professions was reversed:

The talk of the bourgeoisie, not the smoke of the factory, was the defining characteristic of the modern city economy.[41]

Just as the physical proximity provided by urban locations offered cost-
reducing 'external economies' to industrial producers, so, too, cities
offered a mental proximity which was indispensable to the professional
classes. Indeed, this was Edinburgh's 'comparative advantage'. Associated with it was a congenial cultural milieu, itself further enhanced by
the town council's sponsorship of the New Town development from 1765
which provided both a considerable infrastructural investment and a
form of subsidy to the middle and upper-middle classes who took up residence there.

Before the New Town was built, the physical extent of the built-up area
of Edinburgh had changed little since medieval times (fig.1.1).
Reincarnated, medieval merchants would have been able easily to find
their way around eighteenth-century Edinburgh, the second ranked
British city in terms of population. The city remained a compact settlement along a 1,500 yard spine, the High Street, and from which ran
almost 300 narrow alleys known as 'closes' or 'wynds', which on the south

[39] E. C. Sanderson, *Women and Work in Eighteenth Century Edinburgh* (Basingstoke 1996),
168–72; Houston, *Social Change*, 101–2 and 214–33; S. Nenadic, 'The small family firm
in Victorian Britain', *Business History*, 35, 1993, 86–114.
[40] C. J. Simon and C. Nardinelli, 'The talk of the town: human capital, information and the
growth of English cities 1861–1961', *Explorations in Economic History*, 33, 1996,
384–413.   [41] Simon and Nardinelli, 'The talk of the town'.

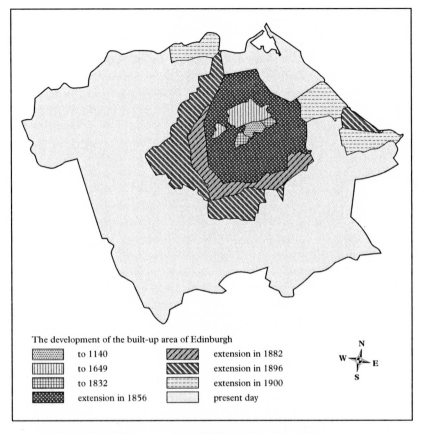

The development of the built-up area of Edinburgh

▦	to 1140	▨	extension in 1882
▥	to 1649	▧	extension in 1896
▦	to 1832	▤	extension in 1900
▦	extension in 1856	☐	present day

N
W — E
S

Figure 1.1 The expansion of Edinburgh 1140–1914

Source: Map of Edinburgh Tramways by W. & A. K. Johnson 1920.

connected to a secondary thoroughfare, the Cowgate (fig. 1.2).[42] Old Town tenements housed a society segregated on a vertical basis, with the lowest classes on the ground and attic floors and the more well-to-do in first floor flats.[43] While the common stair and street entrances provided only a very limited degree of social intermixing, the condition of the poor was an inescapable feature of tenement life for all sections of Old Town society. Though New Town apartments were finely stratified to take account of different income and status levels, and notwithstanding the

[42] M. Lynch, *Scotland* (London 1991), 176; J. Gilhooley, *A Directory of Edinburgh in 1752* (Edinburgh 1989).
[43] T. C. Smout, *A History of the Scottish People 1560–1830* (London 1972), 370.

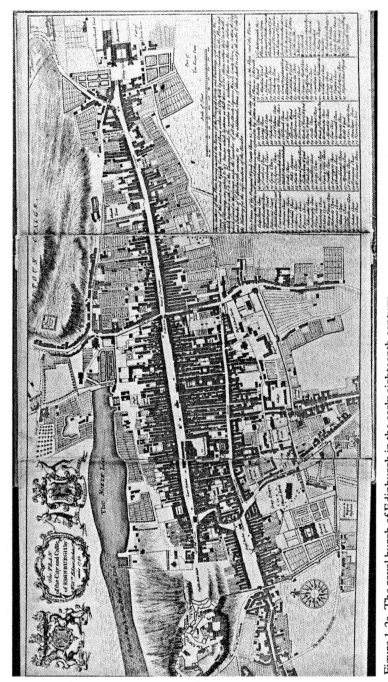

Figure 1.2a The royal burgh of Edinburgh in the early eighteenth century

Source: Edinburgh City Libraries, William Edgar's 'Plan of the city and castle of Edinburgh', 1742.

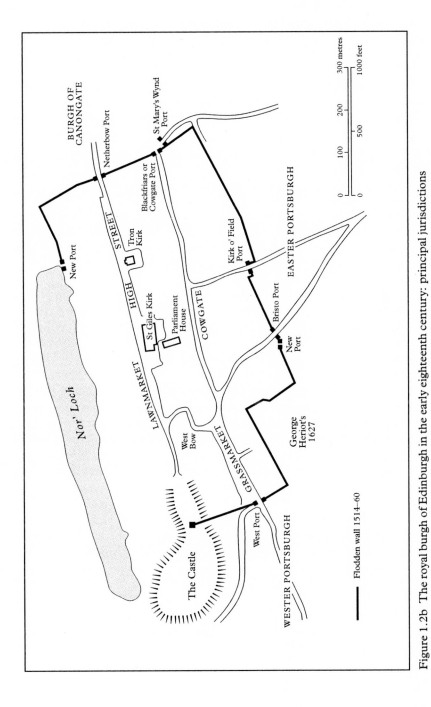

Figure 1.2b The royal burgh of Edinburgh in the early eighteenth century: principal jurisdictions

Source: redrawn from R. Houston, *Social Change in the Age of Enlightenment: Edinburgh, 1660–1760* (Oxford 1994), 106.

numerous subdivisions of flats in the 1820s or the commercial activities which took place in the mews and back lanes, the New Town offered a 'gentility quotient' or cultural haven for residents, a significant number of whom were annuitants. In effect, the New Town was a municipally sponsored suburb built between the 1760s and the 1820s before the concept, far less the reality, was far advanced in London or other English cities (table 1.1). By 1830, therefore, the 'capitalists, bankers, professional and other educated' individuals who constituted the middle class in table 1.1 were already well established in the New Town, and the process of social stratification was so highly developed that in the Old Town and Canongate only one in twenty could be described as middle class.

For the city as a whole the power and influence of the Edinburgh middle classes is difficult to exaggerate. They represented 20.8% of the population of Edinburgh in 1830 – more than three and a half times the proportion in Glasgow (5.9%), and throughout the nineteenth century approximately one male in eight was employed in professional work, again far more than in any other Scottish, or indeed British, city.[44]

Salaried employment was almost synonymous with security of employment. Security of employment meant stability of income, which in turn meant the predictability of expenditure, particularly that associated with rent agreements. So even if the gross annual incomes for wage and salary earners were identical, the predictable rhythm by which the salaried employee was paid meant that his average affordable rent was above that of the waged worker. As a result, the standard of accommodation of the salaried worker was higher, domestic space more generous, and this improved physical environment meant that his children were heavier, taller and less susceptible to a range of medical conditions. Even among the different echelons within the working classes the relationship between the way pay was phased and family welfare was evident. For example, the schoolchildren of the regularly paid skilled working classes of Broughton were one to three inches taller than the offspring of the unskilled, casually employed and irregularly paid parents in the North Canongate.[45] So the composition of the workforce, and particularly the important salaried component, was a critical element in the socio-spatial character of the city and in the physical well-being of its residents. It was a relationship which

[44] *PP 1833 XXXVII*, Census of Great Britain 1831, 970–3. N. J. Morgan and R. Trainor, 'The dominant classes', in W. H. Fraser and R. J. Morris, eds., *People and Society in Scotland*, vol. II (Edinburgh 1990), 106, cite the percentage of the employed male workforce aged over twenty as 20.4%. However, this includes Leith. As for Scotland as a whole, the middle classes represented 5.3%.

[45] City of Edinburgh Charity Organisation Society, *Report on the Physical Condition of Fourteen Hundred Schoolchildren in the City together with Some Account of their Homes and Surroundings* (London 1906).

Table 1.1 *Social segregation in Edinburgh 1831 (middle-class concentrations by parish)*

Parish	% middle class	% shopkeeping handicraft
Extended royalty (New Town)	40.0	42.9
St Mary's	62.7	25.2
St Stephen's	44.2	34.8
St George's	34.4	42.2
St Andrew's	26.5	60.5
Ancient royalty (Old Town)	5.5	65.0
Lady Yester's	10.7	62.5
High Church	9.3	72.2
Old Church	7.2	58.9
Tolbooth	7.2	64.3
Canongate[a]	6.2	69.6
New Greyfriars	6.1	49.4
New North	5.5	62.4
Old Greyfriars	3.8	67.9
College	2.8	70.6
Tron	1.2	64.2
Suburbs – St Cuthbert's[b]	21.8	55.1
Edinburgh average	20.8	55.5

[a] Canongate was, strictly, another 'suburb' but as an extension of High St/ Cowgate is treated as part of the ancient royalty here.

[b] St Cuthbert's was described as 'suburban' in 1831 and as neither in the ancient nor the extended royalty. There was a very substantial population of over 70,000, however, with over 20,000 added in the 1821–31 years.

Source: PP 1833 XXXVII, Census of Great Britain 1831, 970–2.

applied with equal force, if differing local conditions, in Glasgow and Aberdeen, as it did, too, in England.[46]

The salary 'bargain' in contrast to the wage bargain meant not only higher incomes but also different terms of engagement – regular hours, notice of termination, payment in lieu of notice, pension entitlements in certain professions, an element of discretion regarding deductions for unpunctuality and censure rather than sacking over minor misdemeanours. In addition, a degree of regulated entry by means of educational

[46] Dundee Social Union, *Report on Housing, Industrial Conditions and Medical Inspection of School Children* (Dundee 1905), and Scotch Education Department, *Report as to the Physical Condition of Children Attending the Public Schools of the School Board for Glasgow* (HMSO 1907), Cd 3637.

qualifications, articles, ordination and probationary service insulated the professions further against the vagaries of the trade cycle and the over-supply of labour in their field. As one commentator remarked in 1885:

The city has a calm, steady character in keeping with the predominance of legal, educational, literary and artistic pursuits, from which it derives its chief mainte-nance, and contrasts boldly with the fluctuations, excitements and mercantile convulsions which produce so much vicissitude in manufacturing towns.[47]

This cyclical insulation was enhanced by secular growth, that is, as the service sector in Edinburgh also expanded to meet the needs of a matur-ing industrial economy. By 1911, commercial clerks were the single most numerous occupation for men, and for women were second only to domestic service.[48] But the ranks of those on steady incomes were swelled by the inspectors and managers of municipal departments and public utilities such as gas, water, fire, police, building control, licensing, slaugh-terhouses and tramway operation, as well as by the more specialist staffing associated with Victorian institutional administration in prisons, asylums, sanatoria, hospitals and public health.[49] The quantitative and qualitative impact of professional employment on Edinburgh were defining characteristics:

There can be no doubt that it was the metropolitan role of Edinburgh which gave the Lothian economy its structural similarity to the south east of England.[50]

The significance of this hard core of professional occupations extended far beyond their own class since the strength and stability of demand for a broad range of goods and services had multiplier effects for the local economy. Edinburgh, as one observer noted in 1885, was 'the greatest retail shopkeeping centre out of London'[51] and so 'small-scale crafts, catering for a "luxury" market, constituted an important part of this employment'.[52] So, too, were printing, lithography, book-binding, por-traiture and picture-framing, watchmaking, jewellery, precious metal-working, the furniture trades, bespoke clothing and a host of other highly specific activities, including house repairs and maintenance, hairdressing, gardening and domestic service itself, each of which was heavily depen-dent upon the consumption patterns of Edinburgh professionals.[53]

[47] F. H. Groome, ed., *Ordnance Gazetteer of Scotland* (Edinburgh 1885), 354, quoted in R. Q. Gray, *The Labour Aristocracy in Victorian Edinburgh* (Oxford 1976), 18.
[48] *PP 1913 LXXX*, Census of Scotland, 1911, tables D, E, 10–11.
[49] R. Rodger, 'Employment, wages and poverty in the Scottish cities 1841–1914', in G. Gordon, ed., *Perspectives of the Scottish City* (Aberdeen 1985), 25–63.
[50] C. H. Lee, 'Modern economic growth and structural change in Scotland: the service sector reconsidered', *Scottish Economic and Social History*, 3, 1983, 115–35.
[51] Groome, *Ordnance Gazetteer*, 517.   [52] Gray, *The Labour Aristocracy*, 21.
[53] These included, for example, in 1881, artificial flower makers (8); bird and animal

The symbiosis of secure white-collar incomes, highly skilled handicraft and finishing trades and numerous independent and small-scale units of production meant it was not just the households of the middle classes and 'labour aristocracy' of Edinburgh which enjoyed predictable incomes and dependable standards of living. The entire tone of the local economy displayed a greater measure of stability compared to other urban centres and unskilled industrial workers and general labourers such as porters, messengers, watchmen, carters and even street vendors experienced a limited gain from 'trickle-down' effects.[54] This extended to the poor in Edinburgh who in the 1870s received three times as much parochial medical aid per 1,000 population as in Glasgow, and were the recipients of approximately £0.25 million of annual assistance from 150 charities in the 1900s.[55] These were yet further indicators of the comfortable lifestyles in the capital, and for whatever motives, of middle-class efforts to improve marginally the comfort of others.

The industrial interests of Edinburgh were almost invariably presented as weak and the assessment in a guide book of 1849 was not untypical: Edinburgh's 'manufactures are few and on a limited scale'.[56] Another mid-Victorian observer explained the prosperity of different cities on the basis that 'twas cotton that did it' for Liverpool and Manchester, 'twas pig-iron that did it' for Glasgow, whereas 'twas quarrels that did it' for Edinburgh.[57] The capital city was perceived as 'a huge manufactory of litigation'.[58] Yet this overlooked the fact that three in five men and two in five employed women worked in industrial occupations (table 1.2). In mid-century, textiles and clothing occupied 13 out of every 100 in the workforce, food and drink occupied 8 workers and engineering, a crucial source of support and innovation for a wide range of industrial and commercial activities, throughout the century employed 6 out of every 100

stuffers (15); baby carriage manufacturers (29); billiard table makers (4); cabinetmakers (167); carvers, gilders and picture framers (46); fishing tackle makers (16); gunmakers (8); gardeners (75); hotels (90) and refreshment rooms (67); musical instrument makers (29); photographers (43); pocketbook/jewel casemakers (16); umbrella makers (16). See *Edinburgh and Leith Post Office Directory*, 1881.

54   *PP 1913 LXXX*, Census of Scotland, 1911, table D, 10, shows that there was an 18% increase in employment for this group in contrast to a general decline between 1901 and 1911.

55   S. Blackden, 'The poor law and health: a survey of parochial medical aid in Glasgow 1845–1900', in T. C. Smout, ed., *The Search for Wealth and Stability: Essays in Economic and Social History Presented to M. W. Flinn* (London 1979), 262, and H. L. Kerr, 'Edinburgh', in H. Bosanquet, ed., *Social Conditions in Provincial Towns* (London 1912), 56–8.

56   T. and W. McDowall, *New Guide to Edinburgh* (Edinburgh 1849), 10. See also Kerr, 'Edinburgh', 55.

57   J. Heiton, *The Castes of Edinburgh* (Edinburgh 1861), 281–2.

58   Heiton, *Castes*, 177.

Table 1.2 *Occupational structure of Edinburgh 1841–1911[a]*

	% employment by sector							
	Males				Females			
	Profes-sional	Dom-estic	Comm-ercial	Indus-trial	Profes-sional	Dom-estic	Comm-ercial	Indus-trial
1841	13.3	6.5	14.1	63.3	1.9	70.4	2.7	23.6
1861[b]	14.5	2.4	14.4	57.6	3.5	52.3	6.2	35.5
1871	12.7	3.7	16.4	63.9	4.2	55.2	5.3	34.3
1881	14.9	3.9	16.4	63.2	10.8	49.3	2.7	36.6
1891	15.6	2.6	18.8	61.5	10.7	45.9	3.8	39.3
1901	11.1	1.9	22.8	62.6	8.0	42.5	6.8	42.4
1911	15.5	2.5	15.9	64.2	9.7	39.8	2.4	45.0

[a] For comparisons with Glasgow, Dundee and Aberdeen see R. Rodger, 'Employment, wages and poverty in the Scottish cities 1841–1914', in G. Gordon, *Perspectives of the Scottish City* (Aberdeen 1985), 25–63, reprinted in R. J. Morris and R. Rodger, eds., *The Victorian City 1820–1914: A Reader* (Harlow 1993), table 1.
[b] Data for 1861 is compiled on a slightly different basis and includes dependants.
Sources: based on Census of Scotland, *PP 1844 XXVII*; *PP 1852–3 LXXXVIII* pt II; *PP 1862 L*; *PP 1873 LXXII*; *PP 1883 LXXXI*; *PP 1893–4 CVIII*; *PP 1904 CVIII*; *PP 1912–13 CXIX*; *PP 1913 LXXX*.

workers.[59] By 1911, employment in the preparation and sale of provisions accounted for 10% of male workers and nearly 8% of women; printing occupied 6.5% of men and 7% of women, and the manufacture of iron and iron products engaged 5% of male workers.[60]

Edinburgh, therefore, throughout the nineteenth and into the twentieth century had a very powerful and varied industrial sector. What it did lack was a single, dominant, staple industry such as cotton, shipbuilding, woollens or steel manufacturing, and consequently lacked the spectacular boom to bust cycles which characterised such places as Sheffield, Bradford, Dundee – in fact, the majority of manufacturing centres. No single influence, no curtailment of foreign supplies or sudden tariff impositions, no new industrialising nation threatened the lifeblood of Edinburgh. Diversity and complementarity were the guarantees of stability and local prosperity.

The character of the Edinburgh economy with its complementary industrial specialisms and diverse middle-class employment possibilities

[59] Rodger, 'Employment, wages and poverty', 36, table 5.
[60] *PP 1913 LXXX*, Census of Scotland, 1911, table XXIV, 36.

Table 1.3 *Population of the city of Edinburgh 1801–1911*

	Population		Population growth (av. annual growth % compound)
1801	67,288		
1811	82,624	1801–11	2.07
1821	111,235	1811–21	3.02
1831	136,054	1821–31	2.03
1841	138,182	1831–41	0.16
1851	160,511	1841–51	1.51
1861	168,121	1851–61	0.46
1871	196,979	1861–71	1.60
1881	228,357	1871–81	1.49
1891	261,225	1881–91	1.35
1901	298,113	1891–01	1.33
1911	293,491	1901–11	−0.16

Note: for 1801–51 population figures refer to the city and extended royalty; from 1861 figures are for the parliamentary burgh, excluding Musselburgh. The parliamentary and municipal burgh populations were identical for 1881–91, but boundary extensions in 1896 and 1900 (Portobello and Granton, mainly) have been deducted from the population of the parliamentary burgh (316,837 in 1901; 320,318 in 1911).
Source: Census of Scotland 1931, City of Edinburgh, table 2, 20.

in the professional, administrative, educational and financial establishments of the city proved an employment lure (table 1.3 and fig. 1.3). Like many British cities, the highest rates of population growth in Edinburgh were achieved in the early decades of the nineteenth century, with the years 1800 to 1830 registering an annual compound rate of growth of 2.37%, three times (0.71%) the annual rate of growth for the years 1830 to 1860, and double (1.12%) that of the half century from 1860 to 1910.[61]

The diverse employment structure was also sufficiently flexible as to be able both to retain much of the natural increase of population in Edinburgh during the nineteenth century and to lure migrants to the city (figs. 1.4 and 1.5). For example, work on the canal basin at Port Hopetoun between 1816 and 1822 provided work for navvies and attracted considerable numbers of Irishmen as well as Scots from rural backgrounds. As elsewhere in urban Britain, in-migration in the 1840s was associated with famine in Ireland and by 1851 one in sixteen (6.5%)

[61] All of these are compound, not linear, average annual rates of growth and are based on census data.

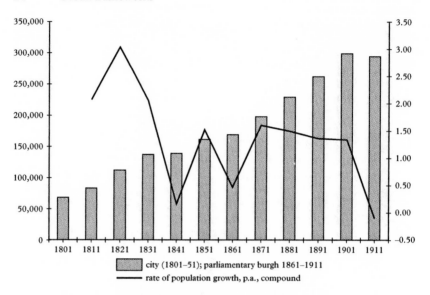

Figure 1.3 Population growth: Edinburgh 1801–1911

Source: Census of Scotland, 1931, City of Edinburgh, table 2, 20.

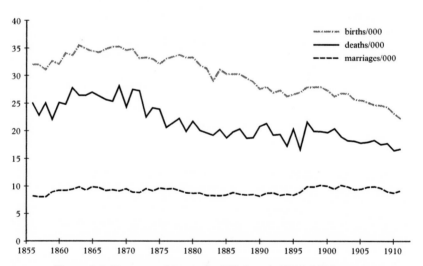

Figure 1.4 Demographic trends: Edinburgh 1856–1911

Source: Registrar-General for Scotland, *Annual Reports*, 1855–1914.

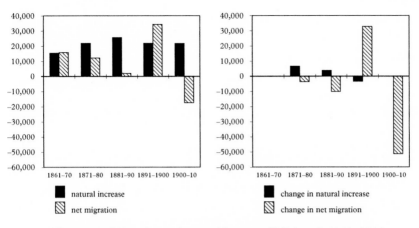

Figure 1.5 Migration and natural increase: Edinburgh 1861–1911

Sources: Registrar-General for Scotland, *Annual Reports*, 1855–1914;
Census of Scotland 1911, Cd 6097, vol. I, table VI, 16.

Edinburgh residents was Irish born.[62] The power of the Edinburgh
economy to retain natural increases in population and attract immigrants
continued in the last third of the nineteenth century, too, when the excess
of families over the total housing stock in the 1870s, 1880s and 1890s was
amongst the highest in urban Scotland.[63]

Birth rates in Edinburgh began their long-run decline from a plateau
established in the 1860s, as did death rates (fig. 1.5). No great instability
was introduced either in the volume of demand or labour supply from this
source, though the levels of in-migration did prove to be more volatile in
the quarter century before 1914. Only in these restricted years was the
ebb and net flow of migrants to the Empire a destabilising force in the
manner described by proponents of an alternating flow of home and
foreign investment – 'Atlantic economy' thesis.[64] By the nature of its

---

[62] *PP 1844 XXVII*, Census of Great Britain, 78; *PP 1852–3 LXXXVIII*, pt II, 1038.

[63] Censuses of Scotland, 1861–1911. Amongst the largest thirty-five burghs in Scotland,
the proportion of excess families to housing stock was greatest in Edinburgh in 1891. In
1881, Edinburgh had the fourth greatest excess (Montrose, Inverness and Dumbarton
had a higher proportion) and in 1901, Edinburgh was ranked third (behind Montrose
and Inverness).

[64] A. K. Cairncross, *Home and Foreign Investment 1870–1913: Studies in Capital Accumulation*
(Cambridge 1953), 12–36; B. Thomas, *Migration and Economic Growth* (Cambridge
1954), 83–122; J. P. Lewis, *Building Cycles and Britain's Growth* (London 1965), 164–85;
J. W. R. Whitehand, *The Changing Face of Cities* (Oxford 1987), 11–29.

diverse employment base, Edinburgh was insulated from cycles of economic activity which were often pronounced in other British cities.[65]

Organisation

The book is arranged around three interconnected sections: urban frameworks, both legal and institutional (chapters 2–5); building enterprise and
housing management (chapters 6–10); complementary visions of society:
housing provision by co-operative and council initiatives (chapters
11–13), followed by a conclusion.

The story, for it is that, of Part 1 begins in the 1590s. It is concerned
with a well-known problem of the Stuart kings – debt. The role of George
Heriot, 'Jinglin' Geordie', as the Stuart's jeweller, pawnbroker and
moneylender for over thirty years from the 1590s may seem a distant and
unrelated point of departure for a study of nineteenth-century land, property and trust. And so it would have been had Heriot bought the land, as
he once intended, at Gosford in East Lothian, now covered by golf
courses from Longniddry to Luffness and its more famous neighbour,
Muirfield. But Heriot's death empowered his trustees. It was by their
shrewd judgement that more than twenty tracts of land were acquired in
the immediate vicinity of Edinburgh between 1626 and 1707. Not only
did this fundamentally affect the balance of power within the city, it
meant that other trustees who sought to follow Heriot's model by using
rents to fund their charitable foundations, mostly educational, were
obliged to buy property all over Scotland, from Peterhead in the north-
east to Kelso in the borders, in order to generate the revenue needed to
sustain the benefactor's 'hospital'. This recycling of property revenue,
which is examined in chapter 2, had profound consequences for
Edinburgh, and for Scotland. 'Who owned Edinburgh?' is an important
point of departure for the study and enables the Victorian inheritance to
be better understood.

Legal changes are not produced in a vacuum. If the New Town, begun
in 1767, was to expand and retain architectural coherence then it was
imperative that property owners be reassured about the character and
future use of buildings in which they had invested heavily. To do otherwise was to risk blight and to compromise future property revenues. After
a series of court cases, some of which were decided in the House of Lords,
the uncertainty was finally removed in 1818. Thereafter, to define the

---

[65] A. G. Kenwood, 'Residential building activity in north-eastern England 1863–1913',
Manchester School, 31, 1963, 116–28; S. B. Saul, 'Housebuilding in England 1890–1914',
Economic History Review, 15, 1962, 119–37; R. Rodger, 'Scottish urban housebuilding
1870–1914', University of Edinburgh PhD thesis, 1975, 90–183.

tone and social exclusivity of an area highly specific clauses in feu charters
were essential. Property owners were reassured: development was
encouraged; finance was forthcoming in advance of construction. Feuing
was an ingenious system, which, though long-standing in its essential features, was developed and embroidered by nineteenth-century landowners and 'superiors'. Unlocking capital for infrastructure investment
ensured that long-run urban development would not be compromised by
seemingly attractive short-term returns.

How legal and institutional frameworks adapted to changing circumstances is reviewed in the later stages of Part 1 (chapters 4 and 5). For
annuitants, trusts and institutions such as educational endowments, the
right to receive a feu-duty in perpetuity was a dependable source of
income. That income streams in the future could be converted into lump
sum payments in the present meant that, on the basis of their property
interests, trustees like private individuals became financial intermediaries.
How they functioned, what strategies they adopted and under what constraints they operated is considered in chapter 4 in connection with the
activities of the Church of Scotland and a variety of private trusts. How the
flow of capital affected the development of an area is considered in a
detailed case study of one area, Trinity, and the activities of the Trinity
Land Company and its antecedents, between 1828 and 1900. Other supplies of capital for housebuilding are also examined and their ebb and flow
is shown in chapter 5 to have had destabilising effects on the building
industry.

A set of interconnected influences – land availability, institutional
agendas, tenure and the feuing system and supplies of capital – are
explored in Part 1 in relation to Edinburgh. But the processes and relationships were valid throughout Scotland. Indeed, the geographical scope
of the hospital foundations administered by the trustees of Mary Erskine,
George Watson and Daniel Stewart extended their tentacles as landowners to many parts of Scotland, as did the Church of Scotland which functioned as a major moneylender in the Edinburgh property market from
the 1860s to the First World War. So, though worked out in Edinburgh,
Part 1 establishes the principles of urban development in Scotland.

To identify demand and supply influences, and to relate these to the
operations of the law of property, provides one level of analysis. How
these forces worked out in practice can only be explored through the
activities of the developer, builder and landlord. Part 2 attempts this
through a detailed analysis of the building firm of James Steel. From
bankrupt to millionaire, James Steel's career almost exactly coincided
with the period of rapid development in Edinburgh. Steel was the largest
builder in Edinburgh and, at his death, the largest private landowner.

Each of his property acquisitions and building developments is analysed and so provides a long-run view of building and the housing market in Edinburgh. This time-series perspective is complemented by what might be termed several 'core' or cross-sectional studies of particular neigh-bourhoods – Tollcross, Sciennes, Dalry, Coates and Edinburgh's 'Belgravia', and Comely Bank. They each demonstrate the existence of several housing sub-markets, with blurred and overlapping boundaries and characteristics. To identify these and to respond to them defined a builder's longevity in a notoriously volatile industry, and chapters 6–8 identify how Steel achieved this. Several complex and overlapping strate-gies of housing development and estate management are identified in Part 2.

The analysis of tenants' strategies (chapter 9) adds a further layer of complexity into the landlord's and builder's decision-making process since occupation, social class, rent level and proportion of spinsters and widows each contributed to differential levels of persistence at a particu-lar address. Indeed, to avoid empty property was the landlord's highest priority and the composition of a neighbourhood according to each of these social characteristics affected the vacancy rate. The number and spread of Steel's rentals in both spatial and social terms contributed to a diverse portfolio which could withstand setbacks in one segment by gains in another. But even this conclusion overlooks the admixture of rich and less well off within certain neighbourhoods, as Charles Booth discovered in his poverty maps of London. Within very limited geographical areas, and even within tenements, considerable social diversity existed which made the application of uniform management strategies by landlords hazardous.

In Part 3 the provision of housing by other agencies is addressed. Co-operation and self-help were intertwined in several schemes undertaken by the Edinburgh Co-operative Building Company from the 1860s and which by 1914 were scattered in more than a dozen locations throughout the city. These co-operative endeavours are examined in chapter 11, and those of the public authorities in chapter 12 where the attitudes and motives of civic officials to slum housing and clearances is also explored. Their response, in the form mainly of an Improvement Trust to demolish defective housing and to drive new streets through overcrowded 'no-go' areas left a distinctive mark on the urban landscape. The municipal endorsement of 'Scots baronial' architecture associated with the City Improvement Trust proliferated new physical forms in the city in a romanticised national style. However, it was not just public officials who annexed the icons of authority and nationalism. Private enterprise (chapter 13) soon took up the idea and from the 1870s thistles and saltires were carved on the external walls of tenements with crow-stepped gables and pepper-pot turrets as representations of an imagined Scottish identity. Lest the flexibility of legal and institutional frameworks and the achievements of Steel be regarded as unequivocally successful, Part 3 shows how dissatisfied certain groups were in Edinburgh with the nature and quality of housing in the city. This in turn relates to the wider discourse of property relations which considers how sacrosanct property was in the nineteenth century and under what circumstances public interest transcended private benefits.

2   Institutional power and landownership: the nineteenth-century inheritance

Queen Anne, James VI and I's wife, was devoted to her dogs. Only in her purchases of jewels was she more obsessive. In March 1606 she fused both interests by spending £4.75 on silver to 'garnish' six royal dog collars and a further £0.75 for silver lace so as to reduce the friction of the collars on the necks of her dogs.[1] The workmanship brought the total bill to £8.10 – equivalent to about £1,800 in the prices of 2000. In itself, the transaction concerning the ornate dog collars had little bearing on the growth and development of Edinburgh, but taken together with other similar transactions they had a fundamental effect.

The supplier of silver dog collars, appointed as Her Majesty's jeweller in 1597 and goldsmith to the king in 1601, was George Heriot (fig. 2.1) who had followed the royal court from his Edinburgh base to London after the Union of the Crowns in 1603.[2] Heriot was not surprised by the queen's commission in 1606. Ten years earlier Her Majesty owed him almost £4,000; ten years later her debts to him had risen to £11,000 (about £1 million in the prices of 2000).[3] The queen's passion for new jewels and expensive settings together with her extravagant gifts to favourites and fondness for expensive masques produced levels of indebtedness to George Heriot which required him to arrange considerable levels of credit for her.[4] On one occasion Heriot observed that he was under 'the extreame burden of interests wherewith he is borne downe . . . and which

[1] NAS GD421/1/3/32, George Heriot's Trust, itemised account of the jewels supplied to the queen by George Heriot, 9 Mar. – 20 Sept. 1606; GD421/1/3/44, accounts and vouchers relative to the jewels furnished by George Heriot to Anne of Denmark, queen of King James VI, 1605–15. Decimalisation has been used throughout in place of £ s d.
[2] NAS GD421/1/2/35, letter of appointment, 23 July 1597.
[3] NAS GD421/1/3/9, 44, accounts for jewels supplied, June 1596, and 21 Dec. 1605 to 18 Jan. 1614.
[4] B. P. Lenman, 'Jacobean goldsmith jewellers as credit-creators: the cases of James Mossman, James Cockie and George Heriot', *Scottish Historical Review*, 74, 1995, 166–73. I am grateful to Amy Juhala for bringing this to my attention. See also D. Scarisbrick, *Anne of Denmark's Jewellery Inventory* (Devonshire 1991); D. Stevenson, *Scotland's Last Royal Wedding: The Marriage of James VI and Anne of Denmark* (Edinburgh 1997), 75.

Figure 2.1 Portrait of George Heriot (?1563–1624), artist unknown

he must shortlye paye, or perish'.[5] Only when the royal debts became intolerable to his business operations did Heriot apply for payment, prompting the queen either to pawn to him as security those jewels in which her interest had waned, or to direct the chamberlain to pay him in gold, or to issue a bond payable at a specified future date.[6] So intense was the pressure on his liquidity as a consequence of the queen's alternation between pawning and payment that Heriot eventually summoned up the courage to propose, successfully, an alternative system of allowances based on the Crown assigning taxes on refined and unrefined sugar to him and without which 'I must undoubtedly perish which I hope her gratious Ma[jes]tie will not suffer in regaird to my long and loyall service.'[7]

The pattern of conspicuous consumption was evident soon after the coronation in 1590. In May 1593, Queen Anne purchased a pair of 'hingeris for lugis' (earrings) with seven dozen rubies, a five pointed diamond ring, 'ane pair of braislettis of gold and perle' and a ring set with rubies around a single diamond – evidently fashionable since several other purchases used this combination of stones – and a number of other items. The queen's jewellery bill was £2,580 in May. In the next three months a further seventeen transactions had swollen her jewellery purchases by another £3,740, a total in four months in excess of £0.5 million in present-day prices. Seldom did a month pass when a few hundred crowns were not added to the queen's account, though it was not always for jewellery. Cash advances were also sought, often when a trip was planned:

George Heriott, I ernestlie dissyr youe present to send me tua hundrethe pundes vithe all expidition becaus I man best me auay present lie -Anne R.[8]

So extensive were George Heriot's dealings with Queen Anne that a specific apartment was prepared in Holyrood Palace for the transaction of his business as jeweller and cashier.[9] In the ten years before the Union, Heriot supplied at least £38,000 sterling in jewels to Queen

---

[5] NAS GD421/1/3/37/2, petition to the queen for payment of debts, c. 1610. There is a reference to twenty-four years service to the royal family.

[6] NAS GD421/1/3/51, itemised accounts of jewels redeemed from pawn by the queen, 1 May 1609–18 Nov. 1616.

[7] NAS GD421/1/3/52, letter from George Heriot, undated. In return for an allowance Heriot offered to return all the jewels pawned by the queen. See also GD421/3/33 enrolment of payments to Office of Pipe, London, 1623, for his farm of impositions on sugars. The queen's income from sugar was stated by E. C. Williams, *Anne of Denmark* (Harlow 1970), 185, to be £13,000 annually, in addition to her other allowances of £24,000 per annum.

[8] NAS GD421/1/3/4, letter from Anne R to George Heriot, no date.

[9] W. Steven, *Memoir of George Heriot with the History of the Hospital Founded by Him in Edinburgh* (Edinburgh 1865 edn), 7. Subsequent references are to this 1865 edition. George Heriot also had frequent audiences in London as noted in W. Scott, *The Fortunes of Nigel* (Waverley Novels, XIV) (London 1868 edn).

Figure 2.2 Portraits of James VI and I and Anne of Denmark, attributed to Adrian Vanson 1595

Anne, equivalent to £4.3 million in present-day prices.[10] In the next eighteen months to Christmas 1605 another £5,000 of jewellery was purchased by Queen Anne, and from 1605 to 1617 over £37,750 of 'dyamentis, imerodis, turquassis, and rubies' were set in rings, brooches, pendants and clasps of various kinds for her to keep or to bestow upon her courtiers and retainers.[11] All told, between 1593 and 1617, at least £81,000 of gems were supplied by George Heriot to the queen alone, with a substantial additional amount of business obtained from the king, Princes Henry and Charles and other nobles, including the Earl of Somerset and the Duke and Duchess of Buckingham.[12]

The queen's obsession with jewels was such that Heriot could not meet her demands. His acute labour supply problems prompted a national call, issued by the Earl of Suffolk in 1609, to all workmen – 'you and every of you, to bee ayding and assisting unto him [Heriot]' – to report for employment at the customary wage rates to George Heriot.[13] Far from being 'a King's man to the core'[14] and despite the fact that the king ran up debts[15] amounting to £10,000 with him, George Heriot's wealth depended primarily upon Queen Anne's fixation with jewellery. It was she who first appointed him to a retainer as the queen's jeweller, not King James, and it was her business which brought him regularly to her chambers, and gave him access to the royal family and members of the court.

George Heriot and 'lasting benefits' to Edinburgh

The significance for Edinburgh of George Heriot's business with the House of Stuart was impossible to anticipate. Though comfortably based in a town house at St Martin-in-the-Fields and a country house near London at Roehampton, Heriot retained his Edinburgh property, continued his moneylending activities to the Scottish nobility throughout his

---

[10] NAS GD421/3/5–6, 9–14, 16–17, 19–21, 23, itemised accounts of jewels supplied by George Heriot. In the years 1593–1603, the total for jewels supplied was £38,127. This differs from the rounded though unsubstantiated figures of £50,000 stated by Steven, *Memoir*, 7, and £48,000 by Williams, *Anne of Denmark*, 69. Since it is difficult to be certain that all of Heriot's accounts survive, the figure of £38,127 should be treated as a minimum.   [11] NAS GD421/1/3/24–30, 44–5, itemised account of jewels.

[12] NAS GD421/1/3/47–48, 67, itemised account of jewels supplied to the king, Apr. 1615 – July 1616, to Charles, Prince of Wales, 22 Feb. 1616, to Duke of Buckingham, May 1622 – July 1623, and Duchess of Buckingham, Dec. 1620 – Jan. 1622; GD421/1/1/5, account of George Heriot's jewels, 6 Sept. 1623. See also T. V. Wilks, 'The Court culture of Prince Henry and his circle 1603–1613', University of Oxford DPhil thesis, 1987, chapter 4.

[13] NAS GD421/3/34, warrant 15 Mar. 1609, to all Mayors, Sheriffs, Justices of the Peace, etc., to assist George Heriot in hiring extra workmen 'for the better expediting' of 'worke for Hir Ma[jesty]'s use & service'.

[14] B. P. Lenman, 'Jacobean goldsmith jewellers', 163.

[15] NAS GD421/2/33/12, copy of the king's debts (£10,091) owing to George Heriot, June 1617.

Figure 2.3 Loving cup; only remaining example
of George Heriot's work

extended residence in England and clearly communicated his intention to
buy an estate in the vicinity of Edinburgh.[16] In 1616, his lawyer Adam
Lawtie expressed sympathy for Heriot's recent illness and noted that 'it
would pleis His Ma[jes]tie to put in your hairt to cum hame & be an scottis
man'.[17] By 1621, George Heriot's resolve to invest in Scotland was much
stronger, and he admonished his cousin James Lawtie for his inability to
clinch a suitable purchase. Pilrig, near Edinburgh, had been in his sights,
as was Gosford, though Lawtie claimed that Pilrig was mortgaged, and
the East Lothian estate too expensive. Lawtie noted that 'ther ar bargains
anewe, and daylie rysing', and urged Heriot to sign a warrant so that he
could deal on his behalf.[18] Lawtie's judgement 'that bargains neir
Edinburgh are hard. Bott if ye will goe to the countreye, I shall be ansuera-
bill for bargains for twentie thowsand pundis shortlie' resulted in explora-
tory talks in 1622 with Lords Newbattle, Yester and Lothian, and the laird

[16] Some of the more prominent financial dealings were with the Earls of Nithsdale,
   Roxburgh, Marquis of Hamilton, Lord Elphinstone, Lord Erskine, lairds of Spott,
   Bombie.
[17] NAS GD421/1/4/31, letter from Adam Lawtie to George Heriot, 23 Sept. 1616.
[18] Steven, *Memoir of George Heriot*, 28–9.

of Pilrig over their lands within a mile or two from Edinburgh's High Street. Had any of these estates been the subject of George Heriot's investment in the 1620s then the face of nineteenth-century Edinburgh would have been fundamentally different.

Heriot's move on the Edinburgh property market was prefaced by his purchase of mortgages at 9% and of superiorities at Canonmills and Canongate.[19] Networking at court in London made this possible, since the superior was the Earl of Roxburgh, uncle to the laird of Broughton whose property George Heriot considered a potential purchase. Worsening health in 1623 prevented the personal inspection of property urged by his representative in Edinburgh, and no sale was agreed before Heriot's death in February 1624.

However, in failing health the inability to conclude a purchase was exceeded by a greater determination to endow a charitable 'Hospitall and Seminarie of Orphans, for educatione, nursing and upbringing of youth, being puir orphans and fathirles childrene of decayit burgesses and freemen of said burgh, destitut and left without meanes'.[20] Explicitly modelled on Christ's Hospital in London where another priority was 'for the ease and comfort of such poore people as are overburthened with many children who are not able to feede them', George Heriot laid out the principles of the foundation in September 1623 which then formed a template for subsequent charitable institutions in Edinburgh.[21] The foundationers were

to be keipte at schole and pious exercise . . . as the Provost, Baillies and Counsale of the said burghe for the tymeshall think expedient, aye and whill thai be full fyfteine yeiris of age competent . . . they may be [set] furth in prenticeschips to learne some honest trade or occupatione, or utherways send to colledgis or universities . . .[22]

Without surviving male heirs George Heriot was determined that his niece, Francischetta de Cesaris (later Crerar) could not challenge his will successfully and thus thwart his public-spirited intentions.[23] It was an anxiety his legal advisers understood, noting in different letters on the same day that 'the feir ye haif consaved that upone the deid-bed' it was

[19] NAS GD421/1/4/32–4, letters from Adam Lawtie to George Heriot, 23 Sept. and 30 Dec. 1622, 14 Mar. 1623.
[20] NAS GD421/1/1, Disposition and Assignation, 3 Sept. 1623; GD421/1/3, Testament of George Heriot, 10 Dec 1623, reprinted in Steven, *Memoir*, Appendix V–VI, 10–54.
[21] ECA MC/MMH/box /2/3 folder 3. George Watson's will charged his trustees to follow 'as near to the rules of the foundation and management of Heriot's Hospital' as possible. See also GD421/3/11, Operation of Christ's Hospital, London.
[22] NAS GD421/1/1, Disposition and Assignation by George Heriot of his Property to the Town of Edinburgh, 2 Sept. 1623. The document is printed in Steven, *Memoir*, Appendix V.
[23] NAS GD421/1/5/21–33. An extended (1624–8) but unsuccessful challenge did ensue as his niece sought to establish her claim.

impossible to guarantee the desired outcome 'for the secluding [*sic*] of your Neyce ffra all succession'.[24] Without exception, the legal opinions were that Heriot's will was drawn up 'according to the solid rewills of our law quhilk cannot be questionabill'.[25] The legal counsel concluded with a finality which also recognised that as death approached Heriot felt a strong sense of public duty:

> as the outwart man decayes, so the inwart man may grow in the graces of his Spirit
> ... and to crowne your w[orschipfull] with immortalitie in the lyfe to cum.[26]

George Heriot's immortality was indeed achieved through the pages of Sir Walter Scott's *The Fortunes of Nigel* in which 'goodness of heart and rectitude of principle' were shown not to be the preserve of the nobility.[27] Scott also commented on the 'lasting benefits he [Heriot] has bestowed on his country'. These 'lasting benefits' were achieved by the use of Heriot's wealth of £23,625 (£2.25 million in 2001 prices) to establish a hospital, and the judicious purchase of several estates to generate an income to sustain it.[28] These interdependent strategies had significant implications for the growth and development of Edinburgh.

The Heriot Trust and estate development

The restrictive nature of trusteeships meant that their investment strategy was largely predetermined – the acquisition of estates and related property investments and the deployment of revenues generated from them to the charitable purposes specified in the will. Heriot's representatives embarked upon an odyssey of land acquisition and consolidation which within a few years positioned the Heriot Trust as a major landowner, and which in succeeding centuries generated a substantial income upon which George Heriot's educational objectives could be realised.

The process began in 1626 when the purchases of eighty-six acres in Broughton from Thomas Flemyng and thirty acres north of the burrow-loch (Meadows) from James Maxwell were approved by the principal officers of the town council, all of whom were appointed as trustees for George Heriot.[29] In the following year, the incestuous relationship with the town council continued when land recently acquired by them was resold to Heriot's.[30] In effect, the councillors as the trustees drew up a

---

[24] NAS GD421/1/4/42, 65, letters from Adam Lawtie and Alexander Ramsay, both 24 Oct. 1623.   [25] NAS GD421/1/4/65, letter from Ramsay, 24 Oct. 1623.

[26] NAS GD421/1/4/65, letter from Ramsay, 24 Oct. 1623.

[27] Scott, *The Fortunes of Nigel*, introduction, xxii–xxvi.

[28] For a brief account of George Heriot's life see *The Bee* or *Literary Weekly Intelligencer*, 9 Nov. 1791, 1–4; 'Biographical sketch of the life of George Heriot', *Scots Magazine*, 1802, 95–9.   [29] NAS RH4/152/1, Hospital Minute Book, vol. 1, ff. 69, 71, 80, 82, 90.

[30] NAS RH4/152/1, Hospital Minute Book, vol. 1, f. 151, 13 June 1627.

sale with themselves for a six acre site described as 'most fit, commodious, spatious and pleasant' on which to build the Hospital itself (fig. 2.4) – the ground was broken in June 1628 by gangs of workers, some of whom were shackled prisoners, including women, and the foundation stone laid at a ceremony on 1 July following a sermon.[31] Within a few months of taking possession, Heriot's trustees granted tacks or leases for farms on the Broughton estate, and payments per acre were set in bolls of wheat and barley at levels determined by them.[32] To the initial modest levels of agricultural income the trustees also received considerable interest payments on loans made by George Heriot during his lifetime to the Marquis of Hamilton, the Earl of Roxburgh and other nobles.

In a fifteen year period beginning in 1634, the governors of Heriot's Hospital initiated an unprecedented phase of land acquisitions (table 2.1). A critical acquisition was made in 1636 when after conveyance and reconveyance, the Earl of Roxburgh disposed of land in Broughton to Heriot's and superiorities in Canongate and North Leith to the town council. In the first twenty-five years of the Trust, as the governors themselves acknowledged, 'scarcely an acre in the neighbourhood [of Edinburgh] came into the market which they did not instantly acquire for the benefit in perpetuity of the Heriot Trust'.[33]

Further land acquisition was interrupted by the occupation in 1650 of the almost completed Heriot's Hospital by Cromwell's men wounded at the battle of Dunbar, by the lessees' attempts to secure a reduction in rents to Heriot's to compensate for crop taken by the army, and by Cromwell's threat to take over the income of Heriot's on the contrived grounds that the trustees, including the town council, had not adhered to George Heriot's will.[34]

During the occupation by Cromwell's forces and with land purchases interrupted, the Hospital governors reviewed their strategy concerning agricultural rents. Many of the farm buildings on the Broughton estate were in a dilapidated state when taken over by Heriot's in the 1630s and 1640s, and some reductions in rent had been conceded when tenants objected to the governors. Robert Gray at Canonmills, for example,

[31] NAS GD421/5/1, Treasurer's Accounts, 1626–32. Steven, *Memoir*, 61, notes that since there were no prisons then magistrates punished convicts with forced labour.
[32] NAS RH4/152/1, Hospital Minute Book, vol. 1, ff. 191, 199, 210, 212, covering tacks 3 Dec. 1627 – 29 Mar. 1630; f. 220, Minute, 10 Jan. 1631, notes that 'council ordanes the pryce of fermes of broughton and lochflatt to be this year'.
[33] ECA Preface to the Lists of Superiorities belonging to the Governors of George Heriot's Trust, 1897.
[34] The 'sick sodgers' were eventually removed to the Canongate in March 1658. See NAS RH4/152/1, Hospital Minute Book, vol. 1, ff. 432–3. See also NAS RH4/152/1, Hospital Minute Book, vol. 1, ff. 343, 353.

Figure 2.4 George Heriot's Hospital 1628

Table 2.1 *Land accessions by governors of George Heriot's Hospital 1626–1707*

Date	Acres	Location	Vendor	Price (£stg)
1626	88	Broughton	Thomas Flemyng	1,876
1626	30	Lochflatt[a]	John Maxwell	1,033
1627	6	Hospital site	Town council	
1634	18	Broughton	John Scot	343
1634	15	Restalrig	John Tailzeour	422
1636	87	Broughton	Earl of Roxburgh[a]	10,500
1637	4	Canonmills, Lochflatt	William Rutherford	113
1637	30	Broughton (east, west)	John Oliphant	844
1641	12+	Fleures lands, Broughton	Robert Glen	250
1642	3	Gallowlee, north side of	James Sanders	76
1644	35	Quarryholes, Easter, Wester	William Rutherford	1,828
1644	4	Restalrig	William Rutherford	
1644	40	Broughton	John Hamilton and Lawrence Oliphant	79
1646	?	Broughton	John Stewart	844
1647	10	Broughton	Robert Logan and Robert Mathieson	343
1647		Howacre, Scabbit lands, St Ninian's acre, Sickman's acres, Ferguson's croft	James Murray	281
1649	6	Quarryholes	James Gillies	270
1649		Guid-barnes croft, Ironside, Broksboag	Peter Barber	383
1649	27	Broughton	Sir John Coupar	909
1657	?	Heriot Bridge (Grassmarket)	John Ormiston	73
1703	8	St Leonard's Hill	James Murray, Elizabeth Thomsone	gift
1704	200	Coates	Earl of Rosebery	4,972
1706		Warriston	Robert Gray	2,846
1707		Broughton	Kay lands	gift

[a] Superiorities also bought out in 1626 and 1661.
Sources: NAS RH4/152/1, Hospital Minute Book, vol. 1, ff. 251, 281–2, 293, 297, 307, 323–4, 330, 332, 337, 351, 358–9; RH4/152/2, vol. 4, ff. 26, 33–4, 46–8, 58, 61, 64, 66; RCAHMS PP59.

claimed in 1657 that the ruinous state of his dwelling was such that his family 'dare not bide anight theirin but with hazard of their lives' and pleaded also for Heriot's as landlords to 'calsay a little sluck' (pave a dirty area) in front of the mills since it was 'like to swallow both man and horse in wintertime' and indeed that he had recently lost a horse in the mud.[35]

[35] NAS RH4/152/1, Hospital Minute Book, vol. 1, ff. 417–18.

Such issues of estate management were a lesser consideration in the efforts by Heriot's to increase the yearly revenue of their Broughton property which the governors noted had been let previously to 'several poor tennants'.[36] Though their rents could not be increased while the nineteen year leases were in force, the governors discovered that 'the lands may be handsomely divided into parcils' which some of the better tenants were prepared also to let. Where tenants refused to pay their rents or to adhere to the terms of the tack, the Hospital governors 'appoint[ed] the baillies to conveen such persons before them . . . and to incarcerate them till satisfaction be made'.[37] If this was not the clearest of indications that the Heriot's Hospital governors, who by George Heriot's will included the entire town council as members, used their leverage over the burgh officials to advance their estate development strategy, then an order of the town council one month later was further confirmation. In the space of just forty years the Heriot's Hospital had established its power and authority in Edinburgh.

The relationship was not entirely one way, however, with Heriot's trustees also functioning as an instrument of the town council. Arguably, the councillors manipulated Heriot's governors, as was implied in 1637 in a letter from one of George Heriot's own nominees as a trustee, Robert Johnstone, who enquired from the town clerk how much of the Heriot estate was by then in the hands of the town council.[38] The implication that the councillors' agenda differed from that of the Hospital governors, and that as appointees they were in effect a Trojan horse within the Hospital's management, was not unfounded. Prior to the sale of Broughton to Heriot's by the Earl of Roxburgh, Johnstone advised the town clerk that if the city did not purchase the Broughton property itself then 'the intended worke wil bee ruined for the poore can not live upon the aire of superiorite and jurisdiction', a clear reminder that the ancient royalty was congested, and some expansion desirable.[39]

Heriot's Hospital also acted informally as bankers to the town council. By forgoing rents and advancing sums to the council the trustees entered into a flexible arrangement to extend credit. It was a mutually convenient arrangement, though not without friction. For example, in 1674 with Hospital funds stretched to meet their educational commitments, the trustees first limited and then reduced the number of scholars while also suspending further loans to the town council.[40] By 1693, however, the cumulative debt of the town council to Heriot's stood at over £2,500, sufficient to give rise for concern to the governors who instructed the

---

[36] NAS RH4/152/1, Hospital Minute Book, vol. 1, ff. 426–7, 443–74.
[37] NAS RH4/152/1, Hospital Minute Book, vol. 1, f. 543.
[38] NAS GD421/1/6/59, letter from Robert Johnstone to the town council, 22 May 1637.
[39] NAS GD421/1/6/55, letter from Robert Johnstone to Alexander Guthrie, 6 Feb. 1636.
[40] Steven, *Memoir*, 99.

Trust's treasurer to obtain a bond from the council for the sum due.[41] In agreeing to the terms of the bond, the town council extracted an undertaking from Heriot's trustees to admit a further six boys, equivalent to a 5% addition to the school roll. By 1701, however, when the trustees authorised the treasurer 'to lend out to the good toun of Edinburgh the soume of 20,000 merks scots and what more he could spare' it was no more than a resumption of Heriot's Hospital's role as a banker to the town council.[42] The financial power of Heriot's Hospital, therefore, could be neutralised to some extent by the political leverage and authority of the town council and, though there was considerable overlap in the personnel of both institutions, they were by no means invariably hand in glove with one another.

Once the intense years of property acquisition came abruptly to a halt in 1649, it was over half a century before the portfolio of land was increased by substantial purchases from the Earl of Rosebery for Coates in 1704 and from Robert Gray for Warriston in 1706.[43] So short of cash was the Earl of Rosebery as a result of his overdrawn account (£3,000) at the Bank of Scotland that while conducting negotiations over his estate the Hospital trustees loaned him £500, and then subsequently were approached to increase this when the deal was delayed.[44] The Coates estate provided a valuable buffer to the main body of Heriot's land acquisitions, and, by contrast, a vector of fragmented landownership to the south and west of the Castle enabled industrial and commercial development to take root in what became Fountainbridge and Dalry.

The addition of the Coates and Warriston estates in 1704 and 1706, together with a small addition at Broughton in 1707, marked the conclusion of major land acquisitions which were of as fundamental importance to Heriot's as they were to the development of the city (see fig. 2.5). 'Scarcely an acre' of land in the vicinity of Edinburgh had not been purchased, the governors noted, 'for the benefit in perpetuity of the Heriot Trust'.[45] Empowered by George Heriot's will and the financial scale of his estate, and also by the complicit agreement of the town council, Heriot's

---

[41] NAS RH4/152/2, Hospital Minute Book, vol. 3, ff. 90–1, act for lending £30,485 8s to the good town and bond, 6 Nov. 1693.

[42] NAS RH4/152/2, Hospital Minute Book, vol. 4, f. 6, Warrant, 20 Oct. 1701. Hospital Minute Book, vol. 4, f. 74, 2 June 1707, notes that the debt had been reduced to just over £900.

[43] NAS RH4/152/2, Hospital Minute Book, vol. 4, ff. 33–4, 46–8, 58, 61, 64, 66. In 1703, property at St Leonard's Hill was given in perpetuity by Elizabeth Thomsone and her second husband, James Murray of Lewchar to 'be consolidate with the superiority therof ther with to remain inseparably with [the Hospital] as their own proper heretage in all tyme comeing' (vol. 4, f. 26).

[44] NAS RH4/152/2, Hospital Minute Book, vol. 4, ff. 38, 46.

[45] ECA Preface to the Lists of Superiorities belonging to the Governors of George Heriot's Trust, 1897.

trustees had encircled the city by a series of judicious land purchases. Moreover, the consolidated estate possessed well-defined boundaries, always important in the defence of a property development strategy. The Water of Leith provided a natural frontier to the north and west, the shores of the North Loch formed another such barrier and the Lochflatt lands between the cliffs of Salisbury Crags were bounded by the royal Holyrood Park and the boroughloch (Meadows) and possessed a strategic importance in that they lay in the route of any southwards expansion. The key access route to the port of Leith was controlled on both sides for some length by the trustees, and, importantly, Leith was all but encircled, even more so by the Warriston purchase, and accordingly the trustees' and the town council's strategies coincided.

Territoriality: Heriot's v. Merchant Company

On a memorable day, 25 March 1707, when the Scottish parliament last met in Scotland, they approved as their penultimate bill the appointment of the trustees for the Merchant Maiden Hospital.[46] In fact, the Hospital proposed by Mary Erskine in 1694 'for the maintenance of burgess children of the female sex' and supplemented by private subscriptions organised by the Merchant Company had been active for a decade when the parliament finally approved the trust arrangements (see fig. 2.7a).[47] One trustee and the treasurer to Mary Erskine's Hospital, George Watson, had the strongest of credentials after some years discounting bills, dealing in foreign exchange, and from 1695 as treasurer to the newly established Bank of Scotland.[48] After a highly lucrative career and close associations with the Merchant Company, George Watson left £12,000 in 1723, approximately £1 million in 2000 prices, also 'to raise a hospital for entertaining and educating of the male children of decayed merchants in Edinburgh'.[49] Just three trustees were empowered 'to compose and adjust the rules' which were 'to be as near to the rules of the foundations and management of Heriot's Hospital and the Merchant Maiden Hospital as the nature of the thing will

---

[46] Act of the Scottish Parliament, 25 Mar. 1707.

[47] ECA MC/MMH/box 2/3, quoting Merchant Company Minutes, 'Record Volume', 1681–96, 6 June 1694. See also E. S. Trowill, 'Minutes of the Trades Maiden Hospital', *Book of the Old Edinburgh Club*, 28, 1953, 1–43, and 'Minutes of the Merchant Maiden Hospital', *Book of the Old Edinburgh Club*, 29, 1956, 1–92.

[48] A. Heron, *The Merchant Company of Edinburgh: Its Rise and Progress* (Edinburgh 1903), 86. Watson was also treasurer to the Society for the Propagation of Christian Knowledge in Scotland.

[49] J. Harrison, *The Company of Merchants of the City of Edinburgh and its Schools 1694–1920* (Edinburgh 1920), 17, and also H. L. Waugh, ed., *George Watson's College: History and Record 1724–1970* (Edinburgh 1970), for brief summaries of the founders' lives. See also ECA MC/GWH/box 3/1, Inventory of Estate of George Watson, 1722.

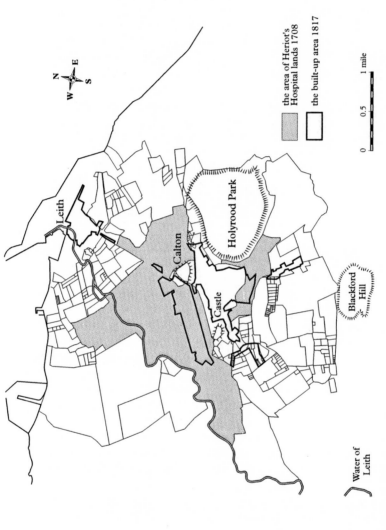

Figure 2.5 Heriot's Hospital lands *c.* 1708.

Note: the map shows property boundaries and the built-up area at the completion of land acquisition by Heriot's trustees, 1708.
Source: based on NAS RH4/152/27–31, Records of George Heriot's Hospital and Trust; Scottish National Library, Map Room,
Maps of Edinburgh by J. Cooper 1759 and James Kirkwood 1817.

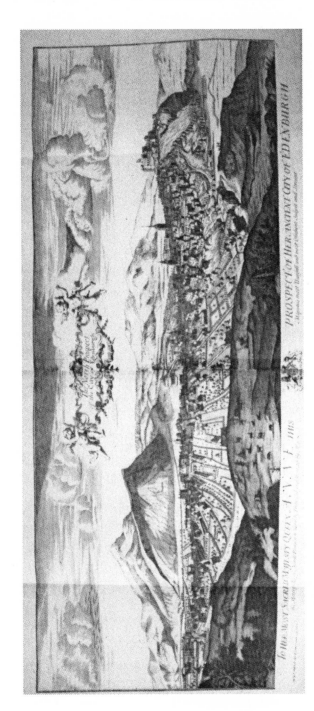

Figure 2.6 Edinburgh from Heriot's northern lands *c.* 1708

Source: NLS, Northern Prospect of Edinburgh, early eighteenth century.

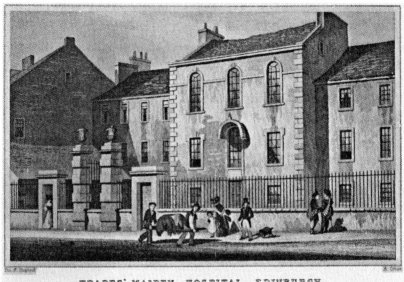

TRADES' MAIDEN HOSPITAL, EDINBURGH.

Figure 2.7a Merchant Company Hospitals: Trades Maidens Hospital
c. 1704

Note: two of many 'hospitals' founded to educate the orphaned and
disadvantaged children of Edinburgh.
Source: T. H. Shepherd, *Modern Athens* (London 1829).

allow'.[50] It was an explicit acknowledgement both of the careful drafting
undertaken by Walter Balcanquhall, one of George Heriot's executors
and the person solely responsible for drawing up the administrative principles of Heriot's Hospital a century earlier in 1627, and of the estate
development practices of the Heriot trustees.[51]

Charged with the responsibility of emulating Heriot's Hospital, the
trustees of Mary Erskine's and George Watson's Hospitals also entered

[50] ECA MC/GWH/box 3/3A, Litigation in Connection with George Watson's Will. In a
further parallel with George Heriot, George Watson's will was also challenged, though on
this occasion under the procedure which allowed any testamentary writing to be contested within sixty days of death. As fifty-eight days elapsed between signature and death,
a challenge was possible, but Watson got his niece and heir to sign a Ratification of
Mortification. As the individual with most to gain from challenging Watson's will, her
reaffirmation of its terms meant that a challenge was unlikely to succeed. Other beneficiaries, though, obtained a 'brieve of ideotry' in an effort to declare her insane and her
actions invalid. The case was contested in the Court of Session. No alteration to Watson's
will was authorised, and the action may well have been dropped.

[51] ECA MC/GWH/box 3/6, Hospital Statutes; Steven, *Memoir*, Appendix VII, 55–84. See
also H. M. Dingwall, *Late Seventeenth Century Edinburgh: A Demographic Study*
(Aldershot 1994), 264–5; R. A. Houston, *Social Change in the Age of Enlightenment:
Edinburgh 1660–1760* (Oxford 1994), 246–50.

GILLESPIE'S HOSPITAL, EDINBURGH.

Figure 2.7b Merchant Company Hospitals: James Gillespie's Hospital 1801

the market for land.[52] The town and harbour of Peterhead were acquired by Mary Erskine's Hospital in 1728 following its forfeiture by the Marischall family after the Jacobite rebellion of 1715 and conveyance to the Fishery Board, a form of eighteenth-century economic development agency which itself was soon in financial difficulties.[53] In 1729 financial pressures induced John Lowis to sell both his Merchiston and Cockburn estates to the trustees of George Watson's Hospital who, in the mid-eighteenth century, added farmland in East Lothian and Roxburghshire to those in Midlothian purchased from Lowis.[54] Land acquisitions continued for over a century from 1750 under the auspices of the different Hospitals and endowments, as was the case with James Gillespie's trustees (fig. 2.7b) who acquired extensive farmland in 1799 to the south of Edinburgh on the edge of the Pentland Hills and contiguous to the original snuff mill owned and operated by Gillespie. This pattern, of redeploying agricultural rents for the education of the Edinburgh bourgeoisie, was still in use in 1861 when Daniel Stewart's trustees acquired almost 900 acres in West Lothian. Only very modest purchases of land in Edinburgh

[52] J. R. Kellett, 'Property speculators and the building of Glasgow 1780–1830', *Scottish Journal of Political Economy*, 8, 1961, 211–32, makes similar points in a splendid account of Hutcheson's Hospital in Glasgow.
[53] ECA ACC 264, Merchant Company Institutions, Notes and Plans for the Use of the Governors, 1891.   [54] ECA MC/GWH/box 3/7, Merchiston miscellaneous.

itself – part of Bruntsfield by Gillespie's trustees (1799), Orchardfield (1801) by George Grindlay's, part of Dean by Daniel Stewart's (1836) or indeed a few individual premises, as at Bristo (1707) by the Mary Erskine's or the Merchant Company's own headquarters at 1 Hanover Street – were undertaken by the institutions which ultimately became consolidated within the Merchant Company, and administered by it after 1886. So, though the Master of the Merchant Company noted proudly at the opening of the new Merchant Hall in 1879 that 'Our Company holds nearly 8000 acres of lands, these estates being in five different counties',[55] their geographical fragmentation meant that they lacked the financial power base of the Heriot Trust with approximately 1,700 acres concentrated in Edinburgh (see figs. 2.8 and 2.9).[56]

Why Heriot's trustees did not express an interest in the Merchiston property on the southern fringe of Edinburgh is unclear. Certainly Heriot's lands were more extensive beyond the North Loch, but they also controlled the southern approaches through the Pleasance and Potterrow. Three possibilities may explain the free run which George Watson's trustees enjoyed. First, the sale of the more distant Currie estate of Cockburn was linked to the disposal of Merchiston, and Heriot's had no interest in agricultural property some eight miles from the city centre. Secondly, they misread the situation in relation to the long-term strategic importance of Merchiston as a suburb in the belief that it, also, was too far removed from the city and their existing interests. Thirdly, that their own activities so preoccupied them that they could not contemplate further expenditure on land acquisition, and that the cash-rich Watson's trustees might in any event bid up the price to obtain a toe-hold in the Edinburgh property market. There is no evidence for the first or second possibilities, but considerable material to support the third. For example, Heriot's trustees had appointed a committee in 1723 to consider the purchase of land near Bonnington Mills, and though they had 'impowred' the treasurer to bid for it in 1725, the sale stalled and was about to go to auction when Myreside, part of the Merchiston estate, also became available in 1728. Bonnington was a contiguous property; Myreside was considerably detached.[57] It was not surprising that Heriot's preference lay in the Bonnington estate, and this preoccupation with their own lands could only have been increased by a proposal in 1723 to drain the North Loch,

[55] ECA MC/box 2/1, Proceedings at the Opening of the Merchant Company's New Hall, 9 July 1879.
[56] Exact acreages for each of the acquisitions are not always available. The figure of 1,700 acres is derived from measurements of the area of the polygon based on the map of Heriot's estate by W. and A. K. Johnston.
[57] NAS RH4/152/2, Hospital Minute Book, vol. 5, 15 Apr. 1723, 7 June 1725, 24 Feb. 1729.

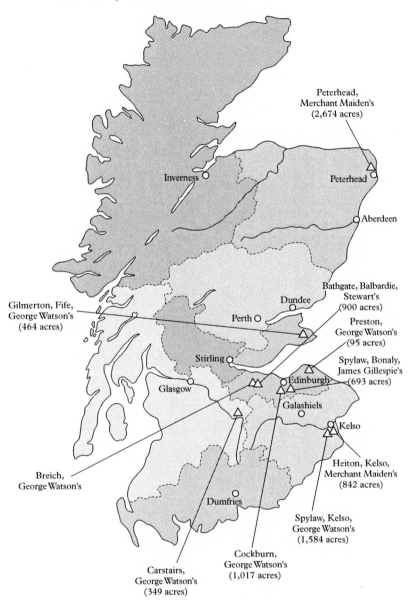

Figure 2.8 Merchant Company lands *c.* 1850

Note: extensive landholdings throughout Scotland first produced
agricultural then urban rents to sustain the charitable purposes of the
benefactor.

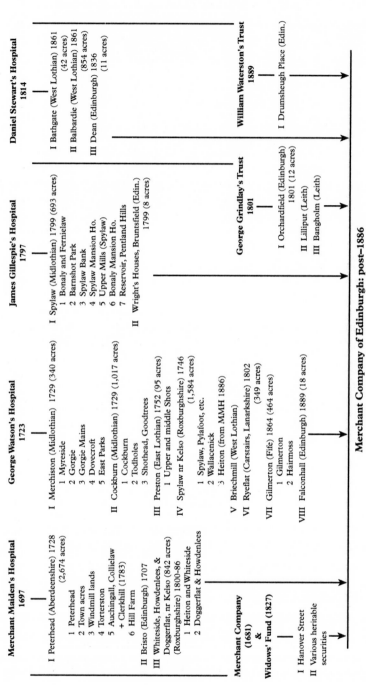

Daniel Stewart's Hospital
1814

I Bathgate (West Lothian) 1861
  (42 acres)
II Balbardie (West Lothian) 1861
  (854 acres)
III Dean (Edinburgh) 1836
  (11 acres)

William Waterston's Trust
1889

I Drumsheugh Place (Edin.)

James Gillespie's Hospital
1797

I Spylaw (Midlothian) 1799 (693 acres)
  1 Bonaly and Fernielaw
  2 Barnshot Park
  3 Spylaw Bank
  4 Spylaw Mansion Ho.
  5 Upper Mills (Spylaw)
  6 Bonaly Mansion Ho.
  7 Reservoir, Pentland Hills
II Wright's Houses, Bruntsfield (Edin.)
  1799 (8 acres)

George Grindlay's Trust
1801

I Orchardfield (Edinburgh)
  1801 (12 acres)
II Lillipur (Leith)
III Bangholm (Leith)

George Watson's Hospital
1723

I Merchiston (Midlothian) 1729 (340 acres)
  1 Myreside
  2 Gorgie
  3 Gorgie Mains
  4 Dovecroft
  5 East Parks
II Cockburn (Midlothian) 1729 (1,017 acres)
  1 Cockburn
  2 Todholes
  3 Shothead, Goodtrees
III Preston (East Lothian) 1752 (95 acres)
  1 Upper and middle Shots
IV Spylaw nr Kelso (Roxburghshire) 1746
  (1,584 acres)
  1 Spylaw, Pylafoot, etc.
  2 Wallacenick
  3 Heiton (from MMH 1886)
V Briechmill (West Lothian)
VI Ryeflat (Carstairs, Lanarkshire) 1802
  (349 acres)
VII Gilmerton (Fife) 1864 (464 acres)
  1 Gilmerton
  2 Hairmoss
VIII Falconhall (Edinburgh) 1889 (18 acres)

Merchant Maiden's Hospital
1697

I Peterhead (Aberdeenshire) 1728
  (2,674 acres)
  1 Peterhead
  2 Town acres
  3 Windmill lands
  4 Torterston
  5 Auchingall, Collielaw
    + Clerkhill (1783)
  6 Hill Farm
II Bristo (Edinburgh) 1707
III Whiteside, Howdenlees, &
  Doggerflat, nr Kelso (842 acres)
  (Roxburghshire) 1800–86
  1 Heiton and Whiteside
  2 Doggerflat & Howdenlees

Merchant Company
(1681)
&
Widows' Fund (1827)

I Hanover Street
II Various heritable
  securities

Merchant Company of Edinburgh: post-1886

Figure 2.9 Merchant Company institutions 1697–1889

Sources: ECA MC/box 2/5-7, Factors' Reports, 2/13 Notes on Company and its Institutions, 2/16-17 Historical Notes, 2/27 Lists of Heritable Properties, 3/16 Reports of Visits to Estate; Merchant Company Institutions, *Landed Estates* (Edinburgh 1891).

financed by an additional levy on beer in 1724, and the likely implications for the expansion of the city northwards into the existing Heriot lands.[58]

The Heriot Trust was also absorbed in the early eighteenth century in two controversial issues with ramifications for their long-term welfare. The newly appointed Hospital physician was 'a violent Jacobite', an Episcopalian vehemently opposed to the Church of Scotland, and in an open letter in 1713 highly critical of the head master of Heriot's Hospital.[59] Eventually, the trustees succeeded in dismissing their physician but the damaging dispute dragged on for three years. At the same time, Heriot's trustees were challenged as to the title of Bearford's Park, an extensive and strategically important portion of land bordering the North Loch and ultimately forming the west end of Princes Street. Robert Hepburn claimed he held Bareford's Park direct from the Crown and not from charters issued by Heriot's from 1641 onwards.[60] Heriot's trustees lost the case in the Court of Session but won on appeal in the House of Lords in 1715.[61] In a volatile political climate in which the Jacobite cause cut across alliances, the Heriot's trustees were involved in high profile cases and, together with financial pressures which obliged them to reduce the number of scholars from 130 to 120, were understandably reluctant to get drawn into an auction for Merchiston.[62]

Territorial conflict based on land spilled over into areas which sustained real and imagined conflicts between Heriot's and Watson's for two centuries. At the centre of the conflict was the decision in 1736 to feu seven acres of Heriot's Croft to George Watson's Hospital, on which Watson's Hospital itself was built.[63] With one Hospital beholden to the other, the two educational institutions faced each other across Lauriston Place. Given the established power and influence of Heriot's and the embryonic status of Watson's, it is not difficult to imagine friction between the two institutions and between the scholars. Indeed, this was evident half a century later. In a protracted dispute with the trustees of the Middle District of Roads, George Watson's protested that their concession of a portion of land for 'the express purpose of widening the road' was in fact used by the Roads authority as a depot for stones, and sought

---

[58] I. D. Grant, 'Edinburgh's expansion: the background to the New Town', in K. Cruft and A. Fraser, eds., *James Craig 1744–1795* (Edinburgh 1995), 12–13.

[59] NAS RH4/152/2, Hospital Minute Book, vol. 4, ff. 233–4.

[60] NAS RH4/152/1, Hospital Minute Book, vol. 1, f. 482, Infeftment of Johnes Hepburn of Bairfurde of twenty acres of Lochbank (Hackerstone's Croft), 8 Aug. 1659.

[61] For a brief account of the case see Steven, *Memoir*, 113–14. This was not the first disputed title. See RH4/152/2, Hospital Minute Book, vol. 3, f. 87, 18 Sept. 1693, case of John Gibson.

[62] Steven, *Memoir*, 119n, notes that the number of boys in the Hospital doubled from 60 to 120 between 1686 and 1694.

[63] ECA MC/GWH/box 3/9, Heriot's Croft. The Royal Infirmary, Lauriston Place, now occupies the site.

to have it removed.[64] This 'very great annoyance' to George Watson's
Hospital was increased because the disputed area

is used as the playground for the boys . . . and the easy command of the small
stones in the depot afforded to idle boys of their own age and those belonging to
the opposite Hospital [Heriot's] a constant opportunity of interrupting the boys
of Watson's Hospital in the course of their amusements and provoking them to
that species of warfare in which boys at certain periods of life are too apt to
indulge and which is often attended with mischief.[65]

Though stone throwing was suspended some years ago, sporting derbies
between Watsonians and Herioters, as well as the social and professional
networking amongst lawyers and accountants in the city, derive much of
their edge from this eighteenth-century territoriality.

An exclusion zone was imposed on Edinburgh by the activities of the
Heriot Trust's property acquisitions in the years 1626 to 1706; it was
simply impossible, thereafter, for an individual or institution to acquire
sufficient property within the immediate vicinity of the city to challenge
the dominance of the Heriot Trust. When other wealthy endowments
sought to copy the precepts of George Heriot in relation to educational
provisions based on revenue derived from property income, then the
available estates were necessarily at some distance from the city (fig. 2.8).
Where the Merchant Company institutions did hold limited urban
estates then their developmental value also lay at some distance in time,
either once suburbanisation in Edinburgh had achieved a degree of
momentum, as after 1860, or once economic development began to
embrace the townships of Peterhead and Bathgate sufficiently to unlock
their developmental value. Thus the consequences of the Heriot trustees'
land consolidation rippled outwards to affect distant parts of Scotland,
and from where rents and duties were redirected to the parent institutions
– George Watson's, Mary Erskine's and, later, Daniel Stewart's Hospitals
– in Edinburgh. It was a parasitical relationship which the final lines of the
Merchant Company song acknowledged:

> The Leddies o' Peterhead bloomin and fair,
> Wi' Bathgate and Merchiston Lairds weel may pair
> While Auld Reekie's Merchants hold princely domains
> For her sons and her daughters, her wifies and weans.[66]

[64] ECA MC/GWH, Minute Books, vol. 5, 26 June 1786; NAS RHP10232, plan, Roads in
the Middle District of Edinburgh, 1828.
[65] ECA MC/GWH/ box 3/9, Heriot's Croft. George Watson's trustees were unable to establish the depot as a nuisance, and the police authorities were not interested. Eventually, the
roads trustees applied for a turnpike act to obtain compulsorily the corner site which they
sought.
[66] ECA MC/box 2/8, Merchant Company songsheet. The 'Leddies o' Peterhead' refers to
the girls of the Merchant Maiden Hospital, and 'Bathgate and Merchiston Lairds' to the
boys of Daniel Stewart's and George Watson's Hospitals.

Heriot's Hospital lands and the emergence of the feuing system

At its simplest, Heriot's administrators may just have been too busy to contemplate further acquisitions or to contemplate a contest in 1728 with George Watson's Hospital over the Merchiston lands. From the 1690s a new phase in Heriot's property management activities developed. Before then, the trustees' management concerns were mostly of a routine kind – renewal of tacks, the installation of heirs and successors to farms and the collection of fees associated with such authorisation, as well as setting rentals and authorising repairs to cottages. The trustees differed little from agricultural factors and, in view of their preoccupation with property matters, relegated their educational responsibilities to a position of secondary importance.[67]

Evidently, there were administrative diseconomies from the scale and complexity of Heriot's property interests. However, even as the property portfolio was being extended with the Coates–Warriston acquisitions in 1704–6, Heriot's itself began to feu land. That is, rather than receive a rent from a tenant for a fixed term, the land was conveyed by Heriot's as the 'superior' to a 'vassal' or feuar for his use in perpetuity, on condition that a small annual feu-duty was also payable 'for all time coming'.[68] In essence, feuing was akin to a freehold sale, though there were some crucial differences which distinguished Scottish land tenure in fundamental ways from that of England (see chapter 3). Feuing was a device which offered security of tenure and thus little risk of loss for improvements to the feuar – something which Irish tenant farmers and Scottish crofters in the late nineteenth century coveted. To Heriot's, and indeed landowners generally, it unlocked some of the obstacles to estate development while relieving the trustees of the considerable management costs associated with the duties of landlord.[69]

In the early decades of the eighteenth century the monthly meetings of Heriot's trustees were almost invariably confronted with property related business. Increasingly this was to dispose of feus, rather than tacks or leases, and not infrequently to consider the transfer from one form of

---

[67] Steven, *Memoir*, 123.
[68] ECA Lists of Superiorities belonging to the Governors of George Heriot's Trust, 1897; NAS RH4/152/27 Cartularies of George Heriot's Hospital, vols. 1–2. The first feu charters were issued in 1644 and occasionally thereafter. The most significant, perhaps, was that to Trinity Hospital, vol.1, f. 222, 10 Oct. 1681, for Quarryholes, straddling the present Easter Road and extending to Abbeyhill. See also ECA plans, bundles 16B/P34, 17/Q5–6.
[69] NAS GD421/9/25, 27, 29–31, 33, 35–6, Estate Papers and tacks; and GD/421/9/45, church and miscellaneous petitions relating to the granting of tacks and their terms *c.* 1700–28.

tenure to the other.[70] In the 1690s, the number of feus granted by Heriot's Hospital was greater than in all preceding years and this pattern continued during the years 1700–20. As feuing business increased, that concerned with tacks correspondingly diminished.[71] The trustees were not content to leave the land market to itself entirely, and in 1698 a sub-committee visited Broughton 'and having perambulated the same it is their opinion that it will be a great advantage to the hospital and improvement of the rent that the same be imparked and inclosed with a dyke'.[72]

In some respects the Heriot's trustees acted as an agricultural improver before the concept existed. The 'imparked' or 'inclosed' land in conjunction with a greater security of tenure, as represented by the gradual transition from tacks to feus, produced a long-term framework within which their vassals could operate. Consolidation resulted. Before 'improvement' many leases were for just two or three acres, but even where tacksmen such as George Home, John Moody, Robert Hill and Alexander Corse leased forty to fifty acres, the terms of the agreement continued to identify individual field boundaries and acreages. On Moody's forty-seven acre tack the fourteen fields averaged a little under 3.5 acres; each of these was reckoned in acres, roods, falls and elns and the rent in bolls, firlots and pecks per acre, or parts thereof. After 'improvement' and under a feu granted 'in perpetuity', not only was there was no need for detailed measurements and payments to be replicated in subsequent leases, but also there was no need for the field boundaries to be retained by the feuar since they could be consolidated into a single holding. Gradually, therefore, as the practice of feuing became more common, the lands of Heriot's which gave the appearance of a consolidated entity became just that, rather than merely contiguous parcels of fields within their overall control.

The imperative of improved agricultural revenues to sustain the educational mission of the founder produced procedural changes in the 1690s in the way lands were owned. This in turn had implications for the subsequent development of the burgh, first, because tacksmen were replaced by an increasing number of titled individuals and merchants who acquired feus presumably with the intention of holding them as long-term investments, and secondly, because the subsequent urban expansion was less inclined to be incremental, that is, field by field, since holdings

---

[70] NAS RH4/152/2, Hospital Minute Book, vol. 3, f. 92, 4 Dec. 1693 'lands belonging presently possest by the said John Patersone by virtue of the foresaids tacks to be disponed to him in feu likeas [the Hospital] unannimously sell annuaillize and dispone to the said John Patersone etc.'.   [71] ECA Lists of Superiorities, 1913–14.

[72] NAS RH4/152/2, Hospital Minute Book, vol. 3, f. 171, Broughton to be parked, 11 July 1698.

were consolidated in feus and thus amenable to a more coherent strategy.[73] These estate management strategies and tenurial changes implemented by Heriot's trustees were not without important ramifications for both rural and urban Scotland.

Half a century before James Craig's plan for the New Town with its Hanoverian street names was taken to London for George III's approval in 1767, Heriot's Hospital trustees had introduced administrative and legal changes which, as fig. 2.10 shows, were beginning to display signs of long-run increases in income from land. Given the realignment of Heriot's property strategies in the early eighteenth century, together with the internal distractions of pro-Jacobite sentiments from the Trust's physician and charges of corruption *c.* 1715 on the Board of Governors, then the tactical decision not to acquire Merchiston was understandable, if short-sighted.

The trustees' decision in 1760 to feu land to the town council, however, opened old wounds and was no formality; it resurrected concerns amongst the Heriot's governors concerning councillors' conflict of interests in relation to the city and in their role as Heriot's trustees. These doubts were articulated most powerfully in an earlier episode in 1715 concerning the title to Bareford's Park, and again in 1736, when the town council sought first to take a feu so as to create Middle Meadow Walk and open access to the south, and then to obain additional land in the St Leonard's area.[74] The propriety of declining the highest bid for Heriot's land called into question the impartiality of councillors who attended Heriot's Hospital meetings. They should not, it was claimed 'sit as judges and decree their own lower offer' since this contradicted the founder's wishes. It also exposed the governing body to charges of maladministration.[75] A breach of trust was at issue and thus the risk to Heriot's of a law suit not far behind.

When, in 1759, the city applied to Heriot's for a thirty to forty acre feu beyond the North Loch, identical arguments were advanced in a protracted dispute amongst the trustees and in which the Merchant Company and Incorporated Trades joined forces to oppose the city

---

[73] A. J. Youngson, *The Making of Classical Edinburgh 1750–1840* (Edinburgh 1993 edn), xii, also makes this point, though for a somewhat later period.

[74] NAS RH4/152/3, Hospital Minute Book, vol. 7, ff. 52–77, Minutes of 11 Oct., 6 Dec., 20 Dec. 1736, 29 Jan., 22 Aug., 24 Aug. 1737.

[75] NAS RH4/152/3, Hospital Minute Book, vol. 7, 26 Aug. 1737. Though just a few years earlier Heriot's trustees had feued five acres to the city in 1730 at Broughton Loan (Picardy Place) for the settlement of immigrant cambric weavers from Picardy, and in 1716 feued thirty acres at Bareford's Park, special circumstances justified the disposal of land in these cases. See RH4/152/2, vol. 4, ff. 308–9, 326, 329, charters, Lochbank purchase, 4 June 1716, 29 July, 12 Aug. 1717; RH4/152/2, vol. 6, f. 93, petition of town council, 20 Mar. 1730.

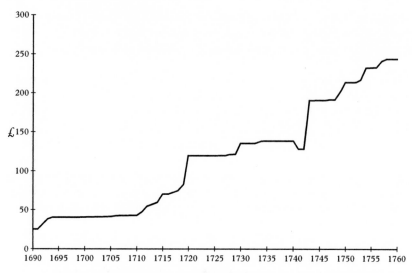

Figure 2.10   George Heriot's Hospital feu-duty income 1690–1760

Source: ECA George Heriot's Roll of Superiorities, 1913–14.

council, charging them with favouritism towards Heriot's and charging Heriot's governors with the abdication of their responsibilities as trustees. Heriot's standing orders were suspended, divisive votes cast, reports compiled and vituperative attacks launched from both sides in a public relations war conducted by pamphleteering.[76] 'After much warm discussion' – impressive for its understatement – the trustees' approval was given in 1760 to the proposals to feu land (fig. 2.11) to the council for the New Town, though legal actions including an interdict (injunction in England) then followed which held matters up for six years before thirty-four acres were feued to the city.[77]

Heriot's liaison with the city over the proposed New Town was no rushed affair. It was a marriage of convenience, for as Walter Scott later identified, the benefits to the town were not at the expense of Heriot's but of mutual gain.[78] Civic aspirations associated with the extended burgh involved substantial expenditure – the acquisition of properties from other superiors, legal expenses associated with a parliamentary bill, levelling and laying out roads, and important jurisdictional issues to be settled over tax and police matters. The front-loading of these costs, that is,

---

[76] See Steven, *Memoir*, 148–54, for a brief account of the dispute, and for a list of pamphlet titles.

[77] NAS RH4/152/3, Hospital Minute Book, vol. 8, ff. 387–8, 28 Nov. 1759, and 416–19, 423–33.   [78] W. Scott, *Provincial Antiquities of Scotland* (Edinburgh 1826), 268–70.

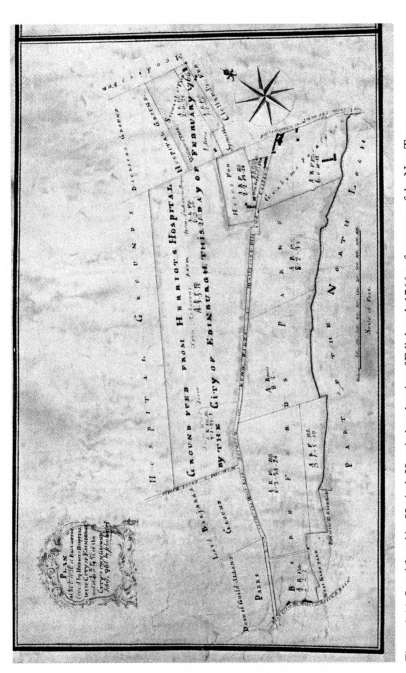

Figure 2.11 Land feued by Heriot's Hospital to the city of Edinburgh 1766 to form part of the New Town

Source: RCAHMS, George Heriot's Hospital Collection, PP6 (560487), Plan of Broughton by John Laurie feued by Heriot's Hospital to the city of Edinburgh.

before building development generated a feuing income, was beyond Heriot's financial resources and the involvement of the city fathers generated considerable momentum for the project. The drainage of the North Loch, largely finished by 1763, and the completion of the North Bridge in 1772 after seven years of construction work, involved public costs substantially beyond those affordable by Heriot's, even if they had been able to persuade a majority of the trustees that this was a legitimate activity for the Hospital.

The civic initiatives of the 1760s conveyed substantial external economies to many Edinburgh interests, none more than the future income and property development prospects of Heriot's. However, when the foundation stone of the first house built in the New Town was laid in October 1767 it symbolised a shift in the balance of power in the city. Nowhere was this better embodied than in an exchange between the respective treasurers of Hospital and city when, with a surplus of £1,000 available for investment in 1768, the treasurer of Heriot's was informed by his opposite number that 'they had no occasion for it and wanted to pay back the £500 of the Hospital's money lent them last year'.[79] Indeed, charitable foundations in general were under something of a cloud, as indicated by the introduction of a Mortmain Act in 1773 which, though it failed, sought to oblige trustees to dispose of their lands and property and to reinvest the proceeds in government stock.[80] The shift in the balance of power within the city was already visible in the 1740s as the feu-duty income which the town council obtained from its lands exceeded that of Heriot's Hospital, and for almost a century both the rate of growth and the absolute amount of the city's feu-duties exceeded that of Heriot's trustees (fig. 2.12). The anxiety which the trustees expressed, therefore, when approached by the town council in 1759 to grant them feus was understandable, especially since the distinction between the long- and short-term benefits for the trust were difficult to determine. In addition, in the long shadow of the Darien disaster, conservative investment was easier to justify than speculative adventure.

When Heriot's granted feus in the eighteenth century there were no restrictions attached to them. Indeed, restrictions or real burdens were virtually unknown and even legal reference works made no mention of them.[81] In other words, no attempts were made to regulate the future use of land, or to protect the interests of the superior or of neighbours.

[79] NAS RH4/152/3, Hospital Minute Book, vol. 10, f. 4, 25 Jan. 1768.
[80] The Merchant Company Hospitals co-operated with Heriot's Hospital to oppose this proposal.
[81] Erskine, *Institute of the Laws of Scotland*, II, 3, 19, and Bell, *Principles*, 868. K. G. C. Reid *et al.*, *The Law of Property in Scotland* (Edinburgh 1996), 378 n. 7, identifies how few cases there were over real burdens.

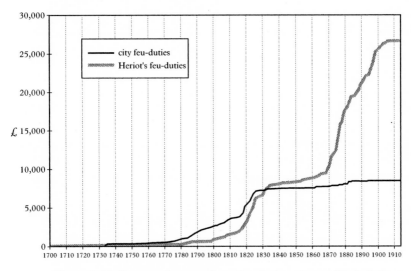

Figure 2.12 Property incomes from feu-duties: George Heriot's Trust and city of Edinburgh 1700–1914

Sources: ECA Roll of George Heriot's Superiorities, 1913–14; ECA City of Edinburgh Superiorities, 1914.

Heriot's feus were unconditional disposals of land, so long as payments of the annual feu-duty were made. To feuars this was, of course, their attraction. Development was uncontrolled.

However, as the New Town building programme accelerated after 1767 with a large number of individual sales then, in the absence of a planning code, no effective guarantees to investors existed that their house, its value and outlook, would not be compromised by the actions of other builders, or by their neighbours' actions. Indeed, it was precisely to protect property interests that a system of burdens or obligations was introduced, and its importance to the development of tenure in Scotland 'is difficult to exaggerate'.[82] As the rest of Europe attempted to dismantle feudal obligations between 1789 and 1848, Scotland was in the process of trying to reconstruct them, and Edinburgh property owners were in the vanguard.[83] Heriot's were instrumental, both directly and indirectly, in

[82] Reid *et al.*, *The Law of Property*, 377. I am grateful to Kenneth Reid for his helpful and patient advice on several aspects of the law of property in Scotland.

[83] The Blythswood estate, feued by Hutheson's Hospital under an act of parliament in 1792, was in effect a parallel New Town development for Glasgow. In this case, however, sub-infeudation was prohibited because the estate was entailed. There was a provision to obtain an increased feu-duty if the vassal subdivided the plot, but in effect the development was not unlike the feu dispositions used for Princes Street and first New Town development in Edinburgh. See *Campbell* v. *Dunn*, Court of Session, vol. IV, 1828, 679. Kellett, 'Property speculators'.

the development of property restrictions and in the creation of tiers of feudal obligations between a superior and his vassals. Redefined, property relationships in the early nineteenth century assumed a new dimension, enabling and accelerating urban expansion in Scotland. How, then, did this transition in property relations and burdens take place?

The initial development of the Edinburgh New Town took place on town council land obtained from Heriot's in 1766 and from several other owners, with building moving east to west along the rectangles formed by Princes, George and Queen Streets.[84] Whether it was due to inexperience, or to the need to generate interest in the project, or simply because the town council followed custom and practice as far as legal procedure was concerned, or a combination of all three influences, the feu charters contained little reference in their short five page length as to obligations other than that owners should maintain sewer connections and cellar supports.[85] In short, the symmetry and unity achieved in executing James Craig's plan for the New Town was not the result of detailed specifications in the conveyancing documents but of the town council's enforcement of a signed contract in which the feuar agreed to adhere to a two-dimensional feuing plan on display in the Council Chamber and 'shewn to all purchasers and feuars of building-ground'.[86]

Thus, the law of contract, not Scots property law, was the critical instrument in the development and uniformity of the Edinburgh New Town. Contract law, of course, only had force in the initial construction phase; how control could be enforced when changes of use were contemplated, or when different versions of the plan were in force, was unclear. Subsequently, the architectural rape of Princes Street in the nineteenth century was possible because such stipulations as to facades and changes of use were not embedded in the initial feu charter. That the original feuars had adhered to the Craig plan for the New Town was no impediment to fundamental changes and rebuilding as proposed by later generations of owners.

In contrast to the brief, vague feu dispositions issued by the town council for their New Town properties and in the absence of controls under Scots property law over the future use and appearance of buildings

---

[84] Houston, *Social Change*, 116–17, gives a brief account of land acquisitions by the magistrates.
[85] ECA Chartulary Extended Royalty, vol. 1, 1768–77, vol. 2, 1777–82. See, for example, charters with Thomas Hill, ff. 42–5, 9 Dec. 1772; Robert Scott Moncrieff, ff. 88–90b, 30 Mar. 1773; Sir William Forbes, ff. 156–8, 8 Feb. 1776; vol. 2, James Reddie and John Wilkie, ff. 37–40b, 4 Mar. 1778; Thomas Braidwood, ff. 114b–18b, 17 Nov. 1779; David Reid, ff. 155–9b, 18 Aug. 1780. Boundaries and feu-duty payments were the principal concerns of the charters, not restrictions on building or use.
[86] *John Young and Company* v. *Forrest Deuar*, Court of Session cases, 17 Nov. 1814, 23.

on their land, Heriot's trustees were increasingly specific, as their feuing interests developed, in respect of the design, form and use of buildings that could be constructed on their property. Developmental control by means of contract was apparent, for example, in an agreement between Heriot's and the city in 1806 covering the Bellevue area and 'land still westward' which remained in the hands of the Heriot's Hospital.[87] The agreement was not retrospective – it did not affect lands already held by the town council from Heriot's. The contract was fifty pages in length and the clauses were highly specific. The houses in Heriot Row and the west end of Abercromby Place fronting Queen Street were to be two storeys only, not exceeding forty feet on the front above the street level and the projection of the roof was not to be more than fifty-one feet at the ridge. Indeed, roofs were to be in line. Dublin, Scotland, Nelson, Duncan, Dundas, Pitt, Howe, St Vincent and India Streets were allowed to have a forty-six foot maximum street height.[88] Clause 4 prohibited stone windows or raised breaks in the roof 'in the French style' except in Cumberland, Dundas and five other named streets; except in Jamaica, London, Dublin, Scotland and seven other streets, clause 5 stated that all houses were to have a sunk storey of broached ashlar or rock work while above the stone was to be polished, droved or broached ashlar with a blocking course fifteen inches high and slates were not to project more than three inches. In twelve identified streets, sunk areas in front with railings and a ten foot wide pavement were to be constructed; the sunk area was to be twelve feet in breadth and houses could project over it by eighteen inches.[89]

This degree of detail was a reflection of Heriot's efforts to defend the social tone and extend the monetary value of their estate development by means of highly detailed clauses in the contracts issued by the Hospital's trustees. Perhaps most crucial of all, the contract stipulated the minimum price per foot of street frontage (table 2.2) at which properties could be feued. Setting the price of land certainly went a considerable way to determining its use even if, ultimately, the feuing conditions remained

[87] ECA Town Court Books, 3 Mar. 1806; NAS GD421, Contract between the City of Edinburgh and Heriot's Hospital, 12, 13, 28 Feb. 1806. A feuing plan by William Sibbald and Robert Reid covered the area of Bellevue held by the city from Heriot's, as superior. Any departure from the plan by either party required the approval of the Lord President of the Court of Session, the Lord Chief Baron of the Court of Exchequer and the Lord Advocate of Scotland, and so the parties were locked in to an expensive judicial process should they consider any departure from the feuing plan.

[88] The same heights were to apply to Drummond Place, Drummond Circus, Royal Crescent, Fettes Row, London Street, King Street, Mansfield Place, Bellevue Crescent and Cornwallis Place. Northumberland Street maximum height was to be thirty-three feet.

[89] Clause 6 allowed for different measurements, but the streets in which such departures were permissible were identified.

Table 2.2 *Prices of feus: New Town streets 1806*

	Shillings per foot
Cumberland, Jamaica, Spenser Streets	4
Royal Crescent, Fettes Row	4
Northumberland Street	5
Heriot Row	5
Dublin, Scotland, Nelson, Duncan, Dundas, Pitt, Howe, St Vincent, India Streets	5
Drummond Circus	7
Mansfield Place, Bellevue Crescent, Cornwallis Place	7
Drummond Place	7

Source: NAS GD421/XX, George Heriot's Hospital, Contract between the City of Edinburgh and Heriot's, 12 Feb. 1806.

subordinate to the authority of the feuing plan. By 1806, therefore, Heriot's had recognised how important it was to have much tighter control over building development on land. In so doing they anticipated the structural shift in feuing practice and shaped the feuing conditions which governed urban development from the 1820s.

The process of asserting urban feudalism was an extended one and began in the 1770s, within five years of the first foundation stone being laid in the New Town. Sixteen proprietors, amongst whom David Hume was the best known, were concerned for the amenity of the 'pleasure gardens' of Princes Street and their unrestricted view of Edinburgh Castle. They contested the town council's right to feu land for building on the south side of Princes Street.[90] The council's motives were purely financial – to generate more income from their feus – and they sheltered behind the authority of Craig's plan 'from which they were not at liberty in any degree to depart therefrom'.[91] The Court of Session upheld the town council's claim in 1772, though this was reversed subsequently by the House of Lords.[92] With an appeal tabled and the buildings almost finished, a compromise was agreed in 1776: building westwards beyond the line of the present Waverley steps would not be permitted but those

[90] ECA Princes Street Sederunt Book, vol. 1, 1816–19, ff. 51–119, provides an excellent summary of the issues. See also J. Hamilton, 'The evolution of Princes Street and Princes Street Gardens', MA dissertation in Economic and Social History, University of Edinburgh, 1974, 14–21; Youngson, *The Making of Classical Edinburgh*, 86–91. The properties at issue were cleared in 1895 as a preliminary to the construction of the North British Railway hotel.   [91] ECA Princes Street Sederunt Book, vol. 1, 1816–19, f. 68.
[92] *Deas* v. *Edinburgh Magistrates*, 1772 Pat 259, House of Lords.

properties under construction were to be completed 'in proper taste'.[93] In the event, the proprietors' concerns for the social tone of Princes Street were fully justified. Once completed, flats were available on the disputed south side of Princes Street for as little as one tenth of the rental of properties on the north.[94] The site, later to become the 'N.B.' and now the Balmoral Hotel, was the nodal point of early commercial and residential access between the Old Town and Princes Street (fig. 2.13). The compromise in 1776 preserved, therefore, the amenity of Princes Street Gardens by prohibiting building in the future but, more importantly, it established for almost half a century until it was over-turned in 1818 that once buildings were completed disputes were governed by the original feuing plan.[95] Craig's plan was itself a legal instrument, the arbiter of disputes.

The central legal problem was that in the absence of restrictions (or real burdens) in the feu charter itself, then how could the actions of individuals prejudicial to the interests of others be limited? The intended coherence of Craig's New Town plan and interpretations of what constituted conformity with the plan formed the basis of what could be built in New Town Edinburgh for over forty years following the decision in 1772 by Lord Mansfield concerning the disputed Princes Street site.

By 1800, with dozens of plots already constructed and building moving westward towards Charlotte Square, a number of disputes arose over the interpretation of the feuing plan.[96] One of these concerned James Gibson who refused to pay his feu-duty in 1809 because he claimed the plot had been purchased on an understanding, shown in a feuing plan, that Heriot's would demolish an old tenement in York Place.[97] That case was still unresolved when, in 1812, John Young and Company proposed to build in the rear of their Princes Street plot and to which the surgeon Forrest Dewar rather belatedly objected once he realised that the buildings would be above the height of the boundary wall.

---

[93] The limitation on building did not apply west of the Mound. Thus, in 1789–91, a feu to Jamieson resurrected the issues and building was begun. In 1824–7 various plans were under consideration for improved access between New and Old Towns and the issue of building on the south side of the Mound resurfaced. See ECA SL/63/4/2 and legislation: 56 Geo III c. 41 1816, Sections 3, 13; 7 & 8 Geo. IV c. 76, Section 53; 1 & 2 Will. IV c. 45, Section 56.

[94] ECA SL35/15, Stent Rolls, ff. 1–23. This is based on averages for Princes Street, Canal Street and St Ann's Street for 1784–5.

[95] See Reid *et al.*, *The Law of Property*, for a table of cases.

[96] *Colquhoun* v. *Lindsay*, 17 Feb. 1803; *Riddell* v. *Moir*, 28 June 1808; *Gordon* v. *New Club*, 11 July 1809; *Dirom* v. *Butterworth* and *Young* v. *Dewar,* Court of Session, both 17 Nov. 1814.

[97] *Heriot's Hospital Governors* v. *Gibson* (1814), HL 2 Dow 301. In this case James Gibson eventually lost the case on appeal by Heriot's because the obligation of demolition was of a prospective nature, and not part of the contract.

Figure 2.13 Contested development: North Bridge from Register House *c.* 1890

Note: this site was the subject of a dispute which involved David Hume and other Princes Street proprietors who objected to the development. It marked a half-century period of uncertainty over property rights only clarified in 1818.
Source: Edinburgh Central Library 92021/9/10.

The Craig plan, Dewar argued, gave no authority to build anything other than stables and coachhouses at the lane-end; Young contended that the plan was not even mentioned in the title deeds. The decision of the court favoured Dewar:

the original plan of the buildings is, by the act of council and advertisements referring specifically to that plan, proved to have been acted upon and . . . recognised by repeated decisions of the Court . . . and held to have established a common law right to insist on its being adhered to.[98]

Emphatically, the judge, Lord Bannatyne, reasserted the supremacy of the feuing plan in cases of disputes and signalled his preference for the *status quo*:

[98] *Young* v. *Deuar,* Decisions of the Court of Session, 17 Nov. 1814, 25–8.

I consider this as one of the most important cases that was ever before us. The rights of the whole New Town of Edinburgh depend on it. If every man is entitled to build as he likes, what would be the situation of the city?[99]

In what was a slow-motion replay, the test of adherence to Craig's plan was already under consideration in the case of *Gordon* v. *Marjoribanks* when the decision over *Young* v. *Dewar* was delivered. Of crucial importance for Edinburgh and for Scottish development more generally, the House of Lords in 1818 came to a different view.[100] It was a watershed and the circumstances reveal why.

The town council feued a plot with a frontage of 42½ feet on the south side of St Andrew's Square to David Ross, later Lord Ankerville, in 1784. The feu charter restricted the future use of the gardens in the Square to which Ross had communal access, and forbade Ross or his successors from converting his property into a brewery or other commercial uses. Like his neighbours, Ross built a house on the plot fronting the Square and outhouses, stables and a coachhouse with a chimney to the rear. A gentlemen's club, the New Club, bought the property in 1809 and sought to make alterations, including the addition of water-closets which were then not standard in early New Town properties. To these alterations the New Club's neighbour, Charles Gordon, was opposed even though his uncle and father had never objected previously to the smoke emissions from the coachhouse chimney-stack. In a series of legal exchanges, the New Club were limited in their building work at the rear to the height of the adjoining wall. Then, in 1813, they sought to convert the stable and coachhouse into a kitchen, billiard room and warm baths, connected by a covered passage to the main house and extending six feet above the level of the party wall. As in the *Young* v. *Dewar* case, petitions were duly submitted to the relevant building authority, the Dean of Guild Court, and the neighbours on either side informed. No objection was forthcoming from one, Dr Gregory, but the other, Gordon, opposed the plans on the grounds that they would contravene the original plan and were a nuisance. After a site inspection, the Dean of Guild Court rejected the claimed nuisance, approved the proposed change of use, but prohibited the increased height of the passageway. Both parties were displeased. Both parties initiated legal proceedings. Eventually, the House of Lords allowed Marjoribanks and the other New Club members to proceed with their plans. Predictably Gordon appealed.

The issues were complex. As no buildings were identified on the rear areas of plots were these always intended to be gardens? If so, why were the communal gardens (in St Andrew's Square) identified explicitly, but not other private gardens? The Craig plan did not specify how far the

---

[99] *Young* v. *Deuar*, 23–31.   [100] *Gordon* v. *Marjoribanks* (1818), 6 Dow 87, 1408–17.

principal houses should extend to the rear, nor even that they should be separated by walls, far less what the height of walls should be. And how could the height of a party wall be represented on a two-dimensional plan, anyway? As the elevations of the facades of early New Town buildings varied and were not interpreted as a departure from the plan, how could this be more relevant for adjoining rear walls not specified in the plan? If these details were not specified on the plans, how, then, could outhouses and stables be prohibited since the charter did not exclude them; in fact, the phrase 'or others built thereon' was conceivably an expectation that there would be such extensions.

Lord Eldon's judgement noted first that where burdens or restrictions exist in Scots law they must be expressly created, and secondly, that this could not be done retrospectively. He then affirmed the previous judgement that Marjoribanks and the 300 New Club members could have their baths on the grounds that Craig's plan was ambiguous and unsafe as a basis to determine what could be built on a plot. Lord Eldon stated that

to infer such a contract from the exhibition of such a plan, would be as violent a stretch in judicature as ever I met with in the course of a long professional life.[101]

In what was a landmark judgement as far as Scottish urban development was concerned, the Lords ruled that no obligation was deemed to have been created simply by showing the Craig plan to the feuars.

The decision fundamentally recast feuing practice. From 1818, the feuing plan was unreliable as an arbiter of what could be built on a lot and so control over future developments could only be achieved by different means. This meant spelling out in considerable detail what restrictions or real burdens applied to a property, and the laborious transcription of these by legal clerks each time a property was transferred, subdivided or refinanced so that the limitations applied to each vassal.

In effect and certainly by 1800, Heriot's had anticipated this legal shift through their increasingly specific feu charters and, by virtue of their more restrained release of land between 1767 and 1818 compared to the city council, were well placed in the nineteenth century to take advantage of the Lords' decision.[102] By creating restrictions and real burdens on their estate, Heriot's trustees had created property itself, not in the form of plots of land but in the form of rights or claims, enforceable in the courts and thus legitimated by society.[103] Dissatisfied with the elusive

---

[101] *Gordon* v. *Marjoribanks* (1818), 6 Dow 87, HL, 1415.

[102] The feuing conditions of 1806 which referred to streets in the northern New Town related to a plan by Robert Reid and William Sibbald dated 1801.

[103] C. B. Macpherson, 'Liberal democracy and property', in C. B. Macpherson, ed., *Property: Mainstream and Critical Positions* (Oxford 1978), 202.

meaning of property rights as embodied in the Craig plan, Heriot's had discovered how to create property obligations and to derive future revenues from them in the form of feu-duties, occasional or 'casualty' payments and repossession where feuars did not adhere to their property obligations.

Even if there was a lag of almost fifty years, the law of property was adapted to suit the changing needs of the social elite and of the powerful institutions whose income flow depended upon property revenues. Managing the market and regulating the city, therefore, was the implicit aim of the merchants, lawyers and trustees who formed the basis of social and economic power in the city. The Craig plan had served its initial purpose, providing a basis in contract law to encourage momentum in the early phases of New Town development. But, once rooted, the new suburbans in the New Town conceived their property rights as organic and sought to adapt the form and function of their buildings. Craig's plan produced contradictory interpretations of property rights where changes of use were proposed and, though it was a positive force in the initial stages of development, for twenty years before its legal force was undermined in 1818 it was an impediment to development, the scale of which was obscured only because wartime interest rates and commercial uncertainty were more obvious restraints on the pace of expansion in the New Town.

Thus Youngson's acknowledgement[104] that he had 'underestimated' the importance of the feuing system to the development of Edinburgh's New Town was incorrect; in fact, he had fundamentally overstated its importance since the feu dispositions were unconditional and the social tone of the New Town was indefensible. What Youngson had underestimated was the importance of the feuing *plan*, sight of which was deemed sufficient until 1818 to imply compliance by builders but which had no force concerning future property use and alterations. Accordingly, much of the first New Town was completed under the law of contract. Until controls over future use and amenity were more explicit, Heriot's were obliged to protect their estate development by means of detailed stipulations regarding the character and appearance of buildings on their property. In this respect their feuing proposals for the area to the north of Queen Street Gardens, drawn up by Robert Reid and William Sibbald in 1801, anticipated the comprehensive nature of feuing conditions and servitudes which became common after 1818 once the feuing plan had forfeited its legal supremacy.

Adjoining this northern development was the Earl of Moray's Drumsheugh estate, acquired from Heriot's in 1782 but only developed

[104] A. J. Youngson, *The Making of Classical Edinburgh 1750–1840* (Edinburgh 1975, 2nd edn), xii.

after 1822. As with Heriot's New Town estate, the Earl of Moray's articles of roup (sale) for building lots were highly specific.[105] His feuars were not at any time permitted to convert their houses 'into shops or warerooms for the sale of goods or merchandize of any kind; but to use them as dwelling houses only'.[106] Superficially, the documents were not unlike those drawn up by Heriot's in 1801. But in effect, whereas Heriot's knew that their feuing conditions were subordinate to the law of contract, the Earl of Moray knew by 1822 that as a result of the Lords' decision in 1818 estate development could not be controlled by contract law and the feuing plan. Realistically, from the date of the Lords' judgement it was the detailed feuing conditions that governed future developments on the Earl of Moray's and others' estates, even if their rights to create and enforce such burdens and restrictions took another generation and yet another House of Lords decision to confirm it.[107] The impact on the Moray estate was that once potential buyers were reassured as to the future use and amenity of property then the plots sold quickly and, despite a recession in the Edinburgh property market generally after 1826, virtually the entire estate was feued by 1836.

The status of the feuing plan had been usurped; it was not replaced instantly but rather more gradually from the 1820s by increasingly elaborate feuing stipulations, enforceable under Scots property law as eventually confirmed in 1840 by the House of Lords. The legal changes were socially and economically constructed, the product of property owners' and developers' need under rapidly changing market conditions to have their rights and obligations clarified. That process was begun in 1772 and culminated in a judgement in 1818 which dismantled the authority of the feuing plan and was a necessary condition for the future development of urban Scotland. How feuing operated in the nineteenth century and how it contributed to the development of Edinburgh and, more generally, Scotland forms the basis of the next chapter.

[105] A. Mitchell, *No More Corncraiks: Lord Moray's Feuars in Edinburgh's New Town* (Edinburgh 1998), 2. The architect was James Gillespie Graham.

[106] Mitchell, *No More Corncraiks*, 2–3.

[107] This was the crucial decision in 1840 concerning the *Corporation of Tailors of Aberdeen* v. *Coutts* (1840), HL 1 Robinson 296. In 1823, the trustees of the Incorporated Tailors of Aberdeen decided to feu land at Crabeston at a public sale. This formed Bon Accord Square and a number of detailed feuing conditions were stipulated. The Incorporated Tailors maintained that Adam Coutts, advocate, Aberdeen and his heirs were obliged to conform to all the details of the feu charter, specifically the construction of a pavement, iron railing and a dwarf wall in Bon Accord Square. With some complications regarding the nature of the tenure, and counter claims by the superior that 'under cover of night' Coutts had made connection to the main sewer, together with appeals, the case was only resolved in 1840 when Lord Brougham delivered the Lords' judgement that there was a real burden upon the property in question, and is binding on the defender' (344), Coutts.

3 Victorian feudalism

The Scottish framework of property rights was based on the feudal system.[1] All rights to land were derived from the sovereign who made grants of land to the nobles and who, in turn, were bound to him by oaths of loyalty, attendance at court in peacetime and by military service during war. These nobles made subordinate grants of parts of their territories to their vassals who were bound to observe the conditions stipulated by their superior. In decay from the fifteenth century, the Clan Act, 1717, finally commuted military obligations to annual payments of money or grain, though the exclusive use and possession of property did not extinguish the dependent status of the vassal which remained a central feature of land tenure in Scotland until 1974. One consequence of this hierarchy of Scottish property relations was the requirement that a landowner or superior be informed of and agree to a change of vassal and from 1617 (1681 in the burghs) the Register of Sasines, a register of land titles and property obligations, provided a written record accessible to the general public with a considerable measure of transparency in property relations.[2] It was, furthermore, 'an efficient system of registration' and afforded 'a degree of security not excelled under any other system'.[3] Certainly the absence of a land registry in England, except in Yorkshire, Lancashire and Middlesex, rendered problematical any attempt to verify titles and restrictions on property.[4]

[1] For an account of the Scottish system of tenure see *PP 1917–18 XIV*, Royal Commission on the Housing of the Industrial Population of Scotland, Rural and Urban, Report, paras. 1482–522; and also the SLEC, *Report* (London 1914), chs. 22–4.

[2] See R. Rodger and J. Newman, 'Property transfers and the Registers of Sasines: urban development in Scotland since 1617', *Urban History Yearbook,* 1988, 51–2, for an account of and extensive references to the history of English and Scottish practices of land registration. For further material on land rights and tenure see K. G. C. Reid *et al.*, *The Law of Property in Scotland* (Edinburgh 1996). For contemporary explanations see A. M. Bell, *Lectures on Conveyancing* (Edinburgh 1822, 3rd edn), vol. II, and J. Craigie, *Scottish Law of Conveyancing: Heritable Rights* (Edinburgh 1899, 3rd edn), 55–62.

[3] *PP 1917–18 XIV*, Royal Commission, *Report*, para. 1508.

[4] F. Sheppard, V. Belcher and P. L. Cottrell, 'The Middlesex and Yorkshire Deeds Registries and the study of building fluctuations', *London Journal,* 1980, 176–217; W. E. Tate, 'The five English district statutory Registries of Deeds', *Bulletin of the Institute of Historical Research,* 20, 1944, 97–105.

In England and Wales, the two principal forms of tenure were freehold, the outright sale of land, and leasehold, the rental of land for a fixed term. In certain areas of England, freehold restrictive covenants conveyed to landowners some of the same powers as in Scotland to limit use and to create burdens on property, but whereas in Scotland these powers were almost universal, in England they were exceptional. Restrictive covenants were also unenforceable until 1848, and indeed after, since the absence of a centralised land registry until 1862 and its voluntary nature thereafter ensured that there was no effective means by which to record and monitor restrictions on English property.[5]

In Scotland, land was feued – sold outright by the vendor who relinquished all title to it, subject to the receipt of a fixed annual levy (feu-duty) in perpetuity, and other occasional payments (casualties). Though it had existed for centuries, the elaboration of the feuing system received a stimulus after 1818 when the House of Lords rejected the primacy of the feuing plan as an arbiter of what could be built on a plot (see chapter 2). Thereafter, landowners and property developers relied increasingly on the skills of legal draughtsmen to write detailed clauses in feu charters to control the nature and future use of property and the buildings erected upon it. So protected, property owners were able to exploit and develop the intrinsic features of feuing, as explained below, and were able to respond to opportunities associated with Scottish urbanisation as they unfolded in the course of the nineteenth century.

Feuing possessed several unique features, each of which tended to push up the price of land (see fig. 3.1). First, since the vendor or superior was liquidating an irrecoverable asset there was a tendency to withhold land in the expectation that the market price would rise – a not unreasonable assumption under eighteenth- and certainly nineteenth-century conditions of population increase and urbanisation. In essence, the motive of maximising receipts from land was no different from that of England, but the methods employed were significantly different and had important implications for the way in which urban development took place.

The superior's entitlement to an annual feu-duty was a second distinctive feature of Scottish land tenure. Since the superior was entitled only to a sum fixed forever in monetary terms and so could not adjust the annual figure to take account of the long-run shifts in the market value of his land, he was not encouraged 'to give his ground for a reasonable feu-duty' but compensated for the inevitable erosion of the real value in the long term by creating high priced feus. In effect this produced a degree of

---

[5] W. S. Holdsworth, *A History of English Law* (London 1972 edn), 185–8; A. W. B. Simpson, *A History of the Land Law* (Oxford 1986, 2nd edn), 282. For the statutes on land registration, see 22 & 23 Vict. c. 3, and 25 & 26 Vict. c. 53.

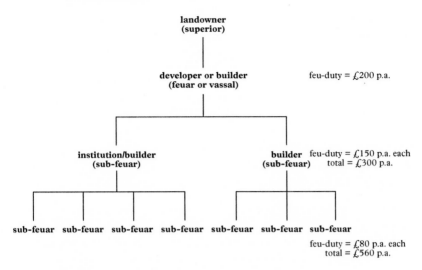

Figure 3.1 A pyramid of Scottish property relationships and obligations

'front-loading', that is, a particularly onerous duty initially.[6] As the Scottish Land Enquiry explained:

Under the feu system ... the superior's natural endeavour is to fix his original conditions of feuing so as to get as large a return as possible, once and for all. It is very probable also that the preponderance of tenements of three and four storeys in height in Scotland as compared with England is attributable in part at least to the high ground rents.[7]

Thirdly, feuing entitled the superior to a number of additional, though occasional payments, equivalent to a second or even third feu-duty in certain years, and this distinguished Scots land law from almost all others. Where the successor to a feu was the heir of a previous vassal a payment of 'relief' was due, equivalent to the annual feu-duty. Furthermore, the superior was bound to accept a successor who was not the heir if a 'composition' payment was made, a sum equivalent to the annual net rental value of the property. The feu contract frequently stipulated 'duplicands' or double feu-duty in specific years, often every nineteenth year, and if new 'composition' and 'relief' burdens could not be created after 1874, then these duplicands were used more frequently.[8]

[6] SLEC, *Report*, 307–12.   [7] SLEC, *Report*, 293.
[8] The Conveyancing and Land Transfer (Scotland) Act 1874 stipulated that the creation of new 'casualty' payments was not possible.

A fourth characteristic of Scottish tenure was the practice of 'sub-infeudation'.[9] The right to exact an annual feu-duty passed successively with the transfer of land from the original landowner, to developer, to builder, to house factor and then to house purchaser (fig. 3.1). A potential compound levy was, therefore, built in to the transfer of land, and land-lords and house factors who were the last in line in the right to exact a feu-duty accordingly passed on the final, cumulative, feu-duty to their tenants. As each individual in the chain of sub-feuing was liable person-ally for payments to his immediate superior then a considerable incentive existed to ensure that this obligation could be met. Consequently, succes-sive tiers of the feuing pyramid (fig. 3.2) tended to be increased significantly to cover this obligation.

A critical characteristic of feuing was that the annual duties were a first charge on an estate at death or bankruptcy. Accordingly, they were a highly desirable security; other creditors had to wait. With such armour-plated assurances, feus were a security upon which banks and individuals would lend, content in the knowledge that they would have first call on the estate in the event of financial difficulty. Thus future feuing income was the collateral used by landowners, builders and developers upon which capital was raised. As a basis for advances of capital, feus were themselves highly sought-after financial instruments, and no doubt increased in price as a consequence. 'Feu-farming', the process of continuously bidding up the annual charge on land, became an accepted practice in Scotland, as James Gowans, a prominent Edinburgh builder during the 1860s and 1870s and chairman of the Dean of Guild Court, the principal municipal body responsible for approving building plans, explained:

A builder looks forward to the town increasing, and he takes up a lot of land from the superior at £50 an acre, and then by re-feuing or building himself he works it up to £200 an acre. That has been done within this city and large fortunes have been made out of it.[10]

As if this device was insufficient, another method of 'farming' was available to Scottish builders and developers. Additional land burdens could be created. A particular type of annuity, 'ground annuals' was developed originally on land where sub-infeudation was prohibited, but by mid-Victorian times ground annuals were becoming additional to

[9] R. Rodger, '"The Invisible Hand" – market forces, housing and the urban form in Victorian cities', in D. Fraser and A. Sutcliffe, eds., *The Pursuit of Urban History* (London 1983), 190–211. J. R. Kellett, 'Property speculators and the building of Glasgow 1780–1830', *Scottish Journal of Political Economy*, 8, 1961, 219, notes that sub-infeudation had been abandoned in England in the thirteenth century.

[10] *PP 1884–5 XXX*, Royal Commission on Housing of the Working Classes, Scotland, on Evidence of Gowans Q. 18893.

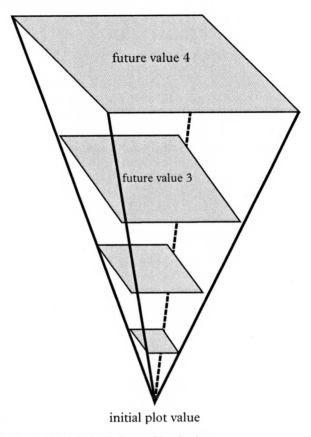

initial plot value

Figure 3.2 Sub-infeudation and land values

feu-duties. The Scottish Land Enquiry Committee explained how the system worked, and why it had become so attractive:

[Ground annuals] are perpetual annual payments on the property and are not redeemable. As soon as they are created they can be sold. And this is precisely the explanation of their existence. The builder commonly disposes of them for cash as soon as they are created, and so finances his operations: he obtains his money at an earlier stage in building the premises and also secures this money at a lower rate of interest than a bond or mortgage.[11]

This practice alone, it was estimated, could add 10–14% to the gross rental of tenement property. The attractions to landlords were undeniable; the implications for tenants were inescapable.

[11] SLEC, *Report*, 308.

So the sale of the right to exact feu-duties, compounded at between twenty to thirty years purchase of the annual value depending on the buoyancy of the housing market, or the raising of a bond secured on the expectation of this income, represented an important source of working capital for builders. But for speculative builders, without a guaranteed sale, there were often great difficulties in selling these sub-feus or in raising bonds on them if the housing market was depressed; incomplete dwellings offered little prospect for obtaining a rental income. Thus the state of the housebuilding cycle had a significant bearing upon the extent to which feu-farming could proceed, and builders needed great skill to match bond maturities if they were to avoid bankruptcy. The Scottish tenurial system provided the financial foundation to building and urban development, but it also tended to exaggerate fluctuations, since the sale-ability of feus released considerable advances for further building devel-opment, and unsaleable feus choked off capital supplies. The amplitude of nineteenth-century housebuilding fluctuations and urban develop-ment was accordingly much more pronounced than in England and Wales.

For security of tenure, as protection against loss for improvements to land and property, and as a means of releasing the intrinsic value of land to finance property development, Scots law had much to commend it. Weighed against these advantages were the incremental duties payable as successive interests acquired a stake in the development process, and inflated prices which resulted from the possibilities for raising working capital, for building or other investment purposes, which such rights to annual income conveyed. Ultimately, tenants paid dearly for the contin-ued protection of feudal property rights. Diagrammatically this relation-ship can be represented as in fig. 3.3.

Though the positions and gradients of the demand curves in both Scotland and England are only schematic, the outcome was that less space was affordable for a given rental in Scottish burghs compared to that of English towns and cities. The implications for Scottish urban form were considerable. Compared to equivalent English plot sizes, Scottish land had to be more densely built to cover land charges. The 'plot loading' ratio had to be higher.[12] To achieve such property densities, higher buildings and smaller floor areas within buildings were essential. For residents, the implications were obvious, and potentially serious in

---

[12] M. Conzen, *Alnwick, Northumberland: A Study in Town-Plan Analysis* (London 1969), 123. M. Freeman, 'Commercial building development: the agents of change', in T. R. Slater, ed., *The Built Form of Western Cities* (Leicester 1990), 258–61, notes in a 1960s context that office developers and retailers believed it imperative to increase plot density to offset the property prices of central city sites.

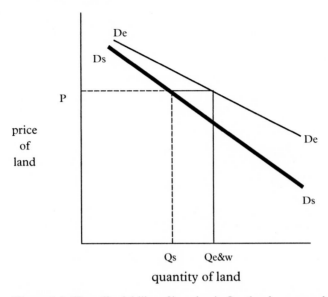

Figure 3.3 The affordability of housing in Scotland compared to England and Wales

relation to health and welfare. Though other factors compounded this outcome, for example, Scottish building costs, laws governing the letting of property and the nature of employment and the composition of demand, the result was that 53% of the Scottish housing stock was of one- or two-roomed houses whereas the corresponding English figure was 7% in 1911; in the same census year, 45% of Scots lived at a density of more than two persons per room which contrasted dramatically with a figure of only 9% for Englishmen.[13]

Topographically, urban sites in Scotland displayed as much variety as in England. Indeed often the same strategic, economic and ecclesiastical considerations on both sides of what was a moveable border for much of the medieval period influenced town foundations and urban development. Nor were cross-border differences in climate or cultural preferences so marked in, say, Carlisle and Dumfries as to justify divergent forms of housing. What was unique to Scotland was not how the towns were founded or the streets laid out, but what was built upon them, and during the nineteenth century, 'The tenement of three, four and in certain cases five or more storeys represent[ed] the final development of housing . . . in the great majority of the larger Scots burghs.'[14] This

[13] R. Rodger, ed., *Scottish Housing in the Twentieth Century* (Leicester 1989), 29.
[14] *PP 1917–18 XIV*, Royal Commission, Report, para. 396.

distinctive Scottish urban form was 'so different from the two-storey self-contained cottages which form the prevailing type in English towns'[15] that conventional definitions of 'house', 'tenement', 'overcrowding' and other legal terms in British statutes proved inapplicable in Scotland.[16]

By producing a distinctive income stream to property, Scottish feudal tenure influenced the time horizon of estate development. There was, of course, a degree of circularity about the way the process operated. Inflated by the effects of the feuing system, the price of Scottish land necessitated the construction of high rise property to spread the land charges, but the prospect of such building densities added considerably to the value of land. This was the process which even enabled 'very high prices [to be] charged on the borders of Scottish towns for access to land' and produced the apparent anomaly of four-storey blocks of flats surrounded by green fields.[17]

The trajectory of Victorian property development

Judged by annual changes to feu-duty revenue received by three major landowners in the city, Heriot's, the town council and Trinity Hospital (see fig. 3.4), there was an approximation to a long-run or Kondratiev cycle in Edinburgh's property development. Low levels of development in the 1750s were replaced by a rapid upsurge in the first New Town phase 1767–89; the growth of income from property development continued, though more intermittently during the war years 1789–1815, to be replaced by an upsurge to 1825, and then by a progressive decline in the rate of property development as the financial crisis of 1825–6 deepened, and as property owners recognised an oversupply in land which, though feued for building, remained undeveloped. From the mid-1820s, the amount of new property feued declined precipitously until another financial crisis in the mid-1840s had run its course.[18] Only from the 1850s did the release of land resume a markedly upward trajectory and it was only then that the emergence and exploitation of real burdens and sub-feuing contributed significantly to the development of the city.

While the Edinburgh town council by 1815 had all but exhausted the land available to it in the rectangle formed between Princes and Queen

---

[15] *PP 1917–18 XIV,* Royal Commission, Report, para. 396.
[16] G. F. A. Best, 'Another part of the Island', in H. J. Dyos and M. Wolff, eds., *The Victorian City: Images and Realities*, vol. II (London 1978, pbk edn), esp. 392–5.
[17] SLEC, *Report,* 326
[18] R. Saville, *A History of the Bank of Scotland* (Edinburgh 1996), 279–99; R. Michie, *Money, Manias and Markets: Investment, Company Formation and the Stock Exchange in Nineteenth Century Scotland* (Edinburgh 1981), 39–48, 77–124; C. W. Munn, *The Scottish Provincial Banking Companies 1747–1864* (Edinburgh 1981), 80–100.

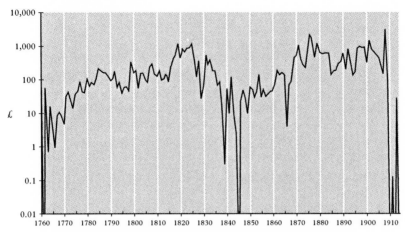

Figure 3.4 Property development: Edinburgh 1760–1914

Note: vertical axis shows annual value of new feus created (£).
Sources: ECA George Heriot's Roll of Superiorities, 1913–14; ECA
City of Edinburgh Superiorities, 1914.

Streets, Heriot's trustees' involvement in the first wave of New Town
development was limited. Accordingly, they were significant beneficiaries
of the House of Lords' decision as swathes of their Broughton, Warriston
and Coates estates in north and west Edinburgh remained unfeued in
1817 (fig. 3.5, plots 34, 55 and 121).[19] Where feuing had taken place on
the northern slopes of the New Town, it was in proximity to the power
source provided by the Water of Leith with its many mills and potential
for washing, dyeing and related industrial processes which first induced
Heriot's trustees to feu the lands of Canonmills and Silvermills.

The disruption of wartime, the banking collapse and the resulting
depression in the property market are all evident from the number of feus
granted by Heriot's. To a large extent, property development only began
its weak recovery in the 1850s and 1860s when the assurances which
feuars were able to obtain in their feu dispositions strengthened interest in
residential development on land controlled by Heriot's trustees (fig. 3.6).

Relatively rapidly, the main New Town thoroughfares and residences on
them were constructed on the town council's feu. That it took many years
to complete the remainder of the New Town is widely known[20] and while

[19] Most of the land held by Heriot's to the south of Edinburgh had by then been feued.
[20] See, for example, A. J. Youngson, *The Making of Classical Edinburgh 1750–1840*
(Edinburgh 1966), 97; P. Reed, 'Form and context: a study of Georgian Edinburgh', in
T. A. Markus, ed., *Order in Space and Society: Architectural Form and its Context in the
Scottish Enlightenment* (Edinburgh 1982), 127–8.

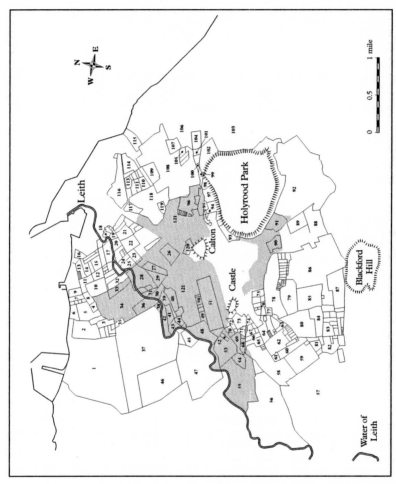

Figure 3.5 The structure of landownership in Edinburgh 1817

Note: numbers refer to individual landowners. The shaded area is that of Heriot's Hospital and plots 34, 53, 55 and 121 show extensive holdings remained undeveloped in 1817.   *Source:* based on NAS RH4/152/27–31, Records of George Heriot's Hospital and Trust; Scottish National Library, James Kirkwood's Map, 1817.

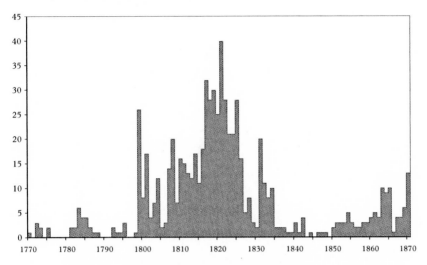

Figure 3.6 Property development in Edinburgh 1770–1870: George Heriot's feus granted (number per annum)

Source: ECA of George Heriot's Roll of Superiorities 1913–14.

fig. 3.7 shows the protracted nature of that development on Heriot's land, it obscures the incompleteness which existed for individual streets. Not only did most streets take a very long time to be completed – decades in some cases – the development of contiguous building stances was by no means the norm. Heriot Row, Northumberland and Great King Streets and Royal Terrace were laid out for feuing but the take-up of the plots rarely proceeded in a neat sequence along the street; feuars identified specific stances as more or less desirable by reason of their size, view and other features, and so cherry-picked their preferred sites. So for some years individual residences in these high status areas stood alone, and only with the passage of time did the gap-toothed appearance of streets give way to a unified and continuous street, just as incisors and molars appear at a variable rate in a child's jaw eventually to produce a complete set of teeth.

This gradual, halting process of physical expansion is represented in fig. 3.7 for just three streets, Heriot Row (1803–19), Northumberland Street (1804–27) and, with less dispersion, Great King Street (1810–24), although it applied to many others including Dundas Street (1802–29), Howe Street (1808–25) and Broughton Street (1824–67).[21] What the protracted development of Heriot's lands also signalled was the street as

[21] ECA Lists of Superiorities belonging to the Governors of George Heriot's Trust, various years.

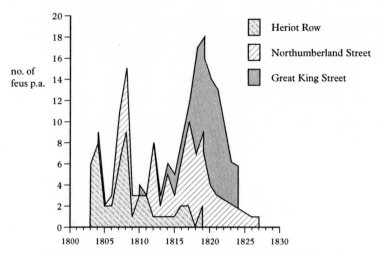

Figure 3.7 Protracted development: partially completed streets on Heriot's property 1800–1830

Source: ECA George Heriot's Roll of Superiorities (various years).

an ongoing building site, and of the mud or dust according to the season. The unified street, with elegant exteriors and apparent social order, as represented by Thomas Shepherd in 1829 and engravers subsequently, belied the noise of construction and the incompleteness of streets for some years.

That there was a clearly developed pecking order in the desirability of feus can be seen from the sequence by which stances were feued in Heriot Row (fig. 3.8). Those which proved most attractive were located towards the centre of the street plan and thus away from the corner lots with Dundas, Howe and India Streets which had small, awkwardly shaped and overlooked gardens to the rear. The preference for the eastern side of Howe Street was determined by the absence of mews property to the rear, and so numbers 10–16 had open vistas to north and south. In later years, as the pace of property development picked up and Heriot's feuing embraced more streets, the trade-off between a lower status corner lot on a high status street and a higher status stance lower down the hill posed difficulties. Nor were these perceived residential hierarchies, within and between streets, confined to the New Town; the same subtleties and dilemmas confronted the petite bourgeoisie of Comely Bank and Learmonth at the end of Victoria's reign (see chapter 9).

Nowhere was the protracted development more evident than in Royal Terrace where thirty feus were released over a forty year period between

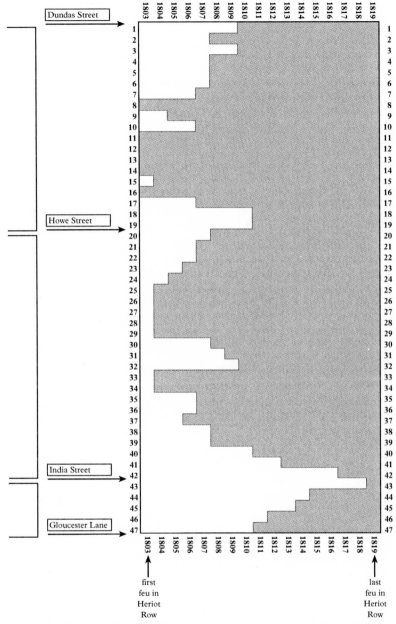

Figure 3.8 Residential hierarchies: the feuing sequence in Heriot Row
1803–1819

Source: ECA George Heriot's Roll of Superiorities (various years).

1821 and 1865.[22] No sooner had these elevated building stances on the north of Calton Hill been drawn up than the effect of the banking crisis arrested development, as it did for the neighbouring Regent and Carlton Terraces, and for Playfair's feuing plan for the streets between Leith Walk and Easter Road where only a few properties were constructed in Brunswick and Windsor Streets.[23] In the event, it was over half a century before the area covered by Playfair's plan was feued and covered with tenements in Albert, Brunswick, Dalmeny and Iona Streets though by then the coherence of the residential plan had long been compromised by the arrival of the North British Railway Company's spur to Leith and its associated goods depot and marshalling yards.

Arrested development

The interruption to property development caused by the financial crisis in 1825–6 affected all types of landowner in the city, and all parts of the city. Interest rate increases, a preference for government bonds as a natural haven for investment rather than loans to developers, and a glut of post-Napoleonic feuing and construction combined to erode investor confidence and the property market and the housebuilding industry together entered a period of inactivity. Terraces were left incomplete, as in Saxe Coburg Place, where house frontages display a vertical crenellated effect and even now await, in vain, further building on the neighbouring lot.

Two consequences of this arrested development were, first, that population growth brought about by natural increase and rural to urban migration was accommodated in a housing stock more suited to seventeenth-century population levels; and secondly, that the resulting overcrowding produced insanitary and defective housing in the Old Town – 'a contagion of numbers'[24] – the scale of which only public intervention could address (see chapter 12). Arrested development in the property sector between 1825 and 1850 was, therefore, of fundamental importance in shaping the long-term character and physical appearance of Edinburgh.

[22] RCAHMS PP108, Royal Terrace, feuing plan Playfair 1820; ECA Lists of Superiorities belonging to the Governors of George Heriot's Trust, 1913–14.

[23] NAS RHP 213, Plan of Windsor Street and Leopold Place, part of plan of Grant's feu, 1756, by Robert Stevenson 1833; RHP 212, Building Plan of Elm Row and Leopold Place by William Playfair 1822; RCAHMS, PP26, Feuing Plan of Brunton Place and Hillside Crescent (Playfair) 1823; PP213, Windsor Street and Leopold Place. Plan of Grant's feu, 1756. Robert Stevenson 1833.

[24] J. A. Banks, 'The contagion of numbers', in H. J. Dyos and M. Wolff, eds., The Victorian City: Images and Realities, vol. I (London 1977 edn), 105–22.

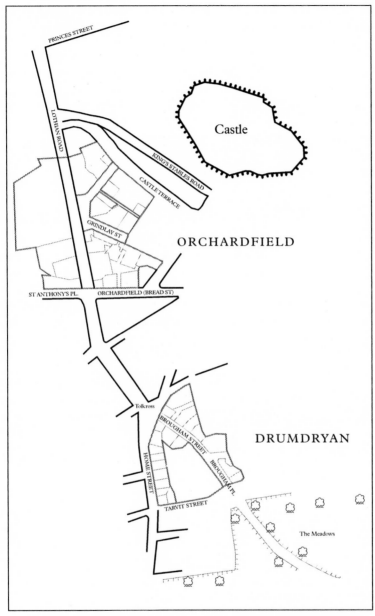

Figure 3.9 Arrested development: Drumdryan and Orchardfield
estates in the 1820s

Sources: based on MC, Drumdryan Chartulary, and ECA MC/GG,
Orchardfield Chartulary.

Areas of the city such as at Tollcross and Lothian Road which lay in the path of western expansion were brought to an abrupt halt by the collapse of property investment and feuing in 1825–6. James Home Rigg sought to participate in the expansion of the 1820s when he feued eleven building stances for tenement construction on his Drumdryan estate between 1824 and 1826.[25] These properties on the east side of Home and Leven Streets were feued according to charters in which Rigg tried to steer an intermediate course following the landmark judgement of 1818 which challenged the force of the feuing plan as an instrument to control future development (see fig. 3.9).[26] On the one hand Rigg stated in the feu charters that he would

not be obliged to execute the feuing plan . . . any further than I please . . . and I reserve full power and liberty without the consent of [the feuars] . . . either to make such alterations on the said feuing plan . . . and even totally to abandon the same.[27]

Nothing could have been more calculated to increase uncertainty amongst potential feuars. In addition, for thirty years the unfeued plot in Home Street eventually taken by Baird in 1852 (see fig. 3.10) created uncertainty as to the eventual line of the access road from the Drumdryan estate to the main thoroughfare.[28] On the other hand, Rigg introduced limited real burdens by prohibiting the feuars from building 'on the back ground' above the height of seven feet, and feuars were on 'no account to erect or set up steam engines or carry on any trade or manufacture' and the usual obligations to 'uphold and maintain the street, causeways and common sewers, side pavements and rails' were also incorporated.[29] After the spurt of feus granted between 1824 and 1826, a quarter of a century passed before another charter was issued in 1852, with two more in 1853. Only in the 1860s was there a revival of interest in building, but by then the collapse of building development in the years 1825–50 and the limited interest in plots in the 1850s and early 1860s meant that there was little prospect of an integrated development of the estate. No builder took on more than a single lot and, in a buyer's market, because potential developers were able to cherry-pick their lots to the detriment of the long-run development of the Drumdryan estate.[30]

[25] MC, Drumdryan Chartulary, vol 1, ff. 18, 26, 36, 45, 56, 64, 67, 74, 90, 98, 105, 110.
[26] *Gordon* v. *Marjoribanks* (1818), HL 6 Dow 87. See chapter 2 for the background to this decision.
[27] MC, Drumdryan Chartulary, feu charter to Thomas Buchanan, 16 Apr. 1825, vol. 1, f. 38.
[28] MC, Drumdryan Chartulary, feu charter to Alexander Baird, 16 Apr. 1852, vol. 1, ff. 201–7.   [29] MC, Drumdryan Chartulary, vol. 1, ff. 18, 32, 38.
[30] For further information on the Drumdryan development see chapter 6.

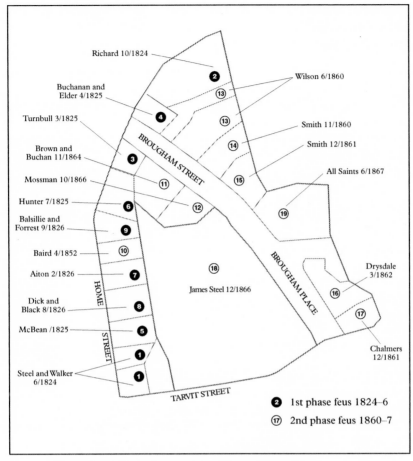

Figure 3.10 Drumdryan estate of James Home Rigg

Source: based on MC, Drumdryan Chartulary.

The arrested development experienced by the trustees of George Grindlay on their strategically located Orchardfield estate (Castle Terrace to Lothian Road, now occupied by the Usher Hall, Lyceum and Traverse theatres, and nearby streets) was a further confirmation, if any was needed, of the slump in the property sector in the second quarter of the nineteenth century. The Orchardfield estate straddled the principal southern access road from Edinburgh's west end. It was the communications pivot between the New Town and the Old Town. To the east of Orchardfield and below the crags of the Castle, the road to Queensferry, the Forth ports and the north skirted the Grindlay property, and the premier route to Glasgow, Lanarkshire and the Forth–Clyde valley left the West Port or 'Main Point' as it was called, as a street called 'Orchardfield' which bounded Grindlay's estate on the south. In the path of urban expansion from both New and Old Towns, the pace and character of this estate illuminates the process of arrested development in the Edinburgh townscape during the second quarter of the nineteenth century.

George Grindlay's wealth as a leather merchant was based on tanneries in Portsburgh and in Leith where with his brother he owned what was later considered to be 'one of the very largest and most valuable works of the kind in Scotland for the production of heavy leather goods'.[31] When George and William Grindlay bought the Orchardfield property in 1782, the eleven acres they obtained represented the largest undeveloped property holding in central Edinburgh still in private hands. Apart from Bangholm Bower and Lilliput, small estates acquired in 1799 on the Edinburgh–Leith boundary and which generated only farm rentals for almost a century, no other property acquisitions were made by the Grindlays.[32] More surprising than the fact that George Grindlay made no other foray into the property market and yet managed, perceptively, to identify a strategic development site was the inability or unwillingness of major developers with first hand knowledge of such activities in the New Town to do so. However, it might be argued that, given only steady agricultural rentals from Orchardfield, Heriot's and Watson's trustees like other potential property investors recognised market saturation and gave Orchardfield a wide berth. Watson's trustees were heavily preoccupied with agricultural estates following half a century of purchases in Midlothian, Roxburgh and East Lothian, while Heriot's 'wait and see' strategy as far as the progress of the New Town was probably a deterrent to any additional acquisitions in 1782.

As a well-connected businessman and merchant it is inconceivable that George Grindlay was oblivious to the opportunities which the Orchardfield estate offered between 1782 and 1801. These last twenty years of his life coincided with his period as a member of the Merchant Company – his abilities were so highly regarded after a spell as an Assistant he was shortlisted in 1798 for the position of Master of the Merchant Company. He served on the Board of George Watson's Hospital and the Merchant Maiden Hospital, and was familiar with the property investment strategies which sustained these and other educational institutions, and to which his own Trust and Disposition eventually

---

[31] ECA MC/GG/box 3, Accounts for the Years ending November 1811 and 1812; MC, Minutes, 14 Dec. 1876, f. 126.

[32] ECA MC/GG, Orchardfield Chartulary, Inventory of Title Deeds of the Lands of Orchardfield, ff. 47–50 and 400–3.

contributed.[33] Developmental capital was not in short supply – the estate was worth £26,000 – yet, almost certainly, Grindlay's decision not to lay out Orchardfield for feuing reflected his caution during wartime since almost 50% of his assets were committed to a portfolio of bank stocks and a limited amount of government bonds. Not unconnected to this assessment of risk, uncertainty and yield was the fact that in the 1780s, the westwards progress of the New Town was still some distance from Orchardfield, and until the 1830s poor communications with the Old Town represented a disincentive for the professional and business elites to locate at the foot of the Castle rock.

After Grindlay's death there were two further legal reasons why Orchardfield remained a stalled building development for twenty years after 1801.[34] First, without a clear legal mandate before 1815 because of a contested claim to the trustees' rights as feudal superiors, clear and unchallengeable titles to land were impossible to establish. The legal challenge to the trustees lasted over four years following Grindlay's son's death in 1810, and stemmed from the feudal superior's claim that the trustees were an arm of the Merchant Company, and as such a corporation whom he as superior was not bound to accept.[35] That it took so long to initiate development on the Orchardfield estate was complicated by a second legal matter, namely by John Grindlay's joint purchase of the property and his entitlement to half of the proceeds.[36] Initially, the trustees sought to assign crop revenues from specific parts of the estate, but only after some years recognised the impracticality of this, opting for the

---

[33] A. Heron, *The Merchant Company of Edinburgh: Its Rise and Progress* (Edinburgh 1903), 156.

[34] ECA MC/GG/box 3, Trust Disposition and Settlement, 18 May 1801. George Grindlay stipulated that the George Watson's and Mary Erskine's Hospitals should benefit from his estate in the event of his son not reaching the age of majority. Grindlay's post-natal provision for his son did not match his ante-natal concern: his wife's poor health during child-bearing was claimed to be a direct result of their accommodation, and she left the marital home first for the sea air at Leith and then for her father's house in Ramsay Gardens, and it was her father who bore the medical expenses of the birth, which Margaret then claimed against the trustees when her husband died in 1801. See ECA MC/GG/box 3, claims against trustees, 15 Feb. 1802.

[35] ECA MC/GG/box 11, letter from Sir William Forbes to Master of the Merchant Company, ff. 7–8, 9 Feb. 1815; also Report to the Master, Assistants and Treasurer of the Merchant Company, 14 Aug. 1867. The superior received casualty payments, i.e. another feu-duty when an heir or nominee assumed the title. Thus to accept the trustees as *de facto* representatives of the Merchant Company meant that the superior would forgo this source of income. The trustees offered an inducement of two years rent and a double feu-duty every thirty years to the superior, but it was only following the intervention of Sir William Forbes as the nominee of the Merchant Company and his personal connections with the superior that the objection was eventually dropped.

[36] ECA MC/GG/box 3/3, Answers for the Master and Assistant of the Company of Merchants to the petition for David Grindlay, 16 Oct. 1811, ff. 1–2.

simpler approach to halve the revenue from the entire estate. This was a strategic decision which, crucially, treated the estate as an integral development, not as two divisible parts, and so an overall estate plan could only be drawn up when the matter was resolved, as it was in 1820.[37]

Without a feuing plan until 1820 the development of the Orchardfield estate was directionless.[38] Indeed, until 1820 Orchardfield remained an agricultural estate at the foot of the Castle rock (fig. 3.9). In 1812, farming produced £207 gross income against which expenses for ploughing, harrowing, seeding and hoeing potatoes cost £192, a net income of just £15[39] even though an earlier estimate considered that the value of the land could be systematically developed to increase feu-duty income from £60 p.a. to an eventual figure of £1,440, which was itself subsequently revised upwards to £2,005 p.a.[40]

By the time the trustees had resolved their legal rights in the courts and had developed an estate plan, the opportunity to place the Orchardfield estate in a pivotal position in the future development of Edinburgh had passed. Some of the vigour had gone out of the residential building boom by the time the first feu charters were signed in 1822–4 for properties in Bread Street, Lothian Road and Castle Barns (fig. 3.11).[41] The property market and building activity declined abruptly, and commercial encroachments were difficult to oppose, not least due to the completion nearby of the Union Canal in 1821. As if these difficulties were not enough, several years of further uncertainty caused by proposed transport improvements around the base of the Castle and affecting two sides of Grindlay's property stifled feuing development until the issue was resolved in 1828.[42] In addition, the agreement between the town council and Grindlay's trustees required three sums of £1,000 to be paid by the trustees for the King's Bridge and other amenities of which they were beneficiaries. The formula for the payment of these sums was triggered by the pace at which the Orchardfield estate enjoyed increased feu-duties,

---

[37] ECA MC/GG/box 3, Minutes of Trustees, 24 Feb. 1820, f. 7. Playfair failed to submit plans and so those of William Burn were adopted.

[38] ECA MC/GG/box 3/3, Minute for the Master and Assistants of the Merchants of the City, 28 Oct. 1812; MC/GG/box 3/3, letter by William Burn to Mr Jollie, 1 Nov. 1820.

[39] ECA MC/GG, Orchardfield Estate, Accounts of Charge and Discharge for Whitsunday 1812, ff. 146–7.

[40] EPL, Report to the Master, Assistants and Treasurer of the Merchant Company relative to their Estate of Orchardfield and others, 14 Aug. 1867, provides a brief, though in some details inaccurate, summary of the feuing operations; ECA MC/GG/box 3/3, Report on the Lands of Orchardfield, 24 Jan. 1816, MC/GG/box 11, meeting of trustees, 24 Feb. 1820.

[41] ECA MC/GG, Orchardfield Chartulary, vol. 1a, ff. 8, 23, 81, 89, vol. 2, f. 356, vol. 3, f. 320.

[42] ECA MC/GG Orchardfield Chartulary, vol. 1a, ff. 505–10. See also 7 & 8 Geo. IV c. 26.

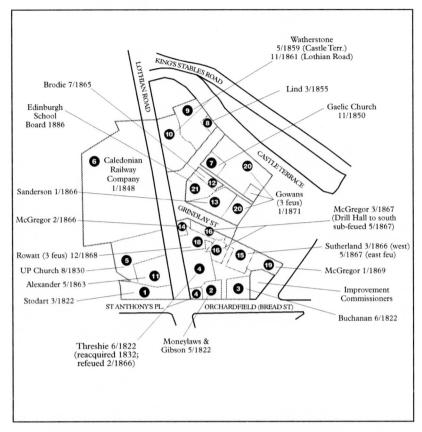

Figure 3.11 Orchardfield: George Grindlay's Trust land

Sources: NLS, Map Room, Merchant Company Lands, George
Grindlay's Trust, and ECA MC/GG, Orchardfield Chartulary.

but this gave little incentive to the trustees to feu their property in a slack
market. This was lessened further by the city fathers' insistence on polished ashlar, droved stonework and elevations similar to those in Downie
Place for the properties fronting Castle Terrace, even if they were less
concerned for the other streets on the Orchardfield estate. All things considered, it was not surprising that property revenues from feuing and
from rentals showed a resolutely stagnant trajectory for a generation (see
fig. 3.12).

Between 1822 and 1849 only two feu charters, both for non-residential
uses, were issued by Grindlay's trustees: one in 1830 was for the Lothian
Road United Presbyterian church, and the other in 1848 to the

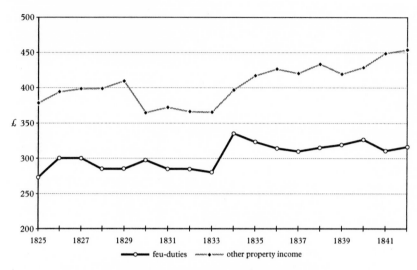

Figure 3.12 Property receipts: Orchardfield 1825–1842

Source: ECA MC/GG box 3, Accounts of Charge and Discharge, annually 1812–42.

Caledonian Railway Company for the property that subsequently formed the 'Caley' hotel, station and goods depot at Lothian Road, and provided the Caledonian Railway with access to the heart of New Town Edinburgh.[43] The purchase price, £7,000, was a bargain, equivalent to just 15.5 years of annual feu-duty payments, and a measure of how weak the landowners' market position was in the city.[44] Indeed, the state of the property market in the second quarter of the nineteenth century was described to Grindlay's trustees as 'a long period of great depression in the building trade of Edinburgh ... and it was not until 1849 that the trustees received another offer to feu'.[45]

On the Drumdryan and Orchardfield property to the south and west of the city property development was on hold for a quarter of a century after the banking crisis of 1825, and gaps remained between the tenements built on Rigg's and Grindlay's lands. On Heriot's extensive property in north Edinburgh the experience was similar, and serrated courses of stonework and the gap in Saxe Coburg Place still testify to the abruptness with which workmen downed tools when funding dried up. Ambitious

[43] ECA MC/GG Orchardfield Chartulary, vol. 2, f. 329, 13 Aug. 1830, vol. 3, ff. 41–84, 18 Jan. 1848.
[44] A figure nearer twenty years purchase was not uncommon before this date, and from the 1850s was normally over twenty years, rising in some cases to twenty-six or twenty-eight years purchase. See below, chapter 5.
[45] ECA MC/GG, History of feuing operations, ff. 14–15.

plans for a crescent were curtailed and transformed Malta Crescent into a mere Terrace.[46] However, long before building revived, the opportunity to create an elegant neighbourhood to the south of the New Town had long since evaporated since neither James Home Rigg nor George Grindlay's trustees grasped how essential it was to defend the social tone of an area through strictly defined conditions in the feu charter. Consequently, commercial development, principally associated with the Union Canal and the Caledonian Railway terminus, encroached on the western margins of the area, whilst the spectre of civic improvement in the form of a 'new west approach' road skirting the Castle rock added yet more uncertainty and a Regency form of planning blight.

Planning blight and feuing prospects

The prospects for property development to the south and west of Edinburgh were never the same again from 1824. A hint of development was underway in the early 1820s with the early stances on Drumdryan and Orchardfield feued for building, but an improvement plan and a dramatic fire in the heart of the Old Town at the junction of Old Assembly Close and the High Street provided the spur to a fundamental reassessment of the communications by the town council. Public decisions redefined private feuing prospects, and if these could not be immediately implemented because of financial conditions and oversupply in the housing market, then superiors began to eye the potential windfall themselves by laying out feuing plans and preparing for the upturn when it did eventually materialise.

On Sunday 21 November 1824, with the embers of a major fire still warm, the Rev. J. Peddie preached on 'The hand of God in public calamities' using as his text Numbers, x, 6: 'Let your brethren . . . bewail the burning which the Lord hath kindled', and littered his oration with biblical references to the spiritual good which came from temporal evil.[47] As for moral evil, that is, crimes against society and sins against God, he observed: 'when may it not be said there is moral evil in the city'.[48] From a pulpit nearby, the Rev. J. A. Haldane used another text to the same purpose in an attempt to assist his congregation to comprehend why God took vengeance, and encouraged his flock to atone for their sins.[49] The collections in the kirks of Edinburgh brought in £1,500 that Sunday

---

[46] I am grateful to Jean Grier for information on this point.
[47] J. Peddie, *The Hand of God in Public Calamities* (Edinburgh 1824).
[48] Peddie, *The Hand of God*, 8. Peddie distinguished between moral and natural evil – the latter being defined as poverty, destitution and hunger – and his text for such a distinction was, 'For the poor shall never cease out of the land', Deut., xv, 11.
[49] J. A. Haldane, *The Importance of Hearing the Voice of God* (Edinburgh 1824).

specifically for the relief of those affected by the fires, and soon the Relief Fund stood at £5,000.[50]

The fires started in a printer's premises within a seven-storey High Street tenement, and spread quickly through the continuous roof spaces of nearby tenements of mixed residential and commercial uses.[51] Gable walls collapsed as the fire extended southwards towards the Cowgate. Just as the fire was brought within control and the flames subsided after more than twelve hours, sparks ignited the steeple of the Tron Church. The heat was so great that the lead roof and the two ton church bell were melted and the firemen forced to retreat. After another twelve hours of fire-fighting, a third fire, unconnected to the others since it was upwind, broke out in an eleven storey tenement in Parliament Square 'in a house occupied by a woman of bad character named Macdonald'. Newspaper accounts were vivid, and the subsequent engravers' versions graphic:

the appearance from the Cowgate was singularly *terrific* – torrents of flame bursting with irresistible fury from every aperture . . . rising to an amazing height . . . brightly reflected in the sky while the red glare which they shed on adjacent buildings and on the battlements of the Castle were at once picturesque and awful.[52]

The scene was 'of a city sacked and burnt by an enemy'.[53] Ten people died from falling gables and roofs, 400–500 were estimated to be homeless, and damage was assessed at a minimum of £200,000. The activities of the Lord Advocate, Lord President and Lord Justice-Clerk as relief firemen in place of the exhausted employees of the fire insurance companies were reported as inspirational to others around them for their 'zeal and intrepidity'.[54]

The Lord Provost, magistrates and police officers also 'exerted themselves with the greatest activity' and no doubt the heroic actions of these public servants served to strengthen an impression of their trusty stewardship of the common good.[55] Two days before the fires and after months of

[50] *Report of the Proceedings of the Committee Appointed for Distributing the Subscriptions Made for the Relief of Sufferers on the Occasion of the Calamitous Fires in Edinburgh* (Edinburgh 1825), 5–13.

[51] Edinburgh Annual Register, 1824, *Chronicle*, 239–45; *Report of the Proceedings of the Committee Appointed for Distributing the Subscriptions*, 5–11; R. Chalmers, *Notices of the Most Remarkable Fires in Edinburgh from 1385 to 1824* (Edinburgh 1824), 54–74; T. R., *The Fire: A Poem* (Edinburgh 1827); Anon., *Account of Great Fires which Have Happened in Edinburgh from 1700 to the Late Awful Burnings* (Edinburgh 1824), 9–16. See also Edinburgh City Libraries, illustrated collections of the fires.

[52] *Report of the Proceedings of the Committee Appointed for Distributing the Subscriptions*, 9.

[53] *Report of the Proceedings of the Committee Appointed for Distributing the Subscriptions*, 13.

[54] Edinburgh Annual Register, 1824, *Chronicle*, 242.

[55] *Report of the Proceedings of the Committee Appointed for Distributing the Subscriptions*, 11. The dragoons from Piershill Barracks, artillerymen from Leith Fort and cavalry of Edinburgh Yeomanry also assisted the private fire appliances of the Sun, Caledonian, North British, Friendly and Royal Exchange fire insurance companies.

Figure 3.13 'Great Fire' at the Tron Church 1824

Source: Edinburgh City Libraries, J.M.W. Turner, Conflagration at the Tron Church Edinburgh 16 Nov. 1824, lithograph by Robertson and Ballatine.

discussions, the town council had reached agreement to submit a bill to parliament to raise a 2% levy for ten years so that various thoroughfares could be cleared and transport access improved.[56]

In the early nineteenth century the principal transport artery through Edinburgh remained the ancient line along the Cowgate and Grassmarket to the West Port. It was an extremely constricted route and since it was one of the lowest points in the city, there were steep gradients to access the High Street. Thomas Hamilton, the architect responsible for the feuing plan for Grindlay's Orchardfield estate in 1820, together with William Burn presented a report for a new approach road on the south of the city and to which other prominent architects and engineers, W. H. Playfair, Thomas Leslie and Robert Stevenson added their weight.[57] Burn and Hamilton appealed to public interest, therefore, by proposing that a western approach road would bypass this narrow and obstructed route, and which at the West Port was so steep that 'it is almost impracticable to wheeled carriages and isolates . . . the Castlehill, Lawnmarket and that portion of the High Street above the Bridges from these districts'.[58]

The real purpose of the proposal, however, was that it opened up the property around Bristo Place, Lauriston Place, Teviot Row, George Square and Buccleugh Place which, 'rendered readily accessible from every quarter, will become much more valuable'.[59] Cleverly, the architects also identified that the Charity Workhouse 'must become a very desirable and eligible situation for building' and so the city as owners would gain in feuing value and thus recoup some of the cost of street improvements. In an undisguised appeal to landowners to the south of the Meadows, the proposal also included a new Greyfriars gate, pinnacle and tracery to improve its appearance, and a gate at the Meadows to improve the 'consistency and give further importance to these improvements'.[60] The plan was an echo of the improvement forty years earlier when, as a result of the construction of the South Bridge 'the town shot out to more than a mile of length, while to both east and west it remained nearly within its ancient limits'.[61] Public disbursements for private property interests were in 1824 again at the heart of the proposal, and one sceptical New Town resident saw through the plan:

[56] ECA SL63/4/2, Minutes of a Meeting of a General Committee relative to the New Improvements in Edinburgh, 13 Nov. and 27 Dec. 1824.
[57] ECA SL63/4/2, Report Relative to the Proposed Approaches, 18 Nov. 1824. There were previous versions in the spring, 1824. See also Description by Thomas Leslie, 16 June 1824.   [58] ECA SL63/4/2, Report Relative to the Proposed Approaches, f. 1.
[59] ECA SL63/4/2, Report Relative to the Proposed Approaches, f. 1.
[60] ECA SL63/4/2, Report Relative to the Proposed Approaches, f. 1.
[61] ECA SL63/4/2, Statement relative to the Improvements of the City of Edinburgh (Edinburgh 1826), 2. See also Youngson, The Making of Classical Edinburgh, 111–32.

the measure will . . . bring into immediate usefulness various large districts which
tho' lying close around the town are now as much disconnected from it by the
nature of the ground as if they were separated by distance.[62]

As a politically astute document, Burn and Hamilton's report presented a powerful case to all property owners and appealed to enlightened
citizens. Owners of houses at the High Street and West Port would find
their values increased; the business decline of the Old Town would be
arrested; New Town residents would have improved access to the High
Street; refuse areas would find 'a value will be conferred on ground which
is at present little better than a receptacle of filth'; demolitions, though
limited, would remove poor quality structures and health hazards; and
aesthetically the entire city would benefit.[63] The spirit of improvement
was in effect a challenge to its critics to deny progress; to object to
progress was to deny the spirit of a Scottish enlightenment.[64]

The first attempt to obtain parliamentary approval failed in 1825.
Objectors materialised at all turns. Existing house proprietors objected to
the imposition of a tax from which they would not benefit, and which by
prompting further feuing, would tend 'to diminish the value of their property'.[65] So strongly did they hold their views that they petitioned the
House of Commons to protect them from a tax which was 'neither necessary, nor desired by them' and whose 'real object' they claimed was
'under the pretext of taste and ornament to enhance the value of property
in the line of the projected streets'.[66] The legitimacy of the council to tax
for purposes of improvements beyond the boundaries of the city was
questioned.

Factionalism emerged to delay a revised bill: Playfair acknowledged
advantages to the University; the incorporated trades identified job
creation as the likely outcome but were anxious about Irish immigrant
labour; New Town residents opposed a tax subsidy to the Old Town;
landlords were anxious about the likely fall in rents in the areas to be
cleared.[67] The piazza for Parliament Square and Flemish style proposals

---

[62] ECA SL63/4/2, letter from Thomas Allan, 15 June 1824.

[63] ECA SL63/4/2, *Statement relative to the Improvements of the City of Edinburgh*, 4.

[64] For the context of enlightenment see, for example, R. A. Houston, *Social Change in the
Age of Enlightenment: Edinburgh 1660–1760* (Oxford 1994), 11–13; T. Markus,
'Introduction', in Markus, ed., *Order in Space and Society*, 1–10; D. Daiches, 'The
Scottish Enlightenment', in D. Daiches, P. Jones and J. Jones, eds., *A Hotbed of Genius:
The Scottish Enlightenment 1730–1790* (Edinburgh 1986), 1–42.

[65] ECA SL63/4/2, Petition to Parliament of the Eight Southern Districts, 15 Apr. 1825.

[66] ECA SL63/4/2, Petition to Parliament of the Eight Southern Districts, 15 Apr. 1825. Sir
John Sinclair subsequently stated that the city would argue that improvements to Princes
Street and St Giles Cathedral would constitute a 'public good' and thus tax could be
assessed to all inhabitants. ECA SL63/4/2, Sinclair to Drysdale, 16 Mar. 1827.

[67] *Edinburgh Advertiser*, 24 Oct. and 19 Dec. 1826.

for the Lawnmarket drew accusations of architectural vandalism. The improvement plan was also claimed to have blighted property development since 'there has hardly been a feu charter granted in Edinburgh since the improvement plan was published'.[68] Very specific objections delayed matters too – the line of the proposed new bridge (George IV Bridge) and whether it would be dog-legged past the Bank of Scotland headquarters or sweep through in a straight line down the Mound to Princes Street. Most contentious of all was the resurrection of the city's wish to feu to the south of Princes Street, as well as at the Meadows and Bruntsfield links in order to recoup expenses associated with the civil engineering costs of bridge building and road making.[69]

The destiny of Edinburgh's southern development was brokered at the committee stage of the revised bill in May 1827.[70] The southern and western approach proposals were accepted by a majority of a Commons committee to which it was referred, but unanimously they insisted on the insertion of an amended clause in the bill 'to restrain the Magistrates and Town Council of Edinburgh from building upon any part of the ground called the Meadows and Burntsfield Links [*sic*]'.[71] It was Lord Shaftesbury who left the Edinburgh delegation in no doubt about the prospects of the Improvement Act when in a private meeting he stated that 'the clause could not pass the House of Lords' if the amendment protecting the Links 'was not assented to by the Lord Provost, Magistrates and Council, the proprietors of the ground'.[72] The Edinburgh delegation took note of the heavy hint from Shaftesbury and acceded to the additional clause.[73]

Feuing potential

The population of Edinburgh doubled to 120,000 between 1790 and 1827, a rate of growth judged to be 'unexampled in the three kingdoms'

---

[68] ECA SL63/4/2, Considerations submitted by a Committee of Inhabitants, 26 Feb. 1827. For positive views see SL63/4/2, Statement by the Committee of Magistrates and Inhabitants of the City of Edinburgh, and, Case in support of a Bill entitled 'A Bill for carrying into effect certain Improvements within the City of Edinburgh'.

[69] *Edinburgh Courant* and *Edinburgh Advertiser*, both 9 Dec. 1826, provide background to the progress of the revised bill.   [70] *Edinburgh Observer*, 15 May 1827.

[71] *Edinburgh Observer*, 15 May 1827; see also *Scotsman*, 16 May 1827. The clause stated that: 'and be it further enacted that it shall not be competent to, nor in the power of, the Lord Provost, Magistrates and Council of Edinburgh, or any other person or persons, without the sanction of Parliament obtained for the express purpose, at any time hereafter to erect buildings of any kind upon any part of the ground called the Meadows and Burntsfield Links, belonging in property to the said Lord Provost, Magistrates and Council'.   [72] *Edinburgh Observer*, 15 May 1827.

[73] *Edinburgh Observer*, 15 May 1827. Only the Lord Provost refused to agree to the amendment.

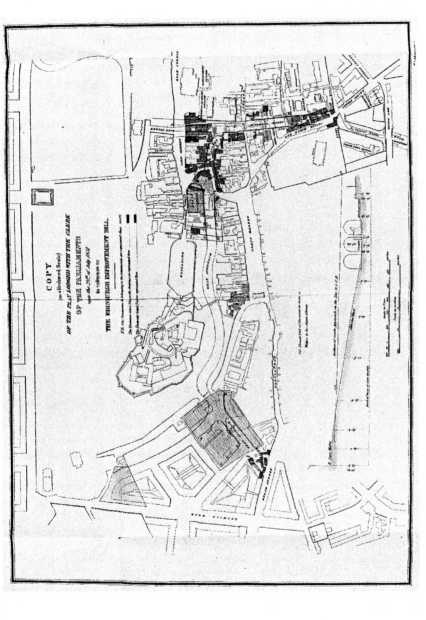

Figure 3.14 Improvement Scheme 1824–1831

Note: after several different versions, the improvement plan that was eventually approved shows the new 'west approach' road (now Johnston Terrace) linked with the Lawnmarket. A southern access road was created by the construction of George IV Bridge. Note the reorganisation to the west (now Castle Terrace) which affected George Grindlay's Orchardfield estate. *Source*: ECA SL63/4/11, Improvement Scheme, map 1831.

of Britain.[74] Overlooking the hyperbole, this numerical growth averaged approximately 30% per decade, and though *The Scotsman* anticipated continued growth, in fact it came to an abrupt halt in the 1830s when the decennial increase dropped to just 2.5%. The feuing inertia which resulted cumulatively from the mid-1820s banking crisis, an overextension to feuing in the post-Napoleonic years and the uncertainty caused by the improvement proposals 1824–7 was reinforced by weak aggregate demand growth as reflected in low population expansion in the 1830s. Thus blighted, the property market was unable to respond vigorously to the short-run development possibilities created by bridge and road building associated with the Improvement Scheme, or the replacement of fire damage.

The potential expansion to the south and south-west did not materialise, and no new residential feus were issued on either of the strategically located Drumdryan and Orchardfield estates. Building work on the embryonic southern suburb of Newington came almost to a standstill in the late 1820s, and the feuing plan drawn up by David Cousin in 1825 for the Grange, an extensive southern estate owned mainly by the Dick Lauder family, was suspended until 1852, when it was then revised.[75] A little beyond the Drumdryan property, the Merchiston lands of George Watson's Hospital, like the remainder of their farms, experienced an actual downturn in rents in 1827–8.[76] Indeed, the stagnation of the Edinburgh property market seemed to be typified by the Merchiston estate where, between 1831 and 1851, much of their land remained committed to agricultural uses.[77]

The downturn in the housing market provided an opportunity for a band of institutional land acquisitions to the north and west by James Donaldson's Hospital, John Watson's Hospital, the Orphan Hospital, Daniel Stewart's Hospital and Fettes' College which was, in later years, greatly to constrain the northwards development of the city, reinforced by the publicly owned barriers to housing development represented by the Botanical Gardens, Rocheid's Inverleith Park (a public park from 1893) and to which were later added Craigleith Poorhouse and extensions to the

---

[74] *Scotsman*, 27 July 1827. It was acknowledged that faster growth might have occurred in those towns where the economy was heavily based on a specific industrial product.

[75] M. Cant, *Edinburgh: Sciennes and the Grange* (Edinburgh 1990), 80–1; C. J. Smith, *Historic South Edinburgh* (Edinburgh 1978), vol. I, 28. NAS RHP 85, feuing plan of Newington 1806 is missing.

[76] ECA MC/GWH/box 3/1, General View of the Revenue and Expenditure of George Watson's Hospital 1823–9; ECA ACC 264, George Watson's Hospital Estate Reports, vol. 2, Report and Valuation of the Farms of Myreside and Gorgie Mains, 1826, f. 19.

[77] ECA MC/GWH/box 3/1, Lists of the different Heritable Properties, 1831 and 1851. For details of the estate, see NAS RHP 20578, 20583, 20584.

Royal Victoria Hospital. Crucially, each trust was set up in the period 1814–40 and acquired property when housing demand was exerting less pressure on the land market. Consequently, it was not difficult for trustees to implement the testator's wishes. This was so for Fettes' trustees who were instructed in 1836

> to purchase or feu a proper situation, as soon as you conveniently can, in the neighbourhood of Edinburgh, and to erect thereon a building for the maintenance, education and outfit of young people, whose parents have either died without leaving sufficient funds for that purpose or who from innocent misfortunes during their own lives are unable to give suitable education to their children.[78]

In the Fettes case, the trustees were the governors of the British Linen Bank, and after a review of the existing educational endowments in Edinburgh, concluded 'that the class of persons for whose assistance in the upbringing of their children the least provision had been made were those of the professional classes'.[79] Whereas Heriot's, Watson's and other trustees had identified orphans and the children of 'decayit burgesses' who had fallen on hard times as worthy recipients of charitable income, Fettes' trustees 'were strongly impressed' with the argument that the children of professional classes should be supported. While Fettes' Trust would provide the building, they explicitly required the parents of such pupils to pay for their education and thus the running costs of the school. The trustees' object, in short, was 'the establishment of a public school with a charitable foundation for its basis but with . . . nothing either of gratuity or charity'.[80] In 1864, after twenty-eight years of deliberation, the foundation stone for Fettes College was laid on a ninety-two acre site in Comely Bank, acquired in 1800 by Sir William Fettes. The trustees were the fifth largest landowner in the city of Edinburgh, excluding the Crown.[81]

While the property market and housebuilding remained flat in the 1840s, however, preparations were made for an eventual upturn. Watson's trustees were aware of the feuing potential of their property. Their architect, David Rhind, in terms which summarised the quintessential attractions of suburbia, considered the Merchiston property especially suited to villa development (fig. 3.15). He explained why

---

[78] ECA MC/box 2/18, Trust Disposition and Settlement, and eight codicils by Sir William Fettes, Bart., 5 July 1830, 30 Nov. 1831, 28 Feb., 27 Mar. and 6 Apr. 1835, 24 Feb., 9 Mar. and 19 Apr. 1836. NAS Books of Council and Session, 2 June 1836.

[79] ECA MC/box 2/18, Fettes Trustees' Memorandum, p. 3.

[80] ECA MC/box 2/18, Fettes Trustees' Memorandum. See also ECA MC, Report in regard to Sir William Fettes and his Endowment for the Education, Maintenance and Outfit of Young People, 27 Nov. 1883.

[81] *PP 1874 LXXII* pt III, Owners of Lands and Heritages, 1872–3, 66–9.

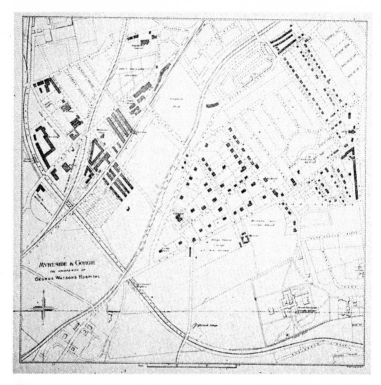

Figure 3.15 Merchiston Park and the development of George Watson's feu, 1862 (centre)

Source: NLS, MC Plan IV, Merchiston and Gorgie. See also NAS RHP 20587.

It [Merchiston] is admitted by those most competent to form an opinion . . . to be in the mildest district around Edinburgh; it is within easy walking distance of the New Town. The views from the different parts of the property are of great beauty and variety; the East Park commanding a most delightful and extensive prospect towards Edinburgh, Corstorphine hill and the Firth of Forth; the Dovecroft park, for those who prefer being entirely shut out from Edinburgh commanding an equally fine and varied prospect towards the Pentland and Craiglockhart hills. The Edinburgh Water and Gas already pass along the roads to Merchiston and Morningside and the district has become sufficiently populous to admit an hourly communication with Edinburgh.[82]

Rhind did 'not think the governors would better advance the interests of the Hospital than by feuing the ground for villas' on 0.25 acre plots,

[82] ECA MC/GWH/box 3/7, Report by David Rhind, 23 July 1844, ff. 2–3.

sometimes as double villas to encourage modest speculation, and with inducements to feuars in the form of lower annual feu-duties for those first to commit themselves to Merchiston.[83] Acutely aware of public utilities and amenities, Rhind also recommended that all plans had to be approved by the governors, and that given there were no trees on the Dovecroft Park and few in East Park then 'it would be desirable to have the ground planted, as it would tend greatly to add to the natural beauty of the situation for villas'.[84]

The market assessment of Watson's architect in 1844 – 'the most desirable situation for a villa residence with which I am acquainted in the neighbourhood of Edinburgh'[85] – could hardly have been more accurate, and in 1852 the Articles and Conditions of Feu spelled out the basis of future development.[86] Together, the feuing plan and terms of feuing anticipated the upturn in property development in south Edinburgh in the 1850s and 1860s, and in both these decades Watson's feued over seven acres, to be followed by twenty-five acres at increased rates of feu-duty in the five years 1870–5.[87] The pent up demand for housing which had been inhibited by market conditions before 1850 eventually burst and was expressed in an intense demand for both flatted apartments and suburban villas. This mid-century Edinburgh participation in suburbanisation was confirmed in the particularly rapid uptake of feus on the extensive Grange estate, also in south Edinburgh, where almost the entire area was feued and villas built in two decades (fig. 3.16).[88]

In defence of their potential feuing income and in recognition of its importance to their educational mission, Watson's governors opposed vigorously the proposed encroachments of the Caledonian Railway. Only 16% of their Merchiston land had been feued when in 1875 the railway company announced plans on land contiguous to Watson's for a station and thirteen acres of sidings. Watson's trustees stressed the residential advantages of their property and, more generally, the appeal of suburbia:

---

[83] ECA MC/GWH/box 3/7, Report by David Rhind, 23 July 1844, f. 4.
[84] ECA MC/GWH/box 3/7, Report by David Rhind, 23 July 1844, f. 10.
[85] ECA MC/GWH/box 3/7, Report by David Rhind, 23 July 1844, f. 13.
[86] ECA MC/GWH box 3/7, Articles and Conditions of Feu of the Dovecroft and East Parks of Merchiston, 28 June 1852. The conditions were subsequently amended somewhat in 1855, 1868, 1874 and 1897.
[87] ECA MC/GWH box 3/7, Brief against the Caledonian Railway Bill, 1875. For indications of that expansion, see NAS RHP 20587, Merchiston Park feuing plan, and ECA Plan Bundle 13/M4, Merchiston East Plans and section of roads 1870.
[88] NLS maps, Grainger and Miller, 1825; Cousin Feuing Plan of the Grange 1851; Lancefield 1871, all in The Grange Association pamphlet (privately printed).

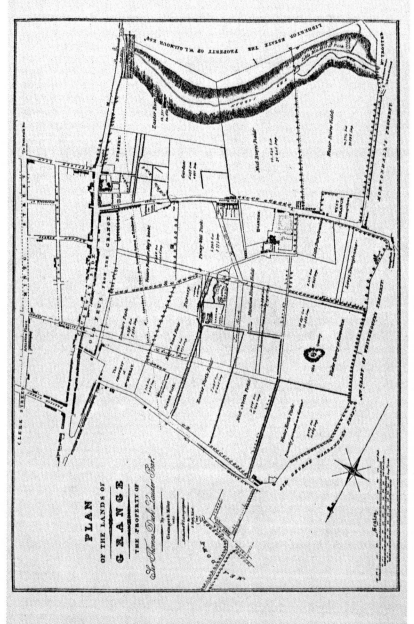

Figure 3.16 Southern suburbanisation: Grange 1825–1868
Estate plan of Grange, 1825

Source: J. S. Smith, *The Grange of St Giles* (Edinburgh 1898), 381.

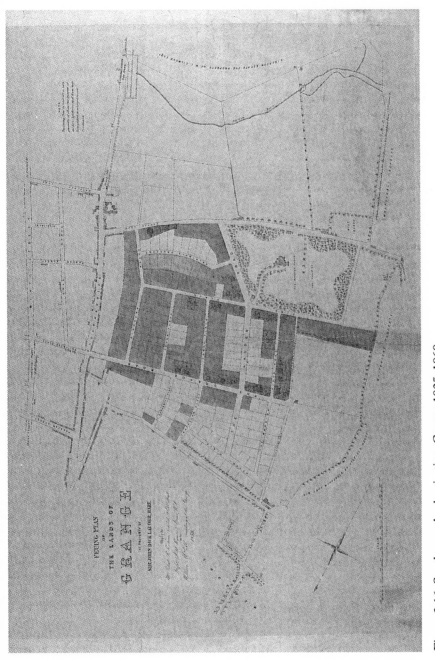

Figure 3.16 Southern suburbanisation: Grange 1825–1868
Feuing plan, 1858

Source: ECA SL145/4/6, Feuing Plan of the Lands of Grange.

Figure 3.16 Southern suburbanisation: Grange 1825–1868
Street plan, 1868

Note: within the space of ten years a major southward migration had attracted middle-class residents to the Grange.

Source: Edinburgh City Libraries, *Post Office Directories of Edinburgh and Leith,* 1868.

[Merchiston] is of a very valuable description. It has been feued off almost exclusively for the erection of large villas or self contained dwelling houses with garden or pleasure grounds which are occupied by the upper and middle classes of the city and also by parties of independent means who have come from Glasgow and other parts of Scotland attracted by the salubrious locality and its proximity to Edinburgh with the many advantages which that city affords its residents.[89]

Merchiston reeked of exclusivity, fostered by the trustees' efforts to defend the social tone against the incursions of commercial development. For example, Watson's argued that the proposed railway sidings would be of 'a most objectionable nature and would entirely destroy the amenity of the district' and claimed that 'no mere money compensation . . . would in anyway represent the loss the governors would sustain'.[90] Migration from north Edinburgh for the healthier and quieter environment in the southern suburbs would be compromised since 'by both day and night there would be continual shunting', and in a revealing line of argument Watson's trustees offered further opposition to the proposal on the grounds that it 'would occasion a large number of employees coming to the district' to work, and disingenuously claimed their opposition to this was because they, too, created more noise and smoke.

By feuing land under strict burdens and conditions for development, Watson's and Heriot's trustees, like private landowners too, set in motion a process of building development within a coherent framework. The suburban development of south Edinburgh and the northern New Town expansion on Heriot's and town council lands was substantially completed before the Dean of Guild Court's jurisdiction over building byelaws was extended to these areas in 1879.[91] This disciplined view of development, as Watson's trustees indicated in their opposition to the Caledonian Railway's proposals, was essentially in defence of their own future feuing revenues, which in turn were not unconnected to the sub-feuing possibilities facing builders. Feu-farming or sub-infeudation enabled developers to cover their obligation to their superior while generating an additional annual sum to which they were entitled, and using this prospective future income to obtain cash advances to undertake building work. For example, on the Drumdryan estate, James Steel feued property from James Home Rigg for the equivalent of £205 p.a., subdivided the building stances, built some himself and sub-feued to others and within two years the same area generated £370 p.a., a profit of 80% to be used for the next project.[92]

[89] ECA MC/GWH/box 3/7, Brief, 1875.   [90] ECA MC/GWH/box 3/7, Brief, 1875.
[91] R. Rodger, 'The evolution of Scottish town planning', in G. Gordon and B. Dicks, eds., *Scottish Urban History* (Aberdeen 1983), 71–91.
[92] For further details see chapters 6 and 7.

Particular impetus to sub-feuing was injected by a buoyant demand for new housing since this meant that, faced with a limited period before they had to pay the full feu-duty to their own superior, developers had to ensure that a sufficient number of plots were taken by builders to cover their own feu-duty obligations. Conversely, when demand for new houses was weak, as in the second quarter of the nineteenth century, then a developer himself could build the house, with less pressure to sub-feu. From mid-century, and especially from the 1870s, cumulative population pressure, deferred demand in the period 1825–50, rising real incomes on a previously unknown scale and significant boundary extensions in 1856 and 1879 produced an amalgam of circumstances which boosted housing and sub-feuing.

The revival in property development in Edinburgh can be dated from the late 1860s (see figs. 3.4 and 3.6). Few areas of the city were excluded, and institutional and individual landowners both participated in the revival (fig. 3.17). Whereas in the 1850s and 1860s feuing development and building was restricted to what Watson's surveyor called 'the upper and middle classes' and 'parties of independent means', and spatially confined to the western New Town and southern suburbs, by the late 1860s and 1870s, the development of the industrial suburbs of Dalry and Abbeyhill–Easter Road was underway (see chapters 7 and 11).

In the last quarter of the nineteenth century few other developments in Edinburgh surpassed the pace of expansion than that between Leith Walk and Easter Road. For two centuries following Trinity Hospital trustees' feu of land in 1681 at Quarryholes for an annual payment of £0.24 to Heriot's trustees, property development had been dormant. As noted previously, the Playfair plan for the area stalled in the 1820s, and as *The Scotsman* observed:

Thereafter there came the great crash in the building trade which stopped operations in this quarter for half a century. When building was resumed the original scheme of square and crescents had been cut up by railway lines running through the district while fashion had meanwhile shifted its quarters to the west end of the city.[93]

In a revealing demonstration of how strict feu charters and the introduction of real burdens after 1818 themselves could blight development, a Court of Session decision was necessary to release the superior from an undertaking to feuars to maintain the price at which his land was feued.[94] Real burdens, therefore, restricted both superior and vassal from degrading the site. Allen's trustees, like other property owners in the area, had expected the Playfair plan for crescents and squares to result in another

[93] *Scotsman*, 22 Oct. 1883.   [94] *Scotsman*, 22 Oct. 1883.

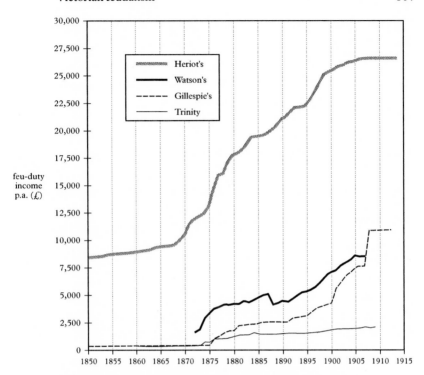

Figure 3.17 Property development: Edinburgh 1850–1915

Sources: NAS GD421/5/5–15, George Heriot's Hospital and Trust
Accounts; ECA City of Edinburgh Superiorities, 1913–14; Merchant
Company of Edinburgh, Annual Reports, 1850–1909.

exclusive New Town style development, and had assured feuars that, in
defence of the social tone of the neighbourhood, a minimum price of land
would be set. It was an undertaking which, under all market conditions
other than buoyant demand, blighted development and only when the
Court of Session revoked the obligation in 1880 was the way clear for
rapid tenement building in the vector defined by Leith Walk and Easter
Road. Heriot's, who still retained unfeued portions of land on either side
of Easter Road, and their vassal, Trinity Hospital, were the principal
beneficiaries, and as fig. 3.17 shows, their feuing incomes accelerated
accordingly. In east Edinburgh, therefore, the years 1885–93 were ones of
intense building activity and, for example, the firms of Andrew Hood,
David Heron, James Slater and Lawrie and Scott feued multiple stances
from the Heriot Trust and Trinity Hospital.[95]

[95] ECA George Heriot's Hospital, Roll of Superiorities, 1913–14, ff. 58–84.

Table 3.1 *Principal builders in east Edinburgh 1885–1905*

Builder	Feu charters (no.)	Feu-duties payable	Tenements (no.)	Principal streets
J. B. W. Lee	7	749	65	Leith Walk, Iona St
Andrew Hood	21	603	64	Brunton Terr. and Gdns, Montgomery St
James Anderson	11	555	55	Easter Rd, Montgomery St
Kinnear, Moodie	2	483	17	Leith Walk, S. Buchanan St
James Slater	6	483	34	Easter Rd, Bothwell St
Lawrie and Scott	11	410	31	Hillside Cresc., Brunton Pl.
William Finlayson	2	407	16	Dalmeny St, Easter Rd
Francis Briggs	2	338	24	Leith Walk
James Kinnear	5	314	14	Hillside St, Easter Rd
William Orman	3	304	41	Elgin St, Iona St
David Heron	11	277	27	Montgomery St, Wellington St
Charles Lawrie	7	263	24	Wellington St, Hillside Cresc.
Joseph Park	3	253	23	Leith Walk, Brunswick St

Sources: ECA George Heriot's Hospital, Roll of Superiorities, 1913–14, ff. 35–82, and ECA City of Edinburgh Superiorities, 1914.

For Trinity Hospital, administered by the magistrates of the city, the feuing income which between 1770 and 1870 had grown gradually from £150 to £300 p.a. increased tenfold between 1870 and 1900.[96] Heriot's overall feu-duty receipts increased threefold between 1870 and 1900; that of George Watson's and, from a lower threshold, James Gillespie's Hospital both increased fivefold (fig. 3.18). As suburban development moved southwards so Watson's feued remaining portions of the Merchiston estate and the eighteen acres of the Falconhall estate in Morningside, acquired in 1889 (see fig. 3.19).[97] Gillespie's trustees found an increasing interest in their Colinton and Spylaw property nestling under the lower slopes of the Pentland Hills and outside the city boundary.[98] However, before they embarked upon 'an extensive system of feuing' in 1877 they sought the opinion of counsel as to their powers to feu and thus to grant unchallengeable titles, a matter which had concerned them when between 1869 and 1874 they feued their limited city

[96] ECA City of Edinburgh Roll of Superiorities, annually.
[97] MC, Falconhall Estate, Chartulary, vol. 1.
[98] MC, Chartulary of James Gillespie's Hospital, vols. 2–4.

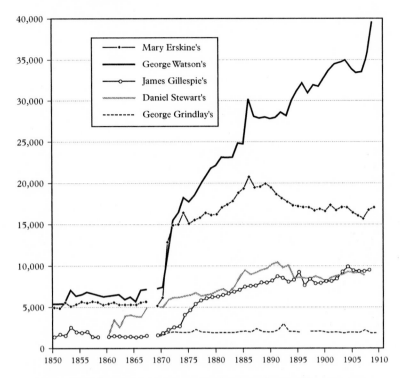

Figure 3.18 Merchant Company institutions: income from property 1850–1910

Source: MC, Annual Reports, 1850–1909.

property at Bruntsfield.[99] Gillespie's trustees were sufficiently reassured by their counsel's advice. They were charged

to administer the trust lands in the most advantageous manner for the trust . . . and it would not be good administration to let the property on agricultural leases when a better and permanent return can be obtained under a system of feuing. Accordingly, when in course of time the land becomes available for building stances we hold that the memorialists are quite entitled to take advantage of this new feuing value and to grant feus for building purposes, assuming always that as fair return is obtained and the land is not prematurely brought into the market. Such feus . . . are not alienations of the trust lands but are lawful acts of adminis-tration.[100]

[99] MC, Chartulary of James Gillespie's Hospital, vol. 1, f. 226 (Gillespie Crescent: W. and D. McGregor), vol. 2, ff. 126–32, 137–44. For further details on Gillespie Crescent, see ECA MC/JGH/box 3/3, Report, 5 July 1852, and Agreement with W. and D. McGregor, July 1869. The Scottish Lands and Building Company also took feus in the Bruntsfield area.

[100] ECA MC/JGH/box 3/8, Memorial as to Feuing of Colinton Estate, 28 July 1877, f. 19.

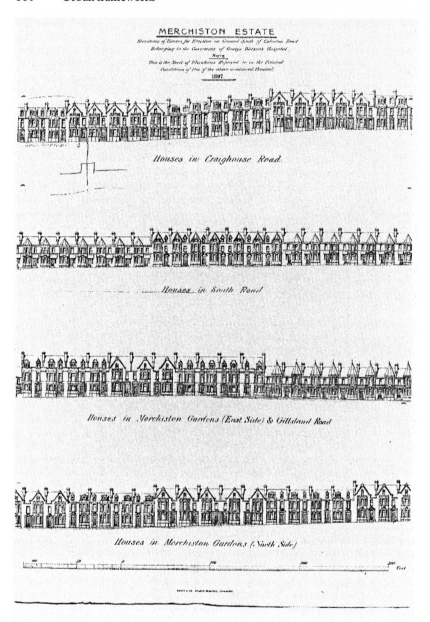

Figure 3.19 George Watson's Merchiston estate elevations 1897

Source: ECA Dean of Guild Court Registers.

Thus emboldened, though not advised to release land too soon or too quickly, Gillespie's trustees set about feuing and found the distinguished Scottish architect, R. Rowand Anderson, willing to take a number of the stances, on which the trustees stipulated detached houses priced at a minimum of £1,600 were to be built.[101]

Feuing and schooling

Realisation of the feuing potential of the Merchant Company Hospitals financed a revolution in the educational provision of Victorian Edinburgh. Educational deficiencies within the Merchant Company Schools, which had been acknowledged even before the 1860s, prompted an internal enquiry and the resulting report in 1868 urged the transition of the residential Hospitals into day schools.[102] The influential political contacts of Merchant Company members were used to press for the passage of the Educational Institutions (Scotland) Act 1869, and with the Home Secretary's approval of the changes, the rolls of the five large fee-paying day schools rose tenfold in a little over three years, from 394 to over 4,000 by 1872, and the number of teachers from 23 to 216.[103] This abrupt increase in the number of pupils educated at the Merchant Company Schools was sustained as a consequence of the judicious feuing development of suburban south Edinburgh, as controlled by Watson's and Gillespie's trustees, and by the meteoric expansion of the herring fishing industry in the north-east and the prosperity of the shale oil and coal industries of West Lothian which enabled both Mary Erskine's and Daniel Stewart's trustees to develop the feuing potential of their property holdings in Peterhead and Bathgate respectively.[104] In short, economic development and local prosperity elsewhere in Scotland were relayed to the restructured Merchant Company and then deployed to the benefit of the Edinburgh middle classes by means of expanded day school provisions.

Edinburgh Hospitals constituted 41.6% of all Scottish educational endowments in 1880.[105] Compared to Watson's (9.2%), Mary Erskine's (6.6%) and Gillespie's (2.9%), Heriot's alone accounted for 22.2% of all Scottish educational endowments. From the 1830s, that is, long before the Merchant Company institutions used their feu-duty incomes to fund

---

[101] MC, Chartulary of James Gillespie's Hospital, vols. 2–4.

[102] S. S. Laurie, *Reports on the Hospitals under the Administration of the Merchant Company, Edinburgh* (Edinburgh 1868); ECA MC/GWH/box 3/4, letter from William Gallaway to the Master and Members of the Merchant Company, 17 Aug. 1841, identified some thirty years earlier that celibacy and the monastic regime of Watson's Hospital as adversely affecting the educational standards achieved.

[103] R. D. Anderson, *Education and Opportunity in Victorian Scotland* (Edinburgh 1983), 179.

[104] MC, Annual Reports, 1850–1909.

[105] *PP 1881 LXXIII*, Return of Endowments in Scotland, 2, 17–19.

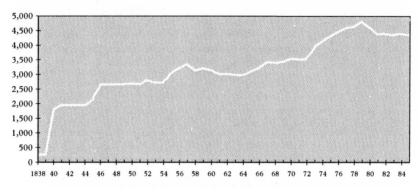

Figure 3.20 Heriot Foundation Schools: pupils 1838–1885

Source: NAS GD421/5/7/7–9, Heriot Trust Accounts, 1852–85.

the expansion of day schools, Heriot's trustees used this source of revenue to expand decisively their contribution to education in Edinburgh (see fig. 3.20).

By broadening the interpretation of George Heriot's will in the late 1830s so as to embrace the education of children in all areas of the city, the trustees constructed a system of feeder schools for the main Hospital School.[106] One of the architects of the scheme explained that the aim was 'to make Heriot's Hospital a great civic school for clever boys and girls selected from elementary schools' in what has been described as 'Heriot's empire of working class education'.[107] Accumulated property surpluses based on feu-duties were used to construct and operate schools and the first of these 'Foundation Schools', at Heriot Bridge in the Grassmarket, was opened in 1838. Five further schools enrolled pupils in 1840. By 1841, over 2,000 Edinburgh boys and girls, 95% of whom were from the most congested areas of the Grassmarket, Cowgate and High Street, were being educated by Heriot's on the basis of feu-duty income recycled from New Town building stances.[108] In all, thirteen Juveniles Schools and eight Infants Schools[109]

[106] 6 & 7 Geo. IV c. 25 An Act to Explain and Extend the Powers of the Governors of the Hospital in Edinburgh, Founded by George Heriot, Jeweller to King James the Sixth.

[107] J. B. Mackie, *The Life of and Work of Duncan McLaren* (Edinburgh 1888), vol. II, 192, quoted in Anderson, *Education and Opportunity*, 184.

[108] W. Steven, *Memoir of George Heriot with the History of the Hospital Founded by Him in Edinburgh* (Edinburgh 1865 edn), 259–61.

[109] These were Heriot Bridge (1838); Cowgate, High School Yards, Old Assembly Close, Borthwick Close, High School Yards Infants (all 1840); Old Assembly Close Infants (1841); Brown Square (1846); Rose Street and Rose Street Infants (both 1848); Broughton and Broughton Infants (1855); Victoria Street Infants (1866); Abbeyhill, Grindlay Street, Arthur Street (all 1874); Abbeyhill Infants (1875); Davie Street and Davie Street Infants (both 1877); Stockbridge and Stockbridge Infants (both 1878).

with an average roll of 3,300 were financed from Heriot's property revenues between 1838 and 1885, and at its height these Foundation Schools educated almost 5,000 or 13% of all Edinburgh schoolchildren in 1881.[110]

Approximately similar numbers were enrolled on the attendance registers of the reformed Merchant Company, and thus the instruction of over a quarter of all children in Edinburgh in the early 1880s was funded by trust revenue based on feu-duties. The dominance of the private endowments, and particularly that of Heriot's where there was a much stronger presence of pupils from artisanal families, undermined the autonomy of the Edinburgh School Board system. Not surprisingly friction developed, fuelled by arguments over the accountability of private endowments and their educational performance as demonstrated by a Victorian version of educational league tables, and after protracted resistance from the trustees, the Heriot Foundation Schools were absorbed in 1886 into the municipally administered school system.[111]

Composition of landownership

The intensification of Scottish Victorian feudalism after 1820 was devised to generate income from property, and the creation of real burdens 'in perpetuity' was the means by which this was achieved. Heriot's and Watson's Hospitals, as the first and third largest landowners in terms of the annual value of property in 1770, stood to gain considerably from tighter feuing conditions, but the benefits of enforceable feu charters applied to all landowners, large and small, institutional or private.[112]

As for the trusts themselves, their powerful position was reflected in the fact that five of the six largest landowners in Edinburgh were Hospitals or Trusts in 1770 and these five alone constituted 3% of owners and 30% of the annual value of property in the burgh.[113] Overall, trusts comprised 19% of all landowners in Edinburgh in 1770 and 39% of the annual value

[110] *PP 1883 LXXXI*, Census of Scotland, 1881, vol. II, table XII, 125.
[111] *PP 1880 XXIV*, First Report of the Commissioners on Endowed Institutions in Scotland, xlii–lxxi, and evidence of F. W. Bedford, and W. W. Waddell; *PP 1880 LV*, Educational Endowments in Scotland; Paper relating to George Heriot's Hospital, 3–37. For further background see Anderson, *Education and Opportunity*, 162–88. Pass rates in various subjects and percentages of scholars presented for examination in Heriot's Schools were compared to those of the School Board.
[112] NAS E/106/22/4, Abstract from the Cess Book of the County of Edinburgh 1771–2. For a long-run view of the structure of landownership in Edinburgh see NAS E/106/22/6, Valuation Book or Roll of the County of Midlothian or Edinburgh 1814, ff. 4, 6–10, 25, 29–33, 38–54, 106.
[113] The outlying areas of Liberton, Colinton, Corstorphine, Duddingston, Cramond and North and South Leith are excluded for the basis of the calculations for 1770.

of property.[114] The remainder – four out of five landowners – some 156 private individuals owned three-fifths of the annual value of land in Edinburgh. So the performance and feuing prospects of Heriot's and the Merchant Company Hospitals were of more than passing interest to a battery of smaller trusts which provided the annuities that sustained the widows and heirs of the Edinburgh middle classes.

Feuing income, of course, was inversely related to the amount of land retained since the release of land to a vassal produced greater feuing income but left less of the estate available for future development. Not surprisingly, therefore, a survey of landownership one century later revealed a number of changes in the structure of property ownership in Edinburgh.[115] For example, the penetration of the railways into the city centre had meant that they had become significant landowners by the 1870s with between 4% and 7% of the total acreage of the city[116] – though by no means was this as intrusive as in other British cities where railways sometimes accounted for 10% of land; in Glasgow the figure was 12%.[117] Company landownership, generally, had changed appreciably since 1770 as firms moved from family organisation to partnerships, joint stock and limited liability forms of business with offices, warehouses, workshops and factories owned by the company itself, and no longer held in the name of an individual. Indeed, whereas in 1770 it was difficult to distinguish between premises used jointly as a residence and a place of work, by 1870 approximately 17% of the area of Edinburgh and 39% of the property values were owned by companies, some of which moved to green field sites in land extensive developments at Abbeyhill and Dalry in the 1860s (see chapter 1). There were nearly fifty firms who owned at least one acre in the 1870s.[118]

While for many widows and legatees an annuity based on feu-duties was the *raison d'être* of property ownership, they were a source of income which also sustained an emergent breed of absentee landowners in the nineteenth century. Approximately 6% of the largest landowners, that is, those with a holding of at least an acre and who accounted for 18% of the

---

[114] These figures are based on the Valuation for 1771–2 with the Crown property in the King's Park valued at £2,542 excluded from the calculations.

[115] *PP 1874 LXXII* pt III, Owners of Lands and Heritages, 1872–3, iii–iv, 66–9.

[116] Only the largest 240 owners with property in excess of one acre were identified individually. There is a possibility that the railway companies owned other properties of less than one acre. If so, their 156 acres would be divided by 3,738 (the total acreage of the city = 4%) or by 2,558 (the amount of acreage held by the top 240 owners = 7%). The percentages for 1872 in this and subsequent calculations exclude the value and acreage of Crown property since Holyrood Park and the area of Arthur's Seat were not available for construction.

[117] J. R. Kellett, *The Impact of Railways on Victorian Cities* (London 1969), 290; N. Morgan, 'Building the city', in W. H. Fraser and I. Maver, eds., *Glasgow*, vol. II: *1830–1912* (Manchester 1996), 19.   [118] *PP 1874 LXXII* pt III.

Figure 3.21 Heriot Foundation Schools 1838–1885

Note: Stockbridge (St Bernard's), Davie Street, Cowgate and Holyrood Schools were four of thirteen schools financed by Heriot's Hospital trustees between 1838 and 1885 for the schoolchildren of all districts in the city. Each school still retains references in the stonework to George Heriot's crest or initials.

acreage and 8% of the value, were not resident in Edinburgh in 1872. These included such powerful figures as Sir Thomas Dick Lauder and Lt-Colonel Alexander Learmonth, who both lived in London on the proceeds of respectively sixty-eight and eighty-six acres in Edinburgh, and the trustees of Charles Rocheid's Inverleith estate (ninety-six acres), superintended from Oxford. The strategically important Edinburgh properties of James Home Rigg were administered from Fife, where the Earl of Moray also lived on the proceeds of his sixteen high status acres in the New Town. The seed of absenteeism was planted, therefore, with the commodification of property values after the House of Lords' decision[119] in 1818 which hastened the creation of real burdens and feu-farming. In turn, this stimulus to Victorian feudalism increasingly sustained both an absentee metropolitan and a gentrified lifestyle.[120]

Feu-duty incomes were 'exported' to London, Dublin, Oxford and, less predictably, to smaller towns such as South Shields. One absentee, Mrs M. C. Agnew, who owned forty-one acres at East Warriston and lived in Bristol, was also a member of an increasing cohort of female property owners in nineteenth-century Edinburgh. In 1772, property ownership amongst women accounted for 3.6% of all owners but only for 0.25% of the property values; by 1872, this had risen to 6.5% of the number of landowners though still only 1.3% by value.[121]

Institutional landownership assumed an increasing importance, too, with expanding civic functions and government responsibilities for Ordnance, the Board of Manufactures and other agencies each with land hungry demands. By 1872, the town council alone owned 8% of the acreage of the city (see table 3.2) and together with other institutional appetites, including public utilities and cemetery companies, this category of landownership accounted for 11% of the 3,738 acres in Edinburgh and 16% of annual land values.

Corporate and institutional landownership expanded as technological changes in the nature and scale of production and distribution fuelled their demands for extended sites and as a result of which private property owners decided to feu land to them. Consequently, whereas in 1770 approximately 80% of owners were private individuals who controlled 60% of land in Edinburgh, by the 1870s and amongst those who owned more than an acre, they had shrunk to 56% of owners in control of 41% of acreages and 36% of annual property values. Trust property, too, had

---

[119] *Gordon v. Marjoribanks* (1818), 6 Dow 87. See also chapter 2.
[120] Only in Glasgow and Dundee were levels of absentee landownership lower than in Edinburgh in 1872.
[121] NAS E/106/22/4, Abstract from the Cess Book of the County of Edinburgh 1771–2; *PP 1874 LXXII* pt III.

Table 3.2 *Landownership in Edinburgh 1872*
(first twenty ranked by acreage)

Landowner	Acres (no.)	Gross annual value (£)	Value of holding per acre (£)
Heriot's Hospital	180	4,770	27
Edinburgh town council	167	6,983	42
North British Railway Company	111	23,199	209
Trustees of Charles Rocheid, Inverleith	96	698	7
Trustees of Sir William Fettes, of Comely Bank	92	1,241	13
Lt-Colonel Alexander Learmonth, of Dean, MP	83	2,455	30
Sir George Warrender, of Lochead, Bart.	74	908	12
Sir Thomas N. Dick Lauder, of Fountainhall, Bart.	68	1,066	16
Watson's Hospital	53	1,718	32
Caledonian Railway Company	44	10,363	236
Caledonian Insurance Co.	42	1,561	37
Mrs M. C. Agnew of East Warriston	41	489	12
James Walker, of Dalry	36	856	24
Duncan McLaren, MP	35	1,513	43
John Hope	29	1,748	60
Richard Trotter, of Mortonhall	25	288	12
Thomas Nelson	24	182	8
Donaldson's Hospital	21	750	36
Trustees of Mrs Begg, of West Warriston	20	1,423	71
Mary Jane Falconer and Mrs Craigie, of Falconhall	20	537	27

Source: PP 1874 LXXII pt III, Owners of Lands and Heritages, 1872–3, 66–9. Crown lands excluded.

contracted somewhat in the course of the century as land had been feued to railway, business and public interests, but still it represented 33% of all acreages and 14% of all values amongst the larger landowners (table 3.3).[122] However, trust incomes stood on the threshold of a major expansion in 1872 when the survey was undertaken. With control of a third of the area within the city boundary still in the hands of hospitals, charities and private trusts, as well as a considerable number of acres just outside the city, trust incomes were set to enjoy an extended period of buoyancy (see figs. 3.4, 3.16).

The number of landowners expanded dramatically in the nineteenth century partly because the city boundaries were extended in 1809, 1832, 1833 and 1856 to colonise the surrounding areas and bring a larger

[122] *PP 1874 LXXII* pt III.

Table 3.3 *Composition of larger Edinburgh landowners 1872*
(owners of >1 acre)[a]

Type of owners	Number	Total acreage	Total value	% acreage	% value
Private	135	872	82,572	34.1	32.6
(Women)	(15)	(113)	(3,274)	(5.3)	(1.4)
Trusts	52	704	32,922	33.2	14.5
Institutions	5	179	22,449	8.4	9.9
Business	47	366	89,763	17.3	39.4
total >1 acre	239	2,121	227,706	100.0	100.0

[a] Crown lands in Holyrood Park (and elsewhere) excluded.
Source: *PP 1874 LXXII* pt III, Owners of Lands and Heritages, 1872–3, 66–9.

number of landowners within the taxable arm of the burgh.[123] Though in many cases landowners retained the right to receive a feu-duty, and in that sense still remained as superiors, it was the new occupants whose responsibility it was to pay local and parishes taxes on the basis of the annual valuation of the property. That there were 11,545 owners of property on the Valuation Roll for 1872 in addition to the Crown, as compared to only 192 in 1770, was an indication of the extent to which both the city had expanded and how properties had developed beyond the ancient and extended royalties of the eighteenth century. The composition of landownership in 1872 is presented in table 3.3. This group of 239 landowners constituted only 2% of all landowners yet owned more than two-thirds (68.4%) of the acreage of the city and 20% of its annual property values.

Of course, some continuities existed between 1770 and 1872 – Heriot's and Watson's Hospitals remained highly ranked; the Dick Lauder family remained prominent landowners in south Edinburgh; sizeable areas of the Dean estates remained intact but were transferred from the Nisbet to the Learmonth family, and the Inverleith estate of Alexander Kinloch was administered by the Rocheid trustees. Another consistent feature over the years 1772–1872 was the continuing presence of owners of small plots of land of less than an acre. Numerically, these were overwhelmingly the most common – 98% of landowners had less than an acre in 1872 (appendix 3.2). Owners of lands in the congested ancient royalty straddling the High Street and those who had feued plots for flats in the Extended Royalty or New Town were numbered in this category, and typically were sub-feuars from the major private and trust owners such as Heriot's Hospital, the Earl of Moray and the town council.

[123] ECA map of Edinburgh city boundary extensions. Further extensions later took place in 1882, 1896, 1900 and 1901. I am grateful to Richard Hunter for supplying information on this point.

The creation of Victorian feudalism in Scotland empowered all land-owners, whether private, trust or corporate, large or small. Each was enabled to deal in land, to create real burdens and to generate long-run income on the basis of the feu-duties and casualties created. The ability to raise capital to finance development and building, or as a capital injection into manufacturing businesses, or to secure entry to professional training, or simply to sustain styles of life to which the landed class aspired was facilitated through the creation and farming of feu-duties. Significantly for the development of Edinburgh, as for other Scottish burghs, the sale of heritable securities produced cash *ex ante* or up-front under the feuing system, rather than *ex post* in the form of reversionary values under the English leasehold system, and in this respect feuing ingeniously unlocked the future development value of property as a means by which to finance its development.

The development of a land tenure system based on feu-duties was a necessary condition to encourage landowners to release their land for development. However, feu-duties were accompanied also by 'feu-farming' which encouraged layer upon layer of feu-duties to be imposed upon a plot of land. Indeed, this was the central tenet of a property development strategy by which Heriot's, the Merchant Company, the Church of Scotland and an array of smaller educational, private and charitable trusts financed their activities. It was not, however, without serious implications for the quantity and quality of housing accommodation produced. The initial effect was to impose cumulative land charges and legal costs which in turn reduced the purchasing power of urban Scots and impaired the ability mainly of working-class households to rent sufficient housing space. The proportion of rent attributable to land was sometimes twice that of central London rents.[124] The consequence was environmental damage, defective sanitary provisions and hazardous living conditions. The morbidity of poor Scots households was not exclusively caused by the legal system, but it was a sufficient factor to cause the creation of feudal casualties to be outlawed from 1875, and contributed to subsequent and insistent demands for reform to the Scottish systems of land tenure and registration of property titles.[125]

---

[124] *PP 1917–18 XIV*, Royal Commission on the Housing of the Industrial Population of Scotland, Rural and Urban, Appendices CXXI, CLXVII, and Report, para. 592; W. Thomson, *The Housing Handbook* (London 1903), W. Thomson, *Housing Up-To-Date* (London 1907), 43–59.

[125] SLEC, *Report*, 331; *PP 1884–5 XXX*, Royal Commission, Evidence of Gowans, Q. 18892–3, Colville, Q. 19085; R. T. Younger, 'Landownership in Scotland', *Proc. of the Philosophical Society of Glasgow*, 20, 1888–9, 177–92; *PP 1893–4 XII*, Select Committee on Feus and Building Leases (Scotland), 1894, c. 477, 2nd Report, iii–vii; *PP 1910 LVIII*, Royal Commission on the Registration of Title in Scotland, 1910, Cd 5316; *PP 1917–18 XIV*, Royal Commission on the Housing of the Industrial Population, Report, paras. 1982–3.

Appendix 3.1 *Composition of landownership in Scottish burghs 1872*

	Landowners with >1 acre (%)			Landowners with <1 acre (%)		
	No. of owners	Acreage	Annual value	No. of owners	Acreage	Annual value
Edinburgh	2.1	68.4	19.5	97.9	31.6	80.5
Perth	2.5	70.2	31.6	97.5	29.8	68.4
Glasgow	2.8	62.4	26.8	97.2	37.6	73.2
Aberdeen	3.7	42.9	27.3	96.3	57.1	72.7
Dundee	4.2	87.7	39.6	95.8	12.3	60.4
Kilmarnock	5.4	87.6	30.3	94.6	12.4	69.7
Leith	5.8	78.0	44.1	94.2	22.0	55.9
Greenock	9.0	87.0	45.2	91.0	13.0	54.8
Paisley	9.8	80.0	43.5	90.2	20.0	56.5
Major burghs	3.5	72.1	28.6	96.5	27.9	71.4

Source: *PP 1874 LXXII* pt III, Owners of Lands and Heritages, 1872–3.

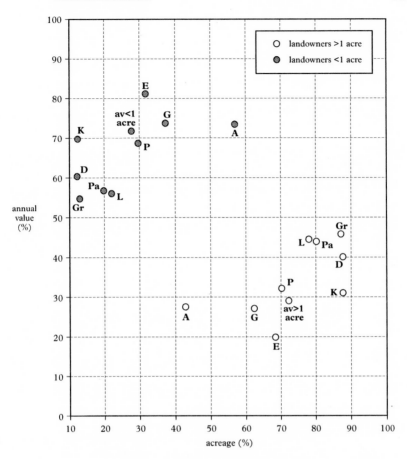

Note: A = Aberdeen; D = Dundee; E = Edinburgh; G = Glasgow; Gr = Greenock;
        K = Kilmarnock; L = Leith; P = Perth; Pa = Paisley

Appendix 3.2 Acreages and values of landowners in Scottish burghs
1872

Source: PP 1874 LXXII pt III, Owners of Lands and Heritages, 1872–3.

Appendix 3.3 Landownership in Edinburgh 1872

	Number of landowners								Percentage of landowners					
	<1 acre	1–5 acres	6–10 acres	11–25 acres	26–50 acres	50+ acres	all		<1 acre	1–5 acres	6–10 acres	11–25 acres	26–50 acres	50+ acres
Owners	11,306	173	28	23	6	10	11,546		97.9	1.5	0.2	0.2	0.1	0.1
Acreage	1,180	364	226	380	227	1,361	3,738		31.6	9.7	6.0	10.2	6.1	36.4
Value	1,041,364	123,150	29,772	15,216	16,530	68,299	1,294,331		80.5	9.5	2.3	1.2	1.3	5.3

Source: PP 1874 LXXII pt III, Owners of Lands and Heritages, Return of 1872–3, 66–9.

4   Building capital: trusts, loans and the kirk

Against the grain of nineteenth-century European history, Scotland reasserted the feudal structures of superior–vassal relations and sub-infeudation by means of increasingly strict conditions on land use and development, as specified in the feu charter or contract. It was not that labour servitude was reintroduced in a formal sense; it was the degree of financial servitude which was intensified. As urbanisation gathered momentum so the opportunity within the land tenure system to create successive tiers of financial obligations introduced more Scots to financial vassalage.

A central feature of the feuing system was that a fixed annual payment or feu-duty had to be paid by the vassal to his immediate feudal superior. Periodically duplicands and 'casualty' payments doubled the annual feu-duty received by the superior. For spinsters, widows and heirs, for charities and churches, as well as for a great number of individuals and institutions this assured income stream formed the annuities on which living standards and charitable purposes depended. Since feu-duties constituted a right to a perpetual income stream they were a negotiable financial instrument, that is, an entitlement to future revenue which could be sold for a lump sum. At this point the interests of annuitants and builders intersected. Individuals and institutions with funds for investment in property sought to buy 'heritable securities', the right to future feu-duties; builders and developers, who had obtained land from superiors, created a further tier of feu-duties on portions of the property and sold the right to receive the feu-duties to annuitants, trusts, institutions and individuals. By creating and mortgaging their future feu-duty rights, builders and developers obtained an essential cash injection for their construction activities while annuitants and trustees strengthened their property portfolios. It was a relationship which worked to their mutual advantage since both parties participated in the role of superior.

As population growth and urbanisation proceeded in nineteenth-century Scotland so the 'terms of trade' or balance of advantage for

superiors improved and, by creating additional tiers of financial obligations, the additional feu-duty burdens ultimately paid by tenants did
nothing to improve the purchasing power of the poor. Affordable space
was reduced and housing standards suffered accordingly. In an expansive
phase of urban development, as existed for much of the nineteenth
century, a seller's market for urban land developed in which higher prices
and additional tiers of feu-duty worked to a superior's advantage to such
an extent that the power to create greater financial servitude had to be
restrained after 1874.[1]

The feu charter was central to building development. Stemming from
the *Gordon* v. *Marjoribanks* decision in 1818, feu charters influenced
directly the character of the built environment through stipulations prohibiting specific noxious activities and by their detailed requirements
concerning building design and materials. Indirectly, but of perhaps
greater significance, was the power to create burdens and to commute
feudal payments for a cash sum which was embedded in the feudal
system. However, since there were no reversionary rights, as in England,
landowners and developers in Scotland were obliged to make very careful
calculations before they relinquished their valuable asset, property. For
example, Grindlay's trustees obtained £7,000 in 1845 from the
Caledonian Railway for the site of the Lothian Road terminus, but had
they waited twenty years the going rate would have yielded them at least
£10,160.[2] Against this had to be weighed the administrative advantage of
a single transaction, and the benefits of an income stream over twenty
years on £7,000 which at 3.5% interest would have realised £12,275.
Rationality and optimisation were simultaneous equations which were
difficult to solve especially since the time horizon was not simply the long
run but 'in perpetuity'. How different strategies were employed by property interests forms a central theme of the present chapter.

An overview of the complex structure of Scottish property relationships is presented in fig. 4.1. The lower part of the diagram makes a fundamental distinction in property tenure between house owners and
tenants and traces the differing pattern of payments of rents and rates
which stemmed from this tenurial divide. Proprietor–landlord–tenant
relations are considered in more depth in chapter 9. The upper part of the
diagram concentrates on the superior–vassal relationships as between
landowners and developers, and in which dotted lines represent the payments made for obligations incurred between the various parties (solid
lines). In fig. 4.1, the development of a plot involves four levels of

---

[1] The Conveyancing and Land Transfer (Scotland) Act 1874 stipulated that the creation
of new 'casualty' payments was not possible.
[2] ECA MC/GG, Orchardfield Chartulary, vol. 3, f. 41.

PROPERTY RELATIONSHIPS

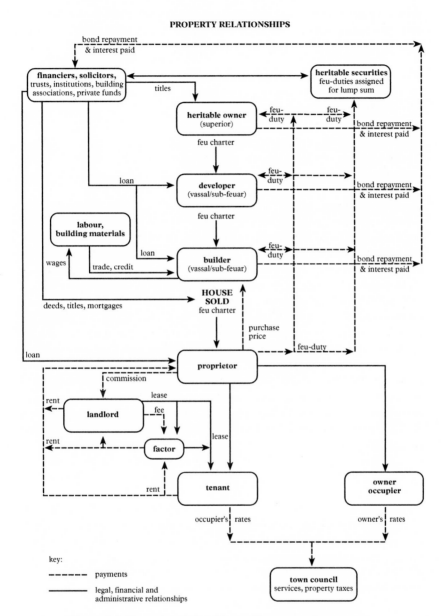

Figure 4.1 Property relationships: a diagrammatic summary

subinfeudation – heritable owner, developer, builder and house proprietor – as represented by the granting of a feu charter between each tier.
The assumption here is that the plot remained intact throughout, though
the resources needed to develop and build on land were commonly
beyond the means of a single agent. The linear presentation of the relationships in fig. 4.1, therefore, more accurately would have had several
lateral branches at each stage in the hierarchy of feudal relations. Each
sub-feuar was liable to his immediate superior for the full amount of the
feu-duty on the property though, in practice, the superior tended to
assign portions of the overall feu-duty to each vassal. At every stage in fig.
4.1, therefore, the vassal must pay a feu-duty to his superior, shown as a
dotted line. In the case of a builder, his own feu-duty revenues from proprietors were used, first, to pay his own feudal superior and secondly, to
finance repayments and interest on bonds obtained previously as working
capital for the building project. A third option was to sell his future rights
to feu-duty income (known as heritable securities) and receive a capital
sum which could then be used to finance further development or extinguish some of his own obligations.

Since every property was subject to feudal rights and obligations, these
had to be recorded in the land registry, the Register of Sasines, where bat-
talions of legal clerks transcribed entries supplied by ever greater armies
of clerks in solicitors' offices. The law practices, therefore, were at the
heart of the feudal system. If, as noted above, the builder sought to sell his
rights to feu-duties, it was lawyers who found buyers from their institutional, trust and private contacts. It was solicitors who acted as go-
betweens in arranging bonds so that builders obtained the necessary
working capital to develop plots. It was solicitors who drew up the terms
of loans, who drafted titles and recorded transfers of deeds and mortgages
in the central land registry. These relationships were complex,
intertwined. They are not, therefore, suited to two-dimensional linear
representations. Fig. 4.1 goes only some way to show the complexity of
Scottish tenurial and financial relationships and their interconnectedness
with nineteenth-century building development.

The functions of landowner, developer and builder could be concentrated into the hands of a single individual, though more frequently it was
the roles of developer and builder which were combined. Building itself
was financed from a number of sources – by trade credit obtained from
suppliers of building materials; by cash advanced from the eventual proprietor in stages as the house was completed; by loans advanced from
building associations or societies on behalf of their members; by loans
from property companies who advanced money speculatively from
share capital subscribed by investors; by private contact with influential

individuals; and by means of contacts established with solicitors who acted on behalf of trusts and institutions anxious to acquire heritable securities for investment purposes.[3]

Each of these sources of building capital is explored in the present chapter by subjecting the activities of institutions, the Church of Scotland, land and finance companies, building associations and the role of private trusts to examination. Sources of capital were diverse and the motives of the lenders no less so. The Church of Scotland, for example, recognised feu-duty revenue as a secure income stream for its city missions and rural ministries; it deepened the reservoir of building finance. In suburban Trinity, almost the entire range of factors affected development by a land company. This chapter also exposes the diverse and often idiosyncratic nature of property development in Edinburgh and Leith as individuals' and trustees' decisions developed their investment portfolios to include land and property elements as part of an agenda about family wealth and inheritance strategies. Methods of financing urban development were not static and the chapter concludes with an exploration of innovations in the last third of the nineteenth century which were a product of the constraints experienced as a consequence of the power of law firms over supplies of capital and an urgent need to extend and deepen the reservoir of building capital.

The Church of Scotland and building finance

Though Christ's expulsion of the moneylenders from the temple formed the text[4] for many ministers on the Sabbath, on the other days of the week the Church of Scotland was one of the foremost investors in heritable securities in Scotland. It was a particularly important indirect source of funds for builders and developers in Edinburgh in the half century before 1914.

In the immediate aftermath of the Disruption in 1843 the Church of Scotland established an enquiry whose terms of reference were to formulate a strategic response to the state of the ministry throughout Scotland in 1846.[5] Their report drew attention to 'the deficiency of pastoral superintendence' in the Church of Scotland in previous years, and to the 'exertions made by various bodies of dissenters' which in effect rendered

---

[3] R. Rodger, 'Speculative builders and the structure of the Scottish building industry 1860–1914', *Business History*, 21, 1979, 226–46.   [4] Mark, 11, v 15.

[5] NAS CH1/34/1, Church of Scotland General Assembly's Committee on the Endowment of Chapels of Ease, ff. 1, 11–13, 20–39, and the Church Extension Committee, f. 23. C. G. Brown, *The People in the Pews: Religion and Society in Scotland since 1780* (Dundee 1993), 11–18, identifies diverse schismatic forces in the Protestant Church before 1843.

Table 4.1 *Churchgoing in Edinburgh 1835 and 1851*

By denomination	1835 (%)	1851 (%)
Established Church of Scotland	44	16
Presbyterian dissent		
Free Church		33
United Presbyterian	30	27
Congregationalists, Baptists, Reformed Presbyterian, others	12	10
Non-Presbyterian		
Roman Catholic	5	5
Scottish Episcopal	5	5
Methodist	3	2
Others	1	2
	100	100

Sources: based on *PP 1837 XXX*, 12–13, and *PP 1837–8 XXXII*, 13, Royal Commission on Religious Instruction; *PP 1854 LIX*, Census of Scotland, 1851: Religious Worship and Education; and adapted from C. G. Brown, *The Social History of Religion in Scotland since 1730* (London 1987), 61.

church building by the established Church of Scotland as 'no longer necessary'.[6] So energetic had been the efforts of dissenters (see table 4.1) that instead of being used as an excuse for the apathy of the Church of Scotland, the report commented that it 'ought to make us heartily ashamed of such apathy'.[7] Indeed, the report continued, the inactivity of the Church of Scotland 'might well be held to denude her of the character of a Church of Christ' and so challenge her right as the established Church.[8]

Stung by the evident success of other denominations, the Church of Scotland resolved through its Church Extension Committee to embark upon a more energetic ministry after 1846. Exhortations were mainly biblical. Textual references to letters from Paul to the Romans, Ephesians and Corinthians littered the efforts to mobilise a campaign to found new churches. Central to this campaign was the precept that 'every member of the church has been assigned a definite ministry for the good of the whole',[9] and as the Church Extension Committee's report proclaimed:

[6] NAS CH1/34/1, Church Extension Committee, 19 Oct. 1846, f. 26. See more generally C. G. Brown, *The Social History of Religion in Scotland since 1730* (London 1987), 28–44.
[7] NAS CH1/34/1, Church Extension Committee, 19 Oct. 1846, f. 26.
[8] NAS CH1/34/1, Church Extension Committee, 19 Oct. 1846, f. 26.
[9] NAS CH1/34/1, Church Extension Committee, 1846, f. 28.

'Undeniably it is the doctrine of the New Testament that the Church is one body in Christ.'[10]

Spiritual destitution had many causes but one of them was the inability of the poor to support a church themselves, and consequently the Committee report appealed to the wealthy to subscribe so that new charges could be founded. The tone of the appeal for money was overtly that of the gospels: 'Shall we be excusable, then, if we thus shut up our own bowels of compassion against our brethren?', but it was also conveyed in language which had something in common with that of Friedrich Engels.[11] The attention of the wealthy urban elite was drawn to the fact that 'many of those for whom the Church wishes to make a more adequate spiritual provision are their immediate dependants – men whose industry has largely contributed to their affluence and in whose welfare, therefore, they must be deeply interested'.[12] The language of Dr Thomas Arnold, headmaster of Rugby School, was also adopted:

When we look at the condition of our country . . . at the poverty and wretchedness of so large a portion of the working classes, at the intellectual and moral evils which certainly exist among the poor, but by no means amongst the poor only, and when we witness the many partial attempts to remedy these evils – attempts benevolent indeed and wise so far as they go [but] utterly unable to strike to the heart of the mischief, can any Christian doubt that here is the work for the Church to do; that none else can do it.[13]

The dereliction of its Christian duty was addressed by the Church of Scotland through a programme of additional church building – 'a stone and lime extension in conjunction with an equally extended efficient pastoral superintendence'.[14] Part of this strategy involved the upgrading of many Chapels of Ease to full status in the Church of Scotland, in contrast to the under-funding and impermanence which before the 1846 report had consigned them to 'a painful sense of ecclesiastical inferiority' with no elders and thus no leadership or voice in the governance of the Church as a whole.[15] To fund the new corps of the Church Extension movement in the second half of the nineteenth century subscriptions were sought and obtained from prominent individuals. In this way a new model army of urban missionaries was funded.[16]

[10] NAS CH1/34/1, Church Extension Committee, 1846, f. 28.
[11] F. Engels, *The Condition of the Working Class in England* (London 1969 edn), 51–5.
[12] NAS CH1/34/1, Church Extension Committee, Minutes, 19 Oct. 1846, f. 35.
[13] NAS CH1/34/1, Church Extension Committee, f. 36.
[14] NAS CH1/34/1, Church Extension Committee, f. 24.
[15] NAS CH1/34/1, Statement on Chapels of Ease, 8 June 1846, f. 21.
[16] NAS CH1/34/1, Sub-Committee on Chapels of Ease, Minutes, 8 June 1846, f. 4; CH1/34/2 subscriptions, f. 203; CH1/34/3–4, list of legacies.

Subscriptions, Sunday collections and legacies were remitted directly or by presbyteries from all over Scotland and used by the Church of Scotland's Endowment Sub-Committee on Finance to purchase 'feu rentals' or heritable securities.[17] Thus, in 1854, the Committee had placed at their disposal an assurance of £120 p.a. from the Wishaw presbytery, and endowments of £40 p.a. from Lord Belhaven, £4 p.a. from Jane Houldsworth and £5 p.a. from a Member of Parliament, Alexander Cochrane of Lamington.[18] These and other receipts were used to fund a succession of purchases which entitled the Church of Scotland to receive feu-duties, and this in turn was redirected to establish new ministries in urban areas and to convert preaching stations to full charges in the counties where if anything religiosity was in even steeper decline.[19] Thus the Wishaw presbytery's endowment and that of private individuals were recycled in 1854 to purchase the entitlement to receive feu-duties at Ladhope, near Melrose, and properties in Claremont Street in Edinburgh. In due course this income was used to make a 50% contribution to the stipends of ministers in new charges, and augmented local funds for improving the fabric and furnishings of small charges.[20]

In the 1850s, the Endowment Committee concentrated mostly on purchases of feu-duties in Edinburgh[21] and then in the 1860s switched to a variety of estates in Glasgow – at Dowanhill, Donaldshill, Hyndland, Meadowflatts, Newhall, Broomloan and Cowcaddens.[22] By 1870, therefore, 150 new parishes had been endowed in the previous nine years from the proceeds of feu-duty revenues, and it was 'confidently reckoned' that 'the same average rate of progress' would be maintained in the ensuing period which saw an increasing reliance on feu-duty receipts as a means

---

[17] The initial subscription list in June 1846 included donations of £1,000 by the Marquis of Bute, £150 from James Kerr of Dunfermline, and £100 each from Sir Charles Ferguson, Sir Ralph Anstruther, A. Pringle, John Macfie, John Stewart Hepburn of Coquhaibrie, William Kinnie of Dunfermline. A number of smaller donations were also made.

[18] NAS CH1/34/2, Endowment Committee, Minutes, 20 Nov. 1854, f. 210.

[19] NAS CH1/34/2, Endowment Committee, Minutes, 9 June 1854, f. 331, indicate an approved financial system to show feus and sums available for rental.

[20] NAS CH1/33/4, Association for Augmenting the Smaller Living of the Clergy, Feu Register and Appropriation Book; CH1/34/6, Endowment Committee Minutes, 5 Jan. 1915. See also Brown, *The People in the Pews*, 14–15, 30–2; R. J. Morris, 'Urbanisation in Scotland', in W. H. Fraser and R. J. Morris, eds., *People and Society in Scotland*, vol. II: *1830–1914* (Edinburgh 1990), table 9, 92.

[21] These were in Saxe-Coburg Street, Claremont Street, Drummond Street, Roxburgh Place, Coltbridge, Kirkgate, Constitution Street (Leith), Wellington Place (Leith), Canaan Lane and Tollcross. NAS CH1/209, Endowment Committee Minutes, 1859–65.

[22] NAS CH1/5/209–11, Endowment Scheme Reports and Finance Committee Reports. For another dimension on the Glasgow property market in the 1860s see N. Morgan, 'Building the city', in W. H. Fraser and I. Maver, eds., *Glasgow*, vol. II: *1830–1912* (Manchester 1996), esp. 22–6.

Table 4.2 *Church of Scotland Extensions financed from feu-duties 1875–1905 (%)*

	1875	1885	1895	1905
Feu-duty revenue as a % of total expenditure on new charges	34.5	68.7	68.0	72.7

Source: NAS CH1/19/74–7, Endowment Committee Annual Accounts.

of financing the Church of Scotland's Extension (see table 4.2).[23] So successful was the property investment strategy that the stipends of 420 ministers scattered throughout Scotland were supported by an average of £68 for the year 1910 by the proceeds of feu-duty incomes (fig. 4.2).[24]

Though George Heriot's Hospital was the largest holder of feu-duties in nineteenth-century Edinburgh, its status was increasingly rivalled by the Church of Scotland. In the 1880s, the Church of Scotland's revenue from feu-duties was 80–90% of that which Heriot's received, though this had fallen back to about 75% in 1914.[25] But whereas Heriot's received their feu-duty income as superiors from land already held by them, the Church of Scotland owned little property other than churches, manses and glebe lands. During the second half of the nineteenth century, however, and particularly after 1870, the Church of Scotland bought heritable securities, or as the treasurer termed them in the annual accounts, 'feu rentals'. By investing substantial capital sums between 1870 and 1914 amounting to over £700,000 or the equivalent of £38 million in 2000 prices, the Church of Scotland brought their cumulative investment in heritable securities to £1,180,000 (£65 million in 2000 prices). From this investment, the Church of Scotland obtained an annual feu-duty income of almost £40,000 in 1914 – approximately £2.2 million in 2000 prices – which was used 'to support the erection of new parishes' in much the same way as Heriot's used its property revenues to support educational initiatives.[26] Over the very long run, from its inception in 1854 in fact, Church of Scotland investments had yielded, therefore, an average of 4.28% p.a., equivalent to a very healthy 1.5–2.0%

---

[23] NAS CH1/34/2, Meeting of the Sub-Committee of the Endowment Scheme, Report, 4 May 1870, ff. 387–8.

[24] NAS CH1/19/77, Endowment Committee Accounts, Factor's Intromissions: Stipends Chargeable on Feu Duties, ff. 11–17.

[25] NAS GD421/5/5/1, George Heriot's Hospital and Trust Accounts; CH1/19/74–7, Endowment Committee Annual Accounts; ECA Lists of Superiorities belonging to the Governors of George Heriot's Trust, 1913–14.

[26] NAS CH1/34/6, Minutes, 5 Jan. 1915.

Table 4.3 *Church of Scotland property investments 1854–1914*

	1854–1914	1874–1914
Edinburgh	54.9	68.7
Glasgow*a*	28.6	19.0
Dundee	0.7	2.2
Aberdeen	8.6	0.9
Other burghs	7.2	9.4
Total	100.0	100.0

a Lenzie is included in figures for Glasgow.
Source: NAS CH1/19/74–7, Endowment Committee Annual Accounts.

premium on gilt-edged securities, and a reflection of the attractiveness of property generally and heritable securities specifically to long-term investors.[27]

Although the agent for the Church of Scotland's investments took an interest in local property markets in burghs throughout Scotland, and indeed bought feu-duties in Oban, Inverness, Montrose, Broughty Ferry, Cupar, Kirkcaldy, Inveresk, Port Glasgow and in each of the four cities, 69% of new investments after 1874 were in Edinburgh properties (table 4.3).[28] This geographical concentration in the investment portfolio was well underway before the collapse of the City of Glasgow Bank in 1878 created intense liquidity problems for property interests in the west of Scotland. Between 1874 and 1878, that is, before the bank failure, the proportion of Church income derived from Edinburgh property increased by 43%, and if there was something of an interruption to this rising geographical concentration of Church investment in 1878–9 caused in part by the echo effects of the banking crisis centred in Glasgow, there was a continued small and steady upward drift from 1880

[27] Calculated as follows: (Gross Revenue/Investment)*100 = (£39,541/£923,637)*100 = 4.28%. The estimate of gross yield is very conservative. If casualty payments for compositions and duplicands were to be included, of which there were over 3,700 payments between 1872 and 1910, then assuming duplicands every nineteen years (or an additional 5.26% to annual feu revenue) and compositions and other occasional payments at half that rate (2.63%) then gross revenue of £42,660 would produce a gross yield of approximately 4.62% p.a. for forty years.

[28] Over the long run boundary problems haunt definitions of urban places. Church investments in Govan and Partick were undertaken in some cases when these burghs were independent and similar problems arise in Edinburgh. For simplicity and because it does not change the argument except in details, Edinburgh is taken to include Portobello and Leith, and Glasgow to include Partick and Govan. Lenzie has been treated as if it were in Glasgow.

Table 4.4 *The changing landscape of Church of Scotland property investments 1874–1913*

Heritable security income from	1874	1880	1913
Edinburgh	33%	52%	60%
Glasgow	50%	35%	25%

Source: appendix 4.1.

in the proportion of investment income derived from the Church's Edinburgh properties (table 4.4, and appendix 4.1).

The impact of the banking crises on the Glasgow building industry was spectacular with some two-thirds of builders forced out of business but it was also important for the Edinburgh building industry because of the investment vacuum created by the depressed property prospects in Glasgow.[29] Furthermore, the Endowment Committee which made decisions concerning the terms and conditions of new feuing investments, though it reported to the General Assembly and drew representatives from parishes all over Scotland, inevitably possessed an Edinburgh bias through their monthly meeting which invariably took place in Edinburgh's New Town. Not surprisingly, the Church's agent was best informed about Edinburgh heritable securities, a predisposition which was reflected in the 140 investments made by the Church of Scotland after 1878 and before the First World War, of which only 14 (10%) were in Glasgow, and four of these were between 1910 and 1914 (fig 4.2).

Events in Glasgow, therefore, reinforced existing property investment preferences in the Church of Scotland's portfolio. Very considerable sums, obtained from gifts, special fund-raising activities in the parishes themselves and increasingly from the reinvestment of property income itself provided the means for the extended portfolio of annual feu-duties which the agent managed. Though the typical investment was £5,020, between 1870 and 1914 there were over 120 decisions (70%) by the Church of Scotland's Endowment Committee to approve purchases of heritable securities at lower amounts (see table 4.5). Such diversity added a measure of security to the portfolio, though in reality the proliferation of these small investments reflected less an attempt to spread risk and more the relative infrequency with which large blocks of heritable securities came on the market. Also, superiors recognised that though there were

---

[29] Glasgow Municipal Commission on the Housing of the Poor, *Evidence* (Glasgow 1904), Q. 7011.

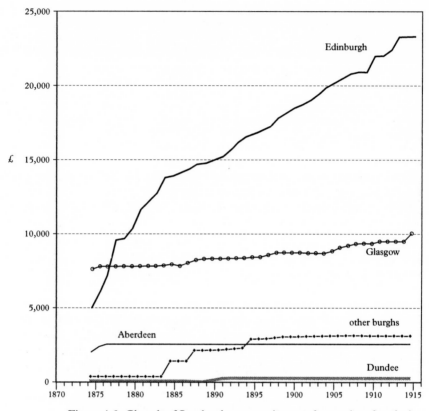

Figure 4.2 Church of Scotland property income from urban feu-duties 1874–1914 (£)

Source: NAS CH1/19/74–7, Church of Scotland Endowment Committee Annual Accounts.

some sizeable institutional buyers, the break up of their own rights to feus into smaller and more manageable amounts enabled a broader spectrum of private individuals, trusts and institutional buyers to express an interest. The modest scale of many trusts suggests that superiors and their financial advisers judged the market accurately and that in parcelling up small blocks of feus for sale they broadened the basis of demand to which they appealed.

Over the long term the attractiveness of property investment varied considerably. An indicator of this was the number of years purchase of feu-duties which potential investors had to pay. The Endowment Committee

Table 4.5 *Size distribution of Church of Scotland property investments to 1914*

Investment ($£$)	Number
100–999	41
1,000–5,020	87
5,021–9,999	31
10,000–14,999	9
15,000–19,999	7
20,000–24,999	7
25,000+	2
Mean = $£5,020$	184

Source: NAS CH1/19/74–7, Endowment Committee Annual Accounts.

sometimes declined otherwise attractive property investments, for example in the New Town, 'believing the price to be too high'[30] and not infrequently refused to bid at or even attend a public roup for heritable securities if the number of years purchase was thought to be too high.[31] At a sale in 1867 the agent was instructed to conclude a purchase but to do so 'without entering into strong competition with other buyers'.[32] More subtly, the agent was instructed to negotiate privately with heritable superiors in an effort to conclude a deal without going to auction.[33]

Property investors used the number of years of purchase to multiply annual feu-duties obtained from a property to calculate a capital sum for the heritable rights. Dominated by property activity in Edinburgh, the 195 transactions which the Church of Scotland entered into between 1870 and 1914 form the basis of figs. 4.3 and 4.4. These show how the number of years purchase indicator moved in almost half a century before the First World War. The annual observations are derived from the

[30] NAS CH1/34/6, Sederunt Book of the General and Acting Committee on the Endowment of Chapels of Ease, Minutes, 3 Feb. 1869.
[31] NAS CH1/34/2, Endowment Sub-Committee, Minutes, 10 Mar. 1863, 19 May 1865, 22 Nov. 1865, 19 Feb. 1866, 11 May 1866, 8 Jan. 1867, 23 Apr. 1867, 1 Apr. 1868, 3 Feb. 1869, 6 Oct. 1869, 4 May 1879, 7 Dec. 1870, ff. 153, 158, 174, 195, 210, 248, 264–9, 308–9, 344, 364, 383, 390.
[32] NAS CH1/34/6, Minutes, 28 Oct. 1867, f. 282.
[33] This was the case over the purchase for £60,000 of the largest single block of feu-duties at Newington. The agent sought to reduce the initial asking price in a series of enquiries, and though there was little movement on the part of the superiors, the bargain was eventually concluded. See Sederunt Book of the Acting Committee of the Endowment Scheme, NAS CH1/34/4, Minutes, 12 Feb. 1873, f. 6, 12 Mar. 1873, f. 8, and 29 Mar. 1876, f. 91.

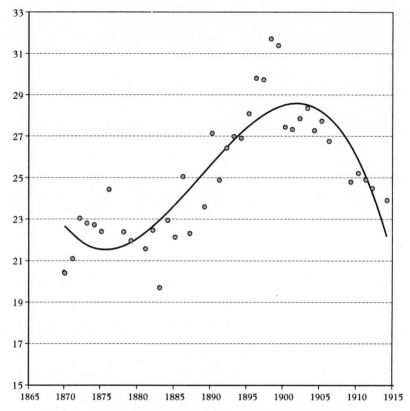

Figure 4.3 Purchase price of heritable securities in Scotland
1870–1914 (in number of years)

Source: NAS CH1/19/74–7, Church of Scotland Endowment
Committee Annual Accounts.

weighted average of property investments transacted in each year on
behalf of the Church of Scotland.[34] Broadly speaking, the pattern of purchase prices for heritable securities in the 1870s remained fairly static if at
a level a little above that of the 1860s. In the 1870s, a vendor could be
almost certain of 22–3 years purchase, but by the late 1880s the figure
had risen to 25–6 and by 1895–6 to obtain 28–9 years was not

---

[34] Though this includes purchases in other Scottish burghs this is justified on the grounds
first, that otherwise there would be several gaps in the data since purchases did not take
place in every year in every burgh; secondly, because there is an almost identical pattern
to the Edinburgh and non-Edinburgh data; and thirdly, because it is useful to develop a
series which has relevance to other Scottish burghs.

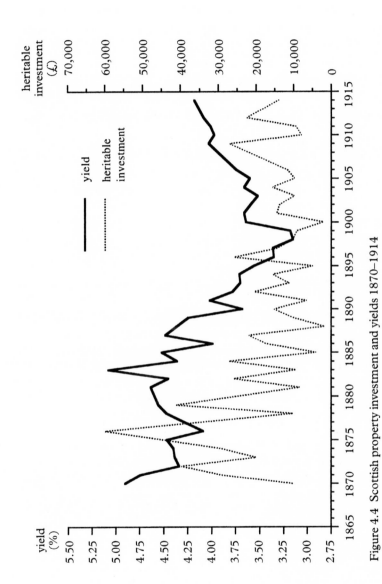

Figure 4.4 Scottish property investment and yields 1870–1914

Source: NAS CH1/19/74–7, Church of Scotland Endowment Committee Annual Accounts.

uncommon. Though this multiplier of annual feu-duties remained above 27 until 1905, thereafter it slipped back to 23–5 by the eve of war.

In effect this meant that feu-duties on property in Gilmore Place, Edinburgh, which produced £69.80 annually could be compounded and sold for £1,454 in 1879, as indeed they were, for £1,577 in 1885, for £1,845 in 1892, for £2,021 in 1903 and for £1,710 in 1912.[35] Correspondingly, and inversely, the yield declined as fixed incomes inevitably did when capital values were rising (fig. 4.4). But since even fixed incomes rose appreciably in real terms during the period due to a significant fall of about 40% in the level of general prices in the last quarter of the nineteenth century, property owners gained doubly, that is, assuming that they had not themselves borrowed heavily and were thus required to pay rising real rates of interest.

The purchase of feu rentals or heritable securities by the Church of Scotland was of considerable importance for the development of Edinburgh. First of all, the Church through its factor collected the feu-duties of a considerable number of Edinburgh citizens, as the map (fig. 4.5) of Church holdings indicates. As opportunities arose, so there developed strong local concentrations of purchases – almost £27,000 was spent on acquiring feu-duties in the Forrest Road–George IV Bridge area between 1871 and 1873, and a similar sum was used to buy heritable securities in the Tollcross area between 1874 and 1879. Portobello was the target for £37,000 of Church of Scotland investment between 1879 and 1885, and in the south Edinburgh middle-class suburbs of Morningside and Merchiston, the Church invested almost £100,000 spread over the entire period 1870–1914 to obtain the rights to receive feu-duty payments.[36] The single largest spatial concentration, however, was obtained in 1876 with the purchase of heritable securities in the Newington area for £60,000 paid over two years to the British Linen Company to whom the feu-duties had previously been assigned.[37]

The significance of the Church of Scotland's investment role, in addition to its internal agenda of church extensions, was the considerable injection of capital into the Edinburgh building industry. This was not in the direct sense of making available advances to builders and developers for working capital, but indirectly since by assigning the feu-duty revenues in perpetuity to the Church of Scotland, builders and developers received a lump sum for relinquishing their entitlements. Once the

[35] The number of years purchase for these calculations, successively 20.83, 22.60, 26.44, 28.96 and 24.50 are based on actual sales in the Gilmore Place area in these years.
[36] Based on calculations from NAS CH1/19/74–7, Endowment Committee Annual Accounts.
[37] NAS CH1/34/4, Endowment Committee Minutes, 29 Mar. 1876, f. 91. See also Minutes, 12 Feb. 1873, ff. 6–8.

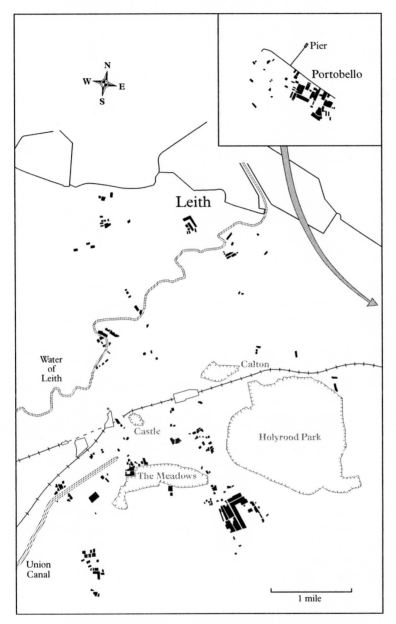

Figure 4.5 Feu-duties in Edinburgh assigned to the Church of Scotland 1870–1914

Source: NAS CH1/19/74–7, Church of Scotland Endowment Committee Annual Accounts.

buildings were substantially completed, and feus assigned to individual flats, a process which often required the superior's agreement, then the real burdens were created and the Church of Scotland's agent bought the future income stream from the feu-duties thus created. Commonly, the lump sum paid to the developer or builder was then used as working capital for the next project.

It was the Church of Scotland, therefore, which in 1869 paid James Steel £8,150 to transfer the right to feu-duties over his property in Drumdryan Street, and which thus provided the financial launchpad for subsequent building activity to the south of the Meadows at Sciennes.[38] Nearby, it was the Church of Scotland which took over the feu-duties on Leven Lodge and Valleyfield, paying almost £21,000 and injecting a welcome improvement to the cash flow of W. and D. McGregor, builders.[39] It was the Church of Scotland which between 1878 and 1880 competed successfully with other institutional and private interests to secure the feu-duties created by the builders Thomas Miller, Andrew Donald, John Muir and William Watson over their properties in Fowler Terrace, Dundee Street and Yeaman Place, and by the joiners and developers John Shackleton, David Johnstone, George Cairns and William Macdougall, also in the same North Merchiston and Dalry areas.[40] The Church injected £18,580 into these building businesses to obtain the rights to feu-duties in perpetuity.

Through its Endowment Committee alone the Church of Scotland invested almost £1.2 million in the property market between 1854 and 1914. Often, however, established parishes outside the Extension Committee's remit to support new charges themselves sought directly to invest in heritable securities in order to provide a steady annual income for their own projects. It was the trustees of Flotta church in Orkney and Ladybank church in Fife, together with those of St Kiaran's and Heatherlie churches, which provided the investment funds to buy the feuduties for Crichton Place and neighbouring sections of Leith Walk.[41] In so doing, these churches financed directly the building operations of J. W. B. Lee in 1899. Similarly, Southwick parish church in the presbytery of Dumfries paid £2,195 to generate £160 annually from the feus created by the Trinity Land Company in 1894 and thus infused the building activities of H., T. and R. Montgomery and others.[42]

[38] NAS RS108/7.79, Register of Sasines, Edinburgh, 11 Feb. 1869.
[39] NAS CH1/34/4, Endowment Committee Minutes.
[40] ECA ACC 282/2–3, North Merchiston Registers, ff. 178–83.
[41] ECA List of Superiorities belonging to George Heriot's Trust, 1913–14, f. 85.
[42] MC/TLC, Chartulary no. 1, 14 May 1894. I am grateful to John Lunn, Morton, Fraser and Milligan for permission to consult this material.

Such instances of parish church investments in heritable securities, like those of the Church of Scotland's Endowment Committee itself, were based on subscriptions and donations from all over Scotland, and increasingly from feu-duty revenues ploughed back into property investment (see tables 4.2, 4.3). It was a demonstration of the geographical recycling of Church investment funds between outlying Scottish communities and Edinburgh not unlike the recycling of Heriot's and Merchant Company feuing income for educational purposes.[43] The relationship was a symbiotic one in which small burgh and rural parishes participated in the rising property values and financial opportunities of the capital city while Edinburgh builders and developers obtained substantial cash injections for their businesses. In effect, heritable security investments were akin to land banks: the depositors (the Church of Scotland, the parish churches and trustees generally) provided capital specifically for property finance, and could cash in their investments at any time, though not always without incurring a penalty if the number of years purchase had declined since their initial deposit.

Trust, trusts and trusteeships

The Church of Scotland was a relative newcomer in the 1860s in recognising the appeal of feu-duty revenues as a secure and predictable source of income. These were precisely the features which, for some time, had been of critical importance to private trusts administered either personally or by legal and accountancy firms as agents. Where annuities of any kind were required to provide for marriage contracts, widows' allowances and annual legacies to family members, then the twin characteristics of security and dependability associated with heritable securities and loans secured on property titles proved of enduring appeal to trustees. So entrenched were trust funds in heritable property that Edinburgh was described in 1883 as 'honeycombed with agencies for collecting money'.[44]

Trustees were obligated to 'hold and administer the trust estate'[45] and were empowered to sell assets, grant feus and leases, evict tenants, borrow on security of the estate, to recover and discharge debts, invest in bonds and other assets, to distribute income and capital to beneficiaries and ultimately to wind up the trust. Experience and personal integrity, therefore, were central to the execution of these responsibilities and where a trust was established as a result of death, family members, personal friends and

[43] See chapter 3.
[44] A. B. Baxter, *Banking in Australia from a London Official's Point of View* (London 1883), 81.
[45] J. B. Wardhaugh, *Trust Law and Accounts* (Edinburgh 1928, 3rd edn), 1.

business associates were in that order most commonly appointed as trustees, together with an accountant or lawyer as professional advisers concerning legal technicalities and trust management.[46] After top-slicing assets for the settlement of funeral expenses and 'mournings', the trustees paid other 'privileged' small debts associated with the sickbed expenses of the deceased – medicine, attendance and related bills. Then, where appropriate, the trust provided initial advances for beneficiaries and settled to the implementation of the longer term principles set out in the Trust Disposition.

To cover regular payments it was crucial to ensure annual income from the estate was sufficient to meet the terms of legacies, annuities and other claims. Property, together with a portfolio of low risk investments such as debentures, fixed income equities including municipal, railway and public utility bonds, and government stock formed the backbone of trust assets. Reliance on these investments coupled with opportunities to switch between them so as to take advantage of changing market opportunities were the guiding principles of financial management for trusts whose powers of investment specifically excluded bearer securities.[47]

In making decisions about investments the trustees were influenced by conditions in the property market. However, their own decisions had not inconsiderable implications for the supply of finance which found its way into housebuilding. The supply and terms of funds available for property investment filtered through from landlords to builders, ultimately influencing the volume of new housebuilding and, if property slipped in the trustees' esteem, the cumulative effect on building and housing was not to be taken lightly.

Typically, trustees blended three different strategic approaches to property to produce an income stream for annuitants. Each deepened the reservoir of finance capital available to the building industry, though some more directly than others. The first strategy, as the Church of Scotland discovered, was to buy heritable securities and obtain a twice yearly income from feu-duties at Whitsunday and Martinmas, together with any rights to casualties such as duplicands – occasional double feu-

---

[46] G. R. A. Howden, *Trusts, Trustees and Trust Acts in Scotland* (Edinburgh 1893).

[47] Wardhaugh, *Trust Law*, 22, notes that where dealings were specifically authorised by the trust deed, the power to deal was not to be vested in a single trustee. In none of the trusts encountered were powers to deal in shares conveyed to the trustees. Legitimate investments included: government stock; Bank of England stock; securities whose interest is guaranteed by parliament; railway company debenture stock; railway company preference stocks (dividends not dependent upon profits, and where these have been paid for at least ten years); municipal stocks secured upon the rates; Scottish local authority redeemable stocks; stocks of the Metropolitan Board of Works and, later, London County Council, East India and colonial stock; feu-duties and ground annuals; loans secured upon any of the stocks; heritable securities.

duties – and 'composition' and 'relief' payments, when a new tenant was related to or nominated by the previous one (see above and chapter 3). Fixed incomes obtained in this way were particularly attractive against the trend of falling prices in the last quarter of the nineteenth century.[48] By creating and compounding feu-duties, builders and developers mortgaged their future interest in revenue-producing obligations on the property and in return received lump sum cash injections to their businesses which they used to finance construction. The second strategy, adopted by both individual investors and trusts, involved making loans to builders and developers out of trust funds, secured against property. For builders it was imperative that they repay the loan or refinance it on maturity otherwise they risked seizure by the trust as lenders. A third strategy which the trust could adopt was to manage existing or buy further properties and to rent them. The trust extended its role to that of landlord rather than simply as investor. For the trust this produced a stream of rental income but involved considerable deductions, perhaps as much as one third, for repairs, insurance, local taxes and management charges, either directly by employing a factor as rent collector and intermediary, or indirectly by devoting personal effort to dealing with tenants. For the building industry, further involvement by trusts in the rental market increased the likelihood of a house sale, greater liquidity and, in turn, this meant existing loans could be paid off and new ones contracted. From all three strategies, though by different routes, trust funds swelled the reservoir of available finance available to builders and developers.

Death produced a steady stream of business for lawyers, but it also hastened a restructuring of asset portfolios. More specifically, the processing of estates produced a degree of temporary liquidity and trustees considered advances on security of property as a highly desirable investment. In the longer term, the appeal of property investments whether as loans, for rent, or as heritable securities owed much to the rationalisation of assets by trustees and lawyers in their efforts to streamline management and minimise risks. For the trustees, there were onerous responsibilities, personal risks, disputes and occasionally law suits over their actions.[49] In addition and by their very nature, the time horizon of trusts was long term. Trustees were stewards, responsible for overseeing financial arrangements so as to generate over two or three generations sufficient income to cover marriage contracts, lifetime annuities to family members and one-off legacies to faithful retainers and deserving charities. For

[48] Conveyancing and Land Transfer (Scotland) Act 1874, 37 and 38 Vict. c. 94.

[49] See, for example, ECA ACC 322, Trust Disposition and Settlement of Sir James Forrest, 1860; ECA Shelf 86, Charles Raitt's Trust, Sederunt Book, letter from Baxter to William Anderson, 1 Aug. 1828.

non-professional fund managers this had to be conducted over and above their own personal and business interests; for lawyers and accountants, it was often one of dozens of such obligations which their professional practices discharged.[50] A web of legal networks existed which were not without benefits to builders and developers as they sought to dovetail maturing loans with new ones.

Under pressure of time and motivated by practical considerations it was not surprising, then, that the first meeting of the trustees of John William Walker decided to liquidate various holdings including stocks of the Oriental Bank, place them on deposit and direct their legal agent 'to advertise and otherwise take means for getting the funds invested on heritable property'.[51] Legal networking clearly functioned efficiently, however, since within the space of four months in 1876 valuations were obtained on high status property in the city and the trustees had invested £9,600 equivalent to 53% of the realised value of Walker's estate, at between 4.25% and 4.5%.[52] The trustees also staked £1,100 in Northern Securities Investment Co. Ltd, a type of property based unit trust, thus divesting themselves of management in this arena too.[53] Though annual interest from stocks selected by Walker still produced a significant amount of the revenue for the annuities due to his wife and five children, the balance of the portfolio was shifted decisively towards property.[54] The trustees had invested in only seven properties geographically distributed throughout the city, at fixed rates and terms, with little possibility of loss and virtually no management requirements.

Business efficiency and risk minimisation were the predominant considerations amongst both legal firms and trustees.[55] As a first charge on a bankrupt or other estate, heritable property was an armour-plated security and this coincided with the interests of the trustees, disposed as they were to caution but charged with security. Miss Elizabeth Gray Robertson's trustees contended 'that many of them [investments] were unsuitable to be held by the trustees . . . [who] resolved to consolidate the

---

[50] S. P. Walker, 'Occupational expansion, fertility decline and recruitment to the professions of Scotland 1850–1914', University of Edinburgh PhD thesis, 1986, 23–6, and 'Anatomy of a Scottish CA practice: Lindsay, Jamieson and Haldane 1818–1918', *Accounting, Business and Financial History*, 3, 1993, 127–54.

[51] ECA ACC 314, John William Walker's Trust, Minutes, 26 Jan. 1876, vol. 1, box 3, f. 30.

[52] ECA ACC 314, Walker's Trust, Memoranda as to the Securities held by the Trustees, Martinmas 1878. This had risen to £13,400 two years later.

[53] ECA ACC 314, Walker's Trust, Minutes, 4 Jan. 1878.

[54] ECA ACC 314, Walker's Trust, Minutes, 4 Jan. 1878. The trustees successfully contested a case in the Court of Chancery, were awarded £5,000 and used the interest to fund annuities.

[55] See also S. P. Walker, 'The defence of professional monopoly: Scottish chartered accountants and "satellites in the accountancy firmament" 1854–1914', *Accounting, Organisations and Society*, 16, 1991, 257–83.

portfolio and identify a list of investments to be realised'.[56] In fact the portfolio was far from adventurous with twenty-four certificates distributed in a mix of railway and shipping shares, utilities such as the London Gas Light Company, bonds issued by the city of Edinburgh, and a sizeable representation of shares in colonial funds, investment trusts, banks and insurance companies such as the London Chartered Bank of Australia, the Scottish American Investment Company and the Phoenix Life Assurance Company.[57] Yet the trustees sought to dispose of twelve of these, arguing unsuitability, though in reality simplifying their management responsibilities.[58] Almost the first act of Miss Robertson's trustees, therefore, was to move into property by agreeing to a proposal to lend £2,000 to a builder on security of property in Brunswick Street valued at £3,100, a proposition put before them by the Trust's lawyers and backed up by a formal valuation.[59]

Widows had an indefeasible legal right during their lifetime to draw on one third of the annual income of a trust. John Chesser's son explained to his mother the relative attractions of the annuity of £350 (rising to £450 once the mortgage on the family home was paid off) provided for in her husband's will[60] as compared to her right to one third of the estate:

You are . . . entitled to ignore the will and claim certain rights at law. These rights are that you can claim one third of the *free* moveable estate as your own. The moveable estate is the life insurances, cash in bank, shares, furniture etc. but subject to all debts and you can also claim one third of the rents from year to year. I find that Dad's rental for the last year was over £2200 but that there are deductions for feu-duties, taxes, insurances, interest, poor rates, repairs etc. to be allowed for to say £600, leaving £1600 as the free income from rents. One third of this is over £500 a year, but you would have the rent of a house and taxes to pay yourself and the house to furnish yourself and you would run the risk of the property not letting or being destroyed by fire, which would reduce your third, whereas under the will your £350 or £450 will be paid off the first of everything and there would be practically no risk about it.[61]

---

56 ECA ACC 313, Miss Elizabeth Gray Robertson's Trust, Minutes, 25 Mar. 1886.
57 ECA ACC 313, Robertson's Trust, Funds and Estate, 2 Dec. 1884. With an estate of over £11,600, the highest individual holdings were in the Guardian Life Assurance Co. (£1,474), Colonial Company debentures (£1,400), Phoenix Assurance (£1,160), Highland Railway (£1,000), Caledonian Railway (£900), Hamilton Provident and Loan Society (£800), English, Scottish and Australasian Bank (£870), the Agra Bank (£700) and the Gas Light and Coke Co. (£700). There were a number of smaller holdings of between £200 and £500.
58 ECA ACC 313, Robertson's Trust, List of Shares, 23 Jan. 1880.
59 ECA ACC 313, Robertson's Trust, Minutes, June 1886; valuation by Thornton, Sheills and Thomson.
60 ECA ACC 322, John Chesser's Trust, Trust Disposition and Settlement, 28 Dec. 1891.
61 ECA ACC 322, Chesser's Trust, Sederunt Books, box 3, Chesser to his mother, 8 Feb. 1892.

Top-slicing the trust income could be achieved by an alimentary or *jus mariti* settlement in the will in favour of the widow, a device which meant her annuity would not be subject to actions by creditors for recovery of debt from the trust.[62] Indeed, great care was taken in setting up trusts to provide for female family members, often on terms preferential to daughters compared to their brothers. This should not be misconstrued; that Victorian fathers sometimes discriminated in their wills and trusts in favour of their daughters reflected the custom and practice of the Scots law of inheritance rather than a sudden Victorian awareness of equal opportunities.

Trustees took their responsibilities very seriously, not least because they were open to legal suits if they did not. This applied as much to the legitimacy of expenditures charged against trust income as it did to the investments themselves, regardless of the period. Thus the woman who had attended Charles Raitt during his final days in 1828 was informed by the trustees' agent that her claim for further recompense was unwarranted and that the trustees 'do not consider themselves authorised to pay you any more' and threatened that 'if you bring your claim before any court . . . they will resist it'.[63] When Dr Logan submitted his bill for £50 for attendance and medicine during Raitt's final illness, the trustees stated that 'they conceive that half the sum is amply sufficient' and instructed the lawyer to offer twenty-five guineas, and if this was declined, to require a detailed bill from Logan which would be submitted to an independent medical authority. Both sides lined up their expert counsel, medical and legal, together with an 'umpire or overman', and fought an out of court compromise – thirty guineas.[64]

Not to resist spurious claims was to milk the trust, jeopardise the ability to pay annuities and to diminish the pool of funds for investment in the property market. When in 1903 Sir William Forrest sought to defray some of his household expenses from the proceeds of the Comiston sandpit, his father's trustees brusquely informed him that they 'can find nothing to indicate that the late Sir William Forrest intended the sand to be treated as

---

[62] ECA ACC 314, Walker's Trust, Trust Disposition and Settlement, 28 Dec. 1870; ACC 316, Samuel Gilmour's Trust, Disposition and Assignment by Samuel Gilmour, 4 Apr. 1792; ACC 315, James Kirkwood's Trust, Codicil, 29 Mar. 1897, to Trust Disposition and Settlement. For an account of these and other provisions see A. McCrum, 'Inheritance and the family: the Scottish urban experience in the 1820s', in J. Stobart and A. Owens, eds., *Urban Fortunes: Property and Inheritance in the Town, 1700–1900* (Aldershot 2000), 79–107.

[63] ECA ACC Shelf 86, Raitt's Trust, Sederunt Book, letter from Baxter to Mrs Logan, 24 Jan. 1828, f. 34. For an extended analysis of Charles Raitt's trust see R. Rodger, 'Stewardship in the long run: Edinburgh trusts c. 1770–1870', *Hume Papers on Public Policy*, 7(3), 1999, 61–73.

[64] ECA ACC Shelf 86, Raitt's Trust, Sederunt Book, f. 25, letter from Baxter to Duncan, 31 Jan. 1828, ff. 34–5, 36–7, 39, 40.

a source of revenue falling to the liferenter'.[65] In another expression of trustees' power, when in 1911 Stennet Chesser wanted to take advantage of an investment opportunity which yielded 5% but was 'normally only available to directors' in the Pumpherston Oil Company he invoked a clause in his father's trust settlement which enabled the children to borrow at 3% from the trust. But the trustees were agitated by this:

the purpose for which a further advance is desired is not one which the trustees in the exercise of the discretion entrusted to them consider to be a proper purpose for which to make a further advance.[66]

The trustees justified their decision by stating that the proposed investment was 'prejudicial to the return obtainable on other trust funds'. As if this invocation of their responsibilities might prove insufficient, the trustees reminded Stennet Chesser of this, adding in a final twist that the education of his sons might be a more appropriate justification for the advance.[67]

It was the costly education of Dr Inglis' boys at Wellington School which, his widow claimed, justified her request in 1874 that the trustees transfer bonds to her name so that she might use the income generated directly for the sons' benefit. Though more subtle in her approach than Stennet Chesser, Mrs Inglis received similar treatment.[68] In refusing the request the trustees stated that the trust deed and settlement contained 'no such documentation and that they [the bonds] are accordingly part of the estate'. Blocked by her inability to administer the funds for herself, Mrs Inglis then repeatedly submitted vouchers to the trustees for clothing, school fees and pocket money for her sons. The friction was evident:

The trustees with great reluctance agreed to sanction the extra payments which have been recently made for expenses incurred by Mrs Inglis and her sons, and resolved that for the future no such extra expenses shall be allowed . . . and declined to allow the account of £6 referred to in Mrs Inglis' letter.[69]

The formidable Mrs Inglis was clearly undeterred for over the next three years she continued to request sums beyond the not inconsiderable annuity of £400 to which she was entitled. The admission in 1879 of one son to the Indian Civil Service and the other to the Royal Artillery were ideal opportunities to reclaim her expenditure on their uniforms, new clothes and other personal items. The trustees agreed to pay the claim for a combined expenditure of £191, but 'expressed themselves as very much

[65] ECA ACC 322, Chesser's Trust, Statement for the Guidance of the Trustees, 1903.
[66] ECA ACC 322, Chesser's Trust, Minutes, 20 Nov. 1911, ff. 250–2.
[67] ECA ACC 322, Chesser's Trust, Minutes, 20 Nov. 1911, f. 250.
[68] ECA ACC 119, Dr Inglis' Trust, Minutes, 18 May 1874.
[69] ECA ACC 119, Inglis' Trust, Minutes, 1 Nov. 1876.

surprised and dissatisfied at the large demands now made'. Furthermore, they were 'of the opinion that the expenditure on the additional outfit has been injudicious and extravagant . . . and a great many charges in these accounts are for repeated supplies of the same articles and . . . are not properly chargeable out of the allowance fixed for Mr. Harry's maintenance and are not matters of outfit at all'.[70]

In administering the assets of the trust, Edinburgh professionals, therefore, wielded considerable power over the families for whom they acted. Where reluctant or uncertain, they invoked the Testator's trust deed, sheltered behind its provisions and, invariably, pursued a conservative interpretation of the use to which trust funds could be put. Even on the rare occasion when they did contemplate overstepping their original terms of reference, the trustees resorted to law to protect themselves.[71] Simultaneously, trusts and the trustees who managed them were disinclined to authorise frivolous expenditure and resisted beneficiaries' efforts to invest in areas other than in property. Indeed, as shown above, trusts and the law firms that managed many of them had a vested interest in consolidating investments and directing them towards the property sector. These 'internal economies' stemmed from the central position of lawyers in whom the various functions of executors, trustees, accountants, estate agent and building society were concentrated.

Trustees and a mosaic of property investment strategies

The complexity and longevity of trust administration coupled with a strict adherence to legal principles ensured property was the dominant source of income from which trustees paid annuities.[72] This was just as valid for trusts at opposite ends of the inheritance spectrum: for the trustees of Alexander Hay whose heritable securities produced an annual income of £50 in the 1830s compared to over £4,700 annually available to James Steel's trustees from 1904.[73] William Reid's estate had only £995 at their disposal to generate annuities compared to James

---

[70] ECA ACC 119, Inglis' Trust, Minutes, 31 Dec. 1879.

[71] ECA ACC 314, Walker's Trust, Minutes, 2 Jan. 1898, f. 216, and Minute of Agreement among Beneficiaries and Letter of Indemnity, May 1897, ff. 212–13. This degree of caution was unusual. Trust deeds usually contained a comprehensive indemnity to protect trustees, and where it did not explicitly, then case law (*Thomson* v. *Campbell* 1838, 16 S. 560) did so. Section 30 of the Trusts Act also protected them against actions for breach of trust so long as the trustees advanced up to two-thirds of the value of heritable property, the valuation to be by an accredited independent valuer.

[72] The average length of life for trusts was just over thirty years for almost forty cases examined in detail.

[73] ECA ACC 334, Hay Borthwick factory, State of feus, Martinmas 1835, Whitsunday 1839.

Kirkwood's estate, valued at £60,000.[74] Even where the trustees were inclined to invest in property bonds and heritable securities wider business and personal considerations affected their ability to do so. In both Reid's and Kirkwood's cases, for example, much of the family wealth was in the form of share capital and to divide up the estate or move into heritable property to obtain an annuity amongst respectively four and six sons would have been to sacrifice the income generating prospects which the businesses themselves promised.[75]

Bankruptcy inevitably distorted the intentions of the testator since the financial basis of annuities was destroyed and had a serious effect on property investment too. This was so for Samuel Gilmour, a ropemaker, who owned a few flats on the third, fourth and garret storeys in a new tenement in the Grassmarket (Moses' Well, Gilmore's Close) and invested judiciously in fourteen acres at Lochrin in 1800, then still a short distance outside the city and feued from the 'hospital founded by the crafts of Edinburgh and Mary Erskine' (the Trades Maidens' estate).[76] The property remained undeveloped with only three feus granted by 1803 and then, on his death, the property passed in 1805 to Gilmour's son, also Samuel.[77] Soon after the death of his father, the cash flow problems of the ropeyard and the inability to sell off further plots during wartime resulted in 'the affairs of Samuel Gilmour having gone into confusion'.[78] Gilmour was forced to borrow heavily, first £2,100 and then over £3,000, on adverse terms from the three Misses Vans Agnew on security of the Lochrin property.[79] However, Gilmour's failure to pay the lifetime annuities of £100 to each of the spinsters resulted in an 'arrestment' and in the sequestration and auction of the estate in 1807. During the 'running of an half hour glass' at the public roup in the Royal Exchange, the 'highest offerers' were able to obtain property at the equivalent of only eighteen years purchase of the annual feu-duties, and the capital sum so obtained was sufficient for the trustee to repay the Misses Vans Agnew.[80]

---

[74] ECA ACC 314, Walker's Trust, Trust Disposition and Settlement, 10 Sept. 1847, ff. 48–9; ECA ACC 315, Kirkwood's Trust, approximate valuation of estate, 4 June 1901, f. 62.   [75] ECA ACC Shelf 86, William Reid's Trust, Minutes, 10 Nov. 1843, f. 36.

[76] ECA ACC 316, Samuel Gilmour's Trust, Disposition and Deed of Settlement, 23 Aug. 1784, and Disposition and Assignment, 4 Apr. 1792; NAS RS27/486.27, reference to 1 Mar. 1800. Gilmour's name was spelled in various ways though the Gilmore form has been retained in Edinburgh street names.

[77] NAS RS27/565.104, confirmed 10 Sept. 1806.

[78] ECA ACC 316, Gilmour's Trust, Discharge and Renunciation by Robert Forrester to John Crawford, trustee, 10 Nov. 1808.

[79] NAS RS27/568.127, 27/568.247 and 27/581.17, 21 and 28 July 1806 and 7 Mar. 1807. ECA ACC 316, Gilmour's Trust, Discharge and Renunciation (three processes) by Margaret, Frances Georgina and Anna Maria Vans Agnew, 25 Jan. 1809.

[80] ECA ACC 316, Handbill of Public Roup, 1807; NAS RS27/629.150, 27/629.159 and 27/629.169, 30 Jan. 1809.

The break up of the estate punctured the exclusivity of the area since the roup of eleven lots at Lochrin meant that ownership became fragmented and without unified control of the estate the homogeneity and social tone were thereafter difficult to sustain.[81] To some extent, the property development strategy had been compromised by Samuel Gilmour (senior) as a result of his relocation of the ropeworks in Gilmore Street (now Place) but the injudicious loans taken out by his son under great financial pressure condemned it. The bankruptcy of Gilmour, further sub-infeudation and a superior (Trades Maidens Hospital) concerned more for short-term revenues than long-term exclusive housing development guaranteed the area as a 'mixed bag of houses' and industrial uses.[82] Ironically, this was the prelude to the arrival of the Union Canal, a development which certainly would have rescued Gilmour from his exposed balance sheet. Within ten years, construction was underway on property previously held by Gilmour for the terminal and warehousing facilities associated with the canal.

Direct investment in property by the trustees took many forms but an important one was in the purchase of property for rent. Walker's trustees were advised by a valuer that the Marchmont Road properties 'were in excellent order and let to respectable tenants . . . the locality good . . . houses let well and the additional tramway line recently introduced will tend to maintain values'.[83] Sufficiently reassured, the trustees switched from Australian to domestic investment, even though they lacked experience in property management and subsequently incurred repair bills on a scale which impaired their ability to meet the annuities payable to Walker's beneficiaries. John Chesser's trustees, by contrast, were pro-active and successful managers of the properties they administered to cover annuities and legacies. Successively master carpenter, superintendent of works and architect, Chesser used his expertise in the building trades and his status with his employer, George Heriot's Hospital, to good effect to purchase a series of high quality and strategically located properties between 1866 and 1883. His first purchase, in the newly laid out Chalmers Street in 1866, was almost opposite Heriot's Hospital and involved Chesser in building on his own

---

[81] ECA ACC 316, Gilmour's Trust, Articles of Roup, 5 Nov. 1807, Discharge and Renunciations, 10 Nov. 1808 and 25 Jan. 1809, and Charter of Confirmation and Clare Constat, 7 Mar. 1817. See also NAS RS27/586.227, 27/588.133, 27/589.175, 27/589.246, 27/602.181, 27/606.129, 27/612.31, 27/616.2, 27/616.256, 27/617.15, 27/618.123, 27/620.99, 27/620.109, 27/628.118, 27/631.111, 27/633.159, 27/633.164, 27/636.199, 27/637.204, 27/661.147, 27/664.18, 27/672.51, 27/673.81.

[82] J. Gifford, C. McWilliam and D. Walker, *The Buildings of Scotland: Edinburgh* (Harmondsworth 1988), 503.

[83] ECA ACC 314, Walker's Trust, Report on Heritable Subjects, ff. 213–15.

account.[84] Rentals from the Chalmers Street flats and other properties financed a series of high class property purchases in the New Town – Cumberland Street (1873), Rutland Street and Rutland Place (1875), building stances on the westward fringes at Coates Gardens (1876) and 1 Erskine Place (1883) – which in turn were used as security for further property investment.[85]

Whereas Walker's trustees embarked on the role of landlord in a rather limited way, did so when the initial southwards suburban drift had begun to lose impetus, and had no experience of landlordism, there was never a question raised amongst Chesser's trustees that they should not continue the successful property letting which had produced a gross rental income of £2,200 in 1891.[86] The rental portfolio had a degree of complementarity: the New Town provided flats for an upper-middle social class, Rutland Place and Maitland Street were mainly shops, and Erskine Place a mixture of houses, shops and offices. But the most important single element in the rental income was the Rutland Hotel which annually produced £500 gross, itself sufficient to meet Ann Chesser's annuity. The trustees were active, though not aggressive, in the management of rental income, increasing the annual rent when the leases permitted. Nor were they mesmerised by John Chesser's portfolio of properties; they sold the Chalmers Street property in 1892 – virtually their first act – then in 1900 undertook a more fundamental restructuring by selling three Coates Crescent properties, separately, and buying twelve flats in St Vincent Street. Though this tripled the number of tenants and added to management costs, it also reduced the Trust's exposure should one of the prestigious Coates Crescent tenancies fall empty.

Where trusts themselves bought existing properties outright it represented an indirect source of capital to the building industry. That is, trust purchases enabled the vendors to repay loans which in turn facilitated further reinvestment in property. Like all houses purchased by landlords, trusts added to the reservoir of property finance.

A more direct form of finance for the building industry resulted from advances by trusts to builders themselves, secured on heritable or other property. James Steel used the loans obtained from twenty-two transactions with trustees to raise almost £100,000 to fund his building and property development activities between 1867 and 1910 – equivalent to

[84] ECA ACC 322, Chesser's Trust, Sederunt Book, Minutes, 19 Feb. 1892, and Notarial Instrument, box 3, ff. 92–5.
[85] ECA ACC 322, Chesser's Trust, Sederunt Book, Notarial Instruments, box 3, ff. 80–2, 89–91, 96–8, 99–104, 108–9; Chesser's Trust, Minutes, 6 June 1900, f. 241, notes that Chesser borrowed £2,000 from both the trustees of Thomas Cook, 16 May 1878, and William Menzies, factor, Kincardine, 15 Nov. 1880.
[86] ECA ACC 322, Chesser's Trust, Minutes, 20 Nov. 1911, f. 252.

Table 4.6 *Sources of mortgage finance: James Steel's house sales 1869–1914*

Funds advanced by	Number of loans	Amount (£)	Average loan (£)	% of total advances
Trusts	69	123,460	1,789	48.6
Private individuals	100	90,045	900	35.3
Building and friendly societies	68	30,051	442	11.8
Institutions	15	10,611	707	4.2
All	252	254,167	1,009	100.0

Source: NAS RS108, Register of Sasines, Edinburgh, 317 entries, 1869–1914.

24% of all his external financing.[87] Often private loans were negotiated by lawyers acting on behalf of their clients, that is, as representatives if not technically as trustees and in Steel's case another 22% of his building development work was funded in this way.

Lawyers acted as financial conduits for trusts in another context by channelling mortgages for private house purchases to builders. This was the case when Mary Orr bought eight flats within the tenement at 18 Dean Park Street from James Steel in 1902, presumably to obtain a rental income for herself, and obtained a mortgage of £1,200 or two-thirds of the purchase price by a private arrangement with the trustees of Elizabeth Ball.[88] Besides sales to small landlords, numerous villas and flats for the middle classes were financed by advances obtained from trusts, as was the case in the western New Town developments of the 1870s and 1880s. Almost two-fifths of the prestigious properties in Douglas Crescent and half those in Eglinton Crescent were bought with trust funds advanced as private mortgages to buyers.[89] An indication of the importance of trust funds as a source of mortgage finance can be obtained from the largest residential builder in late Victorian Edinburgh, James Steel, half of whose house sales (48.6%) were financed from trust funds (table 4.6).

Legal firms brokered house purchase through the provision of mortgage finance garnered from trusts, marriage contracts and reservoirs of private investment capital in search of a predictable return. However, the asymmetric information available to buyers and sellers required mediation and lawyers provided this by arranging transactions between borrowers and

---

[87] NAS RS108, Register of Sasines, Edinburgh, 1867–1914.
[88] NAS RS108/4138.9, 6 Nov. 1902.
[89] NAS RS108/862.132, 108/751.48, 108/757.13, 108/755.141, 108/890.81, 108/890.84, 108/1508.19, 108/1503.157, 108/1491.32, 108/1620.24, 108/1729.105, 108/2167.179, 108/1821.174, 108/1988.13, 108/3584.17. See also B. Elliott and D. McCrone, 'Urban development in Edinburgh: a contribution to the political economy of place', *Scottish Journal of Sociology*, 4, 1980, 25 n. 36.

lenders.[90] Mortgage finance arranged in this way worked reasonably satisfactorily in the cosy and confined legal world of early and mid-Victorian
Edinburgh. But the growth of the city in the second half of the nineteenth
century, the proliferation of builders, lenders and of legal and accountancy
firms, too, made an already partial system of information about the market
for building finance much less reliable. As with other products, personal
contact and the assessment of risk associated with creditworthiness was
increasingly problematic in an ever-expanding, urbanising world.
Matching borrowers and lenders assumed greater risk in an increasingly
impersonal business milieu.

Financing property development: the Trinity Land Company

The development of Trinity in north Edinburgh straddled most of the
nineteenth century and demonstrates the mechanics of property development in almost all its elements. This is not to claim that this is a model
or that all property development followed the same path. But the variety
and nature of relationships and processes are revealed through the activities of the Trinity Land Company. The interaction of the feuing system
and building finance, the importance of tightly defined feu charters to
defend the social tone, the imprimatur conveyed by the involvement of
powerful institutions such as the Church of Scotland and the Merchant
Company are each elucidated in the context of a specific example. The
Trinity Land Company was a property developer. It was an agent. It did
not itself initiate building but was acutely aware of the circumstances
which did. So market factors as well as institutional ones are vital in any
understanding of the process of property development and these, too, are
examined here.

The construction of regency style town houses in Leith after 1815, as in
Edinburgh, was principally aimed at a wealthy middle class. Though
these classical style buildings were still being constructed into the 1830s
and 1840s, a number of modest mansions existed as early as 1815 in an
embryonic suburban settlement to the west in the Trinity and Newhaven
area.[91] The fragmentation of ownership in this area meant that individual
decisions could be made about upgrading properties and from the 1820s
to the 1860s most of the villas in the area were enlarged, modernised and
in some cases an additional property was built within their grounds.[92]

---

[90] M. Casson, 'Institutional economics and business history: a way forward?', *Business History*, 39, 1997, 152–71; S. R. H. Jones, 'Transactions costs and the theory of the firm: the scope and limitations of the new institutional approach', *Business History*, 39, 1997, 9–25.
[91] J. Wallace, *Further Traditions of Trinity and Leith* (Edinburgh 1990), 5–22.
[92] NLS, Kirkwood's Map, 1817.

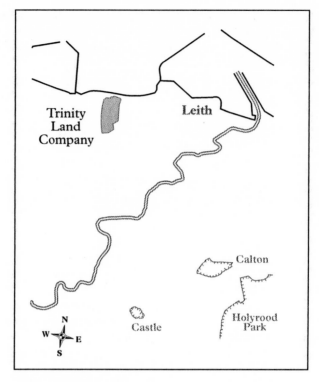

Figure 4.6 Trinity area

Source: MC/TLC, Chartulary vol. 1, Inventory of Writs, 1/91–121, and folio details of individual feu charters.

The modest scale of villadom in Trinity was reflected in the fact that twelve of the largest fourteen landowners in 1873 possessed between just one and five acres, and the other two nine and twelve acres respectively.[93] Fragmented ownership, therefore, permitted flexibility and responsiveness to changing demand conditions and, if one landowner was absolutely opposed to a greater density of building, then there was almost certainly another for whom it was an appealing option.

The sale in 1828 of Trinity Mains or Victoria Park by Trinity House was not the stimulus for sustained suburban development.[94] Much more extensive than the neighbouring fragmented properties, effective development in

---

[93] *PP 1874 LXXII pt III*, Owners of Lands and Heritages, 69–70.
[94] The Masters and Mariners of Trinity House, Leith, bought the land from Queen Anne's representative in 1713 and sold the property to Major General Alexander Murray McGregor on 26 Dec. 1828. See NAS RS27/1235.140, 12 May 1829. McGregor was already a Trinity landowner, RS27/1144.174, 28 Nov. 1826.

this case necessitated an estate development strategy for Trinity. This entailed expense, specifically a surveyor and architect to lay out the estate, and was dependent upon a decision concerning the size of plots. In turn this revolved on an assessment of the market and of the size, growth and composition of demand. Though located at the northern limit of ribbon development from Inverleith and enhanced in amenity by its proximity to the newly resited Botanical Gardens, the abrupt downturn in new building in the mid-1820s in Edinburgh was not the most propitious moment to launch the development of Trinity and so it remained, for over forty years, a nursery on the northern fringe until transport developments and accumulated demand prompted estate development.

The Trinity estate was purchased by William Wilson in 1869. No development had taken place when Wilson sold the land in 1874 to the Property Investment Society (PIS) of Scotland, of which he was himself a director.[95] Four months later, in February 1875, the PIS in turn sold the property, still undeveloped, to the Trinity Land Company (TLC) whose directors again included William Wilson.[96] This series of Trojan horse manoeuvres protected Wilson's interest, enabled the PIS to make a quick if modest profit and, by placing the responsibility for development on the TLC, insulated Wilson and his co-directors from potential losses. The TLC issued bonds in favour of the vendors with both Wilson and the Property Investment Society accepting these as part of the purchase price of £3,000.[97] Such an investment was gold-plated for Wilson and the PIS, while for the TLC it allowed them to side-step the need to raise the full purchase price immediately.

With an initial debt of £18,000 the TLC's pressing need was to develop the estate quickly to generate income to service the interest payments, establish their financial credibility and smooth the negotiations to refinance their debts when bonds matured. Not to do so was to risk their principal, indeed their only, asset and the repossession of the estate. Within two months a feuing plan was prepared by Robert Morham and the first twenty-eight lots were feued as a block in April 1875 to an Edinburgh solicitor, W. E. Armstrong, for a feu-duty of £253 p.a. in two equal payments at Whitsunday and Martinmas.[98]

---

[95] NAS RS108, 17 May 1869.

[96] MC/TLC, Chartulary no. 1, 1875–99, f. 737, writs 1/91–1/97; NAS RS108, 29 Oct. 1874, 26 Feb. 1875. See also books of Session and Council, 18 June 1879.

[97] MC/TLC, Chartulary no. 1, 1875–99, f. 739, writ 1/103. The procedure of part payment in the form of a loan by the purchaser to the vendor was not uncommon. See NAS RS27/2609.59, 2609.67, RS108/2717.10, and MC, Drumdryan Chartulary, vol. 2, f. 175, Charter with James Steel, 28 Dec. 1866. Steel paid £500 in cash and obtained a bond of £4,000 from the vendors/superiors. See also chapter 6.

[98] MC/TLC, feu charter by the TLC to William Elliot Armstrong, 9 Apr. 1875, ff. 1–9.

Edinburgh builders, no doubt encouraged by the general state of the housing market in the early 1870s, were quick to take up the lots which Armstrong sub-feued in only two months.[99] In this their first and relatively short conveyance, the TLC directors had enough expertise as a result of their involvement with the Property Investment Society of Scotland to set Conditions of Feu, the stipulations about the type of development and quality of the buildings. Armstrong's sub-feus combined the lots on the feuing plan in such a way as to produce wide frontages and this enabled affordable, semi-detached villas to be built with ample gardens around them.[100] In so doing he had set the tone for the development, adding considerably to the character of the area by ensuring no perceptible boundary existed between the TLC land and East Trinity with its spacious and self-contained mansions dating from the previous two or three decades.[101] Variety, individuality and privacy were characteristic of the houses built on Armstrong's feus in Trinity Road and in a new street, Lomond Road. At £1,800 or approximately two-thirds the price of a new house on the north-western fringes of the New Town, the price, too, did much to insulate the social tone of the area.[102] Deliberately or otherwise, Armstrong had capitalised on the cachet of the neighbourhood and attached this firmly to the TLC. Their future developments owed much to the social tone set in part only by the Conditions of Feu and it was a lesson which the TLC learned quickly, attaching ever greater specificity in the feu charters as they sought to eliminate any possible development which might jeopardise exclusivity in future development prospects. A decade later, in addition to the Conditions of Feu, thirteen very precise restrictions had been embedded in the conveyancing documents.[103]

To defray interest charges on loans obtained by the TLC from private individuals and the Property Investment Society required income of over £720 annually. By mid-1876, that is, after only fifteen months, though the mortgages obtained by the TLC by means of giving bonds on security of the Trinity lands had all been renegotiated, they were by then entirely in institutional hands.[104] The Scottish Equitable Life Assurance Company,

---

[99] MC/TLC, feu dispositions by William Elliot Armstrong to Alexander Shepherd, 9 June 1875; Kenneth Stewart, William Ligertwood, Robert Hyman, and George Fortune, each 10 June 1875; Alexander Craw, 16 Sept. 1875, ff. 37–57; 65–96.

[100] MC/TLC, feu disposition to Alexander Shepherd, 9 June 1875, f. 57.

[101] The tactic of broad frontages to allow semi-detached villas to be built in their own gardens had been widely used in English suburban expansion but was not as common in Scottish cities.

[102] MC/TLC, feu disposition by George Fortune to Wilhelmina Thom, 13 May 1878, f. 98, and see, for example, feu charters for Douglas Crescent, NAS RS PR 1876: 642.93, 862.132 and 656.76.

[103] MC/TLC, feu contract with Robert Robertson, builder, 8 Nov. 1887, f. 226.

[104] MC/TLC, Inventory of Writs, 1/101, 1/104, 1/108, bonds and dispositions, 27 Feb. 1875 and 16 July 1876.

the National Property Investment Company and the Property Investment Company of Scotland held bonds for £18,000 issued by the TLC. Though these three companies were in business to obtain sound returns on heritable securities, they also took advantage of repossessions to improve their balance sheets. The TLC was no longer in the cocooned environment of personal friends and private investors.

Even though the arrangement with Armstrong had produced a highly satisfactory outcome, annual interest charges exceeded TLC income and so development had to proceed at some pace to avoid repossession when loans matured. Long-term and short-term horizons needed to be integrated. The TLC achieved this by means of a threefold strategy: first, by the continued disposal of individual feus to secure an annual income; second, the sale of heritable securities, that is, the transfer of the right to receive future feu-duties; and third, the outright sale of a feu for a cash sum with only a nominal feu-duty created. The second and third strategies proved critical to the success of the development. Where plots were sold outright they provided an immediate cash injection, as with the Newhaven Parish Manse, sold for £1,010 in 1876.[105] Yet such transactions were occasional – it was three years before the next sale of this type. Meanwhile the debt problem mounted. Two pivotal lots were feued in 1877 but the annual feu-duties which accrued to the TLC as superior made only a small dent in the interest charges and none in reducing overall indebtedness. The two conveyances, however, were significant in another sense since they reasserted the determination of the TLC after an interval of two years not to be panicked into hasty short-run income generation but to take the long-term view of property development.[106] On the site of the oldest property, Trinity Lodge, and on the north-east boundary of the estate, the feuing conditions were explicit and reflected the continued determination of the TLC to defend the social tone of the area:

and it is specially provided and declared that . . . having been feued for the erection of a villa it should not be competent . . . to erect upon any portion of the said subjects any buildings of any other description than a villa or double villa . . . [and that] plans of any such dwelling houses . . . proposed to be erected hereafter shall be first submitted to and approved of by us or the superiors.[107]

The sale of what became known as Lomond Park for £3,155 as a recreation ground for the boys of a nearby school offered a glimmer of financial hope and the cash payment was used within the week to discharge the

---

[105] MC/TLC, feu disposition with Trustees for Newhaven Manse, 29 May 1876, f. 10.
[106] MC/TLC, feu disposition with Robert Hamilton, 24 July 1877, and Andrew Jamieson, 2 Oct. 1877, ff. 23, 32.   [107] MC/TLC, f. 32.

TLC's liability to one of the property companies.[108] However, two years later, in 1881, it was the sale of the superiority of Armstrong's and Jamieson's land for £6,264 to the Merchant Company's Widows' Fund which vindicated the TLC directors' strategy and established firmly the prospects of the company.[109] This was the equivalent of twenty-two years of feu-duties in one lump sum and quite apart from the impact on the TLC balance sheet, it did much to raise the profile of the Trinity development. For the Merchant Company, the heritable securities from the Trinity development provided an assured annual income from which to pay pensions.

As an endorsement, the involvement of the Merchant Company could not have been bettered. It signalled a confidence in the area and thereafter a steady trickle of feu contracts was negotiated in the 1880s. As before, these were either with merchants and professional men who intended to live in Trinity and bought a plot on which to build their house, or directly with builders who used their initiative as middlemen, buying the plot, developing the site, building one or two villas and then selling to customers to recoup their costs. By 1887, five of the ten 'segments' created by the feuing plan were completely feued, two others to the north of Primrose Bank were substantially feued and a strip of three segments on the western boundary of the TLC property were completely undeveloped (fig. 4.7).

The third TLC strategy for estate development was also initiated in 1887. The approach, not novel in itself, was to feu contiguous plots to a single developer imposing tight building controls in an effort to secure the coherence of the houses. The directors took particular care over the development of a plot on Trinity Road which was the first point of contact with their properties when approached from Edinburgh (fig. 4.7). Even though the plot was located on Trinity Road the TLC renamed the stretch of the street as Strowan Terrace, seeking to distinguish it and thus protect the rest of their Trinity development which was of a more exclusive character. The feu charter specified that Robert Robertson, the builder from Jessfield, Leith, was:

bound to erect . . . and to maintain in all time coming . . . a terrace fronting southward of not less than 12 nor more than 14 self-contained houses not exceeding two storeys in height with attics of a villa class . . . the total annual value of at least quadruple the total feu-duty after specified . . . bound to build and have ready for occupation at least two of said houses prior to the term of Martinmas and at least two houses additional every succeeding year . . . the whole of said terrace shall be erected and completed ready for occupation prior to the term of Martinmas 1893.[110]

[108] MC/TLC, disposition to Rev. D. C. W. Darnell, 13 June 1879, f. 103, Writs, 1/102, 19 June 1879.
[109] MC/TLC, disposition to the Trustees of the Widows' Fund of Company of Merchants of the City of Edinburgh, 10 Nov. 1881, f. 131.
[110] MC/TLC, feu contract with Robert Robertson, 8 Nov. 1887, f. 226.

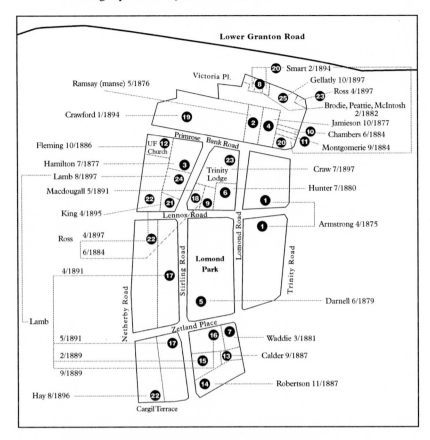

Figure 4.7 Trinity Land Company: street development

Source: MC/TLC, Chartulary vol. 1, Inventory of Writs, 1/91–121, and
folio details of individual feu charters.

By scheduling completion as they did, the TLC ensured that Robertson
could not defer construction should he be inclined to do so for his own
business reasons or by delaying development in an attempt to gain from a
longer term inflation of land values. By tying him to a particular type and
number of houses the TLC directors contained any hopes Robertson
might have nurtured to increase his own revenue by building more
intensively on the plot. The TLC was careful also to specify how close to
the street the houses could be built and, before beginning work, Robertson
had to construct a 'a good ruble [*sic*] wall averaging 15 inches thick 7 feet
high . . . with a rounded dressed stone coping 10 inches thick'.[111] There

[111] MC/TLC, Chartulary no. 1, feu contract with R. Robertson, 8 Nov. 1887, f. 227.

were thirteen restrictions in addition to the general terms laid out in the Conditions of Feu. Such was the bargaining power of the TLC that they could stipulate their terms and conditions; and did so. Anxious to clinch the deal, the builder, Robertson, agreed to take down an existing wall and form part of a new road, Stirling Road, costly activities which would normally be apportioned between the superior and the builder. The only concession the TLC made, though it was one offered elsewhere by superiors in the city, was to stagger the dates by which the full feu was payable on the plot – in Robertson's case it was set at a modest £8.33 in the first year, rising each year also by £8.33 to achieve the full feu-duty of £50 after five years.

Much the same principles of site development applied to the extensive properties developed between 1889 and 1893 by R. Lamb and Co., an established firm of Edinburgh builders that feued strips of land from the TLC along Stirling Road, in Zetland Place and along the east side of a new street, Netherby Road, the boundary of the TLC property (see fig. 4.7).[112] The terms the TLC were able to insist upon in their feu contracts were an indicator of both the desirable nature of the Trinity development and the buoyancy of this segment of the housing market and accordingly attracted such reputable firms as Lamb and Co., H., T. and R. Montgomery (Merchiston) and George Fortune (Leith).[113] Unlike the inner suburban areas around Tollcross and Sciennes, builders came from all over Edinburgh and Leith to undertake just one or two villas on the Trinity Land Company's estate.

Despite twenty years of carefully controlled development the gross revenue from TLC activities remained resolutely in deficit in relation to their mortgage liabilities. As fig. 4.8 shows, this was transformed during 1894 with the sale of heritable securities to two buyers. The trustees of the Endowment Committee of the Church of Scotland paid £8,963 for the right to receive annual payments from eleven feus which were earmarked to finance Chapels of Ease and the trustees of Southwick parish church in the presbytery of Dumfries paid £2,195 for six feus from which they sought to generate an annual income of £160.[114]

---

[112] MC/TLC, feu contracts with R. Lamb and Son, Bellevue and Logie Green, Edinburgh, 28 Feb. 1889, 2 Sept. 1889, 28 Apr. 1891, ff. 258–78, 287–309.

[113] Not all firms were quite as successful as Lamb and Co., Fortune or Robertson. Some went into liquidation. For example, two builders who undertook villas on Armstrong's feu went bankrupt, William Ligertwood almost immediately in 1877 (see listing 7/3/1877 A10100), and Alex Craw in 1885 (29/6/1885 A14931). In Craw's case it was just an interruption – he resumed building activities in Edinburgh until just before 1914. See *Edinburgh and Leith Post Office Directories*, 1875–1914.

[114] MC/TLC, disposition to Trustees of Church of Scotland, and to Trustees of Southwick Church, both 14 May 1894, ff. 344–60, 361–75.

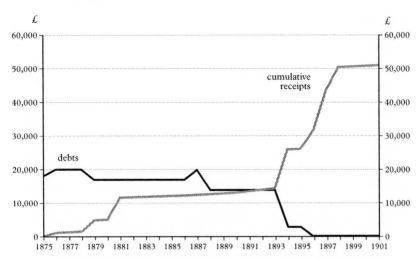

Figure 4.8 Trinity Land Company: receipts and debts 1875–1901

Source: MC/TLC, Chartulary vol. 1, Inventory of Writs, 1/91–121, and folio details of individual feu charters.

Significantly, the Church of Scotland obtained their heritable securities at the equivalent of 25.5 years purchase whereas for Southwick parish consolidation the price was 28.5 years purchase. The bargaining position of the TLC and demand for housing in the 1890s had strengthened appreciably since the initial lifeline which the Merchant Company sale (22.1 years purchase) represented in 1881. It was a position which continued to improve when in 1897 a further sale of superiorities to the trustees of the prominent Edinburgh builder, William Watherston, was calculated on the basis of 29.5 years and yielded a lump sum of £4,670. By contrast, the TLC's pressing need for cash in 1881, the leverage exerted by the Merchant Company and the state of the housing market in Edinburgh combined to depress the number of years of purchase. In 1894 the bargaining power of the Church of Scotland compared more favourably to that of a parish church and so commanded an 11% discount – 25.5 years compared to 28.5 years – for the more powerful disciples. Clearly the state of the property market and its relative attractiveness compared to shares and government stocks was a factor in strengthening the appeal of property investments in the last twenty years of the nineteenth century, but in nurturing their estate over a quarter of a century the TLC showed great care and attention to its long-term income generating possibilities.

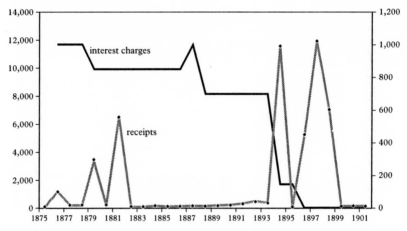

Figure 4.9 Trinity Land Company: revenue and interest charges
1874–1901

Source: MC/TLC, Chartulary vol. 1, Inventory of Writs, 1/91–121, and
folio details of individual feu charters.

The TLC achieved a considerable surplus – the cumulative revenue
was over £51,000 when the company was wound up in 1901. This was
equivalent to average annual gross receipts of £1,965, against which
interest charges of £588 annually had to be offset. Though debts were
not synonymous with expenditure, in practice the TLC recouped site
development charges and architects' fees through the terms and conditions of the feu charter. But as fig. 4.9 shows, TLC average revenue
figures were highly misleading since the viability of the entire venture was
dependent on tunnelling through long periods of low returns in the
expectation that in the long term – in this case a generation – a few lucrative deals would materialise. An offer to buy superiorities must have
created a high degree of nervous tension amongst the directors since the
entire financial future of the TLC depended on it, as figs. 4.8 and 4.9
show.

The recipe for successful development which the TLC used had
several ingredients, of which skilful financial management was just one.
Another, evident from the outset, was the adherence to an estate plan
and strict insistence on the terms for building, whether this related to
materials, boundaries, design or the density of building. Associated with
this was a careful monitoring of building stances as they were developed,
and indeed afterwards. The TLC as superior achieved this by requiring
builders to submit for the directors' approval an allocation of feus, that

is, a summary of how much the individual owners would pay to cover the overall feu-duty which the builder as vassals had to pay to the TLC.[115] At one level this might be seen as interference, but it had the effect of sign-posting the continuing interest of the superior which was to seek a relatively even distribution of feu-duties to preserve the coherence of the development and to avoid undue burdens falling on a particular property.

This concern with the long-term prospects of the estate was enshrined in the TLC's management more generally. When ground was sold for the purpose of building a church, the feu charter anticipated that should the church not be built, or at some time be demolished, then only villas could be constructed on the site.[116] To a degree this was window-dressing, a public relations tactic to reassure those who had already built houses in the area and was designed to appeal to potential customers as evidence of the quality of the local environment. This consideration was never far from the surface of the decision to feu the central area as a playing field for the Cargil schoolboys.[117] The TLC was quick to accept the cash on offer for this plot, not least because of their own vulnerable finances in 1879, but also because they could not in the future then be pressurised to donate land for public purposes since a park already existed. Furthermore, by agreeing to the sale at such an early stage of their activities, the TLC directors added value to the unfeued plots in the neighbourhood. The directors could afford to be in more magnanimous mood when in 1898, with no further ground to be feued or superiorities to be sold and on the point of winding up the company, they were petitioned by twenty-eight owners with properties overlooking Lomond Park. The residents, alarmed that the imminent disappearance of the TLC might lead to a cash offer from a developer so attractive that a sufficient number of residents would suspend their objections to the development of the Park, sought and obtained a reiteration of the original terms of the feu which was binding upon them all.[118] Henceforth, the Park would remain, or at worst would be covered with villas of a quality consistent with that of the neighbourhood. Though it was no concession to the TLC and came at the very end of its

---

[115] See, for example, MC/TLC, Minutes of Allocation of Feu Duty, ff. 101, 102, 127, 130, 255, 279, 333, 507.

[116] MC/TLC, feu charter with James Fleming, 27 Oct. 1886, f. 189.

[117] MC/TLC, feu charter with Rev. D. C. W. Darnell, 13 June 1879, f. 103.

[118] MC/TLC, Assignation by the Trinity Land Company to themselves and others, 4 Mar. 1898, f. 561: 'the said purchasers and feuars have requested us [TLC] to convey to them a joint and several right to insist upon and enforce the burdens, stipulations, conditions and restrictions in the foresaid disposition'.

activities, it was indicative of a commercial philosophy which had governed its long-term business decisions.

Long-term development prospects were assisted by a ploy which strengthened the boundaries of the estate and thus defended its inner social composition. It was achieved by laying out the estate with only limited access to its inner areas. The TLC property extended northwards to Lower Granton Road which skirted the shores of the Firth of Forth at Wardie Bay. To state that TLC villa developments were on a cliff-top overlooking the shoreline road would be to exaggerate the height of the cliff, but for building purposes there was an appreciable drop. The TLC utilised the topography of the site to sanction tenements along the seafront. In so doing they acknowledged some pre-existing development of this nature and took account of the implications which proximity to the sea inevitably meant for commercial developments and the probable impact on seafront property. The cliff and the tenements combined to produce a natural and an artificial barrier to the rest of the estate. To reinforce the exclusivity of the main plateau area of TLC property various feus on the north-eastern corner were sold for a terrace of villa housing at an early stage. Strowan Terrace on the southern edge, a terrace of villas in Netherby Road and a cul-de-sac on the north-western fringe completed the defensive posture of the development. Since the earliest suburban villas had been developed to the east, greater advantage was derived from a more porous relationship with this area, and the orientation of the TLC development in some ways reflected this. Thus financial acumen together with a sound estate plan and implementation served the TLC well.

Where a land-rich but cash-poor interest found property development beyond their resources then the solution was to embrace investors willing to advance funds to lay out the estate and to facilitate building. This happened all over Edinburgh in the half century before the First World War. To the west of Murrayfield Station and north of Corstorphine Road Ebenezer Chalmers sold twenty-six acres to the Murrayfield Real Estate Company in 1898 specifically to unlock the development value of property which was beyond his own means and energies to do so. Though the agreed purchase price was £36,750, in effect Chalmers, who was also a director of the company, provided a £22,000 mortgage and so only £14,750 had to be paid in cash and shares.[119] The Company's prospectus described the area as 'one of the most charming residential quarters . . . completely outside the business parts and yet within easy reach of these

---

[119] NAS GD327/508/4, Kemp Papers, Prospectus of the Murrayfield Real Estate Company, Apr. 1898.

and the centre of the city'. With florid prose the beauties of the area were extolled:

It commands an extensive, varied prospect of the surrounding country, embracing some of the most prominent features . . . the whole ranges of the Braid and Pentland Hills, and the loftier summits of West Lothian and Lanarkshire. The north boundary is a belt of trees, which by arrangement will be maintained for the sake of amenity by the proprietors . . . in all time coming, and immediately beyond these trees lies the Murrayfield Golf Course.[120]

No less important in the prospectus were the amenities and recreational potential of the Murrayfield area: 'A new cable car route, with its regular and continuous service skirts the area' and Murrayfield Station was nearby; the villas were well away from the business districts, but accessible to them; to placate potential buyers over the capital costs of installation it was noted that the 'electric light mains are already carried out'; and 'in addition to the Murrayfield Golf Club, there are bowling and tennis clubs already established in the vicinity'.[121]

Chalmers thus obtained a capital transfusion to develop his property, yet should the Company fail, the mortgage arrangement protected his interest in the land – a reworking of Wilson's 1869 Trojan horse manoeuvres with the TLC. For a modest stake averaging £3,500 the other directors – George McRae, the Edinburgh city treasurer, Sir J. A. Russell, A. B. Mackenzie, an Edinburgh magistrate, and the builder James Alexander – obtained access to the development opportunities and profits on twenty-six acres of prime residential land. As the report by a firm of independent architects noted, 'it would be worth the consideration of the directors whether they should not themselves undertake the building of villas as this venture would prove a considerable further profit to the company'.[122]

Layers of feu-duties, each adding successive amounts to the cost of land, were a central feature of Scottish land tenure. Sub-infeudation, the process of creating these tiers of feu-duty payments, was a heavy penalty for ultimate users, tenants, in the form of rents so high that they approximated those of central London and required more stringent Rent Control measures in the twentieth century than anywhere else outside the capital. But for landowners, developers and builders the opportunity to create financial instruments was an important means of financing urban development and what transpired in Edinburgh was typical of processes which affected a majority of Scottish burghs in the nineteenth century.

[120] NAS GD327/508/4, Prospectus.
[121] NAS GD327/508/4, Prospectus.
[122] NAS GD327/508/4, Report by Dunn and Findlay, architects.

Financial innovations

Urban expansion, which resumed in Edinburgh with some vigour from the 1860s, was itself the stimulus for structural change in a market for building finance determined to break out of the lawyers' stranglehold. Instead of privately arranged deals in legal offices, various agencies provided a more systematic access to funds which increasingly replaced, though never supplanted, personal legal contacts. Building societies and associations together with property investment and heritable security companies, therefore, functioned as formal financial institutions supplying both mortgages to house purchasers and finance for construction.

One pragmatic, small-scale and highly localised approach to building finance was the emergence of building associations from the late 1860s. The Glen Street Building Association and seven others with confusingly similar names – Lauriston, Lauriston Gardens, Lauriston Place, Lauriston Park, North Lauriston Gardens, West Lauriston Place and South Lauriston Building Associations – were, in essence, groups of would-be neighbours in specific streets near Tollcross who combined their resources to finance building. Almost ninety building associations were active in Edinburgh in the years 1869–74 (see appendix 4.2) and on the southern fringes of the Meadows and within a stone's throw of one another, the Hope Park, Bower, Meadow, Meadow Park, United, Livingstone, Melville and Sciennes Building Associations each operated simultaneously as private clubs.[123] Up to a dozen or twenty members each agreed to purchase a flat in a tenement or street. Though their advances did not entirely finance the builder's construction work, the prospect of sales guaranteed on completion strengthened a builder's bargaining power when seeking further loans. In effect, by pooling their commitment to purchase flats and providing a limited amount of start-up capital to the builder, these associations were equivalent to terminating building societies and, as the highly specific names indicate, they were often concerned only with a few tenements in a single street.[124]

---

[123] S. D. Chapman and J. N. Bartlett, 'The contribution of building clubs and freehold land society to working class housing in Birmingham', in S. D. Chapman, ed., *The History of Working Class Housing: A Symposium* (Newton Abbot 1971), 221–46, provide an English dimension.

[124] Although the list of Edinburgh building associations would be very long, the highly localised nature of these relatively short-lived institutions included: Bower (Sciennes); Bruntsfield; Cricket Park; Drumdryan Street; East London Street; Falconfield; Fettes; Fountainbridge Church; Gillespie Crescent; Greenhill Grove; Grove Park; Harrison Park; Hillside Crescent; Hope Park (Sciennes); Imperial; Leamington; Livingstone; Meadow Park; Melville; Polwarth; (South) Grindlay Street; Southern; Stockbridge; United (Sciennes); Wellington Place (Leith).

The mutual principles of the building association were taken a stage further by building societies. Whereas the building association was a closed group in which members and beneficiaries were the same, in building societies investors' subscriptions and savers' deposits were made available to others so as to deepen and extend the reservoir of mortgage finance.[125] More commonly, however, building societies combined their conventional role of borrowing from and lending to private individuals with the more entrepreneurial activities of an investment society. That is, they advanced depositors' money to speculative builders and developers, as was explicitly acknowledged in the many company names which included the term 'property investment company and building society'. The Amicable Property Investment Building Society, Edinburgh Mutual Investment Building Society, Fourth Provincial Property Investment and Building Society; Heritable Security and Mortgage Investment Co., Old Edinburgh Property Investment and Building Society, and Permanent Scottish Union Property Investment Society were just some among many Edinburgh companies that made loans available directly to builders and developers and who were not content simply to act as a valve regulating the transfer of savings from one group of private individuals to the mortgages of others. Nor was it an approach confined to property investment and building societies since the Union Bank and the Life Assurance Company of Scotland were amongst other financial institutions which were active in lending directly to developers. And in another version of the recycling of building finance, out of town companies which included the Kirkcaldy Property Investment Society and the Musselburgh Building and Investment Society also found it profitable, in the last quarter of the nineteenth century, to redirect local savings into the Edinburgh building industry.[126] Country cousins were astute enough to participate in the returns to buoyant building conditions in the major urban centres.

---

[125] These included Amicable Property Investment BS; Edinburgh Conservative Friendly BS; Edinburgh Mutual Investment and BS; Fourth Edinburgh Property Investment and BS; Grange Provident Building Society; Musselburgh Building and Investment Society; Old Edinburgh Property Investment and BS; Permanent Scottish Union Property Investment BS; St Bernard's Friendly Society and Oddfellow's Lodge; Stockbridge Mutual Investment and BS; New Scottish Property Investment BS; Edinburgh House Proprietor's Company Ltd; Edinburgh Property Investment Society; Edinburgh Railway Access and Property Company; Fourth Provident Investment and BS; Improved Edinburgh Property Investment Company; Provident Association of London; Scottish Equitable Life Assurance Society; Scottish Legal Life Assurance Society; Scottish Metropolitan Co. Ltd; Heritable Investors' Company; New Scottish Friendly Property Investment Company; Scottish Provident Institution; Union Heritable Securities Company Ltd; Town and Country Heritable Trust.
[126] NAS RS108/4204.13, 3811.11, 2153.141.

When the Union Bank or Fourth Provincial Property Investment and Building Society combined mortgage business and advances to builders it was part of a property investment strategy which sought to spread risk in relation to expected yields. Trusts, too, recognised the benefits of a portfolio of investments, as Walker's or Chesser's trustees demonstrated by shifting the emphasis between home and foreign investment or between heritable securities and heritable properties. The Edinburgh Heritable Security Co. Ltd, established in 1874, also acknowledged the importance of investment flexibility to achieve a spread of risks and stated in their Articles of Association that their objective was 'to afford persons who have money to lend facilities for safe and profitable invest-ment . . . and to advance or lend money on security of land, houses, and heritable property'.[127] Similarly, the Edinburgh House Proprietors Co. Ltd, founded in 1896, explained in their Articles that their intention was 'to create feu-duties or ground annuals . . . to sell any of the heritable rights . . . [and] to act as owners, lessors and factors of heritable prop-erty'.[128] In the event, the company's emphasis was largely that of land-lord and factor, purchasing properties and subletting shops and houses in Leith Walk, Gorgie and Bryson Roads, as well as properties in the New Town, Merchiston and Morningside. Though not themselves immune to miscalculations, such companies functioned like unit trusts specialising in property investment and altering the balance of the port-folio as circumstances changed and opportunities in their specialist sector arose.[129]

Property investment strategies, then, were a subtle yet complex amalgam of motives which sought by different routes to achieve a balance between risk and yield. Just how complex property finance arrangements were was evident in the development of Gillespie Crescent, an 850 foot strip of land feued by the trustees of James Gillespie's Hospital to a prom-inent Bruntsfield building firm, W. and D. McGregor, in 1869.[130] The feu charter set aside an earlier plan of 1852 for villa housing and the full annual feu-duty of £400 became operational from 1875.[131] The builders

---

[127] NAS BT2/547, Edinburgh Heritable Security Co. Ltd, Articles of Association, clause 3.

[128] NAS BT2/3236, Edinburgh House Proprietors Co. Ltd, Memorandum of Association, clause III/1–3.

[129] NAS BT2/575, BT2/652 Land Feuing Company; General Property Investment Company (see also chapter 7).

[130] MC/JGH, Chartulary of James Gillespie's Hospital, vol. 1, f. 266, vol. 2, ff. 189–99, 266–78. The spelling of McGregor is inconsistent in documentary evidence but is stan-dardised here.

[131] ECA MC/JGH/box 3/3, Report for Feuing Grounds of James Gillespie's Hospital, 5 Jan. 1852.

more than covered their feu-duty obligations to their superior, Gillespie's trustees; they raised some working capital first by subdividing the land into a number of building plots and assigning feu-duties to each, and then, by creating another tier of property burdens, ground annuals, collected further revenues to be used as working capital. Some of the building stances were developed by W. and D. McGregor themselves using profits obtained from an earlier development fronting Bruntsfield links (Glengyle Terrace), but they also sub-feued land to trustees of the Bruntsfield Building Association (BBA) who then re-engaged the McGregors to build five tenements for them. Individual flats were assigned by the BBA according to their Articles of Association.[132] For tenements adjoining those of the BBA an almost identical arrangement was negotiated between W. and D. McGregor and both the Leamington Building Association and the Gillespie Crescent Building Association. However, matters were made even more complicated when several members of the Gillespie Crescent Building Association were unable in 1872 to pay the remainder of the purchase price of their flats and had to seek loans from the Heritable Securities Investment Association (Limited) (HSIA) who, as mortgagees, then held the title to the flats.[133] In a web of financial relations, W. and D. McGregor, therefore, were simultaneously feuars and superiors, developers and contractors, as well as builders.

As builders, W. and D. McGregor were drawn into negotiations first with the building associations and then with a property company (HSIA) to generate working capital. Similarly, and almost simultaneously, another builder, James Steel, entered into agreements with the Heritable Estates Company between 1876 and 1881 to improve his liquidity position and reduce his exposure to loans obtained substantially from trusts (see table 4.6). The Heritable Estates Company was more than a finance company – it actually bought properties either through a series of capital advances to builders while property was still under construction, or by payment of a lump sum on completion.[134] Once acquired, however, the Heritable Estates Company quickly sold their property to private individuals and trusts. Such an arrangement provided either a drip-feed of capital to builders or an assurance of a capital transfusion on completion; either way, it enabled debts incurred in the construction process to be paid off, and for the purchaser there was a specialist mortgage company from whom funds could be borrowed.

[132] MC/JGH, Chartulary, vol. 1, ff. 280–319.
[133] MC/JGH, Chartulary, vol. 1, ff. 320–9.
[134] NAS RS108/1208.70, 1212.49, 1193.183, 1257.52.

There were no simple model by which housebuilding and property development were financed. A mosaic of different agencies emerged. Specialist intermediaries used share capital and deposits by investors to make loans available to house buyers, and the People's Bank, St Cuthbert's Co-operative Association and a growing number of building, friendly and property investment societies emerged to fulfil a function which was well known in England but which until the last quarter of the nineteenth century had been stifled in Scotland because of the powerful leverage exerted on the mortgage market by the legal profession.

In the quest for new and increased funds to finance construction, builders turned relatively less often to law firms and more towards alternative sources of capital. These were responsive, none more so than companies specialising in loans secured against future feu-duty income. For the Trinity Land Company, as in many other developments, the importance of heritable securities was considerable. The Church of Scotland and the Merchant Company were large institutional fundholders, but opportunities for small trust funds and individual investors to participate in property investment were provided in the 1860s and 1870s by an emerging formal financial sector concerned with such investments. For example, the Edinburgh Heritable Security Company Ltd, established in 1874, specified in its Articles of Association that it intended 'to afford persons who have money to lend facilities for safe and profitable investment . . . and to advance or lend money on security of land, houses and heritable property'.[135] Set up in the aftermath of limited liability legislation, these heritable security companies concentrated specifically on investing subscribers' share capital to purchase feu-duties and then used the revenue these produced to pay dividends to shareholders. In 1862 the Heritable Securities and Mortgage Investment Association recognised that such market niches existed and in 1867 was followed by the Scottish Heritable Security Company. A decade later, the assets of these two companies together exceeded £2 million and their proportion of expenses to revenue was between just 4 and 6%.[136] Consequently, the ratio of profits to expenses was between 2–4:1 – that is, profits were double or even quadruple the expenses of the firms.

The creation in Edinburgh of seventeen heritable security limited liability companies in the 1870s was accompanied by reported assets worth £5 million in their combined balance sheets in 1879. Of course, not all investments were in Edinburgh feu-duties, though there can be no

---

[135] NAS BT2/547, Edinburgh Heritable Security Company Ltd, Articles of Association, Clause 3.
[136] *Edinburgh Property Review*, 26 Apr. 1879, 73.

doubt of the considerable widening and deepening in the reservoir for property investment in the city between 1860 and 1880. In addition, heritable security companies generated £2.40 profit for every £1 of expenses incurred.[137] On the basis of dividend to price, therefore, the Alliance Heritable (15.75%), Caledonian Heritable (13.63%) and Scottish Provident Investment (10.25%) were substantially ahead of the property company sector average (8.50%) in the late 1870s, which in turn was 2% above overseas investment companies – yields for Scottish railway and bank stock and for public utility companies such as gas and water undertakings were in the 4–6% range, while the Bank of England's discount rate was 2%.[138] The appeal of the heritable security companies to both investors and builders was understandable.

Under Scots law, sub-infeudation combined with greater activity in the building industry to create circumstances suited to heritable security companies. The central need to create real burdens to control the use and subsequent development of property, clarified in 1818 but effectively held in suspense during the interruption to building in the second quarter of the nineteenth century, became more effective as population pressure, middle-class demand preferences for suburbia and the gradual elimination of excess supply from the earlier phases of New Town development brought the market into partial equilibrium.[139] Attempts to respond to these pressures produced ideal opportunities for superiors to create new tiers of burdens for their vassals, and then to commute that obligation in return for a capital sum, which in turn might be used as the start up capital for estate development and building work. However effective professional and social networking was amongst legal firms, the demand for new housing in the final third of the nineteenth century meant that neither the volume of building finance nor the volume of available investment funds could be handled efficiently through firms of lawyers. The emergence of heritable security companies, property investment and building societies was an indication that Edinburgh law firms were insufficiently responsive to changed market circumstances and in the vacuum which resulted, new financial institutions flourished.

[137] Calculated from *Edinburgh Property Review*, 26 Apr. 1879.
[138] *Edinburgh Property Review*, Stock and Share list, 26 Apr. 1879, 328.
[139] *Gordon* v. *Marjoribanks* (1818), HL 6 Dow 87. See also chapter 2.

Appendix 4.1 *Church of Scotland income from property: revenue from heritable securities in various burghs 1874–1914 (%)*

	Edinburgh	Glasgow	Dundee	Aberdeen	Other burghs
1874	33.1	50.5	0.4	13.4	2.6
1875	36.0	46.8	0.3	14.4	2.4
1876	39.9	43.3	0.3	14.2	2.2
1877	47.0	38.2	0.3	12.5	2.0
1878	47.2	38.1	0.3	12.5	2.0
1879	49.0	36.8	0.3	12.1	1.9
1880	51.9	34.7	0.2	11.4	1.8
1881	53.0	33.9	0.2	11.1	1.7
1882	54.1	33.1	0.2	10.8	1.7
1883	56.0	31.9	0.2	10.4	1.6
1884	53.7	30.7	0.2	9.9	5.5
1885	54.3	30.1	0.2	9.9	5.5
1886	54.3	30.4	0.2	9.7	5.5
1887	53.0	29.8	0.2	9.3	7.8
1888	53.0	29.9	0.2	9.2	7.7
1889	53.1	29.7	0.4	9.1	7.7
1890	53.2	29.3	0.8	9.0	7.7
1891	53.8	28.8	1.0	8.9	7.6
1892	54.5	28.2	1.0	8.7	7.7
1893	55.0	27.8	1.0	8.5	7.7
1894	54.1	27.3	0.9	8.3	9.4
1895	54.5	27.1	0.9	8.2	9.3
1896	54.5	27.2	0.9	8.1	9.2
1897	55.0	27.0	0.9	7.9	9.2
1898	55.3	26.7	0.9	7.8	9.3
1899	55.8	26.4	0.9	7.8	9.2
1900	56.1	26.2	0.9	7.7	9.2
1901	56.5	25.9	0.9	7.6	9.1
1902	56.9	25.6	0.8	7.5	9.1
1903	57.5	25.2	0.8	7.4	9.0
1904	57.6	25.3	0.8	7.3	8.9
1905	57.6	25.6	0.8	7.2	8.8
1906	57.7	25.6	0.8	7.1	8.7
1907	57.7	25.8	0.8	7.1	8.6
1908	57.7	25.8	0.8	7.1	8.6
1909	58.9	25.1	0.8	6.9	8.4
1910	58.6	25.4	0.8	6.9	8.3
1911	59.1	25.1	0.8	6.8	8.3
1912	60.0	24.5	0.7	6.6	8.1
1913	60.0	24.5	0.7	6.6	8.1
1914	59.2	25.6	0.7	6.5	7.9

Source: NAS CH1/19.74–77, Church of Scotland Endowment Committee Accounts.

Appendix 4.2 *Edinburgh building associations 1869–1874*

Abbotsford	Lauriston	Rosehall Place
Albert	Lauriston Gardens	St Leonard's
Albert Place	Lauriston Park	St Margaret's
Argyle	Lauriston Place	Saxe Coburg
Bainfield	Leamington	Sciennes
Barcaple	Leven Lodge	South Grindlay Street
Bower	Leven Terrace	South Lauriston
Brougham Place	Livingstone	Southern
Bruntsfield	Lord Clyde	Spittalfield
Burgess	Lorne	Teviot Row
Burns	Lutton Place	Thistle
Caledonian	Mayfield	Trafalgar
Caledonian Place	Meadow	Tynecastle
Commercial Union	Meadow Park	Tynecastle 2nd
Dalry	Meadowside	Union
Douglas	Melville	United Building
Drumdryan Street	Midlothian	United Provident
East London Street	Montague Street	Valleyfield
Forrest Road	Montgomery	Victorian
Gardner	Montgomery Place	Viewforth
Gillespie Crescent	Newington	Waverley
Glen Street	North Lauriston Gardens	Springfield
Glengyle	North Meadowside	Stewartfield
Grange Provident	Oxford Street	West Claremont Street
Grindlay Street	Panmure Place	West Lauriston Place
Grove	Richmond	West Meadow Place
Hope Park	Rob Roy	Windsor
Ivanhoe	Rockville	Working Men's Provident
Kenilworth	Rose	

Source: NAS, Register of Sasines, Abridgements and Index of Names 1869–74.

5   The building industry and instability

The structure of the housebuilding industry is acknowledged to have been a major factor in the instability which builders experienced in Victorian Britain.[1] With no barriers to entry, under-capitalisation, limited book-keeping and cash flow problems strongly associated with a product normally saleable only on completion, builders were particularly vulnerable to bankruptcy. Together these factors produced boom to bust cyclical fluctuations in building of unprecedented severity – at least 70% more pronounced than in the manufacturing sector generally.[2] Year to year variations in the Edinburgh building industry were 40–80% greater than those in English regional cities – Leeds, Liverpool, Manchester and Birmingham – though in many other industrial burghs in central Scotland levels of instability and uncertainty were far in excess of those in Edinburgh.[3]

To identify changes in the size and composition of demand based on trends in household income and demography seemed beyond the competence of most entrepreneurs, and builders were no exception. Builders relied entirely on their own perception of the 'state of trade', a vague term which encompassed the equally inexact gradations of 'dull', 'fair', 'good' and 'busy'.[4] No builders' accounts or bankruptcy papers referred

[1] P. J. Aspinall, 'The internal structure of the housebuilding industry in nineteenth century cities', in J. Johnson and C. G. Pooley, eds., *The Structure of Nineteenth Century Cities* (London 1982), 75–105; R. M. Pritchard, *Housing and the Spatial Structure of the City: Residential Mobility and the Housing Market in an English City since the Industrial Revolution* (Cambridge 1976), 39; C. Powell, '"He that runs against time": life expectancy of firms in the first half of the nineteenth century', *Construction History*, 2, 1986, 61–7.

[2] R. Rodger, 'Speculative builders and the structure of the Scottish building industry 1860–1914', *Business History*, 21, 1979, 226–46; R. Rodger, 'Structural instability in the Scottish building industry 1820–80', *Construction History*, 2, 1986, 48–60; and R. Rodger, *Housing in Urban Britain 1780–1914* (Cambridge 1995), 20–2.

[3] J. McKenna and R. Rodger, 'Control by coercion: employers' associations and the establishment of industrial order in the building industry of England and Wales 1860–1914', *Business History Review*, 59, 1985, 208; R. Rodger, '"The Invisible Hand": – market forces, housing and the urban form in Victorian cities', in D. Fraser and A. Sutcliffe, eds., *The Pursuit of Urban History* (London 1983), table 10.5, 206.

[4] The *Builder* provides numerous examples of such terminology, as does the *Edinburgh Gazette*.

to a quantitative analysis of immigration, natural increase or household formation as a basis for decision-making despite the relative ease with which such components of demand were available in published form. A casual inspection of the censuses between 1861 and 1901, for example, would have shown that relative to the number of families one of the highest and sustained housing deficits in urban Scotland existed in Edinburgh.[5] In the same period the contribution of the twenty to forty-four age group to decennial population growth never fell below 30% per decade, but in the 1890s the expansion of this age group accounted for 52% of the increase in the population of Edinburgh and it would not have taken a genius to deduce that household formation would rise for a time before resuming a more conventional level. Clearly market knowledge was partial, or asymmetric, and business decisions were correspondingly risk-laden.[6]

In the absence of such market research adjustments were always *ex post,* that is, once the trend was already evident, and even newspaper reports of the annual summary of building plans submitted to the Dean of Guild Court made little or no mention of broader demand and supply conditions. The figures for changes in the numbers of houses and tenements came as something of a surprise to builders in the city, and not least to the members of the plans committee themselves. For example, in replying to the vote of thanks accorded to him in 1903 after twenty-eight years public service and on the conferment of his baronetcy, Sir James Steel stated he was 'very much struck' by the statement by the Dean of Guild in which he said the 'building trade was reviving, because some of them had been under the impression that it was falling off. It was very satisfactory to hear that the opposite was the case.'[7]

To an extent, imprecise market analysis was a result of the small scale of production in the building industry. In the forty years before 1914, over half (52.9%) the applications to build houses in 102 burghs in Scotland were on a 'one-off' basis (table 5.1); only one application in six (17.2%) was for a larger project of three or more properties.[8] In Edinburgh, 40% of Dean of Guild approvals for residential building in the decade 1885–94

[5] Censuses of Scotland, City of Edinburgh, 1861–1901.
[6] For recent discussions on historical aspects of information costs to business see M. Casson, 'Institutional economics and business history: a way forward?', and S. R. H. Jones, 'Transactions costs and the theory of the firm: the scope and limitations of the new institutional approach', *Business History*, 39, 1997, 152–71 and 9–25, and also C. J. Simon and C. Nardinelli, 'The talk of the town: human capital, information, and the growth of English cities, 1861–1961', *Explorations in Economic History*, 33, 1996, 384–413.
[7] ECA ACC 264, Guildry Cuttings file, Annual Report of the Dean of Guild, 1903.
[8] Rodger, 'Speculative builders', 231–5.

Table 5.1 *The building industry and the scale of production: Scottish burghs 1873–1914*

	Number	% of housebuilding in projects of 1, 2 or 3+ houses		
		1 house	2 or more houses	3 or more houses
Cities	3	39.6	60.4	21.1
Major burghs	30	53.9	46.1	20.4
Small burghs	69	74.8	25.2	3.6
Scottish burghs	102	52.9	47.1	17.2

Note: major = burghs with >25,000 population in any census 1841–1911.
Source: based on Dean of Guild Court Registers and Plans in each burgh. See R. Rodger, 'Speculative builders and the structure of the Scottish building industry 1860–1914', *Business History*, 21, 1979, 226–46.

were to builders; the majority, therefore, were for applications to build a single property and were made by private individuals on their own behalf, or for institutions, building associations and companies (see table 5.2). Of those Dean of Guild Court permits applied for by Edinburgh builders, one third were for single houses or tenements, and two-thirds of builders applied to construct three or fewer properties. This contrasted with Sheffield, the most detailed English comparison available, where planning permission granted to builders was in only 50% of cases for three or fewer houses.[9] On this basis, at least, the building industry in Edinburgh was more fragmented than that south of the border, and while the theory of the firm indicates that this should have induced market equilibrium, the imperfect information employed by builders destroyed a necessary condition of stability.[10]

'Reaction lags' – belated and then over-compensating adjustments in housing supply – to changed market circumstances were an inherent feature of industries where the product was characterised as 'lumpy', that is, completed on an occasional rather than on a continuous basis.[11] Such over-reactions were particularly pronounced in the Scottish building industry since the construction of a tenement required up to four times more capital than an English terraced house and where a haemorrhaging

---

[9] Aspinall, 'The internal structure of the housebuilding industry', 91.
[10] ECA Dean of Guild Court Registers, 1860–1914; Rodger, 'Speculative builders', table 2, 228.
[11] R. C. O. Matthews, *The Trade Cycle* (Oxford 1959), chapter 6, provides a succinct account of the mechanism.

Table 5.2 *The scale of business operations: Edinburgh housebuilders 1885–1894*

Number of projects	Number of builders	% of builders	Total no. of projects	% building warrants
1	47	37.3	47	9.9
2	22	17.5	44	9.3
3	16	12.7	48	10.1
4	10	7.9	40	8.4
5–9	20	15.9	130	27.4
10–14	6	4.8	70	14.8
15+	5	4.0	95	20.0
Total	126	100.0	474	100.0

Sources: ECA Dean of Guild Court Registers, 1885–94; R. Rodger, 'Scottish urban housebuilding 1870–1914', University of Edinburgh PhD thesis, 1975, 415.

in the supply of funds had a particularly adverse effect given the longer construction period involved for a tenement and the need to complete and sell the property so as to repay loans. Furthermore, the cumulative impact of sub-feuing exaggerated downward spirals, just as it over-heated in the upswing phase of the building cycle.

Edinburgh builders and property interests were not entirely insensitive to changes in the housing market and did try to adjust their scale of operations. This was evident from at least four perspectives. First, the number of new entrants to the building industry who made just a single application for a warrant declined when the industry was in recession.[12] Secondly, the monthly figures for building bankruptcies between 1856 and 1913 showed fewer builders in short-run financial difficulties when cash flow improved.[13] Thus, when each May new rental agreements came into force, sales of newly completed housing to landlords together with maintenance work on old houses provided a welcome spring injection of revenue to building firms. Bankruptcy rates declined accordingly, as they also did each September when a flurry of house completions anticipated the climatic problems posed by the onset of winter; the rate of bankruptcies in the Edinburgh building trades, as elsewhere in Scotland, declined correspondingly to their lowest monthly point.[14] Thirdly, sales of heritable securities showed a decisive cyclical pattern (fig. 4.3) in response to

[12] Rodger, 'Scottish urban housebuilding 1870–1914', University of Edinburgh PhD thesis, 1975, 420.   [13] *Edinburgh Gazette*, 1856–1913.
[14] R. Rodger, 'Speculative builders', 242; and R. Rodger, 'Business failure in Scotland 1839–1913', *Business History*, 27, 1985, 75–99.

landlords' and investors' changing perceptions of the rental market. In effect, the number of years of purchase for heritable securities was the valve which controlled the flow of building finance and builders had little option but to respond to it.

The level of empty houses was the fourth market indicator to which builders responded. The mechanism was based on the observation that when low levels of vacancies existed then housebuilding was encouraged; when stocks of unlet houses were high then this had a deterrent effect on housebuilding. The relationship was explained by the Dean of Guild in relation to gradually increasing levels of empty property in the city after 1900 which by 1906 had exceeded 5,000 houses:

when they [builders] saw the amount of unlet property they could hardly antici-pate any great improvement for at least some time to come. This state of affairs had been gradually increasing for the last few years.[15]

In Glasgow this adjustment process was itself sufficient to induce a strong cycle in housebuilding.[16] Assuming that housebuilding was activated by a 2% level of empty houses and curtailed by a 10% level, then a 'swing in empties . . . could easily be transmitted into a cycle' which, depending on conditions, might be between twelve and twenty-two years. If, for example, net population growth was 1% annually, and net additions to the housing stock averaged 1% p.a. over a twenty year period but regis-tered only half that rate (0.5%) near the 10% ceiling for empties and was double the average rate (2%) when the proportion of vacant houses was at its lowest level, then a cycle of about twenty years would result 'without any change in demand whatever'.[17]

Thus the inner rhythms of the building industry, with its protracted depressions and accelerated upturns, itself contributed much to the instability and business uncertainty which was common amongst build-ing firms. As the Lord Dean of Guild explained in 1893:

the comparative dullness of the building trade which had prevailed in Edinburgh for a few years past [was] a natural result of the period of overbuilding which pre-ceded it. [He] was inclined to think, however, that the building trade had reached its lowest ebb during the past year, and that a certain measure of brisker trade had begun.[18]

---

[15] *Scotsman*, 29 Oct. 1906.
[16] A. K. Cairncross, *Home and Foreign Investment 1870–1913: Studies in Capital Accumulation* (Cambridge 1953), 31. Cairncross' assumptions led him to deduce a minimum of twelve years for the building cycle, though he acknowledged significant local variations were likely. See also B. F. Reece, 'The price adjustment mechanism in Glasgow's rental housing market, 1871–1913: the claim of "sticky" rents re-examined', *Scottish Journal of Political Economy*, 31, 1984, 286–93.   [17] Cairncross, *Home and Foreign Investment*, 31.
[18] *Scotsman*, 24 Oct. 1893.

The central problem which confronted builders as suppliers was the disjuncture between their short- and long-term horizons. It took time – often more than a year – and sizeable capital advances to develop a site and build a tenement, yet it was imperative in the short term to sell houses so as to improve cash flow, to reduce the level of borrowing and to renegotiate loans when they matured to avoid the clutches of the sequestrator.

Cycles and uncertainty

The intrinsically unstable nature of the housebuilding industry can be judged from annual changes in the indices for approved housebuilding plans, new plots feued for building and the tax assessments (rates) levied on residential buildings (fig. 5.1). It was not uncommon for year-to-year changes of 20–50 index points in these series. In general, and from somewhat different perspectives, therefore, the underlying instability of housebuilding in Edinburgh over a sixty year period is revealed through the three series, concerned as they are with land released for development (feu-duty index), planned housing (housebuilding index) and completed construction (rates index). Despite the volatility of these series, that the matrix of correlation coefficients ranged from +0.61 to +0.77 is indicative of strong harmonic patterns between the three indicators of building activity (table 5.3).

Contemporaries went further. According to *The Scotsman*, 'The work of the [Dean of Guild] Court furnished an index to the state of the building trade, just as the state of the building trade was an indication of the prosperity of the city.'[19] It was only to be expected that there would be a close correspondence between the levels of new housebuilding and the demand for building materials, such as the volume of sand supplied from the outskirts of Edinburgh by the Comiston Sand Pit (fig. 5.2), but more generally, there was a strong degree of synchronisation between the level of new residential building and economic activity, as reflected in the planned commercial and industrial building (fig. 5.3). With a correlation coefficient of +0.70 the residential–industrial building relationship was stronger than any of the other building sub-market pairings.[20]

The approximate twenty year periodicity of the building cycle, with its peaks in the late 1870s and on either side of 1900, corresponded with wider national patterns. However, important local variations were also apparent and this depended in no small measure on the levels and

---

[19] *Scotsman*, 23 Oct. 1894.

[20] These correlations included housebuilding–alterations and additions (+0.61); institutional–alterations and additions (+0.61); housebuilding–institutional (+0.49); institutional–industrial (+0.48); industrial–alterations and additions (+0.08).

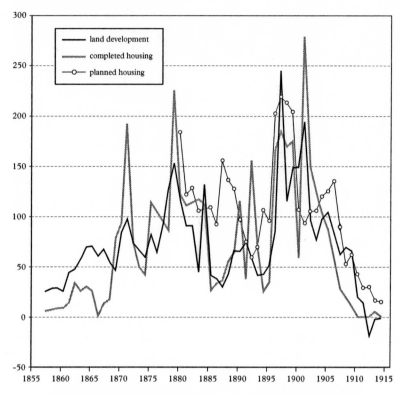

Figure 5.1 Housebuilding and land development in Edinburgh
1855–1914 (av. 1900–9 = 100)

Sources: ECA, Dean of Guild Court Registers, 1880–1914; ECA City of
Edinburgh Rolls of Superiorities, 1875–80, 1882–98, 1900–14; ECA
George Heriot's Hospital Superiorities, 1915; City of Edinburgh,
Municipal and Other Accounts (Edinburgh 1915); City of Edinburgh,
*Statements Respecting Assessable Rentals Local Rates and Net Amounts of
Ordinary Expenditure Charged on the Burgh Assessment 1915–16*
(Edinburgh 1916), ff. 357–68; R. Rodger, 'Scottish urban
housebuilding 1870–1914', University of Edinburgh PhD thesis, 1975,
tables 3.3 and 3.4, fig. 3.1.

composition of income and employment.[21] This was the case, for
example, in the 1880s when middle-class and skilled artisanal incomes in

[21] J. P. Lewis, *Building Cycles and Britain's Growth* (London 1965), Appendix 4, provides
indices for aggregate British and many individual English and Welsh towns and cities.
See also A. G. Kenwood, 'Residential building activity in north-eastern England
1863–1913', *Manchester School*, 31, 1963, 115–28, and R. Rodger, 'The Victorian building industry and the housing of the Scottish working class', in M. Doughty, ed., *Building
the Industrial City* (Leicester 1986), 178–9, for local variations in building cycles.

Table 5.3 *Building indicators: feu-duties, property taxes and planned building correlation matrix 1856–1914*

	Feu-duties	Rates
Feu-duties	1	
Rates	0.77	1
Housebuilding plans	0.65	0.61

N = 59 (housebuilding N = 35)
Sources: as for fig. 5.1.

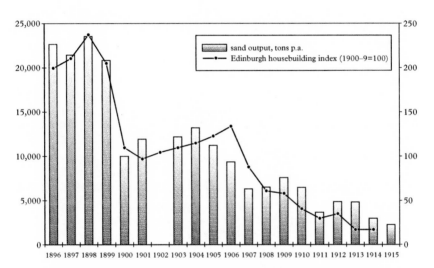

Figure 5.2 Building materials and housebuilding: Edinburgh 1896–1915

Notes
(i) Pit closed 4 Dec. 1915.
(ii) Quarters 1901(2) to 1903(3) missing.
Source: ECA ACC 322, Sir William Forrest of Comiston's Papers, Comiston Sandpit Output ledgers, box 1.

Edinburgh proved resilient to rising national levels of unemployment. Similarly, it was middle-class demand which remained buoyant in the early Edwardian years when landlords and developers lost confidence in property in the face of declining working-class demand and alternative investment outlets, many of them overseas.[22] Though by no means

[22] Cairncross, *Home and Foreign Investment*, 37–64, emphasised Canadian investment.

immune to the 'Atlantic economy'[23] – the inverse cycles of peaks and troughs which affected Britain and America between *c.* 1870 and 1914 – the rhythm of housebuilding in a specific town or city was heavily dependent upon its social and occupational composition. In this respect the disproportionate presence in Edinburgh of the professional middle classes and annuitants, as well as of clerks and artisans, ensured a high degree of insulation against industrial fluctuations and the vagaries of the trade cycle, as was reflected in the levels of villa and detached housebuilding sustained for almost two decades before the Great War (fig. 5.4).[24]

Coping strategies

The hallmark of cycles is their periodicity and if for housebuilding these were a novel feature of the fifty years before the First World War, then the instability of the building trades was not.[25] Using the series for the release of land for building (annual changes in feu-duties) which was shown (fig. 5.1) to bear a close resemblance to variations in housebuilding, then the long-run instability of building in Edinburgh can be seen over the course of a century and a half (fig. 5.5). These year-on-year changes in the value of land feued by the great Edinburgh landowners – Heriots, the City of Edinburgh itself, the Merchant Company and Trinity Hospital principally – are indicative of variations in the housebuilding construction. The development phases for the first and second New Towns, the collapse of interest in building in the 1830s, 1840s and 1850s, and the renewed, if volatile, vigour of the post-1865 years are each clearly identifiable, as is the Edwardian decline. The extreme instability of the years from 1870 to the First World War is particularly notable.

Survival instincts encouraged builders to adopt one or more of a variety of strategies as they sought to contain the effects of instability on their business. For example, some suspended work on their own account and reverted to the status of jobbing builder or master craftsman, a decision which the less volatile levels of alterations and additions work approved by the Dean of Guild Court fully justified.[26] Gatekeepers, caretakers and gardeners lived in a variety of tied accommodation built and financed by railway companies and hospitals, as well as by private individuals and charities, and for a builder to secure a contract in this way was virtually to eliminate risk and uncertainty over the financial resources and final sale associated with housebuilding. Like assured sales, assured sources of

---

[23] B. Thomas, *Migration and Economic Growth* (Cambridge 1954).   [24] See chapter 1.

[25] H. J. Habakkuk, 'Fluctuations in Britain and the United States in the nineteenth century', *Journal of Economic History*, 22, 1962, 198–230, provides a cogent argument for such post-US Civil War timing for building cycles.

[26] Rodger, 'Scottish urban housebuilding', fig. 2.3.

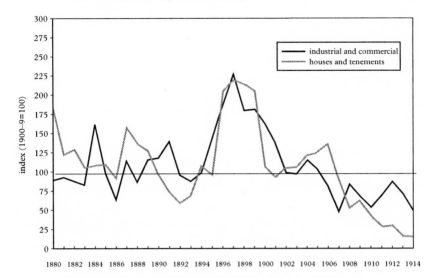

Figure 5.3 Residential and industrial building in Edinburgh
1880–1914

Source: ECA Dean of Guild Court Registers, 1880–1914; see R. Rodger,
'Speculative builders and the structure of the Scottish building industry
1860–1914', *Business History*, 21, 1979, 226–46.

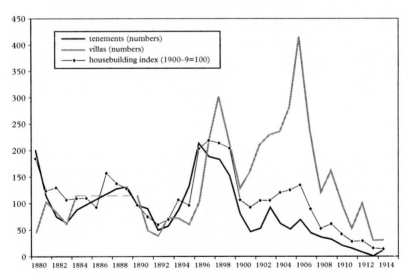

Figure 5.4 Residential building in Edinburgh 1880–1914

Source: ECA Dean of Guild Court Registers, 1880–1914; ECA ACC
264, Guildry Cuttings.

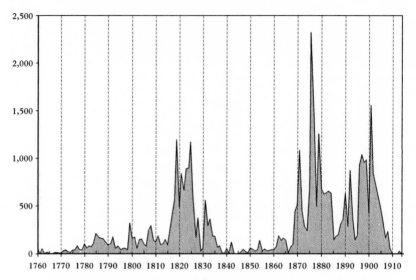

Figure 5.5 Edinburgh building: the release of land for building
purposes 1760–1914 (feu-duties per annum)

Sources: MC Annual Reports, 1850–1909; ECA George Heriot's Roll
of Superiorities, 1913–14; ECA City of Edinburgh Superiorities, 1914.

finance were a lifeline to continuity for builders, and the proliferation of
building associations from the 1860s limited builders' exposure to uncertainty, and thus to bankruptcy. In the years 1885–94, the initiative of
companies and institutions accounted for almost one Edinburgh house in
fourteen.[27] Assured sales to private individuals represented 20% of
housebuilding in this decade, and where builders could secure such commitment, risk was accordingly reduced.

The sale of feus and ground annuals on undeveloped ground, the sale
of heritable securities, that is, of future feu-duty income, extended trade
credit and matching bond maturity dates, together with more question-
able activities such as scamping on the quality of building materials and
departing from the approved house design, repeated bankruptcies and
raising capital on property already mortgaged were tactics which builders
deployed to overcome the business difficulties in which they found themselves. Vertical integration by which builders assumed some of the various
roles of landowner and feudal superior, developer, quarrymaster, builder,

---

[27] ECA, Dean of Guild Court Registers, 1885–94. See also Rodger, 'Speculative builders',
232–4.

financier, landlord and estate agent was another tactic employed to eliminate middlemen, improve profit margins, and thus to limit uncertainty
and restrict risk. Normally these combined roles were only possible for
the larger builders in Edinburgh.

Business tactics and the ingredients for success in the building trade are
the concern of the chapters which follow, seen through the activities of a
building bankrupt and building multi-millionaire – the same individual –
James Steel.

Part 2

Building enterprise and housing management

6   The search for stability

Every week between 1856 and 1913 the pages of the *Edinburgh Gazette* carried lists of names of those who sought to declare themselves bankrupt. Given their number, Edinburgh citizens could be forgiven if, like Victorians generally, they formulated a view of businessmen as sharp operators – fraudulent firms whose owners were not above using bankruptcy proceedings as a device to avoid their debts. Readers of the *Gazette* no doubt consoled themselves with the thought that given the geographical distribution of the notices, ranging as it did from Hawick to Lerwick and from Stranraer to Stonehaven, dubious business practices were not confined to the capital. Had the same citizens been required to read the sequestration documents associated with the Court of Session bankruptcy processes, they might have revised their views more along the lines of business incompetence rather than a presumption of low business morals, since not infrequently bankrupts' accounting procedures were lax; at worst, they were entirely lacking.

In an environment of extreme risk and uncertainty, and where business fluctuations were unsurpassed in their volatility, strategies to diminish instability in housebuilding were essential to business survival.[1] Yet within this objective there was a tension between undue caution and sensible precaution, a tension which on the one hand rendered the business moribund by restricting precisely that entrepreneurial initiative upon which sales and profits depended and, on the other hand, the precaution which by anticipating the vagaries of business fluctuations, insulated the firm and thus enabled it to survive in the long term.

Voluntary liquidation or bankruptcy by definition implied a cash flow problem. This was certainly the case in Edinburgh where, between 1861

---

[1] J. Carroll, N. J. Morgan and M. S. Moss, 'Building by numbers: the life-cycle of Scottish building firms 1793–1913', in P. Joubert and M. Moss, eds., *The Birth and Death of Companies: An Historical Perspective* (Carnforth 1990), 197–214; R. Rodger, 'Business failure in Scotland 1839–1913', *Business History*, 27, 1985, 75–99; and R. Rodger, 'Structural instability in the Scottish building industry 1820–80', *Construction History*, 2, 1986, 48–60.

and 1891, approximately 55–60% of firms had a life-span of three years or less, and in specific products only 5% of firms traded beyond a ten year period.[2] With anonymity increasing as urban expansion progressed, and virtually no barriers to entry to the market, particularly in building, then in a volatile market the business imperative was to make profits.[3] Accountability and business ethics were often of secondary importance. Yet, while many builders accepted this instability as normal, that is, as one of the parameters of business, and accepted that they might change their status from employer to employee as boom changed to trough, for others the financial wreckage created by the radiating ripples of bankruptcy was unacceptable and inherently destabilising. Split between the small firms who rode the crest of the wave with short-run horizons, and those concerns, both large and small, who sought a steady customer base throughout the course of the cycle of boom and bust, the dualism within the building industry was itself a source of instability.

To buttress the firm against such a crisis it was essential to generate trust and business confidence, and in this regard the family performed an important early function. Pre-modern society relied heavily on family and close personal friendships for funding business and trading ventures, and a measure of business discipline and control were exercised through the medium of the family and their close associates, many of whom ultimately became relatives. However, in the nineteenth century, the pace of urban growth, itself initially heavily dependent on in-migration, meant it was difficult to monitor new firms and to be acquainted with an individual's creditworthiness.[4] It was an unstable business environment to which entrepreneurs were exposed, and so they developed a raft of measures to filter business credentials, contain adverse externalities, limit risk and manage the market.[5]

By screening business practice through legal devices and associations of employers an element of stability could be introduced to the market. This was developed much further by ceding supervisory controls to

---

[2] S. Nenadic, 'The small family firm in Victorian Britain', *Business History*, 35, 1993, 90; and S. Nenadic, 'The life-cycle of firms in late nineteenth century Britain', in Joubert and Moss, eds., *The Birth and Death of Companies*, 181–95.

[3] R. Rodger, 'Speculative builders and the structure of the Scottish building industry 1860–1914', *Business History*, 21, 1979, 226–46.

[4] For a development of this argument see D. Reeder and R. Rodger, 'Industrialisation and the city economy', in M. Daunton, ed., *The Cambridge Urban History of Britain*, vol. III (Cambridge 2000).

[5] R. Rodger, 'Managing the market – regulating the city: urban control in the nineteenth century United Kingdom', in H. Diederiks, P. Hohenberg and M. Wagenaar, eds., *Economic Policy in Europe since the late Middle Ages: The Visible Hand and the Fortunes of Cities* (Leicester 1992), 200–19; R. J. Morris, 'Externalities, the market, power structures and the urban agenda', *Urban History Yearbook*, 17, 1990, 99–109.

various municipal agencies. Behind the cloak of civic concern, interventionism was legitimated in fields as diverse as licensing, street trading, nuisances, public order and public health, and edged sideways in a host of interconnected fields of which housing and the regulation of building byelaws were just a part. In this respect, the rise of a technocracy, such as scientific and medical officials and a phalanx of powerful municipal inspectors, each backed by departmental armies of Victorian clerks, as well as self-regulating professional and business bodies, provided a powerful basis for independent advice and control.[6] The emergence of such agencies, whose staffs were 'individually and unconditionally trustworthy . . . and made the modern world possible',[7] was an important ingredient in developing a regulated business framework in the second half of the nineteenth century, even if not all firms were subject fully to the published codes of practice. This transition from family-based trust to impersonal trust, based on contracts and regulatory bodies, denotes a central element in the Weberian preconditions for the transition to a modern capitalist economy.[8] More practically, it constrained the destabilising impact of less responsible operators. Knowingly or otherwise, the municipality created or reconstructed institutions such as the Dean of Guild Court to oversee planning applications and issue habitation certificates for new dwellings, while other agencies vetted sanitary and drainage provisions, and identified areas within the city for redevelopment. In so doing, these institutions offered a mediating mechanism by which tighter order could be established within the city generally, and in the building industry particularly.

How these civic agencies and legal instruments were incorporated into a framework to provide a measure of stability for private builders in Edinburgh is now explored in the context of the development of James Steel's building and housing strategy.

[6] A. Taylor, *State Intervention and Laissez-Faire* (London 1972); V. Cromwell, 'Interpretations of nineteenth century administration', *Victorian Studies*, 9, 1965–6, 244–55; C. Bellamy, *Administering Central-Local Relations 1871–1919* (Manchester 1988), 122, 128, 130, 132, 135; S. P. Walker, 'The defence of professional monopoly: Scottish chartered accountants and "satellites in the accountancy firmament" 1854–1914', *Accounting, Organisations and Society*, 16, 1991, 257–83.

[7] E. Gellner, 'Trust, cohesion and social order', in D. Gambetta, ed., *Trust: Making and Breaking Co-operative Relations* (Oxford 1988), 152; J. McKenna and R. Rodger, 'Control by coercion: employers' associations and the establishment of industrial order in the building industry of England and Wales 1860–1914', *Business History Review*, 59, 1985, 203–31.

[8] M. Weber, *Economy and Society* (Berkeley, edn edited G. Roth and C. Wittich, 1968), 636.

Building a fortune: James Steel's housing strategies

One of the names which appeared in the *Edinburgh Gazette*'s list of petitioners for bankruptcy in 1861 was that of James Steel, builder.[9] The Edinburgh citizenry had little cause to remark on this notice of a meeting of his creditors in Hamilton.[10] For James Steel it represented the nadir of his business life. The fifth of a family of nine children, born in 1829 to James Steel, a tenant farmer at Buchts near Cambusnethan, Wishaw, and his wife, Marion Reid, he had been apprenticed as a mason in the 1840s, saved £50 from his wages and started building in 1853 on his own account in Cambusnethan, and then in 1859 in Glasgow. It was an upward trajectory which enabled him by 1861 to employ twenty-six men, to acquire plant and stock at three quarries to the value of £213, to receive rental income of £300 from houses and shops built and owned in Wishaw and to own two tenements he had built in Garnethill, Glasgow.[11] As a local boy made good and with innumerable relations in the various branches of the family, the loss of face associated with his bankruptcy was immense, and keenly felt. He owed his brother £230, his brother-in-law £80 and his father almost £100. James Steel was discharged as a bankrupt in 1862, and certainly was resident in Edinburgh by the end of the year.[12] If the *Gazette* readers paid little heed to this episode in 1861–2 as bankruptcy proceedings were underway, when his obituaries were printed in 1904, they certainly were aware of one of the most wealthy and powerful figures in Edinburgh.[13] When asked at an enquiry what his income was, he replied '£80,000', and when the questioner reiterated that he had asked about his income not his wealth, Steel repeated his answer, '£80,000', an amount equivalent to an income in excess of £4.5 million per annum in 2000 prices.[14] This 'rags to riches' story of a

---

[9] *Edinburgh Gazette*, 27 Aug. 1861.   [10] *Edinburgh Gazette*, 24 Sept. 1861.

[11] NAS CS318/325, Inventory of estate, 27 Aug. 1861, Census of Scotland, 1861, Enumerators' Books, village of Cambusnethan; NAS RS54, Register of Sasines, Glasgow, 214.186, 214.192, 220.138, 220.191, 227.140, 242.117–18, 1558.256, 1559.28, 1559.51. The referencing system in the Register of Sasines provides a volume number, followed by a page number. This system is followed for subsequent Register of Sasines transactions. The Glasgow properties were at 166 and 172 Bedford Terrace, Renfrew Street and in Wishaw at Cambusnethan and Marshall Streets.

[12] The date is derived from the appearance of his name in the *Edinburgh and Leith Post Office Directory*, 1863–4. Given the lead time required for the compilation of lists, and for printing, late 1862 is not unreasonable, though he may have been in Edinburgh before this. Certainly the date published in his obituaries, 1866, is wrong, and represents another (successful) attempt by Steel to obscure his past. The impressive bust (see p. 349) and grave give no details of his place and date of birth, nor those of any family members.

[13] *Times*, 5 Sept. 1904, col. 4d; *Glasgow Herald*, 5 Sept. 1904, col. 8g; *Scotsman*, 5 Sept. 1904, col. 5a; *Building News*, 9 Sept. 1904, 358.

[14] Anon., *Lord Provosts of Edinburgh 1296–1932* (Edinburgh 1932), 149–50.

migrant, an outsider to the country's capital, culminated 'Dick Whittington-like' with a period as Lord Provost (1900–3) and a knighthood conferred in the city when King Edward VII visited in 1903.[15]

The business career of James Steel provides insights not only into the strategies adopted to withstand the extreme instability of the building industry, but it also reveals key elements by which Edinburgh was reshaped in the years 1860 to 1914 when the Georgian legacy was overwhelmed by a quantity and quality of Victorian tenements and villas which transformed the urban landscape.

In the sequence between the release of an area of land by a heritable owner to the eventual sale or rental to the occupant of a tenement flat or villa, there were many individuals and transactions involved. Sandwiched between landowner and occupant were the estate developer, builder and landlord. Sometimes this was the same person or firm, but the stages by which an area of land was released or feued by a heritable landowner to an estate developer, whose entrepreneurial role it was after the acquisition of the site to draw up a development plan and to sub-feu or sell parcels of land to builders, were complex and financially risky. To adhere to the plan, to phase construction, to schedule payments to suppliers while satisfying the demands of bondholders from whom capital had been raised, and to complete a project so as to ensure sales to individuals and landlords required a business skill which inevitably was beyond the scope of many builders, the majority of whom had had no formal training other than a few years of elementary schooling and the handicraft skills acquired during apprenticeship. For the feuar, to know the builder was as important as to know the price of land itself.

This sequence of estate and building development was common to virtually all properties. But there was a crucial difference in the way it was delivered. On occasions, estate development functions were concentrated in the hands of a single interest, often an institution such as George Heriot's Hospital or Grindlay's trustees, and it was rare, though not unknown, for such institutions to have a building division and to undertake construction themselves. With no pressing need to pay annual feuduties to a heritable owner since institutions were themselves the recipient of such payments then estate development could proceed at a pace consistent with their own priorities. A long-term horizon of estate development was an option in such cases.

This strategy was available only to the larger players on the building stage. The size and location of their property in relation to the path of urban expansion, and their financial leverage enabled them to take the

---

[15] R. Rodger, 'Sir James Steel', in A. Slaven and S. Checkland, eds., *Dictionary of Scottish Business Biography*, vol. II (Aberdeen 1990), 168–9.

long-term view. For the majority of developers this trajectory was impossible. With limited resources, only a modest plot could be acquired, either by a small down-payment or an annual feu-duty. Though a feuar could attempt to raise capital by borrowing on security of the property, to the lender undeveloped plots did not have the same appeal as completed buildings. In exploiting the feu himself, a developer's credit rating also limited the amount of money which could be raised for construction work and so the normal course of events was to sub-feu most of the building stances to other builders, thus securing from them at the outset a sum of money sufficient both to secure the plot with the heritable owner, land company or developer, and to commence building operations on his own account.

This was the strategy adopted initially by Steel in his early phase of independent building development in Edinburgh. However, as might be predicted of a newly discharged bankrupt, James Steel had no capital on his arrival from Lanarkshire. Consequently, in the three or four years following his arrival in Edinburgh, Steel earned a living as a journeyman mason and jobbing builder, based around Tollcross.[16] It was a logical sphere of operations. Apart from the convenience that it was the virtually the first landfall for any migrant from the west, proximity to the canal basin, two railway stations and the principal south-western road transport arteries meant that Steel located himself strategically near the emerging, bustling economic axis of Lothian Road and Fountainbridge. It was an area in which, within a quarter of a mile radius, was to be found the largest concentration of builders in the city.[17] This network of commercial information functioned effectively for Steel, both in his early labouring activities, and subsequently when, as a builder in his own right, he sought to develop a particular site by eliciting capital advances from other building firms who wished to participate in the development of a particular site.[18]

By mid-1866 James Steel had accumulated sufficient capital as a sub-contracted jobbing builder to project himself as an independent operator on to the larger arena of estate development in Edinburgh. Before doing so, Steel bought the Weigh House with its lofts and outbuildings in Bernard Street, Leith, from Andrew Oliver, paid for by borrowing £1,700 from an architect, James Gray, and making a cash advance himself of almost £1,150.[19] Though he may have invested further money in its improvement, the Bernard Street addresses comprising mostly shops and

---

[16] *Edinburgh and Leith Post Office Directories*, 1863/4–1866/7. There were three different addresses for each of the first three years residence in Edinburgh.

[17] *Edinburgh and Leith Post Office Directory*, 1860–1.

[18] See below for the development of the Drumdryan estate of James Home Rigg.

[19] NAS RS27/2587.144 and 147, Register of Sasines, Edinburgh, 16 Aug. 1866, RS27/5633.23.

offices provided a steady commercial rent and, more importantly, collateral for subsequent projects. By 1876 Steel had recouped the original purchase price in rent, equivalent to a rate of return of 11%, then sold part of the property in 1879 for £4,600 and a further portion in 1914 for £1,500, which together with a rental income of £8,750 in the years 1868 to 1914 meant a rate of return of 15.6% p.a.[20]

The complementary uses of the Bernard Street properties were helpful to Steel. There were private residential tenants – labourers, dock workers and seamen, and retailers – many with years of residence at the same address, a diverse class composition underpinned by almost 70% in social classes 2 and 3, but crucially, it was the continuity of commercial lettings which provided a steady flow of rental income. The Caledonian Railway Company paid rent for thirty years, John Waddie and Co. for twenty years, a merchant, Beda Eschnicht, for ten years at two properties, and the shipbroking firm of Stevenson, Ressich and Co. were tenants for eleven years.[21]

The trajectory of Steel's estate development strategy was underpinned by, but not dependent upon, the initial foray into landlordism in Leith. Other initiatives were underway even before the income stream from Bernard Street was available. At the same time, summer 1866, negotiations for another Leith property were in progress. Eventually, late in 1867, Steel bought 8.130 acres of the Bonnington estate at £400 per acre to the north of the Ferry Road, ultimately forming Summerside Street and Place.[22] This was financed by a bond for £3,000 to the same lender, James Gray, as for the first Leith purchase and renegotiated for the increased amount of £5,000 two years later. Rental income from existing properties and prospects for the future development value of the unbuilt portion of the estate – seven sales to sub-feuars were completed in a twelve-month period straddling 1868–9 – justified the increased amount of the bond given by James Steel on security of the estate.[23] By careful phasing and

---

[20] This calculation assumes a 3% annual rate of interest on the £4,600. No adjustments are made for price changes which would increase real income, nor is account taken of local taxes, management and repairs on properties which averaged 11% vacancy rate.

[21] Based on NAS VR100/69–311 and VR55/12–156, Valuation Rolls; *Edinburgh and Leith Post Office Directories*, 1868–1914.

[22] ECA ACC 373, Sir James Steel's Trust, Minute of Agreement between James Steel and Charles Cowan, 13 Aug. 1866, confirmed 14 Nov. 1867; NAS RS27/2678.18, 14 Nov. 1867.

[23] ECA ACC 373, Sir James Steel's Trust, Minute of Agreement, 13 Aug. 1866, f. 4. Under the terms of the feu contract between Charles Cowan and James Steel, houses valued at no less than £500 could be built on the Bonnington feu. The tenant farmer on the property acquired by Steel was Robert Niven who had a lease until Martinmas 1870 and only if compensated at the rate of £5 per acre could this be terminated. In fact, though, he was turned off the farm before being recompensed for the 'loss of crops, unexhausted manure and other claims'.

aided by this rising property market, James Steel ensured that feu-duties owed by him to his superior, Charles Cowan, were matched in amount and timing by those due to him from the future developers of the estate.

The Leith developments which set Steel on his path to fame and fortune were fully two miles from his Tollcross base. The likelihood is that, in the course of his earlier activities as a jobbing builder, he was engaged in work in Leith and became acquainted both with the potential for rental income from Bernard Street and with a sense of the building opportunities which existed with a break up of the former country houses and their surrounding estates – for example, Hillhousefield, Bathfield, Bonnington, Elizafield and Williamfield.[24] None of these estates was so large, nor the aristocratic figures who occupied them so powerful, as to be able to contain the advancing urban sprawl which was underway in Leith in the 1860s.[25] In the event, Steel feued over four acres of Bathfield, more than an acre at Hillhousefield and almost twelve acres at Bonnington.[26] The docks and the home of golf, Leith Links, constrained northern and eastern development and so the small estates to the west were prime targets, to be picked off piecemeal as development dictated. No major Edinburgh figure, nor institutional trustees, seems to have shown much interest, possibly because overbuilding in the capital before 1860 had saturated the housing market. Other disincentives – the payment of feu-duties for land which might remain undeveloped for some years, and the requirement that feuars build sufficient houses within a defined period in order to cover the full feu-duty payable to the superior – required substantial and speculative investment which was unwarranted given the state of the housing market at that time. Even Heriot's Hospital trustees, who might have sought to consolidate the eastern edge of their holdings by mopping up such estates on the northern and western fringes of Leith, showed no interest. So it was left to smaller developers, like Steel, to seize their opportunity, to cherry-pick specific plots and accumulate sufficient wealth so as to be able to embark later on more ambitious projects.

The defining development: Drumdryan

Drumdryan and High Riggs, the estate of James Home Rigg, located at Tollcross was strategically placed in the path of south-western expansion.

---

[24] NAS RHP3283, 83330–1, ECA SL104/4, Hillhousefield Chartulary 1869–89 vol. 1, and SL104/5, Bathfield Chartulary 1891–7 vol. 1.

[25] J. Russell, 'Bonnington: its lands and mansions', *Book of the Old Edinburgh Club*, 19, 1933, 142–88; ECA SL104/4, Hillhousefield Chartulary, ff. 84–90, and SL104/5, Bathfield Chartulary, ff. 11–14.

[26] ECA SL104/4, Hillhousefield Chartulary, ff. 84–90, and SL104/5, Bathfield Chartulary, ff. 11–14.

It was, too, adjacent to the emerging western commercial arteries provided jointly by the terminus of the Union Canal at Port Hopetoun and the nearby western approach road which was eventually approved in 1827.[27] For almost a decade passions had been raised over a ring road to the south of the Castle rock, but the dispute was more over the particular access route to the Mound and the New Town rather than the principle itself. Improved access to the south and west of the city was a certainty of the campaign to improve through access in the early 1820s.[28] Both projects, canal and road proposals, private and public initiatives, added amenity and value to property in the south of the city. The Lauriston and Tollcross areas stood to gain directly.

For landowners, the difficulty was to evaluate short-term gains against long-term development value and thus to judge the character of the development on their estates. Sometimes the matter was taken out of landowners' hands. This was the case across the road from the Rigg's Drumdryan feu, where Samuel Gilmour's twelve acre Lochrin estate promised high status residences when the first few lots were sold in 1803, but his death and his son's bankruptcy led, by 1807, to a fragmentation of lots and a loss of coherent control on the Lochrin property.[29]

Adjacent to Lochrin, the completion of the canal basin in 1821 at Port Hopetoun also crytallised the land use and social character of the area. Rather by default than intent, Rigg's trustees permitted the Drumdryan feu to develop as an essentially commercial area of shops and tenements. Though a feuing plan had been developed by Charles Alison, it was essentially a simple ground plan with elevations and the feu charters subsequently granted were concerned more with limiting Rigg's obligations and requiring feuars at their own expense to undertake work which might affect the public highway. As the conditions attached to the first of the charters specified, it was the builder, Samuel Richard, who was to 'uphold and maintain the street, causeways and common sewers, side pavements and rails opposite to the tenements'.[30] However, this was an echo of the vague early New Town feus; real burdens and restrictions were few and Rigg's legal draughtsmen clearly had not absorbed the implications for feu charters of the House of Lords' decision in 1818 governing the future use of property.[31] There were no detailed stipulations in the feu charters concerning the boundary walls, the nature of the stone or other matters of

[27] See pp. 83–5 for the earlier development of this estate.
[28] ECA SL63/4/2, Report Relative to the Proposed Approaches, 18 Nov. 1824. The area, the report noted, 'must become a very desirable and eligible situation for building'.
[29] See pp. 149–50, relating to Gilmour's business and landholding.
[30] MC, Drumdryan Chartulary, vol. 1, f. 18, feu charter to Samuel Richard, 7 Oct. 1824.
[31] See chapter 2.

detail which offered a measure of assurance about the social tone of a development, and which a feuar might enforce. Only in one case did Rigg's draughtsman explicitly exclude an activity which was regarded as prejudicial to the development potential of the estate. This, however, was an important principle since the feu was granted 'under the express conditions that the said William Dickson and his foresaids shall on no account erect or set up Steam Engines or carry on any trade or manufacture'.[32]

Four other factors determined the character of the development. First, the essentially triangular shape of the Drumdryan and High Riggs feu was constrained by the pre-existing main road, Home Street (fig. 6.1). The triangular shape inevitably produced a number of awkward angles to plots, thereby raising costs, reducing amenity and compromising site development in relation to alternatives nearby. Secondly, there was uncertainty about access from the east where the town council's drainage of the Boroughloch and guarantees about the long-run amenity of this green space complicated the estate development strategy. Thirdly, though Rigg quickly feued the lots fronting Home Street, ten different developers were involved and only two built more than a single tenement.[33] The architectural coherence of these tenements owed more to financial calculations by the builders who judged that to meet the first termly feu-duty it was essential to build quickly and then if possible to sell the flats, or, alternatively, to let properties to defray interest charges and meet feu-duty obligations. Indeed, so anxious were builders to proceed with construction work that some tenements were well advanced by the time the official conveyancing paperwork had been completed in the Register of Sasines. The fourth factor was Rigg's reluctance to lay out the streets outlined in the estate feuing plan. Brougham Street, the secondary street in the development, remained unidentified in maps and plans for over thirty years. This short termism was a false economy and signalled a lack of confidence in the development of the area and an unwillingness on the part of the feudal superior to defend the tone of the area. As Rigg stipulated in one charter, he would

not be obliged to execute the feuing plan . . . to any further extent than I please . . . I reserve full power and liberty without the consent of [Buchanan and Elder] . . . either to make such alterations on the said feuing plan . . . and even totally to abandon the same.[34]

[32] MC, Drumdryan Chartulary, vol. 1, f. 32, feu charter to William Dickson, 9 June 1824.
[33] Samuel Richard took three and the firm of David Steel and David Walker took two building stances.
[34] MC, Drumdryan Chartulary, vol. 1, f. 38, feu charter to Thomas Buchanan and Alexander Elder, 16 Apr. 1825.

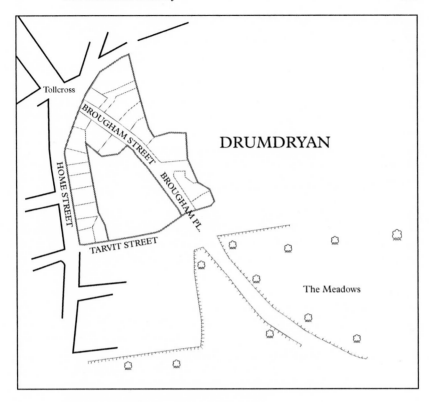

Figure 6.1 Drumdryan feus 1824–1867

Source: MC, Drumdryan Chartulary, vol. 1.

Weak estate development tactics were evident in another respect. Even though local builders had been quick to take up the new stances once they became available – thirteen were feued in twenty-four months from October 1824 – Rigg allowed feuars to choose their plot rather than adopting a more *dirigiste* approach. As a result, three clusters developed with gaps between them. The failure fully to lay out Brougham Street created further doubts about a specific plot which lay vacant for over thirty years and appeared predestined to allow road access to Home Street. From the outset, therefore, a degree of development blight afflicted the remainder of the Drumdryan estate.[35]

---

[35] MC, Drumdryan Chartulary, vol. 1, f. 220. This is confirmed by deviations from the feuing plan. For example, in feuing a corner plot in 1853 the feuing plan and elevations of John Knox Smith are referred to, and thus supersede, the plan of Charles Alison.

Arguably, Rigg's architect got the estate plan back to front. Laying out Brougham Street as the axis of a middle-class residential development with a perspective to the Meadows and Bruntsfield links and their pleasant promenades offered an alternative estate development strategy. Drumdryan House and its gardens might have served as a pleasant focus for more generously proportioned building stances, separated by gardens from the retail developments in Home Street. Short- and long-term development objectives could have been combined; shops and working-class flats above them in Home Street would have provided a short-term annual income, with a more gradual middle-class estate backing on to them. It was a formula which half a century later and in sight of Rigg's Drumdryan properties Sir George Warrender was to develop effectively for his Marchmont estate. However, Rigg and his architect were passive in their vision of estate development. Their preference was to take advantage of perceived existing development opportunities along the ribbon-like transport artery of Home Street; longer term and more ambitious development was not considered. Perhaps the low-lying location of the property together with the effects of prevailing westerly winds carrying the smell of yeast and hops from Drumdryan Brewery adjacent to Rigg's property limited the potential for middle-class housing development. Whatever the possibilities, other than prohibiting steam engines Rigg apparently took no conscious decision about the nature of the estate, trusting to the knowledge of local builders, most of whom lived within a quarter of a mile, to develop tenements according to some intuitive sense of the market.

Following the development decisions of the 1820s no further feu charters were signed for thirty years. The post-war buoyancy and 1820s collapse in the Edinburgh property market were not exclusively a New Town phenomenon; Rigg's stop–go development of Drumdryan encapsulated the experience of property owners throughout the city. A single feu charter in 1852 was followed by another barren period of ten years until, with the death of Rigg in 1860 and the responsibility for the management of the estate transferred to his trustees, the following year initiated another spurt of building, echoing that of 1824–6.[36] Again, builders cherry-picked desirable plots. In 1861 John Chalmers, a coal merchant, selected the site on Brougham Place opposite the proposed Tarvit Street to obtain a relatively uninterrupted view from his flats; Robert Wilson and James Smith, both builders, chose sites which had long back greens and thus possessed a degree of privacy not normally available to tenement dwellers.

[36] NAS RS108/2609.147, 9 Jan. 1867. Rigg's trust set up 19 Nov. 1860.

At his death, Rigg had granted twenty feu charters for what was only a four acre site. Administration of the Drumdryan superiorities was complicated and expensive; hundreds of pages of the Drumdryan Chartulary record the legal issues with which Rigg's agent had to wrestle. For example, the bankruptcy of the building firm of David Steel and David Walker meant that, between 1833 and 1842, Rigg as superior had received no feu-duty on their Home Street tenement.[37] Rigg's agents initiated a legal action to invoke his rights to recover the stance, began another legal process to receive tenants' rents on the property to recoup lost feu-duties, and since there was a bond or mortgage covering the property, Rigg had to unravel this complication too.[38] In all, the rent recouped fell short of the feu-duty due, quite apart from the legal fees incurred. Transactions costs on this Rigg superiority were very considerable.

At its peak in 1866, Rigg's trustees collected the tidy sum of £510 in feu-duties on the Drumdryan estate, though not without difficulty. So it was highly advantageous to them when, in 1866, James Steel offered to buy virtually all of the unfeued Drumdryan lands, 2.052 acres, paid for by a combination of £500 cash and a bond for £4,000 in favour of Rigg's trustees.[39] As a result, the trustees simplified both the legal and managerial aspects of their responsibilities while also securing an outlet for their investment.

For Steel, who took the initiative over Drumdryan, it was a defining moment. As a new arrival in Edinburgh, with only jobbing work in the city and some modest building activity in Leith to his credit, this offered a high profile opportunity not just to build and develop a small estate, but to establish his business credentials and financial dependability with influential individuals – landowners, solicitors and lenders. Alongside Steel's signature to the feu charter were those of James Moncrieff Melville and James Lindesay, both of whom were Rigg's trustees, partners in an

---

[37] MC, Drumdryan Chartulary, vol. 1, f. 226, feu disposition in favour of Miss Douglas Moncrieff, 12 Dec. 1853.

[38] MC, Drumdryan Chartulary, vol. 1, ff. 225–83. A Summons of Declarator of Irritancy *ob non solutum canonem* was raised by Rigg against the trustee of the sequestrated estate of Walker and Steel to re-establish his title. The same process was used to legitimate receipt of the rentals from the property. Miss Moncrieff had advanced £1,000 to Steel and Walker, thus she obtained title by default of repayment, though Rigg remained the feudal superior.

[39] NAS RS27/2609.59, 2609.67, and RS108/2717.10. See MC, Drumdryan Chartulary, vol. 2, f. 175, charter with James Steel. Six months later the remaining lot was also feued to the trustees of All Saint's Episcopal Church, 12 June 1867, MC, Drumdryan Chartulary, vol. 2, f. 180. This cash plus interest bearing bond formula was used widely. See the activities of the Trinity Land Company and Murrayfield Real Estate Company, chapter 4.

established legal office and well connected in Edinburgh social circles through their family names. William Forrester, treasurer to Heriot's Hospital, was the other signatory with powerful business networks. Within three years James Lindesay was acting as Steel's solicitor and in a little over a decade following the Drumdryan transaction had advanced over £30,000 in a dozen separate transactions.[40] This was not dissimilar to a permanent overdraft facility with a merchant bank: whenever Steel needed to refinance maturing loans he could rest assured of a sympathetic hearing from Lindesay who funnelled trust, widows' and marriage contract funds in Steel's direction.[41] On only two occasions and only in the early stages of his Edinburgh career did James Steel step outside the confines of personal contacts, borrowing from financial institutions in 1870 and 1871.[42] The Heriot connection was central to Steel's early property development in north Edinburgh, and the association with Rigg's trustees was so highly regarded that it was they who turned to James Steel when, a decade later, they sought to release the value of their land nearby locked up in Rigg's Dalry estate.[43]

The final development of the Drumdryan feu proceeded with some pace. Steel sold off stances to six different builders who together put up thirty-two tenements.[44] Two building societies, the Bower Building Society, a small group mostly of postal workers, and the Drumdryan Street Building Association also commissioned tenements, and Steel himself built six prominently placed on the axis of the new development, Brougham Place, on behalf of the Improved Edinburgh Property Company in 1868.[45] Within eighteen months of the deal with Rigg's trustees, Steel had not only sold off all feuing stances but the construction work was also well advanced. By the end of 1868 all plots had been built.[46]

---

[40] Based on an analysis of financial instruments in the Register of Sasines associated with James Steel's activities.

[41] After James Lindesay's death, William Babington became a new partner in the firm, and Steel's solicitor. In due course he was also named as one of the trustees in Steel's will.

[42] NAS RS108/117.136, 117.41, bond to Commercial Bank of Scotland, 11 May 1870 and 2 Feb. 1871.

[43] Based on transactions recorded in the Register of Sasines. See, for example, bonds by Lindesay in 1880 over Belgrave Crescent: NAS RS108/1188.114, 1212.114, 1151.66 and 1149.13.

[44] NAS RS27/2618.126 John Omans and Peter Manson, 12 Mar. 1867, RS27/2647.25 Alex. Clunas and Alex. Wilson, 29 May 1867, RS27/2654.77 and 2668.118 Alex. Brown, 28 June 1867 and 5 Oct. 1867, RS108/2690.129 John Omans and Peter Manson, 9 Jan. 1868, RS108/2691.129 William Blake, 16 Jan. 1868, RS108/2695.186 Alex. Thomson, James Muir and Robert McLaren, 12 Feb. 1868, RS108/ 2709.124 Alex. Baird, 18 Apr. 1868, RS108/2710.45 Duncan McRae, Daniel McDonald and Jos. Bennet, 15 May 1868. Given that all financial transactions, reaffirmations of title and other processes were recorded in the Register of Sasines, only the most important entries are cited in footnotes.   [45] NAS RS27/2658.120, 2653.107, 21 July 1868.

[46] *Edinburgh and Leith Post Office Directory*, 1868–9.

Local knowledge was important in Steel's assessment of the risks associated with the Drumdryan development. From his arrival in Edinburgh in 1862 he lived less than half a mile from Rigg's Drumdryan property. At the conclusion of his deal with Rigg, he moved to Drumdryan House itself and remained there for two years, using one of his own tenement buildings across the road in Brougham Street as an office. In effect, he lived on site in 1867 and 1868. Since Rigg's trustees had stipulated that Steel was responsible for laying out the kerbs, drains, roads and nine foot pavements there was some advantage to being *de facto* clerk of works. By dealing with several builders Steel limited his dependence upon the success of any one of them, and by confining their interest to a maximum of five tenements, he ensured that the logistical and financial scale of their operations was not beyond them. Where work was proceeding satisfactorily or indeed completed successfully, then builders might negotiate for a second group of stances. Steel recognised a trade-off between economies of scale and the organisational limitations of large-scale enterprises, a distinction which half a century later local authorities were slow to appreciate as they initiated council housebuilding on an unprecedented scale.[47]

Steel's outlay was £4,500 plus the land development costs associated with street layout. To this were added legal costs involved in drawing up feu contracts with Clunas and Wilson, Omans and Manson, Alex. Brown and the highly visible and respected local firm of W. and D. McGregor.[48] Since a lump sum had been paid to Rigg's trustees, the feu-duty payable by Steel had been fixed at a nominal 1d p.a. So the feu-duties which Steel created on stances in Brougham Street and Place, Tarvit and Drumdryan Streets represented his annual stream of revenue from the development of the feu. There is no sign that Steel had received any such revenue by early 1869 when he sold his heritable securities, worth £370 p.a., for £8,150 – the equivalent of twenty-two years purchase – to the Endowment Committee of the Church of Scotland who thereby received these duties in the future.[49] A gross profit of £3,650 or 81% in the space of two years represented a highly lucrative return by any standard. To this might be added such profit as Steel made himself as a builder in undertaking tenements for the Improved Edinburgh Property Company. Suddenly, highly liquid as the result of the cash injection from the Church of Scotland, Steel was able on the same day to pay off the £4,000 debt to Rigg's trustees as well as a bond for £2,000 given to Melville and Lindesay for an advance secured on a Brougham Street property six months earlier.[50]

[47] S. Marriner, 'Cash and concrete: liquidity problems in the mass production of "homes for heroes"', *Business History*, 18, 1976, 155.   [48] See n. 39 above.

[49] NAS RS108/7.79, 11 Feb. 1869.

[50] NAS RS108/2717.10, 2743.96. See also RS108/7.76, 7.77 11 Feb. 1869.

Figure 6.2 Brougham Place from the Meadows

Note: James Steel lived in the ground floor flat of the corner house (right) on Lonsdale Terrace which he also used as an office after he built over the building yard of the former Drumdryan House. The pillars were erected in 1886 in conjunction with the International Exhibition.
Source: RCAHMS ED/9906 (417136) from an original belonging to the Edinburgh Photographic Society.

Trustees' purchases of heritable securities provided the financial lever for Steel's subsequent activities.

After thirty-six years James Home Rigg had generated £356 p.a. from the Drumdryan estate; in two years Steel had developed the value of a roughly similar acreage to £370 p.a.[51] However disengaged Rigg's interest in Drumdryan might seem, the reality was that there were in the 1820s and 1830s many locations for housing development on the fringes of both the New and the Old Town. It was a buyer's market. After some years of infilling along existing axes of residential development, the second half of the nineteenth century offered a different perspective. Assisted by in-migration and natural population growth, it became a seller's market with new zones of villa and tenement building expanding rapidly to the south. What Steel recognised, however, was that there existed a distinctive

[51] MC, Drumdryan Chartulary, vol. 2, ff. 269–71; NAS RS108/7.79.

housing market for a clerical, artisanal and petit bourgeois component of demand whose own patterns of consumption were in no small measure stabilised by the predictability of middle-class and professional incomes. If these social groups could not afford the panoply of differentiated rooms and generous gardens as in the southern suburbs, housing amenity in inner suburbs for these groups was enhanced in Edinburgh because of its numerous open spaces and hilly sites. These public spaces and vistas conveyed value. Importantly, such 'externalities' could be incorporated in private developments for social classes who sought a measure of gentility without the full costs of suburbia, and in this Steel's assessment of the Drumdryan feus, as subsequently elsewhere in the city, was well judged.

Not only did Drumdryan provide Steel with an opportunity to make a very attractive profit, it also provided excellent contacts for future projects. Most importantly, though, it confirmed his tactic: to concentrate on the lower middle class and petite bourgeoisie, to off-load the extent of his own commitment by involving other builders as sub-feuars and to diversify into other segments of the market only if these represented copper-bottomed ventures. Public amenity and building quality, together with supportive financial networks and clearly targeted markets, were the hallmarks of Steel's building strategy, and Drumdryan represented a highly successful testing ground.

Diversity, complementarity and risk

The expeditious development of Drumdryan – from the signature on the feu charter to the completion of two acres of tenements took only eighteen months – was a powerful endorsement of James Steel's business conduct. Perhaps, too, it reflected a relatively porous social structure in Edinburgh during the 1860s in which a newcomer could so quickly establish his building, organisational and financial credentials. Jobbing work, landlordism in Leith and a putative development off Ferry Road on the Bonnington estate promised much, but the execution of the Drumdryan strategy was faultless. It impressed many, and in no small measure this established Steel's stature in the Edinburgh property milieu. That achieved, his credit rating was secure; though omnipresent, risk and uncertainty were contained, if not eliminated.

Risk management took several forms. Apart from the sound business practices of paying bills on time, of anticipating the renegotiation of bonds and maintaining his liquidity and creditworthiness, James Steel sought to limit his exposure on any particular project. This was achieved, as at Drumdryan, by involving several other builders in the development of building stances, but more generally it developed into a recognition that there were different housing sub-markets as defined by various strata of demand, based on income levels. Like any portfolio of assets, Steel recognised that diversification limited risk, and this could be achieved by developing different types of houses, by building them in various parts of the city and by varying the emphasis between the functions of developer, builder and landlord.

To ensure that each of the various projects was in a different stage of completion was another ingredient of business stability. Thus, perhaps intuitively, a rolling programme of development evolved, and as Drumdryan approached completion, building stances at the Bonnington development (Summerside and Great Wellington Street) were released, and Steel's own building programme there began to produce a rental income where he himself retained properties. Rental income was also forthcoming from the original excursion into property management in Bernard Street, and from 1870 in further forays as a landlord in Leith at Jamaica, Constitution and Charlotte Streets, and across the 'border' in Edinburgh at Antigua Street, where existing properties were also acquired for their rentals.[52]

Further complementarity was achieved with a new project at Sciennes, a little over half a mile east from Drumdryan. Prior to 1860 'there were about half a dozen detached properties in large gardens' on the south-eastern edge of the Meadows, known as Hope Park, and these houses – Westerhall, Sylvan, New Campbeltown, Roseneath, Argyle – were the homes of 'several eminent citizens, artists and men of letters before the area succumbed to the tenement building era of the late nineteenth century'.[53] Not unlike the ring of vulnerable estates in Leith, the modest mansions of Hope Park were picked off in turn by developers. Once leap-frogged by the advance of villadom into the more southerly Grange estate, the resistance of the owners of Sylvan, Roseneath and Argyle was fragile and they surrendered meekly under the assault of tenement development designed to satisfy a mix of housing demands from artisans, widows, shopkeepers and small merchants.[54] Even before the last tenement was completed on the Drumdryan development, James Steel acquired a small plot of land from marriage trustees of the Rev. Robert Borthwick-Brown and his spouse in 1868.[55] As previously, Steel laid off

---

[52] Further land buildings in Leith were rented in Ferry Road (from 1875) and Lindsay Road (from 1877).

[53] M. Cant, *Edinburgh: Sciennes and the Grange* (Edinburgh 1990), 55, 58.

[54] For a summary of ownership of these feus see ECA ACC 373, Sir James Steel's Papers, Inventory of Title Deeds, Hope Park, Inventory of Title Deeds, Sciennes, Inventory of Writs, Melville Terrace and Inventory of Titles, Millerfield Place.

[55] NAS RS108/2741.59, 10 July 1868. A further small plot of land (later known as Tantallon Place) was acquired on 10 July 1868 from Sir Thomas Dick Lauder, head of a prominent family in south and east Edinburgh.

his risk by sub-feuing both to builders and to several local building associations – Hope Park Building Company, Grange Provident Building
Society, Livingstone Building Association, the United Building
Association, Meadow Park Building Association, Melville Building
Association and one with whom he had had previous dealings, the Bower
Building Society.[56] By so doing it was the building associations who
obtained deposits and advances from their membership, and who put up
the capital and commissioned builders to undertake construction. It was
they, not Steel, who shouldered the risk.

With impressive speed, Steel built tenements of shops and flats on his
own account at Gladstone Terrace and Livingstone Place (Sciennes
Road), but the significance of the development far exceeded the modest
number of the properties involved.[57] Steel developed a technique
whereby once the buildings were under construction, he transferred the
legal title to somebody else, in this case a mason, Thomas Morton, on 27
March 1869, who promptly transferred it back to Steel three days later,
on 30 March 1869. It was a device the result of which conveyed the superiority and the ownership to James Steel, and was to be repeated countless
times, so often in fact that in 1888 Steel drafted a *pro forma* version of the
disposition and reconveyance.[58] The practice was laid down by Steel in
his will and his trustees instructed to adhere to the well-worn formula for
estate development, which they did:

I specially empower my trustees . . . to continue the method adopted by me for
creating separate estates of superiority and property of portions of said estate by
granting feu rights and obtaining reconveyances to accept renunciations of feu
rights to allow feuars to redeem casualties and duplicands payable by them.[59]

Though Steel's building costs at Sciennes are unknown, he sold over
twenty flats in 1869 and 1870, payment for which was in excess of
£10,500. The trustees' statement in 1905 to the Surveyor of Taxes that
'he seldom made any profit on the building of tenements'[60] may have

---

[56] NAS RS108/2748.86, 2752.95, 2758.51, 2758.110, 2768.133, 2768.163, 2768.188,
3.195, 6.152, 11.29, 16.80, 21.116.
[57] There were further developments at Millerfield and Tantallon Places, and at Melville
Drive.
[58] ECA ACC 373, Sir James Steel's Trust, Box1/1. Skeleton form of Disposition and
Reconveyance by Hugh Percival to James Steel.
[59] NAS SC70/4/366, f. 246. James Steel, Trust Disposition and Settlement, 9 Dec. 1896.
That the trustees did so is acknowledged in their statement to the Surveyor of Taxes:
'Following the method adopted by Sir James his Trustees erect buildings and constitute
feu duties on the site by entering into Feu contracts with Mr Joseph Inglis W.S. who
immediately dispones back to the Trustees. They accordingly become both superiors and
proprietors of the built on ground, and as proprietors they offer for sale or let the properties erected by them. The Trustees, of course, after a sale of property collect the feu duties
created thereon.' ECA ACC 373, Sir James Steel's Trust, ff. 198–9.
[60] ECA ACC 373, Sir James Steel's Trust, ff. 58–9.

applied in later years, or may have been an attempt to limit death duties, but it seems unlikely that the equivalent of four tenements could have cost more than £6,000.[61] In selling the Sciennes flats Steel gained crucial information at first hand which had not been available to him at Drumdryan, or in his other projects.[62] Whereas at Brougham Place, Drumdryan, Steel had himself built two blocks each of three tenements, they had been exclusively for the Improved Edinburgh Property Company. He had a guaranteed sale. Who the eventual owners were might have been known to him since his own Brougham Place office was directly opposite, and, through a side entrance, gave access to the comfortable five roomed, main door flat, acquired as James Steel's home.[63] In the Sciennes development, however, Steel himself built a higher proportion of the tenements – itself a reflection of his growing financial autonomy – and then sold direct to purchasers. Within two years of the signed agreement with Borthwick-Brown, twenty-one sales had been agreed. The majority of these were with shopowners. Grocers, butchers, a hatter, ironmonger and other retailers outnumbered agents, merchants and manufacturers. The shopocracy of Causewayside, an important retail and commercial artery to the south of the city, had accumulated adequate wealth, and enough confidence, to become owner occupiers.[64] Amongst their number, William Gray (grocer), John Mortimer (butcher) and James Denholm (boot tree maker) became rentiers themselves by buying two or three properties from Steel at the going rate of between £300–£325 per flat.[65] If Ann Watt and Janet Edgar who described themselves as housewives were in a distinct minority amongst purchasers, 19% of Steel's tenants in the Sciennes development were widows, and this, too, was a feature on which Steel drew subsequently as part of his business strategy.[66]

---

[61] This figure is based on the average cost of tenements. See also R. Rodger, 'Scottish urban housebuilding 1870–1914', University of Edinburgh PhD thesis, 1975, 25.

[62] ECA ACC 373, Sir James Steel's Trust, feu charter between Charles Cowan and James Steel, defined a £20 minimum feu-duty which also took the development firmly into the realms of middle-class demand.

[63] NAS RS108/17.14. Steel's home beween 1869 and 1875 was at 1 Lonsdale Terrace, bought for £690 from another builder, Thomas Fullerton, and the office (1869–70) was next door, at 11 Brougham Place, having relocated a hundred yards from 11 Brougham Street (1867–8).

[64] NAS RS108/1868.81, RS108/885.9 and RS108/78.37. Of the first twenty-one sales, only three purchasers required advances from third parties.

[65] NAS RS108/26.18, 15 May 1869 William Gray bought flats in 12 and 14 Gladstone Terrace (now renumbered), RS108/49.80, 18 June 1869 John Mortimer, 11, 12 Gladstone Terrace, RS108/38.104, 21 May 1869 James Denholm for one flat in 12 and three in 17 Gladstone Terrace.

[66] Spinsters represented a further 2% to bring the female heads of household to 21% in Sciennes in 1870.

Apart from its evident short-term financial success, the Sciennes episode provided corroboration of the wisdom of sub-feuing to builders and building associations, both of whom indirectly underwrote Steel's estate development and thereby delimited his uncertainty and risk. The Sciennes development also confirmed both the existence of a reservoir of shopowning and petit bourgeois demand and, in a complementary way, the strategic importance of proximity to a commercial thoroughfare where such interests concentrated. It was an endorsement of strategies first established on the Drumdryan estate and the advantages of access, density and proximity which the pivotal Tollcross interchange provided there. Another lesson learned was that the vulnerability which land-owners displayed in their retrospective and somewhat idealised views of the former glories associated with their estates often placed them in a weak market position. In reality, such properties represented an excellent opportunity for a developer. To say that Steel deliberately set out to iden-tify the weak landowner, crippled by repairs and maintenance to the ancient family home and wounded psychologically by the onset of urban-isation, would be to crystallise his actions and to elevate them to a consid-ered strategy.[67] More likely, and intuitively, Steel recognised through the asking price and his ability to project the developmental potential how high he could go to secure the feu.

If sound construction combined with convenient locations were recog-nised by Steel as the appeal of the inner suburbs, it was not unconnected to organisational considerations associated with his business. From the start of his Drumdryan venture he styled himself as 'builder and quarry master'.[68] By assembling a workforce of sizeable proportions – there were fifteen masons, fourteen joiners, fifty-four labourers, forty-two quarry-men, as well as a carter, a manager, a coachman three blacksmiths, two clerks and two boys in his employment in 1871 within a decade of his arrival penniless in Edinburgh[69] – James Steel recognised it was unsuited to the bespoke building of suburban villa dwellers who sought to custom-ise their house. By definition, villas were physically spread over a wide area and to a builder this was costly in terms of labour productivity. Steel was concerned to develop an early form of system building in which the workforce was fully engaged. Sufficient scale enabled masons, joiners, plumbers, slaters, glaziers and other trades to pursue their specialism, ensuring a minimum level of quality while utilising unskilled labour to undertake earth-moving, carting materials and such jobs.

---

[67] *Edinburgh and Leith Post Office Directories*, 1868, 1871. Steel himself utilised the former mansions of Drumdryan House and Dalry House as his own place of residence, and as his building yard.   [68] *Edinburgh and Leith Post Office Directory*, 1867.
[69] Census of Edinburgh, 1871, Enumerator's Book, 685[4]93.

Specialisation was taken to another level of sophistication by a degree of vertical integration – that is, by combining various stages in the housing market, from quarrying interests in Wishaw and from 1887 at Gunnerton, Northumberland, to building workshops away from the site, and to the housing management dimensions of landlordism.[70] In this Steel was not unique. It had been a feature of housing contractors in England from the 1820s, and was closely connected with the emergence of speculative builders.[71] It was also a central tenet of successful business practice as adopted by the Edinburgh Co-operative Building Company, also in the 1860s.[72] But Steel recognised that a larger scale of building kept the workforce intact, utilised skills and specialisms more fully and, importantly, could only work with volume building. To do this for working-class housing was fraught with difficulty – high numbers of houses might remain unsold, the unskilled working class were more vulnerable to trade fluctuations and bouts of unemployment, and in any case they could often only afford 'made down' or subdivided flats within existing housing. Though more numerous, their effective demand was weaker and fluctuations more exaggerated than in other housing sub-markets, and this increased uncertainty offered less appeal to a builder. Accordingly, Steel identified a lower middle class and petite bourgeoisie as his target groups, but was always alive to opportunities to build for other social classes. Such an opportunity presented itself in Dalry.

[70] ECA ACC 373, Sir James Steel's Trust Papers, lease of quarries at Barrasford between Algernon George, Duke of Northumberland, and lessees, James Steel *et al.*, 24 Dec. 1887.
[71] E. W. Cooney, 'The origins of the Victorian master builders', *Economic History Review*, 8, 1955, 167–76; and E. W. Cooney, 'The building industry', in R. Church, ed., *The Dynamics of Victorian Business: Problems and Perspectives to the 1870s* (London 1980), 142–60.   [72] See chapter 11.

7 Industrial suburb: developing Dalry

Dalry might have been predestined as an industrial suburb. The convergence of the Caledonian Railway with the Edinburgh and Glasgow Railway line on the west end of Princes Street formed a wedge of land use which was unlikely to find favour as a preferred residential setting for the Edinburgh middle class. The availability of northern and western New Town addresses and the suburban exclusivity available to the south in Newington and later, Grange, assigned the vector of land formed by the Union Canal and the main Glasgow road to industrial purposes and to housing for workers. As in other Victorian cities, the lines of railway development shaped subsequent housing development and crystallised existing zones of land use.[1]

In 1842, when the Haymarket terminus and head office of the Glasgow and Edinburgh Railway was opened, there was already an industrial presence in the Dalry and Fountainbridge area.[2] The Canal Basin, opened in 1821, had stimulated many of the carting activities, but there were some larger scale factories too – Lochrin Distillery and Castle Silk Mills being amongst the more conspicuous. The built-up area crept westwards in the 1820s and 1830s, though only slowly, as the arrested development of George Grindlay's Orchardfield estate testified, but it was the sale of 8.396 acres fronting Lothian Road in 1848 by Grindlay's trustees to the Caledonian Railway for extensive yards, sidings and station which guaranteed that there would be no buffer of elegant housing between the industrial and commercial zones of Dalry and the west end of Princes Street.[3]

---

[1] J. R. Kellett, *The Impact of Railways on Victorian Cities* (London 1969). For a recent view of industrial locations see R. T. Simmons, 'Steam, steel and Lizzie the Elephant – the steel industry, transport technology and urban development in Sheffield, 1809–1914', University of Leicester, PhD thesis, 1995.

[2] For a chronology of railway development in Edinburgh see J. Thomas, *A Regional History of Railways*, vol. VI (Newton Abbot 1984 edn), 299–302.

[3] ECA MC/GG, Orchardfield Chartulary, vol. 2, f. 41, feu contract with Caledonian Railway Company, 18 Jan. 1848. The sale was for £7,000. See also Box 11, history of the

In the angle of the industrial wedge, several ancient houses and their surrounding parks came under pressure to sell all or part of their estates, as at Sciennes and North Leith, for the construction of industrial premises and workers' housing.[4] By focusing on Dalry, not only is it possible to explore the role of the heritable owner in the development of the built environment it is also possible to unravel three different types of development strategies. One, the construction by the Edinburgh Co-operative Building Company (ECBC) between 1868 and 1871 of 140 houses using their trademark balcony-access design at Cobden, Bright and the neighbouring 'Scottish' streets – Atholl, Argyll, Breadalbane and Douglas – embraced the self-help aspirations of artisans to provide owner-occupier housing as a means of counteracting the uncertainties of annual lettings. This is examined in chapter 11. Squeezed in between the two coal depots at Haymarket and at Morrison Street, the spectacular success of the Dalry development encouraged the ECBC to pursue two other housing developments in Dalry – North Merchiston Park (1878–84) and Shaftesbury Park (1891–1903).[5] In recognition of its importance as an industrial suburb, the ECBC built 30% of its housing in Dalry.[6]

Two other strategies, those of James Steel and the General Property Investment Company, provide contrasting private enterprise approaches on adjacent sites, and over approximately similar periods. Efficiency, speed and experience in the building industry as demonstrated by James Steel contrasted with delay, fragmentation and indecision on the part of the property development company. The divergent approaches had important implications for tenants' pockets, since there was a direct impact on both the supply and the cost of accommodation.

Three generations of landownership: Dalry and North Merchiston

Three generations of James Walker, each of them sharing the same name and each involved in the legal profession at a senior level, significantly

footnote 3 (cont.)
feuing operations, f. 14, which notes that there were no feu charters between 1830 and 1849. The Caledonian Railway's terminus was at Lothian road initially, where a station was opened in 1848 following the transactions with Grindlay's trustees. In 1870, and nearby, the Caledonian Station was opened, and eventually rebuilt in 1894. See Thomas, *A Regional History of Railways*, 300.

[4] These included Dalry, Bainfield, Brandsfield and North Merchiston. See, for example, J. Smith, 'Dalry House: its lands and owners', *Book of the Old Edinburgh Club*, 20, 1935, 26–59.

[5] The dates refer to the period of most intense building and sales activity. At Dalry 100% of building was in the years 1868–71; at North Merchiston, 94% was between 1878 and 1884; and at Shaftesbury Park, 73% in the years 1891–1903.

[6] NAS GD327/489–91, Papers of C. Norman Kemp. See chapter 11.

affected the development of the western approaches to Edinburgh. From grandfather to grandson, the consolidation and disposal of the estate was governed by twin concerns: to provide a long-term investment for subsequent generations of the Walker family; and, specifically, to protect the position of their wives and daughters by setting up annuities and life-rents based on property incomes from feu-duties.

To some extent the profile of estate development itself represented a cross-section of expansion in nineteenth-century Edinburgh. The initial purchase by James Walker of twenty-five acres in 1798 was entailed with a provision to obtain a considerably increased feu-duty when drawing up contracts to dispose of plots. The extent of the estate was increased in 1820 when the Brandsfield property in Easter Dalry extending to 6.510 acres was purchased from James Home Rigg.[7] James Walker's son consolidated the family's landed interests in the Dalry and North Merchiston area by adding to them in a series of transactions in 1827, 1830 and 1836 for small acreages with the Merchant Company, George Watson's Hospital and with James Home Rigg, from whom an acre of land on the north side of Gorgie Road provided another strategic addition.[8]

Following this consolidation, the development of the Walker estate fell into three phases. The first phase, between 1840 and 1856, was characterised by dealings with transport and public utility interests and was to some extent anticipated by the earlier disposal of a strip of 1.969 acres in 1821 to the Edinburgh and Glasgow Union Canal Company. The Walker property was bisected by the route of the canal and though James Walker, son, received £2,000 in damages, approximately £63,000 in current prices, in addition to the £468 purchase price, subsequent development possibilities were undoubtedly prejudiced.[9] The effect of the sale was to move the boundary of industrial and commercial land use further south, thereby limiting the possibilities for more prestigious residential building. The canal represented a non-negotiable frontier in the spatial development of the city.[10] Perhaps in recognition of the social tone thereby established, further sales of property, all to the north of the line of the canal, were made to the Edinburgh and Glasgow Railway Company, one in 1840 for 8.610 acres and a smaller sale of 0.255 acres in 1845; the

[7] MC, Drumdryan Chartulary, vol. 1, Charter of Resignation and Confirmation 1820, f. 4; see also J. Smith, 'Dalry House: its lands and owners', esp. 45–8.

[8] These were for 1.162, 1.305, and 1.186 acres in 1827, 1830 and 1836.

[9] ECA ACC 282, James Walker's Papers, Registered Disposition by James Walker to the Edinburgh and Glasgow Union Canal, 25 Apr. 1821. The figure was £2,000 with £340 interest accrued.

[10] The canal also formed the basis of social divisions amongst the youth of Edinburgh, those to the north being known as 'keelies'. See A. A. MacGregor, *Auld Reekie: Portrait of a Lowland Boyhood* (London 1943).

Caledonian Railway Company bought over six acres in 1856.[11] Ease of access across largely undeveloped property for this western rail approach governed the route, and as noted by Kellett, the fractured nature of land-ownership assisted the process of acquisition for the railway companies who were again in the land market for an 11.605 acre piece of Walker's estate in 1869.[12]

The northern portion of the Walker estate became the nineteenth-century Edinburgh equivalent of spaghetti junction. Nowhere else in the city did the curves and cuttings converge in such densities. By contrast to the neat geometrical shapes established across difficult terrain in the New Town, to the west, in Dalry and North Merchiston the curvilinear legacy of canal and railway development in the second quarter of the century produced awkward angles and sizes to building plots. As a result, many stances remained unfeued, as with those eventually developed by the Edinburgh Co-operative Building Company opposite Haymarket Station, and landowners such as the Walkers were obliged to forgo housing development and settle where they could for small workshops and storerooms built in the interstices between properties. Long-term and short-term investment horizons were thus frequently in conflict.

The impact of public rights on private interests also affected James Walker, son and grandson, when the route for water piped by the Edinburgh Water Company from the Bavelaw reservoir in the foothills of the Pentland Hills, as approved by an act of 1843, crossed their land in 1850.[13] Access to water was important for many industrial interests and it was these which featured in the second phase of estate development from 1850 to 1867. In recognition of the damage already done north of the Canal, Walker did not oppose Graham Menzies' proposal for his dis-tillery to take water from the Canal by pipe some two feet under the Walker estate, so long as any damage was repaired.[14] In cities throughout Britain uncontaminated water was at a premium and the expansion of William McEwan's Fountain Brewery on Fountainbridge owed much to the conjunction of a high quality water supply and the availability of land; the Walker estate feued two substantial plots to McEwan, one of

[11] ECA ACC 282, James Walker's Trust, Extracts from General Register of Sasines, Dispositions to Edinburgh and Glasgow Railway, 31 Mar. 1840, 10 Mar. 1845, 1 Feb. 1856.

[12] Kellett, *The Impact of Railways*, 4–5; ECA ACC 282, James Walker's Papers, feu disposi-tion to Caledonian Railway Company, 6 Sept. 1869.

[13] ECA ACC 282, Bond of Servitude by James Walker in favour of Edinburgh Water Co. 8 July 1850. Modest compensation was paid and subsequent access to pipes guaranteed to the EWC.

[14] ECA ACC 282, Excerpt of Contract of Feu between James Walker and Graham Menzies 16 May 1855.

4.645 acres in 1866 and a further 8.313 in 1867.[15] These contiguous plots consolidated the Brewery's interests and provided scope for expansion. Located in an area capable of housing significant numbers of workers and with the development of separate sidings at Dalry junction, William McEwan gained a degree of control over the pace and scale of production and distribution as a consequence of his dealings with James Walker, son.

With high class residential development compromised in the north of the estate by railway development, James Walker's son and grandson did not oppose the use of public water by private brewing and distilling companies, and positively assisted it where they could.[16] To them as landowners, the advantage lay in the enhanced prospects for working-class housing development which resulted from such commercial developments and their labour requirements and, in this regard, the feuing of land to institutions complemented their prospects. The Free Church bought 0.731 acres of land on the corner of what were to become Tay Street and Bryson Road, a purchase which though not far from the Fountainbridge Road[17] meant that the church stood at least 200 yards from the nearest structure.[18] Land for the house of God was followed by two sales to house the working classes, one to Rosehall Place Building Association for 0.444 acres in 1865, and another to the Edinburgh Co-operative Building Company for three acres in 1867.[19]

As industrialists set up new plants and expanded existing ones in Dalry in the 1860s then demand for workers' housing in the locality was stimulated.[20] Employees in breweries, bakeries, foundries and in rubber manufacture sought alongside diverse groups of other workers to reside close to their workplace. Accordingly, developers took a keen interest in the strategically placed Walker lands. John Watherston and Sons, builders, feued 3.705 acres in 1868 and James Steel, builder, 13.081 acres in 1869 on what was known as the Easter Dalry feu.[21] In the same year, Walker disposed feus of just over an acre to George Mackay, jeweller, John Oman, builder, and James Carrick and Sons, smiths, and of four acres to Thomas Honeyman, dairyman. Walker's grandson sought specifically to enhance the feuing prospects and income possibilities by various devices, for

---

[15] ECA ACC 282, feu dispositions to William McEwan, 16 Feb. 1866 and 8 Feb. 1867. A small, third plot was feued in 1868.

[16] ECA ACC 282. Another example was the Feu Contract and Disposition to Menzies, Bernard and Co., distillers, 5 Oct. 1868.   [17] Subsequently Dundee Street.

[18] Feu contract and disposition to trustees of the Congregation of Free St David's Church, 8 Nov. 1864.

[19] ECA ACC 282, James Walker's papers, feu dispositions 4 July 1865 and 29 Aug. 1867.

[20] See chapter 1 for a more detailed account of this migration of manufacturing to the suburbs.   [21] NAS RS108/18.186, 15 Apr. 1869.

example, relinquishing his superiority over a corner plot on Caledonian Crescent and Street to James Steel, and, more significantly, by an agreement with Steel to widen a street off Dalry Road since it 'would benefit both parties to widen and extend said road and thereafter preserve it in all time coming as a means of access'.[22]

Less than nine months elapsed between the start of the Sciennes development (see chapter 6) and the agreement James Steel signed with James Walker in 1869 (fig. 7.1).[23] Despite the success of Drumdryan, the rental revenues from the Leith properties and the developing income stream from Sciennes, Steel's own resources were insufficient to undertake the development of the thirteen acre Dalry site acquired from James Walker. So, in just eighteen months, James Steel issued bonds and borrowed £24,500 – about £1.1 million in present-day prices. Secured on a variety of properties, it was an impressive sum and indicative of his credit rating. Significantly, though the powerful liaison with Melville and Lindesay, solicitors, was responsible for raising £4,000, and for a fourth time he turned to James Gray's executors for capital, Steel was obliged to borrow from the formal financial sector, the Commercial Bank of Scotland and the Life Association of Scotland. These were the only two non-private loans taken out by James Steel in almost forty years as a builder in Edinburgh and, rather than desperation, they reflected the scale of capital required for the building and estate development projects underway.

The tactics of development employed by Steel were, predictably, similar to those used on the parallel development of Sciennes. The terms of the contract with Walker phased in the feu-duties: £300 payable in 1871–3, £500 in 1874–5 and £1,000 p.a. thereafter. To delay development was to risk the non-payment of the feu, and Steel, as elsewhere, was prompt in beginning building on his own account, cleverly using the curve of the Granton branch of the Caledonian Railway to define the shape for Caledonian Crescent (fig. 7.1). This maximised the number of building stances, while on the remainder of the estate the layout reserved a proportion for shop developments. By Whitsunday 1871, two years after the legal title had been conveyed, Robert Hislop, John Dickie and several other tenants had moved into Caledonian Crescent. The pattern, initiated at Drumdryan and elaborated at Sciennes, of sub-feuing to

[22] NAS GRS 23/9/1876 and ECA ACC 282, James Walker's Papers. It was Steel, however, who was obliged to shoulder the costs of widening and 'to repair such damage to the road as had already been done'. This was precisely the tactic employed by Walker's father in 1858 when he 'considered it expedient' to enter into an agreement with the Merchant Company and the Caledonian Insurance Company to widen Dalry Road (now Merchiston Avenue) from twenty to forty feet which was 'calculated to promote the accommodation and advantage of the feuars'.

[23] NAS RS108/18.186, 15 Apr. 1869.

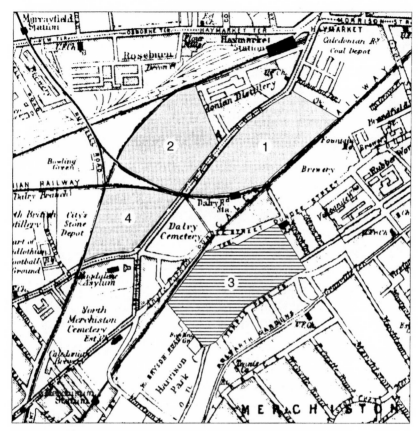

Figure 7.1   Dalry land obtained by James Steel 1869–1878

Notes: the disposal of Dalry lands was as follows
1 1869 Walker to Steel 13.081 acres Easter Dalry
2 1874 Rigg to Steel   15.721 acres Downfield
3 1878 Walker to Hay   36.508 acres North Merchiston
4 1878 Rigg to Steel   9.467 acres Merchiston

builders and property companies was reproduced on the property feued
from Walker in Easter Dalry.[24]

[24] ECA SL104/3/1, Wester Dalry Chartularies, Caledonian Road, Place and Crescent sub-
feuing contracts 1860–70, with f. 1 (John Marshall, mason), f. 10 (James Muir, joiner), f. 20
(David Rutherford, builder), ff. 32–55 (Duncan McRae, joiner), f. 61 (Peter Manson,
builder), f. 92 (Thomas Morton, builder), f. 102 (Thomas Crow, painter), f. 121 (Alexander
Wilson, builder), f. 133 (R. and A. Berry, builders). The streets formed by this development
included Caledonian Place, Road and Crescent, Orwell Place and Terrace, and Dalry Lane.
There were also properties on Dalry Road. D. McCrone and B. Elliot, *Property and Power in
a City: The Sociological Significance of Landlordism* (London 1989), 50, who also look at the
Caledonian Crescent site, note that builders normally put up two tenements.

Figure 7.2 Caledonian Place: typical of early James Steel building
developments at Tollcross, Sciennes and Dalry 1866–1875

The pace of development with which Dalry proceeded in the early
1870s and the rapidity with which Steel's Caledonian Place, Road and
Crescent feus were sold to builders and developed by Steel himself
justified a further excursion into the market place for land in 1874 (fig.
7.1). As with Drumdryan, the superiors were the trustees of James Home
Rigg of Downfield from whom Steel obtained 15.721 acres in 1874.[25]
Even before the acquisition of this area north of Dalry Road, Steel was
ranked fiftieth in a list of the largest landowners in Edinburgh and twenty-
fourth of all private landowners, positions which he had achieved in less
than ten years since his bankruptcy and his arrival in Edinburgh.[26] The
addition of the Rigg land in 1874 on which Cathcart, Downfield,
Springwell and contiguous streets were eventually built served to
strengthen Steel's position as a significant heritable landowner and developer in Edinburgh and, in 1878, he consolidated further his control over
Dalry and the western expansion of the city.

[25] NAS RS108/476.141, 9 June 1874.
[26] *PP 1874 LXXII pt III*, Owners of Lands and Heritages, 1872–3, 66–9. Crown lands
excluded.

Those portions of the Walkers' Dalry estate acquired after the deed of entail in 1798 were not subject to the restrictions of the grandfather.[27] They were conveyed in the normal manner as, for example, in those transactions in 1868 and 1869 to John Watherston and James Steel. However, the remainder of James Walker's Dalry estate was entailed and so the subsequent development of the property had to meet certain conditions.[28] There had to be a public roup or sale; this sale had to be advertised two months beforehand in three Edinburgh papers; the highest bid should prevail; the price should be at least double the rent obtainable for a nineteen year lease; and heirs and successors would be subject to the normal charges. The terms of the entail inclined Walker to sell the land in a single lot. His justification was that 'if feued piecemeal the uses to which some of the feued lots might be put might greatly deteriorate the value of the unfeued ground'.[29] In this Walker was undoubtedly correct, and his own experience as landowner and lawyer was by no means irrelevant to the decision since the fragmentation of the Brandsfield and Dalry feus not covered by the entail had reduced the degree of control over development, while the obligation to search the Register of Sasines and draw up several sets of feu contracts and dispositions was expensive in terms of lawyers' and clerks' fees, and also not without error or potential for dispute.

The piecemeal release of land could be both flexible, yet unstructured. When released in a large parcel, as to James Steel in 1869, a degree of cohesion and integrity was injected into the area. Accordingly, the prospect of a sale to a single buyer was an attractive one and with his previous experience of dealing with Steel, whom Walker described as 'a gentleman of large means', the terms privately agreed between them in 1877 were put to the Lord Advocate for Scotland to ensure that they met the entail stipulations.[30] They did. However, the private arrangement ran aground in January 1878 when as required, the sale of land went to public auction. After several bids, Steel's original offer to feu the 36.508 acres at £2,255 per annum was surpassed and eventually a sale concluded with John Charles Hay for £3,700 (fig. 7.1).[31]

---

[27] For example, John Hay, architect, had had to meet the stipulations when he bought a triangle of land contained by Ardmillan, Angle Park and Henderson Terraces in 1875. ECA ACC 282, feu disposition to Hay, 28 June 1875.

[28] ECA ACC 282, List of Extracts from the General Register of Sasines, 23 Nov. 1805, 14 June 1825 and 30 Oct. 1856 record the transfer of titles and confirm the terms of entail.

[29] ECA ACC 282, James Walker's Papers, Memorandum on behalf of James Walker for the Lord Advocate, 7 Nov. 1877, f. 8.

[30] ECA ACC 282, James Walker's Papers, Memorandum on behalf of James Walker for the Lord Advocate, 7 Nov. 1877, f. 3

[31] ECA ACC 282, James Walker's Papers, Extract of Feu Contract, 16 Oct. 1878, f. 12. This document provides an Inventory of Feus affecting the Walker North Merchiston estate, ff. 51–5.

In the short term, Hay's higher bid – almost two-thirds above that offered by Steel – appeared attractive to the Walker interests, coupled as it was with further stiff conditions governing the development of the estate. For example, Hay had an option to buy out the annual feu-duty, but the formula stipulated twenty-three years purchase of the annual figure – considerably above the level which Steel had managed to generate on the neighbouring Caledonian feus. Also, though the full annual feu-duty payable by Hay was phased in over ten years, the Walker estate was released from all taxes and parochial burdens immediately. Agreement was also forthcoming that by Martinmas 1888 the dwelling houses and buildings erected would 'be sufficient to secure the entire feu-duty' and furthermore, that written permission be obtained from Walker to depart from the stipulation that only 'villas or self contained dwelling houses' could be constructed on the southerly half of the estate.[32] Though defeated at auction, Steel moved decisively to clinch a further substantial land acquisition of 9.467 acres with Rigg's trustees, also in Dalry (Murieston), and virtually opposite the property feued by Hay from Walker (fig. 7.1).[33]

Given that James Walker's grandson was prepared to feu at £2,255 p.a., the sale at £3,700 p.a. seemed a highly satisfactory outcome and a vindication of his grandfather's entail stipulations that a sale should be to the highest bidder at a public auction. It was this assured, long-term income stream which encouraged James Walker's grandson to consider in the early 1880s how best to provide for his three daughters. On the same day in 1882, Walker issued three bonds totalling £40,000 (approximately £2 million in 2000 prices) to three different groups of trustees, secured on the future revenue to be generated by the Dalry estate – £20,000 as a trust fund for his eldest daughter Cecilia as part of a marriage contract agreement, and £10,000 on behalf of the other two daughters.[34] Borrowing to set up a trust fund of these proportions generated a very comfortable annuity of £400 (or about £20,000 in 2001 prices) for the two younger daughters at a rate of interest of 4%, sums consistent with the annuities set up by James Walker's father and grandfather for their wives. The sums were doubled for Cecilia who married into minor East Sussex gentry, something which in her father's eyes warranted a double annuity. In providing for his wife and daughters in this way, James Walker's grandson was able to distribute the product of the family's

[32] ECA ACC 282, Extract of Feu Contract, ff. 41–3.

[33] NAS RS108/857.166, feu contract trustees of James Home Rigg to James Steel, 8 Mar. 1878.

[34] NAS RS108/1361.8, 108/1361.18 and 108/1361.26, 4 Jan. 1882; confirmation, RS108/1641.139, 3 June 1884.

wealth through the female line without disturbing the capital value of the estate itself. As lifetime annuities, whether married or not, the drain on the estate was finite and the capital intact. Hay's successful bid at auction improved the future lifestyle and marriage prospects for Walker's daughters.[35]

The General Property Investment Company

What neither Steel nor Walker knew was that Hay was bidding on behalf of the General Property Investment Company Limited (GPIC) and the Scottish Lands and Buildings Society Limited (SLBS). Simply put, Steel was gazumped by Hay acting as a front for jointly GPIC and SLBS.

The General Property Investment Company was an amalgamation of financial interests with a strong representation from Dundee, where the registered office was also located.[36] Two solicitors and two merchants from Dundee combined with a watchmaker, optician and architect from Edinburgh to set up the company in 1876. Amongst the seventeen original shareholders, all of whom subscribed £2,500 in £10 shares, six only had business interests in Edinburgh, and none had experience in the building trades. Some prominent citizens were involved, including the MP for Dundee, James Yeaman, the provost of Dunfermline, Kenneth Mathieson, and the provost of Stirling, George Christie. Hay functioned purely as a front, neither subscribing as a shareholder nor involved in any other capacity. Like other such property investment companies, the object of GPIC was:

to purchase or acquire heritable property . . . and any heritable rights . . . and to hold, manage, improve, build upon, lend upon, deal with, feu, sell or dispose of . . . with power to borrow money on security of property purchased or acquired.[37]

Experience of development from the sharp end of the operation, that is, as developers, was lacking amongst the directors and principal shareholders of GPIC. Their interests were in the financial aspects of development and most GPIC personnel also held directorships in other investment companies, though Mathieson, Bryson and Curror were the principal directors of the Caledonian Heritable Security Company.[38]

The General Property Investment Company had agreed to pay James Walker's grandson a feu-duty of £1,149 for each of the first five years and then £2,133 for each of the following five years, 1883–8. That is, they had

---

[35] ECA ACC 282, James Walker's Papers, disposition in security by James Walker to trustees, 4 Jan. 1882 in connection with Cecilia, Lillias and Anna Walker.
[36] NAS BT2/652, General Property Investment Company, Memorandum of Association, 3 Feb. 1876.   [37] NAS BT2/652, GPIC, Memorandum of Association.
[38] *Edinburgh and Leith Post Office Directories*, 1875–6, 43.

committed to paying Walker £16,408 by 1888 and a total of £51,557 by 1898. To do so it was clear that the development of the estate needed to proceed rapidly, though this in turn jeopardised feuing rates over the longer term by an oversupply of building in a specific locality. It was precisely this possibility which inclined James Steel to defer his own Dalry development, also acquired in 1878, and for the first time in his career Steel hoarded land, keeping it off the market for almost a decade. Given his track record, credit rating and degree of cross-financing between different projects in Leith, Sciennes and Tollcross, it was a strategy of which GPIC must have been aware but without the resources to copy. Their imperative was to feu and develop otherwise the land would be 'irritated' or repossessed.

Notwithstanding the risk of oversupply, the feuing of GPIC lands began almost immediately – the first plots were sub-feued within the year in Fowler Terrace, a further four were feued in 1879, and then a raft of sub-feus, fourteen in all, negotiated in 1880 and a further ten in 1881, almost exclusively to those engaged in the building trades. While the demand for housing remained buoyant, the GPIC found it relatively easy to dispose of feus to builders, but at the hint of difficulties in the housing market, builders stopped buying stances for housing development. However, the obligation to the feuar, James Walker's grandson, did not cease. This was precisely the attraction of the investment in superiorities to individuals and trustees. Continuity of income was assured and, if an 'irritancy' developed in the form of non-payment, then the superior could reassume and reassign feus at a different price, as Rigg had done when faced with a defaulter on his Drumdryan estate.[39]

The GPIC could dispose of a single feu only in 1882 and that to the School Board of Edinburgh for the Tay Street School.[40] City-wide, the volume of housebuilding fell 23% in 1883 and failed to recover for another four years. GPIC fortunes mirrored this trough. In 1883 no feu contracts were agreed. The next two years were only marginally better, with five feus disposed of in total, mostly for middle- and lower-middle-class housing in Polwarth Gardens. The income stream generated by the GPIC by 1885 only just covered the reduced rate of feu-duties to which Walker had agreed in the original charter, but in 1886 the prospect of generating an additional 45% annual income by the Martinmas 1888 deadline proved to be remote. It was reported that:

[39] MC, Drumdryan Chartulary, vol. 1, feu charter to David Steel and David Walker, 1 July 1825, re-sold to James Fairley, 4 Feb. 1853, ff. 90, 219.
[40] J. W. R. Whitehand, 'The building cycle and the urban fringe in Victorian cities', *Journal of Historical Geography*, 4, 1978, 175–91, points out how public and institutional building frequently occurred in the downswing phase of the residential building cycle.

although the directors have been able to meet the termly payments due at Martinmas, the various creditors who had called up their loans declined to wait any longer and it had been found impossible owing to the impaired credit of the company to replace the loans, the company could not therefore longer carry on its business.[41]

It was the inability of the GPIC to renegotiate bonds due on maturity which triggered the directors' decision on 23 November 1886 to wind up the company. The GPIC had been formed in February 1876 as a limited company with 4,250 £10 shares; £3 was called up by 1880, rising gradually to £5.75 in 1885, and followed by the largest single call for a further capital subscription of £3.25 in 1886 as the problems of the company deepened.[42] At £9 per share, virtually the entire capital had been called up. In addition, the fall in the value of heritable property meant that the company ceased to pay a dividend and was forced to make further calls on capital to meet its annual outlay on debentures and bonds, as well as pay the feu-duties and other termly payments associated with their properties in Dundee, London and those due to James Walker's grandson in Edinburgh. The GPIC were late in paying £1,100 due to the trustees of Alexander McWalter, a Dundee shawl merchant, in November 1886, and £1,200 to the executor for the late Elizabeth Webster, Budleigh Salterton, for interest on a bond due at Martinmas 1885. Various other threats of action were in the air.[43] The combined effect of the capital structure and a dip in property prices accounted for the poor credit rating, and the consequential difficulties encountered in renegotiating bonds. By a strange irony, at the time that the company's affairs were in the hands of the accountant in bankruptcy, the annual value of thirty-five feu contracts disposed of by the GPIC was £2,256, just £1 over the bid made by James Steel in his behind the scenes manoeuvring with James Walker's grandson.

The receivership of the GPIC meant that the official liquidator assumed responsibility for the company's assets and liabilities.[44] With this also passed the responsibility to reassign the superiorities for the feus already disposed. However, within six months, that is, by April 1887 and before officially discharged, the liquidator made a 'Disposition and Assignation' in which the former GPIC directors were 'empowered to sell the real and personal and heritable and moveable property', adjudging that unless the liquidator himself took over the responsibility for disposing

---

[41] ECA ACC 282, James Walker's Papers, Court of Session Extract, 16 Dec. 1886.
[42] NAS BT2/652, Annual Return stating paid up capital, 13 Nov. 1886.
[43] ECA ACC 282, Court of Session Extract, 16 Dec. 1886.
[44] NAS BT2/652, General Property Investment Company. The directors sought to have Thomas Whitson appointed as official liquidator, but the Lords of Council asserted their independence by appointing David Myles, 16 Dec. 1886. Liquidator discharged 25 May 1894.

of plots, then the development of the estate 'could only competently be done' by Thomas Landale and his six other Edinburgh-based associates.[45] Not only was the liquidator authorised to dispose of the company's assets, he could set the price. This is what happened. Landale and his associates 'instantly paid' the £400 price set to assume the mid-superiority, which they had formerly had under the GPIC, and acquired powers to sell superiorities as they saw fit.[46] The Scottish Lands and Buildings Society was unaffected by this and their name continued to appear on legal documents, as a shadow of GPIC.[47] Landale and his associates disposed of feus, styled themselves as 'immediately lawful superiors', presumably to quell any doubts in the locality concerning the authenticity of titles and to reinforce the market value of their properties.[48] By associating the SLBS with these transactions the septet sheltered behind the limited liability which the SLBS offered; while things went well the former GPIC directors benefited, but if anything went wrong, the SLBS would take the fall by providing the limited liability which would contain the financial wreckage as far as the principals were concerned.[49]

Perhaps most important, by 1887 builders and joiners were again prepared to feu property. The last three plots feued before the company was wound up were for better quality properties in Polwarth Gardens, and this trend continued after the liquidation of the GPIC. Five of the first six building stances sold in 1887–8 were in the same street, often for three or four plots each, and so the annual feuing income of Thomas Landale *et al.* resumed its upward course and, by 1889, there was some further interest in the working-class housebuilding prospects for Watson Crescent and Tay Street (fig. 7.3).

By 1892, five years after the GPIC had gone into liquidation, the same individuals offered James Walker's grandson £85,100 to purchase his superiority rights, equivalent to almost £5 million in 2000 prices.[50]

---

[45] ECA ACC 282, James Walker's Papers, ff. 64–6, 68–9. The named individuals were Thomas Landale, land valuator, James Mackay Bryson, optician, John Waddell, railway contractor, Hector Frederick McLean, WS, Alexander Gray, Andrew Rutherford Gray, William John Menzies, WS. Thus the Edinburgh contingent of GPIC shareholders formed a sub-group to buy back the interests and remaining assets of the GPIC.

[46] ECA ACC 282, James Walker's Papers, Disposition and Assignation by David Myles, official liquidator, in favour of Thomas Landale and others, 19 Aug. 1887, f. 3.

[47] Feu contracts and dispositions were prefaced by the names of Thomas Landale and his associates 'as trustees for themselves and the SLBS' or as 'trustees under disposition in their favour by the GPIC now in liquidation'. ECA ACC 282, James Walker's Papers, ff. 71–2, 72–3, 109.

[48] ECA ACC 282, James Walker's Papers, ff. 103–4.

[49] The SLBS continued to function at least until 1914, moving head offices several times in close association with legal interests which were heavily involved in several trusts simultaneously. *Post Office Directories*, Edinburgh, 1870–1914.

[50] ECA ACC 282, James Walker's Papers, North Merchiston Discharged Security Writs.

Figure 7.3 Rear view of the General Property Investment Company development, Watson Crescent, Dalry, taken from the Walker Bridge over the Union Canal

Walker informed the Lord Advocate of Scotland as he was bound to do under the terms of the entail that the trustees of the GPIC 'have intimated to me their intention to [purchase] the lands . . . at the rate or price of twenty-three years purchase of the said feu-duty [£3,700]'. This was the annual feu-duty of £3,700 for which Hay had bid successfully in 1878 and on which an option to buy in a single payment at twenty-three years purchase seemed at the time to be a significant premium compared to the terms Steel had been able to extract on a nearby estate. Landale and his business associates 'instantly made payment' to the three trustees nominated by James Walker.[51]

The former GPIC shareholders generated their lump sum payment by two devices. First, with the sale of further building stances and the associated annual feuing income which ensued, Landale *et al.* could issue

Bonds and Dispositions by Scottish Provident Institution and Standard Property Investment Company show their heavy commitment in making advances to Landale and others in 1892.

[51] By relinquishing his superiority, the properties on which the three bonds for £40,000 were secured to provide annuities for his daughters were no longer under James Walker's control. By choosing to have payment made in this way for the sale of the North Merchiston superiorities he thereby also extinguished his obligations under the terms of these bonds.

bonds and obtain capital from property investment and other financial interests on security of this future income. The creation of real burdens saved them. Secondly, Landale and his associates sold their right to receive feu-duties. Just as Walker had to satisfy his immediate superior with an annual payment, so the GPIC (and later) Landale *et al.* had to fulfil their obligations to Walker. But they too could create sub-feus and did so. The original conveyance from James Walker's grandfather recognised the sub-feuing rights of the purchasers. Rather than hold on to the annual payments in perpetuity, Landale and his associates sold them normally based on a formula of twenty-one times the annual feu-duty. None of the superiorities, thirty-five in total, created by GPIC had been sold when the company was wound up; nor had the next ten building stances sold by the former shareholders between 1887 and 1892. Collectively, Landale and his business associates could exercise their right to compound the annual value of the feu-duty, assigning the right to receive the duty for a lump sum. The decision, therefore, in 1892 to extinguish their obligation to James Walker's grandson for an annual £3,700 feu-duty was financed in May 1892 by selling their rights over a portion of the estate, and by obtaining capital advances from institutions on the basis of the expected income from the remainder of the estate.

Suddenly an opportunity existed in a restricted area of the city to purchase long-run property income. Trusts, institutions and individuals were quick to act. In this first phase, the sale of forty-five superiorities was consolidated in relatively few hands; the Church of Scotland bought the superiority to the first plots created in Fowler Terrace, Dundee Street and Yeaman Place, and the trustees of the Dundee manufacturer James Cox took up some superiorities in Bryson Road, Watson Crescent and the more prestigious Polwarth Gardens.[52] The Paterson and Pape Fund bought superiorities for parts of Bryson Road and on the south-west corner of Yeaman Place (fig. 7.4).[53] In addition to the institutional and trusteeship interests in acquiring long-term and stable incomes on behalf of their clients, individuals also bought superiorities; John Usher consolidated his purchase of superiorities on and around Polwarth Gardens, while Annie Marshall of Ayr, and Mary Black, a widow, living in Oxford Terrace, Edinburgh, bought single superiorities.[54]

[52] NAS RS108/2109.61. James Cox's trustees also bought building stances from James Steel at Springwell Place, 14 Nov. 1888.

[53] Pape's trustees used the income generated to fund the construction of three cottages for widows at Coltbridge from 1894.

[54] Once the immediate reason for selling superiorities had passed, that is, after 1892, the former GPIC directors usually disposed of the superiority at the same time as the sale of the building stance. Though this had the disadvantage of creating a web of ownership and a proliferation of legal documents to dispose of the superiorities, it had the merit that the local market was not flooded with such sales.

(a)

(b)

Figure 7.4 a and b Pape's Cottages, Coltbridge, 1894

Note: George Pape's will provided for these three cottages for widows
'in all time coming' and the trustees used the income from feu-duties in
Bryson Road and Yeaman Place to fund the terms of Pape's will.

Sales of plots with a frontage between fifty-two and sixty feet or plots of approximately 450–500 square yards and a feu-duty of £20–£30 p.a. thus generated cash sums of £425–£600 for the sale of their superiority: that is, the right to receive the feu-duty payable annually on a plot could be compounded and sold for cash. The decision of the former GPIC directors, therefore, to buy back in their own names this right to dispose of the titles for the North Merchiston feus for the paltry sum of £400 seems an act of extreme generosity on the part of the official liquidator.[55] This septet of former GPIC shareholders began quickly to accumulate significant capital.

The receipt of £85,100 by Landale and his SLBS associates for the Walkers' heritable securities provided sufficient cash for James Walker, grandson, to pay off the £40,000 loans obtained on security of this income and which had been used to set up the trust funds for his daughters. However, that was not the end of the Walker interest in Dalry and North Merchiston.[56] The process began again. James Walker used the remainder of the payment from the SLBS to buy twenty-five acres in Merchiston Park. This recycling of property income was an important feature in the long-term sustainability of a private urban estate, the sale of one area releasing accumulated capital gains which were then deployed elsewhere to generate another long-run development prospect.

Urban property and the transmission of wealth

Whereas the father and grandfather had consolidated their estate, the third generation James Walker dismantled it and assembled another asset. The integrity of the estate was retained for sixty years, but ultimately could not resist the intrusive predations of commercial and working-class housing demand for land use. Unless the Walker generations and particularly the grandson were prepared to assume the role of developer in a more forceful manner then a controlled and phased development of the North Merchiston estate was a remote possibility, and given their own legal commitments and professional networks, this was a low priority. Lacking this, the fractures between the differing personal and financial interests which acquired feus ensured that the pace and character of development would be uneven, though the prevailing practice to release land in fairly standard frontages and develop it along similar lines for flatted tenement dwellers indirectly imposed a degree of uniformity on

---

[55] The GPIC directors were initially opposed to the official liquidator, David Myles of Dundee, and suggested their own nominee, Thomas Whitson.

[56] Orwell Terrace and the neighbouring area from the initial land purchases also remained undeveloped.

the spatial development of Dalry and North Merchiston, as was the case elsewhere in the city.[57] In certain essentials, the homogeneity of the nineteenth-century residential areas assumed as great a coherence as the more prestigious New Town addresses, if only because financial constraints ensured a minimum of detailing and flamboyance. The housing market imposed its own discipline on the physical appearance of the city.

Set against this physical coherence was a crazed pattern of financial interests and building development. One superiority, James Walker's, was transmitted to another single agency, the General Property Investment Company, but inexperience and financial stringency caused this to be sold off in ninety-three separate lots between 1878 and 1906, with a few firms only – Duncan Buchanan Ritchie, mason and builder (seven), H., T. and R. Montgomery, joiners (five), and Peter Justice, builder (four) – entering into multiple feu contracts. William Galloway and nine other building trades firms bought only two building stances, and all other builders only one.[58] A fish merchant, bakers' utensil maker, boot manufacturer, flesher, coal merchant and a few solicitors each took one or two stances, never three, and after 1892 this pattern of fragmented ownership and building development was much more pronounced, partly as Landale and his Edinburgh associates could take a more relaxed view of estate development since they themselves were no longer under pressure to produce a substantial annual feu-duty to their superior. Years passed and some streets remained incomplete. Along the entire southern length of Watson Crescent, only two building stances had been developed in 1896, and only four on the north side; and where Watson Crescent formed the southern end of Fowler Terrace and Yeaman Place, again there was no building development at the time of the Ordnance Survey of 1896. Given his record over forty years, it is unimaginable that had Steel's bid for this land been successful it would have produced so few tenements in a twenty year period, and in the sense of restricted supply of housing, working-class tenants were the casualties of the feuing system and its financial implications.

By contrast to the piecemeal and gradual nature of GPIC building development, the sale of superiorities initially enabled property ownership to be recombined by trusts and institutional interests, as well as under the umbrella of personal property portfolios developed by individuals. The mosaic of superiorities provided the secure income possibilities

[57] ECA ACC 282, James Walker's Papers, Articles and Conditions of Feu of parts of the Lands of North Merchiston.
[58] For further elaboration on this point elsewhere in Scotland see R. Rodger, 'Speculative builders and the structure of the Scottish building industry 1860–1914', *Business History,* 21, 1979, 226–46.

sought by widows, spinsters and male investors too. For solicitors, searching for and conveyancing of titles to these properties ensured a steady stream of business, since the Scottish land registry, the General Register of Sasines, required an intensive system of double entry record keeping of every particular, financial and titular, affecting the property.[59]

Of those who developed plots in North Merchiston, 60% were associated with the building trades and most of these lived within half a mile of the building stances they bought from the GPIC and its successor. Where the developer was not a builder, then they tended to live further away from their interests, though this was in part due to the essentially working-class nature of the property being built. A fish merchant, Andrew Dow, lived in the Pleasance, and James Nimmo, a coal merchant, a little further south at Priestfield; two related fleshers, Neil and Duncan Thomson, lived in Irvine and Stirling but through an Edinburgh contact, possibly a solicitor, knew of the opportunities to take building land on adjacent stances in Ritchie Place. These and others who gave no specific occupation were frequently investors, recognising the possibilities for long-term income. Amongst this category were Sophia Bennett and Jane Roberts, both of whom lived nearby, and John Archibald Erskine who, between 1896 and 1899, took on four such investments, always for more than one building plot. Erskine clearly felt that the greater financial security which resulted warranted his move from Goldenacre Terrace to a more substantial villa in Brunstane.

Unlike the highly localised nature of building development, the geographical spread of superiorities was noticeable. Once the GPIC had decided to sell the superiorities, and even taking into account the greater concentration amongst a few buyers in the tranche sold in 1892, there were fifty-two different individuals, trusts and institutions who bought superiorities, and only 40% were from Edinburgh. The others ranged all over Britain, though the Dundee and east of Scotland bias was present (20%). Where those who bought superiorities came from Liverpool, Hampshire and overseas there was usually a family connection with Dundee or with those associated with the GPIC. If this mosaic of ownership in North Merchiston superiorities was revealed through addresses, so, too, it was in terms of social class. In addition to the trusts (40%) who were the largest interest, women (23%), and widows particularly, were the next largest group, holding the superiorities in their own names. Judged by their addresses, some of the widows were of very modest means. Another group included the professionals in medicine and the

---

[59] R. Rodger and J. Newman, 'Property transfers and the Register of Sasines: urban development in Scotland since 1617', *Urban History Yearbook*, 1988, 49–57.

law (12%). Developers and builders, predictably, were also well represented and the MP for Dumfries burghs, a baronet and the Perthshire
widow of another were amongst the landed and titled investors.

Both socially and geographically, the development of the Dalry and
North Merchiston estate touched those near and far. The concentration
of landed interests which had existed in the hands of James Walker's
grandfather had been broken up. To the opportunities created by background economic conditions were added the more specific efforts of individuals – the three generations of James Walker, the speculative
aspirations of the GPIC and its successor, and the individual endeavours
of small builders and investors concerned with individual plots and
narrow margins of error. In the financial powerplay in 1878 which
resulted in a successful bid by Hay and his associates, working-class
tenants were ultimately the losers, since higher land prices and interrupted development both impaired the quality and quantity of affordable
housing in the industrial suburb of Dalry.

Steel and cycles: Dalry recast

Avid readers of the *Gazette* might have identified the trend in building
bankruptcies which showed that between 1878 and 1891 there was a
doubling or tripling in the annual number compared to the previous
twenty years.[60] Even so, this was nothing in relation to the failure of the
City of Glasgow Bank in 1878 which indirectly forced two-thirds of
Glasgow builders into liquidation, voluntarily or otherwise.[61] That it took
James Steel just over ten years (1869–80) to develop the Caledonian feus
was a barometer of weakening working-class demand and there was no
doubt a certain irony that, at the very moment at which he was gazumped
by Hay, the bottom fell out of the market for lower income housing. James
Steel's sensitivity to market trends was in part the result of his own
encampment in the area. As at Drumdryan, where he resided on-site in
the former mansion house, so, too, at Dalry he moved his office in 1871 to
the seventeenth-century Dalry House and then relocated office and home
in 1875 to Torphichen Street, just two hundred yards from the Walker
Caledonian feu. From 1878, the building yard itself was located in
Maxwell Street, in the heart of Steel's Dalry development.[62]

---

[60] *Edinburgh Gazette*, 1856–1913.
[61] Glasgow Municipal Commission on the Housing of the Poor (Glasgow 1904), *Report*,
and *Evidence*, Binnie, Q. 7011.
[62] *Edinburgh and Leith Post Office Directories*, 1866–1905. Steel's development encircled
Dalry House and resulted in it being described as 'a classy villa institutionalised in a back
street'. See J. Gifford, C. McWilliam and D. Walker, *The Buildings of Scotland: Edinburgh*
(Harmondsworth 1988), 508.

It was this degree of business engagement which informed Steel's decision-making process. His integrated approach to the development of Dalry, as elsewhere, enabled sensitive adjustments to be made in the light of changing circumstances. As feudal superior he was acquainted with the ease or otherwise of sub-feuing stances for building; as a builder he was aware of costs of production; and as landlord, the facility with which flats could be rented and vacancies avoided provided a cross-check on the state of the housing market.[63] For those involved in only one of these functions, a lagged response to market changes could, and often did, prove fatal. In the early 1870s, with the cycle in its upswing phase and progress on the Walker feu proceeding satisfactorily, then, consistent with the earlier strategy of having two or even three sites in different stages of development, Steel sought to acquire further land. This he did in 1874 with 15.721 acres – the Downfield site – named after James Home Rigg of Dounfield, whose trustees feued the land to Steel.[64] The site was opposite the Caledonian feu, and if the annual payments to Rigg to which Steel was committed were a little lower than to Walker, this probably reflected the mixed residential and commercial uses, awkward angles and proximity to another complex spaghetti of railway lines. Ironically, perhaps, the feu charter stipulated that Steel's development should cause no nuisance to his neighbours, while at the same time he was prevented from interfering with the flow of sewage in the Lochrin burn, a polluted stream which one of Rigg's tenants used to fertilise a nearby field.

Another of the feu charter clauses required Steel to develop the Downfield area sufficiently to meet the payment to his own superior, Rigg's trustees, before 1881. Since the housing market remained optimistic in the mid-1870s, James Steel had little difficulty after setting out a feuing plan in obtaining sub-feuars to develop the individual stances; an amalgam of builders, trustees, building associations and private developers obtained feus in 1877, either to build themselves, or to contract somebody else to do so. The alacrity of the response was demonstrative of the trust which sub-feuars showed in Steel's judgement of the development potential.[65]

In three respects the development differed from previous Steel enterprises: first, he did not build tenements himself; secondly, there were a number of feus for commercial and industrial premises; and thirdly,

---

[63] For James Steel's activities as landlord see pp. 278 *et seq.*

[64] NAS RS108/476.141, 9 June 1874. The streets formed from this development included Cathcart, Springfield and Downfield Places, Maxwell Street (later Duff Street), Northcote Street and parts of Dalry Road.

[65] ECA SL105, Dalry Chartulary, Search of Incumbrances, ff. 5–8, 10, 12, 14–15, feu charters by James Steel to Robert Finlay, James Maxwell, Alexander White, Robert White, Alexander Petrie, Finlay and Greig, McLeod and Pollock and Alexander White.

institutions such as the Edinburgh School Board and the Free Church
were quick to recognise that they had a role to play in the rapidly expanding industrial suburb of Dalry and obtained land in conspicuous locations
for their purposes. By securing the institutional usages at an early stage of
development, James Steel substantially reduced his risk. Arguably, then,
public building during recessions in housebuilding development may
have owed less to the perspicacity of institutions and more to the private
developers' need to underpin their income from such public and predictable sources.[66] Together, the feu-duties payable by the School Board and
the Free Kirk amounted to 64% of the feu-duty payable to James Steel's
superior in 1877, and 54% over the years 1877–81. It was a priceless
front-loading of the development and even when the full feu-duty became
payable from 1881, these two institutions still produced 27% of the
amount payable by Steel to Rigg's trustees. When, in 1888, James Steel
offered the Downfield and neighbouring feus for sale, conceding thereby
his right to future income for a lump sum in the present, the annual value
of the sale of superiorities was over £1,200, almost 30% above his own
annual payments to Rigg's trustees.[67] It still left a considerable number of
stances either unsold or undeveloped and when, by 1900, most were built
up the developed feu-duty was at least 120% above that payable by Steel
to his superior.[68]

If landing such an institutional catch was of great benefit another tactic
produced a further degree of stability for James Steel. It was a host–
parasite relationship between Steel and his sub-feuars which was
beneficial to both; as host, Steel concluded the major deal with the heritable owner, shouldering the legal and related transactions costs and
taking the ultimate risk – responsibility for the annual feu-duty – and then
broke the land acquired into manageable plots for builders of modest
resources. Taking one or several stances gave a further degree of
flexibility, based on the self-assessment by sub-feuars of their financial
strength and ambitions. Only on a few occasions did Steel's sub-feuars
move with him from one development to the next. As at Drumdryan, in
his various Dalry developments Steel depended heavily upon a number of
highly localised builders – almost 50% of the builders who took sub-feus

[66] J. W. R. Whitehand, 'Land values and land use', in J. W. R. Whitehand, *The Changing Face
of Cities* (Oxford 1987), 45–50.

[67] NAS RS108/2109.161, 2109.181, 2111.54, 2106.89, 2106/19, 2111.54, dated 12 Nov.
1888, show that the heritable securities were bought exclusively by trustees for William
Haig, Edward Meldrum, James Cox and James Davidson. See ECA ACC 282, James
Walker's Papers, List of Feu Duties for Sale, 1888.

[68] The final figure would be at least 141% in excess of Steel's payments to Rigg, once factored in to the calculation are 12.1% for a feu-duty bought out, and duplicands in excess
of those for which Steel was liable to Rigg, divided by twenty-one years to give an annual
figure equivalent to 5.8%.

from Steel in Dalry were local, that is, resident within half a mile of their site.[69] Indeed, many of them moved into the tenements they built, sometimes because, on completion, they had unlet flats since they had missed the critical letting date, Whitsun, from which date leases ran for an entire year.[70] The parasitical relationship did not shield the sub-feuars from bankruptcy, with at least 21% of those engaged in Steel's Dalry development seeking a bankrupt's discharge and others presumably just deciding to cease trading, or resuming their skilled trade on a waged basis.[71]

Though a crucial reorientation of James Steel's activities took place in the mid-1870s, his involvement with the development of Dalry continued into the twentieth century. Within two months of the unsuccessful bid in 1878 for the Walker feu, Steel acquired yet another sizeable portion of land held by James Home Rigg's trustees.[72] This 9.467 acres site (Murieston), like all those developed by James Steel in Dalry, was sandwiched between two railway lines, the Wester Dalry and Haymarket branch lines of the Caledonian Railway, on two sides, and by the main Dalry–Gorgie Road on the south.

Development of the Murieston site reveals Steel's penetrating analysis of the market and his business resolve. For the first time in his career, Steel acquired land and did not develop it. The time horizon of his operations altered and the customary feuing plan followed promptly by a clutch of agreements with sub-feuars did not materialise for decade, an almost exact correlation with the downswing in the Edinburgh building cycle. Indeed, though the feu charter with Rigg's trustees stipulated that by 1883 Steel should complete three buildings to secure the £952 annual feu-duty, there is no evidence that he did so. That he could afford to risk the irritancy (or reversion) of the feu was itself a muscular statement of self-confidence and secure long-term judgement. When, eventually, Steel decided that the housing market warranted further capacity in Dalry, it was as a builder himself that he proceeded in 1886–7. By the following year, with seven tenements producing rents at Murieston Crescent, there was evidence, if proof be needed, that the Murieston feu could be released as elsewhere in Dalry.[73] The development strategy had many of the Steel trademarks – mixed shop and tenement development on the

[69] ECA SL104/3/1–3, Wester Dalry Chartularies. This is based on an analysis of over 120 feu charters on Steel's various Dalry estates, and then compared with those for the Sciennes and Drumdryan developments.

[70] ECA SL105, Dalry Chartulary, Incumbrances, for example, Peter Sinclair, Peter Manson, Alexander Henderson, William Shaw, John Rodgers, Alexander Pringle and Alexander Matthew.

[71] NAS, Court of Session sequestrations, A11553, A11669, A17605, A17798, A23416, A20175.   [72] NAS RS108/857.166, 8 Mar. 1878.

[73] ECA SL104/3/1–3, Wester Dalry Chartularies.

main road frontages, sub-feus to builders, several industrial premises and an institutional presence in the form of the St Cuthbert's Co-operative Association (1888), Evangelical (1893) and Roman Catholic (1894) churches, Salvation Army hall (1897) and town council property (1896). Significantly, in a clear demonstration of the importance of housing to railway development, it was only after the Dalry area was virtually covered in tenements and industrial premises that the Caledonian Railway built Dalry station, opened in 1894.[74]

A significant departure in business strategy, however, was the involvement of James Steel's nephews, James Steel Allan, Alexander Allan and Hugh Percival, and his business partner in the Northumberland quarry, James Turner. Whether, following their marriage in 1883, James Steel was encouraged by his wife to display greater concern for his family, or an indication of a diversification of his activities into politics and company directorships, or even a concern for the continuation of his business dynasty, the motive is unclear.[75] Certainly in setting up his thirty-something spinster nieces after 1885 as lodging house keepers next door to his own Torphichen Street home must have come as a relief to his widowed sister in Lanarkshire. She was relieved, no doubt, at her brother's employment of her son, Hugh, as a clerk. Steel endorsed his other nephews, too. They had obtained apprenticeships in Edinburgh as joiner and mason and, in their mid-thirties, had accumulated sufficient experience to warrant further encouragement from James Steel in the form of assigning them some Murieston sub-feus. The stances fronting Dalry–Gorgie Roads were almost exclusively built by Steel's nephews spread over the years 1888–1902. In fact, the trust shown by Steel in his nephews' ability was considerable, James Steel Allan taking on ten building stances in 1888 with a partner, William Donaldson, whom Steel knew through his earlier building work on Steel's Downfield Place feu, and a further eleven stances in 1889. Altogether, James Steel Allan feued thirty-six building stances in the years 1888–1902 and his brother sixteen plots concentrated in the years 1895–8.[76] No sentimental family favouritism was evident in the arrangement: the nephews had to pay feu-duties to their uncle on a basis comparable with other developers. Even so, James Steel's relationship with his nephews was more than a simple business convenience, with family loyalty working both ways to secure biddable individuals who had much to gain personally from the arrangement.

---

[74] Thomas, *A History of Regional Railways*, vol. VI.

[75] NAS Registers of Scotland 8 Aug. 1883; NAS SC70/4/366, Inventory of Sir James Steel's estate, 19 May 1905.

[76] NAS RS108/222.54, Plots 11 (29 Springwell Place) and 20 (20 Downfield Place) were feued to James Steel Allan in 1887.

Tenement design and the creation of a standardised urban form

Architectural coherence was not dependent upon a formal plan. Visual uniformity was achieved mainly through the 'Conditions of Feu' to which developers agreed when they signed a feu charter with a heritable landowner. This was the same device Heriot's Hospital employed in the New Town and which Steel used effectively in Dalry for working-class tenements. Planning responsibilities were, loosely, within the Dean of Guild Court's jurisdiction but were concerned mainly with existing buildings and disputes over light, noise, smoke and other noxious emissions, as well as with the structural state of buildings as they affected the interest of neighbours.[77] Also, the Dean of Guild Court's jurisdiction was spatially restricted to the boundaries of the ancient royalty and so major areas of nineteenth-century building activity – Dalry, Grange, much of the New Town – were not subject to building control until the Dean of Guild's orbit was extended geographically in 1880. Indeed, despite rapid urbanisation throughout central Scotland and beyond, a regulatory vacuum existed in the burghs in relation to many areas of civic administration. Nowhere was this more so than in public health and housing conditions, and such was the concern that a codified framework of municipal powers was produced in the form of the Burgh Police (Scotland) Act 1862.[78] In Edinburgh, however, many areas of the city were unaffected by the act until the boundary extensions in 1880 brought them within the jurisdiction of the city. By then, many suburbs, both working-class areas such as Dalry and higher social status developments in Newington, had been constructed without reference to civic officials.

As a builder of numerous tenements in the Dalry area, James Steel himself was in a powerful position to introduce a consistent appearance to the streets, but it was the imposition of identical construction materials and design features on others which were critical elements in the homogenised appearance of the industrial suburb. Indeed, such was the degree of standardisation that James Steel drew up a printed list of highly specific clauses.[79] Most fundamental of these was the requirement that tenements were to be 'four storeys high, each storey having ten feet at least between floor and hewn work'[80] – a condition which effectively guaranteed the

---

[77] R. Rodger, 'The evolution of Scottish town planning', in G. Gordon and B. Dicks, eds., *Scottish Urban History* (Aberdeen 1983), 71–91.

[78] See chapter 12 for further discussion of the emerging role of civic government.

[79] ECA ACC 373, Sir James Steel's Trust, Miscellaneous Boxes, Conditions of Feu of the Lands of Parts of Dalry belonging to Mr James Steel, n.d.

[80] ECA ACC 373, Sir James Steel's Trust, Conditions of Feu, Dalry, Clause 1.

uniformity of the roof line and an effect reinforced by the inviolate nature of the building line. There was no possibility of buildings with two or five storeys, nor of structures which jutted out beyond the line of their neighbours' tenement. Superficially, this degree of structural uniformity might suggest a high degree of similarity in the class structure within the tenements, and in some respects this was so, yet there was considerable scope for diversity given the variable size of flats within blocks. The specificity of the external appearance was accentuated by the obligation to build all external walls of stone and the 'openings' – doors and windows – with 'hewn work'; front walls were to be 'built of neatly square-dressed rubble drawn in joints with a key, all the openings having back-set rybats [Scots: margins] or upstarts neatly droved [Scots: horizontal tool-marks]'.[81]

Particular attention was directed to the boundaries of the building stance and to outbuildings in an effort to restrict the capacity for the eyesores associated with unregulated building. 'No outbuilding', the Conditions of Feu declaimed, 'shall be erected on the background rising higher than eight feet', and the roofing materials were clearly specified as 'lead, zinc, or other suitable material'.[82] Plots were to be enclosed:

with a dwarf stone wall twelve inches thick and eighteen inches high, including a stone cope six inches thick, and surmounted by an iron railing of a pattern to be approved by the superior, the railing to be three and a half feet high from the coping – except where the superior shall consider a high wall necessary, in which cases the feuar shall be bound to erect a rubble wall six feet six inches high, with a hammer dressed rounded cope.[83]

The degree of detail increased when the front of the tenement was considered. An iron railing of three feet eight inches was to top a coping stone twelve by eight inches and nine feet from the external wall; the width and quality of the pavement slabs and the size of the whin curbstone were also specified.[84]

To proscribe land use such that 'no trade, manufacture or operation shall be carried on'[85] was as emphatic a form of zoning as anything the Dean of Guild Court could devise and enforce, especially if monitored by a superior who himself was building neighbouring stances, and acting as landlord on those completed. Steel was *de facto* the principal planning agency in Dalry.

Underpinning the Conditions of Feu was a strong moral purpose, informed by a concept of mutuality itself derived from the concept of

[81] ECA ACC 373, Sir James Steel's Trust, Conditions of Feu, Dalry, Clause 1.
[82] ECA ACC 373, Sir James Steel's Trust, Conditions of Feu, Dalry, Clause 6
[83] ECA ACC 373, Sir James Steel's Trust, Conditions of Feu, Dalry, Clause 5.
[84] ECA ACC 373, Sir James Steel's Trust, Conditions of Feu, Dalry, Clauses 8, 9.
[85] ECA ACC 373, Sir James Steel's Trust, Conditions of Feu, Dalry, Clause 7.

'nichtbourheid' which protected an individual from infringements or 'nuisances' from another party. In a regulatory vacuum, at its greatest in the period of most pronounced urban expansion *c.* 1820–80, the contribution of the feudal superior to the quality of the built environment locally was crucial. Even where development was fragmented and loosely monitored, as with the property development company fronted by Hay on the Walker North Merchiston estate, here, too, the prescriptive nature of the Conditions of Feu imposed a strong degree of uniformity in terms of style and external appearance.[86] While the intent might differ – James Steel seeking to use strict Conditions of Feu to define amenity so as to enhance future development value and protect future rental income compared to the General Property Investment Company concerned to define the responsibilities of feuars and superiors for legal and financial purposes – the effect was similar. Conformity in the character and texture of the tenements of Victorian Edinburgh owed much to the discipline imposed on builders by superiors; however, the spectre of repossession for non-compliance with the terms of the feu charter was the only weapon superiors had for enforcement and, like most deterrents sparingly used, it was effective in achieving conformity.

[86] ECA ACC 282, James Walker's Papers, Articles and Conditions of Feu of parts of the Lands of North Merchiston.

The boundaries to the industrial suburb of Dalry, formed by a profusion
of rail tracks to north and south, were impenetrable along their length for
more than half a mile. All traffic, and perhaps more significantly, pedes-
trians, too, were funnelled to and from the city through Haymarket, the
gateway to the western extension to the New Town. The railway lines,
which had done much to define the industrial suburb, also had much to
do with the definition of middle-class zones by acting as a buffer. Whereas
in other Victorian cities encroachments at the margins of high status
residential areas gradually degraded the original coherence of a development through the intrusions of shop and workshop activities, this was less
so in the western suburbs of Edinburgh because of the barrier which both
the North British and the Caledonian railway lines afforded.[1]

Spatially and socially segregated areas of the city were no new phenomenon in Edinburgh. Both the town council and the Heriot's trustees consciously created these essential characteristics when, in the eighteenth
century, they planned and developed an extensive suburb in the form of
the New Town.[2] From 1767, James Craig's plans and feuing practice
combined to segregate the city horizontally in an overt effort to replace an
earlier Scottish form of vertical social segregation in multi-storey tenements.[3] Unlike many British cities, then, where suburbanisation was a

[1] See, for example, D. N. Cannadine, *Lords and Landlords: The Aristocracy and the Towns
1774-1967* (Leicester 1980); D. Olsen, *The Growth of Victorian London* (London 1976);
J. R. Kellett, 'Property speculators and the building of Glasgow 1780-1830', *Scottish
Journal of Political Economy*, 8, 1961, 211-32; and J. R. Kellett, *The Impact of Railways on
Victorian Cities* (London 1969).
[2] G. Gordon, 'The status area of Edinburgh', University of Edinburgh PhD thesis, 1970,
34, shows how clearly defined the social segregation was by 1855.
[3] R. A. Houston, *Social Change in the Age of Enlightenment: Edinburgh 1660-1760* (Oxford
1994), 101, emphasises social cohesion of eighteenth-century Edinburgh: 'The striking
point about Edinburgh in the century before 1760 despite the tensions which existed, the
strands which bound together the fragmented parts of society remained strong.' For an
account of the planning process associated with the formation of the New Town, see I. D.
Grant, 'Edinburgh's expansion: the background to the New Town', and C. Byrom,
'Jewels in the crown: James Craig and the development of Edinburgh's central open
spaces', both in K. Cruft and A. Fraser, eds., *James Craig 1744-1795* (Edinburgh 1995).

relatively new phenomenon when Victoria assumed the throne, for over half a century Edinburgh citizens had been accustomed to both concept and practice.[4]

In a series of moves which proved decisive for the development of north-west Edinburgh in the last quarter of the nineteenth century and indeed for twentieth-century development too, James Steel signed five feu contracts with George Heriot's Trust in fifteen months during 1876–7, and four more in another active fifteen month spell during 1880–1.[5] As important, was his contract with Alexander Learmonth in 1877, and together these west end locations launched Steel into upper-middle-class residential development at a critical moment when demand for working-class housing faltered.[6] Just as a west end address conveyed certain characteristics about the status and respectability of residents, so it did, too, for those who built them, and Steel might as well have displayed the equivalent of a 'By Appointment' insignia above his offices, such was the kudos associated with business transactions with Heriot's Trust.[7]

In various ways the west end acquisitions marked a transition in the property development process for James Steel. There were negotiations with the most powerful landowner in Edinburgh, business dealings with titled and professionally prominent individuals, a high profile site and an excursion into owner-occupied residential building to high specifications and for a social class with whom Steel had not previously been engaged. To be successful it required a flexibility in business practice. This was evident in various respects, for example, in the organic way in which financial resources were marshalled to effect site purchases and to acquire sufficient working capital. The dominant business alliances forged in the 1860s and 1870s with James Home Rigg as heritable owner and James Lindesay as solicitor and source of capital, went into decline and were replaced from the mid-1870s by liaisons with Heriot's and Learmonth as landowners, and with the Earl of Moray as the major source of private finance (see table 8.1). This was to a degree an inevitable consequence of the exhaustion of the developmental possibilities on the Rigg estate.

[4] See F. M. L. Thompson, ed., *The Rise of Suburbia* (Leicester 1982), repr. in R. J. Morris and R. Rodger, eds., *The Victorian City: A Reader in British Urban History, 1820–1914* (London 1993), 149–80; Cannadine, *Lords and Landlords*; R. Rodger, *Housing in Urban Britain 1780–1914* (Cambridge 1995), 38–43, for a summary of the process of suburbanisation.

[5] NAS GD4/152/21, George Heriot's Trust Chartularies, vol. 45, ff. 528, 562, vol. 46, ff. 24, 34, 57, 348, 478, and ECA George Heriot's Roll of Superiorities, ff. 103–6, dated 22 Mar., 18 Apr. and 2 Oct. 1876, and 19 May and 4 July 1877.

[6] NAS RS108/755.168, 16 May 1877.

[7] As a town councillor from 1872, and thus a governor of Heriot's Hospital, James Steel was probably less in awe of the Trust and not unfamiliar with the personnel and procedures.

Table 8.1 *Bonds issued on borrowing by James Steel 1866–1910*

	James Lindesay (i)	Earl of Moray (ii)	Trusts (iii)	Private (iv)	(i)+(ii) as % of (i)–(iv)
1866				1,700	0
1867			4,000	3,000	0
1868	2,000		1,300		61
1869	4,000			2,000	67
1870				7,000	0
1871				7,000	0
1873	2,500				100
1874	4,000		4,000	1,300	43
1876		5,500	3,890	10,000	28
1877	1,800				100
1878	12,000	10,000	6,410	5,000	66
1879			6,360	5,500	0
1880		5,500			100
1881	1,400	10,000	2,500		82
1882		9,000			100
1883		27,000			100
1884		4,500	13,800		25
1885		2,000		3,800	35
1888			2,000	5,600	0
1889		5,500	2,500	23,500	17
1890		1,500		5,000	23
1892			3,000	1,000	0
1893		26,000	1,200	3,700	88
1895				19,450	0
1896				2,500	0
1899	2,700	15,000	6,670		73
1900			12,000	2,000	0
1904		26,000			100
1908				16,000	0
1910		27,000			100
1866–1910	30,400	174,500	69,630	125,050	51

Source: NAS, RS27 and RS108, Register of Sasines, Edinburgh. Based on an analysis of eighty bonds issued by James Steel, 1866–1910.

However, while the principals changed, the principles of property development did not. Nor was the change in personnel abrupt; it was overlapping. From 1876 to 1881, that is, while Steel's building and property development interests were reorientated, the old guard – Rigg and Lindesay – together with the new regime – Heriot's, Learmonth and Moray – all had dealings with him, providing a measure of continuity; once, Lindesay and the Earl of Moray both loaned Steel money on the same day in 1878.[8] In a borrowing programme between 1866 and 1910 which aggregated £398,000 – approximately £22 million in 2000 prices – the importance of private contacts remained crucial with thirty-nine different individuals lending Steel sums which ranged from £300 to £27,000. However, within this group of private financiers two, James Lindesay and the Earl of Moray, accounted for 51% of all Steel's borrowing, various other private male lenders supplied 20%; the remaining 29% was obtained from trust funds (18%), and women (11%) (table 8.1). Though James Steel's opposition to raising finance from formal financial institutions remained implacable, in fact there was little need for him to look beyond the deep reservoir of private funds available in Edinburgh for fifty years before 1914, the valve to which continued to be controlled by solicitors by means of the trust funds at their disposal.

Without substantial personal funds developers were in no small measure dependent upon the goodwill of lenders. Few developers were exempt from this dependency and James Steel was no exception. His cumulative outstanding debt, that is, the overall net amount repayable, excluding interest payments and taking into account occasional loan repayments, is shown in fig. 8.1. From an average monthly debt of almost £8,500 in the late 1860s, the figure soared to £32,780 in the 1870s, and to over £110,000 in the 1880s as Steel assumed loans to undertake the building of west end properties. Interest payments alone amounted to over £3,400 on the average debt of £92,000 in the 1890s, and at this scale of operations the ability to dovetail maturing loans with new borrowing to avoid even the slightest hint of financial weakness was a critical factor in the survival of the firm, and for many suppliers and subcontractors.[9]

How influential the landowner was in determining the social tone and amenity of urban development has been shown to have varied considerably according to highly local factors, the commitment to and concentration of ownership, physical considerations affecting the estate, as well as council policies and industrialists' strategies.[10] One of the most important considerations in exploiting the built-up value of an estate was the role of developers, and the west end of Edinburgh during the last quarter of the

[8] NAS RS108/934.14, 12 Sept. 1878, over 1–3 Belgrave Place and 22–5 Belgrave Crescent.

[9] For this purpose the interest rate is assumed to be a constant or average 3.75%. I am grateful to Alex Moseley for his assistance in these calculations.

[10] See, for example, M. J. Daunton, *House and Home in the Victorian City: Working Class Housing 1850–1914* (London 1983), 74–8; R. J. Dennis, *English Industrial Cities of the Nineteenth Century: A Social Geography* (Cambridge 1984), 154–64; Cannadine, *Lords and Landlords,* 109–23; Rodger, *Housing in Urban Britain,* 13–16, for an overview of these relationships.

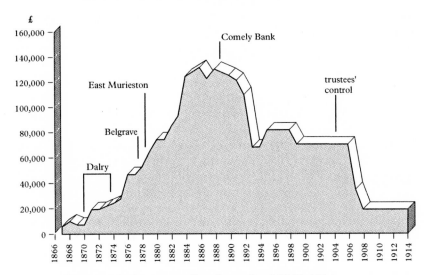

Figure 8.1 Debts outstanding: James Steel 1867–1914

Source: NAS Register of Sasines, Edinburgh. Based on an analysis of bonds issued by James Steel, 1866–1910.

nineteenth century was no exception. For over a century Heriot's had deferred the development of the Coates estate, but with the endowment of Donaldson's Hospital in 1830 to educate deaf and dumb children and its eventual construction between 1841 and 1851 on a site feued from Heriot's in 1835, their interest was awakened. William Playfair's execution of the Elizabethan style specified in the trustees' terms of reference provided magnificent views for new housing, and as the wreckage from the financial panic of 1825–6 receded and the excess supply of housing was mopped up, so new housebuilding was resumed in Edinburgh in the 1850s and early 1860s. Heriot's feuing to the south of Donaldson's Hospital for the development of Hampton, Kew and Osborne Terraces, named to resonate with Playfair's 'old English architecture', reflected that recovery, as did Magdala Crescent to the east. The Magdala properties were feued quickly between 1869 and 1871, some later to James Steel, though in view of 'the unvarying recurrence of oriels' (windows) the architectural judgement of the elevations was highly critical and described by *The Builder* 'as an utter negation of art'.[11]

For Heriot's Hospital, the development of single houses imposed considerable administrative costs. Legal searches, feu contracts, an estate

[11] *Builder*, 1876, quoted in J. Gifford, C. McWilliam and D. Walker, *The Buildings of Scotland: Edinburgh* (Harmondsworth 1988), 372.

feuing plan and frequent site inspections, not to mention the associated clerical work, imposed additional costs on Heriot's. Steel and other developers – the building firms of James S. Roberts, George Roberts and W. Smith and Son – offered administrative economies of scale by undertaking building on several stances, and by collecting and remitting the feu-duties due to Heriot's in a single sum.[12] James Steel offered a track record of sound construction and exemplary financial rectitude, something for which the building industry was not noted as readers of the bankruptcy entries in the *Edinburgh Gazette* knew all too well. Heriot's needed Steel and his like in the same way as they, the developers, needed the careful release of building land. Mutuality underpinned their relationship. So it was not surprising that, with the further development of Dalry impeded in 1878, Steel sought to diversify his operations by developing building stances obtained on Heriot's Coates estate in 1876 and 1877. These, and his acquisition of subsequent sites in 1879 and 1880, led to the construction of substantial portions of Eglinton, Glencairn and Douglas Crescents, and a few properties in Magdala Crescent and Palmerston Place. All were in the prestigious west end.

Unlike institutional landowners such as Heriot's Hospital and the Merchant Company, whose trustees generally operated with a long-term view of their responsibilities and thus a gradual release of land for building development, Alexander Learmonth was hell-bent in the 1870s on liquidating as much of the capital value of his property as possible in the shortest available time. Learmonth's father had bought the lands of Dean in 1826 from the Nisbet family and financed, largely from his own resources, the construction of the Dean Bridge, designed by Thomas Telford and completed in 1832.[13] The bridge significantly improved access to and thus the value of land on the northern side of the Water of Leith. In 1859, Alexander Learmonth inherited this and an estimated gross annual income from property in Edinburgh of almost £5,000, or £0.25 million in 2000 prices. Though born in the same year (1829) as James Steel, their lives diverged markedly until Learmonth's London lifestyle brought their financial interests to a point of congruence. With homes in Windsor and a fashionable London address in Eaton Square in the 1870s, Learmonth's clubs, ex-army social circle and his social status as MP for Colchester almost continuously from 1850 until 1880 made

[12] ECA George Heriot's Roll of Superiorities. Steel secured 25% more building stances than any other contract building firm undertaking multiple contracts, ff. 98–106.
[13] ECA ACC 373, Sir James Steel's Papers, Inventory of Writs and Title Deeds of the Lands and Barony of Dean, 1850, lists the forty-two transactions detailing the transfer of titles from Sir John Nisbett (*sic*) to John Paton, builder, 13 Oct. 1825, and by Paton to John Learmonth, 30 May 1826.

heavy demands on the property income derived from Edinburgh.[14] Indeed, to sustain his lifestyle Learmonth had borrowed heavily against the security of his Edinburgh feu-duties and rents and to refinance these loans his urgent requirement was for capital, not income. Accordingly, he embarked upon a series of land sales for cash.

So cash down was the basis of James Steel's acquisition in 1877 of the Learmonth property, already substantially developed by others, and on which he built upper income residences in streets meaningfully named Buckingham and Belgrave to conjure up elegance, sophistication and metropolitanism. Steel paid £9,750 in cash to Learmonth and in 1878, just a year later, he paid another sizeable sum, £18,000, half in cash and the remainder by repaying £9,000 of Learmonth's loans, for which he obtained the mansion house and over twenty-four acres of farmland fifteen miles west of Edinburgh at Easter Murieston, Midlothian (fig. 8.2).[15] Superficially, it seemed a radical departure, but it was consistent with Steel's search for stability and business independence because, rather than acquiring Easter Murieston for its agricultural revenue or social status, it was the mineral rights which were particularly appealing.[16] As a director of the nearby Broxburn Oil Company, Steel was aware of the prospect of shale oil revenues in the area but it was lime and stone from the quarries on the estate which were the major attraction. With a railway halt at the edge of the estate to transport stone direct to Dalry for the development of west Edinburgh, it meant James Steel was able to meet the strict terms of Learmonth's conditions in relation to building materials while not being dependent on the most prominent quarry companies scattered around Edinburgh.[17] Naming the streets formed on Rigg's Dalry feu, also acquired in 1878, as 'Murieston' was indicative of the importance of the venture to Steel's increasingly integrated building and property development interests.[18]

Between 1876 and 1878, James Steel acquired extensive sites from the Heriot Trust and Alexander Learmonth in the west end. He also acquired

[14] ECA ACC 373, Sir James Steel's Papers, Inland Revenue Succession Duty on real property, 1858, 17 Dec. 1858, f. 263. Learmonth was defeated at Colchester in 1868 and again in 1880, when he retired. He died on 10 Mar. 1887.

[15] NAS RS108/893.131, 17 May 1878. This transaction conveyed the lands of Easter Murieston in the barony of Linhouse, three-quarters of the lands of Dresselrig, Backstonford and Sandygate, in the barony of Calder, lands of Wester or North Torphin in the barony of Marjoribanks and parts of the farm and lands of Keprig.

[16] ECA ACC 373, Sir James Steel's Papers, trunk 1/1, Report and Valuation of the Estate of Murieston, 31 Oct. 1906, Articles of Roup, Murieston, 1907, Tack to Baird and Cunningham, 10 Nov. 1880, Sale of Murieston Lime to Caledonian Railway Company, 21 Oct. 1881.

[17] The feuing conditions stipulated that the Buckingham Terrace houses were to be in line with those already built, using Craigleith, White, Binne, Humbie, Grange, Glasgow or Bannockburn stone.   [18] NAS RS108/857.166, 8 Mar. 1878.

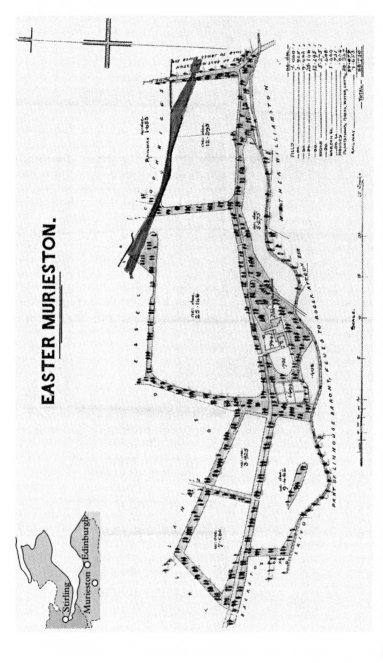

Figure 8.2 Easter Murieston, Midlothian, bought by James Steel from Sir Alexander Learmonth MP in 1878

Note: Learmonth, son of the former Edinburgh Lord Provost, John Learmonth, 1831–3, sold Murieston and his extensive Dean estate (now known as Learmonth and Comely Bank) to sustain his London lifestyle.
Source: ECA ACC 373, Sir James Steel's Papers

farms and quarries in Midlothian from Learmonth. Debts escalated. Thwarted over one Dalry purchase from James Walker, he acquired another substantial property for development in 1878, also in Dalry, from James Home Rigg. Further building stances were acquired from Heriot's in 1879–80. Indebtedness escalated yet again (fig. 8.1). That in a period of faltering housebuilding Steel could finance and renegotiate maturing loans of £50,000 to £120,000 was ample testimony to his credit rating. In the space of three critical years from 1876, Steel had acquired all the building land he required for a decade to keep a rolling programme of development underway.

Adaptation and innovation

The trademarks of James Steel's business success were evident in successive working-class tenement developments at Tollcross, Sciennes and Dalry. Strategic locations, careful evaluation of the site, its layout and feuing rates, and a mixed development with other builders, property investment companies and building associations to spread risk and distribute the burden of financial commitment amongst several parties were each key characteristics of successful building and development practice in the 1860s and 1870s. Taken together with a high priority to complete the site promptly so that financial prospects would not be blighted by an apparent reluctance from tenants, landlords and factors to let and manage properties, then the ingredients of a business strategy were well defined by the final quarter of the nineteenth century. So, to systematise building while sustaining the illusion of customised residences of some distinction and elegance was a business metamorphosis to which Steel responded positively in the west end.

In contrast to all previous developments, none of the building stances which Steel obtained from the Heriot Trust was transferred by him to another builder; he used his own extensive workforce of 190 men by 1881 to construct all of the stances. Always acute financially, Steel recognised that the interest expressed by the Heritable Estates Company in the first group of houses, built in 1876, was a useful guarantee of revenue and in the space of five years he transacted £31,000 of sales to them.[19] As a property company, the Heritable Estates Company bought houses from builders and then arranged the purchase and financing for customers – a Victorian precursor of the one-stop estate agency. It was active elsewhere in the New Town and their business dealings with James Steel provided him with an endorsement as well as an additional sales outlet. It was

[19] NAS RS108/759.181, 827.115, 1215.99, 1278.59, 1273.186.

Figure 8.3 Eglinton Crescent 1876–1877

Note: these properties were developed by James Steel on land feued from
the Heriot's Trust. The external appearance and the interior finish are
for an entirely different income group to previous Steel building projects.

Figure 8.3 Interior window detail, Eglinton Crescent

an arrangement which worked to Steel's benefit.[20] Private sales were an important source of capital for the construction of Coates Gardens and the crescented Douglas, Eglinton and Glencairn terraces on the Heriot feu. It was a system reminiscent of the method employed in English cities whereby builders used sales revenue as working capital for further houses in the terrace (fig. 8.3).

Whatever the competing attractions of the rural idyll in the southern suburbs of Edinburgh, for some the appeal of a town house address remained intact into the final quarter of the nineteenth century. Amongst Steel's purchasers it was those engaged in the law and other professions (42%) and women (17%) for whom the appeal was strongest, with the managerial classes (7%), industrialists (5%) and a scattering of army officers and merchants less susceptible to the allure of a west end property. The average selling price of the Coates houses was almost £3,200 and these substantial three-storey residences, with their basement and

---

[20] See, for example, NAS RS108/1215.99, 1278.59 and 1273.186 which provide details of the sale and mortgage finance from the Heritable Estates Company covering the properties of 15–18 and 20 Glencairn Crescent, 17 May 1880, 11 Nov. 1880 and 17 May 1881.

(a)

Figure 8.4 a and b Buckingham Terrace (begun 1860) and Belgrave Crescent (begun 1874) were both completed by James Steel in 1876–7, as was Belgrave Place

attic flats, offered ample accommodation for family and servants and, judging by the social and occupational profile of buyers, were beyond all but the wealthiest segments of the middle class.

In another characteristic of social exclusivity reminiscent of London parks, residents on the Coates estate overlooked and had access to gated gardens encircled by wrought-iron railings, though even this amenity paled when compared to the elegant 'pleasure gardens' across the steep valley of the Water of Leith to which residents of the Belgrave development had access.[21] These extensive wooded acres bordered the Water of Leith and provided an open prospect to the substantial properties of Belgrave Crescent and to which James Steel added by completing the terrace of houses on part of the Nisbet land acquired from Alexander Learmonth (fig. 8.4). By virtue of this feu contract, the trustees, 'elected from time to time' for the management of the Belgrave Pleasure Gardens, considered the admission of Steel to their exclusive use of the pleasure gardens. The committee agreed that on payment of £600 and £250 respectively, Steel and Andrew Pattison, an advocate for whom Steel had built one of the Belgrave properties, were entitled 'to the use and enjoyment' of the pleasure gardens 'either by themselves or their tenants with

---

[21] P. J. Atkins, 'Elite residence in nineteenth century London', paper to the Urban History Group, Edinburgh, Apr. 1995.

(b)

Figure 8.4 Belgrave Crescent

their respective families, but not both'.[22] A tight concept of amenity, buttressed by the committee's concern to restrict anything 'which will be an eyesore or be seen from any of the houses' and a stated objective that 'it shall not be lawful ... to erect buildings' was the basis on which the management committee controlled admission to the gardens and administered byelaws.[23]

The enforcement of feu charters through an *ad hoc* committee of residents – the phrase 'elected from time to time' appears unjustified – enabled the residents to protect the amenity and social tone of the neighbourhood, as did the initial feuing plan which laid out the streets in such a way as to prevent through traffic. No less important was the protective physical barrier afforded by the ravine through which the Water of Leith passed. Crucially, too, there was a wedge of institutional land use developed earlier on both sides of the ravine – John Watson's Institution (1822–5), Orphan Hospital (1831–3), Donaldson's Hospital (1841–51), Daniel Stewart's College (1845–8), as well as a cemetery (1845, extended 1871) – which offered a solid defence against changes of land use, thereby protecting the western approaches of the high quality properties built by James Steel and others on the former Coates and Nisbet estates (fig. 8.5a).[24]

For such amenity, a high premium was payable. For those Belgrave Crescent properties directly overlooking the pleasure grounds the price was over £5,000; the average for houses built by Steel on the lands acquired from Learmonth was almost £4,000 – double the price of an entire Dalry tenement of eight, twelve or sixteen flats.[25] To unlock a sizeable amount of capital with such a sale, Steel was prepared to be flexible in his business practice. This was the case when the sale of a house in Buckingham Terrace was agreed in the autumn of 1886 with entry at Whitsunday 1887, yet Steel allowed the buyer to obtain the keys six months early 'in order that you may get the papering and painting done and the house made ready for occupation'.[26] Given that the sale was assured and could not under Scots property law be revoked, Steel's agreement to permit tradesmen 'employed by you' (the buyer) to view the

22 ECA ACC 373, Sir James Steel's Papers, Declaration by the Trustees of Belgrave Pleasure Gardens, 14 May 1880, ff. 8–9.
23 ECA ACC 373, Sir James Steel's Papers, Declaration, f. 11.
24 Even though Steel sub-feued stances at Bells Mills, Belford Terrace and Dean Path Mews Lane, this was mostly for stables and some light industrial uses, and as part of the industrial mills and workshops in the valley of the Water of Leith did not constitute a new infringement on the amenity of the cliff-top residents. See NAS RS108/1238.1, 1687.79, 2259.32, 2469.112, 2712.183, 3649.139, 3670.111, 5301.182.
25 This was the average price for houses in Buckingham Terrace and Belgrave Place built by James Steel.
26 ECA ACC 373, Sir James Steel's Papers, letter from Steel's to Robertson, 26 Oct. 1886.

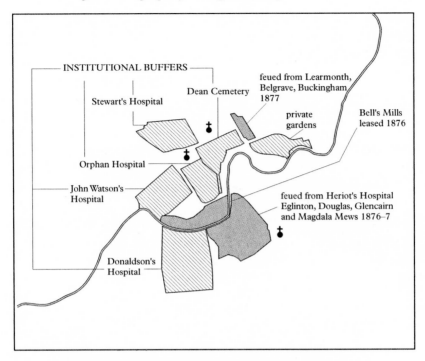

Figure 8.5a West end development: James Steel's property and
institutional landownership

Notes: foundation dates: John Watson's Hospital 1825; Orphan
Hospital 1831; Donaldson's Hospital 1841; Stewart's Hospital 1848;
Dean Parish Church 1835; Bristo Baptist Church 1836; Dean
Cemetery 1845; St Mary's Episcopal Cathedral 1874.

property and 'any deficiency reported to be put in order by me' demonstrated outstanding customer relations.[27]

In many cases private sales were concluded with a cash payment. This
certainly applied to the prestigious Belgrave Crescent houses (fig. 8.4b)
where private incomes were presumably such that recourse to borrowing
was unnecessary, or socially stigmatising. Elsewhere, with average prices
ranging from £3,140 in Glencairn Terrace to £5,480 in Eglinton Terrace,
it was necessary for just over half the buyers (55%) to arrange a loan in
order to complete their purchase, and almost two-thirds of these were
obtained through solicitors either from trust funds or as part of a marriage

---

[27] ECA ACC 373, Sir James Steel's Papers, letter from Robertson to Steel, 26 Oct. 1886,
requested further concessions and elicited a polite, prompt and positive response in a
second letter, Steel to Robertson, 26 Oct. 1886.

Figure 8.5b James Steel's Caledonian and Coates developments

Note: two contrasting phases of housing development can be seen: James Steel's Caledonian feu, 1869 (bottom) and his Coates development at Douglas, Eglinton and Glencairn Crescents, 1876 (top) were separated by the North British Railway line, Caledonian Distillery and Glasgow Road (centre).
Source: RCAHMS C10069 (560213) Haymarket.

contract.[28] Though, understandably, there was a certain amount of variation between individuals and indeed according to streets, on average middle-class buyers put down 27% of the purchase price in cash and took out a mortgage for 73% of the house price.[29] With lawyers so heavily represented amongst the new owner occupiers (27%), it would have been

[28] The figure was actually 62%, and is based upon an analysis of Register of Sasines transactions for properties in the streets concerned.   [29] The range was 68–77%.

surprising if solicitors had not been active in the arrangement of loans, but the 1870s and 1880s probably represented a high-water mark in their control of the mortgage market before building societies and property companies began to make inroads into it during the more active years of house purchase during the 1890s and early 1900s.

Against a background which between 1875 and 1887 not uncommonly described the state of the building industry as 'unsettled' and used various euphemistic phrases to convey despair – 'the building trade has not been in a very prosperous condition' – then a shift of emphasis towards middle-class housing demand made sound business sense.[30] As in portfolios of other assets, hedging risks by switching into gilts or other secure assets when the market proved edgy was a proven tactic, and in this respect the development of the Heriot's Coates estate and the Buckingham and Belgrave properties was James Steel's equivalent. Insulated from the worst vagaries of the trade cycle and numerically powerful in Scotland's capital city, the middle class split their allegiance in the 1880s between suburban estates and town houses and, either way, offered a haven for builders in difficult market circumstances.[31]

The integration of building and housing management

An almost uncanny ability to sense structural shifts in housing sub-markets formed one element in James Steel's successful business strategy. Even the timing of the resumption of building at Dalry (Murieston) in 1887 anticipated changes in the general level of housebuilding by three or so years. By the time the tenements built by Steel himself, his nephews and other sub-feuars had been completed, they were well placed to rent to those tenants most eager and able to afford new flats, and for landlords anxious to avoid the scourge of unlet flats, the attractions of acquiring reputable tenants likely to pay promptly was a considerable attraction.[32]

However, the availability of suitable building sites was limited and this curtailed Steel's activities, just as it did for other developers, including the Edinburgh Co-operative Building Company.[33] Both types of builders, however, also recognised the folly of acquiring land prematurely since even a reduced feu-duty was payable immediately, and on which a number of houses had to built within a stated period under the terms of the feu contract. Excessive land acquisitions, though advantageous in the

[30] NAS GD327/489, Papers of C. Norman Kemp, Annual Reports, 1875–89.
[31] See chapter 1 for details of occupations and social classes.
[32] N. J. Morgan and M. J. Daunton, 'Landlords in Glasgow: a study of 1900', *Business History*, 25, 1983, 264–81; R. Rodger, 'The Victorian building industry and the housing of the Scottish working class', in M. Doughty, ed., *Building the Industrial City* (Leicester 1986), 151–206.   [33] See chapter 11.

upswing phase of development, threatened the continued existence of a builder in recession. The line between sensible anticipation and unwarranted speculation was finely drawn. So given the dwindling activity on the west end estates, and the limited extent of the property remaining in the industrial suburb of Dalry, Alexander Learmonth's bankruptcy in 1886 was timely as far as James Steel's business interests were concerned. It meant that the trustees were obliged to dispose of Learmonth's assets, and since the sizeable and neighbouring tract of land at Comely Bank remained, Steel recognised the opportunity which its acquisition represented. For the Learmonth trustees, previous contact with Steel, his ability to complete a transaction, to pay in cash and to assume responsibility for the repayment of debts incurred by Learmonth in part payment, were powerful commendations and enabled them to resolve several aspects of their duties simultaneously. Apart from the farmland in Midlothian at Easter Murieston, before the Comely Bank purchase Steel's largest land acquisitions for building purposes had been between eight and sixteen acres.[34] In 1889 he acquired almost fifty acres and paid £40,000 for them, approximately £2.3 million in 2000 prices, equally split between cash and the repayment of a bond given by Learmonth to his creditors.[35] Steel raised about one sixth of the purchase price by borrowing from the Earl of Moray, but was forced by the sheer scale of the sums involved to step outside his normal sources of capital by obtaining exactly 50% from Andrew Montague, introduced to Steel as part of the package to transfer the Learmonth lands.

Since there was no feu-duty obligation and thus no pressure from the superior to build houses by a specified date, Steel was at liberty to develop the site in a manner and at a pace determined by himself. It was the ultimate objective of builders. Although the west end developments were completed without off-loading any stances to other builders, the Heriot Trust remained the principal developer there and Steel's role was circumscribed accordingly. Even in Edinburgh's Belgravia, his freedom to develop the site was restricted by Learmonth's original feuing plan for Buckingham Terrace; writs were issued when Steel's architect sought to depart from the plans and elevations of the superior.[36] The Comely Bank site, however, enabled Steel for the only time in his career to pursue his own mature and independent development of an area which by 1914

---

[34] NAS RS27/2678.188 (Bonnington), 18.186 (Dalry/Caledonian), 476.141 (Dalry/Springwell), 857.166 (Dalry/Murieston).

[35] NAS RS108/2158.40, 15 May 1889. The transaction was in the name of one of the trustees, William Hardinge, and the bond due to Andrew Montague.

[36] Gifford, McWilliam and Walker, *The Buildings of Scotland*, 398. The architect was Alexander McNaughton.

extended to fifteen streets, and accommodated 840 households. The principal constraints remained financial – there was a substantial outlay for the acquisition of the site but also significant amounts of working capital were required to develop it (table 8.1). Accordingly, James Steel issued bonds aggregating £200,000 (£11.8 million in 2000 prices) between 1889 and 1910 for these purposes, with exactly 50% borrowed from the Earl of Moray. Overall 87% of Steel's borrowing was from private contacts and 13% from trusts, and so long as Steel met the maturity dates, his sphere of operations remained relatively unconstrained.

A further degree of independence was obtained through the negotiation of a lease to Barrasford Quarries concluded with the Duke of Northumberland on Christmas Eve 1887 (fig. 8.6).[37] The agreement was for nineteen years and with his partners in the venture, William Turner and Sons, the removal of whinstone and basalt meant that the quarry firm of Steel and Turner was subject to a mineral royalty of 6.5d (2.7p) per ton in addition to the rental, with a number of restrictive clauses requiring them to repair environmental damage caused by the extraction of stone. For a city built on rock this Edinburgh variant of 'coals to Newcastle' was not entirely novel as Northumbrian quarries were plundered for Edinburgh buildings in the Victorian version of a border raid.[38] However, with the lease from the Duke of Northumberland, Steel and Turner moved deeper into the North Tyne valley to obtain their supplies, freighted on the Hexham branch of the North British Railway via Newcastle to Edinburgh.[39] Steel's Dalry building yard at Maxwell Street, close to the N.B. Railway Company's Haymarket 'mineral yards', proved a very astute business decision, minimising the amount of trans-shipment and thus the labour costs for this most bulky of products. At the English quarries, too, the designation of a branch line specifically for the Barrasford Quarries, together with a halt to give access to the North Tyne Railway and a main line connection through Newcastle, assisted the transport of building materials to Edinburgh. So the construction of the Comely Bank area owed much to its English influences, both in the Tyne valley for its stone and in London, where Alexander Learmonth's conspicuous consumption drove him into bankruptcy and thus into the financial arms of James Steel.[40]

---

[37] ECA ACC 373, Sir James Steel's Papers, trunk 1/1, Lease of Quarries at Barrasford, Northumberland, 24 Dec. 1877.

[38] Gifford, McWilliam and Walker, *The Buildings of Scotland*, 24.

[39] Northumberland County Record Office, NCRO 493/17, Papers of John Richardson, lime merchant, Alnwick, drawings etc. of sidings at Gunnerton. I am grateful to NCRO staff for their assistance in locating this material.

[40] Information supplied by Colin Shrimpton, Duke of Northumberland's Estate Office, Alnwick Castle.

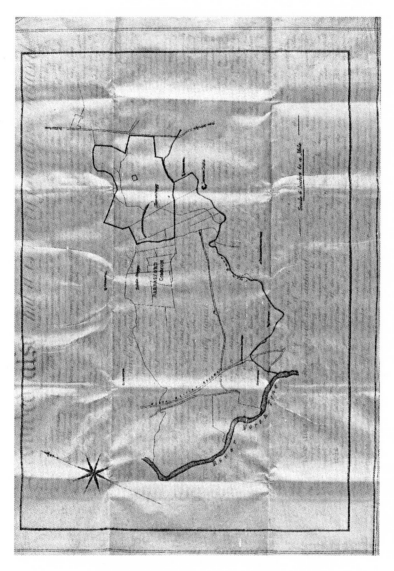

Figure 8.6 Barrasford Quarries near Corbridge, Northumberland, leased by James Steel from the Duke of Northumberland 24 December 1887

Source: ECA ACC 373, Sir James Steel's Papers.

The Comely Bank purchase was the last feu contract entered into by James Steel for the purpose of site acquisition and in certain respects it represented a fitting coping stone to a business career which, after apprenticeship, spanned the roles of jobbing building, builder and developer, quarrymaster and landlord in the second half of the nineteenth century. At its nearest point, the fifty acre Comely Bank site was only half a mile from the west end of Princes Street and Steel's Torphichen Street headquarters. On the opposite side of the trapezoid-shaped site it was about the same distance from the cluster of workshops and industrial premises at Canonmills and Silvermills which provided employment to some of the ECBC residents in the Stockbridge 'Colonies' (fig. 8.7). Not only was there a social polarity on which Steel could base housing development in the Comely Bank area, there was a robust defensive buffer of institutional land to the north and west – the playing fields of the Edinburgh Academy, both Fettes' and Daniel Stewart's Colleges, the Royal Victoria Hospital, the self-styled Scottish equivalent of the MCC, Grange Cricket Club and the extensive property of Inverleith Park, the acquisition of which in 1889 the city council was negotiating at the same time as Steel was finalising the deal with Learmonth's trustees.[41] What development there was in the area was supervised on the Fettes estate and Rocheid's Inverleith properties by a nationally recognised architect, Rowand Anderson, adding thereby further to the social cachet of the area.

Though the Comely Bank–Learmonth estate sloped steeply and presented some challenges in terms of construction, even this had a developmental silver lining, since the higher elevations were nearest to the Belgravia of Edinburgh and offered truly stunning views towards the distant Firth of Forth with the 'Scottish baronial-French gothic masterpiece' of Fettes' College in the foreground (fig. 8.8). At the foot of the incline and closest to the areas of artisanal employment was a gentle gradient conducive to a frequent tram service proposed in various unsuccessful bills in the 1880s and operational from 1888, with a spur to Stockbridge and Comely Bank in 1889.[42]

Perhaps predictably, the initial development of the Comely Bank estate utilised the level stances in closest proximity to the existing built-up area

[41] *PP 1874 LXXII pt III*, Owners of Lands and Heritages, 1872–3, 66–9, shows that Charles Rocheid of Inverleith and Sir William Fettes' trustees were the fifth and sixth largest landowners in Edinburgh in 1873 with respectively ninety-six acres and ninety-two acres, concentrated in the area to the north of Comely Bank.

[42] Gifford, McWilliam and Walker, *The Buildings of Scotland*, 573; D. L. G. Hunter, *Edinburgh's Transport: The Early Years* (Edinburgh 1992 edn), 78.

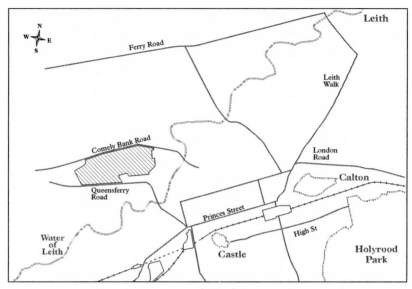

Figure 8.7 (a) James Steel's final building phase: Comely Bank and Learmonth

and along which the transport artery was planned. It was one of the benefits of late nineteenth-century cities generally that their limited geographical extent meant that the acute angles between the radiating spokes of the road network were such that new housing was never more than a few minutes walk in either direction from a major thoroughfare and, from the 1870s, a tram stop.[43] This adhesive housing strategy, that is, of appending new housing to the existing built-up area, conveyed the impression of permanence by enabling new residents to benefit immediately from established shops, services and community facilities. It was a feature which also offered inclusiveness, with ready-made institutions and associations structured around churches and cultural organisations. Though the additions to the housing stock were eventually considerable, they were not sudden. In this respect, and in the availability of a mature social infrastructure lodged in the confined spaces between radiating roads, Victorian Edinburgh avoided the social homogenisation and undifferentiated physical development which characterised the interwar

[43] For a useful survey of Edinburgh tramway development see A. D. Ochojna, 'Lines of class distinction: an economic and social history of the British tramcar with special reference to Edinburgh and Glasgow', University of Edinburgh PhD thesis, 1974.

Figure 8.7 (b) James Steel's final building phase; Comely Bank and Learmonth (centre)

Source: Aerofilms.

years both in municipal housing and in private bungalow developments.[44] To the builder and developer, what was crucial was that overheads such as roads and sewers were often already shouldered by the municipality and that there was little, if any, need to assign valuable portions of real estate to churches and parks in order to establish residential interest in the area.[45]

---

[44] R. Rodger, 'Scottish housing and English cultural imperialism *c.*1880–1940', in S. Zimmermann, ed., *Urban Space and Identity in the European City 1890–1930s* (Budapest 1995), 73–94.

[45] R. J. Morris, 'Externalities, the market, power structures and the urban agenda', *Urban History Yearbook*, 17, 1990, 99–109.

It was impossible, because of the scale of working capital required, and undesirable, because of the consequential oversupply in the housing market, to develop the entire fifty acre site simultaneously. Two-thirds of the acreage purchased from Learmonth remained undeveloped in 1914 and building on the eastern third was carefully phased with most streets completed over several years. One of the first to be developed, Dean Park Street, was begun in 1889 but continued to be under construction for twelve years (table 8.2). But whereas there were gaps in the building line as the development of Dean Park Street proceeded, contiguous plots were built on one side of the main thoroughfare, Comely Bank Road, although they, too, took twelve years of sporadic building to complete this much longer street (fig. 8.9). In the third of the initial street developments, Comely Bank Place, yet another sequence of building development took place as construction swept quickly up one side with all odd tenement numbers 1–49 completed between 1891 and 1895, and then down the other side with the even numbers built in a more concentrated spell between 1895 and 1897.

A fourth variant was employed in Comely Bank Avenue where Steel started building from both ends, though only on one side of the street, meeting in the middle a year and ninety-six tenements later. It was an inspired developmental strategy, latching on at its northern boundary to the proximity of west end addresses and leeching the social tone associated with them into the adjacent streets of the Comely Bank development. James Steel recognised that the illusion of exclusivity was an externality of some value to the entire estate development strategy, and reinforced and indeed protected it by constructing a hierarchy of housing quality on his Comely Bank development which was calibrated according to rental or sale price, with highest value and amenity closest to the authentic west end addresses fronting Queensferry Road. With Comely Bank Avenue (fig. 8.10) suggestively providing a connection to the west end, and a central spine for the entire estate, neighbouring streets reaped the benefit too, so that eventually those areas furthest from the west end provided the locus of twelve and sixteen flatted tenement blocks. A few short cross streets meant that a natural break was introduced into the longer spinal streets of Comely Bank Avenue and Street, so that discontinuities in the social tone were not too pronounced.

The graduated nature of the development was taken to further levels of sophistication by a varied yet flexible street plan for the Comely Bank estate. Most Scottish urban development offset high site values by developing street frontages exclusively with tenements, so that, stockade-like, buildings entirely enclosed a back green. Such a rectilineal pattern was central to the eighteenth-century concept of the New Town and was

Table 8.2 *Building sequence and occupancy: Dean Park Street*

Street number	First inhabited	Order built (rank)	Street number	First inhabited	Order built (rank)
1	1904	17	2	1892	4
3	1904	17	4	1891	1
5	1903	15	6	1895	8
7	1904	17	8	1897	9
9	1903	15	10	1897	9
11	1892	4	12	1897	9
13	1892	4	14	1899	12
15	1891	1	16	1899	12
17	1891	1	18	1902	14
19	1892	4			

Sources: NAS R100, Valuation Rolls, Edinburgh, and RS108, Register of Sasines (twenty-one specific references).

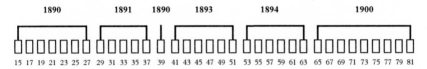

1890   1891   1890   1893   1894   1900

15 17 19 21 23 25 27 29 31 33 35 37 39 41 43 45 47 49 51 53 55 57 59 61 63 65 67 69 71 73 75 77 79 81

Figure 8.8 Building by numbers 1890–1900: the sequence of development in Comely Bank Road

replicated by nineteenth-century developers. Indeed, in constrained spaces in Dalry, James Steel had adopted a series of quadrilaterals as the layout which most efficiently optimised the available building site, as did architects in the thirty years before 1914 on the Warrender and Heriot estates on which so many tenements were built in the Marchmont and Easter Road areas. At Comely Bank, however, Steel adopted a more porous plan in which streets ran off at right angles from one another; the conventional or 'stockade' model was virtually abandoned. To a considerable extent, the spinal characteristic of Comely Bank Avenue predetermined the plan since its quarter of a mile length made a conventional layout impracticable. In effect, then, and once the spine was in place, James Steel used his experience to lay out a series of stepped, parallel terraces which avoided the considerable construction problems posed by the steep gradient.[46] Moreover, rather than being faced with an identical

---

[46] The first two following the development of Comely Bank Avenue were Comely Bank Terrace and Learmonth Gardens, and later ones were Comely Bank Grove and South Learmonth Gardens.

Figure 8.9 Comely Bank Avenue (1893–1895) looking north to Fettes' College (1863)

Note: William Fettes' trustees accumulated substantial revenues from farms at Wamphry and Arnsheen in Ayrshire and Redcastle on the Beauly Firth.

Figure 8.10 Comely Bank Avenue: the spine of James Steel's final housing development

Note: begun in 1893 James Steel built ninety-six tenements in eighteen months, beginning from either end of the Avenue.

tenement opposite residents preferred vistas and so streets offset at right angles from Comely Bank Avenue provided a larger proportion of these than a conventional block layout.[47] Even where more basic tenement accommodation was provided it, too, abandoned the stockade principles and was built in straight lines with more varied street patterns than normally associated with this stratum of the housing market.

The effect of a more open plan was reinforced by the formation of a bowling green at the heart of the development.[48] The Dean Bowling Club, founded in 1900, obtained a ten year lease at a nominal 1d annual rent and formalised a previous undertaking to local residents. The official rules of the club made membership available to Steel's feuars or tenants, and also those of the Dean Building Company.[49] James Steel agreed to pay the wages of the groundsman for a few months, and no doubt in an acknowledgement of the windswept nature of the bowling green which was then on the unsheltered frontier of the built-up area, also agreed that the club would be entitled 'to plant a privet hedge around the bowling green'.[50] In a gesture mixed with gratitude and deference the members recognised Steel's patronage and appointed him as Honorary President, a role which he regarded as not purely ornamental. Certainly, the terms on which they secured the lease were far more favourable than those of another club, the Summerside Bowling Club, from whom Steel had obtained a rental of £20 annually between 1870 and 1899 when they bought the land from him.[51] It is clear that Steel's initial conception of the layout of the estate did not embrace a bowling green and it is arguable that the bowlers' initiative itself did much to crystallise the open nature of the Comely Bank and Learmonth areas. The area which eventually became a bowling green was, between 1890 and 1900, the local building yard for the Comely Bank and Learmonth development, but it was local residents who recognised its recreational potential since a subterranean stream rendered sound building foundations impracticable.[52] While

[47] See, for example, MC, Drumdryan Chartulary, ff. 81–9, 100–1, 26 Dec. 1861 and 12 Sept. 1860.
[48] ECA ACC 373, Papers of Sir James Steel, Box 1/1, letter from J. C. Cantley, secretary, to James Steel, 4 Aug. 1900.   [49] ECA ACC 373, Rules of the Dean Bowling Club, 3.
[50] ECA ACC 373, letter from Cantley to Steel, 4 Aug. 1900.
[51] NAS VR 55/12–69, Valuation Rolls, Leith, 1869–1900, The Summerside Bowling Club also inherited a dispute over the title of the property. See ECA ACC 373, Description of Summerside Bowling Club from Notarial Instrument in favour of the Trustees of the late Sir James Steel, 7 June 1905; Minute of Lease between James Steel and Members of the Summerside Bowling Club, 17 Feb. 1889.
[52] I am grateful to George Baxter and Rory MacLeod of the Dean Bowling Club, and to other members, for their co-operation in providing this information. Amongst the pre-1914 presidents, clerks were the most common occupational category.

James Steel's acquiescence was critical to the success of the Dean Bowling Club's proposal, intuitively he saw the long-run benefit of the proposal put forward by the Bowling Club in terms of the community focus, general amenity and open aspects for the Comely Bank estate in relation to the enhanced value of his own property, and reinforced this by linking the lease to the Bowling Club with the provision of tennis courts, a clear signal of the intended social aspirations of the neighbourhood.

In no sense could it be argued that James Steel came under the influence of garden suburb ideals as proposed by Raymond Unwin and James Nettlefold for English cities, nor is there any indication of the integrated vision of urban life as embraced by Edinburgh's own town planning visionary, Patrick Geddes.[53] The form and function of the housing development at Comely Bank owed less to idealism and more to pragmatism, and Steel recognised increasingly that a modest departure from conventional arrangements would not only be tolerated by residents but was positively sought. The off-set street junctions, stepped terraces, open vistas and a high proportion of main door flats which in their self-contained entrances and small front gardens offered a degree of privacy and individualism not normally available in tenements, each contributed an amendment to the conventional Scottish urban street plan.

The emergence of a property owning democracy

Considerable scholarly attention has been focused on the electoral pledge by Lloyd George in the campaign of 1919 of 'Homes for Heroes', and the role which this promise played in counteracting social unrest associated with both the police and miners' strikes that year.[54] In the west of Scotland, civil unrest during wartime was orchestrated by socialists, many of them women, in a vigorous campaign to resist rent increases and wartime profiteering.[55] Judged by the subsequent responses to council housebuilding programmes on either side of the border in the years

[53] For further explanation of this aspect of English housing development see G. Cherry, *Cities and Plans: The Shaping of Urban Britain in the Nineteenth and Twentieth Century* (London 1988), 64–9, 74–7; M. Miller, *Raymond Unwin: Garden Cities and Town Planning* (Leicester 1992), and for an account of the wide-ranging contribution of Patrick Geddes, see H. E. Meller, *Patrick Geddes: Social Evolutionist and City Planner* (London 1990), 56–79.

[54] M. Bowley, *Housing and the State* (London 1945); M. J. Daunton, ed., *Councillors and Tenants: Local Authority Housing in English Cities 1919–1939* (Leicester 1984); M. Swenarton, *Homes Fit for Heroes: The Politics and Architecture of Early State Housing in Britain* (London 1981), 67–87.

[55] J. Melling, *Rent Strikes: Peoples' Struggles for Housing in West Scotland 1890–1916* (Edinburgh 1983); S. Damer, *From Moore Park to 'Wine Alley': The Rise and Fall of a Glasgow Housing Scheme* (Edinburgh 1989).

1919–39, divergent attitudes to public housing developed. In England the private:public split in new housebuilding was 80:20; in Scotland, it was 20:80.[56] Though there were English boroughs where ambitious council housing programmes were attempted, overall it was a reluctant, even resistant English response which contrasted with a more enthusiastic Scottish embrace.

Why such a philosophical divide developed in the interwar years is problematical. One set of approaches has been to analyse the planning antecedents and ideologies of philanthropic, model and institutional housing which can be shown to have a clear lineage from the 1840s.[57] Public intervention in the property market has been viewed as a logical, necessary and even inevitable extension of Victorian slum clearances and sanitary policy.[58] Such intervention ranged from site clearances in 1866–7 under both the Glasgow and Edinburgh Improvement Trusts, to publicly funded council houses (St Martin's Cottages, 1869) in Liverpool, and purpose built tenement-like block dwellings by the newly created London County Council in the 1890s, some of which generated highly vocal disapproval.

However, there is also a line of argument which rejects the inevitability of council housebuilding programmes, and points to the emergence of garden suburbs and the resurrection of Henry George's 'single tax' under Lloyd George's land tax proposals of 1910 as Liberal Party alternatives in the quest to deliver an urban environment and improved housing in the twentieth century without resorting to subsidies from the public purse.[59]

[56] R. Rodger, ed., *Scottish Housing in the Twentieth Century* (Leicester 1989), 185, 236–7: N. J. Morgan, "'£8 cottages for Glasgow citizens": innovations in municipal housebuilding in Glasgow in the inter war years', in Rodger, ed., *Scottish Housing*, 125–54.

[57] A. Sutcliffe, *Towards the Planned City: Germany, Britain, the United States and France, 1780–1914* (London 1981), 47–87; J. N. Tarn, *Five Per Cent Philanthropy: An Account of Housing in Urban Areas between 1840 and 1914* (Cambridge 1973); R. J. Dennis, 'The geography of Victorian values: philanthropic housing in London', *Journal of Historical Geography*, 15, 1989, 40–54.

[58] J. Melling, ed., *Housing, Social Policy and the State* (London 1980); C. G. Pooley, 'Housing for the poorest poor: slum clearance and rehousing in Liverpool 1890–1918', *Journal of Historical Geography*, 11, 1985, 70–88; J. A. Yelling, *Slums and Slum Clearance in Victorian London* (London 1986); R. V. Steffel, 'The Boundary Street estate: an example of urban redevelopment by the London County Council 1889–1914', *Town Planning Review*, 47, 1976, 161–73; S. Beattie, *A Revolution in London Housing: LCC Housing Architects and their Work 1893–1914* (London 1980); C. M. Allan, 'The genesis of British urban redevelopment with reference to Glasgow', *Economic History Review*, 18, 1965, 598–613; P. J. Smith, 'The housing-relocation issue in an early slum clearance scheme: Edinburgh 1865–1885', *Urban Studies*, 26, 1989, 100–14.

[59] U. Vogel, 'The land question: a Liberal theory of communal property', *History Workshop Journal*, 27, 1989, 106–35; A. Offer, *Property and Politics, 1870–1914: Landownership, Law, Ideology and Urban Development in England* (Cambridge 1981), 283–313, 384–406; M. J. Daunton, *A Property Owning Democracy? Housing in Britain* (London 1987), 40–69.

To some extent the development of Comely Bank provides a measure of support for this interpretation by virtue of an emerging class of owner occupiers able and willing at the close of the nineteenth century to finance their own accommodation rather than rely as earlier on the initiative of landlords.

From the 1890s the appeal of home ownership, the means to afford it and the mechanisms to enable owner occupiers to make regular payments were available, and the result was that many entered into property ownership for the first time. Three-quarters of all James Steel's house sales between 1868 and 1910 were concentrated in the two decades after 1890 and were for the purchase of flats in the Comely Bank, Dean and Learmonth development (fig. 8.11). Between 1890 and 1914 and exactly coinciding with the first completions on the Comely Bank site, fluctuations between new housebuilding and house sales were closely synchronised, unlike the preceding decade when house sales in the crescented Belgrave, Douglas, Eglinton and Glencairn properties purchased by the legal profession and those with private incomes were virtually independent of the trade cycle. In general, from 1890, the turning points in house sales anticipated those in the housebuilding series, confirming the broadly accepted pattern that builders were obliged to complete properties already begun and were also less than sensitive to subtle changes in the demand for new housing than were landlords and private purchasers.[60]

When the sources of mortgage funding are examined, the structural shift in the housing market on either side of 1890 is more apparent (table 8.3). Thus before 1890, individuals relied heavily on private contacts to obtain loans to fund property purchases, with the role of the solicitor marshalling trust funds as a reservoir of mortgage capital on which individuals could call. Over 90% of house purchases were financed in this way, with women advancing almost a quarter of all such loans. The rump of the lending was undertaken by banks, insurance offices and a few specialist property societies prepared to lend on the security of the house itself.

It was an underdeveloped mortgage market, then, until the last decade of the nineteenth century when a number of building societies were formed, but by 1914 the division of mortgage lending was equally distributed in thirds between trust, private and broadly defined building society funds. In this respect, the undoubted success of the Edinburgh

---

[60] A. K. Cairncross, 'The Glasgow building industry 1860–1914', *Review of Economic Studies*, 2, 1934; and A. K. Cairncross, *Home and Foreign Investment 1870–1913: Studies in Capital Accumulation* (Cambridge 1953).

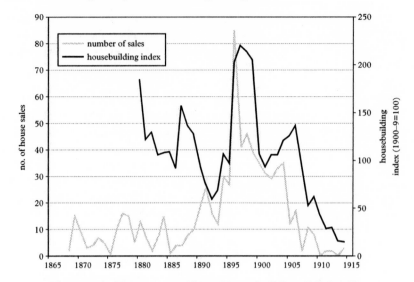

Figure 8.11 House ownership and housebuilding: Edinburgh
1868–1914

Source: ECA Dean of Guild Court Registers, 1880–1914; see
R. Rodger, 'Speculative builders and the structure of the Scottish
building industry 1860–1914', *Business History*, 21, 1979, 226–46.

Co-operative Building Company's 'Instalment Plan' had demonstrated
that weekly payments brought house purchase within the grasp of a
much wider band of incomes. By avoiding substantial lump sum payments which were characteristic of the twice-a-year interest payments
due on bonds raised through solicitors, the greater frequency of payments represented a form of forced saving which those in reasonably
continuous work could afford.[61] This co-operative or mutual influence
was evident amongst the sources of capital accessed by purchasers to
pay for flats built by James Steel; the St Cuthbert's Co-operative
Association and the People's Bank themselves provided almost 30% of
the money borrowed for this purpose (table 8.4). It revealed a developing level of sophistication in the local capital market, and refines earlier
accounts which have attributed an unchanging role in property finance
to the role of lawyers.[62]

[61] See chapter 11.
[62] M. Simpson, 'Glasgow', in M. Simpson and T. H. Lloyd, eds., *Middle Class Housing in
Britain* (Newton Abbot 1977), 59; D. McCrone and B. Elliot, *Property and Power in a
City: The Sociological Significance of Landlordism* (London 1989), 55–6.

Table 8.3 *Sources of mortgage finance: Edinburgh 1868–1914*

	1868–89 (N = 87) %	1890–1914 (N = 317) %
Trusts	41.4	30.3
Private	49.4	37.5
(Women)	(23.0)	(16.1)
Building societies[a]	4.6	25.9
Institutions (banks, life assurance)	4.6	6.3

[a] Includes friendly societies.

Source: based on NAS RS27 and RS108, Register of Sasines transactions for James Steel.

Table 8.4 *Principal building, co-operative and friendly societies: Comely Bank, Edinburgh, 1890–1910*

Name of society (N = 93)	% of lending
St Cuthbert's Co-operative	17.2
Stockbridge Mutual BS	12.9
People's Bank	8.6
Fourth Edinburgh Property Investment BS	8.6
Permanent Scottish Union BS	7.5
New Scottish Friendly Property Investment Society	7.5
Edinburgh Mutual Investment BS	6.5
Amicable Property Investment BS	3.2
Scottish Order of Oddfellows	3.2
Old Edinburgh Property Investment BS	3.2
St Bernard's Friendly Society	2.2
Edinburgh Conservative Friendly BS	2.2

Source: based on NAS RS27 and RS108, Register of Sasines, transactions for James Steel.

Of greater significance, however, was the fact that the building society group of lenders were prepared in nine cases out of ten to lend 100% of the purchase price and, on average, borrowers secured 95% of the purchase price from the societies (table 8.5). This distinguished them from private and trust lending where the amount advanced represented only two-thirds of the purchase price and so borrowers were under pressure to put down a more substantial deposit themselves. To owner occupiers this

Table 8.5 *The structure of mortgage finance: north Edinburgh 1890–1910*

Type of lender	Number	Average loan (£)	Loans as a % of purchase price
Trusts	33	1,172	71.9
Private	59	551	66.5
(Women)	(28)	(360)	(67.0)
(Men)	(31)	(724)	(66.3)
Building societies[a]	74	316	95.2
Institutions (banks, life assurance)	14	646	92.9
Total	180	577	76.0

[a] Includes friendly societies.
Source: based on NAS RS27 and RS108, Register of Sasines, transactions for James Steel.

was a disincentive and it meant that trust and private funds tended to be accessed by a different group of borrowers, that is, by investors who sought a larger advance normally for the purpose of buying an entire tenement block for rental income. Not only were the emerging building societies more disposed to lend to owner occupiers and to advance a larger percentage of the purchase price of a flat, they also did so for significantly smaller lump sums which averaged just over £300, well below the average advances of the other financial intermediaries (see table 8.5). Privately arranged loans to women borrowers were also for more modest amounts. The average loan was £360, half the amount sought by men, but like all borrowers from private sources women, too, found they could only obtain an advance of two-thirds of the purchase price. Even so, women accounted for 47% of Steel's Comely Bank house sales financed by private lenders.

Whether by design or default, building societies as financial newcomers may have been obliged in the 1890s and 1900s to find a niche in the market for home purchase. They certainly did so since in Comely Bank, Learmonth and Dean Park where they focused on smaller flats and first time buyers, providing three-quarters of their advances to home owners buying modestly priced flats at or above the first floor level and about the same proportion (71%) to occupational groups described as class 3 by the Registrar-General. By contrast, trusts, institutions and private financiers directed just over half (52%) their mortgage lending to this social class and about the same proportion (55%) to flats above the ground floor, figures which were swollen somewhat by the borrowing pattern of women, three-quarters of whose advances went to social class 3 and the more modestly priced upper flats.

Pricing differentials between ground and upper floor flats crystallised a vertical housing hierarchy in Comely Bank, as elsewhere in the city and in some respects not dissimilar to that in previous centuries. Exact differentials are difficult to ascertain since the number of flats within a block varied from six to nine in Comely Bank Avenue, seven in Learmonth Grove, nine per block in Comely Bank Place, Street and Terrace, eight or nine in Comely Bank Road, and as many as sixteen flats per block in Comely Bank Row and Dean Park Street.[63] In itself this provided an element of housing variety and choice by which owners and tenants both could adjust their accommodation to their particular household circumstances. Though there were divergent levels of desirability according to individual streets, in general a main door flat, that is, with exclusive use of a front door commanded a significant premium of about one third above the price of first floor flats with a shared entrance, about 40% more than a second floor flat, and about 51–64% more expensive than third floor flats.[64] In those tenements with sixteen flats the top floor ones might be only half the price of the main door flat, though the number of sales of any flat in this type of property was small and conclusions necessarily more tentative. The price differentials of flats and social distinctions with which they were associated are presented in fig. 8.12.

Diversification in the mortgage market assisted access to funds for social classes for whom before the last decade or so of the nineteenth century property owning had been almost inconceivable. For Victorian clerks, artisans and a shopocracy of butchers and bakers, home ownership was achievable in the 1890s. For employees in the offices of the capital's company head offices, the new Scottish Office, governmental administrative agencies, such as the Post Office, and escalating local government bureaucracies, sheltered as they were from the worst vagaries of the industrial fluctuations, predictable income streams enabled many to become householders with a cash down-payment. From the late 1860s many such employees and individuals clubbed together and with their own savings as deposits on flats contracted a builder to put up a tene-

---

[63] Though the floor level is generally clear, the exact location, that is north or south facing, or whether it was the centre flat on the landing, was not recorded consistently by the valuation officials. There were small price differences, too, within the period, mainly in a few years either side of 1900, though overall the sale prices at the end of the period c. 1914 were approximately similar to those in the early 1890s. Thus the figures are best treated as averages, and indicative of the relative desirability and social status of different streets in the area.   [64] NAS RS108, based on sales of 462 flatted tenements.

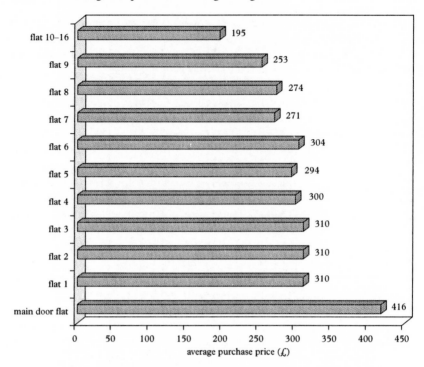

Figure 8.12 Tenement flats and social status: purchase prices in
Comely Bank and Learmonth 1890–1914

Source: based on the analysis of 462 sales in the Register of Sasines and
on information obtained from ECA ACC 373, Sir James Steel's Papers.

ment.[65] But for those who were unable to do so, the emergence of a group
of building societies, mutual and co-operative funds offered a reservoir of
mortgage finance on which they could draw. Less intimidating than a
solicitor's office, they were also the familiar financial organs of a petite
bourgeoisie – savings banks, subscription societies and 'The Co-op'.
Their business tone was of inclusiveness, rather than exclusivity, as
indeed it needed to be to carve out a financial niche in a city of capital.

Just how extensive this development of mortgages was for the petite
bourgeoisie needs more research in other cities, but there were unmistakable signs in Edinburgh of a burgeoning interest within this stratum. The
trend was curtailed somewhat in north Edinburgh by the death of James

---

[65] See appendix 4.2 for a list of almost ninety building associations active in the years
1869–74.

Steel in 1904 and the subsequent interval of two years as the Inland Revenue and his executors sought to defend their legitimate interests.[66] Though the trustees were instructed explicitly to continue with the housing and estate development strategies established by Steel, by the time matters were clarified a more languid period in the housing market had emerged, and the volume of new construction in the Comely Bank area tailed off, as it did throughout the city and in Scottish burghs generally in the decade immediately preceding the First World War.

As tenement flat prices indicate (fig. 8.12), there was considerable diversity in the social tone present in the Dean Park, Learmonth and Comely Bank streets. It was a three dimensional social diversity, since there was a vertical dimension in addition to the horizontal spatial character of housing differentiation. Some streets, particularly those with blocks of sixteen flatted tenements, offered a more basic standard of accommodation on all floors and were relatively similar in their internal layout. But within streets and within tenements there was often a 30–64% variation in the price of flats and this ensured a degree of household and occupational diversity which in turn offered a measure of stability to the area. No single activity, no concentration of employment in one large works existed to expose a pattern of consumption and household expenditure vulnerable to shifts in the factory order book. The class structure of house ownership on the Comely Bank estate showed (table 8.6) a very considerable diversity. These cleavages within home ownership were not unimportant since they denote that property owners were not a homogeneous grouping and that their different perspectives, agendas and social backgrounds may explain why ratepayer politics failed to develop as a cohesive force in the years before 1914.[67]

Not surprisingly, labourers and the unskilled, classes 4 and 5, were not heavily represented amongst the new home owners of Comely Bank; nor were those in industrial employment normally more susceptible than the lower middle class to trade cycle fluctuations. With its clerks, shopkeepers, teachers and local government officials, the occupational composition of Comely Bank was itself a reasonable guarantee of social stability, but the filtering downwards of home ownership through mortgage finance amongst social classes 2 and 3 was a personal financial commitment which reinforced it. In addition, the existence of single family dwellings at the top of the hill, in Learmonth and South Learmonth

[66] ECA ACC 373, Sir James Steel's Trust, ff. 198–9.
[67] M. Weber, *Economy and Society* (Berkeley 1979), 928; Offer, *Property and Politics*; N. McCord, 'Ratepayers and social policy', in P. Thane, ed., *The Origins of British Social Policy*, vol. I (London 1978).

Table 8.6 *Class structure of home ownership: Edinburgh 1890–1914*

Registrar-General's category (N = 95)	%
Class 1	6.3
Class 2	27.4
Class 3	57.9
Class 4	6.3
Class 5	2.1
Total	100.0

Source: based on NAS RS27 and RS108, Register of Sasines, James Steel's sales to private individuals in Comely Bank, Learmonth and Dean Park.

Gardens, populated largely by a professional class, created an illusion of order and stability to which the home owner might aspire, just as the presence of sixteen in a block tenements in Dean Park Street and Comely Bank Row served as a reminder of the past for those who had managed to obtain a mortgage. Though the housing hierarchy might appear to be a dynamic conveyor belt of social aspirations, the reality was that, for many, upward social mobility was financially difficult and the housing hierarchy served mainly to reinforce the *status quo*.

Compared to the direct sale of an entire tenement of flats to a landlord, the cash flow implications of a developing home ownership had little short-term advantage to James Steel. Indeed, fewer large sales reduced transactions costs compared to the paperwork generated by a proliferation of small sales. In the longer term, mixed tenure and social diversity injected an appeal to the area which had a direct impact on the local housing market. In this respect, the Victorian and Edwardian exposure of the Edinburgh petite bourgeoisie to home ownership provided them with a stake in the locality. Permanence replaced transience as the housing experience of many; householders replaced household heads in the Valuation Rolls. The creation of a significant class of home owners in late Victorian Edinburgh, based substantively on the occupational composition of the workforce in the capital and dependent in some measure on the activities of James Steel and the mortgages arranged by the Edinburgh Co-operative Building Company, provided an undertow to subsidised council housebuilding when it was enacted in the 1920s. Rights of collective property as constituted in municipal ownership and the growth of collective goods and services were diluted by a new emphasis on individual property ownership. The culture of home ownership may be too strong a term to describe the mortgage market trends of 1890 to 1914, but the emergence of owner occupancy before the First World War goes some way to explain the unusual preference of Edinburgh city council for central government subsidies for private rather than local authority housebuilding in the 1920s, and the ideological weakness of socialism in Edinburgh when compared both to Red Clydeside and to crimson patches in the surrounding Lothians.[68]

[68] Melling, *Rent Strikes*, 18–26; A. O'Carroll, 'Tenements to bungalows: class and the growth of home ownership before the Second World War', *Urban History*, 24, 1997, 221–41.

9   Landlord and tenant

In Edinburgh, as in Scotland generally, each Whitsunday was a day of drama, even of farce. Cartloads of furniture, bundles of clothes and linen and armfuls of personal possessions were transported from one flat to another. Streets were congested and all types of containers and means of transport commandeered. One government investigation described Scotland's national day of removal as contributing significantly to tenants' stress, particularly since 'the demand for means of conveyance is beyond the supply'.[1]

The annual 'term' day at the end of May was when new leases became operative for the forthcoming year, and was the culmination of a process which began in late January with the 'missive' or letter from the landlord setting out any changes in the level of rent and seeking a tenant's intentions for the coming year. If the terms were agreeable, the bargain for the forthcoming year was often struck in early February. It was in effect a sixteen month rental commitment by Scots. In Edinburgh, because the service sector and artisanal employment offered a measure of stability, judgements about the level of future household income could be made more confidently than in burghs with a high concentration of unskilled, casual and female workers where short time and low pay meant only basic levels of accommodation were affordable throughout the term of the lease.[2] In reality, there was no freedom of contract between landlord and tenant in Scottish burghs and a government enquiry in 1907 endorsed the genuine grievance of tenants with the letting system.[3]

The overwhelming majority of Scottish working-class tenancies – 'about 80%' was the assessment of an official investigation – were

[1] *PP 1907 XXXVI*, Report of the Departmental Committee on House-Letting in Scotland, 3–4.

[2] J. Treble, 'The seasonal demand for adult labour in Glasgow 1890–1914', *Social History*, 3, 1978, 60, appendix 1; R. Rodger, 'Employment, wages and poverty in the Scottish cities 1841–1914', in G. Gordon, ed., *Perspectives of the Scottish City* (Aberdeen 1985), 25–63, repr. in R. J. Morris and R. Rodger, eds., *The Victorian City: A Reader in British Urban History, 1820–1914* (London 1993), 79–98, 107–13.

[3] *PP 1907 XXXVI*, Report, 4. The enquiry discounted the proprietors' contention that 'the agitation for short lets [was] only part of a socialistic programme'.

contracted on the basis of a yearly let and so the quest for reliable tenants who would pay regularly and would not damage the landlord's property was a matter of the utmost importance.[4] Written testimonials concerning a tenant's behaviour were a non-negotiable requirement and without the 'factor's line' as a character reference the prospects of a lease were gloomy. If, for tenants without a 'line' on Whitsunday, the beckoning street was to be avoided then doubling-up with relatives or moving to inferior accommodation or taking in lodgers were the most likely options as households sought to spread housing costs. Shared space meant shared rent; it was a common financial strategy for Edinburgh households. In 1871, between a third and a quarter of all three to eight room houses had lodgers; one fifth of two room houses had lodgers and they accounted for 30–40% of the household.[5] Even in the properties built by the Edinburgh Co-operative Building Company, whose mission was to reduce over-crowding, almost 15% of the households in 1871 and 1891 had a lodger and many more took in adult members of the extended family.[6]

The practice of yearly letting had serious disadvantages for tenants.[7] Approximately 24% of men and about 20% of women in Edinburgh experienced some interrupted employment in the course of the year and so household income could and did vary considerably from week to week.[8] Yet rent, an important element of household expenditure estimated in the 1880s to constitute up to 25% of weekly income, was inflexible since the bargain was struck for a year.[9] Understandably, then, there was a built-in tendency towards overcrowding amongst the unskilled and casually employed since tenancy agreements were governed by affordable rents in the worst, rather than a typical, employment week. Commonly rents were payable monthly in advance, and the landlord often insisted on a 'cautioner' or deposit on yearly lets. Judging the level of rent a family could afford for the next twelve months was not a straightforward matter, therefore, and the penalties for misjudgement were heavy since the accumulation of rent arrears empowered landlords under the Law of Hypothec to seize and then sell a tenant's household effects at a Warrant Sale.[10]

To rents were added rates, occupier's rates. Rates were municipal taxes for council services but there were further charges for police, water and

[4] *PP 1907 XXXVI*, Report, 3.   [5] Census of Scotland, 1871.
[6] Census of Scotland, 1871, Enumerators' Books 685¹70–1; 685²25, 692¹21–2, 24–6, 685¹50, 692²3, 685¹3, Census of Scotland, 1891, Enumerators' Books 685¹129–31, 685³14–7, 692¹25, 27, 685¹82–3, 692²6, 685¹106–7, 685¹123.
[7] Rodger, 'The law and urban change', *Urban History Yearbook*, 1979, 84–6.
[8] Rodger, 'Employment, wages and poverty', tables 9 and 10.
[9] *PP 1884–5 XXX*, Royal Commission on Housing of the Working Classes, Scotland, Second Report, 5, and Minutes of Evidence, Telfer, Q. 19172.
[10] D. Englander, *Landlord and Tenant in Urban Britain 1838–1918* (Oxford 1983), 37–44, 162–83.

poor relief. These charges were collected at different intervals and presented a formidable juggling act for family budgets which often needed to be adjusted downward on food and other essentials to meet them. It was a level of discipline beyond many households and so to smooth out tenants' payments, and to limit their own ultimate responsibility for local taxes in the event of a tenant's non-payment of local taxes, landlords normally combined rents and rates into weekly amounts. Inevitably this led to confusion over how much went to the landlord for rent and how much to the municipality for rates; in turn, this led to suspicion, if not to outright antagonism between landlord and tenant. Unlike their English counterparts, Scottish landlords received no discount on their own tax liabilities for remitting rates to the burgh chamberlain or for acting as unofficial tax collectors to the corporation. Landlords felt aggrieved at such unpaid subsidies to councils.[11]

Despite the protestations of landlords over such irritations, the underlying framework of an annual letting system offered little incentive for Scottish landlords to press for reform, and, unlike England where the balance of landlord–tenant power tilted towards the tenant at the end of the nineteenth century, in Scotland the landlords' position became more secure with summary evictions easier to obtain.[12] Forty landlords and their factors solidly endorsed the *status quo* of long leases when asked in 1907 by a Departmental Committee for their opinion, and the entrenched ideological battle lines were reflected in the unswerving opposition to the system from fifty-two representatives of Trades Councils, trades unionists, miners, tenants' representatives, and a few councillors. Landlord and tenant, capitalist and labourer, rentier and artisan were the unmistakable residential and class antagonisms which the Departmental Committee members revealed in their poll.[13]

For tenants, one consequence of the non-payment of rates was disenfranchisement, but the real sanction was the inability to obtain a factor's line and the ensuing difficulty of securing a home for the family. The rigidity of 'this absurd system'[14] caused the 'missive question', as it was known, to become a contentious political issue.[15] So while the carters might have enjoyed increased demands for their services and street

[11] SLEC, *Report* (London 1914), 476–85, 514–20; *PP 1894 LXXIV pt II*, Royal Commission on Local Taxation in Scotland C.7575; *PP 1907 XXXVI*, Departmental Committee on House-Letting in Scotland, Cd 3715, 1907, Report, 3–6, offer summaries of the local taxation system.

[12] N. J. Morgan and M. J. Daunton, 'Landlords in Glasgow: a study of 1900', *Business History*, 25, 1983, 264–81; Englander, *Landlord and Tenant,* 169.

[13] *PP 1907 XXXVI*, Report, 7–9.

[14] *PP 1908 XLVII*, Minutes of Evidence of the Departmental Committee on House-Letting in Scotland, McBain Q. 5627. The Committee members summarily dismissed the views of the only two individuals who dissented from this view, p. 7.

[15] *PP 1907 XXXVI*, Report, 12–16; Englander, *Landlord and Tenant.*

observers the high drama of Whitsunday, for Edinburgh tenants it was either a matter of great relief to move to another flat or, for others, a sad farewell to the family home. Either way, it meant a 'heavy expense, labour and worry connected with a removal'.[16]

The character of landlordism

A number of issues about landlords and tenants are addressed in this chapter. How difficult were properties to let and did the landlord always hold the whip hand? Were vacancies a cause for concern and were they associated with specific types of properties? How long did residents stay at a particular address? Was continuity at an address associated with social stability in a neighbourhood? Did persistence vary according to social status? How common were female household heads? Did widows and spinsters pursue a different strategy in regard to their housing? Was there a degree of social segregation within tenements? By analysing particular streets of an area is it possible to conclude that the housing market was finely differentiated? Of course, landlords were motivated by an amalgam of factors, just as tenants were.[17] In general, though, the objective was to secure a predictable source of income. How this was achieved and what the implications were for tenants is also examined here?

The motivation of James Steel as a landlord provides a rare opportunity to assess the nature of the house letting and rental markets in Victorian and Edwardian Edinburgh. Steel's activities extended over half a century, involved more than 15,000 tenancies, and covered lettings across a wide social spectrum in fifty different streets in the city.[18]

As a landlord, Steel's strategy had at least two major identifiable strands. At first buildings were acquired and let solely to produce a steady

---

[16] *PP 1907 XXXVI*, Report, 14.

[17] D. McCrone and B. Elliott, *Property and Power in a City: The Sociological Significance of Landlordism* (London 1989), 137–52. Inertia, ego, status, speculative and other motivations are recognised alongside the quest for annuities for individuals, trusts and institutions. For the activities of landlords' agents, see ECA ACC 333/4, Hay Borthwick Factory, State of Feu Duties, Martinmas 1835 and Whitsunday 1839, Annual Statements of Accounts, 1875–94, also ACC 322, John Chesser's Trust, Minutes of Meeting of Trustees, 20 Nov. 1911, f. 252.

[18] NAS RS108, Register of Sasines, and VR100/69–311, Valuation Rolls, annually for 1866–1914 for Edinburgh, and VR55/12–156, for Leith; Edinburgh Voters' Rolls 1890–1914, and *Edinburgh and Leith Post Office Directories*, 1861–1914, form the basis of the nominal and property record linkage on which this chapter is based. These are supplemented by Sir James Steel's will, NAS SC70/1/445 and trust, ECA SL104/1, Ledger 1896–1914, vol. 1, ff. 164–851, which together with details of Feu Charters and Dispositions noted above (RS108) and also contained in Chartularies for Dean, Dalry, Bathfield and Hillhousefield, ECA SL104/2–5, form the basis of the addresses developed, built and retained by Steel for rental purposes. It would be repetitive to cite these sources on each occasion, and impossible to cite all individual Sasines and Valuation Roll folios.

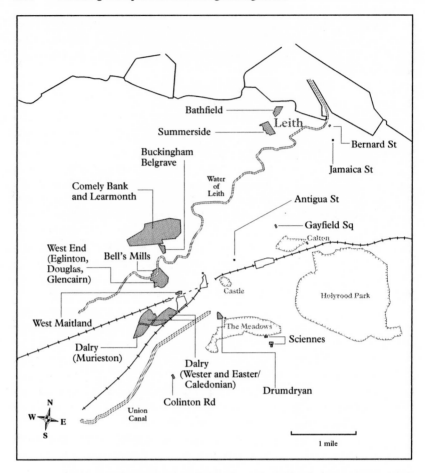

Figure 9.1 James Steel's Edinburgh property development 1868–1914

rental income, though here the similarity with annuitants' motives ceased since the purpose of this income stream was to secure loans in order to finance land acquisition, site development and building. This was the case with properties in Bernard Street (1868) and Jamaica Street (1869) both in Leith, Antigua Street and Gayfield Square (1870–1) off Leith Walk, and a few years later in Constitution Street and Charlotte Street, again in Leith, both acquired in 1875. Indeed, this early revenue-generating strategy was largely concentrated in Leith and indicates that, for an outsider, the 'barriers to entry' to the housing market were not insuperable, and that the permeability of the business elite and rentier elements may have been greater there than in Edinburgh. Overall, Leith rentals accounted for

11% of the number and 7% of the value of Steel's activity as a landlord between 1867 and 1914. These early rent-generating properties were retained throughout Steel's forty year association with the Edinburgh and Leith housing market.

However, based on the substantial capital gain at Drumdryan in 1869, a second and overlapping strand developed in the early 1870s.[19] James Steel suspended his strategy of further additions to the portfolio of existing property since to do so was to tie up disproportionate amounts of capital. Instead, it was replaced by an alternative approach, that of retaining a number of properties, either entire tenements or individual flats within them, on those sites newly built by Steel. This strategy, developed and tested in the early 1870s at Sciennes and Dalry, complemented Steel's preference for house sales which improved the turnover of capital and reduced his dependence on external finance for new building projects. Retaining some properties for rental avoided one of the adverse effects of tenement completion which inevitably brought a number of flats on to the market simultaneously. If no single landlord bought the tenement built by James Steel, to avoid a glut in the market for house sales and inevitable downward pressure on prices, rationality dictated that Steel rent individual flats himself. Locally, and even at the micro-scale within common stairs, the result was the emergence of mixed tenures. Owners and tenants co-existed within the same property: respectability was not conditional upon tenure. For Steel, the strategy of retaining property for rental income to complement sales, tried and tested in the 1870s and extended in subsequent decades, yielded a steady rentier income of £2,000–3,000 annually in the 1870s, which quadrupled in the 1880s, doubled again in the 1890s, and was so successful that by the twentieth century, James Steel derived about £16,000 per year from his rentals (fig.9.2).[20] Steel's rental income in the 1870s was approximately £100,000 and in 1910 over £700,000 in present-day terms.

Embedded within these two central motives were others. In later years, at Murieston and Comely Bank, Steel withheld land in anticipation of even greater future rental prospects. Status and self-confidence were associated with his rental and property development activities, and as early as 1877 he was described reverentially by a prominent landowner as 'a gentleman of means'.[21] Negotiations with landowners and financiers –

[19] NAS RS108/7.79, 11 Feb. 1869, sale of heritable securities to the Church of Scotland yielded 81% profit over two years. See chapter 6.
[20] ECA SL104/1, Abstract of Heritages belonging to Sir James Steel, f. 173, indicates that capital value of the rentals, exclusive of the feu-duties and other burdens due, and calculated at approximately eighteen years purchase, was £246,347.
[21] ECA ACC 282, James Walker's Papers, Memorandum on behalf of James Walker for the Lord Advocate, 7 Nov. 1877, f. 8.

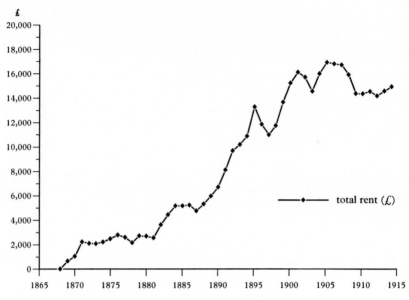

Figure 9.2 Rental income: James Steel 1868–1914

Sources: NAS VR100/69–311, Valuation Rolls, Edinburgh, Valuation Rolls, Leith.

the Heriot Trust, Earl of Moray, Duke of Northumberland, Colonel Learmonth and the Church of Scotland – were generally cordial and business-like, with no particular sign of deference. Indeed, Steel was prepared to enter into disputes if needs be to assert his interest despite the power and status of these influential parties. The terms on which he dealt with builders and sub-contractors as his sub-feuars were inevitably cloaked in legalistic terminology; there was an unswerving clarity and sense in Steel's business purpose.[22]

'Hard to let housing'

Labelled and stigmatised, problem housing estates have been presented as a characteristic of mid- and late twentieth-century British cities and are often considered as synonymous with social deprivation. Residents in Drumchapel or Castlemilk in Glasgow in the 1960s or Craigmillar and,

---

[22] ECA SL104/Box 2, Dalry Conditions of Feu, North Merchiston Feuing Conditions. In Buckingham Terrace Steel attempted to depart from feuing conditions restricting his own activities but duly yielded to the threat of an action before the Lord Advocate. See J. Gifford *et al. The Buildings of Scotland: Edinburgh* (Harmondsworth 1988 edn), 398.

two generations later, Wester Hailes in Edinburgh in the 1980s were labelled according to implicit assumptions.[23] Though there was some substance to the labelling, often the local authorities themselves were complicit in the process by allocating housing space on a points basis according to particular categories of disadvantaged residents.[24]

Problem housing in the public sector, however, was no new phenomenon. The process was apparent in the very first council housing in Liverpool, at St Martin's Cottages in 1869, where the municipality was quick to evict for non-payment of rent.[25] Selecting tenants and ensuring continuity of payment was a critical component of financial success for a landlord, and in London as in almost every British city, certain properties and even districts were 'hard to let'.[26] From the 1890s, London County Council architects attempted to counter tenants' aversion to the block dwellings closely identified with an earlier phase of mid-Victorian philanthropy by developing new designs albeit within the straitjacket of mass housing provision.[27] In the private sector, the thrust of Octavia Hill's housing strategy centred conspicuously on regular rent collection and a very limited tolerance of non-payment.[28] If company and philanthropic housing interests were less aggressive in their eviction policies than was Octavia Hill, their objectives, a mixture of securing labour supplies, appeasing Christian consciences and relieving suffering, relied financially on similar principles of prompt rental payments to secure the desired 4–5% rate of return on capital invested.[29]

[23] For a discussion of housing 'images' see S. Damer, *From Moorepark to "Wine Alley": The Rise and Fall of a Glasgow Housing Scheme* (Edinburgh 1989); R. Dennis, '"Hard to let" in Edwardian London', *Urban Studies*, 26, 1989, 77–89; D. Nash and D. Reeder, eds., *Leicester in the Twentieth Century* (Stroud 1993), 1–22; C. G. Pooley, 'England and Wales', in C. G. Pooley, ed., *Housing Strategies in Europe 1880–1930* (Leicester 1992), 97.

[24] S. Damer, 'Wine alley: the sociology of a dreadful enclosure', *Sociological Review*, 22, 1974, 221–48; S. Damer and C. Johnstone, 'Glasgow housing policy in the inter-war years', unpublished paper to Rowntree Seminar on Social Housing, University of York, 1990.

[25] C. G. Pooley, 'Housing for the poorest poor: slum clearance and rehousing in Liverpool 1890–1918', *Journal of Historical Geography*, 11, 1985, 70–88; M. Barke and M. Callcott, 'Municipal intervention in housing: constraints and developments in Newcastle upon Tyne', in B. Lancaster, ed., *Working Class Housing on Tyneside 1850–1939* (Whitley Bay 1994), 7–38.

[26] Dennis, '"Hard to let" in Edwardian London'; T. Hinchcliffe, 'The housing market in Islington between the wars', University of London PhD thesis, 1991, 17–57.

[27] S. Beattie, *A Revolution in London Housing: LCC Architects and their Work 1893–1914* (London 1980); J. N. Tarn, *Working Class Housing in 19th-Century Britain* (London 1971).

[28] O. Hill, *Homes of the London Poor* (London 1883; repr. 1970); E. Gauldie, *Cruel Habitations: A History of Working Class Housing 1780–1918* (London 1974), 213–35.

[29] J. N. Tarn, *Five Per Cent Philanthropy: An Account of Housing in Urban Areas between 1840 and 1914* (Cambridge 1973); S. M. Gaskell, *Model Housing: From the Great Exhibition to the Festival of Britain* (London 1986), 30–8, 54–8. For a recent review see G. Cherry, 'Bournville, England 1895–1995', *Journal of Urban History*, 22, 1996, 493–508.

Victorians defined 'the housing problem' as one of insanitary working-class housing coupled with moral degeneration associated with over-crowding.[30] It was predicated on a public health based agenda and in England was closely identified with the sanitary reform campaign brilliantly engineered by Edwin Chadwick in a public relations coup in 1842. The 'housing problem' was reproduced thereafter both to legitimate public intervention in the sphere of private property and as part of a moral panic to raise the spectre of epidemic disease.[31] In Edinburgh, which also figured in the Chadwick report, an influential study produced by Dr Henry Littlejohn in 1865 utilised empirical research into mortality and morbidity to raise both the civic consciousness and the social consciences of the Edinburgh middle classes.[32]

The presumption underpinning Victorian investigations was that the housing of the working classes did not represent a sound investment.[33] As *The Builder* commented, 'providing dwellings for labourers has not been found commercially remunerative'.[34] Unruly tenants and damage to the fabric of the property resulted in high maintenance, repairs and factoring charges.[35] James Gowans, a prominent Edinburgh builder and Lord Dean of Guild – equivalent to convenor of the planning committee – commented: 'You have the habits of the people to contend with; you may put a person in a house and he will wreck any sanitation it possesses in a week's time', and as a gratuitous afterthought typical of prejudice elsewhere in Britain observed that 'for the most part they are Irish people'.[36]

Minimising the frequency of unlet property and containing the extent of arrears became obsessive concerns amongst landlords. Thus, as the 'term' day approached, the pressure on landlords with less than desirable

---

[30] A. Macpherson, ed., *Report of a Committee of the Working Classes of Edinburgh* (Edinburgh 1860), 14.

[31] A. Mayne, *The Imagined Slum: Newspaper Representation in Three Cities 1870–1914* (Leicester 1993), 1–16, 57–97; D. R. Green and A. G. Parton, 'Slums and slum life in Victorian England: London and Birmingham at mid-century', in S. M. Gaskell, ed., *Slums* (Leicester 1990), 17–91. See also M. W. Flinn, 'Introduction' to *Report on the Sanitary Condition of the Labouring Population of Great Britain*, by Edwin Chadwick 1842 (Edinburgh 1965), 1–74, for an exemplary contextual analysis, and for another contemporary view by G. Godwin, *Town Swamps and Social Bridges* (repr. Leicester 1972).

[32] *PP 1884–5 XXX*, Royal Commission, Minutes of Evidence, H. D. Littlejohn, Q. 18939–19058, and Appendix A, provides an overview. For the full report see H. D. Littlejohn, *Report on the Sanitary Condition of the City of Edinburgh* (Edinburgh 1865), Appendix 1. See also chapter 12.

[33] Gauldie, *Cruel Habitations*, 221–35; Gaskell, *Model Housing*, 11–12; Tarn, *Five Per Cent Philanthropy*; Glasgow Municipal Commission on the Housing of the Poor (subsequently GMC), *Report* (Glasgow 1904), 16, and *Evidence*, Fyfe, Q. 734, McDonald, Q. 3573, Mann, Q. 8488.   [34] *Builder*, 20 May 1865, 351.

[35] GMC, *Evidence*, Evidence of Motion, Q. 5419, Blackie, Q. 8142, described the 'hustling' policy which Glasgow landlords adopted to move on 'undesirable' tenants.

[36] *PP 1884–5 XXX*, Royal Commission, Minutes of Evidence, Gowans, Q. 18926–7.

Table 9.1 *The rental–house vacancy relationship*

Type of property	Number of streets	Correlation coefficient
Lower rented properties (<£29 p.a.)	23	0.59
Higher rented properties (>£29 p.a.)	10	0.86
All streets	33	0.57

Note: only streets where over 100 tenancies were recorded are included; careful interpretation is required due to the limited number of cases where rentals average >£29. *Sources:* NAS VR100/69–311, Valuation Rolls, Edinburgh, VR55/12–156, Valuation Rolls, Leith.

housing could almost be measured by the extent of repair and maintenance work underway on a property, and it was often only at this time that walls were replastered, distempered, and roofing repairs undertaken. Spring-time brought a brief and frenetic spell of activity amongst jobbing builders, a welcome injection of cash after the difficult winter months, and a decline in the rate of building bankruptcies.[37]

In general, therefore, given the nature of contemporary observations on the 'housing problem', the expectation would be of an inverse correlation between the level of rents and the percentage of unlet property: that is, the lower the rent the greater the susceptibility to vacancies and arrears. Yet the overwhelming evidence of 15,175 tenancies with an average vacancy rate of 5.97% between 1868 and 1914 revises previous versions of working-class housing and the problems which landlords faced. Property by property, street by street, vacancy rates generally were lower in modestly rented accommodation. There was no inverse relationship. The contention that higher rented property was likely to record lower levels of unlet accommodation generally is unsupported (table 9.1). Quite the reverse applied. Vacancy rates were most strongly and positively correlated (+0.86) with rentals at the upper end of the housing market where rents were above £29 per annum and though weaker, were still positively correlated (+0.59) amongst those paying rentals of less than £29 annually.[38]

More specifically, it was those exclusive west end addresses in Buckingham Terrace (30.6%), Eglinton Crescent (21.0%), Queensferry

[37] R. Rodger, 'Speculative builders and the structure of the Scottish building industry 1860–1914', *Business History*, 21, 1979, 242, appendix. The percentage distribution of bankruptcies 1857–1913 recorded the second lowest monthly rate in May, and only in September was the bankruptcy rate lower.

[38] NAS, VR100/69–311, Valuation Rolls. The figure of £29 is used as the weighted mean (to the nearest £) for the rents of Steel's 15,175 properties.

Table 9.2 *'Hard to let' property:*
Edinburgh 1868–1914

No. of consecutive years unlet	N (905)	%
1	352	38.9
2	172	19.0
3	75	8.3
4	76	8.4
5	65	7.2
6	24	2.3
7	91	10.1
8+	50	4.5

Sources: NAS VR100/69–311, Valuation Rolls, Edinburgh, VR55/12–156, Valuation Rolls, Leith.

Gardens (21.7%), Learmonth Gardens (12.8%) and Mews (17.3%), and Belgrave Place (8.8%) which were often significantly above the average level of vacancies (5.97%). For Steel, the Buckingham and Belgrave properties alone accounted for over 15% of the entire rental income and the impact of a single unlet property in this rental bracket was equivalent to ten vacant flats in a Dalry tenement. The assumption, therefore, that working-class housing was intrinsically more problematical for the landlord and that middle- and upper-middle-class property was the safe haven of the property investor needs to be modified significantly.[39]

Specific properties often remained vacant for consecutive years. These 'hard to let' houses were a critical determinant of Steel's activities, as they were for any landlord. The distribution of unlet houses, as shown in table 9.2, reveals that almost four in every ten vacant properties were untenanted for a single year only, but two out of the ten remained empty for a second year, and one in ten for a third year. The remainder, about one third of all empty property, remained untenanted for four or more years. With the exception of some property in Leith where shops, workshops and storerooms were often let in a combined lease with housing, the majority (58%) of this long-run 'hard to let' housing was located in the west end and the highest rented elements of the Learmonth development, in Learmonth and South Learmonth Gardens, and almost two-thirds (64%) of all vacancies in this segment of the housing market were

---

[39] M. J. Daunton, *House and Home in the Victorian City: Working Class Housing 1850–1914* (London 1983), 286–307; and M. J. Daunton, *A Property Owning Democracy? Housing in Britain* (London 1987), 13–15; A. Offer, *Property and Politics, 1870–1914: Landownership, Law, Ideology and Urban Development in England* (Cambridge 1981), 84–9.

concentrated in the years 1908 to 1914. The argument that the crisis in landlordism was associated with the profitability of working-class properties needs to be tempered by the severe and protracted vacancies experienced in the renting of the most expensive addresses, and this in turn may reflect the deferred embrace of detached and semi-detached villadom in peripheral Edinburgh suburbs.

The New Town phenomenon, assaulted by the encroachments of office development, had run its course.[40] The compact Scottish Victorian city, with its residential and social mix, was under pressure at last in much the same way that the mid-Victorian appeal of Sefton, Grassendale and Cressington Parks in Liverpool, to say nothing of the more distant suburbs, dealt a mortal blow to the social tone of Abercromby Square and its surrounding central streets. In Edinburgh, the cumulative effect of suburban developments in Newington and Grange in the second half of the nineteenth century ultimately undermined the confidence of the upper middle classes in town house dwelling and the phenomenon, which persisted only in a weakened form in central London, increasingly left Georgian terraces denuded of their social elite.

'Hard to let' west end flats were affected by another consideration. Family limitation produced a steep decline in completed family size amongst the professional middle classes in Edinburgh in the last third of the nineteenth century.[41] The 1860s were the critical decade in this demographic shift; the average number of children born to Edinburgh professional families fell by 26% between the late 1850s and late 1870s.[42] This was not inconsistent with national British trends[43] towards smaller

---

[40] G. Gordon, 'The status areas of early to mid-Victorian Edinburgh', *Transactions Institute of British Geographers*, 4, 1979, figs. 1–5.

[41] S. P. Walker, 'Occupational expansion, fertility decline and recruitment to the professions in Scotland 1850–1914', University of Edinburgh PhD thesis, 1986, 261.

[42] D. Kemmer, 'The marital fertility of Edinburgh professionals in the later nineteenth century', University of Edinburgh PhD thesis, 1989, 110; Walker, 'Occupational expansion', 262, notes that the decline was established by the mid–late 1870s amongst Edinburgh chartered accountants. See also A. J. Gilloran, 'Family formation in Victorian Scotland', University of Edinburgh PhD thesis, 1985; D. J. Morse, 'Family limitation in Scotland', University of Edinburgh PhD thesis, 1987. *Census of Scotland 1911*, Cd. 7163, vol. III, table P, xxxiv–v, Report on Fertility of Marriage, shows that for women married in their twenties their completed family size was approximately 11% lower than for the twenties' age group whose families were completed just fifteen years earlier, that is, by 1864.

[43] T. H. C. Stevenson, 'The fertility decline of various social classes in England and Wales from the middle of the nineteenth century to 1911', *Journal of the Royal Statistical Society*, 83, 1920, 401–44; J. A. Banks, *Victorian Values: Secularism and the Size of Families* (London 1981), 40–1. For marriages completed in 1881–6 compared to those in the 1850s, Banks shows that for Britain as a whole completed family sizes fell by 33% for the middle classes, 21% for the skilled, 20% for the semi-skilled and 15% for unskilled labourers.

families, and in which skilled, unskilled and mining occupations participated in much diluted measures, but there were two important features as
far as the development of housing demand in Edinburgh was concerned.
First, since the professional and 'allied' groups in the city were 'found to
be occupations of low fertility' this had a disproportionate impact given
the social and occupational composition of Edinburgh; and secondly,
irrespective of the rate of decline, the mean family size amongst Scottish
professionals was itself lower than amongst their English counterparts by
as much as 9–17% in 1911.[44]

The pronounced decline in average family size in late Victorian
Edinburgh together with rising household expenses, particularly those
associated with the costs of servant keeping, prompted west end tenants
to move to smaller apartments or to new and developing suburbs. This
was the case at Colinton, where architect-designed detached housing
with low densities per acre and stipulations in the feu charters about the
minimum selling price were developed for owner occupiers by Rowand
Anderson on the James Gillespie estate.[45] With average yearly rentals of
£135 in Belgrave Place and over £170 in Buckingham Terrace, tenants
could buy detached suburban residences with 'motor houses' for the
equivalent of ten to fifteen years rental. In effect it was the same mortgage
equation which confronted artisans as they considered Edinburgh Co-
operative Building Company's 'Colonies' property scattered throughout
Edinburgh: to lease in the short term or to raise and repay long-term
housing finance in the knowledge that the ultimate prize would be owner
occupancy. Thus in periods of recession, high-rented accommodation for
the wealthier segments of the market was by no means immune to the
general economic climate, even amongst those whose incomes were
derived from the law, accounting, government and financial services.[46]

As landlords, Steel's trustees eventually recognised the vacancy
problem and conceded reductions to the rents for west end addresses.
Initially, however, against a background in 1907–8 of rising vacancies
they displayed a confused market analysis by at first increasing rentals in
Buckingham Terrace by £3 p.a. or 2.2%. A sustained rise in vacancies

[44] Kemmer, 'The marital fertility of Edinburgh professionals', 23.
[45] MC/JGH, Chartulary of James Gillespie's Hospital, vol. 3, ff. 8–16, 46–68, 88–102,
121–44, 148–62, 178, 190–227, 256–346, 355, 362–456, vol. 4, ff. 1–76, 97, 143–90,
202–46, 249–75, 279–96, 300–19, 322–60, 366–82, 392, 408–62. I am indebted to the
Merchant Company for permission to consult this material.
[46] The concentration of unlet properties between 1907 and 1914 was as follows:
Buckingham Terrace – 41%; Belgrave Place – 47%; Learmonth Gardens – 82%; South
Learmonth Gardens – 98%. It should be noted, however, that Learmonth Gardens and
South Learmonth Gardens only became available in stages from 1898 and 1901, respec-
tively.

ensued, only to be followed in 1912 by a swingeing 8.4% reduction in rents which then contributed in the following year to a decline in the vacancy rate to its former levels. Much the same chronology existed in relation to Belgrave Place and South Learmonth Gardens, where a 4.2% increase in rentals in 1907 was eventually reversed by substantial rental reductions of at least £25 (20%) in 1912. Unlet property declined in the next year. However, it would be misleading to conclude that vacancies were price-sensitive, or that landlords fine-tuned rents since a similar profile of rising and then declining vacancies at Learmonth Gardens was accompanied by unvarying rents throughout the years 1898 to 1914. Steel's pattern of rentals provides some corroboration for the view that in the upper ranges of the market at least, rents were inelastic, and that tenants were unresponsive to price changes even when these were substantial in percentage terms. More likely, Steel's trustees' response to changing vacancies was retarded and mirrored the underlying movement in the market; indeed, where they did occur rent reductions provided a windfall gain to the long-standing west end tenants which, at the margin, may have persuaded them not to move, and thus indirectly achieved the landlord's purpose.

By contrast, working-class housing, far from presenting a hostile environment to the landlord, offered predictability. For example, with one exception, in each of the fourteen streets with the lowest rentals, that is, under £20 p.a. or equivalent to 38p or 7s 6d per week, the average vacancy rate during 1867 to 1914 was less than 4% (fig. 9.3).[47] In the Caledonian Place, Road and Crescent tenements of Dalry, part of Steel's development of the Walker estate, the average vacancy rates from the early 1870s until 1914 were respectively 3.7%, 3.0% and 0.12%, and only 2.9% of flats in Dalry Road itself were untenanted over almost the same period. Further along Dalry Road, the tenements in Murieston Crescent and Place recorded only 2.7% and 1.4% vacancy rates during the years 1888 to 1914. On the south side of the Meadows, in his housebuilding activities in Sciennes, Steel experienced vacancy rates in Melville Terrace, Sciennes Road, Millerfield Place and Livingstone Place of respectively 5.9%, 3.8%, 3.8% and zero. In mixed residential and commercial property bought for rental at Bernard Street, Leith (1868), and off Leith Walk at Antigua Street and Gayfield Square (1870–1), the proportion of unlet residential accommodation was in the range 2–4%, consistent with flats at Dean Park Street built for rental in 1891. Spatially, temporally, whether newly built or existing housing, and in both Edinburgh and Leith, flats rented at under £20 p.a. were certainly not the landlord's headache which

[47] The exception was Bernard Street, Leith, where residential and commercial accommodation was mixed and the vacancy rate rose as high as 11% on occasions.

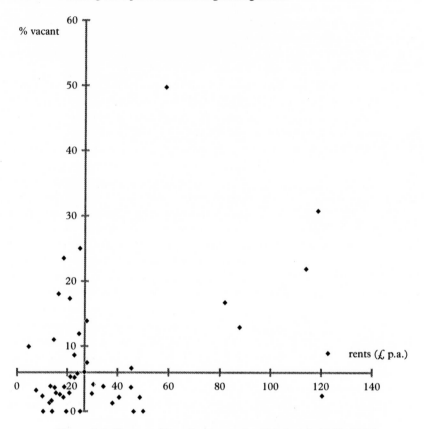

Figure 9.3 Rents and housing vacancies, Edinburgh 1868–1914

Sources: NAS VR100/69–311, Valuation Rolls, Edinburgh,
VR55/12–156, Valuation Rolls, Leith.

working-class housing was made out to be, and the existence of almost
fully tenanted, low rental housing from the late 1860s to the eve of the
First World War indicates that there was a form of long-run equilibrium
in this section of the market. Thus, in Edinburgh at least, fundamental
changes in landlordism were difficult to detect in the second half of the
nineteenth century, and consequently the decline of landlordism was
associated with the years after rather than before 1920, when continuing
wartime rent controls constrained the activities of private landlords and
boosted the prospects for the council as landlord.[48]

---

[48] For an examination of the durability of the rented sector, and of its eventual decline, see
D. McCrone and B. Elliott, 'The decline of landlordism: property rights and relationships in Edinburgh', in R. Rodger, ed., *Scottish Housing in the Twentieth Century* (Leicester
1989), 218–35.

In an analysis of Glasgow housing it was claimed that landlords responded to changing levels of vacant houses by altering rents, and that builders adapted their scale of operations accordingly.[49] The 'evidence for a rental price adjustment mechanism at work' centred on two runs of years – 1871–90 and 1901–14 – and, it was claimed, modified a long-standing interpretation of the Glasgow housing market, as presented by Cairncross, in which he argued that 'rents were more than sticky . . . they were apt to rise quite rapidly just when the number of empty houses was rising rapidly'.[50] This 'stickiness' of rents inhibited adjustments, according to Cairncross, and induced a 'comparative insensitiveness' in the building industry to normal trade-cycle rhythms.[51] Thus rents (the pricing mechanism) were unresponsive and failed to deliver their customary market-clearing function. Cumulative backlogs of housing demand developed and ultimately exaggerated responses levered the housebuilding industry into frenzied activity, over-reactions and excess supply. Internally generated instability in housebuilding was intensified by the 'ebb and flow of labour and capital between Britain and countries overseas' between 1870 and 1914, or, as Cairncross put it, 'the prosperity of the Dakotas . . . brought building to a standstill in Dalmarnock'.[52]

The 'Atlantic economy', that is, the relationship 'between home and foreign investment on the one hand and between immigration of capital and labour on the other',[53] depends in no small measure on the interplay of rents and vacancies. Evidence from Edinburgh suggests that the revisionist Glasgow study is simplistic. This is because, first, there were several distinct housing sub-markets; secondly, aggregation of vacancies obscures considerable neighbourhood variations and the highly localised nature of building activity; thirdly, structural factors within the market produced inherently 'hard to let properties' and others which were invariably fully let; and, finally, where rental adjustments were tried no evidence of a long-run tendency towards an equilibrium could be attributed to such a strategy. Many of these influences are explored in greater detail in the following sections of this chapter.

Persistent tenants: stable communities

Accounts of tramping artisans and influxes of immigrant labour convey an impression of uncertainty and transience in the social fabric of the

---

[49] B. F. Reece, 'The price adjustment mechanism in Glasgow's rental housing market, 1871–1913: the claim of "sticky" rents re-examined,' *Scottish Journal of Political Economy*, 31, 1984, 286–93.

[50] A. K. Cairncross, *Home and Foreign Investment 1870–1913: Studies in Capital Accumulation* (Cambridge 1953), 32.   [51] Cairncross, *Home and Foreign Investment*, 29.

[52] Cairncross, *Home and Foreign Investment*, 25.

[53] B. Thomas, *Migration and Economic Growth* (Cambridge 1954); Cairncross, *Home and Foreign Investment*, 26.

nineteenth-century city.[54] This impermanence, a central tenet of Victorian capitalism with its reliance on the casual and seasonal structure of employment topped up initially by urban in-migration, was captured by a corps of journalists, publicists and social investigators from Mayhew to Mearns and Charles Booth in England, and in Scotland by influential Medical Officers of Health – Russell and Chalmers in Glasgow and Henry Littlejohn in Edinburgh.[55] The expert witness, James Gowans, who preceded Littlejohn in his evidence to the Royal Commission on Housing of the Working Classes in 1885, encapsulated many Edinburgh citizens' fears when he observed: 'We have colonies of Irish who will not come out of those [slum] places, and they are very destructive'.[56] Gissing's *The Nether World* presented no more than an end of century image of fears which had been represented in pamphlets and newspapers for most of Victoria's reign.[57]

One core assumption of industrialisation and urbanisation is of rapid change to production and to employment, and of the disruptions to patterns of daily life and their impact on the home. This was certainly part of the volatile urban experience as represented in small area analyses of Liverpool, Huddersfield, Leicester, Cardiff and London, and in these accounts, the limited duration of jobs, frequent flits of house and home, and the peripatetic nature of labour necessarily involved change.[58] Yet in

[54] C. W. J. Withers, 'Gaelic speaking in urban lowland Scotland: the evidence of the 1891 census', *Scottish Gaelic Studies*, 16, 1991, 103–39; and C. W. J. Withers, 'Class, culture and migrant identity: Gaelic highlanders in urban Scotland', in G. Kearns and C. W. J. Withers, eds., *Urbanising Britain: Essays on Class and Community in the Nineteenth Century* (Cambridge 1991), 55–78, and n. 1; H. Southall, 'The tramping artisan revisits: labour mobility and economic distress in early Victorian England', *Economic History Review*, 44, 1991, 249–71.

[55] D. Englander and R. O'Day, *Retrieved Riches: Social Investigation in Britain 1840–1914* (Aldershot 1995); D. R. Green, *From Artisans to Paupers: Economic Change and Poverty in London 1790–1870* (Aldershot 1991), 181–247; Littlejohn, *Report on the Sanitary Condition of the City of Edinburgh*; J. B. Russell, *Life in One Room, or Some Considerations for the Citizens of Glasgow* (Glasgow 1888); E. Robertson, *Glasgow's Doctor: James Burn Russell 1837–1904* (East Linton 1998).

[56] *PP 1884–5 XXX*, Royal Commission, Evidence, Gowans, Q. 18927.

[57] See, for example, in the context of London, J. Garwood, *The Million-Peopled City: One Half of the People of London Made Known to the Other Half* (London 1853); K. Kirwan, *Palace and Hovel or Phases of London Life* (Hartford, CT, 1871); C. M. Smith, *Curiosities of London Life or Abuses, Physiological and Social, of the Great Metropolis* (London 1853). See also Mayne, *The Imagined Slum*; Gaskell, ed., *Slums*; G. R. Gissing, *The Nether World* (London 1973).

[58] See, for example, R. J. Dennis, *English Industrial Cities of the Nineteenth Century: A Social Geography* (Cambridge 1984), 250–69, for an overall assessment and more specifically; R. J. Dennis, 'Intercensal mobility in a Victorian city', *Transactions Institute of British Geographers*, 2, 1977, 349–63; R. M. Pritchard, *Housing and the Spatial Structure of the City: Residential Mobility and the Housing Market in an English City since the Industrial Revolution* (Cambridge 1976); R. Lawton and C. G. Pooley, 'Individual appraisals of

the short run, the fixed capital stock of workplace and home could change little even if plant and machinery might be decommissioned and labour laid off at short notice. As for social and political organisations, one of the objectives of a governing elite whether in the council chamber, church hall or in the club meeting was to broker change according to their own perceptions; established interests yielded only grudgingly to usurpers whatever office they sought.

Despite many intrinsically conservative forces and their resistance to change, the dislocating experience of urbanisation on community life was recognised. South of the border the absence or under-representation of the Church of England in many industrial centres and low attendance at Sunday worship spurred church building even before the census of 1851 drew attention to the empty pews.[59] Despite a trend towards Scottish religious pluralism between 1760 and 1843, in the second half of the nineteenth century the Church of Scotland reasserted itself, attracting a higher proportion of adherents than before the Disruption and developing an active policy to establish new charges.[60] Social dislocation was addressed by clubs, societies, political parties, works activities and sporting initiatives which provided reference points and social networks in a rapidly changing urban world, and the municipality recognised and fulfilled its civic responsibility with a cultural programme for museums, libraries and galleries, as well as parks, zoos and botanical gardens designed to inform.[61] An urban identity was forged, therefore, through this amalgam of public and private initiatives, and these acted as mental compass points to assimilation. Participation and stakeholding, plurality

nineteenth century Liverpool', Social Geography of Nineteenth Century Merseyside, 3, 1975 (unpublished); C. G. Pooley and J. Turnbull, 'Changing home and workplace in Victorian London: the life of Henry Jacques, shirtmaker', Urban History, 24, 1997, 148–78; M. J. Daunton, Coal Metropolis Cardiff 1870–1914 (Leicester 1977).

[59] For an early assessment of urbanisation and secularisation see H. McLeod, 'Religion in the city', Urban History Yearbook, 1978, 5–22. Updates are provided by C. G. Brown, 'Did urbanization secularize Britain?', Urban History Yearbook, 1988, 1–14; and C. G. Brown, 'Religion in the city', Urban History, 23, 1996, 372–9. See also K. D. M. Snell, Church and Chapel in the North Midlands: Religious Observance in the Nineteenth Century (Leicester 1991).

[60] NAS CH1/34/1 Church of Scotland General Assembly's Committee on the Endowment of Chapels of Ease, ff. 1, 11–13, 20–39, and the Church Extension Committee, f. 23; C. G. Brown, The Social History of Religion in Scotland since 1730 (London 1987), 64–5.

[61] W. Knox, 'The political and workplace culture of the Scottish working class 1832–1914', and W. H. Fraser, 'Developments in leisure', both in W. H. Fraser and R. J. Morris, eds., People and Society in Scotland, vol. II (Edinburgh 1990), 153, 251–61; R. J. Morris, 'Clubs, societies and associations', in F. M. L. Thompson, ed., The Cambridge Social History of Britain 1750–1850 (Cambridge 1990), vol. III, 406–19; H. E. Meller, Leisure in the Changing City, 1870–1914 (London 1976), 6–18, 48–71, 96–116. More specifically, see D. A. Jameson, Powderhall and Pedestrianism: The History of a Famous Sports Enclosure (Edinburgh 1943).

and civility, were central elements of urban tolerance and social stability.[62] A civil society in which associational life flourished was an indication of urban maturity and tolerance but in turn owed much to residential stability.

An input to local organisations apart, permanence amongst tenants contributed significantly towards community stability in tangible ways. Implicit rules amounting to folklore were understandable to long-term residents, but were not always easily understood or remembered by new tenants. Thus, where the key to the back door was kept, who had responsibility for the drying pole, who could use which water-closet might make for neighbourly banter, but the turnover in tenancies also created conflict amongst residents as different protocols took time to absorb. While vacant housing did not in itself increase impermanence since some properties remained unlet for several consecutive years (table 9.2), and even contributed some positive advantages in reducing congested wash day rotas, responsibility for shared amenities such as cleaning the tenement close and sweeping the stairs fell on fewer shoulders. Friction amongst tenants was normally at its most intense over communal amenities and, in Edinburgh, 29% of the housing stock was provided with shared WCs in 1915 and 8% of houses shared a sink.[63] A rapid turnover of tenants disturbed established rhythms, and in sickness, child-minding, mourning, and as a source of borrowed ingredients and general credit, it took time to establish networks of trustworthy neighbours.

The rate of turnover amongst tenancies was, therefore, critical to the stability of an area. If there was a compound 5% change in tenants each year, it would take sixteen years before the population of the entire neighbourhood was replaced; at a turnover of 15%, a little over six years; and if the annual turnover was 25%, the same effect was achieved in just under four years. The implications for club secretaries, branch treasurers, church organisations and other forms of associational culture were evident; their appointment to an executive was likely to be for a considerable stretch of years since arithmetically a high proportion of capable individuals would move out of the locality before a vacancy arose, often leaving those in post unopposed. High rates of turnover amongst the tenants of Comely Bank

[62] K. Kumar, 'Civil society: an inquiry into the usefulness of an historical term', *British Journal of Sociology*, 44, 1993, 375–95. For an overview see J. A. Hall, ed., *Civil Society: Theory, History, Comparison* (Cambridge 1995); J. Habermas, *The Structural Transformation of the Public Sphere: An Enquiry into a Category of Bourgeois Society* (Boston, Mass., 1989); E. Gellner, *Conditions of Liberty: Civil Society and its Rivals* (London 1994); G. Morton, 'Civil society, municipal government and the state: enshrinement, empowerment and legitimacy, Scotland 1800–1929', *Urban History*, 25, 1998, 348–67.

[63] *PP 1917–18 XIV*, Royal Commission on the Housing of the Industrial Population of Scotland, Rural and Urban, Report, para. 571–2.

enabled more individuals to gain access to the Dean Bowling Club by virtue of the residence qualification in the neighbourhood, but the corollary was that low levels of persistence amongst tenants restricted the numbers who could command support as elected officials, leaving owner occupiers tactically well placed in their quest for office. Amongst the first presidents of the club were William Fraser and William Kinsey who resided respectively for eleven and thirteen years in the area, three times the average for Comely Bank, and in stark contrast to the early champions and rank and file members who were generally accustomed to much shorter spells of residence.[64] The oligarchy of the voluntary association committee owed as much to the dynamics of tenancy in a locality as it did to concepts of service, leadership and duty to the membership.

Across the entire spectrum of rented property, James Steel's tenants remained at an address for an average of four years three months between 1868 and 1914.[65] Not all changes of tenancy involved moving out of the neighbourhood. Widows often continued to reside in the marital home after bereavement – this applied to 0.6% of rentals – and there were numerous and sometimes repeated moves within an area which together accounted for 2.4% of changes in tenancy. Adjustments in the calculation of the average tenancy period have been made to take account of such influences, though not for other complicated letting arrangements where despite formal changes in tenancies between unmarried family relations, actual occupancy was continuous.[66] Thus, the average occupancy amongst James Steel's 3,000 tenants was nearer to four years eleven months once account has been taken of such structural factors in the patterns of tenancy. No other Scottish study is available as a basis for comparison, though in English boroughs persistence at a specific address showed about three-quarters of residents at the same address after one year, and about one half to two-thirds still present at the same address after two years. After five years, approximately the same period as the Edinburgh average, in Cardiff, Manchester, York and Liverpool 28–41% of residents were still at the same address.[67]

---

[64] Based on the list of Presidents and Champions, Dean Bowling Club, and on Edinburgh Valuation Rolls, NAS VR100/146–311.

[65] A downward bias on the indicator of residential persistence is artificially introduced both where properties were sold and by the terminal date for this study. Adjustment has been made for this by disregarding all tenancies for two years prior to a sale, and similarly for those properties which changed hands in 1913–14 for the first time.

[66] Cases of continuous occupancy of family members where the head of household changed from one member to another were not rare, but made little impact on the average length of tenancy where a test was conducted. The problem of continuous residency with a change of household head is more problematical where surnames differ, and no attempt to establish a correction factor was undertaken in such cases.

[67] Dennis, *English Industrial Cities*, 257.

Residential persistence – continuities in occupancy relative to the total number of rentals – can be estimated through an assessment of turnover amongst residents. In Edinburgh, the average turnover amongst 3,000 tenants was 15.7%, equivalent to a complete change of inhabitants every seven years.[68] To describe such neighbourhoods as unstable would be to label them much as Victorians did, but there was certainly considerable fluidity in a turnover rate of this magnitude. Various methodologies of residential mobility or persistence have been developed in studies of English boroughs, each with a heavy dependence placed upon tracing individuals identified in the census through the use of directories.[69] Apart from the large numbers of tenancies covered, the strength of the Edinburgh tenancy data is that it is not selected or sampled but is derived from the total population of James Steel's activity as a landlord between 1868 and 1914, and as such it cuts across the social strata. Not surprisingly, considering that there were over 13,000 tenancies[70] widely distributed spatially and according to divergent income levels and housing sub-markets in Edinburgh, and spread across half a century, the averaging process masks local variations, and these reveal important facets of the operation of the housing market in the nineteenth century (see table 9.3). These differing characteristics of housing sub-markets are explored next, followed by a more extended analysis of the Learmonth–Comely Bank area since this was developed and built exclusively by James Steel.

For lawyers and the Edinburgh professional middle classes in general moving home was less common than for other social groups. In part this is because social status was conferred by occupation rather than by residence, and no doubt because the range of housing options which constituted an improvement was for them too limited to warrant the cost and disruption which a removal involved. Residential persistence or stability was four years longer in the west end than for Edinburgh tenants overall; on the south side, it was a year longer than the average. Even within the housing sub-markets, tenants in the higher rented properties of South Learmonth Gardens and Comely Bank Avenue were noticeably more persistent (by one year or 19–26%) than the average of other streets in the

[68] This figure is based on the adjustments for continuity of occupancy despite nominal changes of tenancy resulting from widowhood, family sub-letting and intra-neighbourhood moves.

[69] Dennis, *English Industrial Cities*, 250–69, esp. 250–2, examines the various methodological approaches of scholars.

[70] The number of tenancies upon which this analysis of turnover and tenants' persistence is based differs from the overall number of tenancies by the removal of vacant houses, and by those which were either sold the year following a lease, or where the lease changed hands in 1914. See also table 9.2 above.

Table 9.3 *The duration of tenancies in Edinburgh 1868–1914*

Sub-areas	Average tenancy period (years)[a]					Number of tenancies
	Overall	Males	Females	Spinsters	Widows	
Comely Bank/Learmonth	3.77	3.73	3.89	4.41	3.56	4,660
Leith	3.84	3.52	5.34	6.58	5.04	1,347
Dalry	4.18	4.17	4.20	4.14	4.12	4,307
South side	5.38	5.96	4.33	4.38	4.31	651
West end	8.88	8.35	10.06	6.00	11.21	515
Edinburgh average	4.26	4.25	4.31	4.59	4.20	13,111

[a] This figure has not been adjusted to take account of recent widows', other family members' and intra-area moves.
Sources: NAS VR100/69–311, Valuation Rolls, Edinburgh, VR55/12–156, Valuation Rolls, Leith.

neighbourhood; continuity of tenancy in Learmonth Gardens was double the average of the Comely Bank–Learmonth area (table 9.3). As such, these streets approached the levels of stability amongst their residents associated with the nearby west end properties, and provided evidence of the effectiveness of James Steel's efforts to leech the social tone of 'west-endism' to the nearest Comely Bank–Learmonth streets. Rather than the solidarity of slumdom and the sense of community often attributed to working-class areas, the persistence of the Edinburgh upper middle classes enabled, though could not guarantee, a strong sense of identity to develop. In turn, this persistence reinforced the development of social, cultural and religious networks in middle-class areas of the city and reasserted the *credo* of values on which residential segregation was based originally.

Nor was the industrial suburb of Dalry associated with frequent removals. Indeed the residential persistence in these tenancies was above the average of Steel's properties as a whole. Proximity to work for labourers in the breweries, bakeries, rubber works and railway yards of the district were amongst the explanations for the persistence of tenants at addresses in this area. Another strategic factor was that less than 5% of Steel's Dalry properties fronted the main thoroughfare which converged on Haymarket, and even if some tenements were built in the curves created by the Caledonian Railway, there were tangible benefits of less dirt, noise and disturbance by virtue of their location. Unlike the middle-class residents of the west end where intra-area moves were almost unknown, almost 11% of the changes in tenancies were the result of intra-Dalry moves, and another 2.5% resulted from widows assuming the lease on the death of their husband; in Comely Bank and Learmonth, over 12% of changed tenancies were within the same area. Practical benefits – social and credit networks, occupational ties and strong kinship links – were themselves powerful gains which accrued from continuity within a neighbourhood, irrespective of any formal involvement in church, community or club activities.

Continuity at an address and the community stability with which it was associated depended in no small measure on the gender balance of heads of household in an area. Partly this was because the percentage of women who were household heads varied from one area of the city to another, but was also dependent on their marital status since spinsters' persistence on average was almost 10% longer at four years seven months compared to that of four years two months for widows (table 9.3).[71] In Dalry, spinster heads were relatively uncommon, but in the more exclusive areas of the south side and west end where 25–36% of household heads were women, then they were an important factor in the stability of the neighbourhood (table 9.4). For life-renters and annuitants in these areas, their financial circumstances, age and life-cycle stage were such as to discourage the disruption of moving home if it could be avoided.

As heads of household women assumed responsibilities and roles similar to those of their male counterparts. The 'separate spheres' and gendered space of English suburbia may have had some resonance in the outer villadoms of Colinton and the Grange, but at least in extensive districts within Edinburgh, and presumably in other Scottish burghs too, the frequency of female household headship was not consistent with images of compliance and dependence. The symbolic structuring of space along male/urban and female/suburban lines is, consequently, much too simplistic.[72] Equality there was not, as the failure in 1877 to enact a bill to protect married women's income from real property demonstrated, but amongst widows and spinsters particularly the autonomy conveyed by head of household status was considerable, and a caution against the blanket import of an English *mentalité* of suburban lifestyles to Scotland.[73]

[71] These are crude figures, that is, averages which are unadjusted where widows continued at an address after the death of their spouse.

[72] For male/female and urban/suburban tensions see, for example, B. Schwarz, 'Images of suburbia', in B. Schwarz, ed., *The Changing Face of the Suburbs* (Chicago 1976). See also L. Davidoff and C. Hall, *Family Fortunes: Men and Women of the English Middle Class 1780–1850* (London 1987), 172–92.

[73] M. Vicinus, *Independent Women: Work and Community for Single Women 1850–1920*

Table 9.4 *Female heads of household: Edinburgh 1868–1914*

	Female heads %	Widows %	Spinsters %	Number of tenancies N
Dalry	18.8	14.2	4.6	4,534
Leith	19.5	14.7	4.8	1,666
Comely Bank	23.2	13.5	9.7	5,970
South side	25.3	20.4	4.9	593
West end	35.7	28.0	7.7	504
All tenants	22.1	14.8	7.3	15,175

Sources: NAS VR100/69–311, Valuation Rolls, Edinburgh, VR55/12–156, Valuation Rolls Leith.

Though the construction of the city, in all senses of the term, has been identified as a largely masculine activity, intuitively Steel was aware of the importance of women in the housing market, not simply as heads of household but in terms of the demand for solid construction and the provision of amenities.[74] Significantly, just over a fifth (22.1%) of all Steel's tenants were women, but there were important differences in the preferences of widows and spinsters for one area compared to another. Comely Bank and Learmonth in particular were populated by concentrations of spinster heads of household, and nowhere was this more so than in Comely Bank Avenue where main door flats offered a measure of gentility to which Steel's property development strategy was directed. It was a tenancy pattern which contrasted directly with the west end where widows were proportionately more numerous. In no small measure, distinctions in tenants' persistence in specific streets and areas was a reflection both of the absolute rental level and of the annuitant's resources, which in turn were closely related to marital status. In the west end, it was more likely that widows could continue to live in the marital home because the legacies of their deceased spouse enabled them to do so, and the result was a persistence level almost double that of spinsters in such exclusive addresses. The creation of a petit bourgeois suburb in

(Chicago 1985), 10–45, appears to overlook the autonomy conveyed by household head status. See L. Holcombe, *Wives and Property: Reform of the Married Women's Property Law in Nineteenth Century England* (Toronto 1983), 193. R. K. Marshall, *Virgins and Viragos: A History of Women in Scotland from 1080–1980* (Chicago 1983), is vague on these issues.
[74] S. Saegert, 'Masculine cities and feminine suburbs: polarised ideas, contradictory realities', *Signs*, 5, 1980, 96–111. See also M. Roberts, *Living in a Man Made World: Gender Assumptions in Modern Housing* (London 1991).

Comely Bank indicates how women, both spinsters and widows, in this social class were able to sustain an independent household whereas widowhood in industrial and commercial areas such as Dalry and Leith was likely to lead on bereavement to a removal to lodge with kin.

In late Georgian housing built on the edge of the western New Town, the congregation and persistence of spinsters in, for example, West Maitland and Torphichen Streets, reflected the socially desirable nature of the area and its affordability. The persistence at such an address averaged five years ten months; turnover was 14.4%. On this basis and compared to the overall experience of Steel's tenants (table 9.4) community stability was about 20% greater on one criterion and 9% on the other. For those on fixed incomes, the more manageable size and rentals of properties which shared parish catchment areas with the neighbouring New Town elite was an attractive proposition. Though the ratio of female heads of household favoured widows over spinsters on a ratio of 2:1, where spinsters did outnumber their widowed sisters it was invariably in streets which were on the fringes of desirable areas – Lonsdale Terrace fronting the Meadows, Summerside and Ferry Roads on the rural–urban frontier of Leith, Glencairn Crescent and Torphichen Street on the edges of the second and western New Towns, and in Comely Bank Avenue off Edinburgh's Belgravia. The social cachet of the area apart, for those dependent on trust funds and other fixed incomes, the predictability of household running costs, specifically of domestic staff costs, appears to have been a critical factor in the decision to locate where they did. Rents were not unimportant, but they were a subsidiary factor since these concentrations of spinsters paid about 15s (0.75p) per week, at least 50% above the average of all Steel's rented properties. The key variable for the tenant on a fixed income was to be confident that the annuity would be sufficient to meet household expenses, and in this respect there were pressures not unlike those on low income households where the imperative was to meet weekly rental payments, and a social stigma if they did not. Not surprisingly, the attraction of owner occupancy was diminished for spinsters and annuitants generally since their finite annual resources would then be exposed to the destabilising influences of capital expenditure for repairs, maintenance and local taxes, all of which under a lease were the landlord's responsibility. So it was in Comely Bank and Learmonth where, despite the very strong appeal which the area held for female heads of household who accounted for 23.2% of tenants, only 1.8% of sales were to women, all but one of whom purchased a moderately priced flat on one of the upper landings.

Just as there were preferred streets for spinsters, so within each area developed by James Steel certain streets were favoured by widows too. As reflected in the proportion of residents and their persistence at an address, Belgrave Place, Glencairn Crescent, Dean Park Street and Great Wellington Street in Leith came into this category. Some streets, Melville Terrace, Comely Bank Avenue and Murieston Crescent, for example, appealed to both spinsters and widows. In effect, an implicit housing hierarchy existed at the very local level in which clustering and persistence on the scale observed were not accidental; these were deliberate, strategic housing choices in which price, locus, neighbourhood and familiarity were factored into the decision-making process by female heads of household. In many cases, the crucial determinant for female household heads was price. For widows in Dalry Road, an important thoroughfare, the disadvantage of traffic noise and grime was offset by the social characteristics of the area and by the lower rents to tenants which resulted from shared commercial and residential sites. In Dean Park Street, low weekly rentals around 5s–6s (0.25–0.30p) were an important influence on widows' decision to let property there, as it was for spinsters too. In streets with a highly standardised type of rented accommodation, the low purchasing power of many widows meant that they were attracted there because of the price, the number of flats within their range of affordability and, importantly, because there was less social distinction between the landings from which their apartment was entered. Conversely, in those streets with diverse housing as reflected in a wide dispersion of rents around the average, widows or spinsters who located there were more conspicuous than in the more socially homogeneous streets.

The most important determinant of overall persistence, that is, for male and female heads of household, was rent. The correlation coefficient between this variable and persistence was +0.69. A very weak correlation (+0.17) with the level of vacancies suggests that the presence of empty housing had little to do with whether a tenant renegotiated his or her lease. Nor was the age of the housing stock as defined by whether it was newly built or pre-existing housing an important consideration.

Comely Bank: flats, flits and community stability

The Comely Bank area provides an opportunity to analyse some of the relationships between rents, social class, the gender and marital status of heads of households, and persistence in more depth (fig. 9.4). This arises principally because the estate was entirely developed by James Steel, and not, as elsewhere, as a product of a complicated mosaic of building development. Normally, the fractured pattern of ownership in a city obscures the strategic decisions of landlords and tenants unless it can be assumed that all parties are entirely rational and respond promptly to market

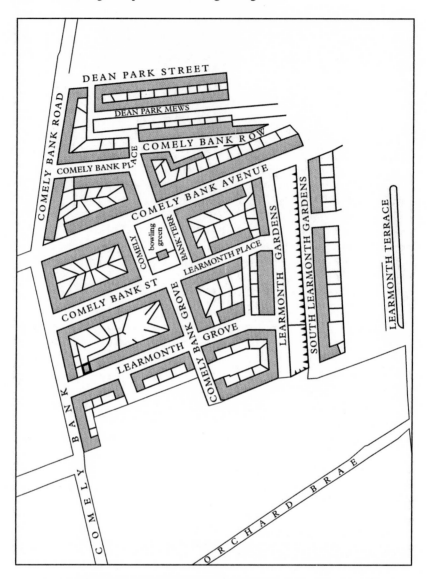

Figure 9.4 Comely Bank and Learmonth streets before 1914

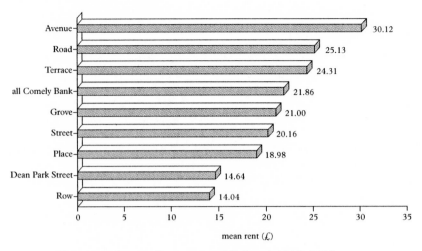

Figure 9.5 Average house rents, Edinburgh 1890–1914

Source: NAS VR100/69–311, Valuation Rolls, Edinburgh.

signals. This is not to claim that the self-contained nature of the Comely Bank and Learmonth estate rendered it immune from city-wide or, indeed, national forces. The population dynamics of the city, the building cycle and fluctuations in the local economy were all underlying considerations, but the conflicting decisions and competing priorities of builders, developers and landlords were inapplicable in a situation where Steel functioned in all these capacities.

The overall profile of the Comely Bank estate is presented in rental terms as a housing hierarchy (fig. 9.5). At one end of this hierarchy were the standardised blocks of sixteen flats in Comely Bank Row and Dean Park Street where rental levels were on average half those of residents at the other end of the hierarchy, in Comely Bank Avenue, where each tenement had a common stair giving access to six and at most nine flats, flanked by two main door or self-contained flats. This subtly graduated pattern of rents enabled different income and social strata to occupy housing affordable in the light of different personal circumstances. Variations in the size of flats and the co-existence of owner occupancy and tenancy within blocks added further dimensions to social diversity, which in turn was reflected in the character of individual streets.

In addition to a housing hierarchy between streets, the social composition within blocks provided another complex overlay. At one end of the distribution there was the standardisation of sixteen-to-a-block tenements in Dean Park Street and Comely Bank Row where the rental, social

Table 9.5 *Vertical variations in rent: Comely Bank Avenue and Road, Edinburgh, 1890–1914*

Six flats in tenement	Ratio flat rent to tenement average	Nine flats in tenement	Ratio flat rent to tenement average
First floor	1.102	First floor	0.985
First floor	1.081	First floor	1.025
		First floor	1.051
Second floor	1.055	Second floor	1.035
Second floor	0.999	Second floor	1.010
		Second floor	1.013
Third floor	0.921	Third floor	1.000
Third floor	0.891	Third floor	0.946
		Third floor	0.927

Source: NAS VR100/69–311, Valuation Rolls, Edinburgh.

class and vacancy rates of ground floor flats were virtually identical to those on all other floors. At the other end of the rental spectrum was Comely Bank Avenue with six, eight or nine flats in a block (figs. 9.6 and 9.7). A superficially similar external appearance belied considerable internal differences within tenements where a vertical housing hierarchy existed. Along the steep quarter mile gradient of Comely Bank Avenue rents for main door flats were routinely 30% above the average of the common stair tenement flat. Yet on different landings within tenements a subtler social grading took place. It was based on a three dimensional rental hierarchy. Rents for first and second floor flats were normally up to 10% above the average of ground floor flats and vacancy rates were generally higher on these landings as a result. Top floor flats were rented at 4.8% below the tenement average, and the percentage of unlet top flats was also lower than in the tenement generally. On each landing a further refinement in pricing accorded front-facing or through flats a small premium of about 2%, and a reduction of at least the same to a small single bedroom flat (table 9.5).

At the top of the hill, closest to Edinburgh's Belgravia, most of these pricing principles also applied to those tenements in Comely Bank Avenue with a more generous six flats in the block. The main door premium was again about 30%, rents for flats on the third landing were as much as 12% below the average of the rest of the tenement, and first and second floor flats were again the most expensive. Third floor flats were at least twice as likely to remain unlet as the first and second floor flats even though the rental was approximately 20% lower.

Figure 9.6 Comely Bank Avenue 1893–1895

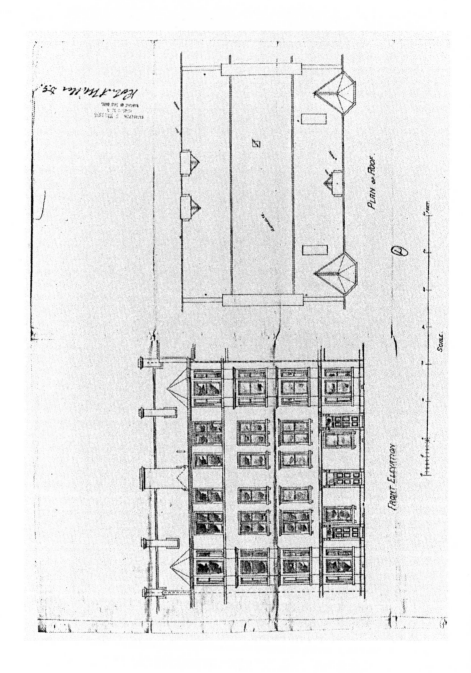

PLAN OF ROOF.

FRONT ELEVATION

SCALE.

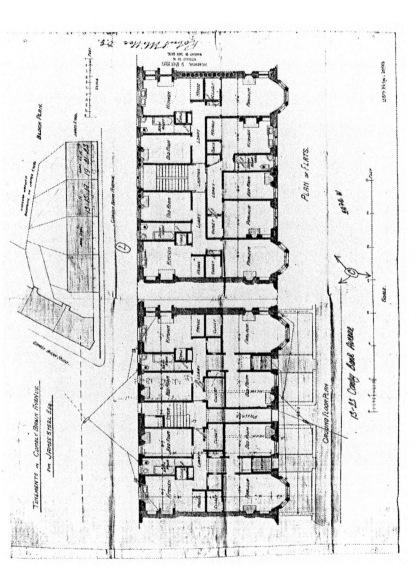

Figure 9.7 Plans and elevations, 13–23 Comely Bank Averue

Note: no. 15 was entered by a common door and had three landings with three flats on each;
nos. 13 and 17 were self-contained ground floor flats with their own entrance.
Source: ECA Dean of Guild Court Registers, 25 Feb. 1893.

The apparent inconsistency reveals a complex mechanism which traded off one set of social values associated with a 'good address' on the upper slopes of the hill, for another set which accorded status to a main door flat in the lower reaches of the street. In some, though not all, cases main door flats could be rented for less than upper floor flats at the opposite end of this prestigious street. Thus, for example, a rent of £26 in 1901 for the main door flat at number 1 Comely Bank Avenue would be consistent with a second floor flat in the upper reaches of the Avenue at number 79; or between 1895 and 1898, rent for the ground floor flat at 37 would have almost covered the rental of an upper floor flat at 63, 69 or number 75.

As new tenements were completed information on them entered the collective knowledge of the neighbourhood. Rent, size and the relative merits of one location were compared to existing accommodation. In some respects, the street, internal position of the flat within the tenement and rent charged were part of a labelling system, a form of tagged social status. Yet depending on the street, these same internal variations within tenements enabled a privacy and social pretence to be maintained.

The nature of this hierarchy of housing was disseminated by word of mouth amongst tenants and evidently understood by them. This was the case with Mrs Mary Alexander who, in 1904–5, lived on the top floor at 10 Comely Bank Grove but was able to obtain better accommodation for an almost identical rent at the first floor level at 34 Learmonth Grove; she then moved on in 1914 to a top floor flat at a more exclusive address, 80 Comely Bank Avenue, in 1914 at £2.50 or 12.5% above her previous rent. Mrs Margaret Dodds, the only tenant amongst owner occupiers between 1896 and 1899 at 69 Comely Bank Avenue, moved from her top floor flat to a main door flat at 81 Comely Bank Road in 1900. Though Mrs Dodds had to pay considerably more for her move because of the tight nature of the housing market in 1900, a few years later Mrs Susan Legg, an embosser, was able to move within the tenement at 2 Comely Bank Street to a ground floor flat and, because of the number of unlet properties at the time, still save almost £1 p.a. or 5% in rent.

This pattern of residential migration demonstrated that vertical mobility could offer a mechanism by which to trade-off affordable rent and social status. Moreover, it was a two way social ladder. By contrast to the upward social mobility and downward vertical mobility for which widows Alexander, Dodds and Legg opted, Mrs Rebecca Hay moved from a ground floor flat at 15 Dean Park Street in 1894 to a top floor one in the next tenement the following year to make a saving of 1.9% on her rent. Hard times forced Mrs Ruth Smith to move from a main door flat at 31 Comely Bank Road to a first floor apartment in Comely Bank Row in

1902, though presumably the reduction in rental of 30% and the loss of social status was an over-adjustment since she then moved again in 1904 to a ground floor flat at an intermediate rent in Comely Bank Grove.

Between the extremes of the housing hierarchy, micro-scale variations in rent, space and the distribution of flats within tenements were evident. Not surprisingly, in Comely Bank Place, commenced in the same year (1891) as tenements in Dean Park Street and Comely Bank Road were under construction, there was a mixture of the dominant designs established in these neighbouring streets – of both sixteen and nine flats per block accessed from the common stair. There were virtually no vertical variations in rents in the sixteen-to-a-block variant, akin to the Dean Park Street housing (fig. 9.8), but elsewhere they were differentiated internally by floor, as in Comely Bank Road. The finely graduated distinctions in price, within and between streets and within and between tenement blocks, enabled an extremely subtle social differentiation to develop.

Externally, the tenement was a vertical version of standardised working- and lower-middle-class English terraced housing, but the reality was that these communal blocks with shared access, collective responsibility and co-operation contributed to a sense of mutuality. At 9 Comely Bank Place, the inhabitants in 1891 included two clerks, a spinster dressmaker, two shopowners, an artisan in the paper and stationery trades, a male shop assistant and a cashier, and an unmarried waitress. Flanked by an architect and an army captain who in 1895 had main door flats at numbers 1 and 5 Comely Bank Avenue, the nine inhabitants of the common stair at number 3 included a cashier, a steward, two drapers and two hairdressers, a traveller, a clerk and a shopowner. In the next common entry tenement, there were four owner occupiers who included a postman and a book-binder, a widow and a spinster with private incomes, and three other tenants – a traveller, a cutter and a clerk. It is difficult to imagine the styles of life and the values associated with them not being discussed privately by residents in these and other tenements where proximity induced both an awareness and conceivably a tolerance of diversity. Privacy and judgementalism, then, were difficult to defend absolutely in tenements, and although the community of the street provided some parallels with those of terraced housing, even the most basic two-up-two-down English arrangement of room space was accessed by a private door. Indeed, the introspective nature of English housing was regarded adversely by a report in 1860: 'The proverb that "an Englishman's home is his castle" contains a very selfish, if not impracticable idea.'[75] Almost by osmosis, the tenement dweller absorbed

---

[75] Macpherson, ed., *Report of a Committee of the Working Classes of Edinburgh*, 17.

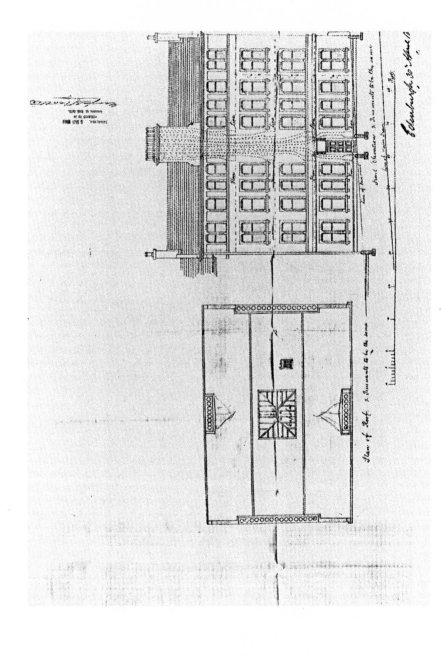

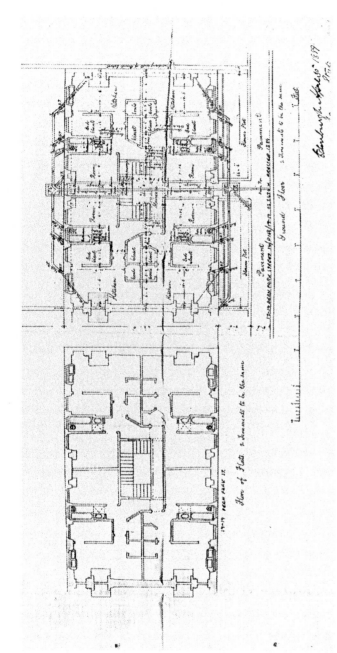

Figure 9.8 Plans and elevations, 17–19 Dean Park Street.

Note: standardised to a simple plan of four flats on each of four floors the construction of the tenement was a complex matter as seen in the room arrangements.
Source: ECA Dean Guild of Court Registers, 30 Apr. 1889.

an awareness of communal interests – what a report in 1860 called
'consanguinity'.[76] Multiplied many fold, at the city level this was sustained by Edinburgh town council, as it was in other Scottish burghs, by
the use of a Common Good account where public interests were recognised to transcend private ones.[77]

Rent variations were an important factor in determining levels of unlet
property on James Steel's Comely Bank development. As seen in those
tenements with sixteen flats, there was no appreciable difference in rent
from the ground floor upwards. Vacancies in such properties were the
lowest, and in streets where the composition of the housing stock was
dominated by properties with sixteen flats, then vacancy levels were correspondingly lower than elsewhere. Equally, persistence at an address in one
these of tenements was shorter than in housing where stairs had only six or
eight flats. Where the dominant tenement type was a common stair with a
large number of flats then the low absolute levels and limited dispersion of
rents was associated with a minimal level of unlet accommodation.

In what must have seemed like a cruel paradox to the overcrowded,
tenants in tenements with the highest rents and thus with most space
were often the only residents on a landing as unlet accommodation was
more common in such properties. Indeed, occasionally the entire top
floor was unlet. Though noise and the disamenities of shared access to
housing were diminished, so, too, were the neighbourly benefits which
came with proximity. Hard to let housing, specifically a number of flats at
13 to 19 Comely Bank Terrace and 2 and 13 Comely Bank Street were
associated after 1905 with a high and persistent level of vacancy, so much
so that social contact and a highly localised sense of a shared residential
experience in newly built homes were more difficult to sustain than in
those fully tenanted flats elsewhere in the area. Across a wide array of
activities – gossip, caring, lending of utensils and ingredients – the reci-
procities of sharing in a communal setting were diminished in those tenements where there was a high proportion of unlet flats. The interaction of
tenants, whether conflictual or consensual, was affected by the frequency
of unlet property just as it was by high turnover rates.

Higher rents bought a number of design features – amenities such as a
kitchen range, copper boiler, internal ornamentation and more space. It
was the quality and disposition of accommodation which a household
head chose deliberately from a position of an assured income whether

---

[76] Macpherson, ed., *Report of a Committee of the Working Classes of Edinburgh*, 17, 18.

[77] T. Hunter and R. Paton, *Report on the Common Good of the City of Edinburgh* (Edinburgh
1905). See also W. H. Fraser, 'Municipal socialism and social policy', in Morris and
Rodger, eds., *The Victorian City*, 258–80.

salaried or from an annuity, and under such circumstances the motive to move house had to be a strong one and suitable alternatives available. Once empty, though, the specificity of the flat and its rental level, particularly on the top landing of tenements with only six flats, meant that it was more difficult to let than almost any other property in Comely Bank. This introduced a tension in the housing market for the landlord, for while higher rented flats were associated with greater persistence amongst tenants, once empty, they were also persistently unlet.

This set of landlord–tenancy relationships is presented in summary form in table 9.6. Inevitably aggregated, many of the subtler variations in the housing market are obscured and yet the overall pattern is clear and, diagrammatically, is presented in fig. 9.9. Predictably, there are some inconsistencies as with Comely Bank Street and Terrace, which though begun in 1898–9 were completed only to coincide with a downturn in the rental market in 1905. Many tenements in these two streets were only half occupied and, arguably, this may have deterred potential tenants. However, the low coefficient of variation in rents confirms that the undifferentiated pricing strategy was also instrumental, a conclusion confirmed both by a vacancy rate of 20% for main door flats almost double that for Comely Bank Avenue and Road (11%), and a consistently high proportion of unlet top floor flats in these eight and nine flatted tenements. The death of James Steel in 1904 meant that it was the trustees who misjudged the market in this instance.

The general symmetry of the housing market elements, as shown in fig. 9.9, provides an indication of consistent relationships between rentals, vacancy and persistence levels. The final column, a summary measure of the social class of a street, offers further confirmation. This is based on an occupational analysis of Comely Bank tenants. Overall, 77% of tenants' occupations were identified and classified using the broad I to V categories for social class deployed by the Registrar-General in the census of 1951.[78] Occupations described as 'professional' constitute social class I; those described as 'intermediate', 'skilled', and semi-skilled were ranked

---

[78] Based on the Registrar-General's categories, Census of England and Wales, 1951, and applied retrospectively. See W. A. Armstrong, 'Social structure from the early census returns', in E. A. Wrigley, ed., *An Introduction to English Historical Demography* (London 1966), 209–37. For assessments of the classification system see R. S. Neale, 'Class and class consciousness in early nineteenth century England: three classes or five?', *Victorian Studies*, 12, 1968, 4–32; R. J. Morris, *Class and Class Consciousness in the Industrial Revolution 1780–1850* (London 1979), 32–6; J. Foster, *Class Struggle and the Industrial Revolution: Early Industrial Capitalism in Three English Towns* (London 1974), 76; Dennis, *English Industrial Cities*, 188–91. G. Routh, *Occupation and Pay in Great Britain 1906–60* (Cambridge 1965), adopts an alternative seven class system.

Table 9.6 *Housing hierarchy: the Comely Bank estate, Edinburgh, 1890–1914*

Comely Bank	Rentals (N)	Mean rent (£)	Coefficient of variation (%)	Persistence (years)	Vacancies (%)	Widows (%)	Spinsters (%)	Social class (score)
Avenue	1,109	30.12	40.27	4.53	7.51	19.3	19.9	2.44
Road	863	25.13	29.77	3.83	8.68	13.4	8.1	2.51
Terrace	123	24.31	10.37	3.13	23.60	13.0	11.4	2.58
Grove	136	21.00	25.22	3.50	2.86	17.6	14.0	2.89
Street	475	20.16	11.11	3.14	18.10	10.4	9.2	2.80
Place	713	18.98	21.02	3.88	2.19	13.6	13.6	2.69
Dean Park Street	556	14.64	19.74	2.79	2.97	10.4	9.2	2.94
Row	459	14.04	3.49	2.61	1.71	13.1	11.4	3.07
All Comely Bank	4,860	21.86	44.92	3.60	7.55	13.7	11.1	2.73

Sources: NAS VR100/69–311, Valuation Rolls, Edinburgh; *Edinburgh and Leith Post Office Directories, 1890–1914.*

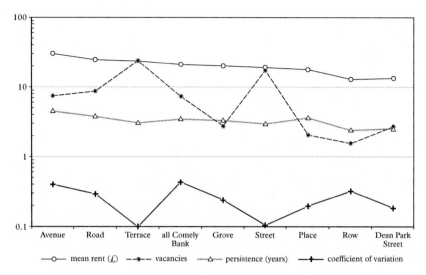

Figure 9.9 Housing hierarchies: Comely Bank 1890–1914

Sources: NAS VR100/69–311, Valuation Rolls, Edinburgh; *Edinburgh and Leith Post Office Directories*, 1890–1914.

II, III and IV, and 'unskilled labourers' as social class V. The figures in table 9.6 provide an average of the social class of the different streets. In general terms the social class scores are consistent with the street profiles developed using rents, vacancies and persistence, though the hierarchy is more in terms of three broad steps than an extended ladder. The scores, which fall around the 2.50s, 2.70s and around 3.00, indicate a generally higher class for Comely Bank Avenue, Terrace and Road, though this itself needs to be treated sensitively. The rough equivalence of the social class score for the Terrace and Avenue should be viewed in relation to the coefficient of variation which confirms that there was a much reduced dispersal of Terrace rents compared to those in Comely Bank Avenue where a small but significant proportion (10.4%) of doctors, solicitors and military officers resided, two-thirds of them in apartments on the more expensive upper slopes of the hill. By comparison, there was a more homogeneous social grouping in Comely Bank Terrace with a quarter of the residents in social class II and two-thirds in class III.

It is possible to detect an important development in the gender basis of the Edinburgh property market in the twenty-five years before the First World War. As heads of household, women assumed an increasing presence in these years, their representation amongst Steel's tenancies rising from 18.3% in the quarter century before 1890 to 22.3% in the years

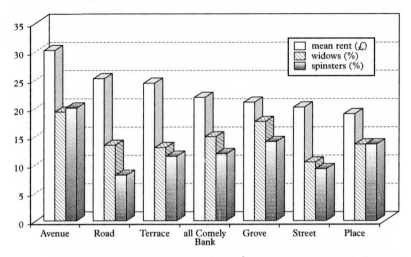

Figure 9.10 Female household heads: Comely Bank Road, Edinburgh, 1890–1914

Sources: NAS VR100/69–311, Valuation Rolls, Edinburgh; *Edinburgh and Leith Post Office Directories*, 1890–1914.

1890 to 1914. The expansion was largely associated with the number of spinsters who assumed head of household status, since the proportion of married women in this category remained almost constant before 1914 at 15%. Before 1890, only 3.1% of all Steel's tenants were spinsters but by 1914 this had more than doubled to 7.5%, with the proportion in Comely Bank accounting for 11.1% of all heads of household. In Comely Bank Avenue, where the highest concentration of spinsters was to be found, they represented 20% of all tenancies, narrowly eclipsing the presence of married women as household heads (fig. 9.10). In no sense, then, did this type of household structure correspond to the highly politicised development of a working-class consciousness as experienced in the west of Scotland where women as rent payers confronted the factor and the bailiff, frequently resisting and certainly delaying his efforts to evict or distrain tenants' possessions in lieu of rent.[79] Nor is there direct evidence to suggest that Steel developed this area of north Edinburgh with women in mind, though his knowledge of trust funds and annuities as the basis of their income, and his personal efforts to set up a household for his spinster nieces together with a lodging house business near Haymarket made him keenly aware of the position of women in the property market.

[79] J. Melling, *Rent Strikes: Peoples' Struggles for Housing in West Scotland 1890–1916* (Edinburgh 1983), 27–34.

One of the reasons for the prominence of women in the Comely Bank area was the number of corner shops. Many of these had living premises attached and even if they did not, the owners and their counter staff often chose in view of the long hours involved in retailing to live nearby. Of the twenty or so rented shops congregated on the corners of Comely Bank Place, Road and Avenue, 39% of shopkeepers between 1890 and 1914 were women.[80] Spinsters overwhelmingly outnumbered their married and widowed sisters three to one.

The diversity of shops was considerable. Amongst the twenty rented premises consistently used as shops during the years 1890 to 1914, competition was greatest amongst the grocers of whom there were three; there were two each of bakers, butchers, dairies, stationer/newsagents and fruiterers. A degree of specialisation was provided with a chemist, china dealer, bootmaker and confectioner, as well as a hosier, draper and clothier. No doubt the absence of the fishmonger reflected the peripatetic nature of the Newhaven fisherwomen with their door to door sales of fresh fish. For residents in the Comely Bank neighbourhood, the considerable variety and longevity amongst retailers offered a measure of dependability coupled with convenience. Some of these retail concerns were almost dynastic. The Buist family ran a grocer's shop in Comely Bank Road and on the death of George Buist in 1898, his widow, Margaret, ran the shop and was succeeded by her daughters. Various members of the Paton family ran confectionery shops in both Comely Bank Road and Place, and the Misses Glen, hosiers, Miss Eliza Chalmers, fruiterer, Misses J. and C. Wilson and Mrs Margaret Aitken, both dairykeepers, were fixtures at their respective shops for over ten years.

Indeed, persistence amongst shopkeepers was a contributory factor to the stability and community of the neighbourhood, the average period being over six and a half years, with vacancy rates correspondingly low at 3.3%. Only in three cases, at 7, 9 and 67 Comely Bank Road, were shops unlet for two consecutive years. Many premises retained the same function even when leases changed hands. Thus, though there were three different tenants at 6 Comely Bank Avenue between 1900 and 1914, the shop remained a stationer's, as did 32 Comely Bank Place despite four changes of tenant. The premises at 7 Comely Bank Road changed hands four times in fifteen years, though the occupants – successively, dressmaker, clothier, tailor and ladies' outfitters – were in much the same line of business. It was rare for the function of a shop to change with a change of lease.

---

[80] Women accounted for 43% of all shop leases.

Table 9.7 *Occupational structure: Comely Bank and Learmonth,
Edinburgh, 1890–1914*

Comely Bank streets	% of employment	Learmonth streets	% of employment
Shopkeepers, workers	16.6	Lawyers	12.7
Clerks	12.0	Clerks	10.2
Travellers	3.6	Stockbrokers	8.8
Compositors, printers	4.8	Other professions	5.9
Joiners	3.1	Military officers	5.9
Teachers	2.7	Merchants	5.6
Butlers	2.4	Coachmen	5.1
Police, local government officials	1.6		

Sources: NAS VR100/69–311, Valuation Rolls, Edinburgh; *Edinburgh and Leith Post Office Directories*, 1890–1914.

The integration of shops within tenements was an established tactic in nineteenth-century Scottish urban development which enabled a degree of cross-subsidisation to take place. Higher commercial rents for street frontages meant a landlord could offer flats at lower rents elsewhere in the tenement, thus attracting interest from a broad range of incomes while still obtaining a sufficient overall income from the entire site to meet feu-duties, local taxes and capital charges. What the market taught the private landlord, however, seemed to be overthrown after the World War when public landlords in the form of local councils built houses without the essential social underpinnings of local shops.[81]

Clerks, shopkeepers and travellers dominated the occupational structure of Comely Bank. Together with the spinsters and widows they defined the petit bourgeois suburb which developed to either side of the spinal column formed by Comely Bank Avenue. On its southern axis and in the closest possible proximity to the earlier, generously proportioned developments bordering Queensferry Road, the predominance of lawyers, stockbrokers and military personnel (table 9.7) articulated an entirely different social tone along the Learmonth streets. Only occasionally was this elite frontier of suburban Edinburgh punctured by the shop-ocracy and artisanal elements which adjoined those of Learmonth. Coachmen, though relatively numerous, were confined exclusively to mews flats, and clerks were concentrated in tenement flats in Learmonth Place and Grove.

[81] ECA Dean of Guild plans, Edinburgh City Council, Lochend, Craigmillar.

Figure 9.11 Tenements and trams: Comely Bank Road, Edinburgh

Note: it took James Steel twelve years to complete the tenements on this street. The occupants were mostly clerks, shopkeepers and skilled artisans. The tram service from Stockbridge and Raeburn Place was extended westwards as the flats were completed.
Source: RCAHMS ED/10237 (560211) from an original by R. S. Henderson.

Learmonth Gardens and South Learmonth Gardens (fig. 9.12) were two elongated terraces of self-contained houses separated by gated gardens accessible only to resident keyholders. In some respects they were an echo of the west end in its earlier pomp, 'a plain version of Buckingham Terrace'.[82] Annual rents of £100 and £115, respectively, were another echo, though still more modestly priced than across Queensferry Road in Belgravia, or south of the Water of Leith in Douglas, Eglinton and adjacent crescents. With modest servants' quarters to the rear (fig. 9.13), both terraces of houses were financially attractive and manageable propositions to an upper-middle-class Edinburgh clientele. Based on occupations, the social class scores were 1.21 for South Learmonth Gardens and 1.34 for Learmonth Gardens, marginally higher than for Belgrave Place (1.44) and Buckingham Terrace (1.61).

Apart from social class, the desirability of Learmonth Gardens was evident from the persistence of its tenants. Learmonth Gardens was built in groups of four or five houses from 1898, and South Learmonth Gardens in a similar way from 1901 (fig. 9.13). So there was little possibility for tenancies to be established for very long. Yet the average persistence at Learmonth Gardens and South Learmonth Gardens was respectively eight and a half years, and five years eight months. Put another way, it was unusual for a tenant to move out of these properties before the First World War, though one resident, Ernest Shackleton, did make the longest known removal by sailing to the Antarctic in 1907.[83] Fine views combined with proximity to the financial headquarters and legal offices in the New Town were the attraction and, accordingly, lawyers dominated South Learmonth (54% of all tenancies, and 50% of sales) and were only slightly less numerous (22%) compared to stockbrokers (28%) in Learmonth Gardens. Moreover, it was the legal elite, advocates and Writers to the Signet, rather than solicitors and other lawyers, who were the residents in these two streets.

Rents, house size and running costs were sufficient deterrents to women who were less in evidence as tenants in this upper-middle-class area than elsewhere in Steel's property portfolio. Women constituted 17% of tenants – about 5% below the average in Edinburgh – and their persistence at an address was appreciably lower than that for male tenants (table 9.8). However, amongst buyers they were well represented. Indeed, lawyers and women were the only purchasers of South Learmonth houses before 1914.

---

[82] J. Gifford, C. McWilliam and D. Walker, *The Buildings of Scotland: Edinburgh* (Harmondsworth 1988), 401.
[83] Even so, Shackleton did not sell his property immediately on his departure.

Figure 9.12 Privacy and exclusivity: South Learmonth Gardens

Note: these elegant self-contained terraced houses were at right angles to Comely Bank Avenue yet formed part of a socially mixed neighbourhood.

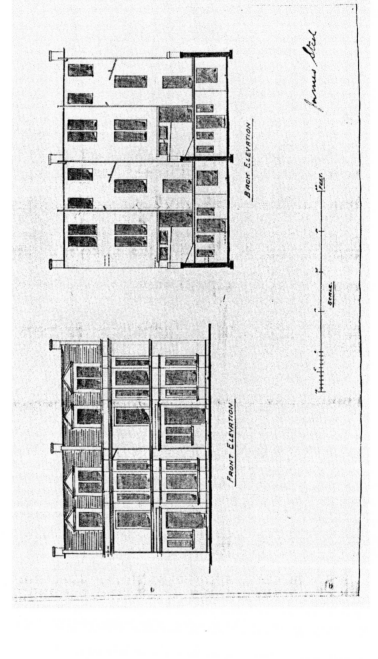

FRONT ELEVATION

BACK ELEVATION

SCALE

FEET

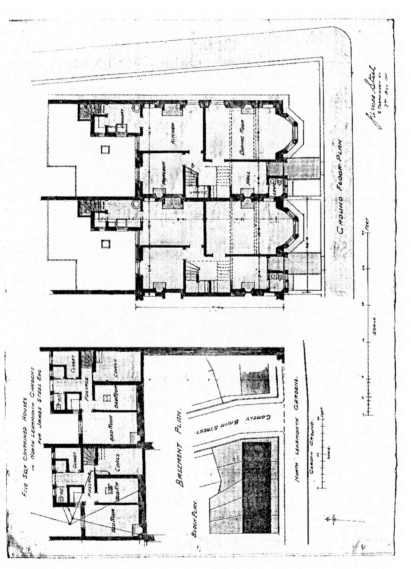

Figure 9.13 Privacy and exclusivity: plans and elevations for North Learmonth Gardens 1901

Note: the plans and elevations for a self-contained residence on three floor were in stark contrast to the flats in Dean Park Street and Comely Bank Road (see 9.8 and 9.11).
Source: ECA Dean of Guild Court Registers, 6 July 1889.

Table 9.8 *Gendered persistence in an elite suburb: Learmonth, Edinburgh, 1898–1914*

	Persistence (years)			Persistence ratio (Female/male)
	Male	Female	Overall	
Learmonth Gardens	8.95	6.80	8.54	0.76
South Learmonth Gardens	6.13	2.00	5.67	0.33

Source: NAS VR100/69–311, Valuation Rolls, Edinburgh.

Table 9.9 *Hard to let elite addresses: Edinburgh*

Street	Social class (average score)	Ranking by rental produced	% of all rental income	Average vacancy (%)	Persistence (years)
Glencairn Crescent	1.00	19	1.46	5.26	12.00
South Learmonth Gardens	1.21	16	1.68	49.57	5.67
Learmonth Gardens	1.34	5	5.62	12.84	8.54
Belgrave Place	1.44	1	11.15	8.79	9.22
Buckingham Terrace	1.61	6	4.25	30.56	8.25
Comely Bank Avenue	2.45	4	8.30	7.51	4.53
Overall	2.00			5.97	4.27

Sources: NAS VR100/69–311, Valuation Rolls, Edinburgh; *Edinburgh and Leith Post Office Directories*, 1890–1914.

For landlords even the upper end of the housing market was not entirely straightforward. When the property sector went into sharp recession after 1905, many lower-rented properties for working-class residents in Dalry were actually immune to vacancies – this was the case in Murieston Place and Caledonian Crescent, and as noted earlier, it was the elite addresses which were most susceptible to vacancies (table 9.9). However, like many streets throughout the city, James Steel's property experienced a meteoric increase in vacancies after 1905; the trustees were unable on 530 occasions to secure tenants between 1905 and 1914. Thus 59% of all vacancies during the years 1868–1914 occurred in this single decade before the First World War. In Comely Bank the figure was higher.[84] Amongst the most prestigious addresses, the rise in the proportion of unlet property

---

[84] It was 70% in Comely Bank and 40% in Leith.

after 1905 was serious – of all vacancies in Buckingham Terrace and Belgrave Place 45–7% were recorded in the years 1905 to 1914.

The private gated gardens, mews flats and separate servants' quarters of Learmonth and South Learmonth Gardens typified an elite residential area. In certain respects, the pricing mechanism which filtered residents and thus defined such areas within cities was predictable and unremarkable. Middle- and upper-middle-class suburbanisation in Edgbaston (Birmingham), Highfields (Leicester), Toxteth (Liverpool) or Headingley (Leeds), as elsewhere in England, reinforced the graduated exclusivity which the pricing mechanism delivered with gatekeepers and regulations to keep out undesirables, however defined.[85] In nineteenth-century Edinburgh, a parallel process of residential exclusivity developed. On one level, the 'English model' of peripheral suburbs of detached and semi-detached residences with private gardens developed and the settlement of Newington (1820s, 1830s), Grange (1850s, 1860s), Merchiston (1870s, 1880s) and Morningside (1890s, 1900s) reflected this in Edinburgh in successive and sometimes overlapping pulses from the 1820s to the First World War.[86] Simultaneously, the New Town phenomenon of exclusive terraced 'Georgian-style' town house residences continued throughout the nineteenth century, and new streets and crescents in the northern and western edges of the New Town, and across the Dean Bridge, testify to this. The development of Learmonth and South Learmonth Gardens demonstrates that, notwithstanding the competing attractions of the semi-rural (or sub-urban) idyll, there was an enduring and sufficient interest in city centre residence to warrant new building until the Edwardian era.

Rents, residential stability and class

For ten years William Kinsey walked uphill most summer evenings from the Dean Bowling Club to his main door flat on the upper slopes of Comely Bank Avenue. No doubt his concern for the affairs of the club of which he was president was a sufficient distraction, but as he ascended the gradient of the Avenue he was no doubt aware of a perceptible change in social class. The green itself, of course, was flat, as were the streets over-

[85] D. N. Cannadine, *Lords and Landlords: The Aristocracy and the Towns 1774–1967* (Leicester 1980); Pritchard, *Housing and the Spatial Structure of the City*; R. J. Dennis, 'The social geography of Victorian Huddersfield', in E. A. H. Haigh, ed., *Huddersfield: A Most Handsome Town* (Huddersfield 1992); P. J. Atkins, 'Elite residence in nineteenth century London', paper to the Urban History Group, Edinburgh, Apr. 1995.

[86] F. M. L. Thompson, 'Introduction', in F. M. L. Thompson, ed., *The Rise of Suburbia* (Leicester 1982), 1–25.

looking it, but as Kinsey began the ascent the average social class score to the north of number 40 was 2.57, and to the south, in the direction he walked, it was 2.19 – a significant difference on a scale of one to five. As he passed, successively, number 51 then 65 and finally reached his own door at 71, so the social class rose further. At right angles to Kinsey's house, were the keyholders' gardens which residents of Learmonth and South Learmonth Gardens used. The social class in these properties averaged 1.34 and 1.21. To the rear, Kinsey overlooked the sixteen-to-a-block flats in Comely Bank Row where tenants paid annual rents half that of his own and, in general, remained at their address for less than half as long as his own Comely Bank Avenue neighbours did. All but two of the flats in the immediately adjacent tenements were privately owned, and one of the owners, Mrs Isabella Canoman, herself owned three flats and sublet them. There were fewer sales to owner occupiers along the entire length of Comely Bank Row than there were to Kinsey's immediate neighbours.

This social diversity was evident in a two dimensional spatial context. William Kinsey like any passer-by could have observed some of the distinctions. Tenurial differences were difficult to detect, however, except in the more obvious self-contained, middle-class properties and main door flats. Internally, tenement design was both standardised, as in Comely Bank Row, and diverse, as in Comely Bank Avenue. As elsewhere in Edinburgh, this was a deliberate strategy developed by James Steel which attempted to reap the benefits of product differentiation. This was achieved through differences in floor space, number and disposition of rooms and the amenities incorporated. Rent levels reflected this in a subtle way. In many Comely Bank tenements, each of the three floors had a one bedroom flat, a two bedroom flat and often a 'through' flat – that is, with front and back views. Often there were nine different rents in a tenement which varied by just a few pence per week, but when considered in conjunction with the disamenities and social status of different floor levels, then the permutations were considerable. As with all new housing, there were no sitting tenants and so there was considerable scope initially to opt for a rent-height-status trade-off which suited the tenant's circumstances. After the initial lettings, there was never quite the same degree of manoeuvre in housing choice.

Scottish urban form, therefore, offered considerable potential for social diversification within a very confined area. Subtly graduated rentals induced residential diversity and, in Edinburgh, James Steel recognised that there was limited demand for undifferentiated accommodation. This was partly because of broader social changes associated with rising real income levels, declining family size and changing tastes and expectations. Heads of household resolved these housing permutations in a multitude

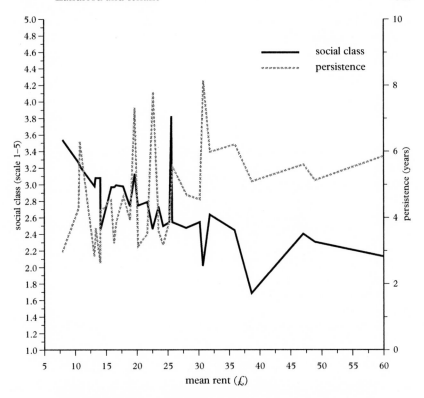

Figure 9.14 Rents, residential persistence and class: Edinburgh 1868–1914

Sources: NAS VR100/69–311, Valuation Rolls, Edinburgh; *Edinburgh and Leith Post Office Directories*, 1890–1914.

of different ways, according to personal circumstances, and across a considerable social spectrum the housing developed by James Steel in Comely Bank and Learmonth provided a suitable locus.

Generalising a multitude of individual housing decisions produces the relationships shown in figs. 9.14 and 9.15. At its most simplistic this merely shows that the higher the rent the more likely a family would reside for several years at an address, and be of a high social class. Rents were positively correlated with persistence ($r^2 = 0.60$) and with social class ($r^2 = 0.70$).[87] The danger is that these reasonably clear relationships

---

[87] The coefficients are developed from all housing, new and existing, built and managed by James Steel between 1868 and 1914 in those streets where there were at least 100 tenancies.

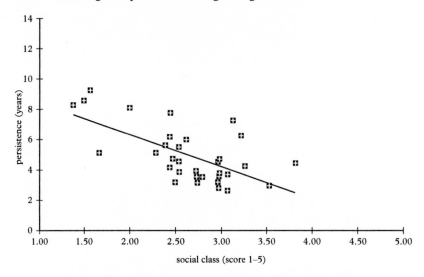

Figure 9.15 Social class and residential stability: Edinburgh
1868–1914

Sources: NAS VR100/69–311, Valuation Rolls, Edinburgh; *Edinburgh
and Leith Post Office Directories*, 1890–1914.

between rent, social class and persistence oversimplify the housing
market and the nature of landlord and tenant decisions. The exceptions
are illuminating and demonstrate the almost infinite variety, and risks,
associated with the housing market. There were instances, as in
Caledonian Crescent and Murieston Crescent, where this three dimensional relationship would break down so that while lower rents were
indeed associated with lower social classes, the permanence at an address
remained higher than average. Structural factors such as the prevalence of
women, and specifically of spinsters, and local employment opportunities
were difficult to judge but each affected landlords' prospects.

At the level of city-wide aggregation, therefore, a matrix of interconnected forces affected the housing market. A snapshot of the housing
market can be seen in rental movements. Demand factors (mainly the
composition and level of employment, and demographic influences)
together with supply factors – mainly based on both landlords' (percentage of vacant houses) and developers' (capital, land, tax and building
costs) assessments of the market – are reconciled in the price of housing,
that is, rents.[88] An analysis based on James Steel's properties (figs. 9.16

[88] Taking real rather than money rents and adjusting for a long-run decline in prices
1873–96 followed by a period of relatively stable prices only marginally affects the pace of

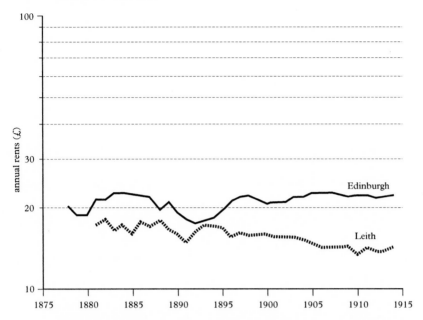

Figure 9.16 Trends in rents: comparative rent levels in Edinburgh and Leith 1875–1914

Sources: NAS VR100/69–311, Valuation Rolls, Edinburgh; VR55/12–156, Valuation Rolls, Leith.

and 9.17) shows the long-run course of average money rents in Edinburgh and Leith in decline, and confirms the city assessor's view that there had been a 7–8% decline in rents in the years 1881–5.[89] The rate of the decline is somewhat more accentuated in Leith compared to Edinburgh. The long-run decline is still unmistakable (fig. 9.17) if the analysis is confined to omnipresent properties in Steel's portfolio (to track the course of rents for this 'older' or 'established' cohort of accommodation) and a threshold of twice the mean rent is used to distinguish unequivocally the middle- and upper-middle-class component of the housing market. Only in the Edinburgh rental series can it at best be said that there was long-run stagnation in the rental market, though to a degree this reflected Steel's perceptive and subtle responses to his opportunity to develop the estate bought from Colonel Learmonth.

this decline. Furthermore, it is arguable that for tenants, fine tuning between changes in real wages and real rents was less relevant that the nominal values for both these series.

[89] *PP 1884–5 XXX*, Royal Commission, Evidence, R. Paterson, Q. 18613.

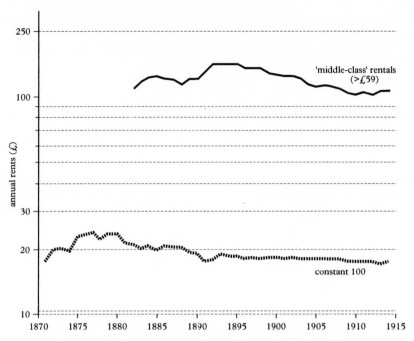

Figure 9.17 Housing sub-markets: Edinburgh 1870–1914

Sources: NAS VR100/69–311, Valuation Rolls, Edinburgh;
VR55/12–156, Valuation Rolls, Leith.

For the tenant, the trend of rents was unquestionably, if unevenly, good news. It represented more and better quality of housing space for money, and confirmed that market-based outcomes, perhaps as much or even more than slum clearances or civic interventionism, contributed to improved living conditions in the four or so decades before 1914.[90] Complaints concerning rising rentals, therefore, may have been confined to central property in the Cowgate, Grassmarket, Pleasance and streets running from them where, in anticipation of compulsory purchase by the local authority for redevelopment, rentals constituted a very high proportion of income.[91]

If, for the shopocracy of Sciennes, the labour aristocracy of Dalry and the unskilled but employed labourers of Leith, the long-run stagnation in rents no doubt held some appeal, then for the landlord the trend

[90] P. J. Smith, 'Slum clearance as an instrument of sanitary reform: the flawed vision of Edinburgh's first slum clearance scheme', *Planning Perspectives*, 9, 1994, 1–27.
[91] *PP 1884–5 XXX*, Royal Commission, Evidence, J. K. Crawford, Q. 18727, 18748; *PP 1917–18 XIV*, Royal Commission, Evidence, Horsburgh Campbell, Q. 18774–6.

represented no strong case to invest in property. Indeed, the existence of faltering rents demonstrated the landlords' weakening market position, certainly from the 1890s in all sections of the market, and even from the mid-1870s in properties affordable by the lower paid. As the terms of trade moved in the tenants' favour, landlords sought to protect their gross income by reducing rents to avoid vacancies and, in property after property, even James Steel was under pressure to do so despite being increasingly insulated by his integrated building operations and considerable financial resources.

This, then, was the financial context which so preoccupied landlords and factors in their evidence to official commissions of enquiry.[92] Faced with declining rents, confronted by increasing management costs and restricted by building regulations as to designs, materials and densities of housing, landlords and builders were disenchanted with property development and management for the lower income groups. Furthermore, since municipal expenditure expanded appreciably in the quarter century before the First World War and burgh assessments and property owners' contributions to local taxation increased correspondingly, then landlords' vigorous defence of the letting system is more understandable.[93] To them the imperative was to obtain reassurances about the occupancy of a property and not to enter into a competition to secure tenants which drove rents down in an effort to avoid vacancies.

The theoretical 'stickiness' of rents – a textbook contention that rents remain unchanged in depression and only rise in more prosperous economic phases[94] – is insupportable in the context of over 15,000 rental bargains in Edinburgh and Leith between 1868 and 1914. For some properties, rents were fixed regardless of the 'state of trade', as at Caledonian Crescent and Livingstone Place where the average rental remained resolutely at £10.60 and £20.00 respectively for almost forty years. By contrast, in Comely Bank Loan, with the exception of only two years, rents declined annually between 1899 and 1914, whereas at Dean Path an increase of £1 to the annual rental in 1904 was maintained until 1914. Another variant existed in Ferry Road, where after a period of stability from the mid-1870s to the mid-1880s, rents reached a peak in the early 1890s when the local economy was still in recession, before falling in 1896, 1907, 1912 and 1913, that is, in all cyclical phases of the economy.

In decisions relating to rent levels James Steel demonstrated a pragmatism and localism which contradicted the existence of 'sticky rents'. At

[92] SLEC, *Report*, 405–7.
[93] *PP 1907 XXXVI*, Report on the Departmental Committee on House-Letting in Scotland, 8, list of witnesses 'against short lets and in favour of the existing practice'.
[94] Cairncross, *Home and Foreign Investment*, 32.

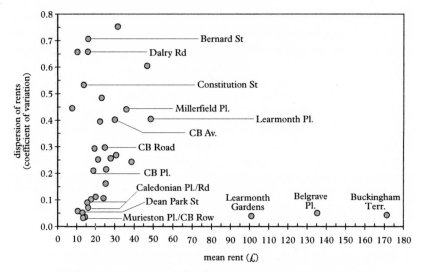

Figure 9.18 Dispersion of rents: Edinburgh streets 1868–1914

Note: the places identified are selected because they occur in the text and relate to different areas and phases of James Steel's building development.
Sources: NAS VR100/69–311, Valuation Rolls, Edinburgh; VR55/12–156, Valuation Rolls, Leith; *Edinburgh and Leith Post Office Directories,* 1890–1914.

the level of the neighbourhood or even the individual street, Steel demonstrated a measure of market sensitivity. The relationship between how homogenised rent levels were in some streets and how diverse they were in others is presented in fig. 9.18. Low coefficients reflect unvarying or inelastic rents. At coefficients below 0.1 were the streets with the lowest and the highest rentals. Steel recognised that pricing variations were largely irrelevant at either end of the income spectrum. For the very rich, demand in Buckingham, Belgrave and Learmonth properties seems to have been unresponsive to price changes and thus no purpose was achieved by marginal rent variations for housing in these areas.[95] For lower income groups in Dalry, locational factors – proximity to employment and the absence of much alternative working-class accommodation in the vector bounded by the railway lines converging on Haymarket Station – meant that rental variations were an unnecessary market

---

[95] Demand may have been backward sloping for this component of demand. That is, the social cachet of the accommodation declined if the quantity was increased or pricing differentials introduced.

complication. Elsewhere, streets were more diverse in their spectrum of rents. In almost three-fifths of the streets in which Steel rented property the coefficient was above 0.2, and in one third it was in excess of 0.4 – double or even quadruple the variability of rents in the poorest and richest neighbourhoods.

Variations in rents perpetuated a Victorian version of the social layering which was identified for an earlier period. In noting that wealthy and noble families in the early modern period lived on the middle floors of High Street tenements with poorer elements above and below them, attention had been drawn to the less socially fractured nature of Scottish urban society which resulted from residential patterns as compared to that of England. In a reference to the Countess of Balcarres' apartments on the third floor, with a fishmonger on the ground floor and tradesmen in the garrets, Smout pointedly observed, 'nobody would have found an English dowager sandwiching herself between a fishmonger and a crowd of tailors and milliners'.[96] In dismissing the English system of housing a report in 1860 noted that 'it shuts out the . . . consanguinity so to speak of . . . a Lord of Session on the first storey and a poor shoemaker on the fourteenth'.[97] Vertical variations in rent and social status were neither as prevalent nor as sharply defined as in earlier centuries, but in Comely Bank, as elsewhere in Edinburgh, they reinforced an earlier awareness and tolerance of alternative lifestyles and values, characteristics which were central to an earlier Scottish enlightenment.

An overview

There is a tension between the general influences on landlords' decisions and the need to recognise that these co-existed with an array of individual decisions. For example, there were powerful general interconnections between rent levels, persistence, the proportion of vacancies and social class. Variations in the level of rents were strongly associated with movements in the others. Persistence was also strongly related to social class; the higher the social class the more likely that a family would reside for a longer than average period at a given address. The vacancy rate was mostly closely correlated with rent levels, then with social class, the percentage of female heads of household and least strongly with persistence. These relationships are presented in table 9.10.

For the individual landlord, however, the problem of aggregation can be most clearly demonstrated by the proportion of female heads of

---

[96] T. C. Smout, *A History of the Scottish People 1560–1830* (Glasgow 1969), 370.
[97] Macpherson, ed., *Report of a Committee of the Working Classes of Edinburgh*, 15–16.

Table 9.10 *A correlation matrix of housing influences*

	Mean rent	Persistence	Social class score	Female head of household
Persistence	.686			
Social class score	−.788	−.695		
Female head of household	−.117	.122	−.113	
Vacancies	.570	.181	−.343	−.243

Note: as the social class variable records a score of 1 as high and 5 as low, the negative signs actually signify a positive relationship in this variable. The same does not apply to other variables.
Sources: NAS VR100/69–311, Valuation Rolls, Edinburgh, VR55/12–156, Valuation Rolls, Leith.

household. In this matrix line, weak relationships are present with all other variables, though it is slightly stronger with vacancies than with other series. Yet, for individual streets, the proportion of women, and even more specifically, of spinsters as heads of household was a crucial factor in persistence, and vacancies. While the general relationship might hold for, say, thirty streets it was inapplicable in several others. It was undeniable that with 33% of household heads as women in Summerside Street in Leith, or 31% in Millerfield Place and Melville Terrace these were important local influences on a landlord's rental income.

For the landlord it was the essence of the problem. While comprehending the general market forces and social characteristics which had a bearing on lettings it was essential to understand the limitations of the system. Local variations could induce miscalculations, and this in turn would undermine profits, or at least introduce a further element of instability. The problems were compounded where landlords were small scale; with few tenements and thus little sense of market indicators, it was possible, even likely, to pick up conflicting signals. So beyond a threshold number of tenement flats the landlord faced fewer problems.

This advantage to the larger portfolios of tenancies was reinforced if property was geographically consolidated. That is, if a few tenements were scattered in various parts of the city then the problem of dependable market signals was considerable. Where tenements were sufficiently numerous in defined areas, then a near local monopoly position might develop in which a landlord could dictate rents and so reduce the risk of unlet flats by redirecting tenants who sought to move away from the area to other properties in their own portfolio. Loyalty worked both ways: to the tenant the assurance of suitable alternative accommodation without

the anxiety of a search and a factor's line was welcome, while the landlord
knew the type of tenant, his or her payment record, and avoided a vacancy
somewhere else in his portfolio. Steel's Leith portfolio demonstrated this
to good effect. The incidence of unlet housing was not simply a distinction between old and new housing, but between a few isolated properties
(in each of Bernard Street, Fort Place, Charlotte Street) and more
consolidated holdings in the Summerside–Ferry Road area and a number
of Bathfield–Lindsay Road tenements where unlet housing consistently
reached only half that of the dispersed holdings (see appendix 9.1).

James Steel moved progressively through the different phases of landlordism. It was not a smooth sequence, and there were overlapping stages
between ownership of a few isolated properties and independent control
of several acres. As a landlord in the late 1860s and 1870s, Steel was
engaged with three types of property. There were, first, his working-class
tenancies in Leith inhabited by a relatively low social class ranging from
3.0 to 3.6, and, secondly, a group of tenement properties in Dalry, built
and rented by Steel himself, where the social class averaged 3.1. Mostly
the residents were skilled or semi-skilled artisans, with a scattering of
unskilled labourers and servants. Apart from the geographical dispersal
of his Leith properties and the consolidated nature of Steel's Dalry property, other compositional factors – the proportion of widows and spinsters, the average rent, and persistence – differed little between Leith and
Dalry (see table 9.3). What distinguished them was that the dispersal of
rents around the mean was significantly less in Dalry. This produced two
important effects: on the one hand, the social class range[98] within the
tenements was four times greater in the Leith housing compared to Dalry
property; and on the other hand, the vacancy rate was three times higher
in Leith than in Dalry.[99] Steel had demonstrated that while it was possible
to build and manage property for the working classes, and even for
unskilled elements within it, the spread of rents and of social classes in
this element of the market exposed him to greater probabilities of vacant
housing. Diversity was not in itself a sufficient condition to spread risk; it
had also to be considered in association with the absolute level of rent and
social class.

If there was any doubt about this dual relationship it was dispelled in
the third of Steel's late 1860s developments. This was in Sciennes, and
though in two streets the social class score exceeded 3.0, there were
enough properties in Gladstone and Millerfield Places and in Melville
Terrace to reduce the overall social class score to 2.7. The shopocracy of

[98] As defined by the coefficient of variation of social class scores, i.e. standard deviation of
social class scores/mean social class score.
[99] The vacancy rate in Leith was 6.3%; in Dalry it was 2.1%.

Table 9.11 *Housing indicators: typical rented housing by James Steel, Edinburgh, 1868–1914*

	Social class score	Social diversity coefficient	Average rental (£)	Female household heads (%)	Vacancies (%)	Persistence (years)
Melville Terrace	2.67	0.26	28.05	31.1	5.91	5.49
Sciennes	2.71	0.27	27.17	21.0	5.97	5.38
All Steel's rented stock			28.51	22.3	5.97	4.26

Sources: NAS VR100/69–311, Valuation Rolls, Edinburgh; *Edinburgh and Leith Post Office Directories*, 1890–1914.

Sciennes offered Steel a glimpse of his future. The rentals in 1869 in Gladstone Place were the first instance of properties both built by and retained for rental by James Steel, but the development also contained sales both to owner occupiers and to other property owners who sought a rental income from them. With a low social diversity coefficient of 0.2 the Sciennes properties enabled Steel to spread risk around a slightly higher social class. Indeed, Sciennes and within it, Melville Terrace, most closely approximated Steel's overall stock of rented housing (table 9.11).

Working-class housing management, therefore, could be successfully undertaken if the property was homogeneous and geographically concentrated, even if the average social class was low, that is, above 3.0. Social class diversity was positively advantageous but not where the absolute social class score was low, when the effect was to increase uncertainty and extend the landlord's risk.

During the late 1870s and 1880s, James Steel switched his attention to building exclusive self-contained neo-Georgian terraces for social class I owner occupiers in the west end. In the majority of cases this property in Eglinton, Douglas and Glencairn Crescents, as well as across the Water of Leith in the Buckingham–Belgrave development, was sold. The concerns of purchasers – principally exclusivity, aesthetics and convenience – were not necessarily those of tenants, factors or landlords. So for Steel, rented property from this phase was residual; it was unsold property and thus less desirable, and in this respect was one of the causes of the 'hard to let' problem experienced after 1905.

By the 1890s and the recommencement of large-scale housing development for rent on the estate purchased from Learmonth, the inter-relationship of rent levels with social class diversity was very fully worked out both within and between streets. This was no social engineering, however. Mixed communities, mixed tenures and social harmony were never hinted at by Steel. Smilesian self-help and independence spliced with a Presbyterian concern for fairness and fair dealing were more appropriate precepts for the kirk elder and were apparent in his stances as city councillor, and in his dealings with his family where duty and loyalty were also ongoing principles. Steel's will, through its provision for building tradesmen in serious distress, acknowledged a social responsibility but approximated a Victorian version of *noblesse oblige* rather than anything more expansive. Accordingly, the development of the Comely Bank estate owed more to market mechanisms and maximising the development potential than to social theory, and Patrick Geddes' *Theory of Social Evolution* would only have been embraced if it was consistent with these.[100]

In view of the highly localised sphere of operations amongst builders and developers, to lay out an estate with a high degree of standardisation would have saturated the equally localised nature of the housing market. James Steel never strayed east of a line drawn from Constitution Street and Leith Walk to Causewayside. East and south Edinburgh were abandoned to other builders and landlords. In his earliest dealings over the development of the Tollcross area centred on Drumdryan, contacts were exclusively with a fraternity of builders and sub-contractors whose addresses were within a quarter of a mile of the site.[101] These highly localised spheres of operations were typical of others in the building industry and housing market. Tacitly and for sound operational reasons, builders reinforced localism since they did not stray into all quarters of the city. Thus a diverse social composition was an essential characteristic by which an area the size of Comely Bank–Learmonth could be developed, and to do otherwise was to risk a high proportion of vacant housing and to compromise private sales. What had been an unintended feature of building in Sciennes had become a critical tool of estate development and property management in Comely Bank.

Thus the emergence of a socially diverse and yet extensive area in north Edinburgh was the only strategy consistent with estate development unless, like an educational endowment, Steel was to take a very long view of his property interests. The absence of direct heirs made such a horizon unlikely. As a result, the purchase and development of the Learmonth

---

[100] H. E. Meller, *Patrick Geddes: Social Evolutionist and City Planner* (London 1990); H. E. Meller, 'City development in turn of the century Scotland', in C. J. Carter, ed., *Art, Design, and the Quality of Life in Turn of the Century Scotland 1890–1910* (Dundee 1982); and H. E. Meller, 'Planning theory and women's role in the city', *Urban History Yearbook*, 17, 1990, 85–98.

[101] *Edinburgh and Leith Post Office Directories*, 1865–1914.

estate punctured the institutional stranglehold in north-west Edinburgh and blazed the way for the construction of private flats in Comely Bank and bungalows in Craigleith during the interwar years. It also revealed how informal planning, articulated by market mechanisms and implemented by the developer, could deliver socially balanced and stable communities. The constraint of market saturation forced such features on James Steel, but where building development was more piecemeal and incremental, then such considerations were beyond the scope of developers.

The Comely Bank–Learmonth development created an entirely new, self-sustaining suburb in the space of a generation. Indeed, it was the second time Steel had achieved this. Dalry was created over an earlier twenty year period during the 1870s and 1880s, and if it lacked the social diversity of his later project, it did not lack for the residential stability of its tenants. Their persistence at a particular address was slightly above that of Comely Bank, though predictably below the Learmonth average. This persistence was encouraged by the development of amenities and social infrastructure, though other than his responsibilities to lay out the roads and pavements, none of this was initiated by James Steel. No parks were laid out in either suburb other than those private gardens associated with the Learmonth properties and for which their owners and tenants paid.[102] Schools and churches were built in both suburbs though only some years after tenants had become established and normally on land sold or leased by Steel at market rates. The Dean Bowling Club in Comely Bank was a private initiative on marginal land, and the swimming club associated with the municipal baths in Caledonian Crescent was another independent organisation.[103] For the most part, then, the provision of social capital by municipal or church-based initiatives – parks, schools, tramways, halls, baths – while they enriched the lives of inhabitants in both suburbs, enhanced the developmental prospects and capital values of James Steel's property through the externalities he enjoyed as a result of the efforts of others.

Notwithstanding this symbiosis between public and private interests, the residential stability and, so far as can be judged, social harmony within the new suburbs were impressive. There can be few British cities where a developer has created two suburbs during his lifetime, and it turned Steel into the largest local taxpayer in the Edinburgh and 'possibly

---

[102] The legacy of a small triangle of green space at Murieston was the result of a cessation in building in the area in the early twentieth century rather than a deliberate creation.

[103] ECA ACC 373, Minute of lease between James Steel and members of the Summerside Bowling Green and Club, 17 Feb. 1889, shows that compared to the Dean Bowling Club, Summerside paid a higher rent, were restricted in the arrears they could owe, and that 'the said bowling green shall not at any time be converted into a public bowling green'.

the largest feuar of land and the largest builder of houses that Edinburgh has possessed'.[104] In the twentieth century, Edinburgh like most British cities pursued another sub-urban approach, rejecting the integrationist character of Comely Bank in favour of socially segregated sub-urban 'communities' in which owner occupancy and local authority rented accommodation polarised more than just the housing stock.

James Steel's reliance on the market mechanisms meant socially mixed housing developments could flourish without the invasive use of mandatory powers of the formal planning process. The crucial difference, of course, was that for those in work and able to afford new housing, whether as tenants or owners, then patience and the market would deliver such solutions.

[104] *Building News*, 9 Sept. 1904, 358; *Scotsman*, 5 Sept. 1904, 5a.

Appendix 9.1 *Landlordism in Edinburgh 1868–1914: principal properties rented by James Steel*

	N	Mean rent (£)	% rental	% vacant	Average social class	Persistence
Antigua Street	395	31.94	3.14	4.13	2.84	5.98
Bathfield (Lindsay Road)	469	7.92	0.92	3.30	3.57	2.95
Belgrave Place	332	135.03	11.15	8.79	1.44	9.22
Bell's Mills	45	98.58	1.10	16.67	2.49	5.00
Bernard Street	531	16.49	2.18	11.06	3.06	3.75
Buckingham Terrace	100	171.10	4.25	30.56	1.61	8.25
Caledonian Crescent	845	10.51	2.21	0.12	3.21	4.25
Caledonian Place	341	15.72	1.33	3.67	2.92	4.52
Caledonian Road	326	16.13	1.31	2.98	3.02	3.52
Charlotte Street	29	25.17	0.18	0.00	3.00	5.80
Comely Bank Avenue	1,109	30.12	8.30	7.51	2.44	4.53
Comely Bank Grove	136	21.61	0.73	2.86	2.89	3.50
Comely Bank Loan	23	19.94	0.10	0.00	2.72	n/a
Comely Bank Place	713	18.98	3.37	2.19	2.69	3.88
Comely Bank Place Mews	37	32.28	0.30	13.95	2.77	3.43
Comely Bank Road	863	25.13	5.39	8.68	2.51	3.83
Comely Bank Row	459	14.04	1.60	1.71	3.07	2.61
Comely Bank Street	475	20.16	2.38	18.10	2.80	3.14
Comely Bank Terrace	123	24.31	0.74	23.60	2.58	3.13
Constitution Street	99	14.08	0.35	3.88	2.88	4.13
Dalry Road	235	16.31	0.95	2.89	2.80	3.19
Dean Park Street	556	14.64	2.00	2.97	2.94	2.79
Dean Path	244	10.72	0.65	2.40	2.91	6.28
Ferry Road	106	30.83	0.81	2.75	2.02	8.08
Fort Place	18	4.97	0.02	10.00	3.50	2.29
Gladstone Place	125	28.05	0.87	11.97	2.64	4.69
Glencairn Crescent	36	163.28	1.46	5.26	1.00	12.00
Great Wellington Street	142	22.65	0.80	5.33	2.41	7.76
Learmonth Gardens	224	100.87	5.62	12.84	1.34	8.54
Learmonth Gardens Mews	143	25.49	0.91	17.34	3.15	4.44
Learmonth Grove	362	23.56	2.12	5.24	2.78	3.32
Learmonth Place	155	48.81	1.88	6.63	2.05	5.10
Livingstone Place	46	19.84	0.23	0.00	2.98	4.6
Lonsdale Terrace	45	41.71	0.47	2.17	2.00	3.75
Melville Terrace	225	25.71	1.44	5.86	2.67	5.49
Millerfield Place	150	35.97	1.34	3.85	2.43	6.17
Murieston Crescent	1,911	17.71	8.41	2.65	3.01	4.65
Murieston Place	782	13.36	2.60	1.39	3.19	3.67
Sciennes Road	102	19.64	0.50	3.77	3.09	7.29
South Learmonth Gardens	59	114.75	1.68	49.57	1.21	5.67
Summerside Road	154	49.95	1.48	1.28	1.61	5.08
Torphichen Street	90	47.07	1.12	2.17	2.29	7.88
W. Maitland Street	734	28.71	8.59	3.67	2.47	5.57
All properties	15,175		100.00	5.97	2.78	4.27

Note: other streets include Summerside Place, Belford Terrace, Eglinton Crescent, Jamaica Street (Leith), Queensferry Gardens.
n/a indicates that these properties were rented only in 1905. Comely Bank Loan was then absorbed into Learmonth Grove, and persistence was calculated along with that street.
Source: NAS VR100/69–311, Valuation Rolls, Edinburgh, VR55/12–156, Valuation Rolls, Leith.

Appendix 9.2 *Rent indices: Edinburgh and Leith 1871–1914 (average 1900–4 = 100)*

Year	Edinburgh rents <£60 p.a.	Leith rents	Rents of existing properties[a]
1871			96.1
1872			109.0
1873			111.0
1874			108.8
1875			126.3
1876			128.0
1877			130.8
1878	94.8		121.8
1879	87.7		128.9
1880	87.7		128.2
1881	101.2	111.0	118.0
1882	101.2	115.3	115.8
1883	106.2	106.1	111.3
1884	106.5	110.4	114.2
1885	105.9	103.2	110.1
1886	103.8	112.9	114.8
1887	102.9	109.2	112.8
1888	91.8	114.9	112.1
1889	99.1	106.2	107.2
1890	90.1	102.7	104.9
1891	85.3	95.4	95.7
1892	82.8	104.0	97.2
1893	84.0	110.2	105.3
1894	86.0	109.6	102.5
1895	91.5	107.9	101.8
1896	98.9	99.5	99.7
1897	103.3	102.9	101.6
1898	104.3	100.9	98.9
1899	100.6	102.1	101.5
1900	97.8	102.1	101.2
1901	98.3	99.9	100.0
1902	98.1	100.1	100.7
1903	102.9	100.1	100.3
1904	102.9	97.9	97.8
1905	106.7	94.3	99.9
1906	106.8	91.4	98.4
1907	106.4	91.1	98.7
1908	105.5	90.9	98.1
1909	103.4	92.2	95.7
1910	104.7	86.8	96.2
1911	104.2	91.1	95.5
1912	102.0	87.9	95.9
1913	102.9	88.4	92.7
1914	103.8	91.0	96.3

[a] properties which were already built and rented when acquired by James Steel.
Source: NAS VR100/69–311, Valuation Rolls, Edinburgh, VR55/12–156, Valuation Rolls, Leith.

10   Postscript: 'firmiter et durabile': the construction of legitimacy

Under examination in 1861 from the trustee in bankruptcy, James Steel identified three major reasons for his business failure.[1] First, others for whom he had done work went into liquidation themselves, as in the case of a Wishaw draper who owed him money, and on a contract at Lochgoilhead where he had lost £600 because of 'the works giving way before the contract was completed'. Secondly, the injudicious speculative ventures in Glasgow tenement building exposed his borrowing strategy as too risky, particularly if, as happened, the market value of the house should not be fully realised. Finally, poor estimating techniques and the failure to keep accounts meant that he was blissfully unaware of his vulnerable position.

The supportive role of the family, however, had been critical in the upward business trajectory of James Steel. The accumulation of unpaid wages to his brother-in-law, the investment of his father and the unsettled trade debts to his brother for joinery undertaken on Steel's property were disallowed by the accountant in bankruptcy because of insufficient documentation, as were a number of other trade debts due to close business associates.

The contrition shown by James Steel over his bankruptcy defined his subsequent business ethos. The characteristics included adherence in meticulous detail to careful estimating for contracts, in book-keeping and in legal records; determination in the negotiation of contracts and feu charters; a rejection of sentimentality in the conduct of business affairs; and loyalty to his family members, particularly those who had assisted his Lanarkshire enterprise and in some cases lost money through his conduct. This was achieved by providing employment as clerks, domestic servants and personal assistants, as well as legacies, for close family members and their children through his trust fund.

Outside the immediate family, but conscious of a wider responsibility for social and moral leadership, James Steel used his wealth to support the

---

[1] NAS CS318/325, Sederunt Book, ff. 39–48.

344

Figure 10.1 Sir James Steel (1830–1904); Lord Provost of Edinburgh
1900–1903

activities of the United Presbyterian Church which received an 8.3% share of the annual income from the trust to be used equally between the Foreign Mission schemes and the building of churches and halls in Scotland, and a further 8.3% share to assist his 'servants, outdoor and indoor clerks and employees', as well as those relations who were not direct beneficiaries of the will.[2] The trustees were empowered to overturn this last provision, remit the money to Trinity Hospital, and to use this share of Steel's estate to render 'assistance to masons, joiners or other workmen connected with the building trade'.[3]

The concept of service and civic responsibility to a city which afforded him first anonymity and then opportunity was almost subconsciously part of James Steel's mentality, reinforced by a strong commitment to the Church. Within ten years of his bankruptcy and arrival in Edinburgh Steel had been elected in 1872 for the prized George Square ward. This he had contested the previous year, achieving some prominence for his vigorous support for the city council's determination to embark on a water supply project from the distant St Mary's Loch.[4] As bailie and then Lord Provost he undertook an active role in the management of the city and served on almost all the committees of council at some stage in his political career.[5] It is difficult to sustain a more cynical view of his involvement in city administration. Steel sought vigorously and often in acrimonious exchanges to alter the constitution and thus the composition of the Dean of Guild Court committee by attempting to disqualify unelected individuals with building, land and contracting interests from the membership of this committee where he perceived there to be a conflict of public and private interest in relation to building development.[6] Steel was not concerned exclusively with the larger issues of urban development, nor solely with the interests of the ward he represented, as he showed in 1885 in his awareness of the needs of commuters and workers by recommending the construction of a convenience and urinal at Slateford Road.[7]

[2] NAS SC70/4/366, Trust Disposition and Settlement, Sir James Steel, 9 Dec. 1896, f. 246.

[3] The trustees frequently considered applications from workmen and awarded relief at the rate of 7s 6d per week. See ECA SL104/1 Sir James Steel's Trust, Ledger, vol. 1, ff. 118–21, 124–7, 133, 140–3, 157.

[4] *Edinburgh and Leith Post Office Directories*, annually, provide a list of elected officials during the period. For a brief account of the St Mary's Loch controversy see J. Colston, *The Edinburgh and District Water Supply: A Historical Sketch* (Edinburgh 1890), and H. Macdonald, 'Public health legislation and problems in Victorian Edinburgh, with special reference to the work of Dr. Littlejohn as Medical Officer of Health', University of Edinburgh PhD thesis, 1971, 175–9.

[5] *Times*, 5 Sept. 1904, col. 4d; *Glasgow Herald*, 5 Sept. 1904, col. 8g; *Scotsman*, 5 Sept. 1904, col. 5a; *Building News*, 9 Sept. 1904, 358 (James Steel obituaries).

[6] ECA ACC 264, Proceedings of the Guildry of Edinburgh, Box 1, Report, 2 Apr. 1878.

[7] ECA SL47/1/6, Streets and Buildings Committee, 20 July 1885.

Figure 10.2 Boroughfield: Sir James Steel's home at 32 Colinton Road 1883–1904

As a businessman, Steel was able to establish sufficiently sound financial credentials as to borrow from the Earl of Moray; the networking which council business inevitably facilitated was superfluous. As a director and chairman of the board of both the Niddrie and Benhar Coal Co. and the Broxburn Oil Co. Ltd, as a director of the National Insurance Company of Great Britain, the Indian Gold Mines Co. Ltd in the 1880s, the Assets Company Ltd in the 1890s, and as a substantial shareholder in the Fife Coal Co., the mechanical and electrical engineering firm of Bruce Peebles and Co. and a range of other locally significant companies, James Steel was able through his own substantial wealth and corporate investments to obtain leverage where he sought to do so.[8] Certainly his position on the governing body of George Heriot's Hospital did him no harm, but it was a position accorded to councillors generally in the context of the relationship between the city council and the trustees, and such information as he did obtain concerning the estate development of Heriot's was virtually common knowledge, since their policy was actually printed in the annual report of feudal income.[9] Through his building interests, he also came into conflict with the governors.[10]

Political and business roles elevated Steel to a position of eminence. During his lifetime, the acquisition of a private landed estate, Murieston in Midlothian, outwardly proclaimed high social status for James Steel.[11] In 1878, a little over a decade after his arrival in Edinburgh, the former Lanarkshire bankrupt bought 88 acres attached to Murieston House and in a further purchase extended this to 201 acres, twice the tenanted acreage his recently deceased father had farmed near Cambusnethan, where Steel also continued to own a few properties. Though there was a hard business edge to this decision – the mineral rights gave Steel a supply of lime, building stone and the possibilities of shale oil deposits – it was also an explicit confirmation of James Steel's respectability, commemorated in his baronetcy, Sir James Steel of Murieston, and in the heraldic motto 'firmiter et durabile'. Unlike other businesses where the third generation of the dynasty migrated to a rural retreat, the estate was acquired in the first generation of the business and, far from retreating,

[8] For Steel's directorships and shareholdings see his will, NAS, CS318/325; Niddrie Coal Company, NAS CB/567, and Niddrie and Benhar Coal Co., NAS CB18/1–6, 14–15; Fife Coal Company, NAS CB3/49–50; Edinburgh Collieries Co. Ltd, NAS CB4002 and 4550; Assets Company Ltd, NAS CB1126/1–3; Rosewell Gas Coal Co. Ltd, NAS CB 1454; Bruce Peebles & Co. Ltd, NAS CB/5383; Indian Gold Mines Co. Ltd, BT2/886, 1721, 2099; and Building Trades Exchange, BT2/3506.

[9] ECA, George Heriot's Roll of Superiorities, 1899–1900.

[10] ECA ACC 373, Report of Commission Steel v. Governors, 24 Mar. 1879.

[11] ECA ACC 373, Report upon Valuation of the Estate of Murieston, 31 Oct. 1906. For Inland Revenue purposes of assessment of death duties the estate was valued at £7,720. See ECA SL104/1, Sir James Steel's Trust, vol. 1, ff. 164, 174.

the newly wed Steel set up his married home in Merchiston in 1883 (fig. 10.2) and forged on with his most lucrative years still ahead.[12]

In the eleven years between the purchase of Drumdryan in 1867 and Dalry in 1878, both from James Home Rigg's trustees, Steel acquired almost seventy-five acres. Had the census of landowning in 1872 been taken in 1878 then Steel would have been in the top three of private land-owners, along with Learmonth and Sir George Warrender, and ahead of Sir Thomas Dick-Lauder.[13] His acquisition of the Learmonth estate in 1889 projected him to the position of the largest private landowner in the city, though his scattered holdings contrasted with the consolidated estates of prominent families. At his death, only the Crown, the city, Heriot's, and the North British Railway owned more land in Edinburgh than did James Steel.

Yet the dynamic quality of the business faltered after his death. The dynastic nature of many family firms was lacking since Steel and his wife, Barbara Paterson, had no children, and Steel's nephews, Hugh Percival, Samuel Forrest Steel and Alexander Allan, lacked their uncle's vision and were content to pursue their own more limited career objectives as architect, rentier and builder. In no small measure, though, it was in the nature of trusts themselves which constrained business development, limited as they were to the management of existing assets rather than empowered to take risk and create wealth. In shaping his Trust Disposition and Settlement so that it was in the hands of trustees, therefore, Steel knew that business drive was limited. In death, his personal wealth of £424,000 (approximately £23 million in 2000 prices) enabled him to distribute largesse to the family members, near and distant, and this has continued for almost a century. A complex formula is still used and, as family members die and relinquish their claim, is revised by the present trustees to calculate the annual distribution from Steel's estate.[14]

The bronze bust of Sir James Steel in the Dean cemetery (fig. 10.1) is the second largest marker in a graveyard which contains a high proportion of the aristocratic, professional, intellectual and business elite of Edinburgh. It proclaims self-importance, but acknowledges no forebears, no origins, nor descendants.[15]

---

[12] For a summary of this argument see P. L. Payne, *British Entrepreneurship in the Nineteenth Century* (Basingstoke 1988).

[13] *PP 1874 LXXII pt III*, Owners of Lands and Heritages, 1872–3, 66–9.

[14] ECA ACC 373, Division of primo and secundo giving effect to the assignation of the late Robert (surname omitted to preserve anonymity) one sixth share, records the following decimal divisions: 0.1428, 0.1667, 0.1794, 0.0949, 0.1008, 0.1369 (twice) and .0104 (4 times) = 1.0. The dissemination of wealth over time and across generations is visible.

[15] ECA SL104/1, Sir James Steel's Trust Ledger 1896–1914, vol. 1, ff. 56–8, notes Lady Steel's irritation over the burial plot arrangements.

Part 3

Complementary visions of society

11   Co-operation and mutuality: the 'Colonies' and the Edinburgh Co-operative Building Company

The history of co-operation accords the Rochdale pioneers' efforts in 1844 an understandable prominence.[1] By then, however, there were already over 100 active co-operative societies though, in Scotland, the 1830s and 1840s have been described as 'an extremely barren time for co-operation'.[2] Even improved legal protection for industrial and provident societies after 1852 did little to foster new co-operative ventures and it was not until the more robust protection provided by limited liability in 1862 that such forms of organisation proved attractive.[3] The objectives of co-operatives were, first, the attempt to counteract abuses associated with employer-controlled factory shops – an attempt to 'rescue from destruction victims of the "tally-shop" system'[4] – which placed employees in a position of dependency, and, secondly, to internalise the advantages of large-scale production in the form of lower costs passed on as lower prices to the membership. For these reasons, co-operatives have been identified amongst the earliest of workers' initiatives to act collectively and as a means by which to challenge the unbridled functioning of the market. The history of co-operation is, therefore, presented as part of an embryonic class or political consciousness and draws on the nature of relationships between the co-operative movement and its financial support for contemporary Labour Party MPs.[5]

[1] *Builder,* 29 Sept. 1860, 617, was amongst the first to enshrine Rochdale with this significance. The Chairman of the Edinburgh Co-operative Building Company acknowledged the Equitable Pioneers Co-operative Society of Rochdale as an important precedent at a public meeting in 1861. See *Edinburgh Courant,* 30 Nov. 1861
[2] J. Butt and J. Kinloch, *A History of the Scottish Co-operative Wholesale Society Limited* (Glasgow 1981), 1–8. For a British dimension, see M. Purvis, 'Co-operative retailing in Britain', in J. Benson and G. Shaw, eds., *The Evolution of Retail Systems c. 1800–1914* (Leicester 1992), 109–18.
[3] Butt and Kinloch, *A History,* 2; M. Purvis, 'Popular institutions', in J. Langton and R. J. Morris, eds., *An Atlas of Industrialising Britain 1780–1914* (London 1986), 195.
[4] Quoted in 'Co-operative societies in 1864', *Edinburgh Review,* 120, July–Oct. 1864, 414. The Edinburgh Co-operative Building Company's 'rows of houses' are also noted, 425.
[5] W. Knox, 'The political and workplace culture of the Scottish working class 1832–1914', in W. H. Fraser and R. J. Morris, eds., *People and Society in Scotland,* vol. II (Edinburgh 1990); G. D. H. Cole, *A Century of Co-operation* (London 1944), 269; Butt and Kinloch,

The formation in 1861 of the Edinburgh Co-operative Building Company (ECBC) was significant for several reasons. First, the ECBC built over 2,300 homes in fifty years and introduced many workmen and their families to both home ownership and share ownership. The ECBC housed as many people as lived in Forfar or Renfrew in 1911; consolidated, its housebuilding would have made it Scotland's twenty-eighth largest burgh on the eve of the First World War. Secondly, the ECBC anticipated the major expansion of co-operatives in urban Scotland and embraced the co-operative principle in the arena of capital projects, so providing a corrective to the history of co-operation written mainly from the standpoint of retailing through such organisations as the East of Scotland United Buying Agency (1863) and the Scottish Co-operative Wholesale Society (1868).[6] Finally, the significance of the ECBC is that it offered a measure of integration to working men and women in a rapidly changing urban society. Through its principles of mutuality and participation, the ECBC provided workmen and their families with the opportunity to acquire a stake in society as householders, as shareholders, as contributors to quarterly meetings and even as directors of the Company. Residents and shareholders were encouraged to submit designs for houses for which a competition panel awarded a 2 guinea prize.[7] By these direct means the ECBC provided an opportunity for workmen to participate in urban governance. Indirectly, the greater average length of time families resided at an ECBC address enabled them to become further involved in community activities and the associational life of the neighbourhood.

The genesis of workers' co-operation in housebuilding

In April 1861 a group of Edinburgh building workers formed their own company (fig. 11.1). That in itself was remarkable. More remarkable still was that in a little over a decade they had planned, built and sold almost a thousand homes. To survive for a decade in any line of business in the nineteenth century was exceptional, especially in the building industry; to construct 'three good sized villages of self-contained houses' in

footnote 5 (cont.)
A History, 254–5; W. Maxwell, *A History of Co-operation in Scotland: Its Inception and its Leaders* (Glasgow 1910), 44–110; J. F. C. Harrison, *Robert Owen and the Owenites in Britain and America* (London 1969); S. Pollard, 'The foundation of the Co-operative Party', in A. Briggs and J. Saville, *Essays in Labour History*, vol. III: *1880–1923* (London 1971), 185–210.
[6] W. Maxwell, *The First Fifty Years of St. Cuthbert's Co-operative Association 1859–1909* (Edinburgh 1909), 40–2.
[7] NAS GD1/777/2, Edinburgh Co-operative Building Company, Minute Book, 9 Feb. and 26 Apr. 1867.

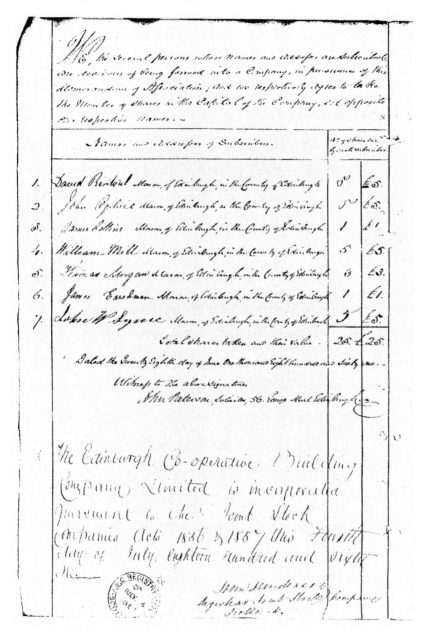

Figure 11.1 The founders of the ECBC 1861

Source: NAS BT2/1970/548/79/1, Memorandum of Association,
28 June 1861.

Edinburgh and 'two similar villages in Leith' in the first ten years of its existence was a major achievement.[8]

Why was a workers' building company formed? The immediate explanation for the formation of the ECBC can be attributed to a building lock-out by employers in 1861. The written request by building trades workers for a reduction in the working day from ten to nine hours was part of a national campaign to improve 'the physical, moral, social and intellectual condition of the working-classes'. This plea was rejected by the employers and for over three months in the spring of 1861 more than 1,200 stonemasons and joiners were denied access to building sites throughout the city. In April 1861, before the lock-out was over, the ECBC had been formed as a limited liability company, the Memorandum of Association of which stated that:

The objects for which the Company is established are the carrying on the business of Building in all its branches, including Joiner-work as well as Mason-work, and in every other work incidental or conducive to the business of Building in all its branches, and that either by Contract or Speculation; including the acquisition, either by Purchase, Lease, or other tenure, of House Property and of Land, for the purpose of erecting thereon Houses and other Buildings.[9]

The first seven shareholders were all Edinburgh stonemasons. By the first anniversary meeting in April 1862 there were 341 registered shareholders of whom 134 or 41% who registered an occupation were stonemasons; collectively, the building trades constituted 55% of the shareholders.[10] If the average number of shares bought by stonemasons was a little lower than for some other trades this probably reflected their straitened financial circumstances following a lengthy period without wages as a result of the lock-out. Solidarity for the co-operative spirit was forthcoming from fifty-five other trades and in some cases several subscribers came from within the same tenements. Seven shareholders gave a Bedford Street address, nine lived in Bristo Street. A quarter mile radius from the Lothian Road and Bread Street intersection housed many of the builders in the city – there were a dozen subscribers living along Fountainbridge. In addition, off the High Street and in a quarter mile radius from the University, there were clusters of tradesmen shareholders sympathetic to the ECBC principles (fig. 11.2). The numerous consecutive share entries by neighbours indicates that they bought £1 shares

[8] NAS GD327/489, ECBC Fifteenth Annual Report, 1876.
[9] NAS BT2/1970/548/79/1, Edinburgh Building Contractors, Ltd, Memorandum of Association, Edinburgh Co-operative Building Company, 1861.
[10] NAS BT2/1970/548/79/4, List of Shareholders, June 1862.

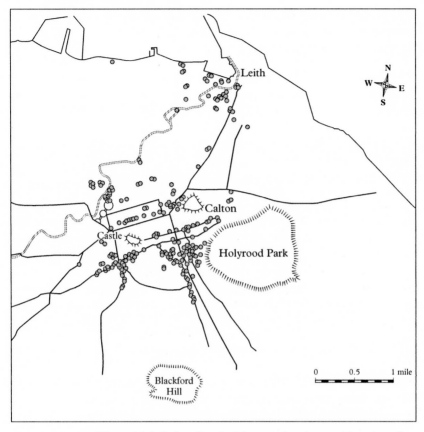

Figure 11.2 Subscribers' addresses: the clustered location of
shareholders in the ECBC 1862

Source: NAS BT2/1970/548/79/4, List of Shareholders, June
1862.

almost out of loyalty and on a basis not unlike present-day fund-raising or
sponsorship. Leithers subscribed 16% of the ECBC capital and in
another illustration of mutuality, a cluster of six engineers and a brass-
founder at Hillhousefield in Leith each bought a £1 stake in the
Company. Trade associations were the largest subscribers – the Co-
operative Plasterers' Society bought fifty shares and the Operative
Plumbers' Society took twenty.

The 'co-operative' spirit shown by the founder members drew strength from its mutual principles and, like the Co-operative Movement generally, the ECBC adopted the motif of the beehive. Embossed on Company documents and inscribed in stone on some of the houses built by the ECBC, the beehive (fig. 11.3) symbolised a community of workers, equal in status and with a common purpose. By building houses in rows, one flat upon another, the ECBC also physically reproduced the appearance of a colony of bees.

While the lock-out provided the opportunity for tradesmen to form their own building company, it was the poor state of housing in the Old Town which was the underlying stimulus to the formation of a company whose stated intention was 'to build comfortable and respectable houses for the working classes'.[11] To appreciate the achievements of the ECBC it is important first to consider the nature of housing in Edinburgh in the mid-nineteenth century.

In the quarter century before 1850 the haemorrhaging of housebuilding had particularly adverse effects on working men and their families since not only was little new housing built specifically for their income range, the virtual cessation of housebuilding for middle-income elements in the city meant that the process of 'filtering-down' was also interrupted.[12] Alternative housing strategies were essential if the social costs of overcrowding were to be avoided. For example, built the same year (1851) both Ashley Buildings at the Tron, High Street and Pilrig Buildings off Leith Walk provided accommodation respectively for seventy and sixty-two families; and in Fountainbridge, artisans' housing in a tenement at Chalmers' Buildings (1854) and the brick-built block known as Rosemount Buildings (1860) nearby were instances of mid-century model dwellings where a room and kitchen, WC and water supply were available for even the lowest rented property in the block (fig. 11.4). Other model dwelling efforts followed (table 11.1). In a brief spell between 1850 and 1865, the model dwellings movement produced a small, though locally significant, addition of almost 850 homes at an average cost of £110 per flat for working-class family accommodation. The gross rate of return on these model dwellings averaged 6.06%.[13]

Private enterprise efforts also recognised a 'model' style, as at Rosebank Cottages near Fountainbridge (1853), where six blocks of

[11] *Edinburgh Courant*, 30 Nov. 1861.
[12] See chapter 3. *Edinburgh Evening Courant*, 24 Oct. 1861, noted that the gap between population growth and housing accommodation had worsened appreciably between 1841 and 1861, to the extent of a further shortfall of 6,000 houses and this is likely to have been greater in the years 1801–31 when population growth was higher.
[13] This figure takes no account of interest payments, management charges and local taxes.

Figure 11.3 The Beehive, Dalry

Note: the motif of the Co-operative Movement was embossed in stone on the walls of the ECBC houses and on Company notepaper and documents.

'flatted cottages' built 'for the better class of mechanics' were built.[14] Company initiatives attempted also to overcome the shortcomings in the housing market, as was the case in a development near Haymarket goods yards at Devon Place, begun in 1861, and developed mainly by the trustees of a coal merchant, James McKelvie, on part of Heriot's Coates estate. This provided workers with 'unpretentious rows of single-storey cottages in stone and brick'[15] even though a report by working-class men

[14] *Builder,* 2 May 1857, 246–7. There were also a number of similar houses built in Dundee and Rutherglen.

[15] J. Gifford, C. McWilliam and D. Walker, *The Buildings of Scotland: Edinburgh* (Harmondsworth 1988), 371, identify 1864 as the beginning of this project, but ECA George Heriot's Roll of Superiorities, ff. 98–100, feu charter dated 4 July 1861 confirms the earlier date for Devon Place, with later charters for 1 Dec. 1864, 20 Feb. 1865. The streets in this development included Devon, Surrey, Pembroke, Carberry, Borthwick, Elgin, Stanhope and West Catherine Places, and Eglinton and Sutherland Streets. For a more general summary of company housing in England, see J. Burnett, *A Social History of Housing 1815–1970* (Newton Abbot 1978), 81–3, 176–8, and for critique and Scottish examples of the system, see J. Melling, 'Employers, industrial housing and the evolution of company welfare policies in Britain's heavy industry: west Scotland 1870–1920', *International Review of Social History,* 26, 1981, esp. 258–80.

Figure 11.4 Rosemount Buildings, Fountainbridge, 1860

Note: this brick built block cost almost £12,000 and originally housed ninety-six families.

Table 11.1 *Model dwellings: Edinburgh 1850–1865*

Name of buildings	Location	Date built	Total cost	Families housed	Average cost per flat (£)	Lowest weekly rent (£)	Gross rate of return (%)
Ashley Buildings[a]	Tron	1851	5,100	70	72.68	0.07	4.94
Pilrig Buildings[a]	Broughton	1851	6,800	62	109.68	0.11	5.11
Chalmers'	Fountainbridge	1855	3,600	29	124.14	0.13	5.64
Dr Begg's[b]	Abbey	1860	6,000	66	90.91	0.13	7.15
Milne's	Tron	1860	2,356	20	117.80	0.16	7.22
Rosemount	Fountainbridge	1860	11,780	96	122.71	0.13	5.70
Croall's	Abbey	1860	3,600	30	120.00	0.10	4.38
Patriot Hall	Water of Leith	1861	4,800	42	114.29	0.19	8.53
View Craig	Pleasance/St Leonard's	1861	15,000	110	136.36	0.14	5.32
Prince Albert	Pleasance/St Leonard's	1863	19,200	132	145.45	0.18	6.65
Blackwood's[b]	Abbey	1863	3,000	26	115.38	0.14	6.37
Prospect Street[c]	Pleasance/St Leonard's	1863	3,600	74	48.65	0.06	6.17
Gillis'	Nicolson St	1863	1,800	12	150.00	0.19	6.67
Clermiston[b]	Canongate	1863	1,750	20	87.50	0.13	8.00
Rae's	Pleasance/St Leonard's	1864	2,500	26	96.15	0.12	6.55
Gladstone	Canongate	1864	2,000	32	62.50	0.06	4.80
Total			92,886	847	109.66		6.06

[a] Water-closets shared between 3 families.

[b] WCs shared between 2 families.

[c] WCs shared between 5 families.

Source: based on H. D. Littlejohn, *Report on the Sanitary Condition of the City of Edinburgh* (Edinburgh 1865), 39.

was less than enthusiastic about this type of design, especially when undertaken in brick.[16]

Philanthropic approaches to housing reflected an essentially moral concern for the consequences of the pressure of space on privacy and decency, a view shared also by many Church of Scotland ministers. Sensational accounts of housing conditions printed in pamphlets and newspaper columns in the 1840s captured the public imagination and, when they were written by a doctor, as with Dr W. P. Alison's *Observations on the Management of the Poor in Scotland and its Effects on the Health of the Great Towns* (1840) or offered in oral testimony to the Poor Law Commission in 1844, these came with even greater authority.[17]

If dearth, debility and disease were linked, so then, it was claimed, were poverty, employment and living conditions. Between 1801 and 1831 in-migration, mainly from Ireland and the highlands, accounted for 66% of the population increase in the Old Town which put further pressure on accommodation there. Nor was Leith spared similar overcrowding. This migration was viewed by Alison as a direct consequence of rural poverty and of an inadequate poor relief system throughout Scotland. The implication was that the Church of Scotland and property owners in rural parishes were unwilling to fund and organise parochial relief – two-thirds of parishes had no such machinery to do so in 1840.[18] Lacking relief from the rural parishes, it was logical that many would make for the cities. This in turn put pressure on the urban social and sanitary system which could only be resolved by a reform of the poor law and its administration.

One approach was to reform the system of poor relief and this was the administrative solution in which the Church of Scotland eventually became involved. By contrast, however, a corps of evangelical Scottish ministers argued that to address the social problems of the 1840s care of the poor should be founded on spiritual relationships, not on bureaucratic and legal obligations. They claimed that the Church was threatened by assuming a secular role in the administration of poor relief, as in England. So, bound up with the state of health in the Scottish cities, and with that of Edinburgh particularly, was the conviction amongst a group of radical ministers that they should provide religious leadership for the community which in turn would have a bearing on the educational, economic and social relationships of their parishioners. In no way was religious instruction separate from other aspects of daily life.

---

[16] *Report of a Committee of the Working Classes of Edinburgh on the Present Overcrowded and Uncomfortable State of their Dwelling-Houses* (Edinburgh 1860), 6.
[17] See chapter 12 for an extended account.
[18] R. A. Cage, *The Scottish Poor Law 1745–1845* (Edinburgh 1981), 112–38; I. Leavitt and T. C. Smout, *The State of the Scottish Working Class in 1843: A Statistical and Spatial Inquiry Based on Data from the Scottish Poor Law Commission Report of 1844* (Edinburgh 1979).

Figure 11.5 Free Church of Scotland ministers Rev. Dr James Begg
(1808–1883) and Rev. Dr Thomas Chalmers (1780–1847)

Note: the relationship between poverty and spirituality, as presented by
the Free Church of Scotland, influenced attitudes to working-class
housing.
Source: Rev. Dr James Begg from a portrait in the Magdalen Chapel,
Cowgate, Edinburgh, and Rev. Dr Thomas Chalmers from the
monument in George Street.

This social radicalism was associated with a strong element of ecclesiastical conservatism. The schism in the Church of Scotland, which in
1843 led to the Disruption and the foundation of the Free Church of
Scotland, was partly the product of this public health discourse centred
on Edinburgh, poverty and insanitary housing. Though both the Church
of Scotland and the Free Church of Scotland acknowledged the 'feck-
lessness' of the poor, they each charted divergent paths to deal with
poverty.

One of the most vigorous campaigners on behalf of the poor and their
housing conditions was the Reverend Dr James Begg who had risen to
national prominence in 1832 at the Church of Scotland's Assembly when
Thomas Chalmers was Moderator (see fig. 11.5).[19] In 1836, Begg toured

[19] See T. Smith, *Memoirs of James Begg*, 2 vols. (Edinburgh 1885); M. M. de S. Cameron,
ed., *Dictionary of Scottish Church History and Theology* (Edinburgh 1993), 68; J. Clark,
'Life of James Clark, DD', reprinted from *The Bulwark*.

the highlands to promote the Church Extension movement, headed by Chalmers. Well connected in the emerging evangelical wing of the Church, Begg and other radical ministers developed a programme to improve housing conditions in the cities which was extensively publicised by Hugh Miller, editor of *The Witness*, even before the schism in the Church led to the foundation of the Free Church of Scotland in 1843.

In 1849, James Begg published two pamphlets: 'Pauperism and the Poor Laws' which set out how to provide more employment for the poor, and another on Edinburgh improvements. In January 1850 Begg developed his radical agenda in an eight point 'Charter'. His proposals were (i) improvement in the quantity and quality of education; (ii) suppression of drunkenness; (iii) better dwellings for working people; (iv) public washing houses and bleaching greens; (v) reform of the land laws; (vi) simplification of the transference of land; (vii) different treatment for crime and pauperism; (viii) greater justice to Scotland in parliament. The Charter points, which were based on the same principles for the moral improvement of society as expounded by Thomas Chalmers, were designed to reduce the price of land for housing and conveyancing costs and to encourage better standards of accommodation.

The stonemasons who founded the ECBC drew much of their inspiration from Free Church ministers. Other influential figures included the messianic Hugh Gilzean Reid who, through his columns in the *Evening News* between 1860 and 1861, did most to inform and reform public opinion, aided by another effective propagandist, Hugh Miller.[20] As a testimony to their formative roles, the ECBC named the first two terraces of houses after them – Reid Terrace and Hugh Miller Place. Indeed, Hugh Miller's contribution to Scottish society generally was so highly regarded that record numbers attended his funeral service and interment alongside Thomas Chalmers in 1856.

From pulpits and lecture halls, in pamphlets and in newspaper columns, these men publicised the view that it was futile to contemplate moral reform without first improving the housing of the working classes. Hugh Miller's comment that 'We must devise some plan by which proper buildings shall be erected, and insure the future well-being of the people'[21] was trenchantly put by James Begg in 1850 during a speech to the founding meeting of the Scottish Social Reform Association:

[20] J. Begg, *Happy Homes for Working Men and How to Get Them* (Edinburgh 1862), 19n., notes that the Free Church of Scotland set up a committee in 1858 to investigate housing conditions and moral reform. See Free Church of Scotland, Committee on Houses for the Working Classes in Connexion with Social Morality, *Report* (Edinburgh 1862), 7–17; H. G. Reid, *Past and Present or Social and Religious Life in the North* (Edinburgh 1871). H. G. Reid, *Housing the People – An Example in Co-operation* (London 1895), 25, noted that the co-operative spirit developed in 'a dingy editorial room in a dingy close'.

[21] H. Miller, quoted in R. Pipes, *The Colonies of Stockbridge* (Edinburgh 1984), 9.

Figure 11.6 Tenement collapse 1861

Note: 'Heave away' was the plea supposedly uttered by rescuers as they sought to uncover the casualties buried by the collapse of a High Street tenement on 24 November 1861.

You will never get the unclean heart of Edinburgh gutted out until you plant it all round with new houses.[22]

The campaign for improved housing conditions gained momentum in the 1850s and masons David Rintoul, John Ogilvie, James Collins and James Colville, the first manager, resolved in 1861 to found the Edinburgh Co-operative Building Company on the basis of mutual help rather than self-help. Further leverage was obtained when a High Street tenement collapsed later that year, killing thirty-five (fig. 11.6). This produced demands for better structural standards which the subsequent Burgh Police (Scotland) Act, 1862 addressed by reinvigorating the Dean of Guild Court (or an equivalent plans authority in those towns which were not royal burghs) to vet housebuilding 'petitions'.[23]

When the building employers eventually conceded that it was 'expedient' to agree to workers' demands over a shorter working day, a spirit of

[22] J. Begg, speech to Scottish Social Reform Association, 18 Jan. 1850, quoted in J. Clark, *Life of James Begg* (Edinburgh n.d.), 7.

[23] R. Rodger, 'The evolution of Scottish town planning', in G. Gordon and B. Dicks, eds., *Scottish Urban History* (Aberdeen 1983), 71–91.

independence allied with mutuality was firmly established amongst Edinburgh workmen, as the occupations of subscribers to the share capital of the ECBC showed.[24] Leaders of this emerging co-operative vision also drew strength from French examples, inspired by the Association of Masons of France, where 200–300 workmen had worked together in 1848 to build their own houses; in Mulhouse workers constructed 692 houses in 'cités ouvrières' during the 1850s. Ideologically, principles of co-operation and mutuality also underpinned early English building societies and, as a Free Church report noted: 'What English men have done to a large extent in the erection of thousands of houses, Scotchmen can do.'[25] These co-operative and political credentials were impeccable.[26]

Rather than remain on the margins of a new industrial order, dependent upon the decisions of philanthropists, builders and a corps of landowners and institutional interests, Edinburgh tradesmen combined to form a limited company, to embrace mutuality and trust and so construct an active role within Edinburgh society. 'The fire wants poking' was how one contemporary described matters.[27] Understandably, the thirty-four Articles of Association made no explicit reference to the Edinburgh Co-operative Building Company as an instrument by which tradesmen would reposition themselves in the social order, but three specific clauses did provide a mechanism by which they might do so.[28] Clause 7 preserved a measure of control over decision-making for workers by stating: 'That the chairman, one of the Vice-presidents, and at least eight of the ordinary directors, shall be building operatives.'[29] In a complex and highly specific formulation, clause 9 weighted voting at Company meetings against large shareholders and, with an exceptional awareness of gender issues, clause 32 assured women of equal treatment within the organisation of the Company by stating that 'notwithstanding any form of expression used herein, the whole conditions hereof shall be binding on females equally as well as male partners'.[30] The transparency of the organisation –

[24] Reid, *Housing the People*, 20; NAS BT2/1970/548/79/4, List of Shareholders, June 1862.
[25] Free Church of Scotland, *Report*, 15.
[26] J. S. Mill, *Principles of Political Economy* (London 1875 edn), 469. See also Reid, *Housing the People*, 6–10. The Social Science Association meeting in 1860 was held in Glasgow where delegates were informed about the Co-operative Societies. For a report of the meeting see *Builder*, 29 Sept. 1860, 617–18, 636.
[27] Reid, *Housing the People*, xi.
[28] The Edinburgh Co-operative Building Company Ltd, *Articles of Association* (Edinburgh 1861).
[29] There were fifteen ordinary directors in 1861, all building tradesmen. The number was subsequently reduced to between ten and twelve.
[30] Voting rights were on a one share one vote basis for holdings of 1–5 shares; thereafter weighting was altered: 6 shares = 5 votes; 7–8/6 votes; 9–10/7; 11–12/8; 13–15/9; 16–18/10; 19–21/11; 22–5/12; 26–9/13; 30–4/14; 35–9/15; 40 shares = 16 votes, which was the maximum. See *Articles*, 8–9, 18.

monthly business meetings, quarterly general meetings, an annual meeting, elections by majority voting and mechanisms for individuals and groups to convene extraordinary meetings in the event of losses sustained by the Company – demonstrated an unusual degree of participation and openness at a time when unionisation in Scotland was weak compared to memberships south of the border.[31]

From its inception, then, an agreed value system underpinned the operations of the Edinburgh Co-operative Building Company. This may be taken to indicate that the social structure of mid-nineteenth-century Edinburgh was 'a stable system in equilibrium'[32] – that is, ordered and consensual, in which common values performed an integrationist role. Put in other terms, the precise form which the ECBC objectives and aspirations took – the provision of sound family housing – was shared by the middle classes and so a commonly posed antithesis based on class tension was suspended in favour of a closer alignment and toleration across social divisions.[33] The integrative role played by shared values as presented by the ECBC thus contributed more generally to social cohesion in the city, an indictment also levelled at working-class organisations for their aspiring respectability and compliance with middle-class values.[34]

Such an interpretation accords primacy to the common value system and shared identity over all other factors, specifically independent social factors, and is based on the assumption that social integration is the objective of the organisation However, a different approach is to present the question of order as a 'problem of how it comes about that social systems "bind" time and space'.[35] That is, the Edinburgh Co-operative Building Company was itself an actor, shaping rather than adapting to an emerging social identity in the city. In such an interpretation, the Company was 'reflexive', constructing its own identity, and not simply cloned on existing values. Both the integrationist and reflexive interpretations of ECBC activities differ from those based on social control, now

---

[31] Reid, *Housing the People*, x, notes that for the quarterly meeting of the ECBC over 300 working men filled the hall. He commented that 'What appeared most delightful [was] that . . . [T]hese men evidently felt that they had some interest at stake.' For an overview of labour organisation and culture see Knox, 'The political and workplace culture of the Scottish working class 1832–1914', esp.138–51.

[32] T. Parsons, *The Structure of Social Action* (Glencoe, Ill., 1949), 389; and also T. Parsons, *Social Structure and Personality* (Glencoe, Ill., 1964), 22.

[33] H. J. Dyos and D. A. Reeder, 'Slums and suburbs', in H. J. Dyos and M. Wolff, eds., *The Victorian City: Images and Realities*, vol. II (London 1978 edn), 359–88; see also R. Rodger, *Housing in Urban Britain 1780–1914* (Cambridge 1995), 38–43.

[34] See, for example, E. J. Hobsbawm, *Labouring Men* (London 1964); J. Foster, *Class Struggle and the Industrial Revolution: Early Industrial Capitalism in Three English Towns* (London 1974). For an assessment see R. Q. Gray, *The Aristocracy of Labour in Nineteenth Century Britain c.1850–1914* (London 1981).

[35] A. Giddens, *The Consequence of Modernity* (Oxford 1990), 14–21; and A. Giddens, *Modernity and Self-Identity* (Oxford 1991), 3–34.

largely discredited, in which working-class organisations are presumed to have values imposed upon them by essentially middle-class interests.[36] The activities of the ECBC are now analysed with these different interpretations in mind.

From 'Colonies' to castles: the Edinburgh Co-operative Building Company Limited

It seems most likely that the designs for ECBC houses were influenced by model housing at Pilrig (1850) and, more specifically, by those for Rosebank Cottages (1853) which were brought to national prominence in 1857 when *The Builder*, one of the most highly respected and influential of Victorian periodicals, reproduced the innovative design.[37] This featured:

> a distinct and independent entrance; secondly a plot . . . for bleaching or for flowers; thirdly a water-closet; fourthly a scullery with washing tubs, bath and hot-water; fifthly a separate access to each apartment from the lobby; and sixthly, ample provision of ventilation and for warming small bedrooms, which have no fireplaces.[38]

Though this design cost £220 and was rather more lavish than that of the ECBC, it was in a form and for the most part to specifications previously unknown to the Scottish urban working classes. Unlike tenement flats which were accessed through a common front door and the shared space of the common stair, the critical features of ECBC housing, like those at Rosebank, were that each family had access to their home through their own front door, and a small garden (fig. 11.7b). As the chairman of the ECBC explained: 'they [residents] enter from both sides; the one has the top flat, and the other the ground flat. That is not the English plan.'[39] By contrast to the undifferentiated space of many two room tenement flats, where cooking and eating activities were by definition undertaken in areas also used for sleeping, the intention was to define room functions and uses more clearly in ECBC houses (fig. 11.7c). However, uniquely, the ECBC design preserved home life on a single

---

[36] See, for example, G. S. Jones, 'Class expression versus social control? A critique of recent trends in the social history of leisure', *History Workshop*, 4, 1977, 162–70; F. M. L. Thompson, 'Social control in Victorian Britain', *Economic History Review*, 34, 1981, 189–208. For a discussion of the integration of the relationship of philanthropic societies in relation to autonomous working-class activities see F. K. Prochaska, 'Philanthropy', in F. M. L. Thompson, ed., *The Cambridge Social History of Britain 1750–1950* (Cambridge 1990), vol. III, 366–75.   [37] *Builder*, 2 May 1857, 247.

[38] *Builder*, 2 May 1857, 246.

[39] *PP 1884–5 XXX*, Royal Commission on Housing of the Working Classes, Scotland, Colville, Q. 19070.

Figure 11.7a Early ECBC houses, Stockbridge, Edinburgh

Source: RCAHMS C40362.

level – one family occupied the ground floor level and another the first floor level, accessed by a distinctive stone staircase with a wrought iron balustrade. The arrangement of rooms permitted through ventilation to both levels, and economised on building costs through shared foundations and roof. Taken together, these design features (fig. 11.7c) were highly original, and as such insinuated a different vision of urban living into the mentality of the Edinburgh working class.

Cautiously, the Edinburgh Co-operative Building Company began its operations in April 1861 on the northern fringe of the New Town in Stockbridge (fig. 11.7a), later more grandiosely described as Glenogle Park, on 1.170 acres of land obtained from the whisky distillers, James

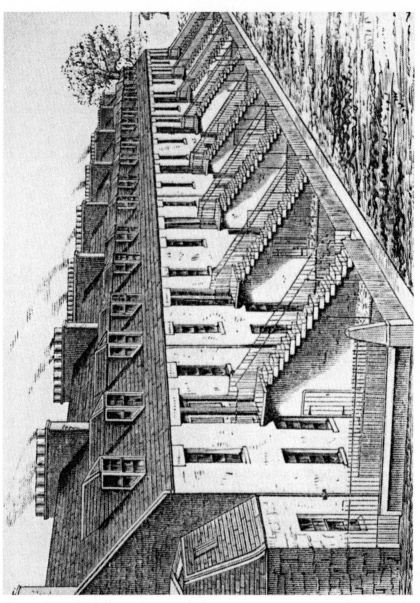

(b)

Figure 11.7b Early ECBC houses at Stockbridge, Edinburgh

Source: lithograph from J. Begg, *Happy Homes for Working Men and How to Get Them* (Edinburgh 1873);

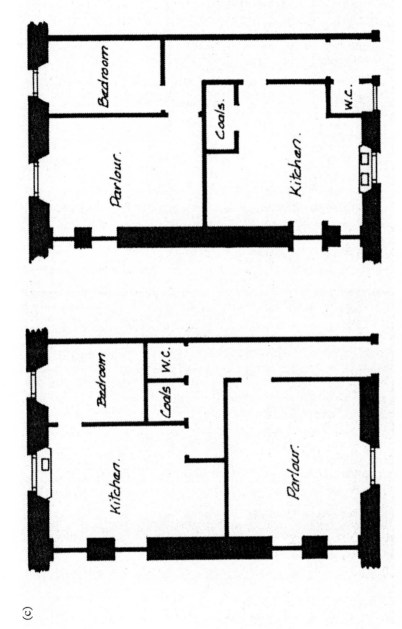

Figure 11.7c Early ECBC floor plans at Stockbridge, Edinburgh

Source: R. Rodger, *Housing the People: The Colonies of Edinburgh* (Edinburgh 1999), 25.

Haig.[40] In laying the foundation stone to Reid Terrace on 24 October 1861, the Reverend James Begg declared that it represented 'a turning point in the history of Edinburgh'.[41] The ECBC engaged its own workmen, supervised by James Colville, and sold the properties to the general public at a price judged to yield a fair return on the outlay. By the date of the first annual meeting, eight houses had been sold; by the third meeting, 120 had been sold.

So encouraging was the interest in the properties that the ECBC obtained a small 1.5 acre site in Leith in 1862 at Hawthornbank, and replicated their building activities there. These houses sold quickly and were so attractive that one of the highest levels of persistence – continuation at the same address – of all ECBC developments was experienced there. By contrast, a few hundred yards distant, a second Leith site on Ferry Road (Henderson Place and Trafalgar Street) proved difficult to sell. Though begun in 1864, three years later, James Colville, the general manager, was still placing adverts in the *Leith Pilot* and attending the 'Show Homes' in person to answer the questions of potential buyers.[42]

There were several reasons for the ECBC difficulties over the Ferry Road project. First, the properties were priced at more than 60% above other Colony houses.[43] Secondly, in Leith, the ECBC built conventional three and four storey tenement flats, abandoning their hallmark external staircase houses. Since they both cost more and were difficult to sell, the Company interpreted the signals accurately and abandoned the construction of this type of accommodation.[44] Thirdly, institutional constraints were powerful and the ECBC had to work within the rhythms and practices of the housing market. For example, the Company's inability in 1865 to complete the Ferry Road houses by the Whitsunday term date, 25 May, when all tenants had to have renegotiated their lets, meant that potential purchasers in effect were required to relinquish their existing accommodation before seeing the new homes which the ECBC were trying to persuade them to move into. Timing was everything. Unsold, the ECBC was forced to become a housing manager with capital tied up in property which they were then obliged to rent to recoup some of their outlay. Despite their mutual efforts, therefore, the

[40] NAS RS27/2354.126, feu disposition, 11 Sept. 1861. See alo R. Pipes, *The Colonies of Stockbridge* (Edinburgh 1998 edn), 16–26, for the background to the Glenogle site.

[41] *Edinburgh Evening Courant,* 30 Nov. 1861. Coins, Edinburgh newspapers, the co-partnery agreement and shareholder list were inserted into a cavity in the foundation stone. Scholars might also wish to note that a statement of the origins of the ECBC was also inserted.   [42] *Leith Pilot,* 26 Jan. 1867.

[43] NAS GD327/489, Annual Reports, 1866, 1867; J. Begg, *Happy Homes for Working Men* (2nd edn, Edinburgh 1872), appendix III.

[44] There were some further tenements at Abbeyhill.

HOUSES AT HENDERSON PLACE AND TRAFALGAR STREET, FERRY ROAD, LEITH

TO be SOLD by PRIVATE BARGAIN, Half-Flat and Main-Door HOUSES situated in Henderson Place, consisting of Three Rooms and Kitchen, Two Bed-Closets, and other conveniences, with large Back Green, the Main Doors having Plots in Front. Prices £250 to £360. Feu Duty £1 1s 6d each.

Two HOUSES Nos. 3 and 6 TRAFALGAR STREET, consisting of Two Rooms and Kitchen, with W.C., and right to Large Back Green. Price £162. Feu-duty 6s.

Also a House No. 6 TRAFALGAR STREET, consisting of one room and Kitchen, W.C., and other Conveniences, with right to Back Green. Price £120. Feu-Duty 5s.

A SHOP and HOUSE No. 3 TRAFALGAR STREET. Price £375. Feu-duty 6s.

Apply to Mr Livingston, House-Agent, 80 Constitution Street, Leith; or to Mr Colville, Hugh Miller Cottage, Glenogle Park, Stockbridge.

Mr Colville will attend at Mr M'Kay's, Baker,. 7 Trafalgar Street, to show the Houses, and give every information required, on Mondays, Tuesdays, Wednesdays, and Thursdays, from Eleven to Twelve, up to 2nd February, when the Houses will be re-let.

Part of the Price may remain on the houses, if desired.   [135.

Figure 11.8 Newspaper advert for ECBC houses in Leith 1867

Source: NLS, *Leith Pilot*, 26 Jan. 1867.

ECBC was unable to buck the market.[45] These initial difficulties stigmatised the Ferry Road development as surely as some council estates
were labelled in the twentieth century, and the consequence was that
James Colville was still available four mornings a week in January 1867
as a sales representative.[46]

The Ferry Road tenements represented a policy U-turn for the ECBC.
Why did the Company abandon its successful Stockbridge colony-style
design? How could it abandon its principles of separate entrances and
family lifestyles so quickly? The explanation probably lies in the extreme
difficulty which the Company faced in obtaining suitable building sites, a
problem which dogged the directors throughout the 1860s and 1870s.
For example, protracted negotiations with Heriot's Hospital over a site at
Ferniehill House, off Leith Walk, were begun in 1865 but in the course of
three years came to nothing despite a deputation of ECBC directors to
the Lord Provost seeking to clarify municipal plans for road developments in the area.[47] On the south side of the city plots of land at
Gladstone Terrace and Brougham Street went in 1866 to higher bidders,
one of whom was James Steel.[48] And even when, after lengthy discussions
with James Walker of Dalry, it was agreed in 1867 to develop three acres
at Morrison Street at a price double that which had prevailed ten years
earlier in Edinburgh, Walker welshed on the deal, preferring to sell the
acres as part of a larger development to another buyer.[49]

During 1866–7 the ECBC was involved, often simultaneously, in
negotiations for twelve sites – Ferniehill, Gladstone Terrace, Brougham
Street, Morrison Street, Maryfield (Abbeyhill) owned by Lady Menzies,
Haymarket (the site obtained from Walker in exchange for the aborted
Morrison Street agreement), four acres at Bonnington owned by James
Steel, three Leith sites at Pitt, George and North Forth Streets, ground
owned by Trinity Hospital also in Leith, and a five acre site at Restalrig
Park. No doubt there were other sites which were considered and
rejected as unsuitable even before negotiations got underway. In short,

[45] NAS GD327/489, ECBC Fourth Annual Report, May 1865. The directors recognised
that a high rate of interest meant that even in Stockbridge the sale of houses in 1865 'had
been slow'.
[46] Thomas Phipps bought eight Henderson Place properties for £2,040 in January 1868
and thereby lessened Colville's duties on this front. NAS GD1/777/2, ECBC Minute
Book, 3 Jan. 1868.
[47] NAS GD1/777/2, ECBC Minute Book, 20 July 1866, 2 and 29 Aug. 1866. The
Ferniehill site, parallel to Leith Walk near Annandale Street, should not be confused with
the modern Moredun area by the same name.
[48] NAS RS27/2609.59, 2609.67, and RS108/2717.10; MC, Drumdryan Chartulary, vol. 2,
f. 175, Charter with James Steel. See also chapter 6.
[49] NAS GD1/777/2, ECBC Minute Book, 10 Sept. 1866; 1 Feb. 1867. Walker's agents
offered £150 compensation to the ECBC but the directors wanted another site, not cash,
as compensation and thus secured the Dalry site opposite Haymarket Station.

land acquisitions were a difficult and unpredictable business and building development depended in part on a variety of purely incidental factors.

The ECBC paid a dividend to its shareholders of 60% in 1864, followed by a more modest 7.5% in 1865. To avoid the impression of instability which variations in dividends might convey, the ECBC also created in 1865 Contingent and Reserve Funds designed specifically to equalise dividend distributions, to 'give stability to the Company', and offer the 'best guarantee the public can have that [the Company] is managed with prudence'.[50] It was a financial tactic associated with the call-up of the remainder of the share capital in 1865, and with considerably more resources at its disposal, the ECBC commenced upon a period of remarkable expansion in the late 1860s. Had the directors looked for a 'golden age' this was probably such a phase.

Financially chastened by the Ferry Road experience, the ECBC resumed its distinctive 'colony-style' of development between 1866 and 1868 in a shrewdly judged phase of expansion associated with three new building sites – at Maryfield (subsequently referred to here as Abbeyhill), Dalry and Restalrig. In addition to the 'continued success' at Stockbridge which 'induced the directors to feu the entire remaining portion of the field, being nearly five acres', the Company acquired 'by way of trial' one acre of land from Lady Menzies at Abbeyhill in 1866. Almost immediately the strategic importance of this site and the energetic interest shown in housing there encouraged the acquisition of a further two acres in 1867, and six more in 1868 since, as the annual report explained, 'the proximity of this ground to the densely populated districts of the Canongate and south east side of the town will greatly facilitate the sale of the houses'.[51] It was less the proximity to an existing population, however, and more the strategic feuing of land in the eye of industrial and commercial development which was the basis of success at Norton Park, Abbeyhill. The ECBC activities were synchronised with the migration of several manufacturers to green field sites at Abbeyhill in the mid-1860s, and with the completion in 1868 of the Waverley–Easter Road rail connection with Leith and the Abbeyhill Station for passengers in 1869 (fig. 11.9).[52]

This formula of feuing and developing land near to railway, foundry and other manufacturing interests was repeated at Dalry Road, where after the Morrison Street episode the ECBC acquired a site of roughly similar size from James Walker in 1867, opposite Haymarket Station

[50] NAS GD327/489, Quarterly Meeting of Shareholders, 27 Nov. 1865.
[51] NAS GD327/489, Annual Reports, 1867, 1868.
[52] J. Thomas, *A Regional History of Railways*, vol. VI (Newton Abbot 1984 edn), 299–302.

Figure 11.9 Industrial estates in the nineteenth century: London Road Foundry, Abbeyhill, 1867

Note: many residents of the Abbeyhill colonies found work not only in this but other foundries, as well as in the nearby breweries, glass works and railway yards.

Source: Edinburgh Central Library, Anon., *Edinburgh Illustrated* (Brighton 1891), 106, Miller and Co. London Road Foundry.

(fig. 11.10).[53] Much the same market judgement of housing prospects was held by James Steel, who just eighteen months later signed a contract, also with James Walker, for thirteen acres adjoining the ECBC land.[54] Even before they were built, enquiries were being made about the ECBC houses and, with the sale of thirty-two houses in the first year, the directors reported that 'this feu has fully borne out the expectations' associated with 'its eligibility and fine situation' and that there would be 'little fear but that the whole of the houses erected will find ready purchasers'.[55]

The third new development, clinched in 1868, was at Restalrig. Relieved by the sale of property on the previous Leith site at Ferry Road, the directors went into paroxysms of purple prose in describing the potential of this acquisition:

It is within ten minutes walk of the centre of Leith, commands an extensive view of Edinburgh and the Forth, and surrounding country, and is so well adapted to the requirements of that fast increasing burgh that the directors have commenced operations by laying the foundations of thirty-two houses.[56]

The confidence of the Company was fully justified. Restalrig contributed significantly in 1869 to all-time record sales – 135 houses and 2 shops. The directors drew considerable satisfaction from this endorsement, especially since the 'great number of practical men in the building trade who are purchasers may be adduced as a guarantee to the general public of the superior class of material and workmanship expended on them'.[57]

Rather like coal mines where seams are in various stages of extraction – under development, highly productive and nearing exhaustion – the ECBC pursued a similar approach to its building sites. As the available land in North Leith was exhausted, first Abbeyhill, then Dalry came on stream; then, as the Stockbridge programme ran its course, so the Restalrig Park area became the backbone of building development. The advantages of such an approach were considerable. The physical distance between the sites enabled the ECBC to tap a reservoir of working-class demand in different geographical areas of the city. The possibilities of market saturation were reduced. Logistically, staged development enabled the Company to employ specialist tradesmen year round, including those machinists and handicraft workers engaged in their own building yard at Balmoral Place, Glenogle Park. In this regard, the directors' practical experience as building craftsmen proved invaluable since they

[53] ECA ACC 282, James Walker's Trust, Feu Contract and Disposition, 29 Aug. 1867, for three acres of land bounded on north, north-east south by Caledonian Railway and on north-west by Dalry Lane.   [54] See chapter 7.
[55] NAS GD327/489, Annual Report, 1868.
[56] NAS GD327/489, Annual Report, 1868.
[57] NAS GD327/489, Annual Report, 1869.

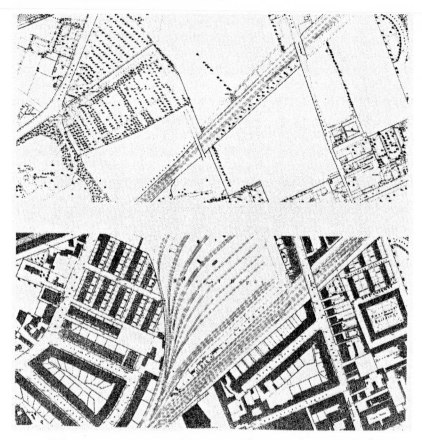

Figure 11.10 Industrial landscape: Dalry transformed in the 1860s

Note: maps of 1853 and 1876 show the before and after effects of new goods yards and freight handling facilities at Haymarket and Dalry. The ECBC Dalry colonies (top left, 1867–70), private Caledonian development by James Steel (bottom left, 1869–74) and the earlier model dwellings (top right) in Fountainbridge (Rosebank (1857) and Rosemount (1860)) are also shown.
Source: NLS, Edinburgh Haymarket Ordnance Survey 1:1056 sheet 38 1853; OS1; 1056 sheet 38 1877.

recognised that improved productivity and cost savings resulted from good labour relations, and that this in turn was founded on steady employment and the regular deployment of practical skills on tasks for which men were trained.[58]

---

[58] The ECBC housing manager, James Colville, was determined to phase building carefully on different sites and on extensions to the same site to take advantage of labour productivity gains. See NAS GD1/777/2, Minute Book, 6 Nov. 1868.

This was precisely the principle on which general contractors had reorganised elements of the English building industry in the 1820s and 1830s, generating productivity gains by employing a regular workforce for specific trades, and moving them to the next house or site where their skills were needed.[59] Delays in the completion of each stage of a house were avoided by the maintenance of a regular contracted workforce. With skills and practical solutions honed on earlier ECBC houses, productivity gains outweighed the higher wage costs associated with a regular workforce. There were financial advantages too. Specifically, cash flow problems were minimised since sales were almost always in the offing at one site or another; furthermore, the reputation of the ECBC houses preceded it with sales agreed and mortgages arranged in advance of completion. For the Company, this degree of continuity did much to reduce the levels of uncertainty and instability which plagued many other building firms. Whereas James Steel's successful housing operations were based on a diversified portfolio of risk by virtue of building for different social classes, the ECBC portfolio spread risk geographically by relying on different sites in various developmental stages at any given time.

By 1872, in just over eleven years of building activity, the Edinburgh Co-operative Building Company had built 914 houses; 96% of them had been sold.[60] Almost £156,000 of business had been done; the average price of dwellings was £171. As the employer of up to 250 workmen, the ECBC was probably the largest building firm in the city in the 1860s, even sub-contracting some of the work to other firms at times. In a single decade, the ECBC had contributed 2% to the entire housing stock of Edinburgh and almost 15% of new housebuilding in the city during the years 1861–71. The activities of the first ten years of the ECBC are shown in table 11.2.

The review of ECBC activities in 1876 on the occasion of its fifteenth anniversary reflected positively on its achievements. It was noted, for example, that between 1861 and 1876 'homes for 6,000' people had been constructed.[61] Yet in the mid-1870s building had virtually ceased. Only eight new houses were completed at Restalrig in 1875; not one was completed in either of the next two years. The final houses on the Stockbridge

---

[59] On English building practices see E. W. Cooney, 'The building industry', in R. Church, ed., *The Dynamics of Victorian Business: Problems and Perspectives to the 1870s* (London 1980), 142–60; H. Hobhouse, *Thomas Cubitt, Master Builder* (London 1971); E. W. Cooney, 'The origins of the Victorian master builders', *Economic History Review*, 8, 1955, 167–76; and Rodger, *Housing in Urban Britain*, 20–2, and 70–83 for further references.

[60] Calculated from Begg, *Happy Homes* (1872 edn), appendix III. The figure takes account of the fact that seventeen of the properties were sold as shops, and a further forty-two were still in the course of erection. Thus only 872 houses were actually capable of being sold for occupancy, of which 841 had been sold.

[61] Begg, *Happy Homes* (1872 edn), 20.

Table 11.2 *Houses built by the ECBC 1862–1872*

Street	Number built	Cost (£)	Average price (£)
Stockbridge			
Reid Terrace	40	4,992	125
Hugh Miller Place	33	4,784	145
Rintoul Place	32	4,866	152
Colville Place	30	5,123	171
Collins Place	30	4,532	151
Bell Place	32	4,830	151
Kemp Place	30	4,940	165
Glenogle Place	8	1,330	166
Glenogle Terrace	8	1,220	153
Avondale Place	30	5,125	171
Teviotdale Place	16	3,295	206
Balmoral Place	24	2,664	128
Dunrobin Place	8	1,440	180
Leith			
Hawthornbank Place	22	3,577	163
Hawthornbank Terrace	22	3,577	163
Henderson Place	43	10,155	236
Trafalgar Street	17	4,040	238

Street	Number built	Cost (£)	Average price (£)
Abbeyhill			
Maryfield	47	7,623	156
Alva Place	47	7,796	162
Lady Menzies Place	46	8,021	174
Regent Place	51	8,172	160
Waverley Place	47	8,038	171
Carlyle Place	47	8,438	180
Dalry			
Cobden Terrace	16	2,655	166
Bright Terrace	16	2,655	166
McLaren Terrace	10	1,670	167
Douglas Terrace	16	2,655	166
Argyll Terrace	16	2,655	166
Atholl Terrace	16	2,655	166
Breadalbane Terrace	16	2,655	166
Breadalbane Cottages	2	420	210
Lewis Terrace	16	3,170	198
Walker Terrace	16	3,780	236
Restalrig			
Woodville Terrace	16	3,140	196
Woodbine Terrace	32	5,273	165
Thornville Terrace	16	2,495	156

Source: based on J. Begg, *Happy Homes for Working Men* (Edinburgh 1872 edn), App. III.

and Abbeyhill sites were under construction, and were completed in 1877. There was a real possibility that the ECBC, for all its evident contribution to the supply of working-class housing, might cease to trade. The signs were ominous, but unmistakable. In an 'unsettled housing market' the ECBC was forced both to retain forty-eight houses at Abbeyhill for rental and to revert to the construction of a limited number of four storey tenements which still proved popular with tenants and landlords.[62] There was even a copycat firm, the Industrial Co-operative Building Company, formed by stonemasons in 1868 which built houses of an identical design in the field adjacent to the Edinburgh Co-operative Building Company's activities at Restalrig (fig. 11.11). By its very name, location and designs, the Industrial sought to position itself in the market on the back of the ECBC's successes, but such externalities were insufficient to withstand difficult market conditions in 1871 as the cost of borrowing rose and the market for workmen's housing in South Leith became saturated. With a subscribed capital equivalent to only 7% that of the ECBC, the Industrial was under-capitalised and was soon confronted with cash flow problems which forced it to suspend building. It went into voluntary liquidation in 1875, though the development was eventually taken over and completed by two of its shareholders, partners in the building firm of A. and W. Fingzies.[63]

For all its earlier successes the ECBC was not exempt from market fluctuations; co-operative zeal and mutual principles could not counter-act variations in wages and employment as experienced by Edinburgh workers generally. When confronted in 1871, therefore, by 'the great flatness . . . in all branches of the building trade', managerial caution dictated that further land purchases were suspended.[64] It was argued that there was little point in saddling the Company with annual feu-duty payments given what the directors perceived as the 'hesitancy on the part of the public to speculate in heritable securities' and symptomatic of which was the preference to rent rather than buy the recently completed properties at Abbeyhill.[65] In short, as the building cycle went into recession, the ECBC maintained its dividends at the lower but acceptable level of 7.5%

---

[62] NAS GD327/489, Annual Report, 1875.
[63] NAS BT2/284, Memorandum of Association of the Industrial Co-operative Building Company (Limited), 8 Apr. 1868, and CS318/49/67, Letter from A. F. W. Fingzies to Wallace and Pennell, WS, 27 Feb. 1901, Inventory and Valuation 6 Mar. 1901, Sederunt Book, f. 32. The streets involved were East Hermitage Place, and Summerfield, Lindean, Noble, Parkvale, Rosevale, Fingzies, Elm, Cochrane and Somerset Places. Alexander Fingzies petitioned for bankruptcy 27 Feb. 1901. Net liabilities were £4,577, but with realised assets of only £182, only £67 or 1.5% was paid to secured debtors. Unsecured debtors (£2,205) received nothing.   [64] NAS GD327/489, Annual Report, 1871.
[65] NAS GD327/489, Annual Reports, 1874, 1875.

Figure 11.11 Aerial view of ECBC developments at Restalrig

Note: three housing developments are shown: top left is the Restalrig
Park development (1868–83); centre left is the Hermitage Hill
development (from 1890); to the right of the continuous East Restalrig
Road is the colony-style development begun by the Industrial Co-
operative Building Company and completed by the firm of A&W
Fingzies after 1875.
Source: RCAHMS B71025.

during the years 1872–5 by virtue of the continuing sales of properties completed in previous years.[66] Since dividend distributions had assumed primacy, so the ECBC had not positioned itself strategically for the cyclical upturn in housebuilding by acquiring building sites suited to working-class demand. As the chairman remarked:

the only real impediment to a lengthened existence in the future seems to be the increasing difficulty of obtaining land in any quantity near the centres of the industries of the city.[67]

The 'unprecedented circumstances . . . of having every available house sold' meant that those who attended the annual meeting in 1877 were advised that the ECBC would in effect be 'brought to a recommencement of operations'.[68] The situation was reversed because of the cumulative effects of industrial migration along the Fountainbridge–Gorgie axis. The Fountain Brewery was established at the western end of Fountainbridge in 1856 and the area became a world renowned centre of rubber manufacture and distribution, especially for vulcanised rubber, waterproof clothing and sheets.[69] Other prominent factories, foundries and distilleries located along the Dalry and Slateford Roads, and workshops and firms supplying component parts and services were also drawn to the interstices – Washington Lane, Grove and Duff Streets – between the major thoroughfares. This process of industrial relocation, along with the proliferation of goods handling at Haymarket, had generated demand previously for workmen's housing at Dalry, but by the 1870s the demand for housing had increased yet again. It was precisely this which attracted James Steel to the Caledonian and Murieston developments at Dalry Road (see chapter 7) and which encouraged the ECBC manager to conclude long-running negotiations with the Merchant Company in 1877 for a site at Gorgie Mains, North Merchiston (fig. 11.12). After a period of ten years when no new sites had been purchased, this purchase rekindled the ECBC's activities in the late 1870s with the construction of over 160 houses at the 'floors' terraces – Myrtle, Daisy, Lily, Laurel, Violet, Primrose and Ivy Terraces – between 1878 and 1884.[70]

The colony-style parallel terraces of the North Merchiston development differed in an important detail from the formula developed by the

[66] NAS GD327/488, Statement of Accounts.
[67] NAS GD327/508/1, Kemp papers. Suggestions affecting the future of the Edinburgh Co-operative Building Company with reference to comments in 15th Annual Report 1876.
[68] NAS GD327/489, Annual Report, 1877.
[69] D. Bremner, *The Industries of Scotland: Their Rise, Progress and Present Condition* (Edinburgh 1869), esp., 362–3; Anon., *A Descriptive Account of Edinburgh Illustrated* (Brighton 1891); Anon., *The English and Scottish Capitals: Representatives of Art, Industries and Commerce at the Beginning of the Twentieth Century* (London n.d); Anon., *Scotland of To-day* (London 1890).   [70] NAS GD327/489, ECBC Annual Reports, 1877–85.

Figure 11.12 ECBC plaques and public proclamations: North
Merchiston Park plaque 1880

Note: typical of almost all ECBC developments, the plaque publicly
proclaimed the achievements of the ECBC.

ECBC on all previous sites. Staircases were internalised. However, the
decision to acquire a small site at Barnton Terrace, Craigleith, also in
1877, produced a much more radical departure from proven principles
by a management still evidently short of suitable sites for housing development. The ECBC acquired nine plots at Barnton Terrace simply
because James Colville was one of the trustees of Robert McNaughton,
builder, and knew that, prior to his death, McNaughton had not developed all of the 3.540 acre site feued from Sir Alexander Maitland in
1871.[71] Not surprisingly, the ECBC's offer of £200 was acceptable to the
trustees and in 1877 construction began.[72] Because the feuing terms set
out by Maitland applied to the entire site and feu-duties were divided

---

[71] NAS RS108/820.57, Feu Disposition, trustees of Robert McNaughton to trustees of the
ECBC, 23 Oct. 1877. I am indebted to Rose Pipes for this information.
[72] NAS RS108/738.103, Notarial Instrument covering lots 13–25, 29 Mar. 1877.

equally amongst the plots, then the ECBC was required, in effect, to emulate the properties already built by McNaughton.[73] Accordingly, at Barnton Terrace the ECBC built self-contained, five bedroom houses; there were no 'high doors' or 'low doors' entrances (fig. 11.13). The selling price of £600 was affordable by the managers, merchants and others of 'a superior class'[74] who bought them – men such as Archibald Blair, a superintendent of various branches of the North British and Mercantile Insurance Company, and Alexander Ross, a grocer and wine merchant in the New Town – sometimes with loans from the Scottish Property Investment Company and the Fifth Provident Property Investment Company.[75] These houses marked 'lines of class distinction' in ECBC activities as reflected in the 'good many enquiries' which were reportedly received from potential house purchasers attracted by the imminent opening of a station at Blackhall.[76]

The excursion into middle-class housing is hardly explainable along the same lines that applied to James Steel (see chapter 7) when in 1878, as working-class demand faltered Steel scaled down housebuilding for this income group at Murieston, Dalry, and switched resources to elite west end developments. By contrast, ECBC activity was reinvigorated by the North Merchiston purchase and the resumption of building in 1878 at Restalrig. More likely, then, is the explanation that the Barnton Terrace site was easily acquired and managed from the nearby Stockbridge yard, while at the same time it provided a modest amount of employment and an opportunity for the workforce to keep skills honed. On these terms, Barnton Terrace was a pragmatic departure based on Colville's networks though, commercially, it was eight years before a sale was made. In the longer term, Barnton Terrace was a diversion from the founders' stated mission to provide housing for the working classes but it enabled the Company to evaluate a number of design features for middle-class housing which were incorporated into subsequent developments. Barnton Terrace – all nine houses – was a significant development in the history of building in Edinburgh, as well as for the ECBC itself.

A critical point was reached in 1883, like 1877, a year in which the last portions of Company lands were built up. For a decade, 1883–93, sales stumbled along at less than twenty per annum, lower than at any time in

[73] NAS RS108/230.34, Feu Disposition, 29 July 1871.
[74] NAS GD327/489, ECBC Annual Report, 1878. When the last Barnton Terrace property was sold in 1900 the price was £1,000.
[75] NAS RS108/539.184, 14 May 1875, 108/333.89, 13 Jan. 1872, and fifteen other feu dispositions for Barnton Terrace.
[76] NAS RS108/820.17, 23 Oct. 1877; A. D. Ochojna, 'Lines of class distinction: an economic and social history of the British tramcar with special reference to Edinburgh and Glasgow', University of Edinburgh PhD thesis, 1974, uses the phrase 'lines of class distinction' to denote those middle-class suburban areas of Edinburgh from where residents used trams (and local railway services) to access the city centre.

Figure 11.13 Design developments: ECBC housing, Barnton Terrace, 1877

Note: as the housing market encountered difficulties in the late 1870s so the ECBC sought opportunities to build houses for different social classes.

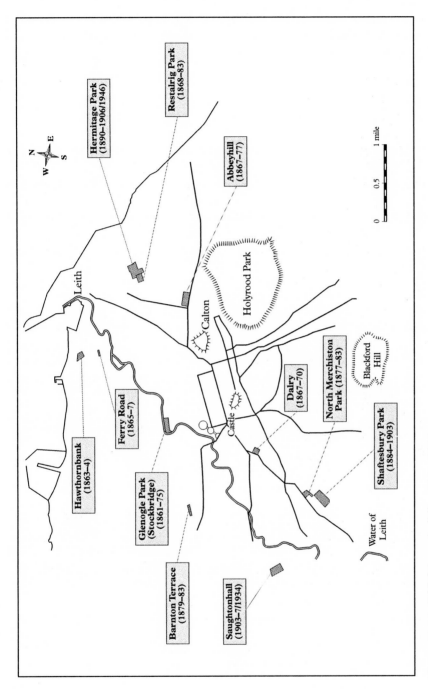

Figure 11.14 ECBC housebuilding 1861–1914

the history of the ECBC.[77] The very features of early success – complementary phases of development and continuity of work for specialist tradesmen – were jeopardised by the haemorrhaging of suitable new sites. Though concerned, the directors confused caution with complacency in the late 1870s and the 1880s, yet presented their strategy to shareholders in 1883 as exemplary:

The directors have been extremely cautious in this matter [of site acquisition] and ... so long as the present dullness in trade continues. [They] ... intend to proceed with the same caution, and only to secure as much ground as will keep them going moderately until the demand for property improves.[78]

Crucially, and symptomatic of the problems facing many of the ECBC's borrowers, the first repossession of one of their houses took place in 1883. 'Owing to the non-fulfilment of the agreement by the purchaser', as the Company rather formally described the default on mortgage repayments, the ECBC had repossessed and resold the property.[79] It was only a more open acknowledgement of the decision taken in the previous year to extend the period of repayments from fourteen to twenty-one years so that mortgages were not 'too great an annual charge on their [borrowers'] means'. Significantly, it was not just one but three repossessions at Restalrig which occurred in 1883; the next year there were four more there, and another at North Merchiston. Thereafter, 'repos' existed for the remainder of the 1880s, most commonly at Restalrig. They signified how, despite the best of intentions and two decades of experience, the ECBC like other housebuilders and landlords remained hostage to the fortunes of the local economy. Continuity of employment remained the most important influence on a workman's ability to pay for housing, whether as rent or mortgage repayments, and the earlier successes of the ECBC depended in no small measure on a buoyant local economy and the structure of employment in the capital.

With the depth and extent of the impending recession unclear and with its supplies of building land exhausted, the Company negotiated with George Watson's Hospital to purchase a ten acre field in 1884 for what became Shaftesbury Park, neighbouring its previous development at North Merchiston (fig. 11.14). By advertising the Shaftesbury Park houses as close to Merchiston Station and so 'conveniently situated for the suburban railway and the tramways', methods of transport not generally used by workmen or their families, the ECBC appealed in a barely disguised way to local government officials, agents and dealers, clerks,

[77] NAS GD327/488, ECBC Statement of Accounts.
[78] NAS GD327/489, Annual Report, 1883.
[79] NAS GD327/489, Annual Report, 1883.

shopkeepers, widows and those on pensions who perceived themselves as socially distinct. Overall, these social and occupational groups accounted for 76% of householders in Shaftesbury Park in 1891, exactly double the average for the rest of the Colonies.

By abandoning the distinctive external staircase of earlier colony developments and providing a separate ground floor door for each house, the ECBC consciously retreated further in both cost and design from its former appeal to workmen. Ashley, Hazelbank and Hollybank Terraces, the first to be built at Shaftesbury Park, marked a change of direction of which, when he retired in 1890, James Colville, manager of the ECBC since its foundation, must have been only too well aware.

The profile of householding in the two final ECBC developments (fig. 11.14) before 1914 reproduced many of the social characteristics evident at Shaftesbury Park. At Hermitage Hill, adjoining the earlier Company housing at Restalrig Park and purchased in 1891–2, the ECBC built what it described as 'continuous villas' on a site 'which for beauty of situation [is] unrivalled in Leith or vicinity'. The ECBC carefully phased the development of 300 houses completed mainly between 1893 and 1907 to a design and quality far superior to those of their earlier neighbours. Whereas at Shaftesbury Park there was a similarity in appearance with the distinctive end-on construction of Colonies terraces to the principal thoroughfare, at the Hermitage site (East Restalrig, Cornhill and Ryehill Terraces, Ryehill Gardens and Avenue) all such pretence was abandoned and houses ran parallel along streets as they did in private developments throughout the city.

The final phase of pre-war construction took place at Balgreen where, on 9.5 acres purchased in 1903, the ECBC built 'continuous villas similar to those erected at East Restalrig Terrace', Hermitage, in the ten years before the First World War.[80] The generously proportioned houses in Balgreen Road and Glendevon Place (fig. 11.15) were the result and though some thought had been given to a few colony-style houses, they never materialised. By the twentieth century the design of ECBC housing was almost indistinguishable from terraces at Willowbrae, Kirkhill, South Lauder Road and other streets built by private enterprise. Distinctive ECBC designs in the 1860s had by 1900 converged with those preferred by many private builders and, in arriving at an alternative to tenement blocks, both private and co-operative builders had resolved the design issues in an almost identical manner: two storey flatted villas. Given their

[80] NAS GD327/490, Annual Report, 1903. The 9.5 acre site was intended for a mixed development of properties 'of a similar class to those built at Shaftesbury Park' and others 'similar to those erected at East Restalrig Terrace'. Though this was the last feu acquired it was not the end of building development which continued in the 1920s.

Figure 11.15 ECBC housing and social aspirations: Balgreen / Glendevon (begun 1903)

Note: the cost-saving external staircase, dispensed with after 1877, was replaced by internal staircases and individual front doors in these developments in an effort to appeal to different social classes.
Source: NAS GD325/505/4, ECBC *Prospectus.*

1860s pedigree, however, there is reason to claim that this was more an ECBC legacy and that it was they who had influenced private builders more than the reverse.

Social integration or *status quo*?

By any standard, the achievements of the Edinburgh Co-operative Building Company between 1861 and 1914 were remarkable. To build over 2,300 houses, to create a class of owner occupiers, the majority of them working-class families, was unknown in the history of the city, or indeed of any Scottish burgh. Of the houses built in Edinburgh between 1861 and 1911, just over 5% were the result of the activities of the ECBC (table 11.3).[81] In the earlier decades it was considerably higher – over

[81] Before 1881, the census definition for a house in Scotland was in fact a tenement. The calculation of the number of houses in 1871 is based on the ratio of families to houses identified by the Registrar-General in 1871, and conservatively used for 1861 as well. This is likely to understate, slightly, the ECBC contribution.

Table 11.3 *ECBC contribution to housing in Edinburgh 1861–1911*

	ECBC housing as a % of total Edinburgh housing stock	ECBC building as a % of the increase in Edinburgh housebuilding
1861–71	1.98	14.6
1871–81	3.10	10.2
1881–91	2.76	1.4
1891–1901	2.74	2.6
1901–11	2.88	5.4
1861–1911		5.2

Sources: based on NAS GD327/488, ECBC House Sales 1862–1917, and Censuses of Scotland 1861–1911.

14.6% and 10.2% respectively in the 1860s and 1870s – and if the percentage additions to housing stock seem modest overall, hovering around the 3% mark, this was because the decennial contributions of the ECBC were inevitably small compared to the aggregate Edinburgh housing stock accumulated over the centuries. However, with almost two in every five of all its properties owner occupied, the ECBC added disproportionately to this category of tenure.

To the founders, ownership empowered the working class.[82] It increased autonomy. Owner occupiers were not necessarily rendered homeless if unemployment struck; nor were old age and infirmity such a threat. Ownership was seen as providing a cushion for family members against the disruptive, short-term effects of unemployment and the long-run consequences of premature death, since the interruption to the income of the breadwinner was less likely to transform the lifestyle of surviving members if they were house owners.

The image of the Company as liberators was a powerful one. If there was a tinge of Samuel Smiles' self-help ethos about it, the co-operative nature of the ECBC was firmly embedded in the Constitution and through the structure of shareownership, with 39% of the original shareholders identified as stonemasons and another fifty-five trades inscribed in the share register.[83] Crucially, the ECBC familiarised many potential buyers with the concept of mortgages, first through a deposit scheme

---

[82] A charming if rather sentimental narrative is provided by Reid, *Housing the People*, 62–9, and again in his *Every Man His Own Landlord* (London n.d.), Edinburgh University Library Special Collection QP656/2, 1–7, in which an imagined dialogue between a couple contemplating their prospects in life is presented.

[83] NAS BT2/1970/548/79/4, Edinburgh Building Contractors, List of Shareholders, 1862.

Table 11.4 *Comparative mortality rates: ECBC housing, Edinburgh and Leith, 1878–1884*

	Average annual mortality/000 ECBC (1878–84)	Average annual city mortality /000 (1878–84)	Balance in favour of ECBC/000
Edinburgh			
Glenogle Park	13.00	19.37	6.37
Dalry Park	13.90	19.37	6.28
Norton Park	14.80	19.37	4.57
Leith			
Hawthornbank	16.60	24.50	7.90
Restalrig Park	15.80	24.50	8.70

Source: NAS, GD327/490, Annual Report 1885.

designed to assist the accumulation of sufficient funds, and then through an instalment scheme which spread house purchase initially over fourteen years, and later extended this in the difficult years of the mid-1880s to twenty-one years.[84] In examining the case of 'A', who bought a house for £220, paid a deposit of £11 (5%) and monthly instalments of £1.36 for twenty-one years, the Company concluded that

anyone who is able to save £4 per annum, out of which to pay the sum additional to rent required for instalments, the feu-duty, and landlord's taxes, need have no hesitation in purchasing a house on these terms.[85]

The ECBC could also demonstrate absolutely better life expectancy in their properties (table 11.4) and were understandably proud of the advantage occupants enjoyed relative to the city as a whole, even once the effect of suburbanisation on city-wide mortality rates was taken into account. The differential death rates, verified by the signed statements of the Medical Officers of Health for Leith and Edinburgh, were a propaganda coup for the ECBC and one which they were not slow to use in their publicity material and reports to shareholders. Improved life expectancy associated with ECBC houses itself, therefore, reduced dependency and was a positive force for empowerment and social integration.

Against a background of concern in the 1840s and 1850s regarding the unhealthy nature of working-class housing in Edinburgh, both physical and moral, those involved in the ECBC could show justifiable pride in

[84] The minimum deposit was 5s and interest accrued at 5%. The deposit scheme was cut back in 1867.   [85] NAS GD327/489, Prospectus 1882, 2–3.

their provision of numerous, well-designed and durable properties. The arrangement for separate access was described as 'an exceedingly novel yet simple contrivance' in securing privacy for the residents, and one which economised on roofing costs while also limiting the degree to which two families under the same roof intruded on one another.[86] Separate access by means of an external stair reduced overall construction costs by a not inconsiderable 20%.[87] The non-negotiable nature of the commitment to provide gardens, shown elsewhere to have been an important leisure activity for workmen,[88] was a distinctive feature of the development, and even the affectionate local term for these properties, 'Colonies', reflected less a sense of dependency and more a spirit of neighbourliness. In the provision of such amenities, the Company directors were sympathetic to the needs of residents, and unlike interwar council housing, recognised that communities required more than purely functional housing.

The benefits of colony-style housing were powerfully conveyed in the story of a courting couple. Arm in arm and soon to wed, John Wilson and Mary Brown, imaginary figures created by one of the Colonies' founders, Hugh Gilzean-Reid, walked towards Glenogle Park in 1861.[89] 'I have resolved' said John 'never to take you to any of those dingy hovels off the High Street, or even to those barrack-like blocks.' Mary replied: 'How horrible it must be to live in those dark closes, and be forced to associate ... with the people one sees there!' She commented on 'poor Mrs Smith' papering her 'dingy rooms' even though the rain would soon run down the walls, on the language of the drunken neighbours and on the hostile conditions in which children grew up there. As they continued their walk John remarked: 'I have been determined, with God's help, to commence life with you in other and better circumstances; and at last the possibility is placed within our reach.' He spoke of his purchase of twenty shares in the ECBC and his intention to buy a house in Reid Terrace. Mary's incredulity was evident: 'John – you must be dreaming.' John pointed out the actual spot they would occupy: 'It seems like a dream but it is as much a reality as our wedding.' John commented on the quality of building, amenities, separate entrance and the mortgage arrangements, and the imaginary episode concluded with the reflection, some years after their wedding, that they had 'for a long period owned their house' and that they

---

[86] *Building and Lands Companies' Gazette*, 1881, quoted in the Edinburgh Co-operative Building Company's details of its instalment scheme, 1 Sept. 1881.

[87] NAS GD327/489, Minute Books, 1867. I am grateful to Rose Pipes for supplying this information which shows that the costs could be reduced by up to £42 by using an external staircase.

[88] S. M. Gaskell, 'Gardens for the working class', *Victorian Studies*, 23, 1980, 479–501.

[89] Reid, *Housing the People*, 62–9.

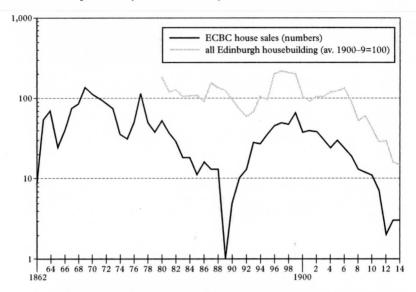

Figure 11.16 Housebuilding fluctuations 1862–1914: ECBC activity compared to all housing construction in Edinburgh.

Sources: R. Rodger, 'Scottish urban housebuilding 1870–1914', University of Edinburgh PhD thesis, 1975, 55, 58–9, 67, NAS GD327/488, Papers of C. Norman Kemp, House Sales 1862–1914.

were 'gradually becoming possessors of other houses for their children'. Gilzean-Reid concluded: 'to all workers . . . the story is full of instruction and hope'.

Yet, in important respects, co-operative principles and workers' autonomy were a smokescreen for a conventional approach to housing supply inherent in the ECBC's activities. Even the language of the reports and committees, the frequent references to the need for 'caution', 'prudence' and the long shadow cast by 'the state of trade', endorse this view of the ECBC as a model of Victorian capitalist conformity. In some respects the Edinburgh Co-operative Building Company even reinforced the *status quo*. The close correlation between the cyclical fluctuations in housebuilding in Edinburgh, Leith and the sales of ECBC property (fig. 11.16) indicates that the Company was unable to break out from the volatile Scottish building cycle of the nineteenth century.[90]

[90] See W. W. Rostow, *The British Economy in the Nineteenth Century* (Oxford 1948); B. Thomas, *Migration and Economic Growth* (2nd edn, Cambridge 1973), Part III; J. P. Lewis, *Building Cycles and Britain's Growth* (London 1965), 164–85. For an overview see R. J. Morris and R. Rodger, 'Introduction', in R. J. Morris and R. Rodger, eds., *The Victorian City: A Reader in British Urban History 1820–1914* (London 1993), 12–14.

Table 11.5 *Share transfers: ECBC 1867–1869*

	Building trades	Other trades	Clerks, merchants	Ladies, and 'no profession'	Company
Sold	445	490	37	135	173
Purchased	156	459	220	282	163

Source: NAS GD1/777/2, ECBC, Report by Finance Committee, 27 Sept. 1869.

Judged by the rhythms of its housing output, the ECBC differed imperceptibly from private builders and landlords. When the labour market tightened and wages drifted upwards, so the ECBC responded by pressing the housebuilding accelerator; when the local economy lost some of its heat the ECBC slowed construction. Rather than search for and buy land in the recessionary phase, the ECBC competed with private sector interests in the upswing phase of the cycle. Heriot's Hospital acknowledged[91] openly that it reinforced the housebuilding cycle in relation to the release of their land and the ECBC did so too (fig. 11.16). As far as these Edinburgh agencies were concerned, or in the pattern of hospital, cemetery, park or golf course provision, there is little evidence that they produced a counter-cyclical rhythm as has been suggested for other British cities.[92]

A considerable shift in the pattern of shareholding, away from stonemasons, building tradesmen and other artisans towards clerks, shopkeepers and a rentier class which included women was indicative of how the pressures of the market induced conformity. The culture of shareholding, of long-term investment horizons, was evidently absent amongst many of the earliest working-class investors in the ECBC and their sales of shares provided new opportunities for petit bourgeois investors in Edinburgh. In late 1860s trading, which saw almost 13% of shares change ownership in two years, it was this social class alone which increased their holdings (see table 11.5). Within a few years, the financial performance, itself an indicator of orthodoxy, was sufficiently robust as to attract non-manual and petit bourgeois investors in place of tradesmen.

Absenteeism and the concentration of shareownership took hold in the ECBC share registers. Already underway by 1870, the infiltration of

[91] ECA, George Heriot's Roll of Superiorities, 1913–14, f. 2.
[92] NAS GD327/506, Report on Ground Feued . . . and Effect of Hospital and Other Institutions on Property Values, GD327/506–7, letters from Kemp to Salmond, various dates 1901; J. W. R. Whitehand, 'Land values and land use', in J. W. R. Whitehand, *The Changing Face of Cities* (Oxford 1987), 45–50.

Table 11.6 *Geographical distribution of ECBC shareholders 1914*

Location	No. of shareholders	Total shareholding	% of all shareholders	% of all shares	Average holding
Edinburgh and Leith	324	7,334	70.0	73.3	22.6
Fife	17	265	3.7	2.7	15.6
Glasgow	15	206	3.2	2.1	13.7
Rest of Scotland	57	1,469	12.3	14.7	25.8
England	36	658	7.8	6.6	18.3
Not known	13	48	2.8	0.5	3.7
Total[a]	463	10,000	100.0	100.0	21.6

[a] One Irish resident omitted.
Source: NAS BT2/1970/548/79/4, Edinburgh Building Contractors, Share Register, 1914.

ECBC shareholding by a petite bourgeoisie was almost complete by the twentieth century and in this respect, too, the ECBC shadowed conventional companies. By 1914, just over 7% of shareholders lived in England, a third of them in London, though only one shareholder, Miss Mary Ingram, a near neighbour in Oak Park, Chicago, of the distinguished American architect, Frank Lloyd Wright, lived outside the United Kingdom.[93] About one shareholder in thirty lived in Glasgow and across the Firth of Forth, another one in thirty of the shareholders in 1914 lived in Fife (table 11.6). To these clusters of shareowners were added others both nearby in the Lothians – from Bonnyrigg, Loanhead, Midcalder, Dalkeith, East Linton and Prestonpans – and a more distant northern representation from Forres, Nairn, Rothes, Dornoch and Wick. Excluding those who lived in Edinburgh and Leith, investors from the rest of Scotland represented one in every five of ECBC shareholders. From Kirkcudbright to Caithness, therefore, modest private savings and trust funds were invested in the ECBC and so facilitated the construction of housing in Edinburgh.

At face value, with almost three-quarters of all shares owned by residents from Edinburgh and Leith, it might seem that control of the ECBC's activities remained local. Indeed 'colonists' themselves comprised one in sixteen (6.5%) of all shareholders and some held resolutely to their certificates and bequeathed them to family members. David Rintoul's daughter and Daniel Kemp's son, for example, retained the shares inherited from their respective founder fathers.[94] Andrew

[93] NAS BT2/1970/548/79/4, Share Register, 1914.
[94] NAS GD1/777/1 and GD1/777/6, ECBC Share Transfer Book, 1865–1922, and Share Ledger, 1897–1944.

Salmond, the ECBC's chairman between 1871 and 1917, lived in the Balgreen development and was the second largest shareholder with 250 shares.[95] Elsewhere, George Forsyth from Carstairs, who had risen through the ranks to become a railway station-master and lived at 20 Myrtle Terrace, used his steady income and money obtained from lodgers to buy £102 of stock in the ECBC. Opposite, Annie Mein used the dividends from her late husband's investment in the ECBC to pay her bills on 40 Ivy Terrace, the house they had bought together from the Company not long after it was built. David Mein was a librarian and, like Forsyth and George Cation, a joiner who had lived at 15 Bell Place for thirty years, enjoyed a secure income sufficient to become both an ECBC householder and a shareowner.[96]

However, as the price of ECBC stock rose, eventually to reach twice the original £1 value, so the original shareholders were inclined to sell their holdings. Judged by the nature of their addresses, it was the comfortably off residing in the New Town and solidly suburban streets in the Grange, Marchmont, Comiston, Morningside, Greenbank and Murrayfield, and to a lesser extent residents of villas in Joppa and Argyle Crescent in Portobello and in the outlying villages of Blackhall, Corstorphine and Davidsons Mains who increasingly bought ECBC shares (fig. 11.17). Sometimes members of the same household each acquired shares in the ECBC. David and John Amos of Lord Russell Street held share certificates numbers 151 and 152 for forty years, and the three Misses McGibbon of 26 Learmonth Grove obtained certificates for 35 shares. Gardener's Crescent, opposite Rosebank Cottages which influenced ECBC designs, was a centre for such investment with Andrew Drummond and his three spinster sisters owning collectively 113 shares and three other neighbours in possession of another 56 shares.

ECBC shares proved increasingly attractive to women. Indeed, two in every five shares in 1914 were owned by a woman; a quarter of all shares were owned by spinsters (table 11.7). Some, of course, lived at a distance and so could not easily attend quarterly Company meetings of shareholders and for a very large number their portfolio of assets was managed by solicitors or other representatives. Of the top twenty shareholders, fourteen were either trusts or women or non-resident in Edinburgh, categories which, judged by the Company's Minutes, were rarely, if ever, present at shareholders' meetings. One who was omnipresent was Andrew Salmond, the ECBC chairman for forty-six years, who undoubtedly in the course of his period of office saw the extent of shareholder involvement in Company policy reduced as executive power became more concentrated in the hands of the directors.

[95] NAS GD1/777/10, Minutes, Special Meeting, 25 Sept. 1917.
[96] NAS BT2/1970/548/79/4, Share Register, 1914; Census Enumerators' Books, 1891.

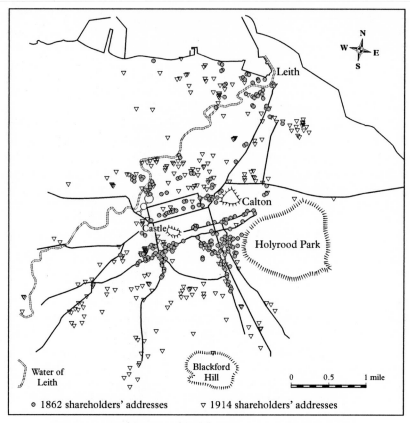

Figure 11.17 The suburbanisation of share ownership: ECBC
shareholders' addresses 1862 and 1914

Almost half the shareholders (44%) controlled only 10% of the shares
in the Company in 1914. Fifty-six individuals or 12% of shareholders
held 50% of the ECBC shares; just 3% of shareholders owned 20% of
shares. As the pattern of shareholding became more concentrated so the
levels of direct engagement in Company affairs diminished. Though
some 'colonists' remained as shareholders, the spatial shift towards the
suburban investor and the spinster with a portfolio of managed investments guaranteed that the early participatory nature of Company meetings would become extinct. It was not a matter of apathy; it was simply
that ECBC investors and their representatives focused increasingly on
dividend distributions and, so long as these seemed acceptable, they had

Table 11.7 *Women as shareholders: the composition of ECBC shareholding 1914*

Type of shareholders	No. of shareholders	Total shareholding	% of all shareholders	% of all shares	Average holding
Widows and married women[a]	77	1,735	16.8	17.4	22.2
Spinsters	112	2,202	24.1	22.0	19.7
All women	189	3,937	40.8	39.4	20.8
Male shareholders	213	4,432	46.0	44.3	20.8
Trusts	61	1,631	13.2	16.3	26.7
All shareholders	463	10,000	100.0	100.0	21.6

[a] It is not possible to distinguish the marital status of these two elements.
Source: NAS BT2/1970/548/79/4, Edinburgh Building Contractors, Share Register, 1914.

little interest in how the profits which generated them were obtained.[97] Short termism and convenience prevailed, and with dividends stable, shareowners cared little about the co-operative *credo* of the ECBC.

Perhaps the strongest indication of the conformist and integrationist character of the ECBC was in its financial dealings. In a letter of unparalleled directness in 1899, one of the long-standing directors and former treasurer, D. W. Kemp, 'confessed' to the chairman 'to being amazed at your timidity', especially over land purchases, and repeated the adage of a respected financier that 'there is nothing divine but dividends'.[98] Dividends mesmerised the directors, and Kemp noted with a degree of irony, that but for the 'steadying' hands of the chairman even more of the 'reserves would soon go to swell dividends'.[99] The Royal Commission on Housing which took evidence in Edinburgh in 1884 heard from the ECBC manager, James Colville, that the Company employed 60–70 workmen regularly, and at one stage this had risen to 250, but there was arguably greater satisfaction in his evidence that the ECBC dividends had averaged 15% over twenty-three years.[100]

The sensitive approach by the Company to borrowers' difficulties over mortgage repayments in 1881–2 resulted in an extension of the

[97] See R. Rodger, *Housing the People: The Colonies of Edinburgh* (Edinburgh 1999), for an account of how this detachment affected twentieth-century activities of the ECBC.
[98] NAS GD327/499, letter from Kemp to Salmond, 14 May 1899.
[99] NAS GD327/499, Kemp to Salmond, 14 May 1899.
[100] *PP 1884–5 XXX*, Royal Commission, Colville, Q. 19070.

repayment period from fourteen to twenty-one years.[101] This sensitivity was lacking in 1895, however, when the ECBC suspended the programme designed to assist small savers to accumulate the 5% deposit necessary to obtain a house and it signalled the Company's increasing concern for shareholders' interests.[102] Again shareholder interests were paramount in 1904 when the ECBC decided to sell its rights to yearly feu-duty and ground annual income. The decision coincided with the onset of a decade of sharp contraction in the housebuilding industry in Edinburgh and consequently the price of such heritable securities fell (see chapter 4). Even so, the ECBC sale of its ground annual entitlements at Shaftesbury Park to the Merchant Company's Widows' Fund produced a healthy cash injection of over £3,000, boosted further by sales of similar heritable securities in Leith between 1900 and 1914.[103] The proceeds were used not to acquire land for development, however, but to issue a 10% dividend bonus. Shareholders, it seems, were to be insulated from the vagaries of the building cycle. Borrowers, by contrast, were more harshly dealt with.

Swept along by the market and unable to unload some of its properties in the 1880s, the ECBC was forced increasingly to act as landlord, tying up its capital and so restricting further its scope for independent action to provide housing for the working classes (fig. 11.18). As early as 1882, when the residential property market was in decline, a perceptible shift in emphasis had developed – the ratio of ECBC revenue derived from house sales to income generated by renting their unsold property fell sharply, and though this recovered in the 1890s, it never again resumed the buoyancy of the first fifteen years.

In view of its reinforcement of the building cycle and of the adoption of financial practices more commonly identified with profit maximising private firms, the activities of the ECBC seemed to confirm a view expressed in 1864 that 'the co-operative principle is that workers are the capitalists'.[104] Constantly looking over their shoulders as to how ECBC business decisions would reflect on the share value and always aware of opportunities in public meetings and through the annual report to add a public relations spin on their activities, the performance of the ECBC directors increasingly resembled that of a well-run private business. The similarity even extended to the problem shared by many other Edinburgh firms, that the continued vigour depended heavily on the ability to replace successfully the founder of the firm, or, in the ECBC case, influential

---

[101] NAS GD327/489, Instalment Scheme Prospectus, 1882.
[102] NAS GD327/490, Annual Report, 1895.
[103] NAS GD327/490–2, Annual Reports, 1904–14.
[104] 'Co-operative societies in 1864', *Edinburgh Review*, 120, 1864, 407.

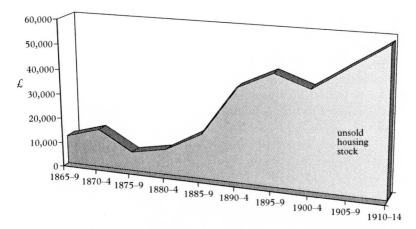

Figure 11.18 Unsold ECBC housing stock and the rise of ECBC
landlordism 1862–1914

Source: NAS GD327/488, Papers of C. Norman Kemp, based on
ECBC Annual Reports.

founders and housing managers, such as James Colville.[105] As another of
the founders remarked in 1895:

of late years the [ECBC] has assumed the character of an ordinary trading
concern, and lost the inspirations of its earlier youth.[106]

The consolidation of house ownership was another indicator of the
conventional character of ECBC operations. Even in Reid's imaginary
household, John Wilson and Mary Brown began to accumulate properties for their children. A few individuals, trustees and property companies
such as the Suburban Feuing Company and the Scottish Metropolitan
Property Company began to mop up colony houses, buying two or three
when they first became available and adding to them subsequently. The
reality was not a honeycomb of private ownership but clustered groups of
properties owned by petty capitalists who derived an annual rental
income from them. Indeed, of colony properties owned in 1911 by trusts,
individuals and companies, 35% were in the hands of owners of two or
more houses.[107] In the street named for the social commentator and
housing campaigner, Hugh Miller, numbers 1–12 and 21–32 were owned

---

[105] See, for example, S. Nenadic *et al.*, 'Record linkage and the small family firm: Edinburgh
1861–1891', *Bulletin John Rylands Library*, 74, 1992, 169–89; and S. Nenadic, 'The
small family firm in Victorian Britain', *Business History*, 35, 1993, 86–114.

[106] Reid, *Housing the People*, xvi.

[107] NAS VR100/33–7, VR100/267–73 and VR55/130, Valuation Rolls for Edinburgh and
Leith, 1861 and 1911.

by Miss C. D. Hamilton and managed by John Hamilton from a suburban Craiglockhart address. It was a pattern of multiple ownership replicated in swathes of Edinburgh housing. Next door to 43 and 44 Alva Place, houses owned by Miss B. Mackie and let for her by an agent in South Clerk Street, were the properties of the absentee owner of number 41 and 42, Mrs E. Evans of Perth, who also owned numbers 2 and 4. In the next street a lawyer, Robert Strathearn, owned 23, 25 and 27 Maryfield. Ownership was mostly in the hands of Edinburgh residents, though H. H. Bayne of the Philippine Islands and Mrs A. M. Hamill, London, were amongst a small number of absentee owners living, in part, on rents obtained from their ECBC properties. As absentee landlords necessarily they employed letting agents, but this practice was also widespread amongst Edinburgh owners, so reproducing the landlord–tenant relations with their inherent conflicts based around the legitimate duties of factors, rent collectors and bailiffs.

Gradually and unevenly, the founders' aspiration of ownership for occupiers was diluted; tenancy status was reasserted in the 'Colonies'. Whereas in Stockbridge, owner occupiers were a majority (55%) of the original residents in the 1860s, by 1911 the percentage had fallen to 28%.[108] More generally, by the eve of the First World War owner occupiers had declined to 25–33% of some 1,500 ECBC houses in Stockbridge, Leith, Dalry, Abbeyhill and Restalrig, and though a minority, it should be stressed this was still at least three times the city-wide average which itself had risen from 8.4% in 1855 to 12.4% in 1914.[109] At the Shaftesbury and Balgreen sites, where houses were built to appeal to clerks, shopkeepers and public officials, owner occupiers accounted for almost 40% of residents; at Hermitage Hill they constituted 70% (see fig. 11.19). By the 1880s, and possibly as early as 1877 when the Barnton Terrace site was acquired, the ECBC de facto had abandoned its former commitment to improve the housing of the working classes.

From its foundation, the stated intention of the ECBC was to house 'the better class of workmen', amongst whom the building trades were strongly represented.[110] This building connection remained a strong and symbolic one, particularly as the initial group of fifteen directors was drawn exclusively from the building trades and their contribution was marked by naming some of the early streets after them. More durable

---

[108] Calculations based on Edinburgh Valuation Rolls, 1911, NAS VR100/267–73, and for 1860s based on Pipes, *The Colonies* (1998 edn), 45–71.

[109] A. O'Carroll, 'Tenements to bungalows: class and the growth of home ownership before the Second World War', *Urban History*, 24, 1997, 223.

[110] The Edinburgh Co-operative Building Company Ltd, *Articles of Association* (Edinburgh 1861), 7; *PP 1884–5 XXX*, Royal Commission, Colville, Q. 19075.

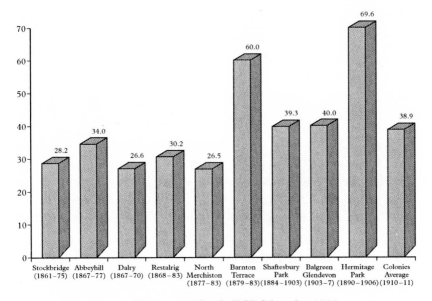

Figure 11.19 Owner occupiers in ECBC housing 1911

Sources: NAS VR100/267–73, Valuation Rolls, Edinburgh, VR55/130, Valuation Rolls, Leith, 1911.

were the stone plaques (see fig. 11.20) of building workers' tools which embellished the end walls of many ECBC streets. Amongst the residents in ECBC houses, however, the presence of artisanal households was visibly diluted in the first thirty years (table 11.18).[111] From the 1860s to the 1890s, clerks (8.9%) were the largest single occupational group amongst household heads, though the retired and annuitants living from pensions and savings were slightly more numerous (9.0%). Public officials such as inspectors, army and navy officers together with managers, teachers, civil and mechanical engineers meant this group of salaried and office workers accounted for approximately 7.3% of heads of household by 1891. A quarter of the residents in the earliest ECBC houses, therefore, were occupied in middle- or lower-middle-class occupations and were living from savings and investments. Commercial activities –

[111] Census of Scotland 1871–91, Enumerators' Books, 1871, 685^{1}50, 685^{1}70–71, 685^{2}25, 685^{2}96, 685^{2}103, 692^{1}21–26, 692^{2}3; 1881, 685^{1}3(L), 685^{1}32, 685^{1}75, 685^{1}100, 685^{1}112–14, 685^{2}31–4, 692^{1}26, 692^{2}4; 1891, 685^{1}6, 685^{1}82–3, 685^{1}106, 685^{1}123, 685^{2}129–31, 685^{3}14–17, 692^{1}25, 692^{1}27, 692^{2}1, 692^{2}6. Subsequent references to family, household and occupational structure in the colonies is based on the schedules from the Census Enumerators' Books, 1871–91.

Figure 11.20 Wall plaques and building trades insignias: ECBC
houses, Stockbridge

Note: clockwise from top left: carter, joiner, painter, mason.
Source: RCAHMS ED/9888, 9890, 9893, 9895.

dealers, agents, salesmen and commercial travellers – provided the
incomes for 6.0%, and drapers, hatters, butchers, bakers and an array of
other shopkeepers and their employees accounted for about 9.3% of
heads of households. Clerks apart, joiners were the single largest group of
artisans (6.4%), and with masons (3.2%), painters (1.8%), cabinetmakers (1.8%) and a group of fourteen building and woodworking trades they
constituted 16.4% of the households in the Colonies in the years

1871–91. Two other elements of the 'better class of workmen' – the railway workers and printers – together contributed about 9.2% of households in the first thirty years of ECBC housebuilding. If, then, as the ECBC manager declared, the intention was to provide housing for 'the better class of workmen' then the reality was very different.

To a mix of tenures was added a mix of occupations and social status in ECBC Colonies. However, identifiable clusters of work-related and social characteristics gave each colony a distinctive status (table 11.8). For example, the Bohemian families of Beithich, Haulfauss, Laiche and Hurch were part of a concentration of glass cutters and engravers at Abbeyhill in 1871 which constituted 4.6% of ECBC households there. Predictably, in Leith incomes derived from maritime activities – deckhands, dockers and 'mariners' mostly – sustained 14.5% of families there, and 4.7% of Restalrig families. In other Colonies, both the sea-faring and glass-cutting activities were insignificant. Railway employment was greatest at Abbeyhill and Dalry; Shaftesbury Park began as a community dominated by shopkeepers, office workers and commercial employees; in Dalry and Stockbridge, building workers were two or three times more common than in the other ECBC Colonies; and at North Merchiston every ninth household head was a pensioner, and in Shaftesbury Park these annuitants and retirees constituted one household in six.

One in seven ECBC homes had a woman as head of household; in Leith and Shaftesbury Park they represented one household head in five (table 11.9). Where there was a woman as head of household, almost two-thirds (65%) were widows, 16% were spinsters and 19% described themselves as both married and head of household. Female-headed households had a number of distinctive characteristics – the average age of fifty-two years was nine years older, the average number of household members was smaller by 1.25 people, and they were three times more likely to have a lodger (40%) – and consequently, the character of individual streets and Colonies was influenced by the frequency of female household heads. Annuitants, of course, had independent means but in providing deposit and instalment schemes to facilitate house purchase, at a stroke, the ECBC improved women's access to mortgages (see chapter 9).

Though in principle the ECBC houses were intended as homes for nuclear families, in practice they sheltered extended family members and lodgers which inevitably affected privacy (table 11.9). Lodgers, of course, supplemented the household income and their frequency in ECBC properties reflected either the pressure in meeting mortgage repayments or tenants' need to boost incomes to meet rental payments. In 1871, one colony house in every seven had a lodger; one in forty had three or more lodgers. Inevitably, there were the horror stories. At 29 Hugh Miller Place

Table 11.8 *Occupational composition of ECBC Colonies households 1871–1891 (%)*

	Annuitant retired	Shopkeepers	Agents, dealers	Government employees, officials	Clerks	Building trades	Printing	Railway employees
Stockbridge	8.7	10.7	3.4	5.0	7.3	23.4	6.3	1.0
Leith	11.0	6.4	6.4	13.3	2.9	6.9	1.7	2.3
Norton Park	5.6	8.3	4.4	4.6	7.5	11.2	5.1	10.9
Dalry	7.9	7.4	8.8	3.7	9.7	27.8	1.9	10.2
Restalrig	9.5	10.0	6.3	13.7	13.7	11.1	1.1	2.6
North Merchiston	12.4	10.6	8.0	6.2	14.2	15.0	0.0	6.2
Shaftesbury	18.0	12.6	15.3	15.3	15.3	7.2	5.4	1.8
All households (N = 1957)	9.0	9.3	6.0	7.3	8.9	16.4	3.9	5.3

Source: Census of Scotland 1871–91, Census Enumerators' Books, Edinburgh and Leith.

Table 11.9 *Household structure: Edinburgh Colony housing 1871–1891*

ECBC development	Female head of household (%)	Households with lodgers (%)	Average household size (persons)		Average age of householder (years)	
			All households	Female household head	All households	Female household head
Stockbridge	14.7	13.5	4.79	3.54	44.5	53.5
Leith	19.9	9.7	4.56	3.82	44.8	47.5
Norton Park	11.7	15.1	4.90	4.31	43.8	52.2
Dalry	12.5	35.1	5.02	4.23	43.3	56.1
Restalrig	11.4	6.8	5.18	3.60	44.1	54.4
North Merchiston	10.3	8.7	4.92	2.77	45.1	53.4
Shaftesbury	18.7	8.1	4.33	3.48	41.0	44.0
All households (N = 1957)	13.8	14.8	4.85	3.78	44.0	51.9

Source: as for table 11.8.

in Stockbridge, four lodgers added unimaginable congestion to William Black's large household of six children, three of whom were over fourteen – a household of twelve persons. In the Dalry development, every third house had a lodger; for the Colonies as a whole in 1871 and 1891 the proportion was one in seven. Even in its flagship development, Stockbridge, where 13.5% of ECBC houses had lodgers this proportion still applied, though in the later developments at Merchiston and Shaftesbury Park lodgers were less common and were in the 8–9% range.

In terms of crude density the most overcrowded ECBC houses were not dissimilar to Old Town flats off the High Street and so despised by moral reformers, but the average ECBC household size of 4.85 persons represented a quantum improvement. Furthermore, the parlour phenomenon or best room in the Colonies permitted a degree of privacy which was impossible in the undifferentiated space of even a two-roomed tenement flat. In this sense, the ECBC properties were indeed 'colonising', that is, not unlike English-style working-class housing which differed fundamentally from Scottish tenement flats by creating private in place of public or communal space. However, unlike English terraced houses, where the scullery, wash-house and kitchen extensions became closely identified with women's space, the gendered nature of space or 'separate spheres' was by the nature of their design more difficult to achieve in ECBC houses.[112]

The floor plan and separate access proved attractive to English settlers in the 'Colonies'. As James Colville commented in 1884: 'most of the English people that come here think very well of them [ECBC houses] and stop in them'.[113] There were very considerable numbers of English immigrants (7.8%), more than from any single Scottish county other than Fife (9.6%), and only exceeded by those born in Edinburgh itself (20.6%).[114] With just one fifth of colony residents Edinburgh born, the ECBC was far from realising another of their stated objectives, that of providing soundly constructed, affordable and self-contained houses as an alternative to High Street hovels for the local working class. Though the inclusion of those born in Leith and the Lothians with Edinburgh raised the proportion of 'local' workmen housed in ECBC properties to 37.8%, the overwhelming majority of households originated from other

---

[112] An exception to this was at Shaftesbury Park where back extensions did reproduce the English terraced pattern more faithfully. For a more extended discussion of space–social relations in Scottish tenements see R. Rodger, 'The Victorian building industry and the housing of the Scottish working class', in M. Doughty, ed., *Building the Industrial City* (Leicester 1986), 163–7.

[113] *PP 1884–5 XXX*, Royal Commission, Colville, Q. 19070.

[114] In ECBC housing in Leith, off Ferry Road and at Restalrig, 17.0% and 13.7% of residents, respectively, were themselves 'Leithers'.

parts of Scotland (table 11.10). These patterns of migration contributed distinctive social and cultural contours to each of the Colonies, even if a degree of assimilation into the host community had developed.

Prior experience was an important influence determining where an immigrant sought work, and the composition of many of the ECBC Colonies reflected this to some degree. For example, no railway engine driver in an ECBC house lived anywhere other than in the Dalry (near Haymarket Station) or Abbeyhill (near St Margaret's Yards) Colonies and almost all were part of a step-wise migration pattern to Edinburgh from smaller urban places in Lanarkshire and Stirlingshire such as Polmont, Cambusnethan and Carluke. Similarly, it was logical for HM Customs officials to prefer proximity to the port and for glass-works at Abbeyhill to attract migrants with such highly specific skills.[115] There were, then, colonies within the Colonies.

By contrast, the varied nature of migration from Fife was reflected in the fact that there were twenty different occupations recorded for the thirty ECBC Stockbridge homes in 1871 whose household head was from Fife. For those who had been born in the borders and south-west Scotland, and from other essentially rural settlements, migrants found work in service, retailing, building, labouring and clerical work and a range of employments where previous experience was helpful but not essential. Predictably, therefore, borderers were fairly evenly scattered throughout ECBC neighbourhoods and 100 different occupations were recorded in the 167 separate households from these areas.

Migrants' journeys to Edinburgh were an important factor in the locational decision. For those migrants from the west, for example, from Stirlingshire and West Lothian, the ECBC Colonies at Dalry and later Shaftesbury Park were in the line of the arrival corridor, and they remained the most common places to settle for such migrants. Sea journeys for Orcadians, Shetlanders and migrants from the north-east meant that their first landfall at Leith encouraged them initially to settle nearby, and the Restalrig and Leith ECBC properties were favoured by comparison with other developments in the city.[116] A quarter of all Fife migrants to ECBC properties settled in Stockbridge and Leith, convenient north Edinburgh locations, but also ones with early housing developments which enabled geographically well-placed 'Fifers' to make an

---

[115] J. Jackson, 'Housing areas in mid-Victorian Wigan and St. Helens', *Transactions Institute of British Geographers*, 6, 1981, 413–32.

[116] C. W. J. Withers, *Urban Highlanders: Highland–Lowland Migration and Urban Gaelic Culture 1700–1900* (East Linton 1998), 109, shows that highland-born immigrants represented just 2.5% of the Edinburgh population in 1891 as a whole, with the north-eastern highlands and Inverness-shire the most heavily represented area.

Table 11.10 *Birthplaces of Colonies' residents 1871 and 1891*

	Stockbridge	Leith	Norton Park	Dalry	Restalrig	North Merchiston	Shaftesbury Park	All Colonies
Edinburgh	22.1	9.3	28.3	19.3	12.8	23.2	15.7	20.6
Leith	1.6	17.0	2.6	2.5	13.7	0.0	1.7	4.8
Lothians	11.5	16.0	9.6	14.8	18.3	8.8	9.1	12.4
Glasgow and west	4.9	3.1	6.2	9.1	5.5	16.0	14.9	7.0
Dundee, Aberdeen & NE	12.8	8.2	8.5	13.2	6.8	12.8	9.9	10.5
Fife	11.3	13.9	7.4	9.1	8.2	8.0	8.3	9.6
Highlands and islands	6.6	10.3	8.1	6.6	9.1	4.0	7.4	7.5
Borders and SW	9.9	8.2	9.1	9.5	8.7	8.0	6.6	9.0
Central	9.3	7.7	7.2	11.5	7.8	5.6	11.6	8.7
England	7.7	5.7	9.6	3.3	6.8	10.4	12.4	7.8
Ireland	1.6	0.5	1.7	0.4	0.9	3.2	2.5	1.5
Non-UK	0.5	0.0	1.7	0.8	1.4	0.0	0.0	0.8
	100.0	100.0	100.0	100.0	100.0	100.0	100.0	100.0

Source: as for table 11.8.

excursion by steamer across the Forth in the 1860s and 1870s to find work in the expanding Edinburgh labour market.

Civil society and the construction of capitalism

A glance at the late twentieth-century map of Edinburgh confirms the design ingenuity and distinctive morphology associated with the ECBC activities in its first fifty years. In this sense, the ECBC contributed significantly to the physical as well as the social landscape of Edinburgh and also provided a model adopted by such small towns as Bonnyrigg and Dalkeith.[117] Central to this achievement was the construction of a radical alternative to the ubiquitous Scottish tenement block. Not only was this achieved in the initial floor plans and elevations of the 1860s, it was reinvented in the 1890s in the form of a continuous row of two storey flatted villas with internal staircases. As an affordable alternative to expensive villadom or west end neo-classicism, the flatted villa solution identified in Shaftesbury Park and refined at Hermitage Hill offered an important variant to Edinburgh's subtly differentiated middle class. As private builders adopted this housing form, too, there was an element of convergence in the urban landscape of Edinburgh in the quarter century before the First World War.

This theme of convergence can be taken further. ECBC houses were not exclusively for working classes and their families; the rhythm of Company housebuilding was identical to, rather than independent of, fluctuations in the private sector; the ECBC management was drawn into debates concerning dividends, profits, speculation and shareowning and accorded them a high priority; and at 5.8%, the percentage of vacant ECBC houses was not unlike that of James Steel's 6.6% vacancy rate for the corresponding years.[118] The ECBC was caught between the participation enshrined in their Articles of Association and the need to secure the viability, and thus the profitability, of the Company. In short, the principles of co-operation and mutuality were in conflict with those of capitalism. Inevitably, compromises were necessary.

[117] The ECBC activities were copied, in a very limited way, in Aberdeen, Glasgow, Dundee and other Scottish towns, and in Liverpool, London and elsewhere in England. In a speech from the chairman of the Liverpool Society in 1868, it was acknowledged that the ECBC was the only one of its type, and in Glasgow, the form of mutuality was disguised in the title of the association, the Glasgow Working Men's Insurance and Building Society. See Reid, *Housing the People*, 19, 44, and J. Begg, *The Health and Homes of Working People in Towns and Cities and How to Improve Them* (Glasgow 1875), 22. See also NAS, Register of Sasines, Abridgements and Index of Names, 1869–74.

[118] The figures relate to the years 1871 and 1891. Stockbridge registered one of the highest rates of empty housing (7.7%) and was exceeded only by Dalry (7.8%) and Shaftesbury Park (8.3%).

Though the first twenty years were successful in both financial terms and in relation to the number of houses built, they were so largely because of the accumulated skilled working-class demand for housing. One indication of this was that despite the fact that 1,000 homes were created in the first fifteen years, it took another thirty-five years to build the next 1,000. Even though the skilled working class in Edinburgh were numerous, diverse and associated with the highest concentration of middle-class consumerism outside London, and their purchasing power was correspondingly higher and more stable than elsewhere, still the fluctuations in employment undermined the volume of demand for ECBC housing from the mid-1870s. If demand for Colonies housing had, therefore, a great deal to do with the structure of employment locally, as radical churchmen and doctors such as Begg and Alison noted as early as the 1840s, then how much more unstable were market circumstances for housebuilders generally in Edinburgh and elsewhere?

For those who did become house owners the words of a contemporary song proclaimed the sentiments of many:

> I hae a hoose o' my ain
> I'll tak dunts frae naebody.[119]

The song extolled the independence which property owning conveyed and this vision of stakeholding in society, of assimilation or social integration, reflected the hegemonic power of liberal values. Ownership confidently proclaimed the message of independence: 'This is mine, no man can raise my rent.'[120] Ownership, replicated many times, provided a mechanism by which the social and moral state of the population at large could be elevated, thus raising 'the whole ground floor of society'.[121] It was an appeal, indirectly, to empower a property owning democracy.[122]

Most importantly, though, the experience gained by workmen in office holding, participation in meetings, public speaking and in management and general business administration was invaluable. Their 'talent for management [was] specially noteworthy'.[123] The educative function was significant, argued contemporaries, and if this had a firm moralising edge initially, the practical effects of saving and sobriety meant that the annual flit at term dates became a thing of the past and an identification with and a commitment to the neighbourhood became embedded as a cultural

---

[119] Edinburgh University Library Special Collections, text of a lecture by J. Begg, 'The health and homes of working people in towns and cities, and how to improve them', Glasgow, Aug. 1875.   [120] Reid, *Housing the People*, x.

[121] Begg, *Health and Homes*, 4.

[122] For an examination of a liberal framework to housing provision in the twentieth century see M. J. Daunton, *A Property-Owning Democracy? Housing in Britain* (London 1987).

[123] Reid, *Housing the People*, 51.

value.[124] Indeed, the same contemporaries saw this as 'a training in self-government' with a long-run contribution towards the development of a concept of civics amongst ECBC property owners.

There was, then, a clearly connected moral sequence in which 'sobriety, economy, self-reliance and mutual trust were essential to success' in relation not just to property ownership, but also to the wider terms of citizenship.[125] Mutual trust and responsibility were values which were central both to the ECBC property owning ethos and to citizenship. By acknowledging how gardens, individual rather than common access, internal space and room function affected human behaviour, and by recognising that the reorganisation of domestic space could have positive effects, the ECBC incorporated the inter-relationship between the physical and moral environment and its consequences for home and family life into its innovative housing designs.[126] If the moral climate which resulted was neither so complete nor so complex as presented by Patrick Geddes' vision of society, it would certainly have been recognisable to him as such.[127]

At another level of mutuality and co-operation, 'since possession is the surest basis of patriotism',[128] house ownership provided a measure of the social cement by which individuals were bound in to the interest of the state.[129] By contrast, dispossession and alienation lay at the heart of rent strikes in the west of Scotland before and during the First World War and which so threatened the stability of the state that rent control was introduced as a consequence.[130] The political contours of urban

[124] Reid, *Housing the People*, 50.
[125] H. E. Meller, 'Urban renewal and citizenship: the quality of life in British cities 1890–1990', *Urban History*, 22, 1995, 63–84.
[126] Such a line of argument is commonly adopted by historians of town planning. However, the ECBC activities and the emerging philosophy of housing c. 1860 in Edinburgh anticipates most genuine town planning efforts. Elsewhere the demands for factory labour were often satisfied in green field sites.
[127] H. E. Meller, *Patrick Geddes: Social Evolutionist and City Planner* (London 1990), 20–85.
[128] Begg, *Health and Homes*, 4.
[129] W. H. Fraser, 'Owenite socialism in Scotland', *Scottish Economic and Social History*, 16, 1996, 61, notes a contrary, though much earlier, view, that private property had weakened community identity.
[130] J. Melling, *Rent Strikes: Peoples' Struggles for Housing in West Scotland 1890–1916* (Edinburgh 1983), 105–15; and J. Melling, 'Clydeside rent struggles and the making of Labour politics in Scotland 1900–39', in R. Rodger, ed., *Scottish Housing in the Twentieth Century* (Leicester 1989), 254–88; S. Damer, 'State, class and housing: Glasgow 1885–1919', in J. Melling, ed., *Housing, Social Policy and the State* (London 1980), 73–112; J. J. Smyth, 'The ILP in Glasgow 1888–1906: the struggle for identity', in A. McKinlay and R. J. Morris, eds., *The ILP on Clydeside 1893–1932: From Foundation to Disintegration* (Manchester 1991). For the British context, see M. Swenarton, *Homes Fit for Heroes: The Politics and Architecture of Early State Housing in Britain* (London 1981), 77–87.

Scotland owed much in the twentieth century to the different trajectories of ownership which were emerging on Clydeside and in Edinburgh before the Great War. However, whether the residents of the Stockbridge Colonies and of Abbeyhill, Restalrig and Shaftesbury Parks enlisted in 1914 in greater numbers to Scottish regiments than volunteers from elsewhere in urban Scotland is not known, but they undoubtedly provided a bridgehead to another, later battle ground, the ideological contest to house Edinburgh workers in the 1920s and 1930s either in subsidised council housing or in private housing partially funded by central government.[131] Arguably the development of the Colonies captured the ideological initiative since, unlike Glasgow and the burghs of the west of Scotland, interwar housing in Edinburgh relied heavily on state funding to private rather than council housebuilding projects.

---

[131] A. O'Carroll, 'The development of owner occupation in Edinburgh 1918–1939', Heriot-Watt/Edinburgh College of Art PhD thesis, 1994. See also A. O'Carroll, 'The influence of local authorities on the growth of owner occupation 1914–39', *Planning Perspectives*, 11, 1996, 55–72. I am indebted to Annette O'Carroll for her helpful discussions.

12 Civic consciousness, social consciences and the built environment

Often a person, group or an event emerges to become defined as a threat to society, its values and interests. The nature of the individual or episode is presented in a stereotypical way by the media, with moral barricades in defence of social norms manned by church, political and civic leaders.[1] Accredited experts pronounce their opinions on causes, effects and solutions, and strategies are developed to mediate the consequences of the condition which may disappear, or it may resurface, sometimes in a more virulent form. The object of panic may be long-standing or a new departure, and if the phenomenon disappears it is still remembered in the collective memory. Where there are more serious implications then policy and the law may be altered permanently. Such concerns form the backbone of an interpretation of panics which is itself dependent on a view that deviants are created by a society which establishes rules and behavioural norms and then sanctions individuals should they infringe them. Infractions of social norms define deviants as outsiders.[2]

The power of the press to intensify public disquiet is a central engine of moral panics.[3] Through a sequence of stages, public concern unfolds first of all through an inventory of disturbing events in a specific arena and is then sensitised by a press aware of the commercial possibilities of public anxiety. Contagious diseases, like criminal activity, drunkenness and prostitution, were such an issue and hyperbole was never far from the surface in contemporary reports.[4] The charge of 'pollution' invoked the strongest possible opprobrium and was used as a 'verbal weapon of control'.[5] Once sensitised, new episodes were classified as part of the phenomenon and previous ones reclassified to conform to the prevailing

---

[1] S. Cohen, *Folk Devils and Moral Panics: The Creation of Mods and Rockers* (London 1972), 9.

[2] H. P. Becker, *Outsiders: Studies in the Sociology of Deviance* (New York 1963), 9.

[3] Cohen, *Folk Devils*, 44–8.

[4] See, for example, R. Sindall, *Street Violence in the Nineteenth Century: Media Panic or Moral Danger?* (Leicester 1990); J. Davis, 'The London garotting panic of 1862: a moral panic', in V. Gatrell *et al.*, eds., *Crime and Law: The Social History of Crime in Western Europe since 1500* (London 1980).

[5] M. Douglas, *Purity and Danger: An Analysis of the Concepts of Pollution and Taboo* (London 1966).

mood of public concern. The sequence of inventory and sensitisation heightened public concern with particular groups labelled as deviants or folk devils and, in a highly charged atmosphere, an often insignificant recurrence produced a vigorous official response including the introduction of corrective measures.[6]

Urban disasters – floods, fires and plagues – normally induce decisive reactions in the form of official efforts to ban combustible materials, develop a new town plan, control river fronts and isolate pestilential blackspots and to an extent such natural disasters represent a special form of panic. The Great Fire of London, successive fires in Edo, Hankow and other Asian cities, and even simultaneous fires in two Swedish towns are some amongst many episodes where disaster has produced changes in the building materials and designs and in the way streets are laid out.[7] Nineteenth-century Edinburgh was not without its share of its disasters which included an extensive fire in 1824, cholera epidemics in 1832, 1848–9 and 1853–4, and fatalities as a result of a collapsed tenement in 1861. Each event was concentrated in the heart of the Old Town and struck at the consciences of municipal leaders whose own conscious migration to New Town addresses and 'flight to the suburbs' abandoned the poorer classes 'to accelerate the descent of the residences in the city centre to slumdom'.[8] It is against such a background that the development of public health policy in Victorian Edinburgh can be evaluated in relation to developments in housing conditions, slum clearance and municipal building, each of which also provides a perspective on the social significance of environmental controversies.

Moral panics, public health and housing

Reports of a tenement collapse in November 1861 stated that there were 35 fatalities and 100 were made homeless.[9] Compared to the 1,065 deaths calculated to have resulted from the cholera epidemic in 1832, or

[6] Cohen, *Folk Devils*, 27–37, 77–84, 161–76; M. Douglas, 'Environments at risk', in B. Barnes and D. Edge, eds., *Science in Context* (Cambridge 1982), 250; C. Hamlin, 'Environmental sensibility in Edinburgh 1839–40: the "fetid irrigation" controversy', *Journal of Urban History*, 20, 1994, 311–39.

[7] These are just a few examples of fire among many. See L. Frost, 'Coping in their own way: Asian cities and the problem of fires', *Urban History*, 24, 1997, 5–16; L. Nilsson, 'The end of a pre-industrial pattern: the great fires of Sundsvall and Umeå in 1888', unpublished paper; S. Porter, *The Great Fire of London* (Stroud 1996), 92–115; R. Porter, *London: A Social History* (London 1994), 66–92; J. C. Weaver and P. De Lottinville, 'The conflagration and the city: disaster and progress in British North America during the nineteenth century', *Histoire Sociale–Social History*, 13, 1980, 417–49.

[8] H. Macdonald, 'Public health legislation and problems in Victorian Edinburgh, with special reference to the work of Dr. Littlejohn as Medical Officer of Health', University of Edinburgh PhD thesis, 1971, 3.   [9] *Scotsman*, 25 Nov. 1861.

550 deaths during the subsequent epidemic of 1848–9 or even 100 deaths in 1853–4, then the loss of life in 1861 was modest.[10] However, it was this relatively minor event which triggered a vigorous official reaction to the public anxiety expressed in various letters to *The Scotsman* in 1861 and 1862. By 1862, a moral panic was underway and the appointments of a Medical Officer of Health and of a reforming Lord Provost were in part a response to quell the public disquiet over the conduct of sanitary policy in Edinburgh. The intervention produced a spate of clearances, many new streets and altered the skyline of the city sufficiently as to provoke accusations of philistinism over the destruction of the historic Old Town.[11]

While responsibility for public health matters rested ultimately with the town council from 1770 until 1856, it was the Edinburgh Police Commissioners who were empowered to deal with sanitary matters. The Cleaning Committee, a sub-committee of the Commissioners with a paid permanent official, was from 1822 specifically concerned with hosing down streets, slaughtering livestock and setting time periods before common lodging house keepers were obliged to report instances of disease; they also stipulated the time period before accumulated dung was to be removed and drew up regulations for the keeping of swine, cleaning of common stairs and the conduct of rag and bone businesses.[12] Alongside such general health measures medical treatment was provided first by public dispensaries established in the Old Town (1776) and New Town (1815) offering free medical advice and home visits to the sick, and secondly by the Royal Infirmary's 'most vital contribution to public health', the admission and thus isolation of fever patients who between 1817 and 1830 numbered over 6,500 persons.[13] Such an expansion of fever cases put immense pressure on the resources of the Infirmary so that additional premises, such as the Queensberry House barracks, were

---

[10] H. P. Tait, 'Two notable epidemics in Edinburgh and Leith', *Book of the Old Edinburgh Club*, 32, 1966, 21–31; R. Christison, 'Account of the arrangements made by the Edinburgh Board of Health, preparatory to the arrival of cholera in that city', *Edinburgh Medical and Surgical Journal*, 38, 1832, ccliv–cclxxxviii; A. H. B. Masson, 'Dr. Thomas Latta', *Book of the Old Edinburgh Club*, 33, 1972, 144–6; Macdonald, 'Public health legislation and problems in Victorian Edinburgh', 19; *Scotsman*, 7 July 1832 and 1 Dec. 1832. The figures for deaths exclude Leith where a further 267 died in 1832.

[11] B. J. Home, 'Provisional list of old houses remaining in the High Street and Canongate of Edinburgh', *Book of the Old Edinburgh Club*, 1, 1908, 1.

[12] *An Act for Watching, Cleansing and Lighting the Streets of the City of Edinburgh* (Edinburgh 1822), 47–58; *An Act for Altering and Amending Certain Acts for Regulating the Police of the City of Edinburgh* (Edinburgh 1832), 1–21.

[13] J. Thomson *et al.*, *Statement Regarding the New Town Dispensary* (Edinburgh 1816); *Annual Report of the Edinburgh New Town Dispensary* (Edinburgh 1832); *Report Respecting the Affairs and Management of the Royal Infirmary of Edinburgh 1836–37* (Edinburgh 1838), 1–12, quoted in Macdonald, 'Public health legislation and problems in Victorian Edinburgh', 6; *Scotsman*, 15 May 1830.

required on an emergency basis, and administrative responsibility was transferred to a Fever Board in 1830. As the 'guardians of the public health', the Fever Board immediately came under extreme pressure with a cholera outbreak in 1832 and a series of typhus epidemics in 1837, 1838 and 1839.[14]

Though the formal administrative structures, medical expertise and voluntary efforts were no worse and probably somewhat better than in many other early nineteenth-century cities, there was public concern at a number of facets of public health policy.[15] In what has been described[16] as the first treatise in English on the subject of public health, an Edinburgh surgeon, John Roberton, argued as early as 1809 for the need for direct municipal intervention to deal with the physical causes of disease, and he proceeded to identify defective water supplies, specific industrial processes and their effluents, and damp and ill-ventilated houses as the immediate targets.[17] It was a version which anticipated Edwin Chadwick's momentous *Report* by concentrating on filth and decomposing matter as the cause of public health problems. However, unlike Chadwick's recommendation, in Edinburgh even at the height of the 1832 cholera outbreak there was no acceptance that a central public health body was desirable, and, according to *The Scotsman*, after the crisis had passed there were 'murmurs' from ratepayers who were disinclined to pay the tax assessment levied to cover the costs of the epidemic.[18]

The town council's stance on public health matters was evident in the proposed New Western Approach in 1824–7 (chapter 3). This Improvement Scheme created new transport arteries – George IV Bridge, Victoria Street and Johnston Terrace – but it was only as an afterthought to enlist public support that sanitary issues and the impact on squalid housing were mentioned.[19] In fact, since most of the inhabitants affected by the clearances lived to the east of St Giles and the improvements were exclusively to the west, then the public health argument was largely cosmetic. It was the feuing prospects, therefore, which particularly

[14] *New Edinburgh Almanac*, 1839, 539; *Scotsman*, 15 Feb. 1837. For the standard general treatment of typhus see H. Creighton, *A History of Epidemics in Britain* (London 2nd edn 1965).

[15] See J. Prunty, *Dublin's Slums 1800–1925: A Study in Urban Geography* (Dublin 1998), 1–40, 62–7, for parallels.

[16] T. Ferguson, *The Dawn of Scottish Social Welfare* (Edinburgh 1948), 240.

[17] J. Roberton, *A Treatise on Medical Police and on the Diet Regimen* (Edinburgh 1809), 230–93; B. M. White, 'Medical police. Politics and police: the fate of John Roberton', *Medical History*, 27, 1983, 407–22.   [18] *Scotsman*, 30 Jan. 1833.

[19] ECA SL63/4/2, Description by Thomas Leslie of a proposed road from the High Street to Haymarket, 14 June 1824; SL63/4/2, Report Relative to the Proposed Approaches from the South and West to the Old Town of Edinburgh, 18 Nov. 1824, f. 1; *An Address to the Public Calling them to Look after their Interests in Regard to the Proposed Improvements* (Edinburgh 1828), 4–9.

appealed to councillors since the improvement proposals opened up the property from Lauriston to Buccleuch – virtually the entire south side of the city – and 'rendered [it] readily accessible from every quarter . . . much more valuable . . . and a very desirable and eligible situation for building'. [20] The knock-on effects for Fountainbridge, Tollcross and parts of the Old Town in terms of increased property values were also noted. So speculators who had purchased ground to the west of the Castle 'found that their purchase would yield no return unless they could succeed in obtaining a road to the High Street', and that 'they boldly proposed to *assess the whole inhabitants of Edinburgh* to build a bridge and carry *their* road along the Castle Rock till it reached the Lawnmarket at the Bow', that is, to connect their building land with the principal thoroughfares of the city. [21] The social consciences of civic leaders could hardly be seen as uppermost in an improvement proposal which was described as 'a fruitful source of favouritism'. [22]

Newspaper campaigns of the 1820s and 1830s sensitised public anxiety over public health matters, and were especially active in connection with the cholera outbreak in 1832, and the 'intense controversy' which surrounded the 'foul burn agitation' of 1838–9 whereby city sewage was disposed of in small open streams. [23] The tone of public concern, however, altered from the 1840s. It was more critical, more persistent, and though the Police Commissioners were able still to shelter behind the expert opinion of prominent members of the medical profession and architects such as Robert Stevenson, William Playfair, William Burn and Thomas Hamilton, the public health campaigns thereafter assumed a greater degree of urgency. [24] Worry had turned to panic.

By national and international standards Edinburgh stood indicted. In 1842 Edwin Chadwick's best-selling *Report* stated that the most wretched living conditions in the country were to be found in the wynds of

[20] ECA SL63/4/2, Report, 18 Nov. 1824, f. 4.

[21] ECA SL63/4/2, Considerations Submitted to the Householders and Shopkeepers of Edinburgh on the Nature and Consequences of the Edinburgh Improvements Bill by a Committee of Inhabitants, letter by W. Drysdale, convenor, 26 Feb. 1827, f. 4.

[22] *Letter to the Citizens and Inhabitants of Edinburgh on the Improvement Bill* (Edinburgh 1827), 5.

[23] *Caledonian Mercury*, 6 Dec. 1824; *Edinburgh Advertiser*, Dec. 1824, 24 Oct. 1826, and 9 Mar. 1827, 17 Aug. 1827; *Scotsman*, 17 Feb. 1827, 15 May and 16 May 1827; *Edinburgh Courant*, 22 Feb. 1827; H. P. Tait, *A Doctor and Two Policemen: The History of Edinburgh Health Department 1862–1974* (Edinburgh 1974), 16.

[24] ECA SL63/4/2, Report by W. Burn and T. Hamilton, 18 Nov. 1824, and letter from W. Burn and T. Hamilton to the Sub-Committee on Improvements, 10 Jan. 1826; Statement by W. H. Playfair, 24 Nov. 1824; letter by Robert Stevenson to R. Strachan, 20 Dec. 1824, and to Lord Provost, 23 Dec. 1824; ECA SL1/211, Town Council Minutes and Edinburgh Police Commissioners Minutes, 22 Dec. 1831, also quoted by Macdonald, 'Public health legislation and problems in Victorian Edinburgh', 14.

Edinburgh, and Friedrich Engels commented in 1844 that the 'brilliant aristocratic quarter . . . contrast[ed] strongly with the foul wretchedness of the poor of the Old Town'.[25] Even before such high profile reports were published, William Chambers, a member of the Edinburgh publishing dynasty, concluded in 1840 that the city was 'one of the most uncleanly and badly ventilated' of locations when compared to British and continental cities.[26] The indictments continued. Despite a 'singularly salubrious situation circumstances and bad taste have gone far to neutralize the benefits that might be expected to arise from its excellent position', and in a vivid phrase to summarise the built form and overcrowding in which 'story was piled on story' (sic), Chambers commented that the narrowness of alleys and wynds meant that 'in many cases a person might step from the window of one house to the window of the house opposite'.[27] The conclusion that 'the construction of the town is radically unfavourable to health' was exemplified by reference to the absence of water-closets either within tenements or in back courts, and so the 'excrementitious matter of some forty or fifty thousand individuals is daily thrown into the gutters, at certain hours appointed by the police, or poured into carts which are sent about the principal streets'.[28] From 'stanks' or pits within the city the 'excrementitious matter' was carted or pumped to Craigentinny where it irrigated the meadows, leaving Restalrig as an island in a sea of nightsoil, and resulting in claims that the men stationed nearby at Piershill barracks and the navvies working on the railway line at St Margaret's were unusually susceptible to disease.[29]

The language of despair – 'the evil is too monstrous for cure by . . . superficial means'[30] – was replicated in a flourishing pamphlet literature and in newspaper columns published in the 1840s. For example, the authenticity of reports by George Bell and Alexander Miller assumed weight by virtue of the authors' professional status as doctors, and Bell in particular described in harrowing terms the debilitating nature of living conditions in Blackfriars' Wynd and the areas nearby.[31] Bell's powerful

[25] F. Engels, The Condition of the Working Class in England in 1844 (London 1936 edn), 34; Chadwick, Report on the Sanitary Condition of the Labouring Population (ed. Flinn), 75. The Edinburgh physician Dr Neil Arnott was Edwin Chadwick's personal physician and wrote the report on Edinburgh for the Report. I am grateful to Bill Luckin for information on this point.

[26] W. Chambers, Report on the Sanitary State of the Residences of the Poorer Classes in the Old Town of Edinburgh (Edinburgh 1840), 1.   [27] Chambers, Report.

[28] Chambers, Report.

[29] Hamlin, 'Environmental sensibility', 311–39; J. Sheail, 'Town wastes, agricultural sustainability and Victorian sewage', Urban History, 23, 1996, 196; P. J. Smith, 'The foul burns of Edinburgh: public health attitudes and environmental change', Scottish Geographical Magazine, 91, 1975, 25–37. See also R. Forsythe, Foul Burn Agitation (Edinburgh 1840).

[30] Chambers, Report, 1.

[31] G. Bell, Day and Night in the Wynds of Edinburgh (Edinburgh 1849); and G. Bell, Blackfriars' Wynd Analyzed (Edinburgh 1850).

accounts of ten consumptive Irish immigrants in a single room, of three generations of women in a single bed in a garret room, of a six foot square space without furniture occupied by a cinder-woman who recycled paper for fish-wrapping, of overcrowding four times greater than in prison cells, captured the public imagination.[32] Newspaper sensationalism in no small measure created the slum. The term was itself invented in the early nineteenth century.[33] Consequently, though insanitary housing was no myth, the 'imagined slum' was, and newspaper sensationalism fed the myth so that in the minds of readers the slum became a reality, and thus amenable to policy initiatives.[34]

The publication of W. P. Alison's *Observations*, reiterated in his evidence to the Poor Law Commission in 1844, marked a shift of emphasis.[35] It also distilled the views of an identifiable 'Edinburgh School' of medical opinion, traceable to Roberton in 1809. Alison contended that the general state of employment was a more fundamental explanation of the incidence of disease and mortality rates than individual behaviour.[36] Dearth, debility and disease were linked. Mounting empirical evidence published by *The Scotsman* together with data on admissions to the Royal Infirmary in the 1830s and 1840s linked fever conditions and overcrowded housing to poverty.[37] More specifically, migrations to Edinburgh between 1815 and 1840 of highlanders and significant numbers of Irish accounted for 66% of the population increase of the Old Town between 1801 and 1831, and were viewed by Alison as a direct consequence of rural poverty and of an inadequate poor relief system. The implication was that the kirk and the heritors (landowners) of rural parishes were unwilling to fund and organise parochial relief – two-thirds had no such machinery in 1840 – and consequently the pressure on the urban social and sanitary system could only be resolved at source, by a reform of the poor law and its administration.[38]

---

[32] Bell, *Blackfriars' Wynd Analyzed*, 10, 12–25.

[33] H. J. Dyos, 'The slums of Victorian London', *Victorian Studies*, 11, 1967, 5–40.

[34] A. Mayne, *The Imagined Slum: Newspaper Representation in Three Cities 1870–1914* (Leicester 1993), 1–17. For a discussion of these issues see A. Mayne, 'A barefoot childhood: so what? Imagining slums and reading neighbourhoods', and D. Englander, 'Urban history or urban historicism: which? A reply to Alan Mayne', *Urban History*, 22, 1995, 380–91.

[35] W. P. Alison, *Observations on the Management of the Poor in Scotland and its Effects on the Health of the Great Towns* (Edinburgh 1840), 1–23.

[36] *PP 1844 XXII*, Poor Law Inquiry, 907–9, Q. 1592–1606; Alison, *Observations on the Management of the Poor in Scotland*, 1–23.

[37] *Scotsman*, 15 Feb. 1837, 7 Jan. and 9 Jan. 1839, 25 Dec. 1839, 8 Nov. 1843; *Edinburgh Evening Courant*, 2 Dec. 1847; *PP 1844 XVII*, Report on the State of Large Towns and Populous Districts, 199, Q. 1.

[38] R. A. Cage, *The Scottish Poor Law 1745–1845* (Edinburgh 1981), 112–38; I. Leavitt and T. C. Smout, *The State of the Scottish Working Class in 1843: A Statistical and Spatial Inquiry Based on Data from the Scottish Poor Law Commission Report of 1844* (Edinburgh 1979).

To such an analysis of systemic weakness in society in relation to the relief of poverty were those who attributed sanitary problems to character defects on the part of the individual.[39] From their standpoint, the sanitary system in Edinburgh was not itself unsatisfactory; it was the inhabitants, especially the 'folk devils' of the Irish and highlanders, whose habits and behaviour created the problems of insanitary housing and fever.[40] These 'chambers of death', as the *Edinburgh News* described Old Town housing, were the result of 'irrational expenditure' and the behaviour of 'constitutional drunkards'.[41]

To address the social problems of the 1840s a corps of Scottish ministers argued that care of the poor should be founded on personal and spiritual relationships, not on bureaucratic and legal obligations as in England. So, bound up with the state of health of the Scottish cities, and that of Edinburgh particularly, was the conviction amongst a group of evangelical Scottish ministers that they should provide religious leadership for the community in educational matters, housing and social services, and that the Church was threatened by assuming a secular, administrative role, as in England in the administration of poor relief. The schism in the Church of Scotland which in 1843 led to the Disruption and the foundation of the Free Church of Scotland was partly the product of a public health discourse centred on Edinburgh and insanitary housing.[42]

The poor were cast as the folk devils. Graphic accounts of deplorable living conditions in the 1840s and 1850s were attributed to individual shortcomings and those who manned the moral barricades cited variously drink, prostitution, gambling, crime and non-attendance at church as the reasons why individuals lived in insanitary housing which prejudiced their life expectancy.[43] In the language of the late nineteenth century Alison's explanation revolved on 'primary poverty' – insufficient income – while the majority of observers emphasised 'secondary poverty'

---

[39] J. V. Pickstone, 'Death, dirt and fever epidemics: re-writing the history of British public health 1780–1850', in T. Ranger and P. Slack, eds., *Epidemics and Ideas: Essays on the Historical Perception of Pestilence* (Cambridge 1992), esp. 128–46; Hamlin, 'Environmental sensibility'; A. Hardy, *Epidemic Street: Infectious Disease and the Rise of Preventive Medicine 1856–1900* (Oxford 1993), 280–9, for the relationship between poverty and health; M. Sigsworth and M. Warboys, 'The public's view of public health in mid-Victorian Britain', *Urban History*, 21, 1994, 237–50, show how in Yorkshire cities explanations other than that of character defects applied.

[40] C. W. J. Withers, *Urban Highlanders: Highland–Lowland Migration and Urban Gaelic Culture 1700–1900* (East Linton 1998), 88, shows that the highland born were just 2.7% of the Edinburgh population in 1851.   [41] *Edinburgh News*, 10 and 17 Sept. 1853.

[42] Hamlin, 'Environmental sensibility', 331.

[43] ECA SL136/1/1, Report by Mr Fraser Relative to the Pensioners on the Society for Relief of Indigent Old Men, ff. 2–11.

– injudicious patterns of expenditure. Apart from temperance, one news-paper provided helpful hints to counteract defective living conditions: the poor were exhorted to counteract perspiration and damp by getting a decent winter coat, by eating nourishing meals and respectfully entered the 'exclusive domain of female rule' with a few remarks on domestic economy:

> Our object is to get the working classes to set about acquiring a knowledge of that department of domestic economy suitable to their wants . . . and to put young and inexperienced housewives in the possession of a vast amount of useful knowledge . . . cannot advise their husbands better than to . . . present them with a copy of Esther Copley's Cottage Cookery, the best guide to a well ordered household that we have ever seen . . . it may be purchased for four ounces of tobacco.[44]

Proof of unwise spending patterns was offered by Bell who observed that 'the poorer the district the more numerous the dram sellers', and the Rev. Thomas Guthrie, founder of the Ragged Industrial Schools, who con-demned the tippling shops and taverns in the Grassmarket and other parts of the Old Town in a series of articles published in the *Sunday Magazine* in 1855. Off the High Street were 'The Grave', 'Coffin' and 'Poet's Corner', eating houses originally but almost entirely devoted by 1850 to the sale of drink or 'lush', and in the case of the 'Poet's Corner' with direct access to a brothel.[45] Predictably, Free Kirk housing reformers such as Hugh Miller, Hugh Reid, and James Begg were vigorous in their condemnation of drink through their columns in the *Witness* and the *Evening News* in the 1850s, as was Henry Johnston in his *Letter to the Lord Provost* in 1856 in which he labelled the poor as 'intemperate, disorderly, sullen, coarse and reckless, respecting neither themselves nor anything human or Divine'.[46]

Moral outrage was expressed in print by influential individuals, and housing conditions themselves, rather than the forces which created them, were their target. All 400 common lodging houses in the city were concentrated in the Old Town – in St Giles, Grassmarket, Tron and Canongate (fig. 12.1). These premises provided accommodation for

[44] *Edinburgh News*, 24 Dec. 1853. For related articles see *Edinburgh News*, 10 and 17 Sept. 1853.
[45] *An Inquiry into Destitution, Prostitution and Crime in Edinburgh* (Edinburgh 1851), reprinted as *Low Life in Victorian Edinburgh* (Edinburgh 1980), 80–3.
[46] H. Johnston, *Letter to the Lord Provost, Magistrates and Council of the City of Edinburgh on the State of the Closes in the Lawnmarket, High Street, Canongate and Cowgate* (Edinburgh 1856), 5; J. Begg, *Happy Homes for Working Men and How to Get Them* (Edinburgh 1862), 19n, notes that the Free Church of Scotland set up a committee in 1858 to investigate housing conditions and moral reform. For other examples of Free Church involvement see Free Church of Scotland, Committee on Houses for the Working Classes in Connexion with Social Morality, *Report* (Edinburgh 1862), 7–17; H. G. Reid, *Past and Present or Social and Religious Life in the North* (Edinburgh 1871).

(a)

Figure 12.1 Dilapidated housing: High School Wynd

Note: Cavanagh's shop at the foot of High School Wynd reflected the
heavy concentration of Irish in central Edinburgh. It was they who were
an easy target and often criticised for the numerous beershops and
brothels in the ill-lit closes of Old Town.
Source: Edinburgh Central Library, Acc 42374, Plate no. 30
(92021/2/9A) High School Wynd by A. A. Inglis.

(b)

Figure 12.1 Dilapidated housing: the Cowgate in the 1860s

Source: Edinburgh Central Library, Acc 42374, Plate no. 25
(92021/1/8A) Cowgate by J. C. Balmain for the Improvement Trust,
1866.

2,560 lodgers, but the moral concern was over shared rooms, lack of privacy, and the shortages of urinals and drinking fountains and not about the underlying causes of these conditions.[47] Symptoms rather than causes were the preoccupation of social commentators and policy accordingly was directed at individual nuisances or specific circumstances which gave offence. Thus an account of destitution in Edinburgh in 1851 recounted many episodes which affronted the readership, including one of a flat in Leith Wynd in which a girl of eighteen wore only a shawl since she had pawned her clothes to buy food. In the neighbouring flat, three girls whilst dressing to go out had consumed a gill of whisky, and in 'painting her face' one remarked 'what's the use of a shop without a sign?'.[48] 'Character deficiency' was the convenient explanation of the Victorian middle classes generally for behaviour which was perceived as abnormal. Yet the girl's reference to her promiscuity should not have shocked the Edinburgh middle classes for in the years 1848–50 a report compiled by the Superintendent of Police indicated that 1,046 thefts had taken place within brothels by prostitutes. Over 90% of these cases were abandoned for insufficient evidence, a higher rate than applied for street thefts by prostitutes, and no doubt a reflection that the complainants did not want to be identified in court as brothel-goers.[49] The double standard of Victorian morality was evident even though the Edinburgh middle classes exclaimed their shock. As one enquiry concluded, 'Destitution, prostitution and crime in Edinburgh may be said to hold high levee on Saturday night . . . and from seven till twelve o'clock is the best time to see the orgy.'[50] Readers were informed that 'congregated on either side of the North Bridge . . . may be seen [the most] disgusting sights possible to conjure up, even in the imagination of those novelists who take strange delight in pouring out scenes of filth and degradation'.[51]

By the 1850s, therefore, insanitary housing was a convenient scapegoat to explain a range of vices. Selective dramatisation had constructed a discourse in which actual housing conditions were elevated to a arena for public policy. Depravity, as described in the press, defined normalcy and to defend this, public intervention was legitimate. In turn, attention was directed to the symptoms, not the causes, of insanitary housing. Consequently, blame was attributed to individual personal failings, an

---

[47] H. D. Littlejohn, *Report on the Sanitary Condition of the City of Edinburgh* (Edinburgh 1865), Appendix, table XII, 61.
[48] *An Inquiry into Destitution, Prostitution and Crime*, 64–5.
[49] Quoted in *An Inquiry into Destitution, Prostitution and Crime*, 116.
[50] *An Inquiry into Destitution, Prostitution and Crime*, 120.
[51] *An Inquiry into Destitution, Prostitution and Crime*, 120.

explanation which suited religious and civic leaders, as well as ratepayers. Where blackspots of disease and high mortality did exist, they could be explained by particular circumstances and ultimately on Irish immigrants, a useful secondary folk devil. Despite the environmental blackspots, with a city-wide death rate which compared favourably to other urban areas, a complacent and self-congratulatory tone amongst medical and civic opinion developed which denied the need for a more interventionist role.[52] The Edinburgh Police Act, 1848, itself illustrated that the conceptualisation of public health issues remained partial and, concerned as it was with individual nuisances, it showed little grasp of the underlying problems of poverty which affected the wider issues of intemperance, prostitution and crime.[53]

No exchange captured this ideological divide better than that in 1849 between Lord Cockburn whose submission to the Lord Provost as to the threat posed by slum dwellers to Edinburgh's beauty drew a withering response from James Begg, the Free Kirk minister of Newington.[54] Begg claimed that Cockburn perpetuated social divisions in the city: 'It is a cruel mockery to speak to the torpid and festering masses of Taste and of the beauties of Edinburgh' and Begg recommended that the poor be granted access to West Princes Street Gardens and Holyrood Park, and that swathes of central property be cleared. He also took some satisfaction from the fact that the increasing costs of poverty meant that the costs of relief fell increasingly on property owners through their rates. More pointedly, Begg later argued that 'many of the higher classes have the notion that it is better to keep the working class in a degraded and subservient state'.[55]

During the second quarter of the nineteenth century numerous pamphlets and newspaper articles raised the awareness of civic bodies and touched the consciences of the Edinburgh middle classes in relation to the sanitary and moral environment within the capital. An 'inventory', to use Cohen's phrase, of events and circumstances had been seared on the public consciousness. *The Scotsman* expressed the underlying fear which prevailed in the 1850s, and to which its own editorial and feature articles had contributed in no small degree:

[52] J. Stark, *Inquiry into some points of the Sanatory State of Edinburgh* (Edinburgh n.d.), 12–14; *Scotsman*, 3 Feb. and 4 Feb. 1846.

[53] A. Murray, *Nuisances in Edinburgh with Suggestions for the Removal Thereof* (Edinburgh 1847); Macdonald, 'Public health legislation and problems in Victorian Edinburgh', 30.

[54] J. Begg, *How to Promote and Preserve the True Beauty of Edinburgh, Being a Few Hints to the Hon. Lord Cockburn on his Late Letter to the Lord Provost* (Edinburgh 1849).

[55] General Assembly of the Free Kirk, Committee on Housing for the Working Classes, May 1862, 3.

A kingdom of darkness, misery and vice has erected itself, and is daily strengthening its fortifications and deepening its trenches. Should such a commotion ever
happen to break up the existence of order in Edinburgh, the High St., the
Canongate, the Cowgate, the Grassmarket, and the West Port would turn out an
array which if not in revolutionary violence, at any rate in terrific appearance,
would not be surpassed by the mass of the 'classes dangereuses' in any city in all
Europe.[56]

Analyses in 1840 from Alison and Chambers and a link with the underlying problem of poverty were replaced in the late 1840s and the 1850s by
alarmist, moralising tracts often using simple statistics to add colour and
a semblance of authenticity to the accounts. Highly sensitised, public
opinion no longer needed epidemic disease but only a few articles and
pamphlets for panic to emerge.

However, a policy void existed. Even though a creeping acceptance of
an enlarged civic role grew in strength, fuelled in part by local opposition
to Edwin Chadwick's proposal to extend the Central Board of Health in
London to Scotland, local initiatives remained limited to specific issues
such as the pollution of the Water of Leith, the closures of cellar dwellings
and controls on lodging houses.[57] So, far from criticising the civic authorities for the administrative procedures and sanitary conditions which prevailed before and after the cholera outbreaks in 1848–9 and 1853–4, there
was an acceptance that a measure of municipal co-ordination in sanitary
matters might be an acceptable local political alternative to the centralising vision of Chadwick.[58] Advocates of expanded civic powers recommended the destruction of insanitary areas and the appointment of a
Medical Officer of Health, but paradoxically the very fear which urged the
demolition of insanitary housing was also fuelled by its consequence, the
prospect of more homeless people on the streets of Edinburgh to molest
its citizens. Consequently, nothing was done for several years.

Crisis, reaction and housing strategies

Civic inertia in the 1850s caused by the tension between the fear of unrest
and the fear of hordes of homeless people was upset by the collapse of a
tenement in the High Street on 24 November 1861.[59] Thirty-five deaths

[56] *Scotsman*, 2 Feb. 1850.
[57] *Scotsman*, 24 May 1854; Hamlin, 'Environmental sensibility', 330–2.
[58] It also coincided with a growing devolution of powers from Westminster to urban authorities in other policy areas and an emerging national self-confidence within the context of
the Union. See G. Morton, 'Unionist-nationalism: the historical construction of Scottish
national identity, Edinburgh 1830–1860', University of Edinburgh thesis, 1994, 227–30,
and G. Morton, 'Civil society, municipal government and the state: enshrinement,
empowerment and legitimacy, Scotland 1800–1929', *Urban History*, 25, 1998, 348–67.
[59] For a report of the incident see *Scotsman*, 25 Nov. 1861.

and numerous serious injuries produced a predictable reaction, an outcry against the housing conditions prevailing in the Old Town.[60] Even before sermons could be preached the following week, *The Scotsman* printed responses from social reformers urging the construction of new housing for the working classes as a matter of urgency. The tenement disaster also provided impetus to the activities of the Edinburgh Co-operative Building Company.[61] A complementary line of reasoning also developed which stressed the need to remove unsafe and insanitary housing. By enlisting the support of the influential Architectural Institute of Scotland[62] and inflamed in the editorial columns of *The Scotsman* by such eye-catching phrases as 'Prevent people inhabiting unsuitable houses'[63] middle-class fear of the Old Town was directed at the Town Council who were 'subjected to the loudest and most savage assault to date for their shortcomings in sanitary work'.[64]

Public opinion and newspaper pressure probably made it impossible to avoid the appointment of a Medical Officer of Health with responsibility for the environmental health of the city. Yet it has been argued convincingly that in 1862 when the town council approved the appointment by the narrowest of margins the decision was a logical outcome of a gradual process of extended council deliberations from the mid-1850s, and not the knee-jerk reaction to events in the High Street the previous year.[65] The subordination of the powers of the MOH to the town council, the retention of the separate posts of Superintendent of Streets and Inspector of Cleaning and Lighting limited the scope of the new appointee, Henry Duncan Littlejohn, and his restricted staff of one policeman and a clerk were indicators of impotence rather than those of an all powerful administrator. Despite the fact that Littlejohn's *Report on the Sanitary Condition of the City of Edinburgh*,[66] published in 1865, was described as 'a classic in the literature of public health'[67] and apart from his role in promoting the Smallpox Vaccination Act, by 1865 'precious little had been done'.[68]

---

[60] H. P. Tait, 'Sir Henry Duncan Littlejohn, great Scottish sanitarian and medical jurist', *Medical Officer*, 108, 1962, 183–90; and H. P. Tait, *A Doctor and Two Policemen*, 17.

[61] *Scotsman*, 28 and 29 Nov. 1861, reporting addresses by Rev. Drs Begg and Nisbet. See chapter 11.

[62] A. Wood, 'The condition of the dwellings of the operative classes in Edinburgh', paper to Architectural Institute of Scotland, 14 Jan. 1862, reprinted in A. Wood, *Report on the Condition of the Poorer Classes of Edinburgh and of their Dwellings, Neighbourhoods and Families* (Edinburgh 1868), Appendix A, 95–115; *Scotsman*, 9 Dec. 1861, 13 Jan. and 14 Jan. 1862.   [63] *Scotsman*, 11 Dec. 1861.

[64] Macdonald, 'Public health legislation and problems in Victorian Edinburgh', 57.

[65] Macdonald, 'Public health legislation and problems in Victorian Edinburgh', 67–72.

[66] Littlejohn, *Report on the Sanitary Condition of the City of Edinburgh*, 20–5, 45–9, 50, 56, 67–71, 76–92.   [67] Tait, 'Sir Henry Duncan Littlejohn', 183.

[68] Macdonald, 'Public health legislation and problems in Victorian Edinburgh', 78.

On the surface, Littlejohn's *Report* contained little that was new. The worst insanitary districts, the nature of public health risks, even the accumulated statistical underpinning, each had been aired in the writings of previous observers. Littlejohn himself had identified the central tenets of his public health principles in earlier pronouncements.[69] The great contrast, though, was that in measured terms and without a particular point to make it was a fully comprehensive study, and readers needed only in the future to study it rather than a trail of partial accounts to derive information on the public health and physical environment of Edinburgh. The *Report* became the authorised 'Bible of Edinburgh sanitary conditions'.[70] Just as important, arguably, by surveying the physical state of every street and close, Littlejohn dispelled some of the fear of the unknown; even if the insanitary conditions were extreme, the extent of the threat was defined.

Demolition and street improvement

Before Littlejohn's *Report* the extent of moral degeneration in Edinburgh was an unknown and feared force. Only a few months after revolutions in France and in central Europe, *The Scotsman* had speculated in 1850 about the possible consequences should the 'classes dangereuses' oppose the control mechanisms to which they were subject in the Old Town.[71] A few years later, *The Builder* urged the public provision of housing for the working classes on the grounds of a latent threat to the state:

Private charity has done much; philanthropists, on speculative principles of moderate remuneration, have also added something; but legislative authority and municipal interposition only can meet an evil which has so increased as to menace the well-being and character of the State.[72]

The extent of depravity and the potential for social unrest were unknown, and successive publications and statistical analyses only fuelled uncertainty often through the pages of the respected *Scotsman*. Since, transparently, the poor law had not resolved the perceived threats associated with the 'folk devils' of criminal and immoral behaviour amongst the very poorest elements in society, then attention was redirected in the 1850s and 1860s to a visible and immovable target, their housing. In powerful and sometimes melodramatic accounts, public opinion was sensitised, and

[69] H. D. Littlejohn, 'On the cleansing operations of Edinburgh as compared with other towns', read to the Social Science Association, 1863, and published under the same title in Edinburgh, 1865.
[70] Macdonald, 'Public health legislation and problems in Victorian Edinburgh', 87.
[71] *Scotsman*, 2 Feb. 1850.   [72] *Builder*, 31 Dec. 1859.

triggered by a particular event, the fatalities associated with the collapse of a tenement in 1861, a momentum developed to validate municipal intervention. Fears associated with 'folk devils' had assumed the proportions of a moral panic in Cohen's terms, and it was only a matter of time before an official response sought to address public concerns.

The definitive nature of Littlejohn's *Report* was used to legitimate public intervention. In particular, the exercise of public authority to expropriate private property by means of compulsory purchases was shown to be justifiable where housing conditions were prejudicial to the collective interest. The comprehensive and 'scientific' nature of the report compiled by Littlejohn, a respected doctor and police surgeon, ensured that municipal intervention was unlikely to be challenged successfully in the courts, and environmental intervention and urban planning thus reaffirmed an ancient set of priorities in Edinburgh whereby 'nichtbourheid' or community issues relating to property were considered paramount to private interests.[73] In addition, the imposition of a more regulated street pattern introduced a different social order upon the urban environment consistent with the changing economic, transport and technological characteristics of the last third of the nineteenth century. In this sense the Edinburgh street improvement proposals in 1867 were not dissimilar to those in Paris where a by-product of Haussmann's plans in the 1850s for improved access was 'the amelioration of the state of health of the town through the systematic destruction of infected alleyways and centers of epidemics'.[74]

Civic vanity, or perhaps jealousy, also prompted the adoption of an Improvement Scheme for Edinburgh. In a reference to the Glasgow proposals for housing clearances to be implemented in 1866, the editor of *The Scotsman* invoked the civic pride of the capital and correspondents then responded by pressing for more extensive demolitions than in Glasgow.[75] It was another instance of the newspaper functioning as a medium to prompt an official response.

Civic pride also motivated William Chambers who was a central figure in the interregnum between the completion of Littlejohn's *Report* in 1865 and the adoption and implementation of its principal recommendations in 1874. Chambers, a retired publisher, had long championed the cause

---

[73] R. Rodger, 'The evolution of Scottish town planning', in G. Gordon and B. Dicks, eds., *Scottish Urban History* (Aberdeen 1983), 71–91.

[74] S. Giedion, *Space, Time and Architecture* (Cambridge, Mass., 1959), 648.

[75] *Scotsman*, 21 Oct. 1865; the estimated cost of the Edinburgh proposals was £0.5 million compared to £1.5 million for those in Glasgow. See also *PP 1884–5 XXX*, Royal Commission on Housing of the Working Classes, Scotland, Evidence of J. K. Crawford, Q. 18706; C. M. Allan, 'The genesis of urban redevelopment with reference to Glasgow', *Economic History Review*, 18, 1965, 598–613.

of housing improvement.[76] He 'had not been in any prominent sense a public man' and took some pride in the claim for his *Journal* that it favoured 'neither party, nor sect'.[77] To break the political impasse which existed within the Council Chamber over the action, if any, to be taken in relation to Littlejohn's *Report*, Chambers was persuaded to stand as a councillor on the clear understanding that his election would then lead to nomination as Lord Provost.[78] However, he consulted widely after his election with previous Lord Provosts, walked 'almost every day' in the closes of the Old Town, sometimes accompanied by the principal city officials – the city architect and Dean of Guild.[79] His ensuing *Statement to the Town Council* represented both a powerful personal *credo* and an endorsement of Littlejohn's *Report*.[80] Chambers' affirmation that diagonal streets cutting through the closes and wynds were most effective in reducing overcrowded and ill-ventilated streets drew on the experience of the sickle-shaped thoroughfares of Victoria Street at the West Bow, formed in 1827, and Cockburn Street in 1856.[81] Chambers' sense of civic duty coincided with an acute sense of a unique opportunity to transform the central areas of Edinburgh, though his motives were questioned by a columnist who claimed that he was 'more anxious to raise a monument to his own Provostship than to confer a benefit on his fellow citizens'.[82]

Four main areas of contention surrounded Chambers' proposals: at which social groups was the scheme directed; could the cost be contained; could those evicted be rehoused at affordable rents; was the scheme over-ambitious? Connected to these issues were many sub-plots: ratepayer opposition was considerable in view of the levies to deal with

[76] See for example Chambers, *Report*; his publications in *Edinburgh Courant*, 31 July 1851, and *Yearbook of the Architectural Institute of Scotland for 1853*; *Improved Dwelling Houses for the Humbler and Other Classes, Based on the Scottish Dwelling House System* (London 1855); *Scotsman*, 9 Dec. 1861, on 'House accommodation in Edinburgh', *Chambers Journal*, 11 June 1864 and 16 Sept. 1865. For publications after his election, see nn. 79 and 80.
[77] *Scotsman*, 11 Nov. 1865.
[78] Macdonald, 'Public health legislation and problems in Victorian Edinburgh', 100, shows that there was no specifically Sanitary Party that promoted Chambers' candidacy.
[79] *The Lord Provost's Statement to the Town Council respecting Sanitary Improvement* (Edinburgh 1865), 2.
[80] *The Lord Provost's Statement*, 3; *Scotsman* 28 Feb. and 9 Apr. 1866. For other statements concerning the views of Chambers see W. Chambers, *City Improvement: Address to the Architectural Institute of Scotland* (Edinburgh 1866); and *idem, Sanitary Improvements: Letters from the Lord Provost to Mr. D. McLaren and Mr. J. Moncrieff, Members of Parliament for the City* (Edinburgh 1866). For detailed proposals of clearances and street alterations see D. Cousins and J. Lessels, *Plan of the Sanitary Improvements of the City of Edinburgh* (Edinburgh 1866).
[81] R. F. Gourlay, *Edinburgh and its Improvement Intended to Illustrate the Science of City Building* (Edinburgh 1851–3). There were eight pamphlets in the series.
[82] *Edinburgh Courant*, 11 Apr. 1866, letter from 'Malcontent'. Chambers refuted the allegation in his address to the Architectural Institute of Scotland in December 1866.

the recent Water of Leith purification; some reformers sought to remove alternate closes only; the architects' (David Cousins and John Lessels) financial estimates were proved by the city accountant to be an under-statement and a more realistic figure doubled their earlier estimates.[83]

The Edinburgh Improvement Act received the royal assent in June 1867, and letters of appointment were sent to the clerk, architect, valuator and other officials in December 1867.[84] Though the act authorised a twenty-two year lifespan, the retiring architect David Cousins considered the principal objectives of the Trust achieved by 1875.[85] By the end of the 1875–6 financial year 74% of the eventual clearance expenditure had been committed, with almost a quarter devoted to property acquisitions, compensation, demolition and street formation associated with College Street and Argyle Square to form the new Chambers Street (fig. 12.2). The Market Street–Leith Wynd clearances accounted for almost a fifth of the entire budget; the formation of Blackfriars and St Mary's Street both swallowed up about a tenth, as did the formation of Lady Lawson Street. The expenditure of £0.5 million in Edinburgh resulted in the clearance of 2,721 homes, though when notifying residents of proposed demolitions, only 500 people could be evicted at any one time and so the trustees implemented a rolling programme of closure notices.[86] Only 340 new homes were built. For the most part, private builders undertook rebuild-ing operations in keeping with the plans specified by Cousins and Lessels, though in Guthrie Street the trustees took an important decision in 1870 to build two tenements and in so doing created the precedent for munici-pal housing in the city.[87]

The scale of the clearances in financial terms was only one third that of Glasgow's Improvement Trust and the time scale to complete the demoli-tion programme was correspondingly shorter – ten years in Edinburgh compared to over thirty years in Glasgow (see figs. 12.4 and 12.5). Consequently, in Edinburgh the Improvement Scheme was 'sanctified' enabling further phases of civic involvement in housing to be accepted,

[83] *Builder*, 22 Feb. and 27 Feb. 1864, 148–9; H. Macdonald, 'Public health legislation and problems in Victorian Edinburgh',116–18; ECA SL1/294, Town Council Minutes, 8 Oct., 27 Nov. and 12 Dec. 1866; Cousins and Lessels, *Plan of the Sanitary Improvements of the City of Edinburgh*; see also *Scotsman*, 22 Nov. 1866, which published Cousins and Lessels *Additional Estimates* and the *Statement by the City Accountant*.

[84] ECA SL64/1/1, Trustees' Minute Books, 4 Sept. 1867; SL64/2/1, Letter Book, 23 Dec. 1867, ff. 1–4.

[85] ECA SL64/1/3, Trustees' Minute Books, 18 Oct. 1875; SL64/1/5, Finance Committee, 22 Sept. 1875.

[86] J. Pollard, *Thirty Years' Sanitary Progress in Scotland* (Edinburgh 1895), 8.

[87] ECA SL64/1/2, Trustees' Minute Books, 6 Dec. 1870. By the terms of the Improvement Trust Act, trustees were permitted only to build temporary accommodation on their own account, and so the Guthrie Street tenements were sold. See ECA SL64/1/3, Trustees' Minute Books, 21 Jan. 1873.

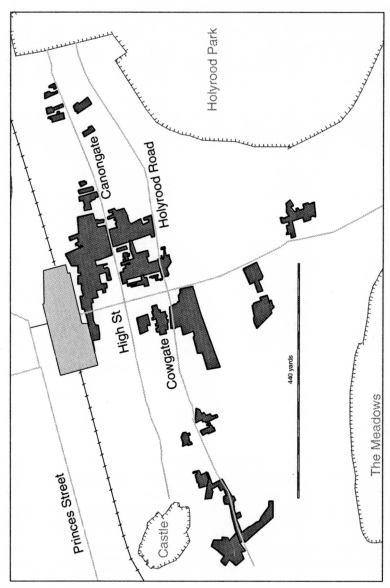

Figure 12.2 Edinburgh Improvement proposals 1866

Source: ECA EDD/331/3/3–8, SL63.

Figure 12.3 a and b Plaques commemorating the Edinburgh Improvements 1867

Note: (a) plaque (junction of High Street and St Mary's Street) with the initials DC/JL dated 1869 for architects David Cousins and John Lessels whose Scots baronial preferences were adopted for tenements in most Improvement Areas in central Edinburgh; (b) by the Blackfriars' Building Association (1871). Note the mason's spelling error in the plaque.

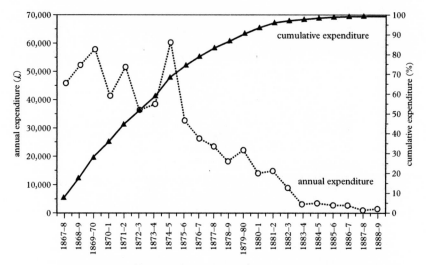

Figure 12.4 Edinburgh Improvement Trust 1867–1889: expenditure on housing clearances.

Source: ECA SL64/3/6, Accounts of the Improvements Trustees.

whereas in Glasgow the extended period of activity poisoned ratepayers' attitudes to such municipal projects and eventually caused prominent politicians to be unseated as a result.[88] Indeed, in Edinburgh, the compression of the clearance programme in the years 1868–75 meant that municipally financed demolitions coincided with a period of considerable private sector housebuilding.[89] The Trust was well aware of the symbiotic importance of private building to public clearances:

> The work of removing so many tenements in so short a time has been made easy by the extensive building for the working classes for some years past in the suburbs; these new buildings give accommodation for a large number of the more provident of the working classes.[90]

By contrast, in Glasgow the Improvement Trust's activities stalled in no small measure because their scale rendered them likely to overlap at some stage with a protracted depression in the building industry, and this further slowed Improvement Trust progress because the private

---

[88] T. C. Smout, *A Century of the Scottish People 1830–1950* (London 1986), 46.

[89] R. Rodger, 'Scottish urban housebuilding 1870–1914', University of Edinburgh PhD thesis, 1975, 95 (table 3), 97 (table 4), 109 (table 5); *PP 1884–5 XXX*, Royal Commission, Evidence of Morrison, Q. 19742.

[90] ECA SL64/1/1, Trustees' Minute Books, 6 Dec. 1870.

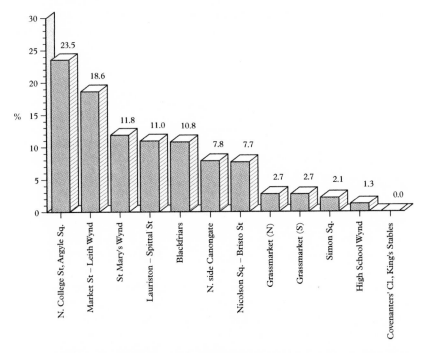

Figure 12.5 Edinburgh Improvement Trust 1867–1889: by clearance area

Source: ECA SL64/3/6, Accounts of the Improvements Trustees.

sector showed little interest in feuing the land when demand was so weak.[91]

The significance of the Edinburgh Improvement Scheme can be identified at several levels. First, the creation of seven new streets and the widening of others altered the townscape.[92] Hardly any part of the Old Town was unaffected. It was 'both enormously expensive and massively intrusive', displaced up to 14,000 people, about 7.5% of the city population, and added 4d in the £ to the local taxpayers' bill.[93] About 30% of the housing stock in the Old Town was demolished with streets leading

[91] Glasgow Municipal Commission (GMC) on the Housing of the Poor, *Report* (Glasgow 1904), 13; Allan, 'The genesis of urban redevelopment', 598–613; R. Rodger, 'Crisis and confrontation in Scottish housing', in R. Rodger, ed., *Scottish Housing in the Twentieth Century* (Leicester 1989), 36–7.

[92] The principal new streets formed are now known as Blackfriars', St Mary's, Jeffrey, Howden, Marshall and Lady Lawson Streets.

[93] P. J. Smith, 'Slum clearance as an instrument of sanitary reform: the flawed vision of Edinburgh's first slum clearance scheme', *Planning Perspectives*, 9, 1994, 1–27.

through the ancient wynds and closes adjoining the High Street most affected.[94] Though acknowledged as a rational and 'healthy recoil from the congested conditions' in which previous generations had lived, there was concern at the nature of 'improvement' measures which had been implemented without 'due regard to historic, literary and aesthetic considerations'. For some this produced a sense of 'isolation' at the 'widespread, ruthless and indiscriminat[e] . . . destruction' of houses and prompted a plea in the inaugural volume of the Old Edinburgh Club in 1908 to 'rescue from the hands of the house-wrecking Philistine' the clearance activities which meant 'that since 1860, two-thirds of the ancient buildings in the Old Town of Edinburgh have been demolished'.[95] (fig. 12.6). Critics maintained that 'rarely has any consideration beyond the most baldly utilitarian been allowed to influence the decision', and in language which would do present-day conservationists credit, it was lamented that 'our most valuable and historic architectural remains [have] been irretrievably lost to the city and to posterity'[96] (fig. 12.1).

A second outcome of the improvement era was that the over-arching plan of the architects Cousins and Lessels imposed a measure of visual uniformity in a Scots baronial style employed previously in 1856–60 in Cockburn Street (fig. 12.7). Superimposed on a medieval warren of wynds and closes, impenetrable except to those familiar with the network, was a simplified street plan increasingly accessible by the end of the nineteenth century to inspectors and officialdom. Porous, pedestrian networks in the early and mid-nineteenth-century city were increasingly replaced by regulated and monitored spaces, streets and buildings.[97] This conflict of ideologies was intensified and given added urgency by the embrace of empiricism through civil registration of births, deaths and marriages after 1855.[98] A statistical revolution quickly developed in which the acquisition of numbers and the use of percentages was an indispensable first step in formulating policy initiatives.[99] Whereas in previous decades public debate was conducted in the columns of the *Edinburgh*

---

[94] *Builder*, 23 Sept. 1878, 1003–4, provided an area by area description of the work of the Edinburgh City Improvements.   [95] Home, 'Provisional list of old houses', 1.

[96] Home, 'Provisional list of old houses', 1–2.

[97] A. Rapoport, *Human Aspects of the Urban Form: Towards a Man-Environment Approach to Urban Form and Design* (London 1977), 289–95; M. J. Daunton, *House and Home in the Victorian City: Working Class Housing 1850–1914* (London 1983), 11–13.

[98] Littlejohn, *Report on the Sanitary Condition of the City of Edinburgh*, 1. The first sentence begins 'When the Act for the Registration of Births, Deaths and Marriages was extended to Scotland in 1855, it first became possible to ascertain with precision the mortality of our cities and towns, and to compare it . . .'.

[99] M. Cullen, *The Statistical Movement in Early Victorian Britain: The Foundations of Empirical Social Research* (Brighton 1975).

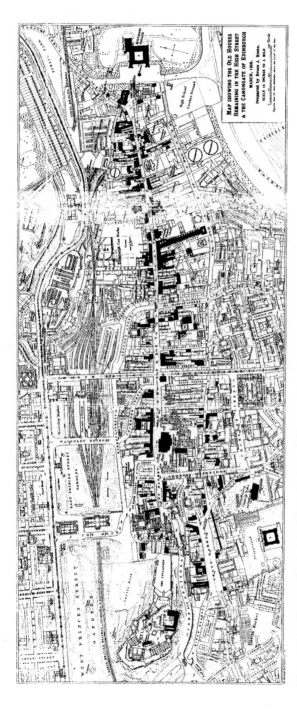

Figure 12.6 Desecration of the High Street c. 1908

Note: the ill-judged demolition of Edinburgh's historical heritage was an issue in 1908, as a century later. The article begins: 'It may safely be assumed that, since 1860, two-thirds of the ancient buildings in the Old Town of Edinburgh have been demolished.' Those that remain are shaded in black here.

Source: B. J. Home, 'Provisional list of old houses remaining in the High Street and Canongate of Edinburgh', *Book of the Old Edinburgh Club*, 1 (1908), 1–30.

Figure 12.7 Scots 'baronial' tenements and Edinburgh Improvements
1867: St Mary's Street–Holyrood Road.

Courant and *The Scotsman,* or in meeting halls scattered around the city, population and mortality data conveyed a sense of immediacy and an impression of objectivity. 'Experts' were created on this rising tide of Victorian quantification. The 'power of knowledge' amongst civic officials was partly a result of the work of the Improvement Commissioners which was then used to mark out administrative territory, to demonstrate the veracity of officials' judgements and to legitimate civic interventionism, not just in public health but in the arenas such as housing and tramway operations.[100]

Thirdly, the Improvement trustees asserted their own will and while Chambers' vigorous leadership jump-started the project, his resignation in 1869 was not unconnected to the persistent criticism of the proposed clearances.[101] In commenting on his energy, *The Scotsman* obituary to Chambers stated that 'probably no Lord Provost of Edinburgh since the famous Thomas Drummond [who presided over the New Town proposals] has effected greater changes on the face of Edinburgh than those associated with the civic reign of William Chambers'.[102] Nor did the cult of the personality elevate Littlejohn particularly, for though his *Report* was highly respected, his daily work remained in public health administration and his limited staff resources constrained the activities, as did the absence of a central co-ordinating committee until 1872.[103]

Fourthly, publication of Littlejohn's *Report* and Chambers' *Statement to the Town Council* within the period of fifteen months, and the passage of the Improvement Act six months later, seized the moment (fig. 12.8). The public mood was transformed; the dimensions of fear were known and considered manageable by the middle classes. Arguably, this was the most important outcome of Littlejohn's *Report.* The anxiety of the directionless 1850s was replaced by detailed information in the 1860s which reassured the civic elite in the 1870s. This was reflected in the confident, self-congratulatory tone in newspaper columns and the Council Chamber which in turn encouraged further public health initiatives. Civil engineering projects were undertaken to bring further fresh water

---

[100] M. Niemi, 'The power of knowledge: public health and policy in Britain and Sweden 1900–40', University of Leicester PhD thesis, 2000.

[101] ECA SL64/1/1, Trustees' Minute Books, 18 Dec. and 20 Dec. 1867; see also Macdonald, 'Public health legislation and problems in Victorian Edinburgh', 150; *Scotsman,* 4 Nov. and 5 Nov. 1868.

[102] *Scotsman,* 21 May 1883.

[103] Wood, *Report on the Condition of the Poorer Classes of Edinburgh,* ix–xi, identified the lack of co-ordination as having an adverse effect upon the poor. See also the editorial in *Scotsman,* 29 Feb. 1868. The consolidation of sanitary responsibilities into a single Public Health Committee was achieved in 1872.

Figure 12.8 Plaque commemorating William Chambers' role in the Edinburgh Improvement Scheme 1867 (St Mary's Street).

supplies[104] from the Moorfoot Hills in 1874 and the introduction of sinks, soil-pipes and water-closets – 1,858 WCs were installed in existing buildings between 1867 and 1870 and twenty-one new drainage schemes initiated in a vigorous application of regulations which previously had had limited effect.[105]

[104] For a discussion of the contentious debate over supplies from St Mary's Loch and the Moorfoot Hills, see J. Colston, *The Edinburgh and District Water Supply: A Historical Sketch* (Edinburgh 1890), 121–91; D. Lewis, *Edinburgh Water Supply: A Sketch of History Past and Present* (Edinburgh 1908), 186–251, 281–309, 368–77, and for political effects, 395–424; ECA SL27/4–5, Lord Provost's Committee Minutes, 1873–4; SL26/1–2, Public Health Committee agenda decisions, 1877–8.

[105] ECA SL1/301, Town Council Minutes, 26 Apr. 1870; *Scotsman*, 27 Apr. 1870. Commonly *The Scotsman* provided *verbatim* accounts of the town council meetings on the following day, and these reports have been used to expand the brief accounts in the

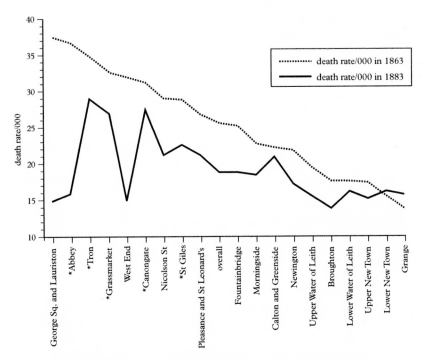

Figure 12.9 Death in Edinburgh 1863–1883: sanitary districts (deaths/1,000)

Note: * Littlejohn described these as the 'Poorest Parishes'.
Source: PP 1884–5 XXX, Royal Commission on the Housing of the Working Classes, Evidence of Dr Littlejohn, Q.18996, Appendix B.

To claim that the decline in the death rate in the period 1863–83 (fig. 12.9) was a by-product of the Improvement Scheme begun in 1867 would be to portray electors and officials as callous. Falling death rates were, certainly, a logical result of slum clearance decisions taken by the civic elite though their motivation was heavily influenced by the fear and uncertainty they associated with the no-go areas of the Old Town. As for mortality levels, for twenty years after formal notification was introduced in 1855, the death rate fluctuated around 25–6 per 1,000, but in the decade 1875–84 it fell by 20% to average just 20 per 1,000, and thereafter continued a general, if gentle, downward drift into the twentieth

Town Council Record, and in sub-committees such as the Public Health Committee where only agenda decisions were reported. For an exception to the argument that fear was dispelled see I. Bird, *Notes on Old Edinburgh* (Edinburgh 1869), in a language reminiscent of the 1850s.

century.[106] By reducing the density of the population per acre in the central districts – death rates fell by 14% in the sanitary districts of Canongate and the Grassmarket, 16% in St Giles and by 43% in the Tron – the likelihood of the transmission of all diseases was reduced, with a consequential impact on death rates.[107] The contribution of the medical profession to this decline in mortality has for long been shown to be marginal[108] and the Edinburgh improvements in the 1860s were an example of how the public health movement and its locally administered preventive health measures played a leading role in combating the congestion and environmental risks associated with industrialisation and urbanisation.

The years 1830 to 1875 have been described nationally as an 'heroic age of pioneering advances in public health activism'.[109] In Edinburgh, civic initiatives were more tardy than in some other British cities, yet public tolerance towards intervention in the sphere of private property to compel closures and clearances in the 1860s eventually spilled over into improvements in the water supply and the introduction of WCs to such an extent that in the last third of the century mortality associated with water-borne diseases was significantly reduced.[110]

The public health initiatives undertaken in Edinburgh between 1865 and 1874 were sufficient 'to engender a mood of silent confidence rather than one of incoherent fear'.[111] Further scares did occasionally break out, as in 1870 when *The Builder,* commenting on a temporary rise in mortality, described Edinburgh as having 'a diseased sanitary core', a 'cancer ... that must be cut out'.[112] Generally, though, if certain diseases such as typhus were in retreat, others, especially typhoid, which was associated with defective drainage and sanitary arrangements, were not.[113] Nor were infectious diseases such as whooping cough, measles and scarlet fever

---

[106] Registrar-General for Scotland, *Annual Reports of Births, Deaths and Marriages,* 1855–1914; *PP 1884–5 XXX,* Royal Commission, Evidence of Dr Littlejohn, Q. 18996, Appendix B.

[107] Littlejohn, *Report on the Sanitary Condition of the City of Edinburgh,* 121; *PP 1884–5 XXX,* Royal Commission, Evidence of Dr Littlejohn, Appendix B.

[108] See T. McKeown and R. G. Record, 'Reasons for the decline of mortality in England and Wales during the nineteenth century', *Population Studies,* 9, 1955, 119–41; T. McKeown, *The Modern Rise of Population* (London 1976); B. Luckin, 'Evaluating the sanitary revolution: typhus and typhoid in London 1851–1900', in R. Woods and J. Woodward, eds., *Urban Disease and Mortality in Nineteenth Century England* (London 1984), 102–19. For a recent historiographical review see S. Szreter, 'The importance of social intervention in Britain's mortality decline c.1850–1914: a re-interpretation of the role of public health', *Social History of Medicine,* 1, 1988, 1–37.

[109] Szreter, 'The importance of social intervention', 21.

[110] Registrar-General for Scotland, *Annual Reports,* 1857–1914, City of Edinburgh. For comparison with trends elsewhere see B. Luckin, *Pollution and Control: A Social History of the Thames in the Nineteenth Century* (Bristol 1986).

[111] Macdonald, 'Public health legislation and problems in Victorian Edinburgh', 194.

[112] See, for example, *Builder,* 12 Feb. 1870, 118–19, and 23 Apr. 1870, 317–18.

[113] A. Hardy, 'Urban famine or urban crisis? Typhus in the Victorian city', *Medical History,*

where children in overcrowded dwellings were particularly vulnerable despite the work of the Improvement Trust.[114] In fact, because of the work of the Trust overcrowding in districts adjacent to those wynds and closes cleared experienced increased occupancy – in the four sanitary districts closest to the clearances population rose by 66% between 1861 and 1881 and by 165% in the Abbey district.[115] The demolitions were likened to the Sutherland clearances, that is, forcible evictions, and the way in which the Trust's officials accepted that tenants found suitable alternative housing was disingenuous.[116] The Trust's secretary explained, improbably, that after bill posting of properties about to be demolished no tenants then remained when the contractors began site clearances and he inferred from this that tenants 'suffer no inconvenience in finding other places of abode'.[117]

Displacement and overcrowding were a consequence anticipated by the Parochial Board of St Cuthbert's drawing on their administration of the poor relief, and by Rev. James Begg who claimed that more not less cheap housing was required.[118] Begg, like Littlejohn, anticipated that the poor should be beneficiaries of public expenditure on housing, and policy instruments were added in 1879 to the blunt weapon of clearances by 'ticketing' houses so as define the acceptable levels of occupancy. This had been done in Glasgow and Paisley, but in Edinburgh it resulted in a battle over medical confidentiality and independence by obliging doctors to notify infectious disease to the Medical Officer of Health.[119] It was an important tactical victory for Littlejohn, and the collection of this information, together with a comprehensive survey in 1885 of 4,600 houses throughout the Old Town, enabled the Public Health Committee to pinpoint those properties they wished to close as uninhabitable and, in an innovative step, obliged owners to show due cause why this should not be

---

32, 1988, 401–25, and Smith, 'Slum clearance as an instrument of sanitary reform', show typhus as active after demolition.

[114] ECA SL1/313, 1/316, 1/318, 1/321, 1/323, Town Council Minutes, 22 Dec. 1874, 18 Jan. 1876, 9 Jan. 1877, 16 Apr. 1878, 4 Feb. 1879.

[115] ECA 16/3/35, unpublished notes on Edinburgh Improvement Act 1867, 53.

[116] *Scotsman*, 22 Feb. 1870, letter from T. Knox with reference to Sutherland clearances.

[117] *PP 1884–5 XXX*, Royal Commission, Evidence of J. K. Crawford, Q. 18712; ECA SL64/1/3, Trustees' Minute Book, 21 Jan. 1873.

[118] Parochial Board of St Cuthbert's, *Report of the Chairman's Committee* (Edinburgh 1866), quoted in P. J. Smith, 'Planning as environmental improvement: slum clearance in Victorian Edinburgh', in A. Sutcliffe, ed., *The Rise of Modern Planning* (London 1980), 99–133.

[119] GMC, *Evidence*, Fyfe, Q. 782–924, Myles, Q. 2150–393, McCallum, Q. 2401–45, Kelso, Q. 3964–4024.

[120] *Scotsman*, 27 Oct. 1885; *PP 1884–5 XXX*, Royal Commission, Evidence of Hannan, Q. 19288, recommended this approach on behalf of the Social and Sanitary Society of Edinburgh.

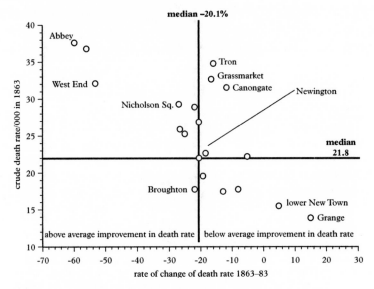

Figure 12.10 Improvements in death rates: Edinburgh sanitary districts 1863–1883

Source: PP 1884–5 XXX, Royal Commission on the Housing of the Working Classes, Evidence of Dr Littlejohn, Q.18996, Appendix B.

the case.[120] As a result, over 1,600 houses were closed as uninhabitable between 1885 and 1890.[121]

Littlejohn continued his public health crusade as Medical Officer of Health into his eighties. His surveys of housing and sanitary conditions in preparation for the Royal Commission on Housing of the Working Classes in 1884–5, coupled with the frequent papers and regular reports to the Public Health Committee and town council only confirmed his belief that significant further advances were possible and desirable. The sanitary districts with the worst death rates in the 1860s were still absolutely the worst in the 1880s, and though St Giles registered the fifth best improvement in mortality, the central districts fell below the median rate of change in the city (fig.12.10).[122] Child mortality, too, showed a slower rate of improvement in the central districts compared to the city average. The evidence, then, is that although there was a high correlation between

[121] *Scotsman*, 27 Sept. 1890; *Annual Report of the Work of the Burgh Engineer's Department for the Year 1893–94* (Edinburgh 1894), 41, gives the figure as 1,400 closures between 1886 and 1894.

[122] *PP 1884–5 XXX*, Royal Commission, Evidence of Dr Littlejohn, Q. 18996, Appendix B; Smith, 'Slum clearance as an instrument of sanitary reform', 7–10.

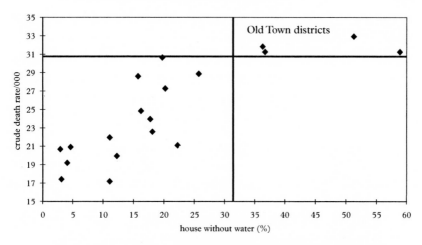

Figure 12.11 Water supply and death rates: Edinburgh wards 1874

Source: ECA SL1, *Return by the Burgh Engineer: Water and Water Closets in the City and their Means of Ventilation,* 16 Feb. 1874.

the clearances and a decline in the death rate (+0.74), 'slum clearance was not a sufficient explanation' for the improvement in mortality in Edinburgh between 1863 and 1883. There can be no doubt, however, that mortality would have been higher without the demolitions, and this has been estimated at over 1,000 lives saved per annum as a direct consequence of the Improvement Trust's activities.[123]

If demolitions were not a sufficient factor in environmental improvement, an important contributory factor in the decline of the death rate in the 1860s and 1870s was the increased availability of running water supplies (fig. 12.11). In 1874, that is, after the demolition of 2,000 of the most insanitary houses in the Old Town, a survey by the burgh engineer revealed that these same districts were the least well supplied with water and with the highest death rates.[124]

The sanitary conscience concerning the condition of housing matured in the 1880s into a more practical, less evangelical approach. Philanthropic initiatives, for example, that by J. R. Finlay, editor of *The Scotsman,* at Well Court were less moralising in tone (fig. 12.12). Other organisations, such as the Health Association (established 1880) which was a propaganda organisation, and the Social and Sanitary Society

[123] Smith, 'Slum clearance as an instrument of sanitary reform', 11
[124] ECA SL1/XX, *Return by the Burgh Engineer: Water and Water Closets in the City and their Means of Ventilation,* 16 Feb. 1874. For the decline of mortality by water-transmitted diseases see Luckin, *Pollution and Control,* 123–4.

(a)

Figure 12.12 Well Court, Dean Village, 1883–1886

Note: this court housing was a £14,000 benefaction by J. R. Finlay, editor of *The Scotsman* to the unemployed villagers and on which Finlay looked down from his cliff top mansion, 3 Rothesay Terrace.

(b)

Figure 12.12 The inscription states 'Be Ye [therefore] wise as serpents and harmless as doves', Matthew, 10, v. 16.

(1884) provided ideas and social analysis; the Social Union (1887), like the Association for Improving the Dwellings of the Poor (1885), offered more direct involvement, buying, renovating and renting properties for the poor.[125] In part, these societies were the conscience of the municipality, reminding councillors of further desirable improvements in the sanitary condition of the city, but the Social and Sanitary Society did not lose

[125] *Scotsman*, 6 Oct. 1880, 22 Oct. 1881 and 29 July 1887, quoted in Macdonald, 'Public health legislation and problems in Victorian Edinburgh', 223.

sight of the fact that sanitary improvement did not imply automatically that social progress followed. Overcrowding was part of fundamental economic relationships associated with the nature of capitalism, yet many poor people also needed sanitary education to overcome habits prejudicial to their health. The rents of new working-class districts put up by Steel and others in Dalry and Murieston were unaffordable and, displaced by clearances but dependent upon the central districts which sustained their itinerant lifestyle and employment possibilities, the poor could only be housed by the renovation of existing central properties, or by the municipal provision of new accommodation at low rents. No Edinburgh witnesses to the Royal Commission in 1885, not even the President of the Trades Council, accepted the principle of municipal housing which 'if every family in the city believed that the town council was responsible' for their accommodation would 'strike at that industry and enterprise that lies at the very root of our national existence'.[126]

The social consciences of several sanitary societies formed in the 1880s increased civic consciousness as to the persistent shortcomings in public health. The statistical evidence of overall death rates and those of specific diseases showed only marginal improvements in the 1880s.[127] Despite the council's opposition to municipal building which had been emphatically stated in the 1880s, the clear definition of Improvement Trust objectives which existed from the 1860s enabled a further wave of clearances to be undertaken in 1893, 1898 and 1900.[128] By 1900, and as a result of almost 1,000 clearances in the three Improvement Schemes, the town council had built 237 deck-access flats for about £160 and rented at between £5.25 and £10 per annum, with another 230 under construction.[129] Though an early municipal housing project was at McLeod Street, Tynecastle, a surburban site a mile further west from James Steel's Murieston development, the main focus of municipal housebuilding was on central sites (fig. 12.13), first of all at High School Yards (1897) and then in the Cowgate at Tron Square (1900). By 1895, the council was also reconciled to small flats, even single rooms, a position which was

---

[126] *PP 1884–5 XXX*, Royal Commission, Evidence of Telfer, Q. 19188.
[127] ECA SL1/355, 1/356, Town Council Minutes, 10 Jan. 1899, 30 Oct. 1900; SL26/1/6, Public Health Committee Agenda decisions, 17 Jan. 1893, 19 Jan. 1897; Macdonald, 'Public health legislation and problems in Victorian Edinburgh', vol. 2, Appendix XXIII, 1–17; *Report of the Public Health Committee on Prevention of Consumption* (Edinburgh 1900), 40–59.
[128] The 1893 scheme schedule 818 demolitions, 28% (228) of these were between the Cowgate and High Street; 25% (202) at Thornybauk (Fountainbridge); 13% (104) at Campbell's Close, Canongate; 10% at both Potter Row and between North Bank Street and the Lawnmarket; and the five further smaller clearances. The 1898 (Stockbridge, Portobello) and 1900 (Greenside, Simon Square) clearances were on a smaller scale.
[129] *Annual Report of the Burgh Engineer of the City of Edinburgh for 1899* (Edinburgh 1900), 6.

Figure 12.13 Council housing: Portsburgh Square 1901 (61 flats)

Note: the first three council housing projects were High School Yards (1897; 56 flats); Tynecastle (1898; 64 flats); and Cowgate (1900; 105 flats).

prompted by a shortage of available accommodation at low rentals, and had conceded that shared WCs were inevitable in the interests of cutting construction costs.[130] Similarly, Cousins' and Lessels' predilection in their 1866 plan for rebuilding in stone and in a Scots vernacular style was abandoned, and by 1900, brick blocks with a balcony access had replaced stone fronted tenements in a style reminiscent of some London County Council building in Islington and Southwark, or that of Liverpool City Council at St Martin's Cottages in 1869.[131]

Perspectives

For most British cities the pressure on existing accommodation and the shortfall in new housebuilding investment was at its greatest in the first half of the nineteenth century, often in the 1830s and 1840s.[132] While the growth of population in Edinburgh during these decades did not match the spectacular levels of many textile and metalworking centres in England, nor of ports and resorts, the financial collapse in the mid-1820s brought a virtual suspension of new building in the second quarter of the nineteenth century, and extreme pressure on the existing housing stock. This reinforced the symbiotic relationship between slums and suburbs identified by Dyos and Reeder: housebuilding investment in new residential zones for the social elites denuded inner city housing stocks of essential capital for repairs and maintenance, and in turn this accelerated both the progressive degradation of the ancient city and further hastened the flight of the wealthy from it.[133]

Significantly, Scottish statistical information on births, deaths and marriages (1855) lagged English registration (1837) by a generation, as did the general thrust of industrialisation and urbanisation. A statistical

[130] *Annual Report of the Burgh Engineer* noted that the North British Railway had also cleared housing in 1895; Macdonald, 'Public health legislation and problems in Victorian Edinburgh', 267.

[131] Smith, 'Planning as environmental improvement', 119; S. Beattie, *A Revolution in London Housing: LCC Housing Architects and their Work 1893–1914* (London 1980), 73, 78–9; C. G. Pooley, 'Housing for the poorest poor: slum clearance and rehousing in Liverpool 1890–1918', *Journal of Historical Geography*, 11, 1985, 70–88.

[132] For an overview see R. Rodger, *Housing in Urban Britain 1780–1914* (Cambridge 1995), 48–9; M. W. Beresford, 'The back-to-back house in Leeds', and J. Treble, 'Liverpool working class housing 1801–51', in S. D. Chapman, ed., *The History of Working Class Housing: A Symposium* (Newton Abbot 1971), 165–220; I. C. Taylor, 'The insanitary housing question and tenement dwellings in nineteenth century Liverpool', in A. Sutcliffe, ed., *Multi-Storey Living: The British Working Class Experience* (London 1974), 41–87.

[133] H. J. Dyos and D. Reeder, 'Slums and suburbs', in H. J. Dyos and M. Wolff, eds., *The Victorian City: Images and Realities*, vol. II (London 1978 edn), 359–86.

vacuum existed in Scotland for longer, therefore, as did anxiety associated with death rates and epidemic disease. Once available in an official form, the evidence on mortality assumed an irresistible authority and efforts to combat epidemic and environmental dangers associated with insanitary housing were forthcoming in Edinburgh. This was a sequence which applied in the second half of the nineteenth century on a world-wide scale. League tables of urban death rates were part of a discourse of national and international comparisons which local officials used to legitimate intervention in the private arena on behalf of the public weal.[134]

In England, local byelaws governing buildings were codified in the Local Government Act, 1858, which provided a set of model public health and building regulations and to some extent the Burgh Police (Scotland) Act, 1862, promoted by the Leith Provost, Lindsay, was a parallel move north of the Tweed.[135] Both English and Scottish measures suffered from being the lowest common denominators, that is, administrative compromises acceptable to the majority of urban authorities. For the larger Scottish burghs the general framework of environmental control under the 1862 act was inadequate and the four cities, Greenock, Leith and a few other burghs adopted a more interventionist approach with slum clearance and eventually rebuilding powers of a more muscular nature than anywhere in England. This flourishing Scottish urban consciousness in the 1860s may have been the result of decisions taken in London in the 1830s and 1840s to cede power to the Scottish burghs and which, it has been claimed, enabled a nationalist dimension within the Union to take root.[136] If Scottish urban autonomy needed a boost it was available as a result of the many Westminster acts which a Royal Commission in 1884–5 discovered were 'a dead letter' under Scots law and so required statutes drafted specifically for Scotland.[137]

Following a protracted campaign in newspapers and privately printed pamphlets in the 1840s and 1850s which informed and alarmed public

---

[134] I am grateful to Alan Mayne for pointing out such similarities in Melbourne, Sydney, Boston, San Francisco and Edinburgh's twin, Dunedin. See also Niemi, 'The power of knowledge'.

[135] S. M. Gaskell, *Building Control: National Legislation and the Introduction of Local Bye-laws in Victorian England* (London 1983). A. S. Wohl, *Endangered Lives: Public Health in Victorian Britain* (London 1983), 166–204, explores local public health initiatives.

[136] Morton, 'Unionist-nationalism', 227 *et seq.*

[137] *PP 1884–5 XXX*, Royal Commission, Report, 4, and Evidence of D. Crawford, Q. 18291, 18443–473, 18489, J. K. Crawford, Q. 18747, Hannen, Q.19289, Morrison, Q. 19745. Though the questions were directed often in relation to the applicability of Artizans' and Labourers' Dwellings Acts, 1875, the existence of this statute came as a surprise to the Greenock burgh surveyor (Turnbull, Q. 20151–3), and the unworkability in Scotland came as something of a shock to the Commissioners. See also G. F. A. Best, 'The Scottish Victorian city', *Victorian Studies*, 11, 1968, 329–58.

opinion as to the criminal and immoral behaviour of the labouring poor, the official statistics for mortality rates which identified insanitary housing as a central cause coincided with a specific disaster in 1861. The appointment of Littlejohn as Medical Officer of Health and his considered *Report* validated an inevitable intervention, and in Edinburgh in 1867, as in Glasgow the previous year, a more comprehensive assault on insanitary housing was launched through clearance campaigns authorised by a private act, the Edinburgh Improvement Trust Act, 1867. Rather than restrict local authorities to dealing with individual properties deemed to be insanitary, as under the Artizans' and Labourers' Dwellings Act, 1868 (Torrens' Acts), in England, or rather than oblige councils to rehouse displaced tenants, as under the later Cross' Acts in England (1875), the Edinburgh town council was permitted to demolish specific areas of the city in a phased manner and then to reconstruct them on a more coherent, planned basis.[138] In a limited way, therefore, the Edinburgh and Glasgow clearances contributed to early town planning thought.[139] While the administrative apparatus in Edinburgh to deal with public health and insanitary housing lagged behind its English counterparts in the 1840s, by the 1860s clearances and housing redevelopment had far surpassed the partial nature of such functions in English boroughs.[140] Perhaps it was a measure of envy as well as a deeper recognition south of the border that more comprehensive powers were needed urgently, but for these and other reasons the Housing of the Working Classes Act, 1890, which enabled both clearances and municipal housebuilding to take place was more actively embraced in English cities compared to Scottish ones where by means of the Improvement Trusts such powers had been available for a generation.[141]

While folk devils and moral panics provide one approach by which to understand the history of the built environment in Edinburgh, it is not the only one. Indeed, it is essential to consider the moral panic as part of the evolving discourse concerning 'verbal weapons of control' used by protagonists to effect policy changes in public health.[142] The language of the slum together with images of slum life were adopted to legitimate housing action. Three other approaches complement explanations based on public opinion

---

[138] See E. Gauldie, *Cruel Habitations: A History of Working Class Housing 1780–1918* (London 1974), Table of Statutes, for a list of housing and related acts. See also J. A. Yelling, *Slums and Slum Clearance in Victorian London* (London 1986).

[139] Smith, 'Planning as environmental improvement', 125–8.

[140] Yelling, *Slums and Slum Clearance*, 9–28.

[141] W. Thomson, *The Housing Handbook* (London 1903); and W. Thomson, *Housing Up-To-Date* (London 1907), provides information on the proliferation of municipal housing schemes under the 1890 legislation.

[142] Pickstone, 'Death, dirt and fever epidemics', provides a useful summary of the issues.

and official responses to it. The first, and most straightforward, is based on 'disaster' theory in which administrative changes are viewed as the direct and immediate consequence of a particular crisis.[143] For example, the fire of 1824 prompted the creation of the first municipal fire brigade, and a certain degree of urban planning with new road and bridge proposals. Though important in the southern extension of the city, the precedent had been created in the eighteenth-century construction of the South and North Bridges, the Waterloo Bridge and within a few years, the Dean Bridge engineered by Telford. Nor should Littlejohn's *Report on the Sanitary Condition of Edinburgh* (1865) be seen as a direct result of the tenement collapse in 1861 since for some time the appointment of an MOH was under consideration and, in any event, it was not until 1872 that a Public Health Committee was constituted to oversee sanitary policy. Other disasters, the loss of life associated with a series of cholera epidemics, for example, did not induce administrative reform in Edinburgh. Public health policy and environmental change seem to have been more evolutionary than revolutionary in response to particular 'crises'.

The second view of administrative development is based on a sequence in which first, interested individuals identified a social problem, which was then followed by prohibition and lax enforcement.[144] Next, further revelations were forthcoming followed by demands for a tighter regulatory code, more specific statistics and the possibility of central government supervision. The fourth stage emerged when existing legislation was shown to be defective, and regulation only partial. With no long-run solution on the horizon, the administrative apparatus became dynamic rather than static with its terms of reference widened and powers enhanced. Finally, the fifth stage of the process enabled executive officers to expand their own powers which had discretionary elements and powers of enforcement, and the expertise of medicine, chemistry and engineering was invoked to legitimate intervention. At this point the era of the expert and the bureaucrat had arrived and the fiefdoms of town clerk and city engineer established.

Though conceived in a different administrative context, the sequence has some validity as far as sanitary and slum clearance policy in Victorian

---

[143] See, for example, B. Luckin, 'Accidents, disasters and cities', *Urban History*, 20, 1993, 177–90; E. Bryant, *Natural Hazards* (Cambridge 1991); K. Smith, *Environmental Hazards* (London 1991).

[144] O. MacDonagh, 'The nineteenth century revolution in government: a reappraisal', *Historical Journal*, 1, 1958, 52–61; H. Parris, 'The nineteenth century revolution in government: a reappraisal reappraised', *Historical Journal*, 3, 1960, 17–37; V. Cromwell, 'Interpretations of nineteenth century administration', *Victorian Studies*, 9, 1965–6, 245–55; S. J. Novak, 'Professionalisation and bureaucracy: English doctors and public health administration', *Journal of Social History*, 6, 1973, 441.

Edinburgh is concerned.[145] The writings of Roberton, Alison, Chambers and many others can be viewed as a protracted initial stage; the enforcement of nuisances and of Dean of Guild powers over new building were expressions of good intent, but ineffectual. Further revelations by Bell and statistics from Stark, together with the revelations in *The Scotsman* in the 1840s and 1850s, and the threatened role for the Board of Health in London as conceived by Chadwick, produced circumstances akin to that of the third stage. Littlejohn's *Report* and its powerful recommendations then produced a climate of opinion which accepted that a new regulatory framework affecting the rights of property owners was inevitable. Finally, the criteria for condemning 'slum' housing, compensation and the projects for housing renewal were vested in panels of experts, in which medical opinion, sanitary engineers and architects were highly influential. By the 1880s, the bureaucratic expansion in this and cognate fields justified the demands for additional office space for the expanded council departments.

The third complementary approach relies on the relationships between the various committees and boards responsible in Edinburgh for the administration of public health. An extensive literature on inter-organisational relationships exists based on the interaction of two or more agencies. One line of interpretation has stressed resource dependency as the basis of interaction resulting from competition for scarce resources, a pattern of interaction largely attributable to the ability of one relatively powerful organisation to allocate and direct the volume and flow of funds to its dependent progeny while enhancing its own position and diminishing its own resource dependency.[146] Other studies have identified a power dependency approach and conclude that, as not all the participant agencies are interested in interaction, a dominant organisation must motivate the network.[147] In early nineteenth-century Edinburgh, the Police Commissioners were empowered by the town council to oversee sanitary and public health matters and received limited funding for the purpose. In this sense they were in a relationship which was dependent on the town council both for its power and resources. The Police Commissioners in turn delegated some responsibilities to the Cleaning Committee, who were thus 'mandated' to

[145] For an interpretation associated with another city see A. R. Neeves, 'A pattern of local government growth: Sheffield and its building regulations 1840–1914', University of Leicester PhD thesis, 1991, 10–12, 254–345, 406–62.

[146] J. Pfeffer and G. R. Salancik, *External Control of Organizations: A Resource Dependence Perspective* (New York 1978); H. Aldrich, *Organizations and Environments* (New Jersey 1979); K. G. Provan *et al.*, 'Environmental linkages and power in resource-dependence relations between organizations', *Administrative Science Quarterly*, 25, 1980, 200–23.

[147] S. M. Schmidt and T. A. Kochan, 'Inter-organizational relationships: patterns and motivations', *Administrative Science Quarterly*, 22, 1977, 22–34.

undertake the duties associated mainly with street cleansing – another approach which refers to an agreement made between organisations for the purpose of mutual benefit where one body is authorised to intervene on behalf of the other.[148] Indeed, the Improvement Trust functioned as a mandated authority, operating in a specific field for a defined period of time to realise objectives shared by public health bodies and the town council.

Interorganisational relations also functioned in the realm of central and local relations, that is, where central government might prove dominant and 'local authorities implement national policies under the supervision of central departments'.[149] This was certainly a fear harboured in relation to Chadwick's vision that the Board of Health in London might oversee public health policy in Scotland, too. Though they proved to be inapplicable in Scotland, the intention to apply the terms of the Artizans' and Labourers' Dwellings Acts (the Torrens' and Cross' Acts) was another, albeit inept, demonstration that centrally driven policies were perceived by some as solutions to local housing problems and the clearance of slum properties.

Another perspective on interorganisational relations has been characterised as an exchange approach where mutual co-operation and benefits have typified the nature of interorganisational interaction, and initiatives are directed towards collaborative relations in the pursuit of mutual gains.[150] The Destitute Sick Society, dispensaries and other voluntary societies together with the Royal Infirmary were active in the treatment of infectious diseases. They defined their own responsibilities based on professional ethics and Christian consciences, and were financed mostly by private subscriptions. Consequently, these bodies were largely independent of the town council. A set of exchange relationships existed, therefore, by which the town council secured public health services from specialist bodies while these quangos in turn could pursue a largely autonomous course of action, untrammelled by codes of practice which the town council could in principle apply. In important respects the Destitute Sick Society was the real though unaccountable public health body in the city. However, by 1830 overstretched resources resulted in a

---

[148] R. H. Hall *et al.*, 'Patterns of inter-organizational relations', *Administrative Science Quarterly*, 22, 1977, 457–74; J. A. Raelin, 'A mandated basis of inter-organizational relations: the legal political network', *Human Relations*, 33, 1980, 57–68.

[149] R. A. W. Rhodes, 'Some myths in central-local relations', *Town Planning Review*, 51, 1980, 270; R. A. W. Rhodes, *Understanding Governance: Policy Networks, Governance, Reflexivity and Accountability* (Buckingham 1997).

[150] K. S. Cook, 'Exchange and power in networks of inter-organizational relations', *Sociological Quarterly*, 18, 1977, 82–8; M. Tuite *et al.*, *Interorganizational Decision Making* (Chicago 1972).

less expansive vision of its role, and public health responsibilities were transferred by the ultimate authority, the town council, to a Fever Board, though funding of £100 annually would hardly seem to suggest that the new body was dependent upon the resourcing of the council. Neither the town council nor the Police Commissioners took much action as far as public health matters were concerned and thus the Fever Board functioned as an agency mandated by them to oversee public health matters in the city. By 1861, the Edinburgh town council had 'failed to provide any systematised or unitary sanitary administration'.[151] The fragmentation of administrative authority was perpetuated even after the publication of the *Report* in 1862 and it was only in 1872 that a powerful municipal committee, the Public Health Committee with a membership which included bailies and experienced councillors, codified the responsibilities of the MOH, sanitary inspector, Dean of Guild, burgh engineer and other administrative posts and co-ordinated their activities. It was the Public Health Committee which motivated the network of sanitary agencies and which thus operated a set of power dependent relationships. Further essential administrative refinements were added in the 1880s, for example, in the obligation on doctors to report infectious diseases, thus binding in yet further elements dependent on the central committee.

These alternative approaches – those of folk devils and moral panics, stages of administrative development and interorganisational relationships – were not mutually exclusive. It is entirely likely that in the development of social consciences concerning the insanitary condition of the housing, the emergence of different organisational structures was deemed necessary as part of the awakening public consciousness. For some observers, the amelioration of housing conditions was itself a sufficient justification for civic intervention; for others, it was a means to demolish fear along with insanitary buildings; and, for yet another increasingly active group on councils in the last decades of the nineteenth century, it was an element in a wider agenda concerning the relationship of the public sphere of operations to private interests.[152]

---

[151] Macdonald, 'Public health legislation and problems in Victorian Edinburgh', 20.

[152] See W. H. Fraser, 'Municipal socialism and social policy', in R. J. Morris and R. Rodger, eds., *The Victorian City: A Reader in British Urban History, 1820–1914* (London 1993), 258–80.

13 Adornment, ego and myth: the decoration of the tenement

Most visitors to Edinburgh encounter Colin Baxter's atmospheric post-cards of the city. The visual imprint has a number of strong images on which to draw, but commonly focuses on an instantly recognisable skyline of castle rock and church spires. Most cities possess distinctive physical features – the serpentine Thames or skyscraper profile of Manhattan are generally sufficient identifiers of place.[1] Postcard images are compressions of time and space, and in Edinburgh the postcard profile captures the relics of a medieval urban order in which the power of the monarch and the church are encapsulated in fort and kirk. Power and social order are explicit messages conveyed through the form as well as by the function of buildings, and despite organic changes in the use of ancient buildings and the intrusion of new ones, still the iconography of the postcard recycles the former systems of power.[2]

Buildings, then, form the ley lines of symbolic power in the city buildings. They were expressions of considerable capital investment and could not easily be downgraded, far less overturned. Lefebvre has noted that capital 'represent[s] itself in the form of a physical landscape created in its own image . . . to enhance the progressive accumulation of capital on an expanding scale'.[3] The sheer scale and durability of construction conveyed continuity to propertied interests. As Harvey observed, 'the geographical landscape which fixed and immobile capital comprises is both a crowning glory of past capital development and a prison which inhibits the further progress of accumulation'.[4]

---

[1] S. Zukin, *Landscapes of Power* (Los Angeles 1991), 221, claims exceptions for Los Angeles and Miami which with no identifiable skyline are then described as post-modern cities.

[2] For an exploration of these ideas see K. Lynch, *A Theory of Good City Form* (Cambridge, Mass., 1981); D. Harvey, *The Condition of Post-Modernity* (Oxford 1989); H. Lefebvre, *The Production of Space* (Oxford 1991), trans. from *La production d'espace* (Paris 1974); T. A. Markus, *Buildings and Power: Freedom and Control in the Origin of Modern Building Types* (London 1993).   [3] Lefebvre, *The Production of Space*, 53.

[4] D. Harvey, 'The geography of capitalist accumulation: a reconstruction of the Marxian theory', in R. Peet, ed., *Radical Geography* (Chicago 1977), 263–92.

However, the perpetuation of existing systems of power and the re-creation of urban space were not inconsistent.[5] Spaces and buildings were instruments in the political process, and in this regard Edinburgh's New Town was a mechanism by which the urban elite detached themselves physically, socially and culturally from the contamination of the ancient royalty while retaining political control.[6] Space was used explicitly by the town council in the eighteenth and early nineteenth centuries as a means to render the social order more explicit. Through the Improvement Commissioners in the 1860s and 1870s, the motives and the medium remained the same even if the means by which they were achieved, slum clearances, differed.

The imprisonment of capital in buildings, to which Harvey referred, resulted from infrastructural investment which was inflexible even in the long term – the heavier the investment then the greater the inflexibility. Victorian institutions – poor law hospitals and workhouses, museums, galleries and libraries, 'museums of madness' for lunatics, infectious diseases hospitals, fire, police and water boards, and many more – were specialised facilities conceived at a specific point in time and incapable of adaptation without considerable public expenditure.[7] Replacement costs for overpopulated and outmoded welfare facilities and public utilities were so substantial that inertia prevailed, particularly as the addition of a wing or block of cells was easier administratively and politically in the light of ratepayers' resistance.

The power of place and of particular buildings to amend individual behaviour has been advanced by observers from Bentham to Foucault.[8] Thus, in the nineteenth century the design of prisons and schools around open courtyards, the 'panopticon' design, to facilitate supervision from observation decks was well known and widely used. Behavioural conditioning was central to nineteenth-century architectural design. But large,

---

[5] D. M. Evans, *Demystifying Suburban Landscapes* (Loughborough Occasional Paper no. 4, 1980), and C. Ghorra-Gobin, 'Les fondements de la ville Américaine', *Géographie et culture*, 1, 1992, 81–8, argue that, in part, nineteenth-century suburban development was based on religious values and moral visions of the 'ideal city', in which women's domestic role was also prescribed.

[6] J. Urry, *Consuming Places* (London 1995); S. Watson, 'Gilding the lily: the new symbolic representations of de-industrialised regions', *Environment and Planning*, 9, 1991, 59–70; R. J. Morris, 'Gentle deceptions: Edinburgh and the making of a cultural identity', in S. Zimmermann, ed., *Urban Space and Identity in the European City 1890–1930s* (Budapest 1995), 96–106; and R. J. Morris, 'Urbanisation in Scotland', in W. H. Fraser and R. J. Morris, eds., *People and Society in Scotland*, vol. II: *1830–1914* (Edinburgh 1990), 77–8; H. J. Dyos and D. Reeder, 'Slums and suburbs', in H. J. Dyos and M. Wolff, eds., *The Victorian City: Images and Realities*, vol. II (London 1978 edn).

[7] T. A. Markus, 'Buildings for the sad, the bad and the mad in urban Scotland 1780–1830', in T. A. Markus, ed., *Order in Space and Society: Architectural Form and its Context in the Scottish Enlightenment* (Edinburgh 1982), 25–113.

[8] Harvey, *The Condition of Post-Modernity*, 201–36; Lefebvre, *The Production of Space*, 44.

indeed monumental, buildings which imprisoned capital also trapped individuals, both inside – their direct intent – and outside – their indirect effect. Changes in the built environment, therefore, have been used to explain changes in social behaviour, sometimes from the perspective of social control.[9] Monumental public building was not the only medium by which power and authority were asserted and behaviour conditioned. The adornment of the urban environment – memorial tablets, park gates, fountains and sculptures, clocks and street furniture – were further conduits by which spatial features attempted to instil social order through the iconography of the state. Embellished by decorative details, can Edinburgh's tenements be described as a four storey equivalent of a medieval wall, and what does such adornment say about builders' perception of the housing market? These themes form the basis of the present chapter.

Habitats and localities

Representations of castle and kirk symbolise the upper echelons of power and authority systems, yet as Foucault noted, 'a whole history remains to be written of spaces . . . from the great strategies of geopolitics to the little tactics of habitat'.[10] In Edinburgh, one of those habitats was the tenement, where, in heraldic fashion, the exterior walls prominently displayed stone shields chiselled with initials, crests, dates, decorative motifs and the occasional homily in splendid examples of the stonemason's craft.[11] Sometimes biblical pronouncements – 'the Lord reigneth, let the earth rejoice' and to the poor of the Cowgate, 'love God above all else and your neighbour as yourself' – together with occasional Latin inscriptions instructed residents.[12] Loyalty was expressed by references in stone to Queen Victoria's jubilees and the coronation of King Edward VII in 1902, and the common motifs of thistle and rose invoked fealty to both Scottish and imperial identities. Apart from 'Edina cottages' no equivalent exists in Edinburgh to those families of floral names – Ivy, Rose, Woodbine Cottages – which by means of name plaques on terraced houses in English cities invoked a supposed rural idyll.

High – three-quarters of all Edinburgh crests were at the second and third floor level (table 13.1) – and highly visible, these decorative shields

---

[9] M. Foucault, *Discipline and Punish: The Birth of the Prison* (New York 1977), is perhaps the foremost exponent of the view that social conditioning results from the nature of the built environment.

[10] M. Foucault, 'The eye of power', in C. Gordon, ed., *Power and Knowledge: Selected Interviews and Other Writings 1972–77* (New York 1977), 149.

[11] *Builder*, 15 Apr. 1865, 258, and 13 May 1865, 326–7, draws attention to the extensive nature of these heraldic and other decorative devices in the fabric of the sixteenth- and seventeenth-century city.

[12] The inscriptions are in Ardmillan Terrace and the Cowgate. Latin inscriptions can be seen, for example, in Cornwall and Dalgety Streets, and Wheatfield Road.

Table 13.1 *Vertical distribution of heraldic plaques on Edinburgh buildings 1860–1914*

Floor level	%
Ground	1.7
First	18.7
Second	28.9
Third	46.1
Fourth and above	4.6
(N = 519)	100.0

Source: based on a census of surviving buildings, July 1997.

were proclamations and cultural expressions of the work of individual builders, organisations and benefactors.[13] Roses and thistles, fans, wreaths and other floral motifs adorned the upper levels of many Edinburgh tenements, with Marchmont and streets off London Road having some of the highest concentrations. Not without their own symbolism these floral tributes (fig. 13.1) constituted over a quarter of all decorative plaques.[14]

The date of the tenement and the builder's initials together decorated one third of all external plaques (table 13.2). Sometimes easily distinguished, sometimes so ornate as to be barely legible and occasionally avant garde as in the numbering employed in Sloane and Dalmeny Streets, off Leith Walk, dates and initials were highly variable in style and form. Simon Henderson's 'SH 1882' in Spottiswood Road and John Pyper's 'JP 1887' in Marchmont Road appropriated the national emblem, and both William Outerston and the building firm of Galloway and Mackintosh in Marchmont and Warrender Park Roads jettisoned a date but incorporated classicism in an attempt to convey rational order and legitimacy. These qualities might have been helpful to '18 A. & W. F 78.', the inscription of the building firm of Alexander and William Fingzies in Industrial Road whose large number of working-class terraced houses on the 'Colonies' model were a prelude to dubious financial practices and bankruptcy.[15] Elsewhere, 'AH' in Brunton Terrace proclaimed Andrew

[13] See D. Hayden, 'The power of place', *Journal of Urban History*, 20, 1994, 466–85; and D. Hayden, 'The meaning of place in art and architecture', *Design Quarterly*, 122, 1983, 18–20.

[14] Before 1827 boys at George Heriot's School 'busked' or decorated the bust of the founder in the form of 'shields, thistles, cornucopias, the crown'. For an account of the ritual see W. Steven, *Memoir of George Heriot with the History of the Hospital Founded by Him in Edinburgh* (Edinburgh 1865 edn), 183.

[15] NAS CS318/49/67, Sequestration of Alexander Fingzies, 18 Mar. 1901, Sederunt Book, ff. 39–67.

Figure 13.1 Scottish nationalism in the built environment: thistles and tenements at Ashley Terrace 1902, JM 1903 (Downfield Place) and Viewforth

Table 13.2 *Heraldic shields and decorative types:*
external detailing on tenements 1860–1914

Decorative type	%	%
Decorated shields		59.2
Dates	18.7	
Initials	8.5	
Dates and initials	4.8	
Floral and other motifs	27.2	
Blank shields		40.8
(N = 519)		100.0

Source: based on a census of surviving buildings, July 1997.

Hood's very active development of Heriot feus between 1884 and 1895 at the east end of London Road and Easter Road, and 'JM 1903' in a combined wreath and thistle announced John Martin's tenements on a plot sub-feued from James Steel in Downfield Place, Dalry (fig. 13.2).[16]

These symbols and images were socially rooted and an integral part of the urban landscape.[17] Reading the runes, like other non-print sources, provides 'a way of seeing what was bourgeois, individual and related to the exercise of power over space'.[18] Three features of this ornamental symbolism should be noted. First, while the date of the building was often recorded, it was a double-edged marketing tool. For a few years, the date of a shield proclaimed the modernity of the building and assisted builders in making a sale, but superseded by later tenement building, it soon acquired the image of older property and saddled landlords with housing which could prove hard to let. Secondly, as two out of every five shields remained blank builders frequently took the decision not to adorn their work. Presumably the imitative effect undermined the advertising message. Where tenements were personalised, then the initials were almost invariably those of the builder, only occasionally those of the architect, and never those of the property owner or landlord. Only some

---

[16] NAS RS108/2111.54, Feu Contract, 16 Apr. 1904; ECA George Heriot's Roll of Superiorities, 1911; NAS GD421/RH/4/152/48, ff. 43, 88, 220, 466, GD421/RH/4/152 /49, ff. 200, 643, George Heriot's Hospital and Trust Chartularies.

[17] C. Geertz, 'Ideology as a cultural system', in D. E. Apter, ed., *Ideology and Discontent* (New York 1964), 394.

[18] D. Cosgrove, 'Prospect, perspective and the evolution of the landscape idea', *Transactions Institute of British Geographers*, 10, 1985, 45–6. Cosgrove also observes (45) that 'the subjective and artistic resonances are to be actively embraced'. On the interpretation of stone inscriptions see, for example, R. Thakur, 'Classification and hierarchy of urban centres in early medieval India c. 750–1200', *Urban History*, 21, 1994, 61–76.

Figure 13.2 Builders' initials, dates: W. and D. McGregor (Glengyle Terrace, 1869); Andrew Hood and Lawrie and Scott (both Brunton Place)

egos were to be memorialised. Thirdly, it was uncommon to find dates and even rarer to find initials on suburban middle-class houses, an indication that both owners and occupiers in this social stratum were deterred by signatures in stone. Nor were New Town properties carved with heraldic devices. James Steel, for all his extensive building activity and market awareness in Edinburgh, never inscribed his tenements, and where decoration was sought it was achieved through simple abstract lines or the suggestion of a floral detail over lintels and around window frames. Steel's financial linkages with Melville and Lindesay and his secure reputation for business efficiency rendered stone signatures redundant as an advertising ploy. Property owners and landlords knew from the Tollcross and Sciennes developments in the late 1860s that Steel's building credentials were not just 'skin-deep', to be proclaimed on the outer layers of a tenement wall. For others, though, and especially those builders who sought to break out of a highly localised market, the stone inscriptions reflected a degree of self-confidence about their work. If, however, advertising was more important than decoration or ego, then the builders' preference for the upper tenement storeys is surprising.

The inscription of street names on stone tablets remained common in late Victorian Edinburgh, and however smoke-encrusted and indecipherable they might become, some of the simpler, date-only tenement tablets presented an element of continuity in this urban tradition, and at little additional cost to the builder. Moreover, shop signs and armorial tablets which in earlier centuries had been common for pawnbrokers, goldsmiths, weavers and an array of retail trades lingered on, and the stone shields were one of the builder's methods of self-advertisement in a world which increasingly accepted this as a legitimate form of competition.[19] No doubt some saw it as a mark of business longevity in an industry noted for its instability and impermanence.

Few inscriptions pre-date 1860.[20] Indeed, there were few inscriptions before 1870 (fig. 13.3) and those were mostly associated with new properties built on land cleared by the North British Railway Company and the town council's Improvement Scheme in 1867. One of the earliest was in Cornwall Street to James Gowans, identifying him as architect for a block, begun in 1868 and described variously as 'astonishing', 'mad', 'hardly believable picturesqueness', and yet still 'large, logical and well-built'.[21]

---

[19] Royal Commission on the Ancient Monuments of Scotland, *An Inventory of the Ancient and Historical Monuments of the City of Edinburgh* (HMSO 1951), 213–16 nn. 150–1, 153–4, 158, KG 55, 117; D. Garrioch, 'House names, shop signs and social organization of Western European cities 1500–1900', *Urban History*, 21, 1994, 20–48.

[20] Some have been added subsequently.

[21] J. Gifford, C. McWilliam and D. Walker, eds., *The Buildings of Scotland: Edinburgh* (Harmondsworth 1988 edn), 263; D. McAra, 'Sir James Gowans (1821–90): romantic rationalist', *Scottish Art Review*, 13, 1972, 23–9.

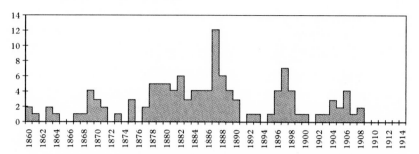

Figure 13.3 Date-stamped buildings: Edinburgh plaques 1860–1914.

Source: based on a census of surviving buildings, July 1997

As a prominent builder and architect, Gowans like Steel had little business need for self-advertisement, and his imprimatur on the side wall of his Castle Terrace block was more egotistical than commercial.[22] Like other builders, Gowans, who was 'obsessed by stone',[23] was in part prompted into decorative action by John Ruskin's *Lectures on Architecture and Painting, Delivered in Edinburgh* in 1858 in which he criticised the monotonous appearance of Edinburgh houses and urged a greater degree of ornamentation to offset this.[24] Within a decade stone inscriptions had begun to appear, and from the late 1870s until 1890 heraldic shields were common additions to the external decoration of property. Since tablets were closely associated with tenement rather than villa 'habitats', then the decline in working-class housebuilding, for example in the early 1890s and after 1905, meant that heraldic shields, too, became scarce especially in the decade before the First World War. Systematic only insofar as it is a comprehensive record of what survives, a survey of stone shields indicates that the two most common individual dates were 1887 and 1897, jubilee years in which builders could fuse an impression of business stability and imperial power (fig. 13.4).

Acknowledgement of public achievements were recognised also in commemorative plaques.[25] Slum clearance and civic improvement in 1867 were accompanied by a flurry of ornamental panels, including in Blackfriars Street the unlikely juxtaposition of the Star of David and the insignia of journeymen masons whose armorial shield bore the inscription

[22] ECA SL12/40, Miscellaneous Items and Deposits, Gowans file, 1867–86, ff. 17, 52, 61, 81, 119. Gowans was councillor, Dean of Guild, and knighted for his work in connection with the International Exhibition in the Meadows.

[23] Gifford, McWilliam and Walker, eds., *The Buildings of Scotland*, 502n. See also N. Taylor, 'Modular rockery', *Architectural Review*, 140, 1967, 147–51.

[24] J. Ruskin, *Lectures on Architecture and Painting, Delivered in Edinburgh* (London 1858).

[25] Only private plaques, that is, those by builders on tenements, formed the basis of the 1997 census.

Figure 13.4 Commemorative plaques: Golden Jubilee 1887
(Ardmillan Terrace); Diamond Jubilee 1897 (Morningside Road);
Coronation 1902 (Ashley Terrace)

'In the Lord is all our trust'. The commemoration of the efforts in 1871 of the Blackfriars' Building Association of eighty-four working men in financing and erecting two tenements on the cleared site was both an admonishment of the town council for its failure to rebuild houses swept away by clearances and a highly public acknowledgement of working-class energy and enterprise to do so (see fig. 12.3b, p. 435). It was a proud and lengthy expression of achievement, of participation and property owning, and drew on the self-confident plaques which the Edinburgh Co-operative Building Company installed in Restalrig, Abbeyhill and their other sites (see figs. 11.12 and 11.20). Significantly, power and personal glory were accorded to the key personnel in these working men's organisations, where in 1868 and 1876 James Colville, manager, and Thomas Field, convenor of the masons, in 1870 had their names inscribed for posterity. Ego trips were not class specific.

Where municipal civil works were involved – the Walker Bridge (1896) across the Union Canal, the Falshaw Bridge (1877) to improve access for 'Colonies' residents to Stockbridge, and nearby a new bridge (1900–1) across the Water of Leith – it was civic officials, normally the Lord Provost and city engineer, who received the plaudits. Expressions of indebtedness to citizens as taxpayers were conspicuously lacking and it is difficult to escape the conclusion that the civic purpose was hijacked to some degree by the incumbents for personal and political aggrandisement. The precedent seems to have been set in the after-glow of the City Improvement Scheme of 1867 by Lord Provost William Chambers in the form of a large and laudatory panel in St Mary's Street (see fig. 12.8, p. 442). In 1886, however, even the physical memorial was dispensed with when the organising committee of the Edinburgh International Exhibition simply proposed a payment of £2,000 to James Gowans for his work as its chairman.[26] One critic denounced the proposal:

without skilful and efficient sub-ordinates no great undertaking can be carried out . . . if a commanding general is handsomely rewarded, the subordinate officers ought also to receive similar treatment . . . there is no call for niggardliness being shown to the workers . . . and it is hoped that a bonus will be voted to all, down even to the sweepers . . . the services of all should be recognised in this way, or else not one should receive a penny above the salary at which he was engaged.[27]

The conflict of interests between civic duty and personal gain should not have surprised the Edinburgh public since Gowans, 'in appropriating part of the garden-ground' opposite his Castle Terrace development in the 1860s had laid out a portion of the land reassigned to the city in 1827 and then basked in expressions of public spiritedness while in fact appropriating

[26] ECA SL12/40, Miscellaneous Items, f. 86. The International Exhibition opened in May 1886 and ran for five months, attracting 2.77 million visitors to the Meadows site.
[27] ECA SL12/40, Miscellaneous Items, f. 101.

amenity and increased value to the residential blocks he was building.[28] Adornment created opportunities for myth, ego and especially profit.

Most elaborate and skilful were the stonemasons' decorative work for schools and public institutions. Their moral and instructive purposes were replicated in stone plaques on most of the Edinburgh School Board buildings where the image of an attentive pupil and a caring teacher (female) were prominently displayed.[29] These were mostly undertaken in the 1890s and 1900s as the Edinburgh School Board inherited over 180 schools on its creation in 1872 and only after a period of rationalisation was new building contemplated. Much more elaborate were the neo-Jacobean confections described as a 'decorated collegiate' style[30] as perpetuated by the Heriot Schools – the intention was one for each of the city parishes – built and developed by the governors of Heriot's Hospital, and operational between 1837 and 1886 when endowed schools were reorganised.[31] The Davie Street, Abbeyhill, Cowgate and Bernard Street schools still exhibit ornamental features borrowed from the original Jacobean building (1628) with elaborate stonemason work to crests, shields and decorative work above windows and doors. Embedded in the most congested areas of the city, the adornment enlivened the drab functionalism of the surrounding urban environment.

Just as literary descriptions and artistic sketches of the cityscape are more than simple descriptions but are informed dialogues with it, then so the buildings and their decorative features convey something of contemporary thinking about that built environment. The iconography of the armorial crests and inscriptions offers a means by which to interpret the human landscape as 'a cultural image, a pictorial way of representing, structuring or symbolising surroundings'.[32] Thus plaques and tablets are not merely decorative but an integral part of the meaning of the built environment and power inherent in property relationships.[33]

---

[28] *Builder*, 7 Aug. 1869, 623; ECA SL12/40, f. 17.

[29] W. M. Stephen, *Fabric and Function: A Century of School Building in Edinburgh 1872–1972* (privately published 1996), 26; D. E. B. Weiner, *Architecture and Social Reform in Late Victorian London* (Manchester 1994), 52–92.

[30] E. R. Robson, *School Architecture* (London 1874; repr. Leicester 1972), see, for example, 301–2, 307.

[31] See *PP 1880 XXIV*, First Report of the Commissioners on Endowed Institutions in Scotland, xlii–lxxi; *PP 1880 LV*, Educational Endowments in Scotland; Paper relating to George Heriot's Hospital, 3–37; R. D. Anderson, *Education and Opportunity in Victorian Scotland* (Edinburgh 1983), 162–201.

[32] S. Daniels and D. Cosgrove, 'Introduction', in D. Cosgrove and S. Daniels, eds., *The Iconography of Landscape: Essays on the Symbolic Representation, Design and Use of Past Environments* (Cambridge 1988), 1.

[33] D. Hayden, *The Power of Place: Urban Landscapes as Public History* (Cambridge, Mass., 1995), 3–6, 15–20, 34–9; Cosgrove, 'Prospect, perspective and the evolution of the landscape idea', 45–62.

Manufacturing myths

It has become accepted as a truism that a city has multiple images. The resonance of the term 'slum', for example, has been shown to have differed appreciably in the nineteenth century given the language and intent of contemporary observers and graphic artists, and according to media representations and ideological beliefs.[34] Manhattan's first skyscrapers presented highly divergent images to users, managers and maintenance workers, visitors, commuters, owners and designers, and reactions depended upon where in the intersection between modes of architectural production and consumption an individual was located. Threatening, phallic, convenient, inspirational, the symbolism of the buildings evoked a range of descriptions to convey different meanings and 'mental markers' associated with multi-storey construction.[35]

So, too, nineteenth-century Edinburgh presented multiple images. Smoke laden 'Auld Reekie' contrasted starkly with 'The Athens of the North', and the subtitle, 'New Buildings, Modern Improvements, Antiquities and Picturesque Scenery' to Thomas Shepherd's drawings of Edinburgh in 1829 encapsulated images of progress counterbalanced by those of rural tranquillity.[36] In the very first sentence of the preface, Shepherd observed that 'The great cities of an empire are ... a species of public property.' However, public property was closely associated with projecting the public image, and the image of the early nineteenth century was, in Youngson's phrase, the 'making of classical Edinburgh' whose citizens were more likely to identify Doric as the language of architectural legitimacy than a regional Scots dialect.

The wars against France were a catalyst for British nation-building. Scotland had participated actively in that process, and, indeed, reinforced it through the integration of the Scottish landed aristocracy into a unitary British nobility.[37] Not surprisingly, then, a sequence of highly visible monuments celebrating Dundas, Nelson, Burns and the National Monument or 'Parthenon' remembering those who had fallen in the

[34] S. B. Warner, 'The management of multiple urban images', in D. Fraser and A. Sutcliffe, eds., *The Pursuit of Urban History* (London 1983), 383–94; A. Mayne, *The Imagined Slum: Newspaper Representations in Three Cities 1870–1914* (Leicester 1993), especially part 2.

[35] M. Domosh, 'The symbolism of the skyscraper: case studies of New York's first tall buildings', *Journal of Urban History*, 14, 1988, 320–45; Warner, 'The management of multiple urban images', 391–3.

[36] T. Shepherd, *Modern Athens: New Buildings, Modern Improvements, Antiquities and Picturesque Scenery of the Scottish Metropolis and its Environs* (London 1829; repr. Newcastle 1969), preface.

[37] F. A. Walker, 'National romanticism', in G. Gordon, ed., *Perspectives of the Scottish City* (Aberdeen 1985), 127–9.

Napoleonic campaigns – the cult of the heroic dead – were neo-classical in form, as were sculptures of Pitt and George IV.[38]

Hellenic ascendancy dominated architectural design in Edinburgh until the 1840s. However, from the 1830s the unitary British state ceded additional powers to town councils and the local bourgeoisie to such an extent that Westminster was not the prime focus of the 'governing' civil society.[39] The degree of local autonomy exercised by the Edinburgh bourgeoisie over the running of institutions, therefore, in part explains the resurgence of a national identity in the built environment of the Scottish capital.[40] Empowered by Westminster and enshrined by statute, a Scottish identity flourished not in opposition to but in association with the British state.[41]

A reaction in the 1830s against the paganism and non-Scottish character of earlier classical monuments is explainable, therefore, in terms of an emerging liberal and pluralist civil society. Where nationalism could co-exist with unionism, then ornamentation which was overtly Scottish could co-exist legitimately with more conspicuously British motifs – lions, unicorns and roses. Nevertheless, there was a period of Scottish decorative ascendancy. An anti-classical faction existed before Sir Walter Scott's death in 1832, but a public subscription for a national memorial to Scotland's most celebrated author of romanticised historical fiction added legitimacy to claims for a non-classical structure, and in 1836 an open architectural competition specified a neo-gothic style for the monument (fig. 13.5). More than anything else it signalled the retreat, though not the final defeat, of classicism; that death spasm coincided with the completion in the 1850s of the Mound complex for the National Gallery and the Royal Scottish Academy.[42] Linearity in intellectual and material progress,

---

[38] ECA SL7/1/211, 45–6, 61–2; SL7/1/192, 176–7; SL7/1/204, 382–3; SL7/1/207, 326–7.

[39] For a discussion of the term 'civil society' see J. Habermas, *The Structural Transformation of the Public Sphere: An Enquiry into a Category of Bourgeois Society* (Boston, Mass., 1989), 32; E. Gellner, *Conditions of Liberty: Civil Society and its Rivals* (London 1994), 98–100; K. Kumar, 'Civil society: an inquiry into the usefulness of an historical term', *British Journal of Sociology*, 44, 1993, 375–95; J. A. Hall, ed., *Civil Society: Theory, History, Comparison* (Cambridge 1995); J. Keane, ed., *Civil Society and the State: New European Perspectives* (London 1988); N. Karlson, *The State of State: An Inquiry Concerning the Role of Invisible Hands in Politics and Civil Society* (Uppsala 1993).

[40] G. Morton, 'Unionist-nationalism: the historical construction of Scottish national identity, Edinburgh 1830–1860', University of Edinburgh PhD thesis, 1994, 227–30; R. J. Morris and G. Morton, 'The re-making of Scotland: a nation within a nation, 1850–1920', in M. Lynch, ed., *Scotland 1850–1979: Society, Politics and the Union* (London 1993). For an English dimension, see L. Davidoff and C. Hall, *Family Fortunes: Men and Women of the English Middle Class 1780–1850* (London 1987).

[41] G. Morton, 'Civil society, municipal government and the state: enshrinement, empowerment and legitimacy, Scotland 1800–1929', *Urban History*, 25, 1998, 348–67; G. Morton, *Unionist Nationalism: Governing Urban Scotland 1836–1860* (East Linton 1999).

[42] *Builder*, 1857, 323.

Figure 13.5 Scott's Monument 1840–1846

Note: partly financed by subscription, the trustees required the monument to be in a neo-gothic style – an endorsement of Scott's romanticism and a rejection of the classical.

Source: University of Aberdeen, George Washington Wilson Collection, E2776.

key elements of the Enlightenment, were modified; plurality, diversity and informality held sway and these values soon found their way into the townscape.[43]

In some respects the Edinburgh middle classes can be exonerated from the charge levelled at their English counterparts, namely, that they failed to develop their own cultural values and merely adopted those of the aristocracy.[44] A new, confident, assertive Scottish nationality emerged and architecture articulated something of that cultural autonomy. This was the context in which Scott's own words were reproduced in *The Builder* in 1865:

> The height,
> Where the castle holds its state,
> And all the steep slope down,
> Whose ridgy back heaves to the sky,
> Piled deep and massy, close and high,
> Mine own romantic town. [45]

In the 1840s, the completion of the Scott memorial (1844) coincided with the entrancement of Queen Victoria with the highlands, culminating in her purchase of the Balmoral estate in 1848. Together these developments legitimised the picturesque in architecture. In an influential parallel development, Landseer's paintings were the harbingers of a new genre in fine art depicting a contented queen amidst settings of her loyal highlands. This fostered images of rural tranquillity and evaded the harsh realities of the Scottish urban environment.[46] This 'invention of tradition'[47] with the queen showing a 'naive acceptance of Sir Walter Scott's romanticism'[48] coincided with technical advances in steel plate engraving and stereography which from 1840 revolutionised printing and, rather like the introduction of modern photocopying, enabled innumerable

[43] M. Glendinning, R. MacInnes and A. Mackenzie, *A History of Scottish Architecture: From the Renaissance to the Present Day* (Edinburgh 1996), 185–214.
[44] M. J. Wiener, *English Culture and the Decline of the Industrial Spirit* (Cambridge 1981), 14, 125–7; C. Dellheim, *The Face of the Past: The Preservation of the Medieval Inheritance in Victorian England* (Cambridge 1982), chs. 4 and 5; M. Barrett *et al.*, 'Representation and cultural production', in M. Barrett *et al.*, eds., *Ideology and Cultural Production* (London 1979); J. Wolff, 'Ideology in the sociology of art: a case study of Manchester in the nineteenth century', *Media, Culture & Society*, 4, 1982, 63–75; J. Wolff and J. Seed, eds., *The Culture of Capital: Art, Power and the Nineteenth Century Middle Class* (Manchester 1988).
[45] *Builder*, 15 Apr. 1865, 256.
[46] T. R. Pringle, 'The privation of history: Landseer, Victoria and the highland myth', in Cosgrove and Daniels, eds., *The Iconography of Landscape*, 142–3, 153.
[47] D. N. Cannadine, 'The context, performance and meaning of ritual: the British monarchy and the "invention of tradition"', in E. J. Hobsbawm and T. Ranger, eds., *The Invention of Tradition* (Cambridge 1983), 101–64. See also E. J. Hobsbawm, 'Introduction', in Hobsbawm and Ranger, eds., *The Invention of Tradition*, 1–14.
[48] A. Dyson, 'Images interpreted: Landseer and the engraving trade', *Print Quarterly*, 1, 1984, 29–43.

copies of the romance with the highlands to be made. The commodification of Victoria received an undoubted boost as a result, to be reproduced in many aspects of product advertising, and no less in commemorative tablets of stone.[49]

The 'ebullient Scotch Baronial style'[50] received an undoubted boost both as a result of an implicit royal endorsement and as a consequence of the Scott phenomenon. If the architectural developments in the 1840s were not pathbreaking in themselves, then in Edinburgh the planning and construction of Daniel Stewart's College (1845–8) and Donaldson's School (1841–51) were indications of how responsive both patrons and architects were to new concepts of the built form. However, 'the main achievement of the period lay not in the set pieces of high architecture, illustrious though they were, but in the sheer *amount* of everyday "architecture" constructed'.[51]

Detailed decoration: embellishing the built environment

The 'sheer *amount*' of everyday architecture with its national overtones was the result of vigorous building activity in the half century before the Great War, and boundary extensions to the city in 1856 and 1879 ensured that such ornamentation was spatially widespread. Nor was it limited to residential building, and was to be found in profusion in the new offices, department stores and civic buildings of the second half of the nineteenth century. Perhaps the most abrupt change was in the roof-line where crow-stepped gables introduced a visual diversity rejected by the clean lines of neo-classical design. Turrets and towers, dormer and oriel windows, castellated pseudo-battlements, corbelling and a range of stone extrusions which played host to animal, vegetable and abstract figures and representations ensured that, at least in some Edinburgh streets, homogeneity would never again be a feature.

These elements of country house or Scots baronial architecture, which were widely adopted in middle-class housing developments, were promptly incorporated in several tenement clearance and rebuilding projects. Demolition in 1853 to enable Waverley Station to be built resulted in a 'prototype Baronial improvement scheme'[52] (Cockburn Street) laid out in 1856 and built between 1859 and 1864 which connected the

---

[49] T. Richards, *The Commodity Culture of Victorian England: Advertising and Spectacle 1851–1914* (London 1990), 73–118.

[50] Glendinning, MacInnes and Mackenzie, *A History of Scottish Architecture*, 243; National Galleries of Scotland, *O Caledonia! Sir Walter Scott and the Creation of Scotland* (CD-ROM, Edinburgh 1999).

[51] Glendinning, MacInnes and Mackenzie, *A History of Scottish Architecture*, 243.

[52] Glendinning, MacInnes and Mackenzie, *A History of Scottish Architecture*, 274.

station with the spine of the High Street. The private act to authorise the
railway company's plans stipulated that they should 'preserve as far as
possible the architectural style and antique character' of the area.[53]
Nearby, at the boundary of the ancient royalty and Canongate, the crow-
stepped gables of Cockburn Street were replicated in St Mary's and
Blackfriars Streets, a product of the municipal improvement schemes of
1867. Scots baronial was a dominant feature in another civic improvement project of the 1860s, Victoria Street, where like the earlier
Cockburn Street 'improvements', rebuilding was generally a private,
speculative venture with the design details outlined by the Improvement
Trust's architects (fig. 13.6). Improvement Commission designs,
however, were not entirely an architectural one-way street since the essentially public buildings in the newly created Chambers Street, which
forged through congested housing in Brown Square to link George IV
Bridge and South Bridge, were designed in an Italianate and neo-classical
style.[54]

Though not directly responsible for their building, therefore, the town
council was instrumental in the events leading to the building of clusters
of tenements in an imagined Scots style. In a pronounced departure from
geometric Grecian form, the broken roof-line accentuated the perpendic-
ular and reinforced the impression of height. Warrender Park and
Marchmont Roads, begun a decade later in the late 1870s, were more
extensive examples of this appropriation of presumed national symbols
and even the otherwise plainest tenement block often sported a pepper-
pot turret or similar baronial decoration on its top-most corner.[55]
Builders deployed such devices to convey a presumed historical authenticity, a manufactured myth; it was also a direct appeal to trust, or, more
potently, a challenge to deny the Scottish national identity.

Though Edinburgh residents were not subjected to a Hellenistic back-
lash, as were Glaswegians in the 1850s and 1860s, there were strong classical continuities in the townscape, however contagious the baronial
influence might be. Most obvious was the enduring uniformity of the
tenement tradition itself. Where bay windows were introduced in tenement housing the effect was, self-evidently, one which broke up the

---

[53] A. Macpherson, *Report of Committee of the Working Classes of Edinburgh on the Present Overcrowded and Uncomfortable State of their Dwelling-Houses* (Edinburgh 1860), 6.

[54] R. J. Morris, 'Death, Chambers Street and Edinburgh Corporation', *History Teaching Review Yearbook*, 6, 1992, 10–15.

[55] *Builder*, 15 Apr. 1865, 256–8, gives extended examples of this sixteenth- and seventeenth-century Scots architecture. On aspects of Scottish national identity and its marketing, see D. McCrone, A. Morris and R. Kiely, *Scotland: The Brand. The Making of Scottish Heritage* (Edinburgh 1995).

plain-fronted homogeneity of the neo-classical Georgian facade.[56] None the less, it introduced another form of regimentation, though the cloning of Victorian terraces of tenements probably had more to do with economics than aesthetics. Reproducing working- and middle-class housing simplified design, maximised labour skills and rationalised drainage, foundations and roof construction. Even where bays were not introduced so that tenements had plain-fronted ashlar facades, builders departed from the Georgian predilection for equidistant windows by grouping them to either side of the common stair.

Another device which distinguished building form in late Victorian Edinburgh from its classical antecedents was the increasing use of different sources of building supplies to produce patterns in stone. This window-dressing – literally drawing attention to the individual stones and courses – not only picked out different functional elements of tenements, they produced a degree of abstraction in stone courses, featured crenellated lines and enlivened gables. Most commonly, this form of expressionism used pinkish-red Dumfriesshire sandstone juxtaposed with grey or buff sandstones produced both locally and increasingly from West Lothian.[57] Such design details, of course, had little to do with a specifically Scottish architectural identity but were indicative of a liberalisation of expression throughout Europe which tolerated diversity in all artistic mediums.[58]

The bespoke nature of the mason's craft in depicting flowers, geometric shapes, dates and personal initials involved costs. It was easier to lay another course of dressed stone than to incorporate a shield or slab with proportions not always consistent with the normal stone courses, and even if only cemented to the tenement fascia, an additional cost was involved. Yet economic rationality was often subordinated to the ornamental. The Edinburgh Co-operative Building Company produced signatures in stone to depict the various building trades – masons, painters, joiners and plumbers. The thistle motif, in particular, was incorporated in

---

[56] Gifford, McWilliam and Walker, eds., *The Buildings of Scotland*, 397, 399, claim that Buckingham Terrace, begun in 1860, was the first of the west end developments to have bay windows, with Learmonth Terrace following in 1873.

[57] G. Y. Craig, 'Topography and building materials', in Gifford, McWilliam and Walker, eds., *The Buildings of Scotland*, 25–6, notes that Locharbriggs, Corncockle and Corsehill were common sources of Dumfriesshire stone, and Binny, Hermand, Dalmeny and Humbie the basis of West Lothian supplies. See also *Builder*, 26 Nov. 1881, 673, and G. Craig, 'On building stones used in Edinburgh: their geological sources, relative durability and other characteristics', *Trans. Edinburgh Geological Society*, 6, 1893, 254–73.

[58] *Builder*, 28 Jan. 1860, 52, carried a verbatim report of the Architectural Association meeting at which a paper was read on 'Coloured material in external design'. The lecturer quoted Assyrian, German and country village and Asian cultural examples to validate such practices.

(a)

(b)

Figure 13.6 Scots 'baronial' architecture
(a) Cockburn Street improvements 1859–1864
(b) Sir Walter Scott's Abbotsford residence near Galashiels (1817–23)

Source: (a) RCAHMS A74563 (417180).

most forms of domestic embellishment from external stone detailing in window surrounds and above lintels, to plasterwork and frosted glass work surrounding main door flats. Where money allowed and status was important, this national iconography was carried further in the railings which marked property boundaries, and internally in plasterwork, where the leaves of indigenous plants and trees were commonly incorporated in the wrought iron or other craft work. Even the Saltire, the cross of St Andrew on a shield or flag, was unashamedly paraded in stone and metalwork.

Exceptional craft skills amongst Edinburgh masons have been attributed to the demands of stoneworking associated with the period of classical ascendancy, but the Victorian age was also one in which craftsmanship was obtainable in a range of mediums at relatively low wages. The middle classes, therefore, found embellishments to their homes affordable, as they did for the additions and alterations, repairs and maintenance, which enhanced the physical fabric.[59] Monumental masons, for example, were not consigned to the production of endless gravestones but undertook ornamental items for gardens and sculpted figures and friezes to adorn buildings. C. & A. Willmott were noted for their artistic metalworking, some of which was for external decoration. One account, written in a whiggish tone around 1900, claimed that 'the whole of the last thirty years or so has been an era of continuous improvement in relation to the effects of modern refinement, culture and improved taste' as reflected in 'the furnishing and general interior equipment' of houses and claimed that this could be 'startlingly illustrated' by contrasting the situation with that 'when the Queen came to the throne'.[60]

Superlatives aside, the composition of demand from middle-class households enabled Edinburgh firms who produced external decorative and artistic works to flourish. This was the case with the Albert Works Co. whose founder, W. Scott Morton, feued property from James Steel at Murieston for his workshops and design studio.[61] Morton drew on his formal architectural training and knowledge of London fashions in architectural decoration to develop his business from its shaky start in the

---

[59] R. Q. Gray, *The Labour Aristocracy in Victorian Edinburgh* (Oxford 1976); J. Holford, *Reshaping Labour: Organization, Work and Politics – Edinburgh in the Great War* (London 1988).

[60] Anon., *A Descriptive Account of Edinburgh Illustrated* (London 1891), 99. The contributor presumably had some literary licence, or difficulty with arithmetic, since it was over fifty, not thirty, years since 'the Queen had come to the throne'. See S. Pryke, 'The eighteenth century furniture trade in Edinburgh: a study based on documentary sources', University of St Andrews PhD thesis, 1995, for an account of the established nature of one of the consumption trades in Edinburgh.

[61] NAS RS108/1605.174, Feu Contract, 12 Apr. 1884, with an additional part of land feued 16 Jan. 1899. Morton paid £500 with combined annual feu-duties of £134.50.

1870s to one of considerable vigour in the last two decades of the nineteenth century.[62] Two features of the business typified the process of conscious adornment upon which the Edinburgh middle classes embarked. The first was the introduction of machines which produced accurate reproductions of works of art – sections of the Elgin Marbles, for example, were reduced to scale from drawings so as to develop templates for tiles, friezes and other ornamental features. The second characteristic of the business was what would now be called interior design, where Morton and his son would 'take a house from the bare walls and complete it ready for the occupant', with all fabrics, wall and other furnishing supplied from the art workshops, and on view in a showroom opposite the works in Ardmillan Terrace.[63]

The diffusion of ornamentation, however, owed much to the increasing mechanisation of building supplies. Building yards from the 1870s increasingly incorporated workshops for steam-powered stone dressing and wood-turning lathes. More specifically, rebates, mitres, tenons, chamfering, beading and tongue-and-grooving were mechanised by 'universal' or 'general' joiners – machines which combined several of these techniques – and specialist saw machines to cut curves and tapers were also gaining popularity in the 1860s.[64] This level of capital investment was justifiable for yards servicing several tenements and multiple contracts, and as builders such as Steel, Cowie, Watherston, Gowans, Hood and others retained an essentially localised presence, then a strategically located yard with expensive equipment acted as the hub for their satellite sites.[65] This was particularly the case with W. & J. Kirkwood, builders, established in 1872 but whose rapid expansion enabled them to employ 300 workers by 1889. Kirkwood's yard accommodated workshops 'replete with machinery and appliances embodying all the latest improvements' and which assisted the 'economical working of the business'.[66] Much the same applied to William Beattie and Sons, builders and timber merchants, whose extensive workshops and sawmills extended 200 yards from High Riggs to Fountainbridge and where a 'fine horizontal tandem engine' provided the power for the turned mahogany, planed deals and ornamental oak which were the mainstay of their business.[67]

---

[62] G. White, 'Tynecastle tapestry at the Albert Works, Edinburgh', in D. C. Thomson, *Fifty Years of Art 1849–1899 Being Articles and Illustrations from 'The Art Journal'* (London 1900), 349–52.   [63] Anon., *Edinburgh Illustrated*, 100.

[64] *Builder*, 14 Aug. 1869, 640. See also *Builder*, 14 Jan. 1860, 19–21, for 'A review of the progress made in the mechanical arts of construction since 1800'.

[65] Anon., *Scotland of To-day: Edinburgh, its Capital and the East Coast Ports* (Edinburgh 1890), 152, 160. In each of these cases the firms were described as having yards amply fitted with machinery.   [66] Anon., *Scotland of To-day*, 138.

[67] Anon., *Edinburgh Illustrated*, 80.

Ornamentation offered a double advantage to large building firms. First, it was they alone who could afford the initial investment in mechanisation, enabling them to cut costs where smaller unmechanised firms continued to rely on handicraft skills; and secondly, as changing taste and architectural fashion dictated that ornamental detailing was almost obligatory, so the ability of small building firms to compete for contracts was diminished, though a new breed of builders' merchants did something to offset this. The cost-reducing effects of mechanisation in the building trade, together with changing architectural taste, enabled even the most basic tenements to have some ornamental details incorporated, even if these were just small, unspecific floral designs or curved lines. Simple motifs of this kind formed the basis of a template which was then drilled to produce the trademark patterns in stone, a degree of ornamentation which was much more easily produced in Lothian sandstones than Aberdeen granites.[68] As the President of the Edinburgh Architectural Association observed in 1872, if mechanisation produced even this level of minimalist ornamentation to the 'utility style' and 'rude grandeur' which necessarily resulted from higher wages and a reduced craft input, then it was desirable.[69]

Decoration had much to do with materials, technical processes and mechanised production. Polished pillars and dressed sandstone decorated the innumerable new facades which were revealed to Edinburgh citizens when the wooden scaffoldings were removed. Before 1850, polished granite was a rare material, but mechanical advances associated with Aberdeen quarries meant that by the 1860s and 1870s it had become more widely adopted as a decorative material.[70] These 'scrapbooks in stone'[71] were complemented by the monuments and memorials made of granite as columns and gate-pillars, as plinths for drinking fountains, horse-troughs and war memorials. Polished granite, durable and ornamental, and with almost none of the features of 'decay' or weathering which concerned architects, became widely used in Edinburgh in the last third of the nineteenth century.[72]

[68] *Builder*, 31 Mar. 1866, 225–56, 7 Apr. 1866, 243–4, and 13 Oct. 1877, 1019–20. The articles note that 'scrolls, coats of arms, panels and many other forms in ornamental and decorative art' can be produced in granite but that it is expensive in both labour and plant.   [69] *Builder*, 23 Nov. 1872, 920.

[70] *Builder*, 31 Mar. 1866, 225–56, 7 Apr. 1866, 243–4, and 13 Oct. 1877, 1019–20. The report in the *Builder* identifies the 1820s as the date at which the technical problems of polishing were resolved, but E. Grant, 'The sphinx in the north: Egyptian influences on landscape, architecture and interior design in eighteenth and nineteenth century Scotland', in Cosgrove and Daniels, eds., *Iconography*, 243–4, claims that the commercial development of polishing only took place around mid-century.

[71] Morris, 'Gentle deceptions: Edinburgh', 97.

[72] *Builder*, 3 Mar. 1860, 132–4, and 10 Mar. 1860, 147–9.

While the organisation of the building industry itself contributed to the ability to deliver decoration in the physical fabric, associated with it were changes in the industrial processes connected with materials themselves. Machine rather than handicraft production across a wide spectrum of products both functional and decorative reduced costs and improved availability and, in turn, this enabled builders to incorporate many items in new tenements geared towards working-class budgets. Sanitary ware, float glass, glazed pipes for drains, moulded plaster work and cast iron cooking ranges were some amongst many supplies where specialisation and factory production delivered household items in wholesale show-rooms where builders could inspect them. Dickson, Walker and Co., glass merchants established in 1859, operated in this way, as did James Watson, founded in 1878 in Leith, who supplied grates and kitchen ranges. Messrs Wood & Cairns, Ltd, general plumbers' merchants, had a spacious ware-house in West Register Street stocked with all kinds of sanitary ware and appliances where 'the newest goods are displayed in the showrooms'.[73] Another supplier of light castings, the revered iron-founding firm of Mushet and Company, produced 'standard sizes' and 'pretty designs' at their Bonnington works for their baths, grates and stoves and 'as there is a steady demand for novelties' were evidently aware of the need to reconcile economies of scale with the decorative and fashionable.[74] The firm of Messrs T. B. Campbell and Co., metal merchants and manufacturers of sheet lead, were the only suppliers in Edinburgh who used hydraulic machinery to manufacture various lead pipes, zinc and other metal sheets. This had considerable significance for roofing materials where zinc ridges, valleys, caps, astragals and other rain water fittings were pro-duced, and in the gas industry where lightweight tin coils and tubes were essential in the production of gas meters.[75]

Specialist producers of building materials expanded appreciably in the fifty years between 1860 and 1910, so much so that there was even a choice between 'off the shelf' heraldic decorations available from Robert Wilson & Sons, a family firm of house painters and gilders established in South Clerk Street from 1867, or C. & A. Willmott, a firm specialising in art metal work but who also produced 'inscription tablets, coats-of-arms and heraldic devices of all kinds' from their Thistle Street premises.[76] 'Builders' merchants', a term unknown in the trade directories of the

[73] Anon., *London and Edinburgh. The English and Scottish Capitals. Representatives of Art, Industries and Commerce at the Beginning of the Twentieth Century* (London n.d.), 137; Anon., *Scotland of To-day*, 128, 164.   [74] Anon., *Edinburgh Illustrated*, 78–9.

[75] Anon., *Edinburgh Illustrated*, 66.

[76] *Builder*, 19 Mar. 1870, 219; Anon., *London and Edinburgh*, 153. Willmott's had also won prizes in the National Trades and Industries Exhibition, one of a number of competitions nation-wide to foster industrial arts.

1860s, contributed thirteen specialist entries by 1910 and were a market response to builders' need to improve their own time management.[77] These 'one-stop' sources of supply also served to update builders as to new products and familiarised them with the potential for incorporating decorative details into their work.

The power of the facade or the facade of power?

In the transition from a neo-classical-dominated programme of building to one in which a romanticised and mythical Scottish identity became highly conspicuous, it would be both plausible to identify the 1840s as a visual changing of the guard and convenient to attribute this to new forms of representation and decision making in municipal and national government in the 1830s.[78] So liberated, Scots' representational forms for the adornment of the built environment were liberalised – a visual form of laissez-faire which permeated Victorian society on both sides of the border. A muscular assertiveness of the national identity – Scots baronial and the parade of statues of Scottish humanists and scientists in Princes Street Gardens – was powerfully insinuated into the mid-century landscape.[79] This paradigm shift in the landscape of Edinburgh was itself subject to a second shift in the 1880s, when, with a measure of autonomy granted through the creation of the Scottish Office and the royal imprimatur on the highlands finessed to represent all things Scottish, the need for national assertiveness diminished. Scotland had achieved that degree of equality with England which it had sought[80] on entering the Union in 1707 and the first International Exhibition in Scotland, held in Edinburgh in 1886, confirmed the position of the city in the constellation of international capitals.[81]

The reinvention of the landscape provided opportunities for 'footloose

[77] *Edinburgh and Leith Post Office Directories*, 1860–1914.

[78] R. J. Morris, 'The middle class and British towns in the industrial revolution', in Fraser and Sutcliffe, eds., *The Pursuit of Urban History*, 300; D. Fraser, *Urban Politics in Victorian England: The Structure of Politics in Victorian Cities* (Leicester 1976), 9–30; J. G. Kellas, *The Scottish Political System* (Cambridge 1973 edn), 26–30.

[79] Excluding the Scott monument, seven prominent sculptures were unveiled in the years 1865–78. ECA TCM, Wilson (professor, moral philosophy), SL7/1/269, 123–4, SL7/1/290, 45–8, 139, 225–6, 270; Ramsay (poet), TCM, SL7/1/281, 119, SL7/1/282, 35, SL7/1/290, 143–66, *Scotsman*, 27 Mar. 1865; Sinclair (novelist/philanthropist), SL7/1/292, 472–4; Chalmers (Free Church minister), SL7/1/302, 410–11, SL7/1/177; Black (publisher, Lord Provost), SL7/1/316, 169, SL7/1/318, 284–5, SL7/1/320, 85, *Scotsman*, 5 Nov. 1877; Livingstone (missionary, explorer), SL7/1/314, 165–6, SL7/1/317, 328, 390–2; Simpson (professor, anaesthetics), SL7/1/212, 237–9.

[80] H. J. Hanham, 'Mid-century Scottish nationalism: romantic and radical', in R. Robson, ed., *Ideas and Institutions of Victorian Britain: Essays in Honour of George Kitson Clark* (London 1967), 143–79; G. Morton, 'Unionist-nationalism', 5–6, 175–90, 227.

[81] R. Hill, 'Architecture: the past fights back', *Marxism Today*, 24, 1980, 21–5, argues that architecture can be used to develop social harmony.

capital'[82] yet it was the availability of trust and heritable income, business and institutional funds which lubricated building development and financed ornamentation in the landscape. In this explanation of visual diversity from the 1840s, the importance of the Edinburgh middle classes and a pluralistic civil society was crucial.[83] Centred as it was in Edinburgh, the Enlightenment and the legacy of intellectual flexibility contributed to a culture which tolerated diversity. Indeed, this may be one explanation of a mid-nineteenth-century phenomenon, recently identified, of different architectural emphases in the east (romantic) and west (classical) of Scotland.[84] Furthermore, the culture of consumption in Edinburgh sustained craft-based industries in furniture and fine arts, pianos and porcelain, and was underpinned by a deep reservoir of expenditure by professional and upper-middle-class households which respected individuality.[85] Variety in the built environment was only consistent with other areas of consumption.

In a contrary direction, visual uniformity was encouraged by certain institutional factors. At one level, feudal superiors insisted on the use of particular materials, and occasionally even on those from specified quarries. In addition, the feuing plans for estate development defined not just street layout and building lines, but insisted in great detail on particular features. James Steel required that 'the whole of the fronts, as well as the ornamented parts, shall be of a style and quality of work to be approved of by the Superiors' and that construction was to be 'in stone from any quarry which in their opinion is suitable in colour and quality'.[86] To disregard these stipulations was to risk 'irritancy', that is, the superior could invoke his rights and reassign the plot without compensation. It was a particularly advantageous device, and a strong inducement to building conformity. Another important institutional factor was the work of the Dean of Guild Court in sanctioning building permits.[87] These medieval foundations were reaffirmed as urban planning authorities in the Burgh Police (Scotland) Act, 1862, and scrutinised plans and elevations

[82] This term for speculative capital is from Zukin, *Landscape of Power*, 220.
[83] A. J. A. Dalgleish, 'Voluntary associations and the middle class in Edinburgh 1780–1820', University of Edinburgh PhD thesis, 1992, identifies the 1810–39 years as those when the number of new voluntary society formations was higher than in the preceding or succeeding thirty year spans. See also N. J. Morgan and R. Trainor, 'The dominant classes', in Fraser and Morris, eds., *People and Society in Scotland*, vol. II, 126.
[84] Glendinning, MacInnes and Mackenzie, *A History of Scottish Architecture*, 317–40.
[85] E. C. Sanderson, *Women and Work in Eighteenth Century Edinburgh* (Basingstoke 1996), 36–40; J. L. Cranmer, 'Concert life and the music trade in Edinburgh c.1780–c.1830', University of Edinburgh PhD thesis, 1991.
[86] ECA ACC 373, Articles and Conditions of Feu of Parts of the Lands of North Merchiston, clause 2.
[87] R. Miller, *The Edinburgh Dean of Guild Court: A Manual of History and Procedure* (Edinburgh 1896); J. C. Irons, *Manual of the Law and Practice of the Dean of Guild Court* (Edinburgh 1895), 11–21.

according to detailed procedures and highly specific requirements concerning materials and standards of construction.[88] Economic rationality encouraged builders to lay foundations and sewers in straight lines, but the building regulations enforced by the Dean of Guild Court defined ceiling heights, chimney and roof construction, the widths of beams and stone walls and a multiplicity of other details which affected the way tenements were built. As tradesmen became familiar with certain methods of working so as to conform to Dean of Guild requirements, so working practices assumed a measure of inflexibility. From the 1860s, therefore, custom and practice reinforced the visual coherence introduced by institutional regulation.

A hierarchy of facades existed. For the rich, the former external decoration, intended to exude confidence and stability as well as to merge the image and reality of wealth in the facade, was in retreat.[89] As privacy gained supremacy in association with suburbanisation, then Edinburgh's new villa residents attached greater emphasis to amenities and interior design than to the mason's elaborate stonework on the facades of Old Town tenements. Nor were Edinburgh's middle-class households attracted by pretentious heraldic devices or other external insignia. Indeed, their architectural hallmark was in the form of 'insistently repetitive bay windows'.[90] It was predominantly in tenements for the working classes that decoration was most commonly, though by no means universally, used to create diversity and visual variety in the urban landscape.

By 1914, Edinburgh's working classes lived in tenements where the facades were the result of mass-produced, machine-dressed stone oblongs. Indeed, more generally, it was recently observed, 'Scotland was the only country in the world where the facade presented by the pre-1914 mass capitalist city was an ashlar-wall'.[91] Confronted by the four storey equivalent of a medieval wall with windows, the eyes of the tenement dweller were drawn particularly to any minimalist decoration in the facade. So the provision by the builder of an heraldic device, date or intertwined initials offered, at a modest level, symbols of his own power and, more ambitiously perhaps, a connection through the representations of thistle and saltire appropriated in the walls of tenements to provide a national identity and a sense of a shared history.[92]

[88] R. Rodger, 'The evolution of Scottish town planning', in G. Gordon and B. Dicks, eds., *Scottish Urban History* (Aberdeen 1983), 71–91.
[89] *Builder*, 13 May 1865, 326–8, provides an account of power in an article 'Street architecture of the Old Town of Edinburgh'.
[90] Gifford, McWilliam and Walker, eds., *The Buildings of Scotland*, 65.
[91] Glendinning, MacInnes and Mackenzie, *A History of Scottish Architecture*, 510.
[92] Pringle, 'The privation of history', 143, argues conversely that the evocation of the myth detaches individuals from history, and from geography by the loss of a sense of place.

14   Conclusion: reinventing the city

The built environment is 'soaked in memories and meanings'.[1] Reactions to and interactions with buildings and spaces produce highly specific mental maps or reference points which enable a resident to navigate around localised parts of the city with the unerring antennae of the animal world. This built environment is part of a visual ideology, a cultural system in stone and an expression of social and political values.[2]

Orientation in the nineteenth century depended on highly localised visual markers yet many of these were swept away and replaced by new intrusions in the landscape. Support networks based on workplace and worship, recreational and political organisations provided points of contact for urban immigrants and continuities for those born in the city. But in a contradictory direction, slum clearance and improvement schemes together with the commercial and financial expansion associated with branch offices and department stores eliminated familiar markers and introduced entirely new ones in the mental landscapes of Edinburgh's population.

If social assimilation was assisted by kinship and family links and by a rich and diverse associational culture, then it was offset by dislocations in the familiar physical landscape. A sense of 'isolation' at the 'widespread, ruthless and indiscriminat[e] . . . destruction' of houses provoked a plea in 1908 to 'rescue from the hands of the house-wrecking Philistine' the clearance activities which meant 'that since 1860, two-thirds of the ancient buildings in the Old Town of Edinburgh have been demolished'.[3] The indiscriminate way in which clearances took place – without 'due regard to historic, literary and aesthetic considerations' – produced trenchant criticisms. 'Rarely has any consideration beyond the most baldly utilitarian been allowed to influence the decision', it was claimed, so

---

[1] K. Lynch, *The Image of the City* (Boston, Mass., 1960), 1, figs. 35–46.

[2] C. Geertz, *The Interpretation of Cultures* (New York 1973), 17–20, 126–8, 193–220.

[3] B. J. Home, 'Provisional list of old houses remaining in the High Street and Canongate of Edinburgh', *Book of the Old Edinburgh Club*, 1, 1908, 1.

that 'our most valuable and historic architectural remains [have] been irretrievably lost to the city and to posterity'.[4]

Superimposed on a medieval warren of Old Town entries and closes, impenetrable except to those familiar with the network, was a simplified street plan increasingly accessible to inspectors and officialdom. A porous and informal network of wynds, closes and vennels in the early and mid-nineteenth century succumbed increasingly to regulated and monitored spaces, streets and buildings by the beginning of the twentieth century.[5] This conflict of ideologies was intensified and given added urgency by the embrace of empiricism which the registration of births, deaths and marriages stimulated after 1855.[6] 'Experts' were created on a rising tide of Victorian quantification which was then used by civic officials to legitimate intervention and the veracity of their judgements.

The reconstruction of the Edinburgh townscape owed much to the creeping imperialism of the Corporation itself. This was, of course, precisely the objective of the Improvement Commissioners who, in the 1860s, sought first to demolish insanitary housing and then to encourage private enterprise to develop the available sites along lines specified by the city engineer's department. Explicitly, the department attempted to shape the nature of the urban environment; implicitly, it redefined the urban landscape. Nowhere was this more conspicuous than in the endorsement of turrets and towers, battlements and crow-stepped gables by the city council in connection with the architecture of the Improvement Schemes and which found powerful echoes in the buildings undertaken by private enterprise in later years.[7]

Only a handful of properties were under council control before 1860, but the number had risen exponentially to 190 by 1884 and to over 650 in 1905.[8] Thus, the presence of the municipality in the landscape of the city redefined the existing fabric and contributed new dimensions in previ-

[4] Home, 'Provisional list of old houses', 1–2, brackets added.
[5] A. Rapoport, *Human Aspects of the Urban Form: Towards a Man-Environment Approach to Urban Form and Design* (London 1977), 289–95; M. J. Daunton, *House and Home in the Victorian City: Working Class Housing 1850–1914* (London 1983), 11–13.
[6] H. D. Littlejohn, *Report on the Sanitary Condition of the City of Edinburgh* (Edinburgh 1865), 1. The first sentence begins 'When the Act for the Registration of Births, Deaths and Marriages was extended to Scotland in 1855, it first became possible to ascertain with precision the mortality of our cities and towns, and to compare it . . .'.
[7] M. Glendinning, R. MacInnes and A. Mackenzie, *A History of Scottish Architecture: From the Renaissance to the Present Day* (Edinburgh 1996), 273–4; A. Macpherson, *Report of Committee of the Working Classes of Edinburgh on the Present Overcrowded and Uncomfortable State of their Dwelling-Houses* (Edinburgh 1860), 6.
[8] ECA SL37/2, SL37/16, SL37/37, ff. 387–449, 450–70, City of Edinburgh Accounts. The figure of *c.* 650 properties in 1905 is a conservative one since another list identified 802. The lower figure is preferred since it excludes a number of very minor properties, such as street booths.

ously undeveloped areas of the city. This was particularly the case with an administrative chain of command for fire and police which relied on local and district sub-stations and brought symbols of authority to all areas of the city. These and other municipal buildings were invested with meanings and memories for local residents, as can be glimpsed by the number of admissions to the 'steamies' – on average 420 people used the Nicolson Square baths and washhouses each week between 1848 and 1853 – and by the resonances such stage and screen productions of this topic have evoked in recent times.[9] The Edinburgh School Board, founded in 1872, initiated an active programme of building throughout the city (fig. 14.1). If not cloned, there was none the less a strong degree of visual uniformity introduced into the built environment by J. A. Carfrae, the School Board architect whose 'heavy, rock-faced classicism'[10] was a distinctive signature in the townscape to which Conan Doyle's description of the London schools as 'Beacons of the future . . . big, isolated clumps of buildings rising up above the slates' seems just as apt.[11]

With the initial phase of gas and water undertakings behind them most municipalities in Britain then turned their attention in the second half of the nineteenth century to important, if less life-threatening, instructional responsibilities – museums, libraries and galleries. In some English cities council building programmes assumed the significance of municipal virility tests with efforts to outdo neighbouring boroughs in the extent and magnificence of their civic creations. Glasgow Corporation might be accused of town hall testosterone but not so their Edinburgh counterparts where delay and confusion characterised the proposed extensions to the city chambers.[12] Scarred by the memory of earlier overextended city projects associated with the New Town which had brought the treasurer's department into acute debt, Edinburgh did not reproduce the cultural clusters of Birmingham's civic centre or Liverpool's William Brown Square.

Buildings on an immense scale became an increasingly familiar part of the Victorian landscape of Edinburgh, as in other cities. Administered by appointees, experts and a scattering of councillors who formed the trustees and management boards for a profusion of Victorian institutions,

[9] *Edinburgh Evening News*, 18 June 1853.

[10] Glendinning, MacInnes and Mackenzie, *A History of Scottish Architecture*, 332.

[11] A. Conan Doyle, *The Naval Treaty*, in W. S. B. Gould, ed., *The Annotated Sherlock Holmes* (London 1969), 179, quoted in W. M. Stephen, *Fabric and Function: A Century of School Building in Edinburgh 1872–1972* (privately published 1996), 20; D. E. B. Weiner, *Architecture and Social Reform in Late Victorian London* (Manchester 1994), 65–82.

[12] *Builder*, 1886, L, 601; 1887, LI, 262, 298, 332, 370, 646; 1888, LII, 209, 299, 311, 330, 341, 380, 384, 386, 390, 394, 398, 402, 406, 406–7, 432–3, 437, 440, 444–5, 472, 476, 480, 483, 493, 499, 500, 510–11, 514–15, 566, 568, 572, 604, 638, 906, 910, 917; 1889, LIII, 234, 562, 568–9; 1890, LIV, 448; 1891, LV, 158.

Figure 14.1 Signature in stone: a plaque typical of those on Edinburgh School Board buildings

Note: each plaque showed a pupil instructed by a caring (female) teacher.

legal responsibility for several aspects of social care fell ultimately upon the local authority. In keeping with the enduring Victorian distinction between 'deserving' and 'undeserving' cases, those adjudged worthy were interned and monitored in extensive and intimidating institutions. Lunatic asylums and workhouses with their associated hospitals ringed the city with only the Royal Infirmary centrally located alongside the medical school and bordering the Meadows. City boundaries dominated the location of hospitals and sanatoria, partly because the central area was already heavily built-up but also, it has been argued, such institutions were so land hungry that only in periods of depressed residential building could the necessary extent of land be afforded.[13] Certainly, the 'buildings for the sad, the bad and the mad'[14] and for the hospital and workhouses of Edinburgh and Leith were built mainly beyond the city boundaries but there is little evidence to support a pattern of institutional building which ran counter to fluctuations in residential construction.[15]

Between 1850 and 1914 almost 1,000 new civic, public, governmental and ecclesiastical buildings were built in Edinburgh. These fundamentally altered perspectives and urban textures. The scale of buildings was monumental; their spires, cupolas and rotundas were unmistakable. Informality succumbed to regulated spaces and the permeable nature of ancient wynds and closes was replaced by the impenetrability of public buildings and reinforced by railway cuttings, extensive warehouses and offices, commonly defended by fortress-like factory walls with their gate-keepers and commissionaires.

Important though this civic and institutional dimension was, by far the most fundamental change to the Edinburgh townscape, and that most relevant to the majority of its citizens, was in the volume of residential building which was completed in the second half of the nineteenth century. In the wake of the financial collapse of 1825–6 relatively little working-class housing was built for over a quarter of a century. With population increases and pent-up demand, then when the upturn in the

---

[13] J. W. R. Whitehand, 'The building cycle and the urban fringe in Victorian cities: a reply', *Journal of Historical Geography*, 4, 1978, 79–96; and J. W. R. Whitehand, *The Changing Face of Cities* (Oxford 1987), 26–9, 36–44, 76–94.

[14] T. A. Markus, 'Buildings for the sad, the bad and the mad in urban Scotland 1780–1830', in T. A. Markus, ed., *Order in Space and Society: Architectural Form and its Context in the Scottish Enlightenment* (Edinburgh 1982), 25–113.

[15] Other institutional building on the urban fringe included: New Craighouse Asylum 1889–94 (now Napier University), Craiglockhart Poor House and City Hospital for Infectious Diseases 1896–1903, Craigleith Poorhouse (Western General Hospital), Royal Victoria Hospital extension 1894, and 1903–6, Leith Public Health Hospital 1893 (Northern General) and Leith Poorhouse 1903–7 (Eastern General). See R. Rodger, 'Scottish urban housebuilding 1870–1914', University of Edinburgh PhD thesis, 1975, 97, for details of cycles in housing and public building.

levels of housebuilding did occur there was a transformation in the townscape from the 1860s. Areas such as Tollcross, Lothian Road and Fountainbridge which had been blighted for thirty years flourished. Ribbon developments on either side of major thoroughfares were completed, and streets such as Leith Walk and Easter Road, where vacant lots had previously punctuated the terraces of tenements, were quickly filled to convey the impression of coherent development. Former country mansions were engulfed by new tenements, and then demolished to make way for more – as at Drumdryan, Roseneath and Sciennes to the south and Hillhousefield, Bathfield and Bonnington in the north.

In the century between 1811 and 1911 the housing stock in Edinburgh increased fivefold; between 1871 and 1911 the increase was 100%.[16] Over this forty year period, the housing stock increased by more than the number of houses accumulated over the entire history of Edinburgh. Doubling the size of any city in 2000 by the year 2040 would be a formidable undertaking yet this is what was achieved in Edinburgh in the forty years before the First World War. Over the years 1871 to 1911 the level of residential investment required is difficult to comprehend but was in the order of £76 million, or approximately £4 billion in the prices of the year 2000.[17] Bearing in mind that public building was very active in these years, too, that industrial investment in new plant and locations was vigorous and that there was a steady and often substantial amount of repair and maintenance work in the form of alterations and additions, then the overall figure was significantly higher – over £165 million in 1911 prices and equivalent to about £8.8 billion for all building work in the years 1871 to 1911.[18]

The drama of this urban development introduced new dimensions into the Edinburgh townscape. Rather than inhabiting the 'made-down' homes abandoned by the wealthy, new housing for the working classes

[16] Before 1881 the census definition considered a tenement as a single house. An exact figure, therefore, cannot be accurately obtained for previous decades. However, by projecting the ratio of housing stock to population on previous census figures for Edinburgh, the housing stock can be estimated. This is certain to overstate the houses in earlier censuses since the density of occupancy used in 1881 was considerably lower than in previous decades. See ECA ACC 264, Guildry cuttings files, and Dean of Guild Court registers.

[17] This is calculated on the basis of an apportionment of new housing on the basis of 36% tenements and 64% villas which is consistent with the Edinburgh data for 1880–1914, and at a pricing of £798 for villas and £4,238 for tenements, again consistent with data for Edinburgh. The unit price of £265 per flat is also close to that for James Steel's Comely Bank portfolio. A price index is applied on the basis of 1911 as the base year and so does not take account of changing price levels between 1870 and 1914. To do so would be arbitrary but would certainly increase the overall levels of residential investment.

[18] Rodger, 'Scottish urban housebuilding 1870–1914', 80. The division of building work was, approximately, residential 46%; industrial 25%; public 15%; alterations and additions 10%. Civil engineering work is excluded from these calculations.

was purpose built virtually for the first time. Granted, this was after 1860 and mostly for the skilled working classes, so the families of the unskilled and casually employed continued to compete for overpriced and defective accommodation in and around the Old Town. Though it took several years to complete some streets, the pace of building was often hectic and entire areas were transformed.

New suburbs developed. Industrial suburbs in Dalry and Abbeyhill, and then at Gorgie and Jock's Lodge, were initially connected to the east–west axis of railway development, though the related warehousing and distribution facilities improved employment prospects for all grades of workers and so acted as a magnet to migrants. Some were accommodated in co-operative colonies, housing plantations located on the urban frontier at Stockbridge, Dalry and Abbeyhill, and like the American frontier as it moved outwards so, too, did settlement to Restalrig, North Merchiston and Shaftesbury Park.

In twentieth-century language, these were housing estates developed for workers on new industrial estates. Economies of scale and technological changes meant that for many Edinburgh factory owners a migration to green field sites was essential to sustain their market position. William Younger's Holyrood Brewery, Nelson's Parkside printing works and several bonded warehouses were relocated on the borders of Holyrood Park. At Abbeyhill, a cluster of large-scale premises included Moray Park Maltings, Miller and Co.'s London Road Foundry, established in 1867, which made wheels for railway stock and papermaking, and the Royal Blind Asylum's Workshops.[19] Holyrood Flint Works employed skilled immigrant glass-workers, some of whom lived in the nearby Norton Park 'Colonies'.[20] In Dalry, the extensive Fountain Brewery, Grove Street Biscuit Factory, established in 1868, and pioneering North British Rubber Company's Castle Mills (fig. 14.2), established in 1843, employed large workforces which were housed in the Edinburgh Co-operative Building Company's properties and the tenements built by James Steel and others on land feued by James Walker and James Home Rigg in the 1860s and 1870s.[21] Other major employers who moved green field sites included Bertrams' at St Katherine Works, Sciennes – the 'largest and best equipped paper-makers' engineers . . . in Britain'[22] – A. M. Fleming and Co., oil refiners, established from 1852 at their extensive Caroline Park works near Granton, and D. Bruce Peebles' Tay Works in

[19] Anon., *Scotland of To-day: Edinburgh, its Capital and the East Coast Ports* (Edinburgh 1890), 98–9; Anon., *A Descriptive Account of Edinburgh Illustrated* (London 1891), 106–8.

[20] Census of Scotland, 1871, Enumerator's Book 685²25; 1891, Enumerator's Book 685³14–17; Anon., *Scotland of To-day*, 132–3.

[21] Anon., *Edinburgh Illustrated*, 46–8, 85–7.   [22] Anon., *Edinburgh Illustrated*, 60.

(a)

(b)

Figure 14.2 Industrial estates nineteenth-century style
(a) Grove Street Bakery   (b) North British Rubber Company's Castle Mills, both Fountainbridge

Sources: Edinburgh Central Library, Anon., *Edinburgh Illustrated* (Brighton 1891), 46, 86.

Bonnington which produced gas meters, governors and valves. Demand for new artisanal housing was generated by a diverse and spatially widespread industrial sector in Edinburgh and builders were not slow to respond to these changes in the housing market.

From the 1860s the process of industrial decentralisation owed much to the diseconomies which many firms experienced in central Edinburgh. The ancient pattern of small-scale production from premises in the Pleasance, Fountainbridge, the Old Town and even in the back lanes of the New Town provided external economies up to a point – proximity to suppliers, sales outlets and commercial information. However, beyond a certain scale of production, central locations were a severe disadvantage – physical limitations to sites, traffic congestion and an undue dependence on road freight in the age of the railway. It was a measure of the maturity of the Edinburgh economy as it shifted emphasis from workshop to factory production that ancient relationships at the workplace were abandoned as inappropriate and relocation of the plant and workforce deemed essential. The multiplier effects of relocation by a few major industrialists on specialist suppliers, services and retailers has been the basis of industrial and regional policy in the twentieth century where industrial estates and New Towns have been developed with a few high profile companies luring small firms in their wake. Victorian industrialists figured out the economics of industrial location for themselves.

While business strategy played an important role in where and when housing development took place in Edinburgh, two other factors were also significant. By 1860 it was evident amongst some elements of the working class that affordable, solid, sanitary and self-contained housing was attainable; amongst philanthropists and ministers it was increasingly evident that a new dimension to housing the workers was essential. So business and housing priorities coincided in the 1860s with a moral dimension injected into the spatial reorganisation of the city.

The second factor was topographical. The east–west axis had been the ancient route by which produce was brought into Edinburgh with the Grassmarket–Cowgate as the principal artery. The reason was simple: in a city of hills relatively easy gradients were essential considerations where heavy goods traffic was concerned – and an important factor in the construction of bridges in the city between 1760 and 1830. Abbeyhill and Dalry were in some respects simply further east and further west – nineteenth-century extensions on the same transport axis. Gradients were important, too, for canal and railway engineers who had utilised even ground to gain access to Edinburgh in the 1820s and 1840s and, logically, the companies sited their goods depots nearby. In the 1860s, industrialists followed this lead to establish new 'industrial estates' and so areas of nineteenth-century working-class housing development reflected, in broad terms, this east–west orientation. By contrast, and somewhat over-simplified, the north–south orientation was the direction which middle-class housing development followed, assisted from the 1870s by tramway routes. As the phrase 'lines of class distinction' implies, on the basis of their fare structure tramcars were essentially a middle-class mode of transport.[23] So steep were the north–south gradients that the uphill effort required fresh teams of horses when pulling Edinburgh trams. In turn, this limited the number of tram routes which operated across the folds of hills and, as a consequence, insulated middle-class areas from invasions by both commercial activities and working-class housing. For a time at least, the spatial extent of the city was constrained, and though occasionally the Merchant Company and other landowners pressed the Edinburgh Tramway Company to develop tram lines into the suburbs the Tramway manager explained cogently that they were not disposed to anticipate property development:

If tramways were to succeed [in financial terms] feuing must precede . . . and tramways would not precede in order that feuing might succeed.[24]

Except perhaps for the New Town, middle-class suburbs were also a new development – to the south in Newington in the 1820s and the Grange from the 1840s, and then successively in Merchiston and Morningside and across the Dean Bridge to the north at Learmonth. While this spatial and social segregation was underway in general terms, the experience of James Steel and the evidence of Valuation Rolls throughout the city suggest that these were by no means socially homogeneous developments; within streets, and even within tenements on different floors, a socially diverse group of tenants lived. Nevertheless, the centrifugal forces which created socially homogeneous middle-class suburbs in English cities were also at work in Edinburgh. Though middle-class flats retained some of their appeal throughout the period, the advance of the ubiquitous English semi-detached villa was difficult to resist and it took a firm hold in the south side suburbs. Even so, compared to English cities of an equivalent size, it proved difficult to dislodge completely middle- and upper-middle-class households from the central districts of Edinburgh. In England, the process of degradation in the central areas was based generally on the subdivision of substantial town houses into several units which then were quickly penetrated by lower income groups.[25] Something of this had taken place in Edinburgh by the 1830s

[23] A. D. Ochojna, 'Lines of class distinction: an economic and social history of the British tramcar with special reference to Edinburgh and Glasgow', University of Edinburgh PhD thesis, 1974, chs. 5 and 6.   [24] ECA SL1, Town Council Minutes, 20 Dec. 1881.
[25] See, for example, the experience of various cities in S. D. Chapman, ed., *The History of Working Class Housing: A Symposium* (Newton Abbot 1971).

and, accelerated by office and institutional demands for city centre space, certainly was well advanced in the New Town along George and Princes Streets by 1850.[26] But the sheer number of neo-classical city centre apartments completed in Edinburgh and the fact that they were in an area physically detached from the principal industrial and working-class districts inoculated the Edinburgh city centre against the very influences which undermined social exclusivity and architectural integrity in major English cities.

With the compression of a considerable amount of housebuilding into a relatively short space of time between 1870 and 1914, it was inevitable that the similarities in materials and architectural details gave an impression of architectural coherence. In fact, the economics of building and the administrative process of petitioning for a permit to build contributed to the effect of standardisation. Laying pipes and foundations, as well as constructing masonry walls and roof lines, were both easier and less costly when undertaken in straight lines and this helped to contain the costs of building and so restrain rents. As James Steel's experience showed, there were considerably lower levels of unlet property at the cheaper end of the rental market and so the characteristics of the building industry contributed to the standardised appearance of housing. Overall, this has caused architectural historians to liken the development of tenements after 1860 to a four storey equivalent of a medieval wall, with windows.[27]

Visual standardisation resulted in no small measure from the influence exerted by landowners through the feu charters. Inexorably, the number of clauses specifying feuing restrictions grew in number and length. The five page charters governing the earliest New Town feus issued by the town council were insufficiently specific and Heriot's trustees from the outset insisted on very detailed feuing conditions concerning pavement widths, cellar dwellings, roof heights and other details, all of which were laid down in feet and inches, with little scope for misinterpretation.[28] Certainly, some of the clauses in these and the feu charters of other superiors were formulaic, but the message that the superior was engaged actively in monitoring adherence to the feuing stipulations encouraged developers to adhere to the letter as well as to the spirit of the agreement. The feuing restrictions imposed by Heriot's trustees to define building quality and design were embedded in their feu charters over a quarter of a century before the House of Lords' decision in 1818 signalled that other

[26] G. Gordon, 'The status areas of early to mid-Victorian Edinburgh', *Transactions Institute of British Geographers*, 4, 1979, 168–91.

[27] Glendinning, MacInnes and Mackenzie, *A History of Scottish Architecture*, 510.

[28] ECA box O, bundle 1/6, Contract between the City of Edinburgh and Heriot's Hospital, 12 Feb. 1806.

superiors would have to follow suit. With this legal ambiguity resolved from 1818 and feuars reassured about the future amenity of their plots, then development could proceed unhindered. The Heriot's feuing conditions were a benchmark for disciplined development and, on their own property and that of others, a high degree of visual uniformity was imposed through detailed stipulations. The principles of urban estate management developed by Heriot's were plagiarised by institutional and private landowners alike who printed copies of similar feuing conditions for prospective developers.[29]

While the legal and institutional apparatus was an important element in the standardisation of the built environment in Edinburgh, it was not inevitably so. There is little doubt that the dominant position of endowed hospitals, principally George Heriot's, limited the scope for irregular frontages and roof lines. Even where the Heriot Trust feued to a developer who then sub-feued to another, then all tiers in the pyramid of development had to conform to the feuing conditions set by Heriot's. The unity of the New Town, largely feued by Heriot's, however, was a reflection of the demand for exclusive housing from surgeons, advocates, merchants, as well as from annuitants and aristocratic family members, often from other parts of Scotland as well as from Edinburgh. It was a seller's market in the last third of the eighteenth century and Heriot's could define the terms of building and protect the value of their assets – building plots. By contrast, in the areas of south Edinburgh which the Heriot Trust owned, no such fierce feuing conditions were set and the boundary lines of Heriot's property are impossible to discern. Partly this is to be explained by the timing of the release of feus. Where these were before c. 1760 then Heriot's, too, were fairly relaxed about the terms of their feu dispositions, only in the mid-eighteenth century converting themselves from agricultural improvers in north Edinburgh to developers as the pace of economic growth and urbanisation quickened and improved the long-term prospects of their estates. In some cases, as at Canonmills, Redbraes, Logie Green and other plots adjoining the Water of Leith, the opportunity to feu was governed by the industrial and commercial possibilities presented by water power. To take advantage of this potential, feus were often fragmented and irregular in shape and predetermined by the meandering river itself.[30] Here, too, demand influenced

---

[29] ECA/MC/GWH/box 3/7, Articles and Conditions of Feu of the Dovecroft and East Parks of Merchiston, 28 June 1852; ECA ACC 373, Sir James Steel's Trust, Miscellaneous boxes, Conditions of Feu of the Lands of Parts of Dalry belonging to Mr James Steel, n.d.

[30] NAS RH4/152/83–5, St Leonard's feus to David Reid (1690) and Andrew Gairden (1691); ECA George Heriot's Roll of Superiorities, 1913, for example, and the feus to Anna Biggar for areas of Buccleugh Street, Arthur Street, both 1737, and St Leonard's, 1757.

the physical appearance of the city in the future and, since the release of feus predated the concept of the regular street pattern of the New Town and because it was inappropriate in an industrial setting to insist on the style and design of such buildings, then Heriot's did not impose strict feuing conditions. The visual legacy was accordingly more irregular.

Irregularity, or individuality, was acceptable to superiors where large detached and semi-detached suburban villas were built in the Grange, Craigmillar Park, Merchiston and Colinton on the estates owned by the Dick-Cunningham family, and by George Watson's and James Gillespie's trustees. For the most part feu charters were unspecific about architectural characteristics but, by stating the value of the house to be built on a plot, the superiors defined the social tone by a different means. In a finely tuned social hierarchy, George Watson's trustees specified in 1897 that 'semi-villas fronting Colinton Road' should be £1,600, Merchiston Gardens, £1,000 or £1,250 depending on which end of the street, Craighouse Road, £1,100, South and Gillsland Roads, £850.[31] The size of the plot itself – often a quarter and sometimes even half an acre – was a device to define the social character of an area and George Watson's trustees explicitly prohibited the subdivision of plots on their Abbotsford and Merchiston Park feus so as to prevent subsequent degradation.[32] The concept of amenity – promoting gardens and preserving trees, open spaces and access to the river – ran through Gillespie's trustees' feuing conditions and this reinforced the minimum price which was used to define the social tone.[33] The preamble to feuing conditions was equally discriminating as to the social cachet of the neighbourhood and in one of the more blatant statements, Gillespie's trustees commented on their most illustrious vassal, Rowand Anderson, a nationally known architect, but elided their Colinton feus not just with his development of several plots but with his social status.[34]

In a terrace of neo-classical housing where irregularity was immediately visible as an interruption to the building line, then feuing conditions tended to be more explicit as to points of detail. Future property values were closely connected with the architectural coherence of the development. However, where individualism was a selling point for estate devel-

---

[31] ECA MC/GWH, Conditions of Feu, Barony of Merchiston, 18 Mar. 1897.

[32] ECA MC/GWH, Charter by the Governors of George Watson's Hospital, Mar. 1855, f. 2.

[33] MC/JGH Chartulary of James Gillespie's Hospital, charter to William Anderson, 14 June 1808, vol. 1, f. 9, charter to J. C. Wright, 16 July 1903, vol. 4, f. 143, charter to Parish Council of Colinton, 16 May 1910, vol. 5, f. 408; ECA ACC 314, Walker's Trust, Minutes, 2 Jan. 1898, f. 216, and Minute of Agreement among beneficiaries and Letter of Indemnity, May 1897, ff. 212–13.

[34] MC/JGH, Box 3/8, Notes on the estate of Spylaw and Bonaly, 24 June 1891, f. 5.

opment, then the feuing documents filtered the social status and wealth of potential buyers by being more specific about gardens, plot size and building costs. Such a degree of flexibility within the feuing system was taken to a greater degree of sophistication by James Steel who preserved the externally standardised appearance of tenements but built flats of different sizes and rental levels within them, thus using internal differentiation to reach various elements of the housing market in his efforts to diversify his product, flats, and to limit risks.

Though the expense of estate layout and road construction fell to the developer, to fulfil the council's public health and public order responsibilities, as well as those of a moral and instructional nature, an extended programme of municipal intervention resulted from housing expansion in the second half of the nineteenth century. The civic mission was only possible, however, because of a fundamental shift in the nature of public finances which in turn was a reflection of a subtly changing relationship between the municipality and property owners. In the eighteenth and early nineteenth century the incidence of local taxes fell mainly on business and commerce with most of the town council's recurrent expenditure financed by tolls, taxes on particular products, customs and excise and, where appropriate, harbour dues. Even in the first half of the nineteenth century it was a system under pressure. The growing scale of civic responsibilities made the reform of this local taxation system essential, and by 1856 a new system was devised, based on property values. Residential rather than commercial interests shouldered most of the burden. At one level this provided a measure of subsidy to business interests as, increasingly, charges for water, roads, police and fire and other civic services fell on private property owners, tenants and landlords. At another level, it set a collision course between the interests of property owners and the obligations of the municipality over the cost and extent of council intervention. After a gentle increase in local taxation of about 30% in the course of twenty years from the late 1850s, the extended boundaries and expanded responsibilities induced a substantial rise thereafter.[35] Between 1880 and 1914, local taxes payable by owners doubled; rates payable by occupiers or tenants increased by 50%.[36] Overall local taxes on residential property increased by almost two-thirds.

In what is a somewhat circular argument, the expansion of housing in Edinburgh financed the growth of municipal services from 1875 to 1914

[35] ECA SL37/1–47, Municipal Accounts, 1857–1915; Parliamentary Papers, Local Taxation Returns, 1857–1916.
[36] These calculations are in money terms. However, though there was a considerable decline in prices in the 1880s and 1890s, the price indices by 1914 had recovered to 1880 levels. Accordingly, the percentage increases to rates are for both money and real terms.

through the rating system. Property interests accordingly enhanced their stature in the Council Chamber – 70–80% of councillors were landlords – and between 85 and 95% of the membership of the three most important council committees were landlords and those with property interests.[37] Yet, on the back of property taxation and in the name of housing improvement, the town council became increasingly involved as a supplier of homes for the very poor. Simultaneously, developments in the private sector were moving in an opposite direction from the 1860s as mortgage companies responded to the interest in home ownership shown by the skilled working class, shopkeepers and clerks, and to which the Edinburgh Co-operative Building Company also contributed. Numerically, the rented sector remained most significant, but this pluralism in the Edinburgh housing market, though not without its own tensions in future years over the direction and balance between public and private provision of housing, was an important mediating force which avoided the confrontational landlord v. tenant, capital v. labour relationships in Glasgow. With the Edinburgh economy pursuing a more gradualist expansion in the fifty years before the First World War based on diverse industrial interests and on significant and relatively stable financial, commercial and professional activities, then the city was cushioned from the economic crises which peppered the Glasgow economy. The trajectory of the Edinburgh economy together with the growth of owner occupancy and mixed tenures within tenements meant that the social tensions associated with unemployment and bankruptcy in Glasgow, which in turn spilled over into the housing market and political polarisation, were much more muted in Edinburgh. Even after 1919, when Scottish local authorities embraced council housing with great enthusiasm, the Edinburgh town council, more than any other, took advantage of treasury subsidies available to private owners.[38]

The power of the Edinburgh landowner was considerably enhanced in the century and a half which followed the founding of the New Town. Partly this was because little scope existed for the development of an Old Town already largely built up, but it was also because the creation of feu-duties was impossible within the ancient royalty. By breaking out of the spatially confined areas of the Old Town and Canongate new possibilities were created for those whose land lay in the eye of residential and industrial development. As with Heriot's, owners and trustees in general discovered that former agricultural lands attracted considerable premiums

[37] D. McCrone and B. Elliott, 'The decline of landlordism: property rights and relationships in Edinburgh', in R. Rodger, ed., *Scottish Housing in the Twentieth Century* (Leicester 1989), 221.
[38] A. O'Carroll, 'Tenements to bungalows: class and the growth of home ownership before the Second World War', *Urban History*, 24, 1997, 221–41.

when building could be anticipated. In its essentials, this differed little from the experience of English and Welsh landowners such as the Bute family (Cardiff), Derby and Sefton families (Liverpool), Fitzwilliam and Norfolk interests (Sheffield) and Ramsdens (Huddersfield) in English cities, or, indeed, of educational endowments such as Dulwich College (Camberwell), Eton College (Chalcots) or St John's College (Oxford).[39] Engulfed by urbanisation, windfall gains accrued to landowners.

In Scotland, though, the process differed in important essentials. Feuing conditions provided an effective mechanism by which to defend the development prospects of an estate since infractions entitled the land-owner, who never ceded ultimate ownership, to insist on compliance on penalty of the repossession of the property (irritancy). The same tech-nique was applied in England through restrictive covenants but proved much less significant there, first because there was no centralised land registry in which boundaries and property restrictions could be entered, and secondly because the enforceability of such covenants was question-able until the decision in 1848 in *Tulk* v. *Moxhay* clarified the position.[40] Even where the Scottish landowner sold his rights to future feu-duty rev-enues, still his agreement was obligatory for developments on the plot. The legal code imposed a strong degree of discipline on builders and developers. A landowner's interest in urban development was acknowl-edged in the additional feu-duties or 'casualty' payments for seemingly arbitrary events, such as the transfer of a property title to an heir or the nomination of a successor to the title of a property, as well as an occa-sional double feu-duty or 'duplicands' normally every nineteenth or twenty-first year. It was an assertion of the superior's power and authority over urban development. However, when, in 1874, landowners conceded the right to create new casualties it was a recognition of public concern about how these increased site costs and so adversely affected housing quality for those on low incomes.[41] The legal framework was not inflexible, therefore, and was responsive to wider concepts of social welfare, though it is more than possible that the use of compulsory pur-chase and, later, municipal housing rendered superiors compliant on this issue.

Discipline and flexibility were combined in the Scottish legal system and this had considerable significance for urban development in Edinburgh, and other burghs. The early challenges in 1772 and 1776 to the authority of James Craig's feuing plan clarified the position and

[39] D. N. Cannadine, *Lords and Landlords: The Aristocracy and the Towns 1774–1967* (Leicester 1980), 41–61.   [40] *Tulk* v. *Moxhay*, 1848, 2 Ph. 774.
[41] R. Rodger, 'The Victorian building industry and the housing of the Scottish working class', in M. Doughty, ed., *Building the Industrial City* (Leicester 1986), 151–206.

reassured potential developers and investors.[42] But when after 1809 additions and alterations, that is, changes of use to existing buildings, were contemplated then the previous decisions were eventually regarded as unsafe and from 1818 feuing conditions were tightened and used as the instruments to regulate what was built on a site and how its use was controlled in the future.

Custom and practice also reflected this mix of discipline and flexibility. Normally, landowners did not press their entitlements too far. They phased in feu-duties, aware that if they did insist upon a payment of feu-duties in full from the outset then they might prejudice the willingness of builders to become involved with them in the future. By means of a process called 'irritancy' landowners could recover control over their property if the developer of builder got into difficulty in making feu-duty payments, or if they transgressed feuing conditions. In a sense, this process provided an insurance premium to the superior and so did not inhibit a degree of risk taking with relatively unknown developers. This was the case with James Home Rigg's willingness to feu to James Steel who was such an unknown quantity in Edinburgh in 1866 that Rigg's trustees did not know of his earlier bankruptcy.

However, the most adaptable element of the process of urban development in Scotland was the creation of feu-duties. They were an ingenious and flexible device. Yet for over a century, from c. 1650 to 1750, a powerful and experienced estate managed by trustees, Heriot's Hospital, rarely feued property, preferring tacks by which to let farms and to derive income from land.[43] Feu-duties were annual payments, based on land, heritable and transmissible across the generations, and guaranteed payment before all other creditors. Feu-duties were payable 'in all time coming' and like other property obligations could be commuted by the payment of a lump sum; property rights could be created by each layer or vassal in the process called sub-infeudation. In short, feu-duties offered security, a means by which each element in the developmental chain – landowner, developer, builder, house owner and each of those amongst whom one of the stages might be shared, for example, when a developer dealt with several builders – could participate in the increased value of land and property as urbanisation proceeded. Each feuar in each tier could create rights and receive annual payments in the future. Since feu-duties were assets, their future value could be discounted and a lump sum realised by an investor or trust, to whom the right to receive the annual payment was transferred. Though this process and its implications are

---

[42] See chapter 2.
[43] K. G. C. Reid et. al., The Law of Property in Scotland (Edinburgh 1996), 378 n. 7, notes how few cases there were over real burdens.

explored in much greater depth in chapters 3 and 4, it is worth repeating that the practice of feuing elicited capital, sometimes in very modest amounts, from widows, shopkeepers and indeed any who sought a steady income, including those who used heritable securities as a means of providing for their pension. In so doing, the reservoir of capital to finance residential development was deepened and the threshold for property investment reduced and less 'lumpy' than in England.[44] In effect, a flexible and responsive legal system used solicitors and the high degree of public trust enshrined in their professional status to create the equivalent of private land banks by receiving deposits and guaranteeing an annual payment to investors. The effect was to unlock the future developed value of a property from the outset and so encourage small private investors, trusts, widows and annuitants, generally, to invest in property.

Thus the feuing system was participatory and 'inclusive'.[45] Instead of a unitary system of ownership, where absolute control to dispose of property was vested in a single individual and there were no restraints on the use of property, the system of property rights in Scotland devolved an interest in land to ever more participants as urbanisation gathered pace. So, though the landowner or feudal superior retained ultimate power and could veto building or other development, the creation of vassals and subsequent tiers of sub-vassals conveyed to them an interest in property, albeit within a framework set by the superior. In turn, the mortgaging of future rights to property income for a cash sum incorporated another group of investors. In each case, the ability of one layer of property interests to pay its feu-duty obligations to another, superior, interest was only possible as the potential of building sites for residential and manufacturing purposes was released. Industrial and commercial expansion bid up the value of undeveloped plots and, at the same time, improved expectations of future annual income streams based on feu-duties encouraged investors to come forward. It was this symbiotic relationship between industrial expansion and urban development which both prompted a change in feuing conditions from the 1820s and was then facilitated by it.

Two value systems – absolutism and liberalism – were in different trajectories. Towards the end of the eighteenth century, at the height of classical liberal thought, the idea of property was at the centre of conceptual schemes of political philosophers and legal theorists.[46] Simple,

---

[44] D. Sugarman and R. Warrington, 'Land law, citizenship, and the invention of "Englishness": the strange world of the equity of redemption', in J. Brewer and S. Staves, eds., *Early Modern Conceptions of Property* (London 1996), 111–43.

[45] C. B. Macpherson, 'Liberal-democracy and property', in C. B. Macpherson, ed., *Property: Mainstream and Critical Positions* (Oxford 1978), 202, uses the term.

[46] For a useful introduction and overview see J. Waldron, *The Right to Property* (Oxford 1988), and Macpherson, ed., *Property*.

unrestrained ownership of property was at the core of this eighteenth-century value system with freedom and equality of status conveyed by an individual's control over property. In several American state constitutions property was identified as one of the natural rights of man, and the French Civil Code defined property as 'the right of enjoying and dispos-ing of things in the most absolute manner'.[47] Absolute and unrestrained rights over property were accordingly at the heart of liberalism and criti-cal to the assault on feudalism with its complex hierarchy of land tenure relationships based on lord and vassal.

During the French Revolution feudal property was abolished. During the American Revolution Jefferson extolled the virtue of a system of land titles unencumbered by feudal restrictions, and in England during the 1760s the foremost jurist, William Blackstone, denounced the archaic nature of feudal tenure.[48] In Scotland, by contrast, the fortunes of feudal tenure were in the ascendant, though not without checks and balances to restrain the power of the landowners. Broadening participation in both heritable property and securities was one mechanism which distributed rising land values to a range of interests – annuitants, widows, small private trusts and institutions – rather than just to landowners them-selves. Another was that as property was feued so the remaining amount of undeveloped land concentrated in the hands of an individual or institu-tion declined. This limited an individual's or institution's potential to direct future development strategy; it also limited the landowners' future gains from rising land values while increasing that of developers and builders to whom the land had been feued.

In those countries where feudalism was in retreat liberal formulations of property were confronted by a paradox. Where property owners had an individual right to the exclusive use and disposal of plots of land, then under free market conditions this resulted in a concentration of owner-ship, resources and power which infringed equality of status, the central tenet of liberalism. The very freedom of contract on which the capitalist market system was constructed could not logically prevent individual and unequal appropriations of wealth and power. This paradox, it has been claimed, can only be resolved by adopting a wider definition of property based on greater participation in property rights and benefits.[49] In nineteenth-century Edinburgh this was exactly what transpired. Though

[47] R. Schlatter, *Private Property: The History of an Idea* (London 1951), 188–9; B. A. Ackerman, *Private Property and the Constitution* (New Haven 1977), 97–167; Macpherson, ed., *Property*; J. R. Macey, 'Property rights, innovation and constitutional structure', in E. F. Paul *et al.*, *Property Rights* (Cambridge 1994), 181–208.

[48] W. Blackstone, *Commentaries on the Laws of England*, 4 vols. (London 1796).

[49] Macpherson, 'Liberal-democracy', 201. Greater inclusivity is not quite synonymous with Macpherson's 'not being excluded from' property rights.

the absolutist powers of the feudal superior were retained, the creation of claims on property filtered down to other tiers in the property hierarchy who in turn benefited from the capital gains and rising rental incomes which were associated with urbanisation. Through solicitors, building associations and heritable security companies, trusts and private investors, including petty capitalists amongst the shopocracy and labour aristocracy, enjoyed greater participation in rising land and property values in the course of the nineteenth century as Scotland developed a unique blend of absolutist and liberal property principles.

Set in the context of an increasing degree of national and municipal autonomy in the early nineteenth century and accompanied by an expanding industrial and commercial base, the evolution of a system of private property rights in Scotland was part of a process internal to the development of capitalism itself. Scottish urban development in the nineteenth century flourished not only as a result of the income generation or demand-led influences which resulted from economic growth, but also because the legal system responded to an urgent need from the professional and manufacturing classes to protect their investment in property. From the 1820s, more specific restrictions were embedded in feu charters to give an increased measure of protection as to the future use and value of property. The advance of capitalism in Scotland, therefore, was closely meshed with the advance of private property rights and tenure: the two phenomena were mutually reinforcing. As with specialisation and the subdivision of manufacturing processes to achieve greater productivity and growth, so property owners subdivided their original ownership rights by granting numerous feus. On the basis of these private agreements landowners created a complex of elaborate and abstract institutions and claims characteristic of industrial capitalism – trusts, bonds, annuities and obligations of various kinds. These subdivisions of property rights were predicated upon the hierarchical feudal relations which existed between lord and vassal, that is, between superior and feuar, and without which the pace, character and urban form of Scottish urban development would have been different.

The subdivision of property rights meant that small investors and trusts were encouraged to place their funds at the disposal of solicitors and, from the 1870s, of property investment companies who then aggregated these to buy heritable securities – the right to receive feu-duties on a property in the future – with a lump sum paid over to the builder or developer. Thus, in a relatively small country with limited financial resources, the investment leakages were contained and the lure of English municipal bonds and imperial bank stocks resisted. Limited supplies of capital were recirculated to enrich Scottish economic growth and urban development.

This was the real significance of the lump sum purchase of future feu-duty revenues by the Church of Scotland which injected capital into James Steel's early enterprises at Tollcross, or of their involvement, jointly, with the Merchant Company in purchasing feu-duties which salvaged a precarious financial situation for the Trinity Land Company.[50] Tactically, the investment strategy was of advantage to institutions, trusts and private investors alike but for businesses, whether in building or in other spheres of production, ownership of property rights provided access to capital. As a consequence, urban development in Scotland was liberated by the feuing system.

There is nothing which so generally strikes the imagination, and engages the affections of mankind, as the right of property.[51]

[50] See chapters 4 and 6.
[51] Blackstone, *Commentaries*, vol. II, 2.

Principal sources

EDINBURGH CITY ARCHIVES

ECA Catalogue of Monuments and Burial Grounds
ECA Chartulary, Extended Royalty
ECA City of Edinburgh Superiorities 1875–1914
ECA Dean of Guild Court Registers. Index to plans: Edinburgh, 1860–1914 (7 vols.); Leith 1877–1914 (2 vols.). See also SL144/52–63 for DGC decisions.
ECA George Heriot's Roll of Superiorities, various years
ECA Index of Maps and Plans. Bundles 1–5
ECA ACC 50, Norton Family Papers 1830s–80s
ECA ACC 58, Titles to nineteenth- and twentieth-century properties
ECA ACC 59, James Allan Papers
ECA ACC 81, Edinburgh Water Supply – newspaper cuttings 1871–81, 4 vols.
ECA ACC 85, Leith Improvement Scheme 1885–1916
ECA ACC 95, Titles to various High St and Nicolson St properties
ECA ACC 100, St Cuthbert's Lodge of Free Gardeners
ECA ACC 119, Dr Inglis' Trust
ECA ACC 221, Miscellaneous legal titles, sixteenth to nineteenth centuries
ECA ACC 230, Mathieson Family Papers 1804–1935
ECA ACC 232, Dr Watson's Trust
ECA ACC 237, Edinburgh Society for Relief of Indigent Old Men
ECA ACC 261, Feu Plans and Maps
ECA ACC 264, George Watson's Hospital Estate Reports, 3 vols., 1802–65; Merchant Company Accounts, 7 vols., 1868–92; Guildry Cuttings file
ECA ACC 282, James Walker's Papers, North Merchiston (5 vols.)
ECA ACC 284, Correspondence of Thomas Lamb, Leith
ECA ACC 300, Titles to property (miscellaneous)
ECA ACC 308, Subscribers to Unemployment Relief Fund
ECA ACC 313, Miss E. G. Robertson's Trust
ECA ACC 314, John W. Walker's Trust
ECA ACC 315, James Kirkwood's Trust
ECA ACC 316, Samuel Gilmour's Trust
ECA ACC 322, John Chesser's Trust
ECA ACC 322, Sir William Forrest of Comiston's Papers
ECA ACC 328, Mrs Matilda Mill's Trust

ECA ACC 333, Legal Papers relating to 36 South Bridge

ECA ACC 334, Hay Borthwick Family Papers

ECA ACC 373, Sir James Steel's Trust

ECA MC/box 2/1–33, Miscellaneous: notes, bequests, properties

ECA MC/DSH/box 3/1–9, Daniel Stewart's Hospital, property papers, 1791–1910

ECA MC/GG/box 11, George Grindlay's Trust: Minute Books, 6 vols., 1801–1909

ECA MC/GG/box 3/1–4, George Grindlay's Trust, estate and property papers, 1801–79

ECA MC/GWH/box 3/1–18, George Watson's Hospital, property papers, 1730–1914

ECA/MC/JGH/box 3/1–8, James Gillespie's Hospital, Colinton estate papers, 1812–1900

ECA/MC/MMH/box 2/5–28, Merchant Maiden Hospital, property and estate papers, 1728–1914

ECA Shelf 48, Canongate Feu-Duty Ledger 1885–1907

ECA Shelf 50, Canongate Land Tax 1839–51

ECA Shelf 59, Princes Street Proprietors' Sederunt Books, vols. 1–3, 1816–30

ECA Shelf 68, Trinity Hospital Records, vols.1–9, 1816–81

ECA Shelf 86, Lindsay's Trust 1836–41

ECA Shelf 86, Professor Dick's Trust, 3 vols., 1866–77

ECA Shelf 86, Charles Raitt's Trust 1827–42

ECA Shelf 86, Robert Allan's Papers, Leith, 1832–7

ECA Shelf 86, William Reid's Papers 1843–50

ECA Shelf 90, Lord Alva's Feu-Duty Ledger 1837–51

ECA Shelf 92, Feu and Tack Leet 1863–5

ECA Shelf 142, Inventory of Charter Deeds and Title Deeds

ECA SL1/181–370, Town Council Record, various volumes from 1820

ECA SL12/35, Deeds of Foundation of Several Charities 1842

ECA SL12/40, Miscellaneous Items and Deposits: newspaper cuttings, Gowans, 1867–86

ECA SL12/169, Sievewright Papers: lands of Dalry and Gorgie, accounts

ECA SL12/210–14, Maps of Edinburgh

ECA SL25/1, Lord Provost's Committee, Minute Books

ECA SL26, Public Health Committee, various volumes from 1872

ECA SL35/15, Stent Rolls, various to 1829

ECA SL37/1–47, Edinburgh Corporation Abstract of Accounts 1864–1915

ECA SL47/1, Streets and Buildings Committee Minutes, various from 1858

ECA SL63/1–6, Improvement Act 1827. Minutes, Letter Books, Financial Records, Miscellaneous, Title Deeds

ECA SL64/1–5, Edinburgh City Improvement Act 1867. Minutes, Letter Books, Financial Records, Legal Records, Miscellaneous

ECA SL65, Edinburgh City Improvement Act 1893

ECA SL66, Housing of the Working Classes Acts 1888–1900 (published reports)

ECA SL104/3/1–3, Wester Dalry Chartularies

ECA SL104/4–5, Hillhousefield and Bathfield Chartularies
ECA SL105, Dalry Chartularies
ECA SL136/1–2, Report Relative to the Pensioners of the Society for Relief of
      Indigent Old Men

EDINBURGH CENTRAL LIBRARY

There is an immense collection of pamphlets and related contemporary literature
on housing and health in the Edinburgh Room of the Central Library and to cite
this material would be to reproduce large sections of the catalogue. Particular use
was made of:
Census Enumerators' Books, Edinburgh and Leith, 1871, 1881, 1891
Edinburgh and Leith Post Office Directories, 1840–1914
Voters' Rolls
Extensive use was made of images contained in the following collections:
Balmain Collection
Begbie Collection
Calotype Club
Inglis Collection
Skene Collection
Visual Index

EDINBURGH CITY ARTS CENTRE

City of Edinburgh Art Collection: catalogue and selected transparencies

NATIONAL ARCHIVES OF SCOTLAND

NAS BT2, Bankruptcy Papers, various
NAS BT2/284, Industrial Co-operative Building Company (Limited)
NAS BT2/547, Edinburgh Heritable Security Co. Ltd
NAS BT2/562, General Property Investment Company
NAS BT2/575; /652, Land Feuing Company
NAS BT2/3236, Edinburgh House Proprietors Co. Ltd
NAS BT2/3506, Building Trades Exchange
NAS BT2/9240, Edinburgh House Factorage Co. Ltd
NAS CB, Coal Board Papers
NAS CH1, Church of Scotland Papers various
NAS CH1/19, Church of Scotland Endowment Committee Accounts
NAS CH1/33, Church of Scotland Feu Register and Appropriation Book
NAS CH1/34, Church of Scotland Endowment Committee Minutes; Sub-
      Committee on Endowment of Chapels of Ease; Subscriptions
NAS CH1/5, Church of Scotland Endowment Scheme Finance Committee
      Reports and Minutes 1859–65
NAS CS, Court of Session – various Sequestrations

NAS E106/1/1 Valuation Roll, 1649
NAS E106/22/4–6, Cess Book of the County of Edinburgh 1771–2; Valuation Book, 1814
NAS GD1/777, Edinburgh Co-operative Building Company
NAS GD327, Papers of C. Norman Kemp
NAS GD327/488–91; /508, Articles of Association, Annual Reports and Accounts of Edinburgh Co-operative Building Company, House Sales 1862–1912
NAS GD421/1–3, Personal Papers and Executry of George Heriot, 1583–1685
NAS GD421/4, George Heriot's Hospital and Trust; Cartularies; Minute Books; Register of feu-duties; Inventory of Titles
NAS GD421/5, George Heriot's Hospital and Trust; Treasurer's Accounts; Abstracts of Hospital and Trust Accounts; Financial Papers
NAS GD421/9, George Heriot's Hospital and Trust; Estate Papers
NAS RH4/152, Records of George Heriot's Hospital and Trust
NAS RHP, Register House Plans – various
NAS RS27; RS108, Register of Sasines, Edinburgh
NAS RS54, Register of Sasines, Glasgow
NAS SC70, Books of Session and Council
NAS VR55/12–156, Valuation Rolls, Leith, 1866–1914
NAS VR100/69–311, Valuation Rolls, Edinburgh, 1867–1914

MERCHANT COMPANY (SEE ALSO UNDER ECA)

ECA MC/box 2/1–33, Miscellaneous: notes, bequests, properties
ECA MC/DSH/box 3/1–9, Daniel Stewart's Hospital, property papers, 1791–1910
ECA MC/GG/box 3/1–4, George Grindlay's Trust, estate and property papers, 1801–79
ECA MC/GWH/box 3/1–18, George Watson's Hospital, property papers, 1730–1914
ECA MC/JGH/box 3/1–8, James Gillespie's Hospital, Colinton estate papers, 1812–1900
ECA MC/MMH/box 2/5–28, Merchant Maiden Hospital, property and estate papers, 1728–1914
MC (Merchant Company archives), Drumdryan Chartulary, 3 vols., 1817–1920
MC, Falconhall Estate Chartulary, vol. 1
MC, Stead's Place, 2 vols., 1864–1903
MC, Warrender Park Crescent Feus, 1881–1913
MC, Annual Reports 1850–1909; Minutes 1696–1704, 1847–1923: box 6/1–3, box 7/14–21, box 8/22–4
MC/GG, George Grindlay's Trust: Orchardfield Chartularies, 5 vols., 1821–99
MC/GWH, Falconhall Estate, 2 vols., 1889–1914
MC/JGH, Chartularies of James Gillespie's Hospital, 5 vols., 1808–1923
MC/TLC, Trinity Land Company Chartularies, 2 vols., 1875–1914
National Library of Scotland, Merchant Company feuing plans

NORTHUMBERLAND COUNTY RECORD OFFICE

NCRO 493/17, Papers of John Richardson, lime merchant, Alnwick

ROYAL COMMISSION ON ANCIENT AND HISTORICAL MONUMENTS OF SCOTLAND

Maps, plans and photographs from the following series: A, B, C, ED, EDD, PB and PP. Specific items of particular relevance include:

A22438, 22450, 22456, 34551, 34554, 37481, 40710, 40712, 45696–7

B20, 21763–4, 27860, 38759, 38818, 49055, 49058, 62320, 63376, 69904–6, 71014–16, 71018, 71036, 78039, 95130

C10069, 48793, 96509

ED3675, 3713, 5814–22, 6907, 6989, 7013, 7475, 7583, 7704, 7721, 7723–4, 9886–9, 9887–9, 9892–3, 9895, 9906, 9985, 10023, 10025, 10237, 10246, 55313, 55316

EDD125, 128, 140, 149, 152, 170, 701, 732, 738, 1107, 1109, 1121, 1171, 5322, 5324, 8613, 29311

PB160–3, 169

PP1, 3–6, 9, 20, 26, 28, 32, 37–8, 44–5, 56–7, 59, 66, 79, 87–9, 98, 103, 108–9, 122, 126, 153, 159, 162–3, 173, 188D, 191–2, 200, 204, 213, 217, 227, 250A–E, 251A–J, 255, 255A, 260A–D

SCOTTISH NATIONAL PORTRAIT GALLERY

Portraits, busts, and miscellaneous correspondence relating to Rowand Anderson, James Begg, David Bryce, Thomas Chalmers, Patrick Geddes, Henry Duncan Littlejohn, Hugh Miller and James Steel, including PG 175, 255, 340, 426, 437, 564, 591, 687, 836, 985, 1042, 1090, 1110, 1305, 1394, 1595, 1649, 1653, 1699, 2028, 2044, 2365.

UNIVERSITY OF ABERDEEN

George Washington Wilson Photographic Archive, various images relating to Edinburgh

GWW 153, 168, 185, 188, 268, 299, 325, 603, 688, 909, 1110, 1171, 1520, 1541, 1589, 1725, 2362, 2366, 2457, 2652, 3040, 3223, 3824, 4565, 4570, 10079, 10084, 10097, 10551, 10560, 10637, 21290

UNIVERSITY OF EDINBURGH

Special Collections, QP656/2, 1–7 H. G. Reid, *Housing the People – An Example in Co-operation* (London 1895), 62–9, and again in his *Every Man His Own Landlord* (London n.d.)

Special Collections, Text of a lecture by J. Begg, 'The health and homes of working people in towns and cities, and how to improve them', Glasgow, Aug. 1875

PARLIAMENTARY PAPERS

Local Taxation (Scotland) III Accounts and Papers 1874–1916
Censuses of Great Britain and Scotland 1831–1911: *PP 1833 XXXVII*, Census
   of Great Britain 1831; *PP 1844 XXVII* (1841); *PP 1852–3 LXXXVIII*
   (1851); *PP 1862 L*, Census of Scotland 1861; *PP 1873 LXXII* (1871); *PP
   1883 LXXXI* (1881); *PP 1893–4 CVIII* (1891); *PP 1904 CVIII* (1901); *PP
   1912–13 CXIX* and *PP 1913 LXXX* (1911)
PP 1844 XVII, Report on the State of Large Towns and Populous Districts
PP 1844 XXII, Poor Law Inquiry
PP 1874 LXXII pt III, Owners of Lands and Heritages, 1872–3
PP 1880 LV, Educational Endowments in Scotland
PP 1880 XXIV, First Report of the Commissioners on Endowed Institutions in
   Scotland
PP 1881 LXXIII, Return of Endowments in Scotland
PP 1884–5 XXX, Royal Commission on Housing of the Working Classes,
   Scotland, Second Report, Minutes of Evidence
PP 1888 LXXX, First Annual Report Crofters' Commission, 1886–7
PP 1893–4 XII, Select Committee on Feus and Building Leases (Scotland), 2nd
   Report
PP 1894 LXXIV pt II, Royal Commission on Local Taxation in Scotland
PP 1907 XXXVI, Departmental Committee on House-Letting in Scotland,
   Report
PP 1908 XLVII, Minutes of Evidence of the Departmental Committee on
   House-Letting in Scotland
PP 1910 LVIII, Royal Commission on the Registration of Title in Scotland
PP 1911 XXXIII, Annual Report of the Local Government Board for Scotland
   for 1910
PP 1912–13 XXXVII, Annual Report of the Local Government Board for
   Scotland for 1911
PP 1917–18 XIV, Royal Commission on the Housing of the Industrial
   Population of Scotland, Rural and Urban

NEWSPAPERS, MAGAZINES AND PERIODICALS

Bee or *Literary Weekly Intelligencer*
Builder
Building and Lands Companies' Gazette
Building News
Caledonian Mercury
Edinburgh Advertiser
Edinburgh Courant
Edinburgh Evening Courant
Edinburgh Evening News
Edinburgh Gazette
Edinburgh News
Edinburgh Observer
Edinburgh Property Review

Edinburgh Review
Glasgow Herald
New Edinburgh Almanac
Scotsman
Sunday Magazine
Times

PUBLISHED REPORTS

City of Edinburgh Charity Organisation Society, *Report on the Physical Condition of Fourteen Hundred Schoolchildren in the City together with Some Account of their Homes and Surroundings* (London 1906)

Dundee Social Union, *Report on Housing, Industrial Conditions and Medical Inspection of School Children* (Dundee 1905)

Glasgow Municipal Commission on the Housing of the Poor, *Report* and *Evidence* (Glasgow 1904)

H. D. Littlejohn, *Report on the Sanitary Condition of the City of Edinburgh* (Edinburgh 1865)

Registrar General for Scotland, *Annual Reports of Births, Deaths and Marriages*, 1855–1914

Scotch Education Department, *Report as to the Physical Condition of Children Attending the Public Schools of the School Board for Glasgow* (HMSO 1907), Cd 3637

Scottish Land Enquiry Committee, *Report* (London 1914)

Index of Edinburgh street names and districts

Abbey 445
Abbeyhill 106, 114, 375, 377, 381, 405, 408, 414, 469, 493, 496
Abbeyhill School 112n, 470
Abbotsford 500
Abercromby Place 61
Albert Place 173
Albert Street 82
Alva Place 402
Angle Park Terrace 219
Antigua Street 206, 282, 291
Ardmillan Terrace 219, 468, 481
Argyle 206
Argyle Square 433
Arthur Street 112n
Ashley Terrace 389, 465, 468
Atholl Terrace 212

Bainfield 173
Balgreen 397
Balgreen Road 389
Balmoral Place 377
Bangholm Bower 86
Bareford's Park 51, 55
Barnton Terrace, Craigleith 384–6
Bathfield 196, 337, 492
Bedford Street 356
Belgrave Crescent 245, 250–3, 269, 338
Belgrave Place 250, 269, 288, 290–1, 303, 322, 338
Bell Place 397
Bellevue 61
Bellevue Crescent 61n
Bernard Street, Leith 194–5, 206, 282, 291, 337
Bernard Street (Stockbridge) School 112n, 115, 470
Blackfriars' Street 467, 476
Blackfriars' Wynd 420
Blackhall 397
Bonnington 48, 195–6, 205–6, 374, 483, 492

Boroughloch *see* Meadows
Borthwick Close School 112n
Borthwick Place 359n
Botanical Gardens 98
Bothwell Street 108
Braid Hills 165
Brandsfield 213, 219
Bread Street 88, 356
Breadalbane Terrace 212
Bright Terrace 212
Bristo 48
Bristo Place 94
Bristo Street 356
Brougham Place 173, 208
Brougham Street 198–9, 374
Broughton 18, 36–8, 41–2, 54, 77
Broughton Loan 55
Broughton School 112n
Broughton Street 79
Brown Square 476
Brown Square School 112n
Brunstane 230
Brunswick Street 82, 109, 145
Brunton Gardens 108
Brunton Place 82, 465
Brunton Terrace 108, 462
Bruntsfield 48, 96, 109, 168–9, 173, 200
Bryson Road 168, 215, 226–7
Buccleugh Place 94
Buchanan Street 108
Buckingham Terrace 245, 252, 256, 287, 290, 322, 338, 477n

Caledonian Crescent 216, 217n, 218, 291, 326, 330, 333, 340
Caledonian Place 173, 217n, 218, 291
Caledonian Road 218, 291
Caledonian Street 216, 217n, 218
Canal Street 63n
Canongate 18, 36, 38, 375, 423, 476
Canonmills 36, 38, 77, 259, 499
Carberry Place 359n

Index of individual building firms

William Beattie and Sons 481
Cowie and Son, 481
A. and W. Fingzies 381, 462
George Fortune 160
Galloway and Mackintosh 462
James Gowans 481, 72, 286, 294, 466–7,
   469–70
Simon Henderson 462
David Heron 107
Andrew Hood 107, 464–5, 481
P. Justice 229
W. & J. Kirkwood 481
R. Lamb and Co. 160
Lawrie and Scott 107, 465
J. W. B. Lee 140

W. and D. Macgregor 141, 168–69,
   465
R. McNaughton 384–5
John Martin 464
H. T. and R. Montgomery 140, 160, 229
W. S. Morton 480
William Outerston 462
John Pyper 462
Samuel Richard 197
D. B. Ritchie 229
Robert Robertson 158–60
James Slater 107
David Steel and David Walker 201
James Steel *see* separate entry
John Watherstone 215, 219, 481

General index

Aberdeen 19, 132, 482
  Bon Accord Square 68n
absenteeism 116, 402
  see also landowners, landownership
accountability 7, 69, 190
accountants 8, 52, 141, 143–4
advertising 464–6
aesthetics of building 79, 80, 438, 477,
    487
agricultural improvement 53–4, 502
  and urban development 54, 86, 502–3
alienation 10, 487
  see also class
Anne of Denmark, Queen 30, 32
annuitants 7, 18, 27, 114, 123, 141, 143,
    146–9, 182, 213, 253, 283, 300, 315,
    318, 405
architects 94–5, 263, 438, 464
  Architectural Institute of Scotland 429
  Edinburgh Architectural Association
    483
architects, individual
  Anderson, R. Rowand 111, 259, 290,
    500
  Burn, William 94–5, 419
  Carfrae, J. A. 489
  Cousins, David 98, 433, 438, 452,
    476
  Gowans, James 466–7
  Gray, James 194–5, 216
  Hamilton, Thomas 94–5, 419
  Leslie, Thomas 94
  Lessels, John 433, 438, 452, 476
  Morham, Robert 154
  Playfair Wiliam 82, 94, 95, 106, 243
  Rhind, David 99
  Stevenson Robert 94, 419
architecture 8, 95–6, 497–8
  council housing 12, 450, 452
  Georgian 477
  historic 438–9, 474–5, 484, 487–9
  Italianate 476

Jacobean, decorated collegiate 470
neo-classical 26, 60, 80, 153, 472, 476,
    484, 489
neo-gothic 472; 'Scots baronial' 28, 259,
    438, 452, 476, 484, 488, features 475;
    Scott monument 472–3
'old English' 243
tenement design 236–8, 476–7
  see also built environment; Scott, Sir
    Walter
Arnold, Dr Thomas 129
artisans 273, 332, 395, 403, 412, 502
  employment 259, 278, 320
  incomes 180, 206
  see also building trades
arts, fine 243, 485
associations 260, 295–6, 487
  employers 191
asylums 491
  see also hospitals
auction, roup 135, 149, 219–20
Ayr 226

banks and banking 7, 13, 171, 269
  Bank of England 171
  Bank of Scotland 42, 43, 95
  banking failure 77, 132
  British Linen Bank 99, 138
  City of Glasgow Bank 132, 231
  Chartered Bank of Australia 145
  Commercial Bank of Scotland 216
  land banks 141, 505
  Oriental Bank 144
  People's Bank 170, 270
  Union Bank 167–8
  see also credit; crisis; finance
Begg, Rev. Dr James 363–4, 372, 412, 423,
    427
betterment 11
Birmingham 174, 489
birth rate 24–5, 175
Blackstone, William 506

364–5, 381, 395, 404, 467, 470, 476, 486; painter 404; plasterer 358; plumber 209, 358; slaters 209
buildings
  commercial 65, 68, 92, 105, 150, 183, 195, 208, 215, 232, 289, 375, 487, 499
  industrial 42, 77, 114, 183, 215, 232, 259, 375, 383, 492–3, 496, 499
  mixed 150, 259, 303
  public 491, 491n, 492; *see also* churches; schools; town council
  residential *see* housing; tenements; middle classes; working classes
  as symbols of authority 460, 488
built environment 124, 268, 454, 459, 475, 480–4
  architectural decoration 460–83, 477, 486
  empire and 461, 471
  ethnography and 464–76
  'imprisoned capital' 461, 486
  memory and 488–9
  modernity and 464
  ornamental symbolism 461–70, 476
  power and 459–60, 464, 467, 486, 487
  scale, monumentality 116, 460, 471, 489, 491
  Scottish nationalism and 461–2, 472, 474–6, 480, 484, 486
  state and nationalism in 13, 28–9, 459, 461, 471
bureaucracy 6, 191, 273
  civil administration 236, 273, 276, 412, 421–2, 460
  theories of 455, 488
business structure 114, 190
  of family firms 4, 149, 348
  of head offices 13
  of small firms 21, 114, 175–6, 190, 203, 496
  see also builders

Cambusnethan 192, 348, 409
Canal, Union 197, 213–14
capital
  human capital 14
  Local supplies 270; *see also* heritable securities
  overseas flows 25, 58, 150, 168, 181–2, 293
  sources of 74, 118, 123, 135, 140, 169, 194, 294
  working 138, 140, 169, 262
  see also building finance
capital costs 58, 95–6

capitalism 3–4, 11, 67, 74, 118, 165, 174, 208, 229–31, 268–9, 280, 292, 294, 353, 394–401, 411, 502, 508
  dynamic nature of 10, 13, 73–4, 118, 166, 171, 184–5, 190, 292–3, 394–401
  house ownership and 210, 268, 280, 394–5
  social structure and 4, 20, 205, 305
  and urbanisation 12, 67, 165, 171, 178–9, 190, 293, 450, 452–3
celebrations, jubilees 461, 468
cellars 60, 428
cemeteries 3
  see also Dean Cemetery
censuses 175
centralisation 3, 5, 116, 414, 428, 455–7, 472
  Board of Health 428, 456–7
Chadwick, Edwin 286, 418–19, 428, 456–7
  Report 286, 418–19, 428
Chalmers, Rev. Dr Thomas 363–4
Chambers, William 420, 428, 431–2, 441, 456
  Report and proposals 432
charities 4–5, 21, 92, 123, 182, 430
  endowed 7, 26, 43, 58, 98–9
  poor relief 21
  see also endowments; hospitials; trusts
children 19, 289
  education of 36, 42–3, 51, 99
  mortality of 444, 446
  see also schools
cholera 416–19, 428, 455
Church of Scotland 7, 51, 91–2, 127–41, 153, 160–1, 170, 172, 203, 284, 294, 362, 421–2
  attendance 127–8, 294, 422
  Chapels of Ease 129, 160
  collections 130; legacies and subscriptions, 130
  Disruption 127, 294, 363, 422
  Endowment Committee 133–4, 136, 140–1, 160, 203
  extension movement 127–9, 131, 138, 364
  heritable securities 7, 27, 127, 130–6, 160, 172, 203–4, 226; geographical distribution 130–3, 138–40
  housing reform *see* Begg, Rev. Dr James; Chalmers, Rev. Dr Thomas; Edinburgh Co-operative Building Company; Free Church of Scotland
  investments 7, 130–41, 172, 226
  moralism and 129, 285–6, 362, 426–7, 496

Printed in the United Kingdom
by Lightning Source UK Ltd.
115505UKS00001B/161